Investigations Operations Manual

FDA Field Inspection and Investigation Policy and Procedure

Concise Reference

Investigations Operations Manual

FDA Field Inspection and Investigation

Policy and Procedure

Concise Reference

Investigations Operations Manual: FDA Field Inspection and Investigation Policy and Procedure Concise Reference

PharmaLogika

PharmaLogika, Inc.
PO Box 461
Willow Springs, NC 27592

www.pharmalogika.com

Author / Editor: Mindy J. Allport-Settle

Published by PharmaLogika, Inc.

Printed in the United States of America. First Printing.

ISBN 0-9821476-2-7
ISBN-13 978-0-9821476-2-7

Contents

Preface

About this Book

This book is first, and foremost, a unified reference source for the United States Food and Drug Administration Investigations Operations Manual. The procedures, guidance documents and some forms have also been collected.

The included *Overview and Orientation* (Chapter 2 of this book) is designed to provide a foundation for understanding the background of the FDA's regulations and FDA's relationship with the individual protectees.

This book was designed to be used both as a reference for experienced industry representatives and as a training resource for those new to the industry.

Included Documents and Features

Investigations Operations Manual

The IOM is the primary guidance document on FDA inspection policy and procedures for field investigators and inspectors.

Exhibits, Appendix, and Sample Schedules

The exhibits support each chapter of the IOM with examples, tables, graphics, and forms. The exhibits available are listed in this book, but the published exhibits are available on the FDA's website.

Reference Tools

Glossaries for each included part and procedure combined in one location

Combined Index for all procedures and addendums to the manual

About the Reference Tools

Overview and Orientation

This overview provides the reader with a brief history of the FDA and explains not only what good manufacturing practice is, but why we have regulations and how they came to be.

The overview also lists all of the parts within Title 21 of the Code of Federal Regulations.

Combined Glossary

The Combined Glossary includes all of the definitions from each chapter listed alphabetically rather than by document.

When a word or term appears multiple times in the regulation and guidance documents, the word will appear multiple times in the Combined Glossary. Each duplicate entry is indented to highlight that it is a duplicate and the earliest reference to the entry is listed first. The source for each entry is bracketed (i.e., [Chapter 4]) for ease of reference. While the definitions are similar from one regulatory or guidance document to the next, they are not always identical.

Combined Index for all chapters and addendums

The index is composed of a list of both words and terms specific to investigations operations. It is a tool that assists in cross-referencing the various guidance (rather than having to rely on reading and comparing each chapter individually).

The index provides keywords and terminology as a tool to easily locate specific references across all chapters and addendums rather than having to rely on memory or paging through the entire manual.

Overview and Orientation

The Food and Drug Administration (FDA)

The United States Food and Drug Administration (FDA) is responsible for protecting and promoting the nation's public health.

The programs for safety regulation vary widely by the type of product, its potential risks, and the regulatory powers granted to the agency. For example, the FDA regulates almost every facet of prescription drugs, including testing, manufacturing, labeling, advertising, marketing, efficacy and safety. FDA regulation of cosmetics, however, is focused primarily on labeling and safety. The FDA regulates most products with a set of published standards enforced by a combination of facility inspections, voluntary company reporting standards, and public and consumer watchdog activity.

The FDA frequently works in conjunction with other Federal agencies including the Department of Agriculture, Drug Enforcement Administration, Customs and Border Protection, and Consumer Product Safety Commission.

Historical Origins of Federal Food and Drug Regulation

Prior to the 20th century, there were few federal laws regulating the contents and sale of domestically produced food and pharmaceuticals before the 20th century (with one exception being the short-lived Vaccine Act of 1813). Some state laws provided varying degrees of protection against unethical sales practices, such as misrepresenting the ingredients of food products or therapeutic substances.

The history of the FDA can be traced to the latter part of the 19th century and the U.S. Department of Agriculture's Division of Chemistry (later Bureau of Chemistry). Under Harvey Washington Wiley, appointed chief chemist in 1883, the Division began conducting research into the adulteration and misbranding of food and drugs on the American market. Although they had no regulatory powers, the Division published its findings from 1887 to 1902 in a ten-part series entitled Foods and Food Adulterants. Wiley used these findings, and alliances with diverse organizations (such as state regulators, the General Federation of Women's Clubs, and national associations of physicians and pharmacists) to lobby for a new federal law to set uniform standards for food and drugs to enter into interstate commerce.

Wiley's advocacy came at a time when the public had become alert to hazards in the marketplace by journalists and became part of a general trend for increased federal regulation in matters pertinent to public safety during the Progressive Era.[1] The 1902 Biologics Control Act was put in place after

---

[1] A History of the FDA at www.FDA.gov.

diphtheria antitoxin was collected from a horse named Jim who also had tetanus, resulting in several deaths.

The 1906 Food and Drug Act and creation of the FDA

In June 1906, President Theodore Roosevelt signed into law the Food and Drug Act, also known as the "Wiley Act" after its chief advocate.[2] The Act prohibited, under penalty of seizure of goods, the interstate transport of food which had been "adulterated," with that term referring to the addition of fillers of reduced "quality or strength," coloring to conceal "damage or inferiority," formulation with additives "injurious to health," or the use of "filthy, decomposed, or putrid" substances. The act applied similar penalties to the interstate marketing of "adulterated" drugs, in which the "standard of strength, quality, or purity" of the active ingredient was not either stated clearly on the label or listed in the United States Pharmacopoeia or the National Formulary. The act also banned "misbranding" of food and drugs.[3] The responsibility for examining food and drugs for such "adulteration" or "misbranding" was given to Wiley's USDA Bureau of Chemistry.[4] Strength, quality, identity, potency, and purity (SQuIPP) are currently the key product safety standards, with only two measures added since 1906 Act.

Wiley used these new regulatory powers to pursue an aggressive campaign against the manufacturers of foods with chemical additives, but the Chemistry Bureau's authority was soon checked by judicial decisions, as well as by the creation of the Board of Food and Drug Inspection and the Referee Board of Consulting Scientific Experts as separate organizations within the USDA in 1907 and 1908 respectively. A 1911 Supreme Court decision ruled that the 1906 act did not apply to false claims of therapeutic efficacy,[5] in response to which a 1912 amendment added "false and fraudulent" claims of "curative or therapeutic effect" to the Act's definition of "misbranded." However, these powers continued to be narrowly defined by the courts, which set high standards for proof of fraudulent intent.[6] In 1927, the Bureau of Chemistry's regulatory powers were reorganized under a new USDA body, the Food, Drug, and Insecticide organization. This name was shortened to the Food and Drug Administration (FDA) three years later.[7]

The 1938 Food, Drug, and Cosmetic Act

By the 1930s, muckraking journalists, consumer protection organizations, and federal regulators began mounting a campaign for stronger regulatory authority by publicizing a list of injurious products which had been ruled permissible under the 1906 law, including radioactive beverages, cosmetics which caused blindness, and worthless "cures" for diabetes and tuberculosis. The resulting proposed law was unable to get through the Congress of the United States for five years, but was rapidly enacted into law following the

---

[2] A History of the FDA at www.FDA.gov.

[3] Text in quotation marks is the original text of the 1906 Food and Drugs Act and Amendments.

[4] A History of the FDA at www.FDA.gov.

[5] United States v. Johnson (31 S. Ct. 627 May 29, 1911, decided).

[6] A History of the FDA at www.FDA.gov.

[7] Milestones in U.S. Food and Drug Law History at www.FDA.gov.

public outcry over the 1937 Elixir Sulfanilamide tragedy, in which over 100 people died after using a drug formulated with a toxic, untested solvent. The only way that the FDA could even seize the product was due to a misbranding problem: an "Elixir" was defined as a medication dissolved in ethanol, not the diethylene glycol used in the Elixir Sulfanilamide.

President Franklin Delano Roosevelt signed the new Food, Drug, and Cosmetic Act (FD&C Act) into law on June 24, 1938. The new law significantly increased federal regulatory authority over drugs by mandating a pre-market review of the safety of all new drugs, as well as banning false therapeutic claims in drug labeling without requiring that the FDA prove fraudulent intent. The law also authorized factory inspections and expanded enforcement powers, set new regulatory standards for foods, and brought cosmetics and therapeutic devices under federal regulatory authority. This law, though extensively amended in subsequent years, remains the central foundation of FDA regulatory authority to the present day.[8]

Early FD&C Act amendments: 1938-1958

Soon after passage of the 1938 Act, the FDA began to designate certain drugs as safe for use only under the supervision of a medical professional, and the category of 'prescription-only' drugs was securely codified into law by the 1951 Durham-Humphrey Amendment.[9] While pre-market testing of drug efficacy was not authorized under the 1938 FD&C Act, subsequent amendments such as the Insulin Amendment and Penicillin Amendment did mandate potency testing for formulations of specific lifesaving pharmaceuticals.[10] The FDA began enforcing its new powers against drug manufacturers who could not substantiate the efficacy claims made for their drugs, and the United States Court of Appeals for the Ninth Circuit ruling in Alberty Food Products Co. v. United States (1950) found that drug manufacturers could not evade the "false therapeutic claims" provision of the 1938 act by simply omitting the intended use of a drug from the drug's label. These developments confirmed extensive powers for the FDA to enforce post-marketing recalls of ineffective drugs.[11] Much of the FDA's regulatory attentions in this era were directed towards abuse of amphetamines and barbiturates, but the agency also reviewed some 13,000 new drug applications between 1938 and 1962. While the science of toxicology was in its infancy at the start of this era, rapid advances in experimental assays for food additive and drug safety testing were made during this period by FDA regulators and others.[12]

---

[8] A History of the FDA at www.FDA.gov.
[9] A History of the FDA at www.FDA.gov.
[10] Milestones in U.S. Food and Drug Law History at www.FDA.gov
[11] A History of the FDA at www.FDA.gov.
[12] A History of the FDA at www.FDA.gov.

Good Manufacturing Practices vs. Current Good Manufacturing Practices

The terms "Good Manufacturing Practices (GMPs)" and "Current Good Manufacturing Practices (CGMPs or cGMPs[13])" are often used interchangeably both in industry and by FDA inspectors.

"Good Manufacturing Practices" generally refers to the legal mandates detailed in Title 21 of the Code of Federal Regulations (21CFR). "Current Good Manufacturing Practices" refers not only to the legal requirements, but to the guidance provided by the FDA and the standards practiced in industry that are not memorialized as law.

Organizational Structure

The FDA is an agency within the United States Department of Health and Human Services responsible for protecting and promoting the nation's public health. It is organized into the following major subdivisions, each focused on a major area of regulatory responsibility:

- The Office of the Commissioner (OC)
- The Center for Drug Evaluation and Research (CDER)
- The Center for Biologics Evaluation and Research (CBER)
- The Center for Food Safety and Applied Nutrition (CFSAN)
- The Center for Devices and Radiological Health (CDRH)
- The Center for Veterinary Medicine (CVM)
- The National Center for Toxicological Research (NCTR)
- The Office of Regulatory Affairs (ORA)
- The Office of Criminal Investigations (OCI)

How does the FDA communicate with Industry?

Code of Federal Regulations[14]

The Code of Federal Regulations (CFR) is the codification of the general and permanent rules and regulations (sometimes called administrative law) published in the Federal Register by the executive departments and agencies of the Federal Government of the United States. The CFR is published by the Office of the Federal Register, an agency of the National Archives and Records Administration (NARA).

The CFR is divided into 50 titles that represent broad areas subject to Federal regulation. Title 21 is the portion of the Code of Federal Regulations that governs food and drugs within the United States for the Food and Drug

[13] The lower case "c" was coined in industry to differentiate between the law, emphasized with capital letters, and the current accepted industry practice not mandated by law.
[14] Available CFR Titles on GPO Access at http://www.access.gpo.gov/nara/cfr/cfr-table-search.html#page1

Administration (FDA), the Drug Enforcement Administration (DEA), and the Office of National Drug Control Policy (ONDCP).

It is divided into three chapters:

- Chapter I — Food and Drug Administration
- Chapter II — Drug Enforcement Administration
- Chapter III — Office of National Drug Control Policy

Guidance Documents

Guidance documents represent the Agency's current thinking on a particular subject. They do not create or confer any rights for or on any person and do not operate to bind FDA or the public. An alternative approach may be used if such approach satisfies the requirements of the applicable statute, regulations, or both. For information on a specific guidance document, please contact the originating office. Another method of obtaining guidance documents is through the Division of Drug Information.

Federal Register

The Federal Register (since March 14, 1936), abbreviated FR, or sometimes Fed. Reg.) is the official journal of the federal government of the United States that contains most routine publications and public notices of government agencies. It is a daily (except holidays) publication.

The Federal Register is compiled by the Office of the Federal Register (within the National Archives and Records Administration) and is printed by the Government Printing Office.

There are no copyright restrictions on the Federal Register as it is a work of the U.S. government. It is in the public domain.[15]

Citations from the Federal Register are [volume] FR [page number] ([date]), e.g., 65 FR 741 (2000-10-01).

Direct Communication and Letters

The FDA interacts with consumers, health professionals, and industry representatives through letters, meetings (requested by either the FDA or the industry representatives), and telephone calls.

While not all questions can be answered over the phone, the FDA prefers telephone interactions over physical meetings (when a teleconference can reasonably replace a face-to-face meeting).

www.FDA.gov

The FDA maintains a website at www.fda.gov that is focused on three key audiences:

- consumers
- health professionals

[15] The Federal Register at the GPO, online in both text and PDF, from 1994 on.

- industry representatives

Through collaboration with users in testing site-wide designs, FDA.gov provides online access to its guidance documents, communication with industry, consumers, and health professionals. Information is categorized by topic, with related subjects consolidated in sections on the site.

Additionally, FDA.gov provides a search engine for Title 21 of the CFR that makes finding keyword references throughout the title more accessible.

Conferences

The FDA routinely sends speakers to industry conferences where they are available to answer questions on their particular area of expertise.

False Statement to a Federal Agency

The U.S. Code of Federal Regulations (CFR) makes it a federal crime for anyone willfully and knowingly to make a false or fraudulent statement to a department or agency of the United States. The false statement must be related to a material matter, and the defendant must have acted willfully and with knowledge of the falsity. It is not necessary to show that the government agency was in fact deceived or misled. The issue of materiality is one of law for the courts. The maximum penalty is five years' imprisonment and a $10,000 fine.

A person may be guilty of a violation without proof that he or she had knowledge that the matter was within the jurisdiction of a federal agency. A businessperson may violate this law by making a false statement to another firm or person with knowledge that the information will be submitted to a government agency. Businesses must take care to avoid exaggerations in the context of any matter that may come within the jurisdiction of a federal agency.

CFR Title 21 - Food and Drugs: Parts 1 to 1499[16]

General

(1) General enforcement regulations

(2) General administrative rulings and decisions

(3) Product jurisdiction

(5) Organization

(7) Enforcement policy

(10) Administrative practices and procedures

(11) Electronic records; electronic signatures

(12) Formal evidentiary public hearing

---

[16] All of the 21CFR regulations can be searched online for no charge at http://www.accessdata.fda.gov/scripts/cdrh/cfdocs/cfcfr/cfrsearch.cfm

(13) Public hearing before a public board of inquiry

(14) Public hearing before a public advisory committee

(15) Public hearing before the commissioner

(16) Regulatory hearing before the food and drug administration

(17) Civil money penalties hearings

(19) Standards of conduct and conflicts of interest

(20) Public information

(21) Protection of privacy

(25) Environmental impact considerations

(26) Mutual recognition of pharmaceutical good manufacturing practice

(50) Protection of human subjects

(54) Financial disclosure by clinical investigators

(56) Institutional review boards

(58) Good laboratory practice for nonclinical laboratory studies

(60) Patent term restoration

(70) Color additives

(71) Color additive petitions

(73) Listing of color additives exempt from certification

(74) Listing of color additives subject to certification

(80) Color additive certification

(81) General specifications and general restrictions for provisional color additives for use in foods, drugs, and cosmetics

(82) Listing of certified provisionally listed colors and specifications

(83-98) [reserved]

(99) Dissemination of information on unapproved/new uses for marketed drugs, biologics, and devices

Foods

(100) General

(101) Food labeling

(102) Common or usual name for nonstandardized foods

(104) Nutritional quality guidelines for foods

(105) Foods for special dietary use

(106) Infant formula quality control procedures

(107) Infant formula

(108) Emergency permit control

(109) Unavoidable contaminants in food for human consumption and food-packaging material

(110) Current good manufacturing practice in manufacturing, packing, or holding human food

(111) Current good manufacturing practice in manufacturing, packaging, labeling, or holding operations for dietary supplements

(113) Thermally processed low-acid foods packaged in hermetically sealed containers

(114) Acidified foods

(115) Shell eggs

(119) Dietary supplements that present a significant or unreasonable risk

(120) Hazard analysis and critical control point (HACCP) systems

(123) Fish and fishery products

(129) Processing and bottling of bottled drinking water

(130) Food standards: general

(131) Milk and cream

(133) Cheeses and related cheese products

(135) Frozen desserts

(136) Bakery products

(137) Cereal flours and related products

(139) Macaroni and noodle products

(145) Canned fruits

(146) Canned fruit juices

(150) Fruit butters, jellies, preserves, and related products

(152) Fruit pies

(155) Canned vegetables

(156) Vegetable juices

(158) Frozen vegetables

(160) Eggs and egg products

(161) Fish and shellfish

(163) Cacao products

(164) Tree nut and peanut products

(165) Beverages

(166) Margarine

(168) Sweeteners and table syrups

(169) Food dressings and flavorings

(170) Food additives

(171) Food additive petitions

(172) Food additives permitted for direct addition to food for human consumption

(173) Secondary direct food additives permitted in food for human consumption

(174) Indirect food additives: general

(175) Indirect food additives: adhesives and components of coatings

(176) Indirect food additives: paper and paperboard components

(177) Indirect food additives: polymers

(178) Indirect food additives: adjuvants, production aids, and sanitizers

(179) Irradiation in the production, processing and handling of food

(180) Food additives permitted in food or in contact with food on an interim basis pending additional study

(181) Prior-sanctioned food ingredients

(182) Substances generally recognized as safe

(184) Direct food substances affirmed as generally recognized as safe

(186) Indirect food substances affirmed as generally recognized as safe

(189) Substances prohibited from use in human food

(190) Dietary supplements

(191-199) [reserved]

Drugs

(200) General

(201) Labeling

(202) Prescription drug advertising

(203) Prescription drug marketing

(205) Guidelines for state licensing of wholesale prescription drug distributors

(206) Imprinting of solid oral dosage form drug products for human use

(207) Registration of producers of drugs and listing of drugs in commercial distribution

(208) Medication guides for prescription drug products

(209) Requirement for authorized dispensers and pharmacies to distribute a side effects statement

(210) Current good manufacturing practice in manufacturing, processing, packing, or holding of drugs; general

(211) Current good manufacturing practice for finished pharmaceuticals

(216) Pharmacy compounding

(225) Current good manufacturing practice for medicated feeds

(226) Current good manufacturing practice for type A medicated articles

(250) Special requirements for specific human drugs

(290) Controlled drugs

(299) Drugs; official names and established names

New Drugs and Over-the-Counter Drug Products

(300) General

(310) New drugs

(312) Investigational new drug application

(314) Applications for FDA approval to market a new drug

(315) Diagnostic radiopharmaceuticals

(316) Orphan drugs

(320) Bioavailability and bioequivalence requirements

(328) Over-the-counter drug products intended for oral ingestion that contain alcohol

(330) Over-the-counter (OTC) human drugs which are generally recognized as safe and effective and not misbranded

(331) Antacid products for over-the-counter (OTC) human use

(332) Antiflatulent products for over-the-counter human use

(333) Topical antimicrobial drug products for over-the-counter recognized as safe and effective and not misbranded

(335) Antidiarrheal drug products for over-the-counter human use

(336) Antiemetic drug products for over-the-counter human use

(338) Nighttime sleep-aid drug products for over-the-counter human use

(340) Stimulant drug products for over-the-counter human use

(341) Cold, cough, allergy, bronchodilator, and antiasthmatic drug products for over-the-counter human use

(343) Internal analgesic, antipyretic, and antirheumatic drug products for over-the-counter human use

(344) Topical OTIC drug products for over-the-counter human use

(346) Anorectal drug products for over-the-counter human use

(347) Skin protectant drug products for over-the-counter human use

(348) External analgesic drug products for over-the-counter human use

(349) Ophthalmic drug products for over-the-counter human use

(350) Antiperspirant drug products for over-the-counter human use

(352) Sunscreen drug products for over-the-counter human use [stayed indefinitely]

(355) Anticaries drug products for over-the-counter human use

(357) Miscellaneous internal drug products for over-the-counter human use

(358) Miscellaneous external drug products for over-the-counter human use

(361) Prescription drugs for human use generally recognized as safe and effective and not misbranded: drugs used in research

(369) Interpretative statements re warnings on drugs and devices for over-the-counter sale

(370-499) [reserved]

Veterinary Products

(500) General

(501) Animal food labeling

(502) Common or usual names for nonstandardized animal foods

(509) Unavoidable contaminants in animal food and food-packaging material

(510) New animal drugs

(511) New animal drugs for investigational use

(514) New animal drug applications

(515) Medicated feed mill license

(516) New animal drugs for minor use and minor species

(520) Oral dosage form new animal drugs

(522) Implantation or injectable dosage form new animal drugs

(524) Ophthalmic and topical dosage form new animal drugs

(526) Intramammary dosage forms

(529) Certain other dosage form new animal drugs

(530) Extralabel drug use in animals

(556) Tolerances for residues of new animal drugs in food

(558) New animal drugs for use in animal feeds

(564) [reserved]

(570) Food additives

(571) Food additive petitions

(573) Food additives permitted in feed and drinking water of animals

(579) Irradiation in the production, processing, and handling of animal feed and pet food

(582) Substances generally recognized as safe

(584) Food substances affirmed as generally recognized as safe in feed and drinking water of animals

(589) Substances prohibited from use in animal food or feed

(590-599) [reserved]

Biologics

(600) Biological products: general

(601) Licensing

(606) Current good manufacturing practice for blood and blood components

(607) Establishment registration and product listing for manufacturers of human blood and blood products

(610) General biological products standards

(630) General requirements for blood, blood components, and blood components, and blood derivatives

(640) Additional standards for human blood and blood products

(660) Additional standards for diagnostic substances for laboratory tests

(680) Additional standards for miscellaneous products

Cosmetics

(700) General

(701) Cosmetic labeling

(710) Voluntary registration of cosmetic product establishments

(720) Voluntary filing of cosmetic product ingredient composition statements

(740) Cosmetic product warning statements

(741-799) [reserved]

Medical Devices

(800) General

(801) Labeling

(803) Medical device reporting

(806) Medical devices; reports of corrections and removals

(807) Establishment registration and device listing for manufacturers and initial importers of devices

(808) Exemptions from federal preemption of state and local medical device requirements

(809) In vitro diagnostic products for human use

(810) Medical device recall authority

(812) Investigational device exemptions

(813) [reserved]

(814) Premarket approval of medical devices

(820) Quality system regulation

(821) Medical device tracking requirements

(822) Postmarket surveillance

(860) Medical device classification procedures

(861) Procedures for performance standards development

(862) Clinical chemistry and clinical toxicology devices

(864) Hematology and pathology devices

(866) Immunology and microbiology devices

(868) Anesthesiology devices

(870) Cardiovascular devices

(872) Dental devices

(874) Ear, nose, and throat devices

(876) Gastroenterology-urology devices

(878) General and plastic surgery devices

(880) General hospital and personal use devices

(882) Neurological devices

(884) Obstetrical and gynecological devices

(886) Ophthalmic devices

(888) Orthopedic devices

(890) Physical medicine devices

(892) Radiology devices

(895) Banned devices

(898) Performance standard for electrode lead wires and patient cables

Mammography

(900) Mammography

Radiological Health

(1000) General

(1002) Records and reports

(1003) Notification of defects or failure to comply

(1004) Repurchase, repairs, or replacement of electronic products

(1005) Importation of electronic products

(1010) Performance standards for electronic products: general

(1020) Performance standards for ionizing radiation emitting products

(1030) Performance standards for microwave and radio frequency emitting products

(1040) Performance standards for light-emitting products

(1050) Performance standards for sonic, infrasonic, and ultrasonic radiation-emitting products

Regulations under Certain Other Acts

(1210) Regulations under the federal import milk act

(1230) Regulations under the federal caustic poison act

(1240) Control of communicable diseases

(1250) Interstate conveyance sanitation

(1251-1269) [reserved]

(1270) Human tissue intended for transplantation

(1271) Human cells, tissues, and cellular and tissue-based products

(1272-1299) [reserved]

Controlled Substances

(1300) Definitions

(1301) Registration of manufacturers, distributors, and dispensers of controlled substances

(1302) Labeling and packaging requirements for controlled substances

(1303) Quotas

(1304) Records and reports of registrants

(1305) Orders for schedule I and II controlled substances

(1306) Prescriptions

(1307) Miscellaneous

(1308) Schedules of controlled substances

(1309) Registration of manufacturers, distributors, importers and exporters of List I chemicals

(1310) Records and reports of listed chemicals and certain machines

(1311) Digital certificates

(1312) Importation and exportation of controlled substances

(1313) Importation and exportation of list I and list II chemicals

(1314) Retail sale of scheduled listed chemical products

(1315) Importation and production quotas for ephedrine, pseudoephedrine, and phenylpropanolamine

(1316) Administrative functions, practices, and procedures

Office of National Drug Control Policy

(1400) [reserved]

(1401) Public availability of information

(1402) Mandatory declassification review

(1403) Uniform administrative requirements for grants and cooperative agreements to state and local governments

(1404) Governmentwide debarment and suspension (nonprocurement)

(1405) Governmentwide requirements for drug-free workplace (financial assistance)

(1406-1499) [reserved]

Part I

Investigations Operations Manual

Foreword

Last Update / Version: June 18, 2009

The *Investigations Operations Manual* (IOM) is the primary source regarding Agency policy and procedures for field investigators and inspectors. This extends to all individuals who perform field investigational activities in support of the Agency's public mission. Accordingly, it directs the conduct of all fundamental field investigational activities. Adherence to this manual is paramount to assure quality, consistency, and efficiency in field operations. The specific information in this manual is supplemented, not superseded, by other manuals and field guidance documents. Recognizing that this manual may not cover all situations or variables arising from field operations, any significant departures from IOM established procedures should have the concurrence of district management.

For 2009, the IOM contains some important changes which clarify or present new procedures.For instance, the LACF/AF Sample Schedule was revised and sample identification procedures were clarified in Chapter 4; additional FDA 483 guidance was added; OEI maintenance instructions reference FMD-130; and additional information related to food, drug, and veterinary products was incorporated in Chapter 5; and current import terminology was updated in Chapter6. Appendix C - Blood Values was completely revised.

As with each new edition of the IOM, please take time to review sections of the IOM for changes which may apply to your work.

Since December 1996, the IOM has been posted on ORA's Internet Website, Investigations Operations Manual. The entire IOM is available there, with all graphics included. Future updates to the IOM will be performed periodically during the year to this on-line version. The hard copy will be published annually. Remember, whether reviewing the "hard copy" or the "on-line' version of the IOM, the most recent version is the document of record.

We are committed to the continual improvement of the quality and usefulness of the IOM. Suggestions for the 2009 edition of the IOM or recommended changes, deletions, additions to the IOM may be sent to the Division of Field Investigations (HFC-130), 5600 Fishers Lane, Rockville, MD 20857 or via e-mail to the Director, DFI. You can also e-mail IOM@FDA.HHS.GOV. If you are recommending a change or revision, please use the IOM Change Request Form available from the web site.

Thank you for your continued hard work and dedication in protecting and promoting the health and well-being of the American people.

Michael A. Chappell, Acting Associate Commissioner for Regulatory Affairs

FDA/Office of Regulatory Affairs

Note: This manual is reference material for investigators and other FDA personnel. The document does not bind FDA and does not confer any rights, privileges, benefits or immunities for or on any person(s).

Vision / Mission / Values

Vision

All food is safe; all medical products are safe and effective; and the public health is protected and advanced.

Mission

Protecting consumers and enhances public health by maximizing compliance of FDA-regulated products and minimizing risk associated with those products.

Values

Values that I believe exist in ORA today:

1. Our mission defines our work and our purpose as employees.
2. We are dedicated to having a meaningful and positive impact on public health.
3. We take pride in our ongoing commitment to excellence in our work products and our contribution to the mission of FDA.

Values that I believe we need for the future:

1. We work as a team and build partnerships with our stakeholders in a global regulatory environment.
2. We invest in our people and processes to target and improve our impact on public health.
3. We continuously improve both what we do and how we do it.

Michael A. Chappell

Acting Associate Commissioner for Regulatory Affairs

December 9, 2008

Chapter 1: Administration

CONTENT		VERSION DATE
Subchapter 1.1	English Language Requirement for FDA Documents	June 11, 2009
Subchapter 1.2	Travel	July 13, 2009
Subchapter 1.3	Leave	June 11, 2009
Subchapter 1.4	Disclosure of Official Information	July 13, 2009
Subchapter 1.5	Safety	July 13, 2009
Subchapter 1.6	Public Relations, Ethics & Conduct	July 13, 2009
Subchapter 1.7	Interdistrict Assignments	July 13, 2009
Subchapter 1.8	Organization Overview	June 11, 2009
Subchapter 1.9	Office of Regulatory Affairs	July 13, 2009
Subchapter 1.10	References	July 13, 2009

1.1 - English Language Requirement For FDA Documents

Definition: the term document applies to official records which are considered to be U.S. Government property regardless of the media e.g. Regulatory notes (electronic and hardcopy), memoranda, inspection reports, e-mails, and official government forms (e.g. SF-71, FDA-482, FDA-483, etc.)

All official FDA documents generated during your routine duties shall be completed in English. This requirement is necessary to facilitate efficiency in the workplace. For instance, many of your work products used in support of FDA's regulatory process are subject to review and auditing by your supervisor, utilized by your co-workers, and others, including the public, in that they are releasable under the Freedom of Information Act (FOIA). The Agency does not have the resources to assure the accurate and timely English translation of documents written in a non English language in order to facilitate their use in the conduct of official business. English is generally considered to be the common language of the U.S., therefore it is necessary to standardize the language utilized in the production of official FDA documents.

Additionally, FDA imposes English only requirements on the public for information submitted to the Agency. For example 21 Code of Federal Regulations section 803.13(a) (English Reporting Requirement) states that " All reports required in this part which are submitted in writing or electronic equivalent shall be submitted to FDA in English."

1.2 - Travel

All official travel must be authorized and approved with a valid travel order (T.O.) using FDA's online travel management program GovTrip. Emergency travel can be approved and the travel order prepared and authorized after the fact. "After the fact" T.O.s should be utilized on a very limited basis.

The federal travel regulations contained in 41 CFR 301, Department of Health and Human Services (DHHS) Travel Manual, and the Food and Drug Administration (FDA) supplements thereto, govern official travel. Become familiar with these documents. All material contained in the Investigations Operations Manual (IOM) must be used in conjunction with, and subject to, federal travel regulations. Additional travel information can be obtained from the Office of Financial Management (OFM) Intranet home page.

For foreign travel, be aware that there are differences in reporting requirements and reimbursable expenses. See the Guide to International Inspections and Travel, Chapter 1, Subchapter 110 - Travel, for specifics.

Effective March 1, 2000, federal employees must put most official travel-related charges on government-issued credit cards, with exceptions only for expenses that are either relatively minor or inconvenient for credit card usage such as parking, local transportation, tips, phone calls, and certain expenses for which credit cards are not accepted.

FDA selected Northrop Grumman's GovTrip as their E-Government Travel Service. GovTrip is accessed at www.govtrip.com. GovTrip will enable FDA travelers and travel preparers to make travel reservations, book hotel accommodations and rental car reservations, and create authorizations and vouchers (including local travel vouchers) in a single web-based system. In addition, GovTrip will interface with the Unified Financial Management System (UFMS) for obligation and payment of travel vouchers. Payments will include direct payment to US Bank for expenses charged to the individual's official government travel credit card. The system incorporates Federal Government travel policies which include the city pair airfare contract program and Federal Travel Regulations and is structured to require justification if you want to deviate from General Services Administration's (GSA) regulations. A policy has been established with the FDA so that your government-issued credit card will be your primary method of billing and payment when you book flights, make hotel reservations, or reserve a rental car. Additional information can be obtained by contacting your Administrative Officer (AO) or visiting OFM's website.

1.2.1 - Common Carrier

Request round-trip tickets when it can be expected you will use them. This reduces paperwork costs, even though there may be no savings on the tickets themselves.

You should cancel reserved tickets if you will not be using them. Failure to do so may result in charges levied by the carrier. Note the date, time of your cancellation, and the name or code number of the agent that you advised. Unused tickets must be returned to your AO or Travel Management Center.

Requirements which authorize you to use cash payments for procurement of common carrier transportation and related expenses, in lieu of your government-issued credit card, or centrally billed account, are specified in 41 CFR 301-72.200 and 301-51.100. Cash payments are generally permitted:

1. To obtain passenger transportation services, in an emergency, for any amount when authorized by your District Director (DD) and documented on your T.O. Otherwise, cash and personal credit cards may not be used for transportation expenses exceeding $100.00.
2. To pay air excess baggage charges up to $15.00 for each leg of a trip.

When cash is used, claim a reimbursement on your travel voucher and submit your ticket stubs or other appropriate receipts. You must also explain the circumstances for using cash on your travel voucher. See IOM 1.2.7 for mandatory statements required on a travel voucher.

1.2.1.1 - Air

It is FDA's policy to require all travelers to use coach class service for official travel. A contract air carrier must be used unless one of three approved exceptions is met and your District Director approves another carrier. See your fiscal clerk for further information. Justification for use of non-contract carriers must be approved on the Travel Order by the Regional Food and Drug Director (RFDD), DD or Administrative Officer, or on the voucher, if "after the fact." Refer to Federal Travel Regulation (FTR) 301-10.107 and 301-10.108 for the mandatory use of a contract city-pair fare.

Exceptions to using City Pair Program are:

1. Contract service is not available in time to accomplish the purpose of your travel
2. Use of contract service would require you to incur unnecessary overnight lodging costs that would increase the total cost of the trip
3. Contract service is outside normal working hours
4. A non-contract carrier offers a lower fare (available to the general public), the use of which will result in a lower total trip cost to the Government
5. Cost effective rail service is available and is consistent with mission requirements

The Associate Commissioner for Management must authorize First Class travel. The use of first class travel must be pre-approved, and such approval will not be granted, even for medical reasons, unless business class is not available.

The National Defense Authorization Act for Fiscal Year 2002, Section 1116 specifically states that federal employees may retain for personal use promotion items, including frequent flyer miles, earned on official travel. Normally it is the policy of the Government that employees generally must travel by coach class accommodations. However, you may upgrade your transportation class to premium service e.g. business class/first-class with your personal funds or your frequent flyer miles based on regulations found in FTR 301-10.123 and 301-10.124.

Accommodations other than coach will be approved if in met in accordance with the FTR and the NTEU-MOU for foreign inspections.

Consistent with FTR 301-12.2, you may be reimbursed expenses related to baggage, but you should be prudent and only request reimbursement for reasonable excess baggage authorized and approved in advance on the travel order.

Please see the FTR on the GSA website for additional information.

1.2.1.2 - Auto Rental

GSA and the Department of Defense (DOD) both provide employees with a nationwide commercial auto rental program. The Federal Travel Directory, published monthly on floppy diskette, contains a list of vehicle leasing companies participating in this program. Agency policy dictates leasing the least expensive auto to satisfy the transportation requirements.

Commercial auto rental is available when specifically authorized by a special or blanket T.O. You will be reimbursed for rental expense when it is properly vouchered and your receipt is attached to your travel voucher.

Optional Collision Damage Insurance known as CDW will not be reimbursed. Participating rental companies have agreed to settle any claim for damages with the FDA. It is important to note that only damages incident to official travel will be covered by this agreement. If an investigation shows your vehicle damage or personal injury was the result of your unauthorized use of a rental vehicle, you may be personally liable for all related costs. See IOM 1.2.2.3 -Liability.

CDW is required for foreign travel and will be reimbursed. See the Guide to International Inspections and Travel, 211.7 - Auto Rental.

Travelers are required to adhere to the same rules and regulations covering government owned vehicles when using a rental car while on official business.

1.2.1.3 - Taxi

Reimbursements for the use of taxicabs will only be allowed when authorized on your T.O. Allowable tips are 15% of the reimbursable fare. Receipts are required for fares over $75.00.

You will be reimbursed for the usual cab and/or airport limousine fares plus tip from your home/office to the common carrier terminal on the day you depart on an official overnight trip, and upon your return. In lieu of cab, you may use your personal car at a mileage rate not to exceed the cab fare plus tip. See your administrative personnel for current mileage rates, the maximum allowable taxicab fares, and other pertinent details.

1.2.1.4 - Accident Insurance

The government will not pay or reimburse you if you purchase accident insurance. Obtaining accident insurance is at your expense since you are covered while on official business by workmen's compensation insurance. See IOM 1.2.1.2 for payment of insurance on rental cars.

Many insurance policies will not cover you if you perform any duties connected with your job while on an interstate transportation carrier. This could affect you if you perform on-board inspections under the Interstate Travel Sanitation Program during a trip.

1.2.1.5 - Gainsharing

The Government Employees Incentive Awards Act, 5 USC Paragraphs 4501-4507, authorizes an agency to pay a cash award for "efficiency" or "economy". FDA in conjunction with the National Treasury Employees Union (NTEU) implemented a Gainsharing Travel Savings Program which rewards you if you save the FDA money while you are on temporary travel (TDY). Your participation is optional. The Agency's gainsharing policy as well as filing instructions for gainsharing claims can be found by accessing OFM's website.

1.2.2 - Government Furnished Vehicles (GFVs)

GFVs are provided for official purposes only. The term "official purpose" shall be interpreted strictly, and not construed to mean mingling of official business with non-official business. Using a GFV for sightseeing, personal business, personal convenience or preference will be construed as unauthorized use of a GFV. The distance involved in any such misuse is irrelevant. The following is an excerpt from the DHHS Travel Manual Appendix A 1-2.6a., dated May 31, 1988 which further defines official purpose:

"Use of Government-furnished Vehicles."

a. "Use limited to official purposes - When a Government furnished vehicle is used by an employee for official travel, its use shall be limited to official purposes (31 U.S.C. 638a) which include transportation between places where the employee's presence is required incident to official business; between such places and places of temporary lodging when public transportation is unavailable or its use is impractical; and between either of the above places and suitable eating places, drug stores, barber shops, places of worship, cleaning establishments, and similar places necessary for the sustenance, comfort, or health of the employee in order to foster the continued efficient performance of Government business."

You are responsible at all times for the proper care, operation, maintenance, and protection of a GFV. If you willfully or knowingly use or authorize the use of a GFV for other than official purposes, you are subject to suspension or removal.

1.2.2.1 - Interagency Motor Pool

GFVs for district operations are furnished by the regional GSA motor pool. Be guided by the district operating procedures in effect for the appropriate regional pool.

Vehicle Operation - You are required to have a valid state, District of Columbia, or commonwealth operator's permit for the type vehicle to be operated, and a valid DHHS identification document (i.e. Agency ID card, credentials, building pass, etc.).

Each district has working arrangements for the repair and maintenance of vehicles, either with GSA contractors or the GSA motor pool. It is your responsibility to adhere to those safety and maintenance checks. Do not operate cars known to be mechanically unsafe. Handle emergency repairs in travel status in accordance with your District and GSA motor pool procedures.

Purchase gas and oil for your GFV with GSA Credit Cards. Make emergency purchases with cash only when the GSA Credit Card is refused. Your receipts are required by the GSA motor pool. Provide for the safe and proper overnight storage of GFVs while you are in travel status, and put the charges on your travel voucher.

You are responsible for all traffic violations, including parking fines, you incur during the use and operation of a GFV. See DHHS Material Management Manual Section 103-38-052.1.

Allowance - While on official business, you may be reimbursed for parking fees or overnight storage charges. Put these charges on your travel voucher. Receipts are required when available.

Bridge, ferry and road tolls may be paid in cash. Put these charges on your travel voucher. Receipts are only required for amounts over $75.00.

1.2.2.2 - Accidents

Immediate Action - Render first aid. If you are injured, obtain emergency treatment. Contact police.

1.2.2.2.1 - Information to be obtained

Information to be obtained:

1. Description of vehicles involved, including license numbers
2. Name, address and other pertinent information about drivers and owners of other vehicles; exchange state driver license information if possible
3. Names, addresses and signed statements of witnesses
4. Names, official affiliation of investigating police officers
5. Photographs of the scene and the damage
6. Make no statements as to responsibility for the accident, except to your supervisor or investigating official.

1.2.2.2.2 - Reporting

Report the accident to the police after rendering emergency first aid to the injured. Telephone your supervisor and the chief of the motor pool from which the vehicle is assigned, unless your supervisor advises you the district will handle it.

1. Complete the following forms and submit as required:
   a. "Motor Vehicle Accident Report" (SF-91)
   b. Copy of an traffic regulations or ordinance which was violated
   c. Results of any trial or disposition of summons if any arrests were made or charges preferred.
   d. "Claim for Damage, Injury or Death" (SF-95) or other written notification of an incident accompanied by a claim. (SF-95 or statement constituting a claim must be date-stamped by the office initially receiving the claim to document the exact date the claim was received.) To be completed by claimant/non-government employee.
   e. Investigation Reports and Policy Reports
   f. Statement of Witness (SF-94)
   g. Itemized receipt of payment for necessary repairs or two itemized written estimates of cost of repairs
   h. Statement listing date of purchase, purchase price and salvage value where repair is not economical
   i. Photographs of damage and/or scene of accident if available
2. File reports to comply with all local and state laws dealing with accident reporting. Keep copies of all reports made and attach them to the federal accident report.
3. Check with your personal insurance carrier for their requirements.
4. Immediately submit to your supervisor any notice, summons, legal paper or claim, which may subsequently arise from the accident.
5. Check with your district safety officer to determine if additional reports or information are needed.

1.2.2.3 - Liability

The Federal Drivers Act (28 U.S.C. 2679(a)-(e)) was enacted to protect government drivers from personal liability while driving within the scope of their employment. This means you must be on official business to be covered. It relieves you from the burden of acquiring private automobile liability insurance for driving while on the job.

The government's exclusive liability provided by this Act is predicated on its status as employer, without regard to whether the vehicle involved is government owned or privately owned.

The Military Personnel and Civilian Employees' Claim Act of 1964 allows for claims against FDA by employees, provided the loss or damage was within the scope of their employment and the employee (claimant) is free of negligence regarding those losses (See IOM 1.2.2.3.1). The Federal Tort

Claims Act provides for claims generally coming from outside the Agency where the activities of the Agency or specific individual employees are negligent and cause death, injuries, or property loss or damage (See IOM 1.2.2.3.2).

Claims should be submitted through your Administrative Office to the Office of Shared Services, Fleet Manager, HFA-720, 12345 Parklawn Drive, Rockville, MD 20857. The claim will be reviewed and forwarded to Program Support Center (PSC) for processing.

1.2.2.3.1 - Military Personnel and Civilian Employees' Claim Act of 1964

Documentation and information is to be submitted as follows for military personnel and civilian employees' claims under the Military Personneland Civilian Employees' Claim Act of 1964.

Claims Involving Household Moves:

1. "Employee Claim for Loss or Damage to Personal Property" (HHS-481)
2. Schedule of Property
3. Household Inventory showing items claims
4. Other documents that may provide evidence of damage or loss
5. Proof of Ownership
6. Cost of Repair (if damage is over $50.00 submit receipt of cost of repair or estimate of cost on company letterhead)
7. Photographs if available
8. Copies of private claims if applicable (claims must be filed seeking recovery from carrier before FDA claim can be filed.)

Claims Involving Property Loss or Damage:

1. "Employee Claim for Loss or Damage to Personal Property" (HHS-481)
2. Schedule of Property
3. Proof of Ownership
4. Cost of Repair (if damage is over $50.00 submit a receipt for the cost of repair or estimate of cost on company letterhead)
5. Photographs if available
6. Copies of private claims if applicable
7. Police report and/or other agency report and witness statements if appropriate

Motor Vehicle Accidents - See IOM 1.2.2.2

1.2.2.3.2 - Tort Claims

Tort Claims can be filed by any individual who states that they have suffered personal injury or property damage or loss resulting from the action of an

FDA employee or Commissioned Officer who was acting within the scope of employment.

Property Damage or Personal Injury

1. "Claim for Damage, Injury or Death" (SF-95) or other written notification of an incident accompanied by a claim. (SF-95 or statement constituting a claim must be date-stamped by the office initially receiving the claim to document the exact date the claim was received.)
2. Investigation Reports and Policy Reports
3. Statement of Witness (SF-94)
4. Itemized receipt of payment for necessary repairs or two itemized written estimates of cost of repairs
5. Statement listing date of purchase, purchase price and salvage value where repair is not economical
6. Photographs of damage and/or scene of accident if available

1.2.2.3.3 - References

FDA Staff Manual Guide 2260.1

Military Personnel and Civilian "Employees' Claims Act of 1964 Directive 495.1 - Claims Under The Military Personnel And Federal Tort Claims Act http://www.law.
cornell.edu/uscode/html/uscode28/usc_sup_01_28_10_VI_20_171.html

HHS and PHS General Administration Manuals (Chapters 4-00, 4-10, 4-30, 40-35)

1.2.2.4 - Use of a GFV Between Your Residence and Place of Employment

Use of government owned, or leased autos between your residence and place of employment, is approved by the Secretary, DHHS, for certain job series as stated in FDA Staff Manual Guide (SMG) 2173.1. The use of a DHHS-16 "Request to use Government Furnished Vehicle for Transportation between Domicile and Place of Employment" is no longer required, however, local management may continue to use the form or establish a verbal approval process, if desired. The Daily Log of Government Vehicle (Form FDA-3369) must be maintained by all approved persons using a GFV, assuring that all items indicated on the form are completed for each trip. The DHHS now requires that each person taking a GFV home, in order to perform field work, must indicate in Column 10 on the Form 3369, the location of their residence. The Daily Log must be kept for at least a period of three years and must be available for audit purposes. The use of Form DHHS-17 "Quarterly Report on use of Government-Owned or Leased Vehicles between Domicile and Place of Employment" is no longer required.

1.2.2.5 - Care & Custody of U.S. Vehicles

GSA has issued instructions on the use and protection of U.S. Government vehicles, Government National Credit Cards, and car keys. The parts of these instructions applicable to you while the car is in your custody are:

1. The car should be locked when parked in public areas, in private lots, or in open government parking areas.
2. The operator is responsible for the keys and the credit card. They should be removed from the vehicle and carried whenever the vehicle is parked.
3. The keys and credit card are returned to the motor pool office when the vehicle is returned. These items should be kept in a safe place at the office if the vehicle is stored at other than a motor pool location.
4. The credit card must be removed when a vehicle is left at a garage or service station and the keys remain with the garage or station attendant.
5. The credit card may only be used to purchase fuel and lubricants or other items listed on the back of the card for the vehicle identified, and not used for other vehicles.
6. Before signing a service ticket, check for accuracy. Be sure the imprinted address is legible, and write the vehicle mileage (odometer reading) on the ticket.
7. The use of tobacco products is prohibited in government-owned or commercial, leased vehicles

1.2.3 - Privately Owned Vehicle (POV)

On official business, you may use your POV instead of a GFV, if authorized. However, reimbursement for mileage will not exceed the cost of using a GFV. You should carry a set of government accident reporting forms whenever you use your POV for official business. See IOM 1.2.2.2.2 for accident reporting requirements.

Allowances - In general, the mileage allowance is in lieu of all expenses of operating your POV, except tolls. Unless otherwise authorized, reimbursement is limited to the cost of travel by common carrier. Standard highway guide mileage may be used in lieu of odometer readings for direct travel from one town to another. Explain any extra mileage on your travel voucher.

1.2.3.1 - Accidents

The Federal Employee's Compensation Act (Workmen's Compensation) protects employees against losses due to personal injuries received while operating POVs on official business.

Under the Federal Driver's Act [28 U.S.C. 2679(a)-(e)], you are immune from any civil liability to other parties for property damage, personal injury, or death resulting from operation of a vehicle within the scope of your employment. This immunity applies whether the vehicle involved is a GFV or POV. The government would defend any such claim or suit, and would pay any damage award to the injured party.

If an accident was caused by your negligent operation of a vehicle, and your vehicle is damaged, the cost of repairing your vehicle will not be paid for by the government. You should look to your own private insurance carrier for reimbursement, payable under the terms of your own automobile insurance policy. You are protected from liability by the Federal Drivers Act. See IOM 1.2.2.3 for further information on this.

If the accident is determined not to have been caused by your negligence, the provisions of the Military Personnel and Civilian Employees Claims Act (31 U.S.C. 240-243) would be applicable. Under this Act, you would be reimbursed for the deductible portion of the repair not covered by your own automobile insurance policy, up to a maximum of $250.00 deductible. (You may also collect from the other party's insurance.) Form DHHS-481, Employee Claim for Loss or Damage to Personal Property, should be obtained from, completed, and submitted to the Office of Shared Services, Fleet Manager, HFA-720, 12345 Parklawn Drive, Rockville, MD 20857, with evidence establishing that the use of a POV was authorized for official purposes and that the accident was not caused by your negligence.

Employee Liability - see IOM 1.2.2.3.

Reporting - Report vehicle accidents as instructed in IOM 1.2.2.2.2.

1.2.4 - Per Diem and Subsistence

Subsistence is the cost of lodging, meals, tips, and the miscellaneous expenses you incur while in travel status. Per Diem is based on the actual cost of lodging, plus a set amount for "Meals and Incidental Expenses" (M&IE), not to exceed the maximum rate for the prescribed city or area. Note: For domestic travel only, report lodging taxes separate from lodging expenses and claim them in the "Other" column on your travel voucher. Foreign travel taxes still remain a part of your lodging expenses.

Lodging expenses should be paid using your government-issued credit card, when possible. The credit card bill will be mailed directly to you. It is your responsibility to pay the bill on time. The FDA will reimburse late charges on your bill only when you can show the late payment was due to late reimbursement of funds by the FDA.

Accurately record all of your expenditures. Document the date of your departure from each point where your duty is performed. Be guided by your district's policy for where to record this information, e.g. in an administrative diary, etc.

Administrative Notes - Your regulatory notes (See IOM 2.1) should not contain notes of a purely administrative nature (documentation of travel, expenses [tolls, sample costs, etc.], fiscal data, mileage, etc.) These administrative notes can be documented in some kind of an administrative diary. They do not need to be kept in a permanent record other than the completed Travel Voucher, Claim for Reimbursement for Expenditures on Official Business, Receipt for Samples, etc. Follow your district's requirements for maintaining this information.

1.2.4.1 - Per Diem Rates

Consult your supervisor or administrative personnel for specific rates for specific locations or at the ERIC website.

Per Diem commences when you depart your home, office, or other point of departure, and terminates when you return to your home, office, or other point. This applies whether you are traveling by auto or by common carrier.

The M&IE Allowance is 3/4 of the daily rate on the first and last day of travel when overnight travel is involved, and the full daily rate for each intervening day.

M&IE may apply where there is no overnight lodging. However, M&IE will not be allowed for periods of time less than twelve hours.

Your work time plus your total commute time must be greater than twelve hours for you to be eligible for M&IE.

1.2.4.2 - Hospitalized In Travel Status

If, while you are in travel status, you become hospitalized by illness or injury not due to your own misconduct, your per diem continues (even if covered by your health insurance carrier) provided you do not receive hospitalization (or reimbursement therefore) under any Federal statute such as Workmen's Compensation, VA, or military hospital.

Your per diem is calculated on the lodgings-plus system, not to exceed the per diem rate allowed. Check with your district supervisor or administrative personnel.

1.2.5 - Change of Official Station

Effective January 11, 2004, the Office of Financial Services, OSS, centralized FDA relocation services with Prudential Relocation Services. Services provided include: entitlement counseling, transportation of household goods, and travel voucher review and preparation. Access the ERIC website to view the online "Agency-wide Relocation Policy Guide" which provides basic administrative information for employees transferring from one duty station to another within the FDA.

1.2.6 - Advance of Funds

You will use your government-issued credit card to obtain a cash advance from an ATM machine, for official government business only. Ensure your Travel Authorization contains a statement that you are authorized to use an ATM to obtain cash advances and the amount authorized. ATM cash advances may be used to purchase samples. There are usually two fees associated with an ATM cash advance. The "Terminal Fee" assessed by the ATM terminal's owner/supplier and the "Cash Advance Fee" assessed by the bank. Currently, the Cash Advance Fee is 1.5% of the total ATM advance; or 1.5% x $(Cash advance amount + ATM Terminal Fee). The Cash Advance Fee is described in your credit card agreement. These amounts must be included on the Travel Authorization/Voucher along with receipts before reimbursement can be made.

If you do not have a government travel card and are required to travel, please see your administrative officer about receiving a travel advance. For further information, see Staff Manual Guide 2343.1 Government Travel Card and ATM Advance Programs.

1.2.7 - Claims for Reimbursement

Within five days after each trip, submit your electronic claim for reimbursement (Travel Voucher) using GovTrip. Expenses for local travel for meetings and/or field work are also claimed using GovTrip. All travel vouchers are processed electronically. See www.govtrip.com for web-based training information.

Travel Voucher Preparation - Clerical procedures vary from district to district, so consult your supervisor or administrative officer for instructions. State all items in chronological order. Show your mode of transportation and if accompanied, the names of the other travelers.

Show your date of departure and return to your official duty station, and when periods of leave commence and end. Show all points where costs are incurred.

Mandatory Statements Required on Travel Voucher - See IOM Exhibit 1-1 for allowable expenses, receipts required, etc.

Leave Taken in Travel Status - If you take any type of leave while in travel status, include a statement on your travel voucher that you apprised your timekeeper of the amount and type of leave taken. The timekeeper must initial your voucher to show that the leave has been recorded.

Reimbursable Expenses - Explain the necessity for unusual expenditures such as rental equipment, stenographic services and emergency charges (See IOM Exhibit 1-1). The following cash purchases are reimbursable when accompanied by necessary receipts (see Documentation below):

Travel costs such as road and bridge tolls, storage and parking for government cars, and handling of official (not personal) baggage.

Costs for samples and the necessary casual labor charges for their collection and packing. (See IOM 4.1.4.1(4) Official Samples.)

Telephone and telegraph expenses. Document that the use was for official purposes. For local telephone calls, show the number of calls only and the total cost each day.

Emergency purchases (flashlights, batteries, photographic film, jars, or dry ice for samples, etc.)

Coveralls or lab coat laundry while in travel status

Personal laundry while in travel status within continental U.S. (CONUS) for four or more consecutive nights

Documentation - Except for samples, all cash payments should be supported by itemized invoices or receipts signed by vendor, if possible. If you are unable to furnish receipts when submitting your voucher, explain that on the voucher.

Receipts for registration fees at meetings are required regardless of the amount. See Exhibit 1-1.

1.2.8 - Telephone Communications

Commercial - Local, official telephone calls are reimbursable. When placing an official call from a non-government phone, use your government-issued calling card, call collect if permitted by your District's policy, or call commercially and claim reimbursement on your travel voucher.

Commercial calls from hotels or motels should be made using your government-issued calling card, whenever possible. If not possible, they should be claimed on your travel voucher and be supported by the phone bill. Calls made using a personal credit card or similar billing arrangements should be claimed on your travel voucher if a receipt is available at the time of voucher preparation. Otherwise, a follow-up petty cash voucher should be sub-mitted, supported by a copy of your itemized phone bill, and certification the charge was for official government business.

Calls To Residence - FDA has established the following guidelines under which an employee in travel status for more than one night within the U.S. may be reimbursed for telephone calls home:

Calls should be made as economically as possible.

Calls should be made on the FTS network when possible. If not possible, calls should be made using your government-issued calling card. Telephone calls made with government-issued calling cards are automatically billed to the FDA. You are reimbursed through the voucher system when a surcharge is imposed for credit card calls from the traveler's motel/hotel room. Refer to Staff Manual Guide 2343.2 to determine the maximum allowable reimbursement for telephone calls home.

Districts that have differing union-negotiated agreements regarding telephone calls home while in travel status should be guided by those agreements.

1.2.9 - Itineraries

Since situations arise which necessitate contacting you while in travel status, provide your supervisor with a travel itinerary listing where and how you can be reached.

1.3 - Leave

Annual, compensatory, and sick leave is charged in one-quarter hour increments. Prior approval must be obtained from your supervisor for all leave, whenever possible. If this is not possible, advise your supervisor within the first hour of your workday when you will not be on duty. Questions relating to leave should be directed to your immediate supervisor.

If it is necessary for you to take leave while in travel status, notify your supervisor immediately. Include a specific statement on your travel voucher that you did so.

Refer to the NTEU Collective Bargaining Agreement dated 10/1/99 or the agreement negotiated at your local site for additional information regarding leave issues.

More leave information is also available at http://www.opm.gov/oca/leave/index.asp compensatory time at http://www.opm.gov/oca/pay/html/comp.htm and credit time at http://www.opm.gov/oca/worksch/html/cred_hrs.htm. Information for Commissioned Corps is located in the officers handbook under Leave and Work Schedules on pages 97-100 at http://dcp.psc.gov/eccis/documents/PAM62.pdf.

1.4 - Disclosure of Official Information

You are not to release or divulge any information obtained during FDA investigative or inspectional operations, unless you are authorized to do so and the sharing (regardless of the manner) complies with FDA's information disclosure laws and procedures. This includes information contained in diaries and field notes, except for official issuance of forms or documents to addressees. Do not release any originals or copies of reports, memos, diaries, forms (e.g.: FDA-483, 484, 464, etc.), or similar investigational documents to anyone outside the Agency without express concurrence of district or regional management and without following FDA's laws and procedures (21 CFR 20.85 - federal, 21 CFR 20.88 -state/local, 21 CFR 20.89 -foreign, 21 CFR Part 20 -Freedom of Information Act (FOIA), and 21 CFR Part 21 -Privacy Act). See IOM 1.4.4.

1.4.1 - Subpoena

If you are served a subpoena (commanding your appearance in court) or a subpoena duces tecum, (commanding the production of any record or testimony, or the giving of information relating to official FDA matters), immediately advise your supervisor. You will be instructed by your District officials as to the proper procedures and actions on your part in complying with the subpoena. See 21 CFR 20.1, 20.2 and the Regulatory Procedures Manual (RPM) chapter 10-9, "Testimony; Production of Records; Certification of Records."

1.4.2 - Requests by the Public, Including Trade

Be guided by IOM 1.4.4 on requests for information desired by the public under the Freedom of Information Act (FOIA). Refer to FDA's "Information Disclosure Manual" (IDM) for procedures for sharing non-public information with federal, state, local, or foreign government officials. (See IOM 1.4.3).

In the case of complaints where a sample has been collected from the complainant, your District may inform the complainant of FDA's findings when an examination is actually made of the sample. When you collect a sample from a complainant, and he asks for analytical results, he may be told that the FDA will advise him by letter of the general nature of the findings. See IOM 4.1.7 and IOM 4.4.6.3 for cautions on collecting this type sample.

1.4.3 - Sharing Non-Public Information with Other Government Officials

If you receive requests for non-public information from officials of other federal agencies or from state, local or foreign government officials, be guided by the current IDM published by the Division of Compliance Policy (DCP) (HFC-230). You may not share FDA non-public information with such officials without being authorized to do so under FDA's procedures.

The procedures contained in the IDM on disclosing information to the public or sharing non-public information with officials from other federal agencies, or from state, local, or foreign governments were formerly found in Chapter 8 of the FDA's RPM. With the publication of the IDM, this material no longer appears in the RPM.

The most current IDM is available on the FDA Intranet by visiting the Office of Enforcement's website. Relevant sections on non-public disclosure may be found in the IDM, Section 4 as follows:

Sharing Non-Public Information with Foreign Government Officials,

Sharing Non-Public Information with Federal Government Officials,

Sharing Non-Public Information with State and Local Government Officials

1.4.4 - Freedom of Information Act

Public Law 89-487, the Public Information section of the Administrative Procedures Act, more commonly known as the FOIA, adopts a general rule that, except where specifically exempt, all documents in government files shall be made available to the public. There are various exemptions in certain areas, and it is these that mostly affect your operations in FDA. The regulations exempt certain information, such as personal privacy, deliberative process, open investigatory, as well as a company's trade secrets or confidential commercial information.

1.4.4.1 - Procedures

Study and become familiar with the general provisions of the FOIA and the regulations in the Code of Federal Regulations (CFR) regarding the release of information to the public. In particular, study 21 CFR Parts 20 and 21, 21 CFR 71.15, 171.1, 314.430, 514.11, 514.12 and others, all of which contain provisions regarding confidentiality in various FDA records and documents. Also, see the IDM.

In addition to the FOIA, various other Acts such as the Federal Food, Drug, and Cosmetic (FD&C) Act, the Public Health Services (PHS) Act, and 18 U.S.C. 1905 each contain information relating to the confidentiality of information in government files, and are of particular interest. Special care should be taken to protect the identity of confidential sources. See IOM 5.2.9 for further guidance.

1.4.4.2 - Requests for Documents

No field FDA employee has authority to deny any request for documents, no matter what form the request takes. Authority to deny requests rests with the Associate Commissioner for Public Affairs.

Each field and district office is responsible for the internal handling of requests. Information disclosure personnel, e.g. FOI Officers, designated by their respective RFDD's, are responsible for coordinating the implementation of the regulations, for development of procedures within their organization to handle requests, and for adherence to Fad's laws and procedures regarding the maintenance of confidentiality of non-public information. If you receive a request for information under the FOIA, advise the requester to write to the Food and Drug Administration, Division of Freedom of Information (HFI-35), 5600 Fishers Lane, Rockville, MD 20857. See DFOI's website at http://www.fda.gov/foi/foi2.htm.

1.4.5 - Internal FDA Documents

FDA records that are intended for internal use only, may contain information protected from disclosure to the public by a FOIA exemption. An example would be "work plans."

Work Plans - Do not divulge district work planning operations without authority from your supervisor.

If you receive requests for internal documents or for parts of them, refer to IOM 1.4.4 and IOM 1.10.2.7.

1.5 - Safety

Safety is a responsibility of FDA employees, their supervisors, and the Agency's management. These responsibilities include:

1. The reporting of any hazards or suspected hazards

2. Taking the necessary safeguards to minimize the opportunity for safety problems.

The Agency cannot permit employees or supervisors to disregard established or otherwise reasonable safety precautions and thereby place themselves and/or their fellow employees and/or the Agency's facilities at risk. Refer to IOM 5.2.1.2 - Personal Safety for additional inspectional safety concerns.

Be alert for problems associated with defective or misused equipment or supplies and their possible impact on patients and/or users. Contact your supervisor and/or the headquarters contacts listed in the applicable compliance program as necessary for assessment. The home district of the manufacturer should be notified of product misuse, so it may be brought to the manufacturer's attention for consideration of precautionary labeling or redesign of the product. Fully document these problems, to include the hazard and/or defect observed and whether user actions could be a contributing factor. Documentation should present sufficient data, such as photos and diagrams, to supplement a narrative describing the situation as well as the collection of samples.

When conducting an inspection or collecting a sample in a facility which requires donning personal protective equipment, guidance should be provided by the firm's management as follows:

1. Information about the specific hazards that may be encountered

2. The potential concentrations of these hazards

3. The personnel protective equipment determined to protect against these hazards

The firm's management should be able to provide you with documentation showing how these hazards were determined, what the expected exposures are and how they relate to the Occupational Safety and Health Administration's (OSHA) Permissible Exposure Limit (PEL). It should also offer information about the personal protective equipment that will protect you against a hazardous exposure. If you have any doubts about the hazards or the equipment recommended or provided to protect against them, do not enter these areas. Your Regional Industrial Hygienist or the Office of Regulatory Affairs (ORA) Safety and Occupational Health Manager may be able to help you evaluate the information provided to you, or furnish information regarding the hazard and the recommended personal protective equipment.

If you do not have the specific personal protective equipment recommended by the firm's management, have your District furnish what you need. In some cases, the firm may be willing to provide the necessary personal protective equipment, however if respiratory protection is required, you should not wear any respiratory protection unless your District has a written Respiratory Protection Program and you have been certified by your District's Respiratory Protection Program Administrator as having currently met the requirements of this program. See IOM 1.5.1. It is ultimately your responsibility to ensure that you do not expose yourself to any hazard.

Disaster conditions present inherently dangerous situations. See IOM 8.5.

Operations in the radiological area also pose special dangers. See IOM 1.5.4.2.3. Obtain advice on protective measures from regional radiological health personnel.

1.5.1 - Protective Equipment

1.5.1.1 - Eye Protection

Wear safety glasses during all inspectional activities in which there is a potential for physical or chemical injury to the eye. These glasses should, at a minimum, meet the American National Standard Z87.1-1989 standard for impact resistance. Guidance should be provided by the management of the facility being inspected as to additional eye protection required. Unvented goggles should be worn whenever there is the potential for a chemical splash or irritating mists. Additional eye protection may be required in facilities that use exposed high intensity UV lights for bacteriostatic purposes, tanning booth establishment inspections (EIs), etc. Follow the manufacturer's recommendation regarding eye protection for any instrumentation generating light in the UV or higher energy wavelength range.

1.5.1.2 - Hearing Protection

You should wear hearing protection in noisy areas. The OSHA PEL for employees exposed to noise ranges from 90 decibels for an 8-hour time-weighted average to 115 decibels for 15 or fewer minutes per day. However, risk factors for hearing loss include personal susceptibility, noise intensity, noise frequency, distance from the noise source, etc. The noise reduction rating is provided by the manufacturer of various earplugs and muffs, but also depends on the appropriate fit. The efficiency of muff type protectors is reduced when they are worn over the frames for eye-protective devices.

1.5.1.3 - Protective Clothing

1. Wear safety shoes on inspections, as required.

2. Wear hard hats in hard hat designated areas

3. Use appropriate gloves to avoid slivers and/or splinters when handling rough wooden cases or similar items. Use protective gloves when handling hot items or working around steam pipes, and when handling frozen products or working in freezers. Use protective gloves when handling lead pigs containing radioactive materials to avoid hand contamination. If you are handling solvents, wear gloves that are impermeable to the solvent. Your regional industrial hygienist or the ORA Safety and Occupational Health Manager can provide guidance in the type of gloves to use for a particular solvent.

4. Plan ahead for the clothing that may be required for a particular location or situation. Such clothing includes coveralls, lab coats, freezer coats, rubber or vinyl aprons, and disposable paper-like coveralls.

1.5.1.4 - Respiratory Protection

If it is possible to perform an inspection without entering areas in which respiratory protection is mandated or recommended, do not enter these areas. If you determine it is necessary to enter an area in which you must wear a respirator, you must have documented evidence showing the requirements of the District Respiratory Protection Program have been met prior to wearing your respirator. Your District shall have a written Respiratory Protection Program, as delineated in IOM 1.5.1.4.1.

1.5.1.4.1 - Program Provisions

In any workplace where respirators are necessary to protect the health of the employee, or whenever respirators are required by the employer, OSHA requires the employer to establish and implement a written respiratory protection program with worksite specific procedures according to the requirements in 29 CFR 1910.134. The program must include the following provisions:

1. Procedures for selecting respirators for use in the workplace, and annual fit testing of each employee wearing the selected respirator(s)

2. Medical evaluation of employees required to use a respirator prior to the employee's use of a respirator, and repeated as specified in the Respiratory Protection Program. A medical evaluation can be obtained by contacting your local Industrial Hygienist or Ann Gallman, SERL, phone (404) 253-2214.

3. Procedures for using respirators in routine and reasonably foreseeable emergency situations

4. Procedures for maintaining respirators

5. Training of employees in the hazards to which they are potentially exposed during routine and emergency situations, and in the proper use of respirators including limitations of their use and fit checking procedures each time the respirator is donned

6. Procedures for regularly evaluating the effectiveness of the program. OSHA requires each employer perform an evaluation of any workplace which may contain respiratory hazards. If these respiratory hazards cannot be removed through engineering controls, the employer must provide respirator protection. Do not enter any area you suspect may contain an unevaluated respiratory hazard. Your training should include a determination of the minimum respiratory protection for each type of inspection you may perform. Your regional Industrial Hygienist or the ORA Safety and Occupational Health Manager may be consulted for guidance in the type of respirator, type of cartridge or filter, and the useful life of the cartridge or filter.

1.5.1.4.2 - Firms with Potential Respiratory Hazards

The following list includes situations, which have been identified as having the potential for respiratory hazards:

1. Feed or drug plants where there is a possible inhalation hazard due to airborne particulates.

2. Fumigation or storage facilities where treated grain or produce is encountered, including trucks, vessels, railroad cars, fumigation chambers.

    a. Do not enter any structure or conveyance or sample any product that is being treated with the fumigants Methyl Bromide or Phosphine. If a sampling area is suspected of having been fumigated with methyl bromide or phosphine, and has not been cleared according to the EPA requirements, contact your local industrial hygienist for guidance as to how to ensure that the area is safe to enter. Do not enter the area until it is appropriately aerated and tested. If entry is required using personal protective equipment, you local industrial hygienist can provide guidance to ensure you are using the appropriate respirator and cartridge, and any other protective equipment necessary based upon the fumigant concentration. See IOM 1.5.3.4, Asphyxiation Hazards, and IOM 1.5.4.2 Factory Inspections, for additional cautions related to fumigants.

    b. Areas and/or products being treated with fumigants are required by Environmental Protection Agency (EPA) to be placarded, and the placards not removed until the treatment is complete (usually 12 hours to 4 or more days) and the areas and/or products are clear of fumigant gases (phosphine <0.3 ppm and methyl bromide <1 ppm).

    c. Self-contained breathing apparatus (SCBA) is generally the only respiratory protection gear approved for use in areas being fumigated. It is necessary to follow many other precautions when working around fumigants. See Note on Methyl Bromide and Phosphine at the end of this section for additional information.

3. Facilities using ozone, or where ozone is produced as a by-product of the manufacturing operation.

4. Facilities where sterilizers utilize ethylene oxide gas (EO) - See IOM 1.5.4.2.2 Factory Inspection

5. Grain elevators or other grain storage facilities that potentially contain aflatoxin in the dust.

6. Spice grinders and repackers that potentially produce airborne respiratory irritants such as pepper.

7. Any rodent-infested area. - See IOM 1.5.5.4 Hantavirus Associated Diseases

1.5.1.5 - Health and Hygiene

Inoculations - FDA provides operating field personnel with various inoculations for protection from infection or injury on the job.

The following schedules of shots are recommended:

1. Domestic Work:
    a. *Tetanus:* Permanent immunity through the Tetanus Toxoid series followed by a booster dose every ten years;
    b. *Typhoid:* No longer required even if working in a contaminated environment. Booster dose may be given every three years if desired and requested by employee;
    c. *Smallpox:* No longer required in the U.S.;
    d. *Other:* As required by your specific job.
    e. *Hepatitis B Vaccine:* a synthetic vaccine has been developed and is available to those employees that may be exposed to the virus during the normal course of official duties. Contact your AO to arrange for this vaccination. Keep in mind a vaccination is not to be considered a substitute for good laboratory/field safety practices. This vaccine is specific for Hepatitis B virus (HBV) only, and not for other blood pathogens.

2. Foreign Travel - Check with your supervisor well in advance of planned foreign travel as to specific requirements of the countries to be visited.
    a. *Typhoid:* recommended for travel to areas where typhoid fever is endemic.
    b. *Cholera:* a primary vaccination or a booster within six months is required for traveling to India and Korea. May also be required occasionally for other nations.
    c. *Other:* as required for specific country.

Physical Examinations - There is no requirement for periodic physical examinations. Even so, it is your responsibility to adhere to good personal hygiene and health practices.

If any firm management demands evidence of recent physical examination before permitting inspection, consult your supervisor. A mere request to examine your hands for sores, etc., is not unreasonable. However, do not accede to a physical examination.

1.5.2 - Automobile Safety

Automobile Condition - See IOM 1.6.2.

Prior to driving, check the following:

1. Tires, check for tread wear, etc
2. Mirrors, for proper adjustment
3. Brakes
4. Windshield
5. Lights, headlight, turn signals and brake
6. Gasoline and oil gauges
7. Spare, jack, lug wrench, first aid kit, flares, etc.
8. Fire extinguishers are no longer required in vehicles
9. Seat belts must be used.

Ensure all volatile solvents, either in the sample collection kit or contained in a sampled material, are sealed to prevent contamination of the air in a closed vehicle. Be especially aware of the hazard of transporting dry ice in a closed vehicle. The concentration of carbon dioxide gas can cause drowsiness, or even an asphyxiation hazard, if the dry ice is carried in an unventilated vehicle. See IOM 1.5.3.4 Asphyxiation Hazards.

1.5.3 - Sampling

When you are collecting samples, always be alert for possible dangerous conditions (e.g., poisonous materials or fumes, flammable or caustic chemicals, high places, etc.)

1.5.3.1 - Sample Fumigation and Preservation

Follow safety precautions when fumigating and/or preserving samples. Guidance is as follows:

1. Whenever possible, freeze the sample. If freezing is not practical, contact your servicing laboratory for alternative fumigants and preservatives.
2. When fumigants or preservatives are used, exercise care to limit your exposure to these chemicals. Contact your servicing laboratory for the appropriate precautions necessary with these chemicals.
3. Material Safety Data Sheets (MSDS) for each of these chemicals must be available at each duty site (e.g., District office, resident posts), and can be obtained from your servicing laboratory. These sheets list the hazards involved with these chemicals and precautions to take for use.

You must read and follow the instructions in the MSDS prior to using the chemical. If a measured amount of chemical fumigant or preservative is present at the time of shipping, enclose a copy of its MSDS with the shipped sample. Again, if you have any questions, contact your servicing laboratory.

4. Avoid excessive heat and open flame.

5. Use glass vials or jars with lined lids whenever possible. Depending on the type of fumigant used, some polypropylene containers can also be used.

1.5.3.2 - Electrical Hazards

Many samples are collected in poorly lighted areas, or in older poorly wired buildings. Be alert for low hanging wires, bare, exposed, or worn wires, and broken or cracked electrical outlets.

When you are using portable power tools, etc., be extra cautious of the shock hazard. See Inspectors Technical Guide # 22 regarding Ground Fault Circuit Interrupters, and use one if feasible.

1.5.3.3 - Physical Hazards

Be alert for dangerous conditions on all sampling operations. If it is necessary to use a flame to sterilize sampling equipment, use extreme care.

All flammable liquids in your sampling kits must be in metal safety cans. See IOM 4.3.6.1.2

Care must be taken when handling sharp objects, e.g.; knives, syringes with needles, glass, etc. If it is necessary to sample such objects, take care in packing the sample to avoid injuring anyone who handles the sample later. Place them in a rigid container, e.g. glass jar, plastic box, etc. In addition, state in the Remarks or Flag Section of the Collection Report (C/R) (FDA-464) that a syringe and needle were collected as part of your sample.

1.5.3.3.1 - Railcars

Railcars:

1. When sampling, make sure doors are propped open to avoid accidental closing if the car is bumped while you are in it.

2. Display a warning flag or similar device to alert others you are in the car. If possible, have a railroad yardman present.

3. When entering the car, make sure the ladder is secure.

4. On hot days, or after a car has been fumigated, it should be aired out prior to entering, preferably by opening both doors.

5. Observe "No Smoking" in rail cars.

6. Don't crawl under railcars - go around them.

7. Avoid any cables between the railroad tracks. These are often used to move cars on sidings. A cable snapping taut can kill or maim.

1.5.3.3.2 - Grain Elevators

Grain Elevators:

1. Prior to use, make sure man lifts are operating properly.

2. Make sure cross-rungs on ladders are safe.

3. When stepping off ladders or man lifts, be sure the floor is actually a floor and not a bin covered with canvas, cardboard, or other temporary non-supportive cover.

4. Make sure walkways between bins are sturdy.

5. Use caution when sampling from high bins or tanks. Wet or icy conditions may prevail, so check these conditions.

6. When brass grain bombs are used to collect bin samples, do not drop the bomb to the surface of the grain. This could cause sparks if it hits the bottom or side of a bin. Lower the bomb gently to the grain surface, then raise it four to five feet and let it fall to the grain surface to collect the sample. Do not use steel grain bombs; use only brass bombs for sampling.

7. Do not use flash units in dusty areas because of the possibility of explosion hazard. See IOM 5.3.4 for additional information.

1.5.3.3.3 - Clothing

Clothing:

1. Do not wear loose fitting clothes when collecting samples or conducting inspections, the clothes could catch on equipment or conveyor belts and lead to injuries.

2. Do not carry notebooks, credentials, etc., in the outer pockets of your inspectional uniform because they could fall into the equipment.

3. Steel mesh gloves should be worn when cutting portions from frozen products such as fish, etc.

1.5.3.3.4 - Trucks

Make sure any truck you enter during sampling and/or inspection will remain stationary while you are in it.

1.5.3.4 - Asphyxiation Hazards

1. Prior to entering closed areas, ascertain if they have been fumigated and, if so, air them out prior to entering.

2. When sampling or inspecting at rendering plants or fishmeal plants, be alert to possible hydrogen sulfide accumulations in dump pits and other areas. These fumes can be deadly.

3. Be alert and take proper safety precautions in plants, silos, bins, pits, and any closed areas where semi-solid buttermilk or other liquid dairy products, silage, or other bulk products are stored. If not properly stored, improperly handled, or decomposing, certain products can produce dangerous amounts of carbon dioxide, or other gases, or may deplete the oxygen supply in these areas.

4. When transporting dry ice or packages containing dry ice in your car, have some external ventilation (See IOM 1.5.4.2.1, 4.5.3.5, and 8.5.3 for additional dry ice cautions).

5. When sampling from the top of a grain elevator, do not jump down on top of grain. There may be a cavity caused by crusted grain which could break and result in you being buried in grain, or being in an atmosphere of fumigating gas.

6. Be alert when entering storage areas having controlled atmospheres, e.g., where oxygen has been replaced by carbon dioxide to prolong fruit storage, added sulfur dioxide for preservation purposes, etc. These areas must either be aerated prior to entering, or Oxygen Breathing Apparatus (OBA) must be used.

1.5.3.5 - Radioactive Product Sampling

The sampling and viewing of radiopharmaceuticals may be accomplished working through a lead shield or viewing through lead glass and using protective clothing latex gloves and tongs to prevent exposure to "unnecessary" radiation.

1.5.3.6 - Chemical Hazards

You may be assigned to collect samples of FDA regulated products involved in a wreck where chemicals pose a threat, or in areas of chemical spills or hazardous waste sites. In such instances, unprotected personnel are not permitted into hazardous zones. You will be permitted into those areas deemed safe, however, consult with the on-site DHHS Coordinator, usually an employee of the Agency For Toxic Substances and Disease Registry (ATSDR), to ascertain if any safety precautions are necessary on your part. Follow instructions provided. See IOM 3.2.12 for further information and for the address and phone numbers of the ATSDR contacts.

1.5.3.7 - Carbadox Sampling

Concentrated Carbadox (above 95%) has a severe dust explosiveness rating, is a flammable solid, and is also carcinogenic. The only approved source of Carbadox in the US is "Mecadox 10", a medicated pre-mix at a 2.2% concentration.

High concentrations of Carbadox (up to 99%) have been found during investigations of illegal bulk drugs. Some have been falsely labeled as Mecadox. Carbadox, in its pure form, is a minute yellow crystal. It is considered dangerous. Do not collect physical samples of any bulk substance identified or represented as Carbadox or Mecadox. The Center for Veterinary Medicine (CVM) will take action on documentary samples.

If there is no labeling and/or a dealer refuses to identify any yellow powder, inform the dealer of the hazards of Carbadox. Contact your supervisor before collecting any samples of suspected Carbadox. If instructed to collect a sample, use extreme caution and proceed as follows:

1. Wear disposable gloves
2. Use a respirator or other effective means to avoid breathing the dust. Paper masks are not adequate
3. Use goggles
4. Do not sample in drafty places
5. Use only plastic bottles with plastic caps
6. Collect only 1-2 oz. per sub
7. Cover material collected with at least an equal amount of distilled or deionized water and gently mix. It is preferable to use too much water than not enough
8. Note on collection report (CR) the approximate amount of water added to the bottle of suspect product
9. Protect subs from excessive heat and do not store in the trunk of car in the sun
10. Store in insulated cartons with ice, if necessary
11. Flag the CR as to possible presence of Carbadox

Notify the receiving laboratory of sample collection.

1.5.4 - Inspections

Many firms pose safety hazards or problems. Some include:

1. Flying glass in bottling plants
2. Explosion hazards from dust
3. Man-lifts which do not operate properly

4. Asphyxiation problems in rendering plants, fish meal plants, fumigated bins in elevators, fumigation chambers and any closed bins or areas

5. Forklifts and other power equipment operated in the plant. Be alert for their presence and avoid being hit.

1.5.4.1 - Man Lifts and Ladders

Many firms have either power or hand driven man lifts for movement between floors. Do not use the man lift if company policy forbids non-employees using them.

Before riding mechanical lifts, make sure safety equipment is installed and operating properly.

When riding power lifts, observe the following safety precautions:

1. Determine ahead of time what floors are serviced by the lift and at which floor you intend to get off

2. Determine safety devices, and how they operate. Check lift for automatic cut off at the top or a safety stop cord

3. Always face the belt when riding the lift

4. Never carry excess equipment or items that protrude and could get caught between floors.

When using hand powered lifts, remember to:

1. Check the foot brake for proper operation

2. Check if control rope is firmly fastened at the bottom

3. If lift has a stop pin which must be removed prior to use or after use, determine how it is used and use it

4. Check counterbalance of lift, and add or remove weights if necessary

5. Never free-fall on the lift when descending; always keep descent in control by using the brake

6. Use gloves to avoid rope burns or slivers from the hemp or metal pull ropes.

Never over-extend a ladder. If possible, have the bottom held by someone while you are using it. Use blocks on base of portable Grain Car Ladders to hold base away from car wall to provide foot space on ladder rungs.

Some mills and elevators have makeshift ladders. Extreme care should be exercised when using these.

1.5.4.2 - Factory Inspection

Inspections of retorts require extra safety precautions. Be alert for live steam and other potentially dangerous heat sources. Do not enter a retort if your safety cannot be assured. When it is necessary to enter a retort, inform plant management. If firm has safety interlock switches, make sure they are engaged and locked. Have a second investigator or plant management stand outside the retort to assure nothing will happen.

1.5.4.2.1 - Thermal

When inspecting freezers, make sure doors cannot accidentally snap shut and lock you inside. Be alert to ammonia leaks while inspecting freezing and refrigerating operations. Note: ammonia under normal operating conditions retains its chemical stability and will not burn or support combustion. An ammonia leak in a freezer can cause explosions if proper air/ammonia mixtures are reached. It can be toxic if inhaled, and can cause eye and throat irritation. If an ammonia leak is discovered during an inspection, leave the area immediately and notify management of the leak. Warning: If an ammonia-contaminated area must be entered, a full-face mask or self-contained oxygen mask or a gas absorbing canister mask must be worn. Protective clothing is also necessary, if the ammonia concentration is high. If you are unable to obtain the use of the mask and protective clothing, then do not enter the area.

Use care when entering areas where large amounts of dry ice are used or stored. Be sure the area is adequately ventilated prior to entering. See IOM 1.5.3.4, 4.5.3.5 and 8.5.3 for additional cautions concerning use of dry ice.

When visiting facilities handling drug products, check with management to determine if any of the articles produced require special handling or protective equipment, such as respirators.

1.5.4.2.2 - Chemical

When conducting inspections of firm's using chemicals, pesticides, etc., ask to review the MSDS for the products involved to determine what, if any, safety precautions you must take. This could include the use of respirators or other safety equipment.

Ethylene Oxide (EO) - EO is a colorless gas or volatile liquid with a characteristic ether-like odor above 500 ppm. Unmonitored and inadequate ventilation will allow EO buildup of extremely high concentrations, especially in facilities utilizing malfunctioning or leaking equipment. Door gaskets, valves, and threaded fittings are typical areas where leaks have been observed. Additionally, exhaust vents from the sterilizer and the sterilizer room should not be located near air conditioning intake vents, or vented directly into work areas. If the odor of EO is detected, ventilation and containment are inadequate. Leave the area and report the situation to your supervisor for further inspectional guidance. Special EO monitoring equipment is available upon request from DFI for investigators" safety monitoring of inspectional site.

OSHA standard regulating employee exposure to EO is presently 1 ppm over an 8-hour day. You should avoid all unnecessary and preventable exposure to it. This gas has toxic (including possible cancer and reproductive hazards), flammable and explosive properties, and must be used and handled with caution. Adhere to any procedures the firm has established for protection of personnel from over-exposure to EO. Where improper venting procedures or defective equipment are observed, take adequate precautions, i.e., do not enter potentially hazardous areas, and/or wear protective clothing and a respirator. Refer to IOM 1.5.1. 29 CFR 1910.134 contains basic requirements for proper selection, use, cleaning, and maintenance of respirators.

1.5.4.2.3 - Ionizing Radiation

Each investigator who visits a manufacturer of radioactive products or tests ionizing radiation emitting products (e.g., diagnostic x-ray tests) must wear a Thermoluminescent Dosimeter (TLD) to estimate external exposure. These are available in each district; personal alarm dosimeters are also available. These can alert the investigator to high exposure areas during visits to manufacturing firms. Make an estimate of the time spent in areas where radiation is present, and estimate exposure during this time from your personal dosimeter. The estimate can be compared to the results from the TLD badges, which would be processed by Winchester Engineering and Analytical Center (WEAC). Contact WEAC for additional information concerning TLD badges.

Experience has shown there is a potential for internal exposure from inhalation of radioactive material, especially in the case of iodine isotopes. Ingestion of radioactive material from contaminated notebooks, workpads, etc. is also possible.

When you are inspecting radiation-emitting devices and substances, take every precaution to avoid undue exposure or contamination. Time, distance, and shielding are important when working around radioactive materials. Adhere to the firm's established safety procedures and precautions. Where employees are required to wear protective apparel, eyeglasses, or monitoring equipment, follow those procedures. Use protective gloves to avoid hand contamination when handling the lead pigs containing radioactive materials.

Monitoring devices must be used whenever exposure is possible. Monitoring equipment must be calibrated periodically in order to be accurate. There are a variety of meters that can be utilized for radiation protection. Film badges are usually used to determine accumulated amounts of radiation, and unless these are analyzed the exposure dosage is unknown. This will be done by WEAC. Dosimeters will provide a reading at the time of exposure.

1.5.5 - Microbiological Hazards

When processes involve potential for microbiological contamination, normal controls and procedures should contain or protect against any possible hazards. The procedures may include routine use of protective clothing and equipment. Precautions mentioned below concerning gowning, masks, gloves, etc., in this section, are also important in the event that accidents, spills or unexpected, uncontrolled contamination occurs while you are in work areas. If contamination is known in advance to be uncontrolled or you must handle contaminated materials, do not enter an area or handle these materials without first consulting with your supervisor.

1.5.5.1 - Animal Origin Products

Caution: It may be necessary to wear gowns, masks, rubber gloves, etc., when inspecting some of these work areas. Be guided by how the firm's employees dress for their work areas, and dress accordingly. Consult with the firm's management and your supervisor regarding dress and precautions to follow.

When inspecting manufacturers, or collecting samples of animal origin products, be alert for possible routes of contamination that could lead to your injury or illness. Some possible vectors of disease exist, in firms that process products, which use animal origin products as raw materials. They include:

1. *Anthrax* - Care must be taken during inspections of processors of bone meal, dicalcium phosphate and gelatin.

2. *Tularemia* - Use caution when inspecting rabbit processors. Be careful of scratches from bone splinters. Use gloves for protection.

1.5.5.2 - Viral and Other Biological Products

Take proper precautions to protect yourself. If necessary, consult your supervisor and/or district microbiological personnel. NOTE: Inspection of vaccine manufacturers may require inoculation in advance of the inspection to adequately protect the investigator. Contact the Center for Biologics Evaluation and Research (CBER), Division of Viral Products, HFM-445, for guidance.

Methods of transmission include aerosols, which may be created by manufacturing operations (e.g., centrifugation, filling, etc.) or spills. Transmission may occur through inhalation; contact with contaminated objects, including equipment, animals, waste materials, reagents, file cabinets and doorknobs. Transmission can occur through ingestion, inhalation, or through broken skin.

1.5.5.2.1 - Protective and preventive measures

Protective and preventive measures include:

1. Precautions listed in IOM 1.5.5.1 and 1.5.5.3

2. Do not touch. This means equipment, materials, reagents, animals, etc.

3. Wear protective clothing. Evaluate the needs for gowns, caps, masks, gloves, and shoe coverings, and wear them where necessary. Protective clothing worn in a work area where a virus or spore bearing microorganism is handled must not be worn into a work area for another product. Leave all used protective clothing at the firm for proper disposal.

4. Wash hands thoroughly after leaving each work area.

5. Determine if the firm has established safety precautions and procedures, and follow them if adequate.

6. If the firm is processing viruses or other potentially infec-tious biological agents during the inspection, determine if it is advisable to enter the work areas. Chances of infection through aerosols are reduced when there is no active processing.

7. Females of childbearing age are advised not to inspect areas where the Rubella virus is actively processed unless immunity has been established. Infection during pregnancy may result in congenital abnormalities.

8. Vaccines are available for your protection against some organisms (e.g., Rubella). For information on inoculations and physical examinations, refer to IOM 1.5.1.5.

1.5.5.2.2 - Viral Hepatitis and Human Immunodeficiency Virus

Precaution - Blood and Plasma Inspections - Viral Hepatitis and Human Immunodeficiency Virus (HIV), the Acquired Immune Deficiency Syndrome (AIDS) virus - Be alert around blood banks or blood processing operations to the possible dangers of these and other infectious agents.

Keep in mind the following warnings:

1. Do not touch. This means do not handle lab instruments, blood samples, containers or reagents in blood bank labs unless absolutely necessary. Wear lab coats with long sleeves. Disposable lab coats that are impervious to blood are best. These should be left in the laboratory area.

2. Do not smoke, drink, eat or have meetings in the blood banks or in the testing areas for Hepatitis B Surface Antigen (HBsAg), HIV, or any other infectious agents.

3. Consider blood samples, the antigen and antigen testing kits and other associated HIV, HBsAg, and other test reagents as potentially infectious.

4. Consider the possibility of aerosol contamination if there is spilling or splashing of test reagents or blood samples.

5. Use care when placing inspectional or personal equipment in lab areas. Wash hands thoroughly after these inspections. Hepatitis can be transmitted by hand to mouth.

6. Use disposable gloves. Spills may be wiped with a 5% sodium hypochlorite solution and/or solutions such as Wescodyne or Betadine. Autoclaving is the preferred method (121 degrees C for 60 minutes) for sterilizing reagents, samples and equipment.

   Note: When accidental spills, etc. occur in your presence, you are not required to participate in cleaning or disposing of materials. This is the firm's responsibility.

7. Use scrupulous personal hygiene at all times in the blood bank and in the testing areas for HBsAg, HIV, and other infectious agents.

1.5.5.2.3 - Precautions for Non-Clinical Laboratory Inspections

Precaution - Non-Clinical Laboratory Inspections - During inspections/investigations of sub-human primate facilities (e.g., Good Laboratory Practices (GLPs), non-clinical laboratory testing facilities, animal holding facilities, etc.) do not enter rooms housing sub-human primates. Monkeys normally housed in these facilities can carry "Herpes-B Virus", "Simian B Virus", or "monkey-virus". During inspections of this type, use the following guidance:

1. Investigators shall not enter any rooms which hold or house subhuman primates. Bioresearch monitoring (BIMO) inspectional information should be derived from personnel interviews and record examinations conducted outside of the primate areas.

2. All study records usually found in the monkey rooms (Standard Operating Procedures (SOPs); protocols; animal housing, feeding, handling, and care records; animal isolation and health records, room environmental records; dosing and animal I.D. records; animal daily observation records; equipment and room cleaning records, et al.) should be reviewed outside of the rooms.

3. Although contact with subhuman primates in the course of an inspection is prohibited, information on animal room activities may be obtained through personnel interviews.

1.5.5.3 - Bacteriological Problems

Take proper precautions to protect yourself. If necessary consult with your supervisor and/or district microbiological personnel. Possible routes of Salmonellosis include dust inhalation in dried milk and dried yeast plants. Thyroid processing plants may also be a source of this problem.

In no case should you taste any item implicated or suspect of causing injuries or illnesses (e.g., consumer complaint samples, etc.). Handle these with extra care since even minute portions of certain items may cause serious illness or even death (See IOM 8.3.3).

1.5.5.4 - Hantavirus Associated Diseases

Rodents and other small mammals have been identified as the primary hosts for recognized hantaviruses. Infected rodents shed the virus in saliva, urine and feces. The time of this virus' survival in the environment is unknown.

Human infection may occur when contact is made with infected saliva or excreta, through inhalation of aerosol produced when the animals sneeze, or contaminated dust particles are stirred up. In addition, infection can also occur when dried contaminated materials are disturbed and directly introduced into broken skin or onto the conjunctivae.

Hantaviruses can present some or all of the following symptoms: fever, headache, muscle aches, nausea and vomiting, chills, dry cough, and shortness of breath.

Investigators/Inspectors may be subject to an increased risk of infection because of unpredictable or incidental contact with rodents or their habitations, i.e., entering various buildings, crawl spaces and other sites that may be rodent infested.

When encountering or suspecting rodent infested areas, the following protective and preventive measures are recommended:

1. First and foremost, DO NOT HANDLE RODENTS - DEAD OR ALIVE.
2. Be careful when moving items around, excessive dust may increase the risk.
3. To prevent eye contamination, wear goggles or a full-face respirator.
4. High-Efficiency Particulate Air (HEPA) filter masks or respirator cartridges are recommended to avoid inhalation of aerosols. Because of the minute size of the virus, dust masks will likely not filter out the organism.
5. Wear coveralls, and handle and dispose of as infected material.
6. Wear disposable latex or rubber gloves. Be careful to avoid hand contamination when removing gloves. Wash hands thoroughly after removal.
7. In addition to these measures, follow any guidance issued by state health departments.

Anyone who develops a febrile or respiratory illness within 45 days of the last potential exposure should immediately seek medical attention. Inform the attending physician of the potential occupational risk of Hantavirus infection.

1.5.6 - Wireless Devices

The following information is provided regarding the use of wireless devices:

1. If you carry a blackberry, cell phone, or other wireless device, always enquire about a firm's policy with regard to their operation within the establishment as they may pose a safety hazard.
2. The General Services Administration's FMR Bulletin B-2 discourages the use of hand held wireless phones while operating Government owned and commercially leased and rented vehicles.
3. FDA policy [Staff Manual Guide 2173.1] discourages the use of hand held wireless phones or other wireless devices while operating government, commercially leased/rented vehicles. Drivers who use cell phones within their scope of work are required to use hands-free cell phones and other hands-free devices.

1.5.7 - Reporting

Automobile Accidents - See IOM 1.2.2.2 - Accidents, for procedures.

Injuries - If you are injured during the performance of official duties, report immediately to your supervisor. If medical aid is required, obtain it as soon as possible. Check with your supervisor on what accident report forms are required and procedures to be followed.

Note: *Supervisors must refer to Chapter IV - Guide 8, Compensation for Injury, of the DHHS Personnel Guides for Supervisors concerning procedures to follow and forms to be filled out whenever an employee is injured.*

1.6 - Public Relations, Ethics & Conduct

FDA's ethics program is administered to help ensure that decisions made by Agency employees are not, nor appear to be, tainted by any question of conflict of interest. The "ethics" laws and regulations were established to promote and strengthen the public's confidence in the integrity of the Federal Government. The ethics program is available on the FDA intranet and standards of conduct are available at http://www.fda.gov/opacom/ethics/hhssoc.html.

1.6.1 - Public Relations (Press, Radio, TV and non-government meetings)

Over the past few years, the inspectional and investigational activities of the FDA have received extensive coverage in the electronic and print media. Regional and District Directors are the spokespersons for FDA in their respective areas. However, investigators and inspectors are occasionally requested by the media to comment or provide information on their individual inspectional activities. Such requests include being interviewed and filmed during inspections, investigations and sample collections. If media representatives contact you, be courteous and helpful, but refer all requests for information, interviews and personal appearances to your supervisor. You may be permitted to appear on camera or be interviewed, but authorization must be gained in advance. Otherwise, your Regional or District office will handle the inquiry, or refer it to the Assistant Commissioner for Public Affairs (HFI-1) at headquarters.

Do not solicit media interviews or on-camera appearances. In those instances where media request you be interviewed or filmed, the request should be tactfully declined and referred to the district office, your immediate supervisor and/or District Director. There may be occasions when management of a firm you are inspecting invites representatives from the news media to observe the inspectional process. Please see IOM 5.1.4.3 for instructions on how to appropriately handle such events.

FDA publications, press releases and talk papers on a wide variety of subjects are available in your district, and are helpful in answering media and public inquiries. In addition, you should refer them to FDA's Internet Web site. Talk papers, press releases, FDA publications, federal register announcements, etc. are on-line at this Web site.

1.6.1.1 - Non-Government Meetings

Speakers and representation at meetings will be provided when such attendance is for official purposes, and consistent with the policies and best interest of FDA. As a public agency FDA must be responsive to public inquiries of all kinds.

Authorization - Attendance must be authorized in advance. Form DHHS 99 is required, unless the primary purpose of attendance is to officially explain, interpret or acquaint the public with FDA programs or activities.

Selectivity - Selection will not arbitrarily favor one sponsoring organization over another.

Fees - Acceptance of payment in cash or kind must be approved in advance. No such payment may be accepted when inspectional or administrative and/or a supervisory relationship exists between the employee and the non-federal organization offering to pay his/her expenses.

1.6.2 - Equipment Care, Custody, And Loss

Care and custody

You are responsible for the proper care and custody of all government property entrusted to you. This includes:

1. Storing government vehicles in protected off-street parking facilities, when possible.

2. Keeping inspectional and investigational equipment securely locked in the trunk of the car while the car is under your direct control. Do not leave valuable equipment in the car's trunk while the car is in for servicing, unless you stay with the car. Do not leave electronic equipment, such as computers, in the trunk of the car for extended periods in extreme hot or cold weather conditions.

3. Storing all property in safe, secure areas.

Your responsibility for government property in your custody is specified in the Staff Manual Guide FDA 2280.5.

1.6.2.1 - Maintenance of Equipment

First-line maintenance rests with you as, the custodian of the items entrusted to you. You are expected to perform, or have performed, the normal maintenance such as checking oil, tires, battery, windshield wipers, etc. on the GFV you are using. Other equipment requires little or no maintenance as such, other than dusting, replacing batteries and bulbs, making minor adjustments, properly packing in carrying cases, and proper protection as necessary. Common sense, and handling the equipment as if it belonged to you, should suffice.

1.6.2.1.1 - Repairs

Any repairs needed, defects, or inoperative equipment observed, should be immediately reported to your supervisor.

When in travel status, necessary minor repairs to equipment may be obtained locally, if possible, and reimbursement claimed on your travel voucher. Major repairs should be cleared through your supervisor.

1.6.2.1.2 - Equipment Calibration

You are responsible to assure equipment assigned to you is calibrated for accuracy. This includes thermometers, pyrometers, balances, scales, stopwatches, etc. Keep a record of the calibration with each item requiring calibration. Calibration of certain inspectional equipment can be done by your District laboratory.

Stopwatches may be calibrated using the atomic clock at the U.S. Naval Observatory in Washington D.C., using the commercial number at (202) 762-1401 or (202) 762-1069. Calibrate stopwatches at several different time intervals within the expected parameters of use. At least three runs should be made at each interval, then averaged for each interval and the correction factor, if any, entered on the record of calibration maintained with the watch. Calibration of your computer's internal clock can be obtained from the same source. Information and software is available on the U.S. Naval Observatory's Website.

1.6.2.2 - Lost or Stolen Equipment

As soon as you discover any government property assigned to you or in your custody is missing, report it verbally to your supervisor. Normally, you must submit a form GSA-3155, "Offense/Incident Report". Your district should have these in stock. This form must be supplemented by a memorandum detailing the circumstances surrounding the loss, including the comprehensive steps you took to recover the items. The procedure is outlined in the Staff Manual Guide FDA 2280.5.

Follow your district procedures for any additional requirements.

1.6.3 - Official Credentials, Badge

Show your credentials to appropriate firm personnel during all non-undercover investigations, inspections, sample collections, recall effectiveness checks, etc.

1.6.3.1 - Delegated Authority

When you are issued the FDA official forms FDA-200 A&B, certain parts of the Commissioner's enforcement authority, as specified in Staff Manual Guide 1410.32, is re-delegated to you. You are expected to use this authority wisely and judiciously. See IOM 5.1.1.2 on cautions against Xeroxing or photocopying your credentials.

Your investigator badge, if you are issued one, is for use in certain situations to reinforce the official credentials when needed. Check your district Staff Manual Guide, FDA 2280.3, 5b, for situations in which use of the badge may be appropriate.

1.6.3.2 - Qualifications for Credentials

FDA employees engaged in general inspectional and investigational operations are issued FDA-200 A&B credentials. By virtue of their position, these employees are recognized as qualified to perform the duties assigned.

FDA Official Credentials confer extensive inspectional authority on you. Exercise the utmost care of your badge and credentials. Carry them in a manner that will assure positive protection against loss. For example, do not carry them in the upper pockets of your clothing where they may fall out if you bend over. You may not only lose your credentials and badge, but they may, during inspections, fall into vats or machinery resulting in embarrassment and possible financial loss to you as well. Also, carrying your credentials and badge in the glove compartment of your car or leaving them in the pocket of an unattended coat or jacket are invitations to loss or theft.

1.6.3.3 - Lost or Stolen Credentials, Badge

The procedure for reporting loss or theft of credentials and/or badge is in the Supervisory Staff Manual Guide, SMG 2280.3. Notify your supervisor immediately, and submit a written report of the loss or theft to him. If instructed, report the loss or theft to local law enforcement authorities and request the police report identification number. Also ask that the number of the lost credentials/badge be entered into the National Crime Information Center (NCIC). Include this information in your report.

1.6.4 - Business Cards

In June 1999, the FDA determined it is proper to use general appropriation funds to purchase business cards for employees whose interactions with outside organizations further the agency's mission. Due to certain restrictions pertaining to the purchase of business cards, employees should consult with local management prior to purchasing such items, to ensure adherence to agency policy and procedures.

1.6.5 - Employee Conduct

As a government employee of the FDA, as few limits as possible are placed on your interests and activities. Nonetheless, certain limitations are necessary to protect the interest of the government. These constraints are covered the Standards of Ethical Conduct for Employees of the Executive Branch, and consult with your supervisor if you have any questions or concerns in this regard. The Standards of Ethical Conduct for Employees of the Executive Branch can be found on FDA's intranet under the Office of Human Resources and Management Services' (OHRMS) ethics laws.

As you work to advance the health and welfare of the public, seek to maintain the highest standards of ethical conduct. The essence of good government is the personal responsibility that each public servant feels for the public trust he/she holds. You are responsible for complying with the regulations, obtaining advice from your supervisor, personnel or AO, and when required, obtaining advanced approval for certain outside activities.

FDA employees must be persons of unrivalled integrity, and observe the highest standards of conduct. Because of FDA's special regulatory responsibility, its personnel must carry on the agency's business effectively, objectively, and without even the appearance of impropriety. Their actions must be unquestionable, and free of suspicion.

The Standards of Ethical Conduct for Employees of the Executive Branch (5 CFR Part 2635) gives concise details on what is expected, insofar as conduct is concerned. In addition, certain subparts, and Appendix A to Part

73 of the HHS Standards of Conduct, remain in effect. Additional information is also available on FDA's internet at www.fda.gov/opacom/ethics/.

1.6.5.1 - Professional Stature

You are the eyes and ears of FDA, and to most of the public you are their only contact with FDA. Your actions may be the basis upon which they judge the entire FDA. The public expects exemplary behavior and conduct from the government employee. This responsibility applies to both on the job and off the job activities. As you inspect or appraise individuals, you are, in turn, being evaluated. Both the industries FDA regulates and the public-at-large are keenly aware of, and are quick to report, what they consider improper actions by government employees.

When you issue an FDA 483, the firm is provided with information as to how to contact the District Office with such reports and information on the Small Business Enforcement Fairness Act of 1996 (SBREFA), which provides regulated industry a means for addressing industry concerns about government agency enforcement activities. See IOM 5.2.3.1.1. You may receive complaints or other questions from the regulated industry during routine field operations, such as sample collections, investigations, import entry reviews and establishment inspections where an FDA 483 was not issued. In these circumstances, provide the firm the "Information for FDA - Regulated Industry" Website "www.fda.gov/oc/industry." Explain there are Small Business links on the webpage and the FDA Ombudsman link is located under the Contact FDA heading and they may also call the District Office. Document this discussion in your regulatory notes and include it in your Establishment Inspection Report (EIR) in the Discussion with Management section, your Memorandum of Investigation, or the remarks section of your collection report.

If the firm does not have internet access, provide the firm the main District phone number.

1.6.5.1.1 - Integrity

This is steadfast adherence to a strict moral or ethical code. It characterizes a person of deep-seated honesty and dependability, with a devotion to accuracy, objectivity and fairness.

Employees may not use or permit others to use official information not available to the general public for gain or to advance a private interest.

You are expected to conduct yourself in a prudent manner, so that the work of the Agency is effectively accomplished. Your job is to gather and present the facts. Accuracy and objective observation are absolutely essential.

The Office of Internal Affairs (OIA), Office of the Commissioner (OC), is responsible for obtaining factual information for the FDA on any matter relating to allegations of misconduct, impropriety, conflict of interest, or other violations of Federal statutes by Agency personnel. If you uncover or suspect any such problems, report them to your supervisor. The District/Region will contact OIA. 21 CFR 19.21(b) requires the facts be forwarded to OIA, HF-9, in writing. OIA will maintain the anonymity of your complaint, if you so desire.

Under the Federal Managers" Financial Integrity Act, it is your duty to report any serious problems of waste, mismanagement, fraud or misuse of Government funds by any personnel from other agencies or government contractors. These problems should be reported to your supervisor, who will, in-turn, notify the Division of Management Programs (HFA-320).

1.6.5.1.2 - Attitude

Be dignified, tactful, courteous and diplomatic. Make your approach firm but not unresponsive. Do not display strong-arm tactics, an air of superiority, an attitude of special authority, or an over-bearing posture. Do not apologize or justify your request for necessary and authorized information.

1.6.5.1.3 - Attire

Good public relations and practical common sense requires you dress appropriately for the activity in which you are engaged. Consult your supervisor for district policy on normal office attire.

Protective clothing is required for many inspectional tasks. The District provides coveralls or other clothing for this purpose. Failure to wear suitable attire, including head coverings, while the firm's employees are so attired, is indefensible. Plastic foot guards over street shoes are required, if walking on raw materials such as bulk grains, bagged material, etc. Prophylactic measures - to guard against the spread of disease may be required during certain investigations. See IOM 1.5.1 and IOM 5.2.10.

1.6.5.1.4 - Employee Prohibitions - Gifts, Luncheons, and Snacks

The Standards of Ethical Conduct for Employees of the Executive Branch, 5 CFR Part 2635, Subpart B, specifically provide that an employee shall not, directly or indirectly, solicit or accept a gift:

1. From a prohibited source

2. Given because of the employee's official position.

Notwithstanding any of the exceptions provided in Subpart B, an employee shall not:

1. Accept a gift in return for being influenced;

2. Solicit or coerce the offering of a gift;

3. Accept gifts from the same or different sources on a basis so frequent that a reasonable person would be led to believe the employee is using his/her public office for private gain.

The Standards of Ethical Conduct for Employees of the Executive Branch cover many aspects governing employee conduct and provide that an employee shall avoid any action, whether or not specifically prohibited by the regulation which might result in or create the appearance of:

1. Holding a conflicting financial interest

2. Loss of impartiality in performing official duties

3. Using public office for private gain.

An area of concern for inspectional personnel is a setting where, during an establishment inspection, you have lunch with plant officials and/or personnel and find your lunch paid for by them, or there is no way you can pay for your portion of the luncheon.

It is always best for an employee to decline any gift, including meals, offered by a regulated company's staff. However, when circumstances arise where refusal is imprudent or impractical, such as finding your lunch paid for by the firm, be gracious, but make it clear the situation cannot be repeated. Always use your best judgment. Modest items of food and refreshment, such as soft drinks, coffee, and donuts offered as other than part of a meal, are excluded from consideration as gifts.

1.6.5.1.5 - ORA Policy

ORA's policy requires you do not use or consume a firm's products at any of the firm's facilities. This can be interpreted as acceptance a product is satisfactory and could embarrass the Agency, particularly in the event of a subsequent regulatory action against the firm.

1.6.5.1.6 - Professional Personnel Contacts

During inspections and investigations, your activities often involve discussions, conferences, and interviews with professional people.

When dealing with top management officials and other professional persons, your presence may often be disruptive to their activities. Many times you may be squeezed into already crowded schedules and your interviews or investigations may, of necessity, be conducted in offices, waiting rooms, or other areas where customers, patients, or employees are present. If you find yourself in this type of situation, be aware your conversations or activities may be overheard by others.

If it is necessary to review records or conduct interviews, conduct your activities in a quiet and dignified manner. Always try to arrange with management for a private area for this work.

If the person becomes unreasonable, and it is impossible to continue the assignment, terminate the interview and consult your supervisor.

1.6.5.2 - Attempted Bribery

Bribery is the practice of offering something, such as money or a favor, to a person in a position of trust to influence that person's views or conduct. Occasionally, FDA employees experience bribery attempts.

Bribery or attempted bribery of a Federal Officer is a crime (18 U.S.C. 201). If you are offered money or anything else of value, pursue the following course of action:

1. Attempt to obtain a clarification of the offer (e.g., Ask questions like, "What is this for?").

2. Do not accept or refuse the offer. Appear to vacillate, and keep the door open for future contact.

3. Calmly terminate the exchange.

4. As soon as possible, prepare detailed notes concerning what transpired.

5. Contact your supervisor as soon as possible. The District should notify the OCI office immediately. You may be asked to assist the OCI and other investigative bodies by accepting proffered money as evidence, under controlled conditions. Do not participate in any such activity, or accept anything of value outside the controlled conditions of an undercover activity conducted by OCI and/or other involved Federal law enforcement agencies.

1.7 - Interdistrict Assignments

See IOM 1.1 English language requirement. This subchapter defines the procedures for issuing assignments between districts and referring information between Districts and ORA headquarters. FDA has put a new data system in place, Field Accomplishments and Compliance Tracking System (FACTS), which includes the ability to generate assignments. This system should be used whenever possible to issue and manage all assignments. You received training on that process during your basic FACTS training. If you have any questions, contact your FACTS Lead User.

1.7.1 - Issuance Authority

FACTS is the preferred method to generate, issue, and manage assignments for all activities. Memorandums must be used when hard copy attachments accompany the assignment. If mail delay for memorandums is objectionable, overnight delivery is authorized. Use the telephone when urgency requires instant communication; however, all assignments must be entered into FACTS as soon as possible. The receiving District can use the "ad hoc" process in FACTS to generate the assignment in urgent situations. The EIR endorsement shall not be used to make assignments, although it may be an attachment to a written assignment. E-mail the receiving district of an assignment if there is any urgency.

Assignments, excluding recall audit checks, must be approved and signed or issued by a first line manager/ team leader, compliance officer, those acting in these positions, or a higher level of management. Recall audit checks may be signed by the Recall and Emergency (R&E) Coordinator.

Assignments involving three or more districts, or requiring more than three working days to complete, shall be approved by the branch director or appropriate manager of the issuing district. Multiple district assignments need to be closely monitored by the issuing district to avoid unnecessary duplication of work.

1.7.2 - Procedures

Each assignment shall contain the following details:

1. Description of the problem and nature of the assignment, i.e., sample collection, records collection, inspection, etc.
2. Full name, address and the FDA Establishment Identifier (FEI) number of the responsible firm. You may also provide the central file number (CFN) if known or available.
3. Program Assignment Code (PAC).
4. Product code and full description of product including lot number(s) and code(s).
5. Home district code.
6. Full name and address of the firm (or firms) and individual(s) to contact to accomplish the assignment.
7. Priority and requested completion date.
8. Name, telephone number and mailing symbol of the contact person who can answer questions concerning the assignment and the person who should be notified of results.
9. Where to send samples, records, reports, etc.

1.7.3 - Assignments and Reporting

If all the data is contained in the FACTS fields, there may be no need for a separate memorandum.

Assignments for fieldwork are to be sent to the accomplishing district(s). Assignment memorandums, attachments, or other documents needed to complete the assignment should be sent to the appropriate branch director in the accomplishing district.

Copies of assignments which involve emergencies, danger to health situations or highly publicized investigations shall be sent via e-mail or Federal Express (FedEx) to the Emergency Operations Center, HFA-615 (301-443-1240). Completion and referrals - A copy of the Establishment Inspection Report (EIR), C/R, memorandum, etc., showing results should be sent to the person specified in the assignment, along with a copy of the assignment. When an assignment is completed, make sure the appropriate FACTS fields are updated/entered as necessary. Copies of responses to assignments that involve emergencies, danger to health situations, or highly publicized investigations shall also be sent to Emergency Operations Center, HFA-615.

In the case of samples going to a non-FDA laboratory or a Headquarters' laboratory, a copy of the assignment should be printed and attached to a copy of the C/R which is included in the FDA-525.

All documents relating to an assignment shall include the FACTS assignment and/or operation number.

1.8 - Organization Overview

A complete description of the FDA's organizational structure and its functional statement is found in various chapters of the Staff Manual Guides (SMG) which are available on FDA's Intranet Website.

The following is a list of internet websites that contain FDA's organizational structure:

1. http://www.fda.gov/oc/ with organizational charts at: http://www.fda.gov/oc/orgcharts/orgchart.html

2. Center for Biologics Evaluation and Research: with or-ganizational charts at: http://www.fda.gov/cber/inside/org.htm

3. Center for Drug Evaluation and Research: http://www.fda.gov/cder/office.htm with organizational charts at: http://www.fda.gov/cder/cderorg.htm

4. Center for Devices and Radiological Health: http://www.fda.gov/cdrh/organiz.html with organizational charts at: http://www.fda.gov/cdrh/organiz.html

5. Center for Veterinary Medicine: http://www.fda.gov/cvm/aboutcvm.html with organizational charts at: http://www.fda.gov/cvm/Documents/cvm1.pdf

6. Center for Food Safety and Applied Nutrition: http:// www.cfsan.fda.gov/~lrd/cfsan4.html with organizational charts at: http://www.fda.gov/oc/orgcharts/CFSAN.pdf

7. Office of Regulatory Affairs: http://www.fda.gov/ora/ hier/ora_overview.html with organizational charts at: http://www.fda.gov/oc/orgcharts/ora.html

The FDA is a part of the Department of Health and Human Services (HHS). An appointed Commissioner who serves at the discretion of the President heads the agency.

There are approximately 9300 FDA employees.

The FDA is a team of dedicated professionals working to protect and promote the health of the American people.

FDA is responsible for ensuring:

Foods are safe, wholesome, and sanitary; human and veterinary drugs, biological products, and medical devices are safe and effective; cosmetics are safe; and electronic products that emit radiation are safe.

Regulated products are honestly, accurately, and inform-atively represented.

These products are in compliance with the law and FDA regulations; noncompliance is identified and corrected; and any unsafe or unlawful products are removed from the marketplace.

1.8.1 - FDA Principles

We strive to:

Enforce FDA laws and regulations, using all appropriate legal means.

Base regulatory decisions on a strong scientific and analytical base and the law; and understand, conduct, and apply excellent science and research.

Be a positive force in making safe and effective products available to the consumer, and focus special attention on rare and life-threatening diseases.

Provide clear standards of compliance to regulated industry, and advise industry on how to meet those standards.

Identify and effectively address critical public health problems arising from use of FDA-regulated products.

Increase FDA's effectiveness through collaboration and cooperation with state and local governments; domestic, foreign, and international agencies; industry; and academia.

Assist the media, consumer groups, and health professionals in providing accurate, current information about regulated products to the public.

Work consistently toward effective and efficient application or resources to our responsibilities,

Provide superior public service by developing, maintain-ing, and supporting a high-quality, diverse workforce.

Be honest, fair, and accountable in all our actions and decisions.

1.9 - Office of Regulatory Affairs

1.9.1 - Associate Commissioner for Regulatory Affairs

The Acting Associate Commissioner for Regulatory Affairs (ACRA) is Michael A. Chappell, and the Deputy Associate Commissioner for Compliance Policy is Steven M. Solomon, DVM, MPH. The Deputy Associate Commissioner for Field Operations is Michael A. Chappell

ORA is under the leadership of an Associate Commissioner known as the ACRA. This office is responsible for the activities and operations of the field headquarters staff and the field staff of FDA. The Headquarters Office Directors and the Regional Food and Drug Directors (RFDD's) report to this office.

This office advises and assists the Commissioner and other key officials on regulations and compliance oriented matters which have an impact on policy development and execution and long-range program goals.

As of November 2008, there were over 3500 employees in the ORA field organization including ORA headquarters. For ORA contact information, see the ORA Field Contacts Directory at the end of this manual.

Immediate office of ORA:

Special Assistant to ACRA - Amy Waltrip

Regulatory Counsels - Carolyn Becker and Anne Kirchner

Senior Advisor for Risk Analysis – Kara Morgan

QMS – Brenda Holman

Senior Advisor for Science – John Marzilli

ORA Executive Operations - Charlotte Christin

1.9.2 - ORA Headquarters Organization

ORA consists of four individual offices which operate independently of each other. However, their functions are related and they support each other. A description of the function of each office is outlined below.

1.9.2.1 - Office of Resource Management (ORM) (HFC-10), James M. Strachan, Director

The Deputy Director of ORM is Michael W. Roosevelt.

ORM is basically responsible for the planning, management, and evaluation of the operations of the field offices. It is also responsible for the computer systems which handle the information generated by the field offices.

The Division of Management Operations in ORM controls the budget for the field's day to day operations. ORM allocates funds as determined by actual needs of the field and headquarters units.

1. The training of personnel stationed in the field is also coordinated by The Division of Human Resource Development in ORM. ORM has the following divisions:

2. Division of Management Operations (HFC-20)
   Director - Richard Garwood

   a. Management Operations and Analysis Group
      Michele M. Berger, Supervisor

   b. Financial and Program Analysis Group,
      Andrea Oliver, Director

   c. Facilities Management Group,
      Randy Higgins, Supervisor

3. Division of Planning, Evaluation and Management (HFC-40), John A. Lechus, Director

   a. Program Planning and Workforce Mgmt. Branch,
      Carrie Mampilly, Supervisor

   b. Program Evaluation Branch
      Lynnette I. Riggio, Supervisor

4. Division of Human Resource Development (HFC-60),
   Gary German, Director
   Vacant, Deputy Director

5. Commissioned Corps Liaison, Diann Shaffer

6. FDA History Office (HFC-24): John Swann, and Suzanne White Junod, Historians.

1.9.2.2 - Office of Regional Operations (ORO) (HFC-100) David K. Elder, Director

The Director of ORO is David K. Elder. The Deputy Director is vacant. Special Assistant to the Director is Kara Lynch. International Affairs Program Manager is vacant.

ORO coordinates and manages all Agency field operations, Team Biologics Core Team, and the Prior Notice Center on behalf of the ACRA; develops issues, approves, or clears proposals and instructions affecting field activities; serves as the central point within the Agency through which headquarters offices obtain field support services.

It evaluates the overall management and capabilities of the Agency's field organization; initiates action to improve the management of field activities. Coordinates nationwide health fraud activities between the field, states, and Headquarters organizations. Coordinates field public affairs and information programs; distributes timely information to the field; coordinates activities with Agency counterpart organizations. Serves as the Agency focal point in developing and maintaining international regulatory policy and activities to assure the safety, efficacy, and wholesomeness of regulated imported products. Coordinates Agency procedures with Headquarters and field offices and is the primary contact with the U.S. Customs Service and others among those offices. Develops and/or recommends to the ACRA policy, program, and plans for applied research relating to Agency enforcement problems; coordinates such research efforts with appropriate agency components. Directs and coordinates the Agency's emergency preparedness and civil defense programs. Provides other Agency components with laboratory support in highly specialized areas.

ORO has the following components:

1.9.2.2.1 - Division Of Field Investigations (HFC-130)

Michael C. Rogers, Director 301-827-5653

Patricia Alcock, Deputy Director 301-827-5653

DFI provides coordination, direction, assistance, and management for the field's domestic and foreign investigative activities. It serves as the Agency focal point for Headquarters/field relationships on investigational and inspection problems, and programs and operations.

It develops and reviews investigative and inspectional procedures, training programs, and prepares and issues investigative and inspectional guidance manuals. The division provides the field investigative and engineering technical assistance and guidance for foreign inspections.

DFI has two branches: Domestic Operations Branch and International Operations Branch. The Division's deputy director manages ORA's National Experts.

Gerald D. Bromley, Jr. is the Director of the Domestic Operations Branch, and Rebecca Ramos Hackett is the Director of the International Operations Branch. They may be reached at 301-827-5653.

The following personnel within the Domestic Operations Branch are available to help you in various program related activities and may be reached at DFI's main number 301-827-5653 or at the numbers below:

James Dunnie	Human Drugs, Veterinary Drugs	301-827-5652
Norman Fogg	Foods	301-827-5645
Vacant	Medical Devices	
Gail Katz	Biologics	301-827-3357
Ruark Lanham	Bioresearch Monitoring, Good Laboratory Practices (GLPs)	301-827-6691
Barbara Marcelletti	Foods, Seafood HACCP	301-827-5635
Vacant	Bioresearch Monitoring, Clinical	
Vacant	Biologics, Microbiology	

Personnel responsible for foreign inspections and trip planning in the International Operations Branch:

Linda Adams	Drugs	301-827-5648
Olaide Akimade	Drugs	301-827-3902
Oumou Barry	Biologics	301-827-3904
Deborah Blanks	Foods	301-827-0943
Barbara Blosser	Drugs	913-752-2466
Dyrene Braswell	Program Assistant	301-827-5659
Luis A. Carrion	Foods	787-474-9520
Lawrence Carter	Drugs	301-827-3903
Doreen Chin Quee	Devices	301-827-5632

Denaja Crutchfield	Assistant	301-827-6884
Olga Duran	Drugs	301-827-5644
Patricia Griffin	Devices	301-827-5668
Attila Kadar	Bimo	301-827-5647
Tania Mercado	Bimo	301-827-5637
Heriberto Negron-Rivera	Drugs	301-827-3901
Irma Rivera	Drugs	301-827-5665
Minerva Rogers	Devices	301-827-5633
Naveen Walker	Foods	301-827-0167
Joyce Watson	Biologics	301-827-5664
Marisa White	Bimo	301-827-5629

The National Experts, stationed at a District office or resident post, are assigned to DFI.

Thomas Arista	DAL-DO Biotechnology	214-253-4920
Regina T. Brown	NWJ-DO Drugs	732-940-8946 x14
Mary T. Carden	NYK/BUF Biologics	716-541-0352
Debra Devlieger	SEA-DO Food/LACF	206-842-0251
Sharon K. Thoma	MIN-DO Drugs	612-758-7159
Brian Hendrickson	DET-DO Food/LACF	317-226-6500 x104
Joan Loreng	PHI-DO Biologics	215-717-3724
Dr. Gerald McGirl	SAN-DO BIMO	510-337-6850
Rebeca Rodriguez	SJN-DO Drugs	787-474-9556
Robert D. Tollefsen	SEA-DO Computer	425-483-4923

David B. Wieneke	MIN-DO Food, Aseptic Processing, Dairy	612-758-7177
Kimberly Lewandowski-Walker	MIN-DO Devices	414-771-7167 x23
Norman Wong	SEA-DO Devices	206-483-4935
Ingrid Zambrana	ATL-DO Food Outbreak and Food Defense	404-253-1284

1.9.2.2.2 - DIVISION OF FIELD SCIENCE (DFS) (HFC-140)

Carl Sciacchitano, Director

Thomas Savage, Deputy Director

301-827-1232

DFS provides a focal point for all aspects of ORA Field Laboratories and serves as the Headquarters' scientific and technical staff. It manages FDA's overall field scientific resources to assure their coordinated, efficient, and effective use; provides coordination between field and center scientific programs, and develops and manages the Science Advisor Program and Department of Defense Shelf life Extension Program.

DFS manages field research programs and the applicability of new, complex, scientific instruments for field analyses and provides scientific and analytical expertise related to laboratory automation, analysis, process control and acquisition of automated data laboratory instruments. DFS manages the scientific aspects of the FACTS. The Division participates in the determination of long and short-range field scientific facility needs and in the formulation, delivery, and evaluation of training and career development plans for field scientists. Program contacts in DFS are:

1. Larry D' Hoostelaere, CBER/CDRH programs contact; Mad Cow and TSE issues
2. Marsha Hayden, CFSAN programs contact
3. Don Lech, CDER programs contact
4. George Salem, CVM programs contact

They can all be reached at 301-827-7605/6

1.9.2.2.3 - DIVISION OF FEDERAL-STATE RELATIONS (DFSR) (HFC-150)

Richard H. Barnes, Director 301-827-6906

Preetham R. Sudhaker, Staff Manager, Contracts and Grants Staff

Catherine M. McDermott, Staff Manager, Public Affairs and Information Staff

DFSR interacts with counterpart State and local officials to promote cohesive and uniform policies and activities in food and drug related matters. It also serves at the focal point for cooperating officials from state agencies that need information, coordination or services from headquarter units. DFSR coordinates efforts between FDA and state and local counterparts. DFSR also provides information to and receives information from state, territorial, and local agencies. Work is completed by cooperating directly with state and local government officials and industry and indirectly through FDA field offices and national regional and state associations.

DFSR manages a contract/grant program with the states benefiting them with technical training, familiarity with federal requirements and more uniform enforcement of consumer laws through cooperation and coordination with FDA. Contracts involve food safety, tissue residues, radiological health, and medicated feeds which allows FDA to enlarge coverage of the Official Establishment Inventory (OEI) and also to redirect resources to other problems. Grants include areas in Food Safety and Food Defense, Health Fraud and small conference issues. Cooperative agreements include areas in FERN and BSE.

DFSR coordinates work between FDA and State and local agencies through Voluntary Work Agreements such as partnership agreements, memoranda of understanding (MOU's) and coordinated operations plan for emergencies (COPE).

DFSR serves as Liaison for Cooperative Programs between headquarters, CFSAN and FDA field staff. Cooperative Programs include the retail food program, milk safety and shellfish sanitation program areas which CFSAN leads the daily responsibility for providing assistance to FDA regional specialists who in turn interact with state specialists. DFSR also provides policy and technical information on medicated feeds and drugs to state control officials.

DFSR is responsible for the commissioning of State officials and oversees the national program which provides authority to state and local officials to conduct investigations and collect samples to enforce the Federal Food Drug and Cosmetic Act. Also included is the sharing of a wide range of Agency documents as well as responding to state and local requests for information on Agency policy or position. DFSR coordinates the activities of FDA Field Public Affairs Specialists (PAS), the first line contact for consumers, health professionals, academia and the media on current and emerging FDA issues. DFSR is responsible for monitoring and maintaining the Public Affairs Reporting System (PAIRS). DFSR is responsible for the State Advisory Fax/Email System (SAFES), a communication system, which allows FDA to send out information including fax and e-mail emergency/priority messages to specific program groups, e.g. State Boards of Pharmacy, State Health Commissioners, State Food Program Directors, and others 24 hours/day.

1.9.2.2.4 - DIVISION OF IMPORT OPERATIONS POLICY (DIOP) (HFC-170)

Domenic J. Veneziano, Director 301-443-6553

Deputy Director, Vacant

This division provides direction, assistance, management and oversight of field import operations. It serves as Agency focal point for contact with U.S. Customs and other Federal Agencies regarding import activities. Develops and reviews agency import policies, procedures, programs, etc. and is responsible for issuing import informational directives (Import Alerts, Bulletins, etc.) and RPM, Chapter 9. DIOP is responsible for the maintenance of the Operational and Administrative System for Import Support (OASIS), including the coordination with program Centers to establish automated screening criteria.

Contact points within DIOP are:

1. Systems Branch (HFC-171)
   Steven Kendall, Director 301-594-1162

2. Operations and Policy Branch (HFC-172)
   John E. Verbeten, Director 301-594-3845

1.9.2.2.4.1 - Prior Notice Center (PNC) (HFC-180)

Laura J. Draski, Director 301-621-7809

Anthony C. Taube, Deputy Director 866-521-2297

The PNC was established as a result of the Public Health Security and Bioterrorism Preparedness and Response Act of 2002 (BTA), specifically related to the prior notice requirements of the BTA. The PNC provides a focal point to the FDA field on all aspects of Prior Notice with expertise in researching import shipments and their related firms. The PNC operates 24 hours a day, 7 days a week within Customs & Border Protection's National Targeting Center to receive, review and provide the appropriate response to information submitted in advance of FDA regulated food products, including animal feed, imported or offered for import into the United States. The purpose of prior notice is to enable FDA to target for exam the highest risk imported foods at the time of arrival, in order to maximize food safety and security in the United States and to prevent products that may be intentionally contaminated and/or may pose a potential significant health risk due to terrorism or other health related emergency from entering into U.S. Commerce.

Contact Points within Prior Notice Center are:

Nabil Anis, Watch Commander

D. Yvette Arline, Watch Commander

Greta Budweg, Watch Commander

Kelli Giannattasio, Watch Commander

Janice Gordon, Watch Commander

Jamie Hughes, Watch Commander

Lonna Potter, Watch Commander

Angel Suarez, Watch Commander

Marilyn White, Watch Commander

All of the above can be reached at 866-521-2297

1.9.2.3 - Office of Enforcement (OE)(HFC-200) Vacant, Director

The Director of OE is vacant and the Deputy Director is Alyson L. Saben.

OE advises and assists the ACRA and other key officials on regulations and compliance policy matters which impact on policy development, implementation and long range goals. OE also coordinates, interprets, and evaluates the FDA's overall compliance efforts and, as necessary, establishes compliance policy and recommends policy to the ACRA.

OE also acts as liaison with other federal agencies on compliance matters, evaluates proposed legal actions, coordinates actions with the Office of Regional Operations (ORO) and the Office of Chief Counsel (OCC) and handles appeals of proposed compliance actions which are disapproved by the centers or OCC.

This office coordinates agency bioresearch monitoring activities and serves as Agency focal point for the Federal Medical Products Quality Assurance Program (GWQAP).

OE consists of the following elements:

1. Division of Compliance Management and Operations (DCMO) and Recall Staff (HFC-210) Vacant, Director

2. Division of Compliance Policy (DCP)(HFC-230) Douglas W. Stearn, Director

3. Division of Compliance Information and Quality Assurance (DCIQA) Staff (HFC-240) Katherine A. Hollinger, Director

1.9.2.4 - Office of Criminal Investigations (OCI) (HFC-300) Terrell L. Vermillion, Director

This office advises and assists the ACRA and other key officials on regulations and criminal violations involving regulated activities and products.

OCI directs and conducts criminal investigative activities in coordination with FDA headquarters units and with other Federal, state and local law enforcement agencies. OCI is instrumental in implementing FDA criminal investigation policy, training, and coordination. OCI interfaces directly with Federal and local prosecutorial offices and participates in grand jury proceedings and judicial actions as required.

OCI has 170 employees in headquarters and the field.

1.9.3 - ORA Field Organization

The ORA field organization is divided into regional offices. The Regional Offices are under the control of Regional Food and Drug Directors (RFDD's) who report to the ACRA. There are currently five regional offices which are located as follows:

Northeast New York, NY

Central	Philadelphia, PA
Southeast	Atlanta, GA
Southwest	Dallas, TX
Pacific	San Francisco, CA

Each regional office directs 2 to 7 district offices.

There are currently 20 district offices located in major cities around the country. Each district office (DO) is usually comprised of four branches or units as follows:

1. Administrative Branch
2. Compliance Branch
3. Investigations Branch - some DOs may have 2 investigations sections, one for domestic products and one for imported products.
4. Laboratory Branch - not all DOs have laboratories

1.10 - References

This subchapter will help you to locate regulatory references and FDA staff.

1.10.1 - Law, Regulation and Guidance

The Public Health Security and Bioterrorism Preparedness and Response Act of 2002 (the Bioterrorism Act), the Medical Device User Fee and Modernization Act of 2002 (MDUFMA), the FDA Modernization Act of 1997, (FDAMA), the International Conference on Harmonization (ICH), the Mutual Recognition Agreement (MRA), national emergencies and initiatives, and other forces continue to impact FDA inspectional operations as changes in law, regulation, guidance and internal procedures issue. As ICH members (Japan, U.S. and European Union) reach consensus agreements, ICH guidelines are adopted by all three governments. In the United States, they may replace outstanding FDA guidance in the medical device, human and animal drug areas. Unless exempted, the Bioterrorism Act and implementing regulations require most domestic food facilities and foreign food facilities who export to the U.S. to register as of December 12, 2003; FDA began accepting registrations on October 16, 2003. The Bioterrorism Act requires that FDA receive prior notice of food imported into the United States, beginning on December 12, 2003. The 2002 MDUFMA authorizes FDA to charge user fees for medical device premarket review; it allows third party medical device inspections, sets out new regulatory requirements for single-use devices, and directs FDA to establish the Office of Combination Products. FDA drug GMP initiative and Process Analytical Technology (PAT) efforts are underway.

In conducting inspections and investigations according to changing policies, in order to be effective, FDA regulators must understand the difference between regulatory requirements and guidance.

Laws or statutes, enacted by Congress, and regulations or rules, promulgated by Federal agencies, contain regulatory requirements.

FDA's guidance documents, on the other hand, have a different legal status and serve purposes different from laws and regulations. The purposes of guidance documents are to:

1. Provide assistance to the regulated industry by clarifying requirements that have been imposed by Congress or issued in regulations by FDA, and by explaining how industry may comply with those statutory and regulatory requirements, and

2. Provide specific review and enforcement approaches to help ensure that FDA's employees implement the agency's mandate in an effective, fair, and consistent manner.

The term "guidance documents" includes documents prepared for FDA staff, applicants/sponsors, and the public that:

1. Relate to the processing, content, and evaluation/ approval of submissions;

2. Relate to the design, production, manufacturing, and testing of regulated products;

3. Describe the agency's policy and regulatory approach to an issue; or

4. Establish inspection and enforcement policies and procedures.

Guidance documents do not include documents relating to internal FDA procedures, agency reports, general information documents provided to consumers, speeches, journal articles and editorials, media interviews, press materials, warning letters, or other communications directed to individual persons or firms. FDA procedures issued for staff to follow, such as the IOM, are internal procedures intended to direct your activities and you are to follow them.

Guidance documents for industry do not establish legally enforceable rights or responsibilities and are not legally binding on the public or the agency. Rather, they explain how the agency believes the statutes and regulations apply to certain regulated activities. For a more detailed explanation of the background to the development, issuance and use of guidance documents see the preamble to the February 27, 1997 Federal Register Volume 62 Number 39. To access 21 CFR 10.115 Good Guidance Practices, see http://www.access.gpo.gov/nara/cfr/waisidx_01/21cfrv1_01.html . Also see http://www.fda.gov/cdrh/ohip/guidance/1323.pdf to access the CDRH Manual for the Good Guidance Practices (GGP) Regulation - Final Guidance for FDA Staff (2/01). For a comprehensive list of FDA current guidance documents, see http://www.fda.gov/opacom/morechoices/industry/guid_edc.htm.

The Federal Register is the official daily publication for rules, proposed rules, and Notices of federal agencies and organizations as well as Executive Orders and other Presidential documents. The Code of Federal Regulations (CFR) is a codification of the general and permanent rules published in the Federal Register by the Executive Departments and agencies of the Federal Government. Most regulations enforced by FDA are located in Title 21 of the

CFR. For a listing of all titles in the U.S Code, see http://www4.law.cornell.edu/uscode/#TITLES.

1.10.2 - Sources of Information

1.10.2.1 - Investigator Training and Certification

ORA's Investigator certification program provides a focused training plan for the ongoing professional development of agency investigators. The program is designed to address the specific needs of agency District Offices by providing a structured mechanism for investigators to maintain the required levels of competency.

Performance certification promotes uniformity in investigator training and experience. The program is designed to promote the efficient use of (ORA) training resources. Investigators who complete the program will be formally recognized as meeting the competencies required at the specific certification level achieved.

Additional information on ORA's Investigator Certification program, including procedure documents and forms for certification in specific commodity areas, is available on ORA U on DHRD's intranet site.

In addition to managing the investigator certification program through ORAU, the Division of Human Resource Development (DHRD) (HFC-60) manages and coordinates with Regions and Districts, the ORA staff's overall ongoing professional development training through in person and web-based courses, broadcasts, and video conferences. For more information on available training on the ORA U, see DHRD's intranet site.

1.10.2.2 - Contacting FDA Employees

Easily finding colleagues you need to contact can make your work life more productive. See IOM 1.9. for the organization of FDA offices, including a directory of ORA field offices and program managers. The Office of Regulatory Affairs organizational directory (blue pages) is available in electronic format. See ORA Directory. At the end of the blue pages, find a listing of District program monitors. For FDA Center staff directories:

CFSAN - See http://www.cfsan.fda.gov/~dms/srchbfd.html.

CBER - See http://www.fda.gov/cber/inside/org.htm

CDRH - See http://www.fda.gov/cdrh/organiz-info.html. For a list of resource staff by topic of specialization in the Division of Small Manufacturers, Consumer and Interna-tional Affairs, see http://www.fda.gov/cdrh/dsma/dsmastaf.html#DSMICA_Staff

CVM - See http://www.fda.gov/cvm/cvmlist.html

CDER - See http://www.fda.gov/cder/directories/reference _guide.htm. For a list of resource staff by topic of speciali-zation, in the CDER Division of Manufacturing and Pro-duct Quality, (HFD-320) see http://www.fda.gov/cder/dmpq/subjcontacts.htm.

To obtain contact information for an FDA employee in your e-mail directory, find the name, then click on "properties" for telephone number and office designation. If the telephone number listed is inaccurate for an FDA employee you wish to contact, call the FDA Personnel Locator at telephone number 301-443-1544 for an update.

You may also search the Department of Health and Human Services electronic employee directory, which includes FDA and all other HHS staff. See http://directory.psc.gov/employee.htm. See IOM Chapter 3 for other Federal agency and State contact information, or to check the Directory of State and Local Officials on the FDA web site, see http://www.fda.gov/ora/fed_state/directorytable.htm.

1.10.2.3 - Internet and Intranet

The FDA Internet Web site at http://www.fda.gov provides access to FDA references in electronic format: laws, regulations, policy, guidance, correspondence, reports and other publications. From the FDA home page link to laws enforced by FDA and related statutes at www.fda.gov/opacom/laws. From there you can access the Code of Federal Regulations, the Federal Register, and FDA Manuals and Publications. Under the heading "FDA Manuals and Publications" is a link to a comprehensive list of current FDA guidance documents at http://www.fda.gov/opacom/morechoices/industry/guidedc.htm.

Two features will facilitate your navigation of the FDA website, For the FDA "Website Index", see www.fda.gov/opacom/hpchoice.html. To access the FDA "Website Map", see www.fda.gov/sitemap.html.

Subscribe to various FDA e-mail lists for updates on web postings. See www.fda.gov/emaillist.html.

FDA libraries are accessible on the FDA intranet site.

1.10.2.4 - FDA on Disk

The FDA Gold Disk is an electronic source of regulatory references maintained on CD-ROM by the Office of Enforcement, Division of Compliance Information and Quality Assurance (HFC-240) Scott Lewis 781-596-7748. To order a Gold Disk, contact San Francisco District, Gwen Wong, 510-337-6890. FDA personnel who do not have access to an FDA network server can use the Gold Disk in an off-line mode. It may also be available on your local district server. Check with your computer support personnel. The FDA gold disk is a convenient source of FDA regulatory references in electronic format when Internet access is not available. It contains, for example, the Federal Food Drug and Cosmetic Act, Title 21 CFR, Compliance Policy Guides, Enforcement Reports, Talk Papers, Import Alerts, Investigations Operations Manual, Regulatory Procedures Manual, selected Compliance Programs, the Food Code, and listings of approved drug products. The Gold Disk is not releasable under FOI and is not available to the public. It is for FDA use only. The subset of the Gold Disk available to state and local agencies (but not releasable under FOI) is the Eureka Disk. To order this, contact Christina Segura-Ramos in the ORA Division of Federal-State Relations (DFSR) at 301-827-2901.

1.10.2.5 - Electronic-Fax Information Systems

The FDA Medical Devices fax information system issues documents twenty-four hours a day, seven days a week on request to 800-899-0381. Follow the directions by the automated attendant to receive a faxed list of references and their order numbers. Next, request specific documents by number as indicated on the index.

Biologics, Human/Animal Drugs and Foods do not have fax information systems.

1.10.2.6 - FDA/ORA Manuals and Reports

ORA headquarters and the OC Office of Information Resources Management support a change to electronic manuals, not paper manuals, because electronic manuals are easier to issue, revise and distribute. As part of the ORA Quality Management System, ORA HQ supports electronic manual dissemination through developing Intranet master lists or indices for directives used by ORA. See the FDA Intranet for more information. During transition from paper to electronic manuals, a limited selection and number of paper manuals will be available as follows:

1. Compliance Policy Guides (CPGs): A limited number of 2000 paper manuals available by contacting OE/DCP at 240-632-6860;
2. Compliance Program Guidance Manual (CPGM): No paper manuals;
3. Data Codes Manual: No paper manuals; for electronic lists of program assignment codes and establishment type codes contact ORM/Division of Program Evaluation and Management
4. Enforcement Reports: No paper reports;
5. Field Management Directives (FMDs) - No paper manual;
6. Guide to International Inspections and Travel - For paper manuals contact ORA/DFI 301-827-5653;
7. Inspection Technical Guides - No paper manuals;
8. International Cooperative Agreements Manual - No paper manuals;
9. Investigations Operations Manual (IOM) - Current edition paper manuals available by contacting ORA/ORO/Division of Field Investigations at (301) 827-5653.
10. Laboratory Procedures Manual (LPM) - No paper manuals;
11. Laboratory Information Bulletins (LIB) - No paper copies;
12. Regulatory Procedures Manual (RPM) - No paper copies;
13. Recalls and Safety Alerts - No paper copies;
14. Staff Manual Guide: No paper manuals;
15. State and Federal Cooperative Agreements: No paper copies.

1.10.2.7 - Forms and Other Publications

The FDA on line Public Forms Catalog contains a list of FDA forms and the information necessary to order them.

Order paper copies of FDA forms from the USDA Consolidated Forms and Publications Distribution Center, Beltsville Service Center at 6351 Ammendale Road in Beltsville, MD 20705. Phone or fax orders will not be accepted. Forms may be ordered electronically. To obtain a customer number necessary to order forms electronically, or for other questions concerning FDA forms, contact:

FDA/Office of the Commissioner/Office of Management/ Office of Management and Programs/Division of Management Systems/Paperwork Reduction and Records Branch

Elizabeth Sands, Forms Management Officer, (HFA-250)
5600 Fishers Lane, Room 6A-22
Rockville, MD 20857
301-827-1480
FAX 301-594-0060
Or e-mail to Elizabeth.Sands@fda.hhs.gov
or Formsmanager@oc.fda.gov.

The Department of Health and Human Services (DHHS) Program Support Center, 16071 Industrial Drive, Gaithersburg, MD 20877 also maintains a limited selection of FDA forms and publications. To search their catalog, see https://propshop.psc.gov/shopping/formspubs.asp#/. For questions, contact Danny Saum at PSC at 301-443-7634.

The INTRANET FDA's Electronic Forms Catalog is another resource. Internal forms related to field operations are located at that site. For example, you can find seals, affidavits, Form FDA 482 Notice of Inspection, and many other forms on which FDA documents its activities related to investigations, inspections and sample collection and analysis. Forms are organized alphabetically as well as by form number.

1.10.2.8 - Regulatory References and the General Public

The general public must make a request under the Freedom of Information Act (FOIA) in order to obtain certain FDA documents requiring redaction. See IOM 1.4.4 (Freedom of Information Act) and IOM 1.4.5 (internal Documents) for additional information on FOIA. For instructions to the public on how to file an FOIA request, see www.fda.gov/foi/foia2.htm.

Many FDA documents are available to the public without an FOIA request. To obtain forms, direct the public to the FDA Public Use Forms web page. The public can purchase paper editions of various agency manuals, such as the Food Code and Compliance Program Manuals if ordered by NTIS item number from the National Technical Information Service (NTIS). Instruct the person seeking a publication to first locate the NTIS item number by calling the NTIS sales department at 800-553-6847. The next step is to enter the NTIS item number in the search box at the NTIS website at www.ntis.gov, and follow directions on ordering the publication. For additional information on NTIS publications, direct the public to contact:

National Technical Information Service
Technology Administration

U.S. Department of Commerce
Springfield, VA 22161
Order Desk: 703-605-6585
Fax: 703-605-6900

The public may also obtain federal publications from the U.S. Government Bookstore on-line or on site. See http://bookstore.gpo.gov/locations/index.html for locations of on-site U.S. government bookstores.

The public may also obtain FDA documents from the CDRH automated FAX information service listed in section 1.10.2.5 of Subchapter 1.10.2. FDA references are also available to the public in electronic format from the FDA website. From the FDA homepage, link to special information for consumers, industry, health professionals, patients, state and local officials. For example, direct industry to the FDA industry web page.

Those regulated by FDA may contact their ORA Regional Small Business Representative (SBR) for an explanation of how FDA requirements apply to specific circumstances.

SBRs also locate relevant references, make referrals, conduct or participate in workshops and conferences, or make non-regulatory audits on request. See http://www.fda.gov/ora/fed_state/Small_Business/regional.htm for a list of SBRs and the regions they serve.

Direct industry inquiries in accordance with District policy either to appropriate District personnel, to the ORA Small Business Representative for your region, to an FDA industry assistance office or the Center Ombudsman, or to the Office of the Commissioner. In CDRH, the Division of Manufacturers, International and Consumer Affairs (DSMICA) staff specializes in industry assistance. For FDA drug manufacturing queries, a list of resource staff in the CDER Division of Manufacturing and Product Quality, (HFD-320) identifies each staff member by area of knowledge. Refer questions about post approval changes to the CDER post approval changes e-mail box at pac314_70@cder.fda.gov. Refer questions about good clinical practice requirements to the FDA's GCP staff.

Refer consumer inquiries to the appropriate District Public Affairs Specialist.

Try to refer appropriately to make your government work more effectively for all concerned.

1.10.2.9 - Acronyms

To access explanations for some of the hundreds of acronyms in FDA references, try the following:

1. CDER Acronym list compiled by the CDER Division of Biometrics III

2. CVM Related Acronyms and Abbreviations

3. CFSAN Abbreviations and Acronyms from the CFSAN Risk Analysis Working Group Report "Initiation and Conduct of All Major Risk Assessments within a Risk Analysis Framework" (3/02)

4. Draft Listeria monocytogenes Risk Assessment report: Abbreviations and Acronyms

5. ORA Glossary of Computerized System and Software Development Terminology

6. Fiscal Year 2001 Performance Plan, FY 2000 Final Performance Plan, and FY 1999 Performance Report Glossary of Acronyms

7. Fiscal Year 2004 Annual Performance Plan, FY2003 Revised Performance Plan, FY 2002 Annual Performance Plan see Appendix F Glossary of Acronyms at http://www.fda.gov/ope/fy04plan/2004pp-mainpage.html.

1.10.3 - Special Regulatory by Product Category

Information including product databases, inspection guides, industry guidance, and regulatory references are available by product category on-line at DFI's intranet site.

Chapter 2: Regulatory

CONTENT		VERSION DATE
Subchapter 2.1	Regulatory Note	June 11, 2009
Subchapter 2.2	Statutory Authority	June 11, 2009
Subchapter 2.3	Reconditioning And Destruction	June 11, 2009
Subchapter 2.4	Consent Decree	June 11, 2009
Subchapter 2.5	Default Decree	June 11, 2009
Subchapter 2.6	Compliance Achievement	June 11, 2009
Subchapter 2.7	Detention Activities	July 13, 2009
Subchapter 2.8	Denaturing	June 11, 2009
Subchapter 2.9	Regulatory Submissions	June 11, 2009

2.1 - Regulatory Notes

Regulatory notes are the contemporaneous, sequential record of your daily investigatory efforts. They record your observations relevant to violations and active cases. They are the vital link between your findings and your subsequent testimony in court. Because of the data, which regulatory notes contain, such as information pertaining to open investigatory files, trade secrets, and personal information protected under the Privacy Act, they are confidential. Regulatory notes are government property. The notes cannot be released to anyone outside the Agency, except with the express permission of your management, and after following FDA's procedures. (See IOM 1.4) See IOM 1.2.4 for guidance on administrative notes.

2.1.1 - Uses of Regulatory Notes

Accurate regulatory notes are to refresh your memory when reporting certain important details of a sample collection, inspection, and investigation. Notes also support the principle of "presumption of regularity", i.e., in the absence of clear evidence to the contrary, courts presume public officers properly discharge their official duties. Regulatory notes are useful as a means to refute assertions by defendants, witnesses or others. Regulatory notes also aid in defending lawsuits against FDA agents. This has been an issue of significance in a number of regulatory cases in the Federal Sector.

2.1.2 - Regulatory Notes Characteristics

See IOM 1.1 for English language requirement. Regulatory notes should be accurate, objective, factual, and free of personal feelings or conclusions. Regulatory notes should be made at the time of the event they repre-sent. Regulatory notes are original contemporaneous, sequential recordings of an activity, and may be handwritten (in ink) or electronic. Do not erase, edit or rewrite original notes. Do not leave excessive space between diary entries. Whether handwritten or electronic, any additions, deletions, or corrections to regulatory notes should be identified by strike through (strike through font for electronic notes) for deletions, brackets [ ] for addi-tions and by initialing and dating your changes.

Electronic Regulatory notes: you should be able to identify and attest the electronic notes were taken by you to ensure document integrity. You should exercise good judgment when deciding if a change is contemporaneous or if change should be initialed and dated. For example, changes or backspacing to correct information ordinarily would not need initialing and dating as long as the changes were made contemporaneously with the activity being documented. Otherwise, you should initial and date the change. Adhere to agency directives and procedures to safeguard and file electronic notes. Regulatory notes can be printed, and each page initialed (handwritten initials) and dated by the investigator. If this procedure is used, the original disk or Compact Disk-Recordable (CD-R) can be identified with the firm name, dates, and investigator's initials; placed in a FDA-525 envelope or equivalent; and then sealed with an Official Seal, FDA-415a. NOTE: See IOM 5.3.3 - Exhibits, for guidance on the identification and storage of electronic data obtained from inspected firms, and used as exhibits for the EIR.

2.1.3 - Regulatory Entries

Regulatory notes should contain sufficient detail to refresh an investigator's memory regarding inspections, investigations and sample collections. They should include objectionable conditions, pertinent information about your activities during an operation, details of a sample collection, etc. If a checklist is used during an inspection, don't repeat that information in your regulatory notes. The checklist should be handled as part of the notes. Likewise, when relevant information is contained on an FDA form, or in an exhibit collected during an inspection, that information need not be repeated in your notes.

Regulatory notes should contain the substance of all significant discussions with people contacted during the activity; e.g., discussions of individual responsibility. When entering a direct quote in a notebook, such as a statement against self-interest, it is important the exact words be used to preserve the original intent of the individual and subject. Every quote of significance appearing in the final report should be in your regulatory notes since they are part of the source documents, which will support any regulatory or administrative action.

Regulatory notes should not contain purely administrative information. See IOM 1.2.4 for guidance on administrative notes.

2.1.4 - Format for Regulatory Notes

Keep your handwritten regulatory notes in a bound notebook. Bound notebooks provide continuity and integrity and also prevent lost or misplaced pages. Loose-leaf and spiral bindings allow easy removal of pages, an invitation to vigorous and heated cross-examination on the witness stand.

Regulatory notes in electronic format are a valuable tool to expediting the conduct of an inspection. They may be stored on computer disk or CD-R, but should be preserved in a manner that ensures data integrity.

Regulatory notes whether written or electronic are subject to audit at any time; must be available for review; and must, on demand, be surrendered to your supervisors or other authorized personnel. Regulatory notes should be identified with your name, telephone number, and address to facilitate their return if lost. To assist in the return of lost regulatory notes, include the following information in the bound book's inside cover or as a placard affixed to the back cover:

This book is the property of the U.S. Government.

If found, drop in mail box.

POSTMASTER: Postage guaranteed

Please return to: [Enter the appropriate district (or resident post's) mailing address here, including the zip code]

Advancing technology may increase the preservation options available. District policy should be followed regarding the preservation of all regulatory notes.

2.1.5 - Retention of Regulatory Notes

Identify your regulatory notes with your name and the inclusive dates they cover before they are turned over for storage. Follow your District's policy regarding the maintenance of regulatory notes.

Based on your district's policy, regulatory notes (including computer disks or CD-Rs) may be kept by you, filed with the final report, or kept by the district in a separate, designated file. At a minimum, retain regulatory notes for the same period of time as the inspection report, collection report or other investigational report, or until all court actions, including appeals, have been adjudicated.

If you leave FDA, or are transferred from your district, identify any regulatory notes in your possession and turn them in to the district you are leaving. Districts are to retain regulatory notes as official records as outlined in the FDA Staff Manual Guide.

Regulatory notes prepared by headquarters' personnel during a field inspection/investigation are official records. Headquarters personnel are to follow their Center's policy regarding the retention of regulatory notes. In general, all regulatory notes should be maintained in the District or Center where the original report is filed.

2.2 - Statutory Authority

Various acts specify the authority conferred on the Secretary of DHHS. This authority is delegated by regulations to the Commissioner of Food and Drugs, and certain authorities are delegated further by him.

2.2.1 - Federal Food, Drug, and Cosmetic Act

This Act, as amended, and its regulations provide the basic authority for most operations.

Examinations, Investigations, and Samples – Collecting samples is an important and critical part of FDA's regulatory activities. While inspections and investigations may precede sample collection, a case under the law does not normally begin until a sample has been obtained. Proper sample collection is the keystone of effective enforcement action.

The basic authority for FDA to take samples falls under the statutory provisions of section 702(a) of the FD&C Act [21 USC 372(a)], which authorizes examinations and investigations for the purposes of this Act.

Section 702(b) of the FD&C Act [21 USC 372(b)] requires FDA to furnish, upon request, a portion of an official sample for examination or analysis to any person named on the label of an article, the owner thereof, or his attorney or agent. In a precedent case, "United States v. 75 Cases, More or Less, Each Containing 24 Jars of Peanut Butter, the U.S. Circuit Court of Appeals for the Fourth Circuit held the taking of samples is authorized under section 702(b) of the FD&C Act [21 U.S.C. 372(b)], since this section "clearly contemplates the taking of samples." See Kleinfeld and Dunn 1938-1949 at 126. The FD&C Act also refers to samples in sections 704(c) and 704(d) [21 USC 374(c) and 374(d)].

2.2.1.1 - Authority to Enter and Inspect

Authority to Enter and Inspect - Section 704 of the Food, Drug and Cosmetic Act [21 U.S.C. 374] provides the basic authority for establishment inspections. This authorizes you to enter, and to inspect at reasonable times, within reasonable limits, and in a reasonable manner, establishments or vehicles being used to process, hold or transport food, drugs, devices or cosmetics. The statute does not define, in specific terms, the meaning of "reasonable". FDA's establishment inspection procedures maintain this authority extends to what is reasonably necessary to achieve the objective of the inspection.

2.2.1.2 - Food Inspections

Authority to inspect food plants resides in the general inspectional authority of section 704 of the FD&C Act [21 U.S.C. 374]. Section 306 of the Public Health Security and Bioterrorism Preparedness and Response Act of 2002 ("the Bioterrorism Act") (PL 107-188), signed into law on June 12, 2002, created a new section 414, "Maintenance and Inspection of Records," in the FD&C Act. Under this new authority, the Secretary of Health and Human Services (the Secretary) may by regulation establish requirements for persons (excluding farms and restaurants) who manufacture, process, pack, transport, distribute, receive, hold, or import food to establish and maintain food records. These records identify the immediate previous sources and the immediate subsequent recipients of food. In addition, section 414(a), "Records Inspection," and section 704(a), "Factory Inspection" authorize the Secretary to access and copy all records related to an article of food if:

(1) the Secretary has a reasonable belief that an article of food is adulterated and presents a threat of serious adverse health consequences or death to humans or animals, and

(2) the records are necessary to assist the Secretary in making such a determination. FDA plans to carry out its authority to inspect all records and other information described in section 414 in a similar manner as FDA's authority to perform inspections of facilities (i.e., upon presentation of appropriate credentials and a written notice at reasonable times, within reasonable limits, and a reasonable manner.) FDA employees will not invoke this authority during inspections unless the requirements for record access under the Bioterrorism Act are satisfied. Further guidance is available at http://www.cfsan.fda.gov/~dms/secgui13.html .

The Infant Formula Act of 1980 added new authority to the FD&C Act. Section 412 of the FD&C Act [21 U.S.C. 350a] extends the definition of adulteration to include specific nutritional, quality and good manufacturing control requirements. It also mandates a firm make available batch records, quality control records, nutrient test data and methodology, and similar documents for examination and copying. Section 704(a)(3) of the FD&C Act [21 U.S.C. 374(a)(3)] gives investigators the right to examine and copy these records.

2.2.1.3 - Device Inspections

Section 704(a) of the FD&C Act [21 U.S.C. 374(a)] provides the general inspectional authority to inspect medical device manufacturers. The Medical Device Amendments of 1976 provided additional authority to inspect records, files, papers, processes, controls, and facilities to determine whether restricted devices are adulterated or misbranded. The Amendments also provide FDA authority, under section 704(e) [21 U.S.C. 374(e)], to inspect and copy records required under section 519 or 520(g) of the FD&C Act [21 U.S.C. 360i or 360j(g)].

2.2.1.4 - Limitations

Section 704 of the FD&C Act [21 U.S.C. 374] provides authority for FDA to conduct inspections of factories, warehouses, establishments, and vehicles, and all pertinent equipment, finished and unfinished materials, containers, and labeling therein where food, drugs, devices, or cosmetics are manufactured or held. This section does not include a provision to inspect records within those facilities, except for inspections of prescription drugs, nonprescription drugs intended for human use, and restricted devices, as stipulated in 704(a)(1)(B) [21 U.S.C. 374(a)(1)(B)], or inspections of infant formula described in 704(a)(3) of the FD&C Act [21 U.S.C. 374(a)(3)].

Keep in mind that several other sections of the Act or of regulations also include provision for inspection and copying of required records. For example, 505(k) provides authority to access and copy records required for new drug applications and abbreviated new drug applications, 512(k)(2) and

512(m)(5) of the FD&C Act [21 U.S.C. 360b(k)(2) and 360b(m)(5)] provide access and copying of records regarding new animal drug and medicated feed permits, HACCP regulations in 21 CFR 123 for fish and fishery products provide for access and copying of required records.

Some firms will allow access to files and other materials for which the FD&C Act does not give mandatory access, but retain the right to later refuse. Management may propose the following alternatives:

1. That inspections to obtain data from these files be made without issuing an FDA-482, Notice of Inspection. You cannot agree to this because the act requires the notice be issued before the inspection.

2. That when data is provided, you are advised in writing it is being given voluntarily. In this instance accept the written or oral statement, and include it as part of the EIR.

Management may insist answers to specific questions be provided by the firm's legal department or other administrative officers. In some instances, management may request questions be submitted in writing. In these cases, try to obtain answers necessary to complete the inspection. Do not submit lists of questions unless specifically instructed to do so by your supervisor.

2.2.1.5 - Electronic Radiation Product Examinations and Inspections

The authority for obtaining samples of radiation-emitting electronic products for testing is provided in Section 532(b)(4) of the FD&C Act [21 U.S.C. 360ii(b)(4)].

The authority to inspect factories, warehouses, and establishments where electronic products are manufactured or held is provided in Section 537(a) of the FD&C Act [21 U.S.C. 360nn(a)]. This authority is limited; FDA must find "good cause" that methods, tests, or programs related to radiation safety (such as noncompliance with a standard) may be inadequate or unreliable. If there is no finding of "good cause," inspections must be voluntary unless another authority, such as Section 704(a) of the FD&C Act [21 U.S.C. 374(a)] for medical devices, exists. The authority to inspect books, papers, records, and documents relevant to determining compliance with radiation standards is provided in Section 537(b) of the FD&C Act [21 U.S.C. 360nn(b)]. The Electronic Product Radiation Control prohibited acts and enforcement authorities are specified in Sections 538 and 539 of the FD&C Act [21 U.S.C. 360oo and 360pp].

2.2.2 - Selected Amendments to the Fd&C Act

The amendments to the FD&C Act are summarized in Regulatory Procedures Manual (RPM) chapter 2-2.

2.2.3 - Other Acts

See IOM 2.2.10 and IOM 3.2.1.3 for special authorities involving detentions under the Federal Meat Inspection, Poultry Products Inspection, and Egg Products Inspection, Acts.

2.2.3.1 - Anabolic Steroids Control Act of 1990

Amends the Controlled Substances Act by adding Anabolic Steroids to Schedule III of section 202(c).

2.2.3.2 - Fair Packaging and Labeling Act (FPLA)

Fair Packaging and Labeling Act (FPLA) is an Act to prevent the use of unfair or deceptive methods of packaging or labeling of certain consumer commodities.

2.2.3.3 - Federal Anti-Tampering Act

Federal Anti-Tampering Act prohibits certain tampering with consumer products (18 USC 1365). See IOM 8.8 for guidance on tampering investigations.

2.2.3.4 - Federal Import Milk Act

Federal Import Milk Act regulates the importation of raw and pasteurized bovine milk and cream from foreign producers.

2.2.3.5 - Federal Caustic Poison Act

Primarily a labeling Act specifying warnings and precautionary statements on labeling of certain household caustic preparations.

2.2.3.6 - Poison Prevention Packaging Act

Provides for special packaging to protect children from serious personal injury or serious illness resulting from handling, using, or ingesting household substances.

2.2.3.7 - Public Health Service Act (PHS)

Public Health Service Act (PHS) - Sampling: For biological products, which are also drugs under the FD&C Act, the sampling authority of both Acts exists.

Section 351(c) of Part F, Title III of the Public Health Service (PHS) Act [42 USC 262(c)] authorizes inspections of biological establishments (vaccines, serum, and blood). Authority to collect samples and records is found in 21 CFR 600.22. Section 361(a) of Part G of the PHS Act [42 USC 264] authorizes inspection and other activities for the enforcement of 21 CFR 1270, Human Tissue Intended for Transplantation, and 21 CFR 1240, Interstate Quarantine Regulations. Part 1240 covers the mandatory pasteurization for all milk in final package form intended for direct human consumption; the safety of molluscan shellfish; the sanitation of food service; and food, water, and sanitary facilities for interstate travelers on common carriers.

2.2.3.8 - Mammography Quality Standards Act of 1992

Mammography Quality Standards Act of 1992 amends the Public Health Service Act to establish the authority for the regulation of mammography services and radiological equipment.

2.2.4 - Code Of Federal Regulations (CFR)

The Code of Federal Regulations is a codification of the general and permanent rules published in the Federal Register by the Executive departments and agencies of the Federal Government. The Code is divided into 50 titles which represent broad areas subject to Federal regulation. Each title is divided into chapters which usually bear the name of the issuing agency. Each chapter is further subdivided into parts covering specific regulatory areas. For example, the specific regulation covering drug GMPs appears as "21 CFR 211", that is, Title 21, Part 211. Regulations enforced by FDA are found in volumes 1-8 of Title 21, parts 1-1299. They are updated as of April 1 of each year. The Federal Register and the CFR must be used together to determine the latest version of a given rule.

2.2.5 - Definitions

The following terms are used in assignments, correspondence, and various procedures described in this manual and used throughout FDA.

2.2.5.1 - Civil Number

A docket number used by US district courts to identify civil cases (seizure and injunction).

2.2.5.2 - Citation (Cite)

The section 305 Notice is a statutory requirement of the FD&C Act. It provides a respondent with an opportunity to show cause why he should not be prosecuted for an alleged violation. Response to the notice may be by letter, personal appearance, or an attorney(s).

2.2.5.3 - Criminal Number

A docket number used by the US district courts to identify criminal cases (prosecutions).

2.2.5.4 - FDC and INJ Numbers

The number used by the Chief Counsel's office to identify FDA cases.

2.2.5.5 - Complaint for Forfeiture

A document furnished to the U.S. attorney for filing with the clerk of the court to initiate a seizure.

2.2.5.6 - Home District

The Home District is the district in whose territory the alleged violation of the Act occurs, or in whose territory the firm or individual responsible for the alleged violation is physically located. The original point from which the article was shipped, or offered for shipment, as shown by the interstate records, is usually considered the point where the violation occurred; and the shipper of such article, as shown by such records, may be considered to be the alleged violator.

Where actions against a firm are based on goods which became violative after interstate shipment was made, or after reaching its destination (such as 301(k) violations), the dealer in whose possession the goods are sampled may be considered the violator, and the location of this dealer determines the "Home District".

2.2.5.7 - Nolle Prosequi (Nol-Pros)

The prosecutor or plaintiff in a legal matter will proceed no further in prosecuting the whole suit or specified counts.

2.2.5.8 - Nolo Contendere (Nolo)

A plea by a defendant in a criminal prosecution meaning "I will not contest it".

2.2.5.9 - Seizing District

The district where seizure is actually accomplished. The seizing district is not necessarily the collecting district, as in the case of intransit samples.

2.2.5.10 - Subpoena Duces Tecum

A writ commanding a person to appear in court bringing with him certain designated documents or things pertinent to the issues of a pending controversy.

2.2.5.11 - Supervising District

The district which exercises supervision over reconditioning lots in connection with seizure actions.

2.2.6 - Seizure

Seizure is a judicial civil action directed against specific offending goods, in which goods are "arrested." Originally designed to remove violative goods from consumer channels, it was intended primarily as a remedial step; however, the sanction often has a punitive and deterrent effect.

For more information on seizure actions consult RPM Chapter 6-1 “Seizures.”

2.2.6.1 - District Recommendation

The district considers all evidence, including any establishment inspection, sample collection, and analytical results. If indicated, seizure is recommended to headquarters.

2.2.6.2 - Headquarters

Except for certain direct seizure authority, district seizure recommendations are referred to the appropriate center for approval. If approved, the case is referred to the Office of Enforcement (HFC-200) which then requests the Chief Counsel to initiate seizure action.

2.2.6.3 - Department of Justice

The Food and Drug Division of the Department's Office of Chief Counsel reviews and forwards the seizure action to the U.S. attorney in whose judicial district the violative goods are located, through the seizing district. The U.S. attorney files a Complaint for Forfeiture addressed to the U.S. district court, setting forth the facts of the case and calling for the "arrest" of the goods. This Complaint is filed with the appropriate district court.

2.2.6.4 - U.S. District Court

The court orders the arrest of the goods by issuing a motion and warrant to the U.S. marshal, directing seizure of the goods.

The marshal seizes the goods, which then become the property of the court. You may be asked to assist the marshal in the seizure. If so, submit a memorandum to your district office covering this activity.

2.2.6.5 - Claimant and Options

Any person who has an interest in the goods may appear as claimant or to intervene, and claim the goods.

2.2.6.6 - Abandonment

If no claimant appears within a specified time, (return date), then the U.S. attorney requests a Default Decree of Condemnation and Forfeiture, in which the court condemns the goods and directs the U.S. marshal to destroy or otherwise dispose of the goods. Usually, the District assists the marshal in determining the method of disposal, and you may be asked to help in the actual disposition. Any disposition must be in accordance with the National Environmental Policy Act of 1969 (NEPA); 42 U.S.C. 4321-4347.

2.2.6.7 - Reconditioning for Compliance

A claimant may appear and propose the goods be reconditioned to bring them into compliance. After the FDA agrees to the method of reconditioning, the court issues a Decree of Condemnation permitting reconditioning under the supervision of the FDA, after a bond is posted. Salvage operations may include:

1. Cleaning, reworking, or other processing,
2. Relabeling, or
3. Denaturing.

2.2.6.8 - Contested Seizure

A claimant may file an answer to the complaint and deny the allegations. The issues then go to trial.

2.2.6.9 - District Follow-up

The district monitors the progress of the seizure and forwards appropriate reports to the headquarters.

2.2.7 - Prosecution

Prosecution is a criminal sanction directed against a firm and/or responsible individuals. They can be pursued at two levels: misdemeanor or felony. A prosecution is punitive, with the view of punishing past behavior and obtaining future compliance.

2.2.7.1 - Section 305 Notice

The section 305 Notice is a statutory requirement of the Act. It provides a respondent with an opportunity to explain why he should not be prosecuted for the alleged violation. Response to the notice may be by letter, personal appearance or attorney.

Under certain circumstances, the Agency will refer prosecution (or for further investigation) without first providing the opportunity for presentation of views in accordance with section 305 [See 21 CFR 7.84(a)(2) and (3)].

The facts developed at the hearing are reviewed, along with other evidence, and the district prepares a recommendation the case be:

1. Placed in permanent abeyance, with no further action, or
2. Placed in temporary abeyance, in which case the decision is delayed pending additional evidence, or for other reasons, or
3. Requests, with RFDD concurrence, ad hoc meeting when there is an indication of potential felony charges or the case is especially unusual, or
4. Forwarded to the Justice Department for prosecution.

The district recommendation is reviewed by Headquarters units in the light of current policy and procedure. If prosecution is indicated, the case is forwarded to the Office of Chief Counsel (OCC) for review. If the Chief Counsel agrees, the matter is forwarded to the Department of Justice (DOJ) where it is reviewed again. If DOJ concurs, the case is forwarded to the appropriate U. S. Attorney. Non-concurrence results in return of the case to FDA.

2.2.7.2 - Information

An Information is a legal document filed in misdemeanor actions identifying the defendants and setting forth the charges. The Information is forwarded to the appropriate U.S. Attorney, who then files the legal instruments. A trial date is set by the court. Ideally, trial preparation is a collaboration between representatives of the U. S. Attorney's office, OCC, the District and the involved Center.

2.2.7.3 - Grand Jury Proceedings

The Justice Department must proceed by indictment in all felony cases. Evidence in possession of the government is presented to the grand jury which decides if it is sufficient to warrant prosecution. If the grand jury returns a "True Bill", and the defendant pleads not guilty at the arraignment, preparation for trial begins.

The deliberations of a federal grand jury are secret, and only those whom the court has placed under Rule 6(e) of the Federal Rules of Criminal Procedure may be privy to the grand juries activities. Consequently, if you have been designated under the Rule, you may not divulge your knowledge of grand jury affairs to anyone, including colleagues or supervisors, unless they, too, have been placed under the Rule. Strict adherence to the rule of grand jury secrecy protects not only the integrity of the government's investigation, and the validity of any indictment the grand jury might return, but the rights of the person accused. See IOM 5.2.2.9 Working with a Grand Jury.

When you are assigned to work with, or for, a grand jury and are instructed as part of that assignment to conduct an inspection or an investigation, do not issue a Notice of Inspection (FDA-482) (See IOM 5.2.2.4 Conducting Regulatory Inspections When the Agency is Contemplating Taking, or is Taking, Criminal Action). Check with district management and the Assistant U.S. Attorney or Chief Counsel attorney involved, prior to initiating this type of assignment. Also, refer to IOM 5.2.2.4, 5.2.2.5, 5.2.2.6, 5.2.2.7, 5.2.2.8 and 5.2.2.9.

2.2.7.4 - District Follow-up

Appropriate reports are made to the Administration when the case terminates. Follow-up may involve inspections either of a routine nature or as directed by the court.

2.2.8 - Injunction

An injunction is a civil restraint issued by the court to prohibit violations of the Act. Injunction is designed to stem the flow of violative products in interstate commerce, and to correct the conditions in the establishment.

Injunction actions must be processed in strict time frames. Therefore, you may be requested to conduct an inspection to determine the current condition of a firm and to obtain specific information required for the injunction.

2.2.8.1 - Temporary Restraining Order (TRO)

Upon presentation of evidence, the U.S. district court may issue an order restraining defendant from certain acts, for a specific length of time. This period may be extended by order of the court.

2.2.8.2 - Hearing for Injunction

Prior to the expiration of the TRO, if one is involved, the U.S. Attorney, assisted by the district, presents evidence to support an injunction.

2.2.8.3 - Consent Decree of Injunction

The defendants may, following conferences with the U.S. Attorney, consent to a decree of preliminary or permanent injunction. If not, the issue goes to trial.

2.2.8.4 - Trial for Injunction

A preponderance of evidence is required to support an injunction. This differs from a prosecution, which requires evidence establishing guilt "beyond a reasonable doubt". Trial is before the district court. There is no trial by jury, unless demanded by the defendant. In violations of injunction (contempt), the action is brought under the Rules of Criminal Procedure.

2.2.8.5 - Preliminary or Permanent Injunction

A preliminary or permanent injunction enjoins a firm or individuals from continuing a specific violation(s). The terms of the injunction specify the steps to be taken to correct the violations at issue.

2.2.8.6 - District Follow-up

Generally, the district will police an injunction to assure the terms of the decree are met. This may include routine inspections or actual supervision of compliance activities dictated by the terms of the injunction.

2.2.9 - Emergency Permit Control

Section 404 of the FD&C Act [21 U.S.C. 344] provides for the issuance of temporary permits prescribing the conditions governing the manufacture, processing or packing of certain classes of foods. It applies to foods subject to contamination by injurious microorganisms, where such contamination cannot be adequately determined after such articles have entered interstate commerce.

2.2.10 - Detention Powers

Sections 402 and 409(b) of the Federal Meat Inspection Act, sections 19 and 24(b) of the Poultry Products Inspection Act, sections 5(d), 19, and 23(d) of the Egg Products Inspection Act, and section 304(g) of the FD&C Act [21 U.S.C. 334 (g)] provides certain detention powers.

In essence, articles subject to the Federal Meat Inspection Act or the Poultry Products Inspection Act that are believed to be adulterated or misbranded under the FD&C Act may be detained. FDA representatives may detain articles subject to the Egg Products Inspection Act, which are suspected to be in violation of that statute.

Devices may be detained under the FD&C Act for a maximum of thirty days when there is reason to believe they are adulterated or misbranded under the FD&C Act.

See IOM 2.7.2 for inspectional procedures, which must be followed, in exercising the detention authority.

2.2.11 - Courtroom Testimony

Effective testimony, whether it be in court before a judge or jury, grand jury or opposing counsel at a deposition, is a result of quality investigative skills; the ability to prepare factual and informative investigative reports; and thorough preparation for being a fact witness.

As a witness, you are required to testify from memory, but you are allowed to refer to diary notes, reports and memoranda, when necessary to refresh your recollection. For this reason, and the fact they are available to opposing counsel, the Agency insists your notes, reports and the like always be accurate, organized and complete.

There is little difference in giving testimony in court, in a deposition or before a grand jury. In a deposition, testimony is given upon interrogation by opposing counsel, under oath, before a court reporter. Be guided by your (the Government's) attorney in preparing for a deposition. Once completed, the deposition is available to all persons interested in the case, and is available for use at trial.

In a grand jury, testimony is given under oath to a group of jurors who determine whether sufficient evidence exists to charge someone with a felony (See IOM 2.2.7.3).

2.2.11.1 - Testimony Preparation

The following suggestions may be helpful in preparing to provide testimony in court, before a grand jury or at a deposition:

1. Carefully and thoroughly reviewing your diary notes, inspection reports and all samples collected.

2. Be neat in your personal appearance; dress conservatively in business attire, and be well groomed.

3. When you take the witness stand, get comfortable, sit erectly and carefully look around to familiarize yourself with the court surroundings.

4. Tell the truth. If asked, do not hesitate to admit you have discussed your testimony in advance with the U.S. Attorney's office.

5. Be sure you understand the question before you answer. If you don't understand the question, request clarification. Take your time. Give each question such thought as required to understand and formulate your answer. Do not answer questions too quickly. Give your attorney time to raise an objection in case it is a question you should not answer. Answer questions clearly and loudly enough so everyone can hear you. Look at the jury and address your remarks to it so all jury members will be able to hear and understand you. Speak directly and authoritatively, and do not use ambiguous phrases such as, "I guess so", "I believe," etc. Do not be afraid to say, "I don't know".

6. Be polite and serious at all times. Give an audible answer to all questions. Do not nod your head yes or no.

7. Do not lose your temper, even if baited by an attorney. Do not spar with examining attorneys; answer questions frankly, factually and confidently, then stop. Do not answer questions, which have been objected to until the court rules on the objection. Do not volunteer information.

8. If you make a mistake answering a question, correct it immediately. If a question can't be truthfully answered with a yes or no, you have the right to explain your answer. If you are asked questions about distances, time or speed, and your answer is only an estimate, be sure you make that clear.

9. If a recess is declared while you are on the stand, keep to yourself. Do not discuss your testimony with anyone except on special instructions from the U.S. Attorney or his/her assistant.

10. Be natural, be yourself. Do not be intimidated by personalities.

2.2.11.2 - Interviewing Persons under Arrest

Miranda Warning - In the Agency's normal course of operation, it is not necessary to read a person their rights, (i.e.: Miranda warnings) because the Agency does not routinely interview individuals who are in custody (under arrest). Miranda warnings are not necessary, during discussions with management when conducting inspections, during investigational interviews, or during a section 305 of the FD&C Act [21 U.S.C. 335] meeting because the individuals being interviewed are not in custody, and are free to leave at any time.

In certain situations, however, FDA personnel may interview someone who is already in custody. In this case, the individual must be given their Miranda rights.

When this situation is encountered, copy page 1 of IOM Exhibit 2-1. If the subject cannot speak/read English, you must arrange for a form in the appropriate language. Read this material to the individual, preferably in the presence of another person, and then have them sign and date the waiver statement. Submit the signed statement with your report. If the individual refuses to sign the statement, indicate this on the unsigned statement, and identify the witness on the document. Submit the unsigned statement with your report.

2.3 - Reconditioning and Destruction

801 of the FD&C Act [21 U.S.C. 334 and 381] provide the legal basis for reconditioning or destruction of goods under domestic seizure or import detention.

Reconditioning and destruction are the means whereby goods are brought into compliance with the law, or permanently disassociated from their intended use. Manpower may not be expended on supervision of reconditioning and destruction of goods except under administrative controls, detention, or emergency and disaster operations. See IOM 8.5 for operations in disasters.

FDA does not seek or condone the destruction of books or other publications. FDA policy and practice tries to be sensitive to the potential First Amendment issues associated with the regulation of books and other printed materials that function as labeling of a product. See Compliance Policy Guide 140.100. In the context of judicial enforcement, disposition of any labeling subject to the court's jurisdiction is determined by the court. In a voluntary compliance situation, the disposition is the prerogative of the manufacturer, distributor, wholesaler, or retailer. Agency policy does not authorize field employees to direct or limit the options for disposition of violative labeling or other printed materials in such circumstances. Good judgment should always be exercised in such matters.

Section 536(b) of the FD&C Act [21 U.S.C. 360ll (b)] provides authority for electronic products to be reworked if FDA determines they can be brought into compliance with radiation performance standards. Therefore, reconditioning of radiation-emitting products must be approved by CDRH, Office of Compliance, prior to implementation to assure compliance with performance standards. If a foreign manufacturer conducts the reconditioning, the district should notify both the importer/consignee and the foreign manufacturer's agent of all FDA actions.

2.3.1 - Definitions

2.3.1.1 - Reconditioning

The reworking, relabeling, segregation, or other manipulation which brings a product into compliance with the law, whether or not for its original intended use.

2.3.1.2 - Destruction

The procedures involved in rendering a product unsalvageable. Destruction may be accomplished by burning, burial, etc.

2.3.1.3 - Denaturing

Decharacterization of a product, whereby it is made unusable for its originally intended purpose.

2.3.2 - Disasters

Reconditioning and destruction of contaminated merchandise in times of disasters can assume national proportions and is handled differently than normal operations.

Instructions for operations pertaining to reconditioning and destruction during non-attack type disasters is covered in IOM 8.5.

2.4 - Consent Decree

2.4.1 - Policy

Seized goods may be released under bond, by court order to be destroyed or brought into compliance. The order normally provides for supervision of the operation by FDA. Release of the bond depends upon your certification the court order has been satisfactorily executed.

Do not undertake reconditioning until you are certain a court order has been entered, bond posted, and goods released by the marshal. Be certain the identity and amount of goods corresponds with that seized. Be sure you are familiar with the terms of the court order.

Reconditioning or destruction may, at times, be permitted without continuous supervision. However, the lot must be checked before operations start, rechecked intermittently and upon completion. Supervision must be sufficient to assure none of the lot was diverted. All of the goods involved in the action, including reconditioned goods as well as discarded material such as screenings, old labels, etc., must be accounted for. If organoleptic examination will not permit a judgment regarding the degree of compliance, collect suitable samples for laboratory examination. If the reconditioning process does not appear to comply with the order, immediately advise the claimant and your supervisor.

2.4.2 - Relabeling

Before permitting any relabeling operation, be sure FDA has approved the proposed new label. Provide an accounting of disposition of the old labels. Submit three (3) copies of the new label and three (3) copies of the old label with your report of the operation.

2.4.3 - Reworking

Before permitting any manipulation, determine the proposed process has been approved by your district. This includes ensuring the facilities and equipment to be used are sanitary and effective for the proposed process. Report the yield of the reworked product.

2.4.4 - Segregation

Thoroughly examine goods set aside as legal, and submit samples for laboratory examination, if indicated. Follow up on disposition of reject material to prevent illegal diversion. Describe the method of destruction of unfit material resulting from the segregation process.

2.4.5 - Destruction

Supervise and describe the method of destruction of goods, labels, labeling, etc. and report the amount destroyed.

2.4.6 - Disposition Of Rejects

Arrange for reject materials to be destroyed in an approved manner, under your supervision. The method of disposition will have already been approved by the District, and in some cases set out in the Consent Decree.

2.4.7 - Release of Goods

Do not authorize release of reconditioned goods, unless specifically directed by your supervisor. Formal release is normally handled by district headquarters.

2.4.8 - Reporting

Promptly submit a detailed report upon conclusion of the operation. Where the operation is prolonged, submit interim progress reports. Include the following information in your report of the operation:

1. Identification of the case (sample number, court number, FDA number, product and claimant).

2. Description of the method of reconditioning or destruction.

3. Disposition of rejects; explanation for unaccounted goods.

4. Findings of field examinations.

5. Exhibits and samples collected. Do not pay for samples collected during reconditioning operations conducted under a Consent Decree.

6. Expenses, including time spent in supervision and travel, mileage, per diem, and incidental expenses.

2.5 - Default Decree

2.5.1 - Policy

When no claimant appears in a seizure case, the court issues a Default Decree of Condemnation condemning the goods. It may or may not specify the manner of disposal. Disposition, whether by destruction, distribution to charitable institutions or sale by salvage must be approved and monitored by the Government.

Primary responsibility for disposition of seized lots following a default decree lies with the U.S. Marshal's Office.

FDA inspectional personnel frequently accompany the marshal to witness the operation. Although you are there in an advisory capacity, assist the marshal in every way to assure compliance with the court order.

2.5.2 - Reporting

Promptly submit a written report of your observations upon completion of the operation. See IOM 2.4.8.

2.6 - Compliance Achievement

2.6.1 - Policy

FDA uses a blend of industry voluntary correction and regulatory actions to help achieve industry compliance.

A voluntary corrective action is defined as the observed voluntary repair, modification, or adjustment of a violative condition, or product. For purposes of this definition, violative means the product or condition does not comply with the Acts or associated regulations enforced by the Agency.

Voluntary destruction in lieu of seizure of small lots of violative goods shall be encouraged, where the proposed method is adequate. Supervision of voluntary segregation and denaturing of violative goods shall not be provided, except where it can be accomplished with dispatch, minimal inspectional resources, and in a manner consistent with procedures outlined in this Subchapter.

The most extensive actions in this area usually occur in disaster situations. Follow instructions in IOM Subchapter 8.5 - Disaster Procedures.

Do not engage in actual destruction, reconditioning, repair, modification, etc. of goods. This is the responsibility of the owner or dealer. You are in the capacity of witness only. Samples should be collected of violative goods prior to voluntary destruction to support subsequent action against the responsible individuals. Take photographs where applicable. See IOM 5.10.2.1 and IOM 2.6.4, 2.6.4.1/2 or reporting requirements.

2.6.2 - Destruction

Before you supervise destruction, be sure management is aware the action is voluntary and that you are acting only as a witness. See IOM 2.6.4.

Witness all destructions personally, making certain destroyed goods are rendered totally unsalvageable for food, drug, device, etc. use. Keep in mind personal and public safety. Exercise proper precautions in dealing with potentially dangerous substances and situations. Comply with local ordinances regarding the disposition of garbage and trash.

Note certain products should not be disposed of in a conventional manner (e.g.: sanitary landfill, flushing down the drain, etc.). In particular, certain products which have been banned in the past (chloroform, methapyrilene, hexachlorophene, PCB, etc.), are classified by EPA as hazardous and toxic substances and may require a special method of disposal by a licensed hazardous disposal facility. Any possible hazardous or toxic substance (carcinogen, mutagen, etc.) should not be disposed of without prior consultation by the firm with the U.S. Environmental Protection Agency and/or the regulating state authority. Refer to 21 CFR 25 and the National Environmental Protection Act for guidance regarding the environmental impact of voluntary destructions.

2.6.2.1 - DEA Controlled Drugs

FDA and DEA have a written policy to permit FDA representatives, in certain situations, to witness the destruction of DEA controlled drugs. The procedures and instructions to follow when these drugs are destroyed are:

2.6.2.1.1 - DEA Approval

FDA and the Drug Enforcement Administration (DEA) have a mutual, written policy concerning witnessing the destruction of drugs under the distribution control of DEA. This provides for FDA, upon receiving a request to witness such destruction, to advise the DEA regional office and obtain approval for the action. If approval is requested by telephone and verbally approved, the approval should be reduced to writing for the record.

2.6.2.1.2 - Procedure

The necessity for FDA personnel to witness destruction of DEA controlled drugs will normally happen only when FDA is already present in the firm, encounters DEA controlled drugs, and is requested to witness destruction, or when DEA controlled drugs are to be destroyed at the same time FDA is witnessing destruction of drugs not under DEA control.

If you are in a firm either making an inspection or to witness destruction of drugs under FDA's distribution control, and the firm requests you also witness destruction of DEA controlled drugs, do not commit yourself. Telephone your supervisor for instructions. You will be advised whether or not to proceed after your district communicates with DEA. In all other situations refer the requester to DEA.

If the request to witness the destruction is approved, observe the destruction, and prepare DEA Form DEA 41 as follows:

1. List each dosage form of each drug on a separate line. Calculate amounts for columns 6 and 7.
2. Line out the inappropriate sentences in the paragraph following line 32.
3. Date and sign the form.
4. Type or print your name, title, and district under your signature.

Prepare the original only and submit it to your district for transmittal to DEA.

2.6.3 - Reconditioning

The supervision of voluntary segregation of violative goods without the regulatory safeguards of seizure should be avoided. Voluntary segregation and destruction of violative lots should be encouraged; but under no circumstances should you supervise the voluntary segregation and salvage of unfit goods, regardless of the nature of the violation or the size of the lot. Be sure management is aware the segregation is its responsibility. Collect samples where indicated, and/or advise the dealer or owner of his responsibilities under the law. If the dealer decides to voluntarily destroy any lot, refer him to the National Environmental Protection Act (NEPA). See IOM 2.6.2.

2.6.4 - Reporting

Report any voluntary correction of a problem unrelated to a district recommendation for regulatory action.

2.6.4.1 - Documenting Voluntary Destruction

Prior to supervising voluntary destruction, prepare a statement on the firm's letterhead or on an FDA 463a, Affidavit, providing the following information.

1. Voluntary nature of the action, with you as a witness.
2. Name of the product, including applicable code marks.
3. Condition of the lot.
4. Amount.
5. Method of destruction.
6. Signature of responsible individual.

2.6.4.2 - Compliance Achievement Reporting

The following are examples of compliance actions to be described in the report, EI Record, and reported into the Compliance Achievement Reporting System in FACTS (Exhibit 5-15) per district office SOP's:

2.6.4.2.1 - Violative Products

Voluntary destruction by the person in possession of any violative product.

2.6.4.2.2 - Destruction by Cooperating Officials

Destruction of violative products by a cooperating food or health official, where such product was discovered by and reported to such official by FDA when those officials were doing work for FDA under contract. Do not report formal condemnation by cooperating officials in the usual course of their independent work.

2.6.4.2.3 - Manufacturer's Raw Materials

Voluntary destruction of manufacturer's raw materials during the course of an inspection. For example, decomposed cream or filthy milk.

2.6.4.2.4 - Capital Improvements

Significant improvements correcting a violative condition such as new equipment, rodent-proofing, etc. These should be reported at follow-up inspections where actual improvement has been accomplished or committed, and the improvement is the result of a previous FDA observation or suggestion and not as a result of a seizure, injunction or prosecution.

2.6.4.2.5 - Correction of GMP Deviations

During an inspection the investigator observes GMP deficiencies have been corrected since the previous EI. These corrections are based on the previous FDA 483.

2.6.4.2.6 - FORMULA/LABEL CORRECTION

Based on a sample analysis, consumer complaint, etc., a product formula or label is corrected.

2.6.4.2.7 - Additional Personnel

Employment of personnel for quality improvement or improved quality control.

2.6.4.2.8 - Educational and/or Training

Initiation of an educational and/or training program among employees or producers, or other general industry movement to improve conditions.

2.6.4.2.9 - Items Not Reported in Facts

Do not report:

1. Recalls, although voluntary, because they are already recorded elsewhere (FACTS).

2. Corrections which are not directly attributable to the efforts of FDA, or states under contract to FDA.

3. Corrections as a result of a seizure, injunction or prosecution.

For products involving the field compliance testing of diagnostic X-Ray equipment, use form FDA 2473a to report these actions, as directed by the Compliance Program. Submit the completed form to your district. Your district will submit a copy to the CDRH, Office of Compliance and maintain a copy for the district files.

2.7 - Detention Activities

2.7.1 - Overview and Authority

The objective of any detention is to protect the consumer by preventing movement in interstate commerce or by removing from interstate commerce a food or device that may be adulterated or misbranded. The specific statutory authorities, as well as specific set of guidelines that would apply to either foods or medical devices are outlined in this section of the IOM. The detaining of foods or medical devices will depend on the product/s involved;

the situation and evidence observed/collected; and which statutory authority is being invoked to accomplish the detention.

2.7.1.1 - Overview

Detention differs from controlling the distribution of violative products in interstate commerce by civil judicial actions such as seizures or injunctions accomplished under a court order (See IOM 2.2.6 and 2.2.8).

Foods or medical devices in "domestic import" as well as "import status" could be detained as described in this subchapter provided they meet the criteria listed below. Normally, however, detention of foods and medical devices in import status are covered separately in IOM Chapter 6 - Imports.

2.7.1.1.1 - Accomplishing a Detention

Accomplishing a Detention can take one or more paths depending on the product/s involved and the actual statutes invoked, which are covered under the "Authorities" section of this subchapter. Some of the statutes under which detentions can be accomplished are under section 304 (Seizure) of the Federal Food Drug and Cosmetic Act (FD&C), including 304(g) and 304(h), which cover Medical Devices and Foods, both human and animal. Other statutes which cover detention are those involving products under dual jurisdiction of the US Food and Drug Administration (FDA) and the US Department of Agriculture (USDA), specifically meat, poultry, and egg products.

2.7.1.1.2 - Detention of Medical Devices

Detention of medical devices believed to be adulterated or misbranded can only be accomplished under one statutory path: FD&C 304(g) - covered under the regulations set forth in 21 CFR 800.55.

2.7.1.1.3 - Detention of Foods

Detention of foods (human or animal) can be accomplished under one of two statutory paths:

1. section 801(a) to detain articles of food in import status. See 21 CFR Part 1, subpart K and FD&C Act section 304(h).

2. Detention of dual jurisdiction meat, poultry, or egg products: Such products that meet the jurisdictional requirements of section 304 of the FD&C may be adulterated or misbranded, and are covered under either sections 402 and 409(b) of the Federal Meat Inspection Act (FMIA, 21 U.S.C. 601 et seq.), sections 19 and 24(b) of the Poultry Products Inspection Act (PPIA, 21 U.S.C. 451 et seq.), or sections 19 and 23(d) of the Egg Products Inspection Act (EPIA, 21 U.S.C. 1031 et seq.

3. Detention authority under the FMIA, PPIA, and EPIA does NOT extend to meat, poultry, and egg products when those products are inside a USDA-inspected facility.

2.7.1.1.4 - Detention Procedural Steps

The procedural steps to be followed in both executing and terminating a detention differ slightly depending on which statutory path is deemed most appropriate and chosen, and agency clearances that are required may differ depending on the type of detention. You should consult your supervisor before detaining dual jurisdiction FDA/USDA products under FD&C section 304 and associated FDA/USDA statutes. You must have the approval of your District Director before detaining any devices under section 304(g). You must have the approval of your District Director or an official senior to such director prior to detaining foods under the authority of FD&C section 304(h).

2.7.1.2 - Authorities

The various Acts described in this subsection provide certain detention powers for FDA. Pertinent sections of the FMIA, PPIA, EPIA, and FD&C Act, and its Regulations pertaining to detention of devices and food, are printed on the reverse of page 1 of the FDA 2289, Detention Notice (IOM Exhibit 2-2).

2.7.1.2.1 - Food Drug and Cosmetic Act

Section 304(g) of the FD&C Act provides FDA with authority to detain a device believed to be adulterated or misbranded. You should become familiar with this section and the regulations implementing it. See 21 CFR 800.55. At the present time, these regulations apply only to devices intended for human use. See FD&C Act section 304(g) [21 U.S.C. 334 (g)].

Section 304(h) of the FD&C Act provides FDA with the authority to order the detention of any article of food that is found during an inspection, examination, or investigation under the Act, if the officer or qualified employee has credible evidence or information indicating that the article of food presents a threat of serious adverse health consequences or death to humans or animals. See 21 CFR Part 1, subpart K.

2.7.1.2.2 - Federal Meat Inspection Act

Federal Meat Inspection Act (FMIA) - Sections 402 and 409(b) provide the FDA with the authority to detain meat products subject to the FMIA, found outside an USDA inspected plant, if the FDA has reason to believe the products are adulterated or misbranded under the FD&C Act. The detention may not exceed twenty (20) days and the items detained shall not be moved by any person from the place of detention until released by the FDA representative.

2.7.1.2.3 - Poultry Products Inspection Act

Poultry Products Inspection Act (PPIA) -Sections 19 and 24(b) provide the FDA with the authority to detain poultry products subject to the PPIA found outside an USDA inspected plant, if the FDA has reason to believe the products are adulterated or misbranded under the FD&C Act. Detention may not exceed twenty (20) days and the items detained shall not be moved from the place of detention until released by the FDA representative.

2.7.1.2.4 - Egg Products Inspection Act

Egg Products Inspection Act (EPIA) - Sections 19 and 23(d) provide the FDA with the authority to detain egg products subject to the EPIA, found outside an USDA inspected plant, if the FDA has reason to believe the products are in violation of the EPIA Act. Detention may not exceed twenty (20) days and the items detained shall not be moved from the place of detention until released by the FDA representative.

2.7.1.3 - Definitions

Regulatory

2.7.1.3.1 - Device

Section 201(h) of the FD&C Act [21 U.S.C. 321 (h)] defines a device as follows: "The term "device" *** means an instrument, apparatus, implement, machine, contrivance, implant, in-vitro reagent, or other similar or related article, including any component, part, or accessory, which is:

1. Recognized in the official National Formulary, or the United States Pharmacopoeia, or any supplement to them,

2. Intended for use in the diagnosis of disease or other conditions, or in the cure, mitigation, treatment, or prevention of disease, in man or other animals, or

3. Intended to affect the structure or any function of the body of man or other animals, and which does not achieve its primary intended purposes through chemical action within or on the body of man or other animals and which is not dependent upon being metabolized for the achievement of any primary intended purposes."

2.7.1.3.2 - Food

For the purpose of detention of food under section 304(h) of the FD&C Act, see section 201(f) of the FD&C Act, which defines food as follows: “(1) articles used for food or drink for man or other animals, (2) chewing gum, and (3) articles used for components of any such article.”

Examples of food include, but are not limited to, fruits, vegetables, fish, dairy products, eggs, raw agricultural commodities for use as food or components of food, animal feed, including pet food, food and feed ingredients and additives, including substances that migrate into food from food packaging and other articles that contact food, dietary supplements and dietary ingredients, infant formula, beverages, including alcoholic beverages and bottled water, live food animals, bakery goods, snack foods, candy, and canned foods.

2.7.1.3.3 - Perishable Food

For the purpose of detention of food under section 304(h) of the FD&C Act, the term “perishable food” means food that is not heat-treated; not frozen; and not otherwise preserved in a manner so as to prevent the quality of the food from being adversely affected if held longer than 7 calendar days under normal shipping and storage conditions. See 21 CFR 1.377.

2.7.1.3.4 - Meat Products and Poultry Products (Dual Jurisdiction)

For FDA purposes, meat products and poultry products are defined as the carcasses of cattle, sheep, swine, goats, horses, mules, other equines, or domesticated birds, parts of such carcasses, and products made wholly or in part from such carcasses, except products exempted by U.S.D.A. because they contain a relatively small amount of meat or poultry products (e.g.; meat flavored sauces, pork and beans, etc.). Examine labels for USDA Shield or coding information to help determine if it is a USDA product.

2.7.1.3.5 - Egg and Egg Products (Dual Jurisdiction)

The term "egg" means the shell egg of the domesticated chicken, turkey, duck, goose, or guinea.

The term "egg product" means any dried, frozen, or liquid eggs, with or without added ingredients, excepting products which contain eggs only in relatively small proportion or historically have not been, in the judgment of the Secretary, considered by consumers as products of the egg food industry, and which may be exempted by the Secretary under such conditions as he may prescribe to assure the egg ingredients are not adulterated and such products are not represented as egg products. This would be done on a case by case basis by USDA.

2.7.2 - Inspectional Procedure

Direct attention to meat, poultry, or egg products only when found during your regular operations; when so instructed in a Compliance Program Guidance Manual; following up on complaints; or, on other assignments as directed by your supervisor.

Detention of food under section 304(h) of the FD&C Act should be considered only when there is credible evidence or information indicating that the article of food presents a threat of serious adverse health consequences or death to humans or animals, and only when approved by the District Director or an FDA official senior to such Director.

In evaluating whether credible evidence or information exists for purposes of detention of food, consider a number of factors, including, but not limited to, the reliability and reasonableness of the evidence or information and the totality of the facts and circumstances.

2.7.2.1 - Criteria for Detention

The criteria listed are for your guidance in judging whether or not the product or products should be detained. Detention may be made when all of the requirements listed for the particular detention authority are met.

2.7.2.1.1 - Devices

For detention of devices under section 304(g) of the FD&C Act, the requirements are:

1. You have reason to believe the device is adulterated or misbranded.

2. There is no reasonable assurance the device will not be used, moved, altered, or tampered with in any manner before the FDA can take appropriate legal action.

3. The device is intended for human use.

2.7.2.1.2 - Food

For detention of food under section 304(h) of the FD&C Act, the requirements are:

1. The article meets the definition of food in section 201(f) of the FD&C Act.

2. You have credible evidence or information that the article of food presents a threat of serious adverse health consequences or death to humans or animals.

3. A "serious adverse health consequences" determination should be made by CFSAN or CVM, as appropriate.

4. The article of food is not a meat, poultry, or egg product inside a USDA-inspected facility. If the article of food is a meat, poultry, or egg product outside a USDA-inspected facility, consult with your supervisor.

2.7.2.1.3 - Meat and Poultry Products

For detention of products subject to the Federal Meat Inspection Act or the Poultry Products Inspection Act the requirements are:

1. The article meets the jurisdictional requirements of section 304 of the FD&C Act and is in commercial channels.

2. The article is located in an establishment which does not have USDA meat or poultry inspection service.

3. The article is intended for human food channels or could be readily diverted into such channels.

4. The article appears to be adulterated or misbranded under the FD&C Act.

NOTE: For any contemplated detentions based on adulteration under section 402(b) of the FD&C Act [21 U.S.C. 342 (b)], check with your supervisor. These detentions should be cleared with the Center for Food Safety and Applied Nutrition.

2.7.2.1.4 - Egg and Egg Products

For detention of products subject to the Egg Products Inspection Act the requirements are:

1. The article, whether or not in interstate commerce, is located in an establishment which does not have USDA Egg Products Inspection Service.

2. The article is intended for human food channels or could be readily diverted into such channels.

3. There is reason to believe the article is in violation of the Egg Products Inspection Act.

2.7.2.2 - Detention Procedure

After assuring yourself the criteria for detention are met, immediately advise your supervisor of the situation. The information you furnish should consist of that requested in blocks numbered 2, 4, 5, 7, 8, 10, 11, 13, 15, 19, 20, 21, 22, 24 and 26 on the Detention Notice, fda 2289. see IOM 2.7.2.3.

For detention of medical devices under section 304(g) and articles of food under section 304(h) of the FD&C Act, the District Director in whose District the device or article of food involved is located, or for foods, an FDA official senior to such director, must approve the detention order in writing. If prior written approval is not feasible, prior oral approval must be obtained and confirmed in writing as soon as possible.

2.7.2.2.1 - Considerations

If the article of food to be detained is in-transit aboard a conveyance, e.g., railcar, truck, or ship, be aware that that detention of food aboard a conveyance may impact other activities of commerce that are dependent upon the ongoing operation of the conveyance.

It is possible that we will allow the detained food to be removed from the conveyance to a storage facility. However, consult with your supervisor on this matter because the determination of whether the food can be moved from the conveyance to another location should be made based on considerations about the nature of the contaminant, security, preservation of the food, and accessibility to the food during the period of detention.

For all detentions, follow the guidance in IOM section 4.3.4 to determine when FDA may examine a package that is in the possession, control or custody of a common carrier. Guidance on resealing a conveyance is also found in IOM section 4.3.4.3.

If your supervisor instructs you to detain the article, proceed as in IOM 2.7.2.3, and 2.7.2.4.

2.7.2.2.2 - Executing the Detention

When you have been authorized to place a detention proceed as follows:

1. Indicate conditions that are to be maintained while the article of food is detained in the "Remarks" section of the detention notice (block #26). If applicable, also indicate that the movement of the food to another facility during detention has been authorized in writing by an authorized FDA representative, pursuant to 21 CFR 1.380 and 1.381.

a. For detention of food under section 304(h), determine the storage conditions required, e.g., refrigeration, and whether movement to another facility is necessary to either provide the storage conditions required or for security purposes. Consult your supervisor for guidance. Indicate conditions that are to be maintained while the article of food is detained in the "Remarks" section of the detention notice (block #26). If applicable, also indicate that the movement of the food to another facility during detention has been authorized in writing by an authorized FDA representative, pursuant to 21 CFR 1.380 and 1.381.

b. Maintain surveillance on the detained in-transit products and after products are placed in storage if possible.

c. Arrange for the custodian to place the product in proper storage if the custodian will agree.

d. If neither (b) nor (c) is possible, place product under detention and remove it to a proper storage facility. Notify the custodian of the place of storage (use block 16 on the FDA-2289) and advise your supervisor of the necessity for including this information in the letter to the owner.

e. After a device is detained, it may not be moved unless specific procedures are followed. Consult your supervisor for guidance.

2. Personally inform the immediate custodian, at the highest management level, that the article is under FDA detention, and if a device, that the record keeping requirements of 21 CFR 800.55(k) are in force. If an article of food is under detention, inform the custodian that the detained article of food may not be transferred within or from the place where it has been ordered detained, or from the place to which it was removed unless a request to modify the detention order has been authorized in writing by FDA.

3. Prepare the "Notice of Detention, FDA-2289", as instructed in IOM 2.7.2.3.1, and issue page 1, the original, to the custodian named. If the product is a device, or an article of food detained under section 304(h) of the FD&C Act, point out the appeal rights of the owner, which are listed on the back of Page 1 of the FDA-2289.

4. Affix a sufficient number of "Detention Tag, FDA-2290" to the article in a manner to assure visibility. If necessary, a label other than the Detention Tag may be used to identify an article of food that has been detained, provided the label includes all the information listed on the current FDA-2290.

2.7.2.3 - Detention Notice FDA 2289

The Detention Notice, FDA 2289, is a pre-numbered five-part snap-out form, constructed and arranged to serve as a Notice of Detention and as a report of the action.

2.7.2.3.1 - Preparation of Detention Notice

Print or type the information in the appropriate blocks. The first page blocks which must be filled in per statute 21 CFR 1.382 are those numbered 1, 3, 6, 9, 10, 11, 12, 15, 16, 17, and 18. Indicate the name and title of the person who approved the detention order and the manner in which the approval was obtained in blocks #17 and 18. For devices mark #24 and #26 N/A. For meat, poultry or egg products not being detained under the authority of section 304(h) of the FD&C Act, mark #17 and 18 N/A. Block 2 should also be completed. Once page 1 is completed, signed, and issued to the custodian, it becomes an official document and the detention period begins.

You should immediately complete the additional pages of the Notice of Detention (2 through 5) and submit them to your supervisor, for processing the action. Blocks to be filled in on these pages are items 13, 14 and 19 through 28. These blocks should be completed as appropriate (e.g. if samples were collected) or according to the product being detained (e.g. device or food) if the pertinent information can be readily determined. See IOM Exhibit 2-2.

2.7.2.3.2 - Preparation of Page 1 (FDA 2289)

Preparation of Page 1:

1. For detention of articles of food, the District Director's email address and fax number must also be included in this block. For detentions under the FMIA, PPIA, and EPIA, this information should also be included.

2. NAME OF CUSTODIAN - Obtain the name of the highest-ranking official of the firm at the place of detention. Page 1 of the FDA 2289 is to be issued to the person named in this block.

3. DETENTION NOTICE NUMBER - This is normally pre-stamped on each form. In the event that an electronic version of the form is utilized in the field, the detention number from a pre-printed detention form must be entered and the original pre-printed form bearing that number destroyed. Any correspondence or subsequent actions should reference this number.

4. TITLE OF CUSTODIAN - Insert proper official title such as president, warehouse manager, etc. Do not use courtesy titles.

5. TELEPHONE NO. - Insert the office telephone number, including area cod.

6. DATE AND HOUR DETAINED - Insert actual date and time you hand the original to the custodian. The period of detention begins when you issue the original to that person.

7. FIRM NAME - Enter the legal name of the custodial firm.

8. ADDRESS - Use complete street name, city, state and Zip Code of custodial firm.

9. MAXIMUM DETENTION ______ DAYS - Enter "20" for detention of meat, poultry or egg products. Enter either "20" or "30", as instructed by your supervisor, for detention of devices, or detention of articles of food under section 304(h) of the FD&C Act.

10. NAME OF DETAINED ARTICLE - Use the actual name of the actual product e.g., "Beef Pot Pies with mushrooms", not just "Pies"; "Dr. Z's Tongue Depressors", not just "device".

11. SIZE OF DETAINED LOT - Indicate number of cases or other type container or article and subordinate containers, e.g., 2000 cases/24/#2 cans, 250 half sides pork carcasses, 500/fore quarters veal, 95 crates/50 lbs. whole fryers, 25/30 lb. cans frozen eggs, etc.

12. DETAINED ARTICLE LABELED - Quote enough labeling so the article can be positively identified. Include product numbers, lot numbers, serial numbers, control codes, grade marks, etc.

13. APPROXIMATE VALUE OF LOT - This is the wholesale or invoice value of the merchandise. Estimate if there is no documentary reference you can quote.

14. SAMPLE NUMBER(S) - List numbers of any samples taken in connection with the detention.

15. REASON FOR DETENTION - Give a brief, general statement of the reasons for detention, i.e., describe the apparent violation and briefly list evidence available to substantiate it. In the case of detention of food under section 304(h) of the FD&C Act, include information about the "serious adverse health consequence" determination. Keep in mind that any classified information supporting the detention of food must be protected from unauthorized disclosure in the interest of national security. Consult with your supervisor for the requirement to protect classified information according to Executive Order 12866. If the product is a device, always state not only the section of the FD&C Act the device is believed to violate, but the particulars of the violation as well. Discuss the reasons for detention with your supervisor when you obtain the permission to detain a device. See page 3 of IOM Exhibit 2-2.

16. DETAINED ARTICLE STORED AT - In most instances this will be the same as the custodial firm indicated in blocks 7 and 8. However, if the product has been moved to another location, enter the name and address of the firm and location where it finally comes to rest and will stay until the detention is terminated. Once the product is detained, it is unlawful to move it without direct authority from FDA, except that devices may be moved and processed under 21 CFR 800.55(h)(2) pursuant to section 304(g)(2)(B) of the FD&C Act [21 U.S.C. 334 (g)(2)(B)]. Articles of food detained under section 304(h) of the FD&C Act may only be moved if FDA approves a request to modify a detention order under 21 CFR 1.381(c).

17. Name and title of person who approved the detention order. For detentions other than detention of food under section 304(h) of the FD&C Act, enter "N/A."

18. Indicate whether approval of the detention order was written or oral. If oral, you must obtain written confirmation of the approval as soon as possible. For detentions other than detention of food under section 304(h) of the FD&C Act, enter "N/A."

    NAME OF FDA EMPLOYEE - Print or type.

    SIGNATURE - Sign the form.

    TITLE - Enter your title.

2.7.2.3.3 - Preparation of Page 2 through 5 (FDA-2289)

The blocks on pages 2 through 5 are identical and completion of these constitutes your report on the detention, unless directed otherwise by your supervisor.

19. In the case of detention of food under section 304(h) of the FD&C Act, if the owner of the article can be readily determined, you must issue a copy of the detention notice to the owner as well as the custodian listed in block #2.

20. NAME AND ADDRESS OF INITIAL SHIPPER OR SELLER - - Enter name and address of person or firm who first shipped or sold the product.

21. NAME AND ADDRESS OF SUBSEQUENT SHIPPERS OR SELLERS - If products have passed through more than one firm prior to coming to your attention, list these firms.

22. NAME OF CARRIERS - List carrier or carriers involved, starting with the one who first picked up the article.

23. DATE LOT SHIPPED - Use date on a shipping document, not the invoice date.

24. NAME AND ADDRESS OF PACKING PLANT - Enter firm name and address of the plant where products were actually packed, processed, manufactured or assembled. For devices or articles of food other than meat, poultry, and egg products, enter "N/A".

25. DATE LOT RECEIVED - Self-explanatory.

26. PACKING PLANT USDA NO. - All plants under U.S. Department of Agriculture inspections are numbered. This number is placed on products packed or processed in that particular plant. Enter the complete number. For devices and articles of food other than meat, poultry, and egg products, enter "N/A".

27. DESCRIPTION OF SAMPLE - Describe sample collected in connection with the detention operations. This will be the same as on the C/R.

28. REMARKS - Elaborate on items wherever necessary. List any recommendations you made to the custodian for special storage such as refrigerated, frozen, etc.

2.7.2.3.4 - Distribution of FDA-2289

Distribution of FDA-2289 - The five-part snap-out is distributed as follows:

1. Page 1, original - Give to custodian and, if applicable, give a copy of page 1 to the owner of the article.

2. Page 2, 3, 4 - Turn in to your district immediately using the fastest means possible.

3. Page 5 - Retain in your possession.

2.7.2.4 - Detention Tag FDA 2290

This tag is a warning and identification device intended to be affixed to the detained products.

2.7.2.4.1 - Preparation

As soon as you have issued the Detention Notice, fill out Detention Tags, FDA 2290, following the instructions below. See IOM Exhibit 2-3.

2.7.2.4.2 - Front of Tag

Front of Tag.

"DETENTION DATE AND HOUR" - Copy the date and hour of detention from block #6 of the Detention Notice.

"DETENTION NOTICE NO. DN" - Copy the exact number from block #3 of the Detention Notice.

"MAXIMUM DETENTION _____ DAYS" - Copy the number of days from block #9 of the Detention Notice.

"NAME FDA EMPLOYEE WHO ISSUED DETENTION NOTICE" - Print or type.

"SIGNATURE" - Sign.

"TITLE" - Enter your title.

"NAME OF THE EMPLOYEE AFIXING TAG (if different from issuing employee)"

"SIGNATURE OF EMPLOYEE AFIXING TAG (if different from issuing employee)"

"TITLE OF EMPLOYEE AFIXING TAG (if different from issuing employee)"

2.7.2.4.3 - Reverse of Tag

Reverse of Tag.

"NAME OF DETAINED ARTICLE" - Enter the name exactly as in Block #10 of Detention Notice.

"DETAINED ARTICLE LABELED" - Copy enough from Block #12 of Detention Notice to identify the product.

"SIZE OF DETAINED LOT" - Copy from Block #11 of Detention Notice.

2.7.2.4.4 - Use of Tag

Complete and affix tags so they are visible on several sides of the lot detained. Use sufficient tags to give adequate warning the lot is under U.S FDA Detention and must not be used, moved, or tampered with, in any manner.

Each tag has a self-locking pin, the point of which should be firmly inserted in an appropriate seam, border, flap, or other area of the container or product, and pulled sharply downward to engage the top curve of the pin. Do not just lay tags on the articles. Secure them to the containers or products. If locking pin cannot be used, tape or tie the tag firmly onto the container or item.

Advise the custodian that Detention Tags have been affixed, and of the reason for the detention. Also advise the custodian that the merchandise may not be moved without written permission of the Agency. In-process devices may be completed without permission. For devices, see 21 CFR 800.55(h)(2) for instructions. For detention of foods, see 21 CFR 1.381(c).

2.7.2.5 - Termination of Detention

When final action has been taken on the detention, you will be authorized to terminate the detention. This will occur when one of the following conditions has been met.

1. For articles of food under detention, the article of food has been destroyed under appropriate supervision.

2. For devices, or for meat, poultry, or egg products detained under authority of the FMIA, PPIA, or EPIA, the product has been brought into compliance, denatured or destroyed under appropriate supervision.

3. For meat, poultry, and egg products detained under authority of the FMIA, PPIA, or EPIA, the USDA, state, county, or local authorities have accepted jurisdiction and control of the article.

4. For meat, poultry, and egg products detained under authority of the FMIA, PPIA, or EPIA, it has been determined there is no significant violation of the FD&C Act, or of the EPIA, whichever is applicable, and the USDA has been notified that FDA intends to terminate the detention.

5. Twenty consecutive days have expired (or 20 or 30 days, for detention of foods and devices), counting from the day and hour of detention of the product.

6. Seizure or other legal action has been accomplished.

7. The district director or the Regional Food and Drug Director order the termination.

2.7.2.5.1 - Removal Of Detention Tags

As soon as you are authorized to terminate the detention, proceed to where the detained material is stored, personally remove and completely destroy all detention tags. Do not merely throw them in the trash.

2.7.2.5.2 - Issuance Of Detention Termination Notice FDA 2291

Issuance of Detention Termination Notice FDA 2291 - As soon as you have removed all detention tags, tell the custodian the article is no longer under detention. Immediately prepare a Detention Termination Notice by filling out blocks 1 through 12, and the bottom of the form to include name, title, and signature. Give the original (page 1) to the custodian. This terminates the detention.

Complete the "Remarks" section to elaborate on pertinent information such as supervision, reconditioning, destruction accomplished, etc. The Detention Termination Notice, FDA 2291, together with Detention Notice, FDA 2289, will, unless instructed otherwise, constitute the complete report on the detention. See IOM Exhibit 2-4.

2.7.3 - Sampling

Official samples of articles involved in this type of operation are collected, prepared, and submitted in the same manner as any other regulatory samples. In the case of food detained under Section 304(h) of the FD&C Act, consult with your supervisor to determine whether the suspected contaminant in articles of food that have been detained makes it necessary to follow sampling procedures that may be different from those followed for routine regulatory samples.

2.7.4 - Supervision of Reconditioning, Denaturing, or Destruction

Methods and procedures for reconditioning, denaturing, or destruction, will be proposed to the district by the owner of the devices or meat, poultry, or egg products. For food detained under Section 304(h) of the FD&C Act, destruction will likely be the only option, and it can only be done after FDA approves in writing a request to modify the detention order. For all detentions, do not take any action on reconditioning, denaturing, or destruction unless you are authorized by your supervisor. The district officials will determine the adequacy of the proposed method. If satisfactory, you will be advised of the procedure and authorized to monitor the action.

When the operation is satisfactorily completed, and when authorized, terminate the detention as indicated in IOM 2.7.2.5.2.

The results of the reconditioning, denaturing, or destruction may be described in the "Remarks" section on the Detention Termination Notice, FDA 2291, if desired. See IOM Exhibit 2-4.

2.7.5 - Reporting

Except in unusual situations, or unless instructed otherwise by your supervisor, the Detention Notice, FDA 2289, the Detention Notice Termination, FDA 2291, and the FACTS Collection Record are designed to provide all information required to report the action from detention to termination.

2.8 - Denaturing

2.8.1 - Objective

The basic purpose of denaturing is to prevent salvage or diversion of violative materials for human consumption.

2.8.2 - Diversion to Animal Feed

Carefully consider any situation before agreeing to diversion of contaminated foods to animal feed. The indiscriminate use of contaminated food for livestock may constitute a hazard to such livestock, as well as humans.

When denaturing human foods for animal feed purposes, contact the Center for Veterinary Medicine, Division of Compliance (HFV-230) at 240-276-9200 to determine if the product may be converted safely to animal feed.

2.8.2.1 - Rodent or Bird Contaminated Foods

Diversion of rodent or bird contaminated foods for animal feed is authorized only when the contaminated product is treated by heat to destroy Salmonella organisms. In the case of wheat and other grains containing rodent excreta, a suitable heat process may be used or the product is examined bacteriologically and shown not to contain Salmonella.

2.8.2.2 - Moldy Food

If processors insist on salvage of moldy grain or foods for animal feed use, it must be done under proper supervision, and provide for:

1. Treatment by dry heating to destroy viable spoilage microorganisms (generally, this will result in grain having a toasted color and odor), and

2. Evidence it does not contain mycotoxins, and

3. Evidence, by animal feeding studies, the product is safe for animal use.

2.8.2.3 - Pesticide Contamination

Foods contaminated by pesticides residues should not be diverted to animal food use unless a determination is made which assures illegal residues will not result in the food animal or their food products, e.g., meat, milk, eggs.

2.8.3 - Decharacterization for Non-Food or Feed Purposes

The choice of methods, should be made by considering the type of the denaturant, the physical properties of the diverted material, and the ultimate use of the article.

2.9 - Regulatory Submissions

Subchapter 2.9 provides information on the procedures for obtaining information and filing applications with the agency. These will be covered by Center. The filing and registration requirements are directed by the FD&C Act and its implementing regulations. They are filed, in most cases, by industry (e.g.: drug registration, LACF registration and process filing, ANDA's, etc.).

2.9.1 - Center for Drug Evaluation and Research (CDER)

The FD&C Act and its regulations require the filing of certain forms by firms which produce human drugs and drug related products. The requirements and procedures for these are described below.

2.9.1.1 - Registration and Listing

Owners or operators of all drug establishments not exempt under Section 510(g) of the FD&C Act [21 U.S.C. 360 (g)] or 21 CFR 207.10, that engage in the manufacture, preparation, propagation, compounding, or processing of a drug or drugs, including blood products, and biologicals, are required to register each such establishment and to submit a list of every drug in commercial distribution, whether or not the output of such establishment or any particular drug so listed enters interstate commerce. Briefly, first time registration, re-registration and updates are accomplished by submitting an FDA 2656 (Registration of Drug Establishment/Labeler Code Assignment). The drug listing and subsequent June and December updating shall be on form FDA 2657 (Drug Product Listing) or form FDA 2658 (Registered Establishments Report of Private Label Distributors).

Registration and Listing is required whether or not interstate commerce is involved. Detailed registration and listing instructions appear in 21 CFR 207.

An establishment shall register on the form FDA 2656 (Registration of Drug Establishment/Labeler Code Assignment) and list on form FDA 2657 (Drug Product Listing) or form FDA 2658 (Registered Establishments Report of Private Label Distributors). The forms may be obtained online at http://www.fda.gov/opacom/more-choices/fdaforms/cder.html.

General information and questions can be addressed by: Phone: 301-210-2840, Mail: Food and Drug Administra-tion, Center for Drug Evaluation and Research, Drug Registration and Listing (HFD-337) 5600 Fishers Lane, Rockville, MD 20857, or e-mail: DRLS@cder.fda.gov. See IOM Exhibit 5-12 for types for drug operations that require registration and listing.

2.9.1.2 - Investigational New Drug Application (IND)

An application which a drug sponsor must submit to FDA before beginning tests of a new drug on humans. The IND contains the plan for the study and is supposed to give a complete picture of the drug, including its structural formula, animal test results, and manufacturing information. Detailed instructions for the submission of IND's can be found in 21 CFR 312.

2.9.1.3 - New Drug Application (NDA)

A New Drug Application is an application requesting FDA approval to market interstate commerce a new drug for human use. The application must contain among other things, data from clinical studies needed for FDA review from specific technical viewpoints, including chemistry, pharmacology, biopharmaceutics, statistics, and anti-infectives, microbiology. Detailed instructions for the submission of NDA's can be found in 21 CFR 314.

2.9.1.4 - Abbreviated New Drug Application (ANDA)

A simplified submission permitted for a duplicate of an already approved drug. ANDAs are for products with the same or very closely related active ingredients, dose form, strength, administration route, use, and labeling as a product already shown to be safe and effective. An ANDA includes all the information on chemistry and manufacturing controls found in a new drug application (NDA), but does not have to include data from studies in animals and humans. It must, however, contain evidence the duplicate drug is bioequivalent to the previously approved drug. Information concerning the submission of ANDA's can be found in 21 CFR 320.

2.9.2 - Center for Devices and Radiological Health (CDRH)

The FD&C Act, its amendments, and the regulations promulgated under the Act, require the filing of certain forms and submission of certain data by those involved in the production (and in some cases the use) of medical devices and radiological products. Within the CDRH, the Division of Small Manufacturers, International and Consumer Assistance (HFZ-220) has been charged with responsibility for providing information and assistance to industry in complying with these requirements. The general requirements are discussed below, as are several issues unique to CDRH submissions.

2.9.2.1 - Device Registration and Listing

Section 510 of the FD&C Act [21 U.S.C. 360] and 21 CFR 807 describe the establishment registration, device listing, and premarket notification requirements and specify conditions under which establishments are exempt from these requirements.

Manufacturers of finished devices (including device specification developers, reprocessors of single use devices), repackers and relabelers, foreign exporters and initial importers of medical devices, are required to register their establishments by submitting a form FDA 2891. After initial submission, annual registration is accomplished by use of the Center for Devices and Radiological Health (CDRH) computer generated FDA 2891(a). Component manufacturers are not required to register if the components are sold to registered device establishments for assembly into finished devices. Registration and listing is required, however, if the component is labeled for a health care purpose and sold to medical or clinical users. Optical laboratories, clinical laboratories, dental laboratories, orthotic and prosthetic appliance assemblers, hearing aid dispensers and others who, using previously manufactured devices, perform a service function for physicians, dentists, other licensed practitioners or their patients, are exempt from establishment registration if they are located in the United States. X-ray assemblers are exempt from establishment registration. An exemption from registration does not exempt an establishment from inspection under Section 704 of the FD&C Act [21 U.S.C. 374].

Each establishment, except initial importers of medical devices, required to register must list their devices. Device listing is accomplished using a form FDA-2892; the same form is used to update listing information.

All foreign manufacturers are required to notify FDA of the name, address, telephone and fax numbers, and e-mail address of their United States agent. The United States agent must reside or have a physical place of business in the United States. Post office boxes, answering services and machines are not allowed.

Establishments are required to register and list, even if interstate commerce is not involved. Foreign establishments must register, list and submit a United States agent notification prior to exporting to the United States. See IOM Exhibit 5-13 for types of medical device operations, which require registration and listing.

An establishment must initially register on the form FDA 2891, and list on form FDA 2892 which may be obtained from:

1. FDA Internet site: http://www.fda.gov/cdrh/reglistpage.html .

2. CDRH, Division of Small Manufacturers, International and Consumer Assistance (HFZ-220), 1350 Piccard Drive, Rockville, MD 20850, 800-638-2041 ext. 102 or 301-443-6597 ext. 102. Please note this is an automated publications' request line. Caller must leave name, address, phone number and publications needed.

A sample United States agent notification letter may be obtained from:

1. FDA Internet site: http://www.fda.gov/cdrh/reglistpage.html .

2. CDRH, Division of Small Manufacturers, International and Consumer Assistance (HFZ-220), 1350 Piccard Drive, Rockville, MD 20850, 800-638-2041 ext. 102 or 301-443-6597 ext. 102. Please note this is an automated publications' request line. Caller must leave name, address, phone number and publications needed.

General information and policy questions can be addressed by:

1. Sending an e-mail message to RLPROGRAM@cdrh.fda.gov.

2. Writing to or calling Food and Drug Administration, Center for Devices and Radiological Health, Office of Compliance/Division of Program Operations, Registra-tion and Listing Program (HFZ-308), 9200 Corporate Blvd., Rockville, MD 20850, 301-827-4555, press 3, then 2.

2.9.2.2 - Investigational Device Exemption (IDE) Regulation

The IDE regulation in 21 CFR 812 contains requirements for sponsors, Institutional Review Boards (IRBs) and Clinical Investigators. Additional requirements are found in 21 CFR 50, Informed Consent, and 21 CFR 56, IRB's. All Sponsors of device clinical investigations must have an approved IDE, unless specifically exempted by the regulation. Sponsors who have an approved IDE are exempt from requirements on labeling, registration and listing, premarket notification, performance standards, premarket approval, GMPs except the design control provisions, banning of devices, restricted devices, and color additives.

Provisions for obtaining an IDE, and the sections of the regulations, with which sponsors, investigators, and IRBs must comply, differ according to the risks posed by the device. Sponsors of nonsignificant risk devices must obtain IRB approval, and are subject to a limited number of provisions; sponsors of significant risk (See 21 CFR 812.3(m)) investigations are subject to the entire regulation.

There are investigations, described in 21 CFR 812.2(c) that are exempt from the IDE regulation. Exempted investigations apply to devices and diagnostics, which meet the criteria in the regulation. These devices are, however, still subject to other regulatory requirements of the Act, such as labeling, premarket approval of Class III devices, and GMPs (as stated in the preamble to the IDE regulation).

A Sponsor who knows a new device is not "substantially equivalent" to a preamendment device, or who is not sure if a device is "substantially equivalent" without conducting a clinical investigation, must obtain an approved IDE to conduct the clinical investigation. After collecting clinical data, a sponsor who desires to market a device must either submit a premarket notification (510k) or premarket approval application to FDA. A premarket notification may be submitted if the sponsor believes the data supports a finding of substantial equivalence.

Certain radiation-emitting electronic devices that are investigational are also subject to radiological health regulations, 21 CFR 1000 through 1050.

Transitional devices, must have an approved IDE in order to be investigated.

Sponsors, Monitors, IRBs, Investigators, and Non-Clinical Toxicological Laboratories will be covered under the Bioresearch Monitoring Program. FDA has the authority to inspect and copy records relating to investigations. Records identifying patients by name will be copied only if there is reason to believe adequate informed consent was not obtained, or investigator records are incomplete, false, or misleading.

2.9.2.3 - Premarket Notification - Section 510(k)

The Medical Device Amendments of 1976 require device manufacturers to notify the CDRH at least 90 days before commercially distributing a device. This is known as a "Premarket Notification" or a "510(k)" submission. "Commercial distribution", for practical purposes, means the device is held for sale. These 510(k) requirements do not apply to Class I devices unless the device is intended for a use which is of substantial importance in preventing impairment of human health, or to any Class I device that presents a potential unreasonable risk of illness or injury. See section 510(l) of the FD&C Act [21 U.S.C. 360(l)].

A manufacturer must submit a Premarket Notification to FDA in any of the following situations:

1. Introducing a device into commercial distribution for the first time.

2. Introducing a new device or product line for the first time, which may already be marketed by another firm.

3. Introducing or reintroducing a device with significant changes or modifications affecting the safety or effectiveness of the device. Such changes or modifications could relate to design, material, chemical composition, energy source, manufacturing method, or intended use.

These requirements do not apply to "custom devices." A "custom device" is a device made exclusively for, and to meet the special needs of, an individual physician or health professional, or for use by an individual patient named in the order of a physician or dentist (such as specially designed orthopedic footwear). A "custom device" is not generally available in finished form for purchase; and is not offered through labeling or advertising for commercial distribution.

Refer to IOM Exhibit 5-13 for types of medical devices, which require 510(k) submissions. The investigator should document for CDRH review failures to submit required 510(k)s.

2.9.2.4 - Premarket Approval

Class III devices are required to undergo premarket approval in accordance with the provisions of Section 515 of the FD & C Act [21 U.S.C. 360e]. Premarket approval for a device is initiated with the submission of an application to FDA. Prior to approval of a premarket approval application (PMA), or a supplemental PMA, FDA has the authority to inspect the applicant's facilities and those records pertinent to the PMA.

Compliance Program Guidance Manual 7383.001 contains specific guidance on performing PMA pre-approval and post-approval inspections.

Inspections of manufacturing facilities are usually required prior to approval of a Premarket Approval Application. A full GMP inspection may not be necessary if there has been a recent satisfactory inspection covering a device similar to the PMA device.

Requests for PMA inspections issue from HFZ-306. The assignments will request the firm be inspected for compliance with the GMP regulations, and with their commitments in the PMA.

2.9.2.5 - Classification of Devices

All medical devices subject to the FD&C Act will be classified as either Class I, Class II, or Class III medical devices.

Manufacturers who have questions regarding the classification of a device can write CDRH under Section 513(g) of the FD&C Act [21 U.S.C. 360c (g)] and request an opinion as to the status of the device.

2.9.2.5.1 - Class I

Class I - General - Devices for which general controls (i.e., the controls in Section 520 of the FD&C Act [21 U.S.C. 351, 352, 360, 360f, 360h, 360i, and 360j]) provide reasonable assurance of safety and effectiveness.

2.9.2.5.2 - Class II

Class II - Special Controls - Devices for which the general controls, by themselves, are insufficient to provide reasonable assurance of safety and effectiveness of the device, and for which there is sufficient information to promulgate special controls, necessary to provide such assurance.

2.9.2.5.3 - Class III

Class III - Premarket Approval - Devices which:

1. Cannot be placed into Class I or II because insufficient information exists to provide assurance of safety and effectiveness, and cannot be placed into Class II because too little data exists to support the promulgation of special controls, and

2. Are purported or represented to be for use in supporting or sustaining human life, or for a use which is of substantial importance in preventing impairment of human health, or

3. Presents a potentially unreasonable risk of illness or injury.

Unless they are determined substantially equivalent to devices distributed prior to the 1976 Medical Device Amendments, devices proposed for marketing after May 28, 1976, fall automatically into Class III. Class III medical devices marketed before May 28, 1976, and the substantially equivalent devices marketed after that date, remain subject to the premarket notification requirements until required to have an approved PMA. Petitioners can request to have such devices reclassified into Class I or II. Transitional devices, those regulated as new drugs before May 28, 1976, are automatically assigned to Class III.

2.9.2.6 - Requests for GMP Exemption and Variances

Section 520f(2)(A) of the FD&C Act [21 U.S.C. 360j (f)(2)(A)] allows manufacturers, trade organizations, or other interested persons to petition for exemption or variance from all or part of the GMP. Filing a petition does not defer compliance with the GMP requirements, and petitions will not be processed while an investigation is ongoing, or while regulatory action is pending.

Some Class I devices have been exempted from the GMP through the classification process. Each classification panel was required to consider the Class I devices reviewed by that panel and recommend if they should be exempt from the GMP. Devices exempted from the GMP by the classification process are published in classification regulations in the Federal Register.

Devices labeled or otherwise represented as sterile are not eligible for exemption from the GMP regulation. A sterile device is subject to all GMP requirements pertinent to sterility and sterilization processes.

No exemptions will be granted from 21 CFR 820.198 - Complaint Files, which requires the device manufacturer to have an adequate system for complaint investigation and follow-up. This Policy extends to 820.180 - General Requirements, which gives authorized FDA employees access to complaint files, device related injury reports, and failure analysis records for review and copying. When FDA has granted a manufacturer an exemption from one or more GMP requirements, the manufacturer still has the responsibility to implement appropriate quality control measures to assure the finished device has the quality it purports to possess, as stated in Section 704(a) of the FD&C Act [21 U.S.C. 374 (a)], and may be subject to regulatory action if devices are adulterated or misbranded.

2.9.2.7 - Medical Device Reporting

The Medical Device Reporting (MDR) regulation and the changes mandated by the Safe Medical Devices Act of 1990 (SMDA) is a mandatory information reporting system. It requires manufacturers, importers, and users of medical devices to report to FDA certain adverse experiences caused or contributed to by their devices. This program is administered by the Center's Office of Surveillance and Biometrics. The regulation requires a report be submitted to FDA whenever a manufacturer or an importer becomes aware of information that its device:

1. May have caused or contributed to a death or serious injury, or

2. Has malfunctioned and, if the malfunction recurs, is likely to cause or contribute to a death or serious injury.

Under the Safe Medical Devices Act of 1990, user facilities must report device-related deaths to FDA and to the manufacturer, if known. User facilities must also report device-related serious illnesses and injuries to the manufacturer, or to FDA if the manufacturer is unknown. In addition, SMDA also requires user facilities to submit to FDA, on an annual basis, a summary of all reports submitted.

The CDRH Division of Small Manufacturers International and Consumer Assistance and the Office of Surveillance and Biometrics should be contacted for further guidance about the MDR regulation. Inspections for compliance with the MDR regulation are conducted following the guidance contained in the Compliance Program 7382.845 - Inspection of Medical Device Manufacturers. When reviewing the manufacturer's complaint files, look for complaints, which are reportable, and have not been reported by the manufacturer.

2.9.2.8 - Radiation Reporting

Prior to introduction of products into commerce, manufacturers of radiation-emitting electronic products must submit radiation safety Product Reports if the product is listed and marked in Table 1 of 21 CFR 1002.1. (Non-medical radiation products have NO registration and listing requirements, but the same type of information is included in these reports.) These are premarket documents but there is no timeframe for review and manufacturers do not have to wait for clearance. However, these documents must be processed by CDRH, Office of Compliance to provide rapid import entry of electronic products. Radiation Product Reports provide technical specifications, how products comply with standards, and radiation testing and quality control programs to support the firm's (self)-certification of compliance of each product.

In addition, manufacturers must file annual reports (if specified in Table 1), defect or noncompliance reports when appropriate (similar to recall notices), and accidental radiation occurrence reports when appropriate (similar to, and sometimes replaced by, Medical Device Reports (MDRs)).

2.9.3 - Center for Biologics Evaluation and Research (CBER)

The requirements for the registration and licensing of biological products fall under both the Public Health Service Act (PHS) and the FD&C Act.

2.9.3.1 - Registration and Listing

See also IOM 5.7.3.

CBER provides industry with registration and listing forms, FDA 2830, Blood Establishment Registration and Product Listing, and FDA 3356, Establishment Registration and Listing for Human Cells, Tissues, and Cellular and Tissue-Based Products (HCT/Ps). Instructions for completing these documents are on the reverse side of these forms along with establishment and product definitions. Registration forms are available through the district office and through CBER's Office of Communication, Training and Manufactures Assistance, and from the CBER website. Registration and listing is required whether or not interstate commerce is involved. (See IOM 5.7.3)

2.9.3.1.1 - Human Blood and Blood Products

Human Blood and Blood Products:

1. Who must register - Section 510 of the FD&C Act and 21 CFR 607 delineate the requirements and exemptions relating to the registration of establishments engaged in the collection, manufacturing, preparation, or processing of human blood or blood products. Registration and listing are required whether or not interstate commerce is involved. Fixed blood collection sites that have supplies or equipment requiring quality control or have an expiration date, e.g., copper sulfate, centrifuges, etc., or are used to store donor records, must register. Temporary collection sites, to which all blood collection supplies are brought on the day of collection and are completely removed from the site at the end of the collecting period (except beds, tables, and chairs) and blood mobiles, are not required to register. All Military blood bank establishments are required to register. (MOU with Department of Defense [Federal Cooperative Agreements Manual] Regarding Licensure of Military Blood Banks.) Brokers, who take physical possession of blood products, such as in storage, pooling, labeling, or distribution, are required to register. Blood establishments located outside of the United States that import or offer for import blood products into the U.S. are required to register with FDA. They must also provide the name of the United States agent, the name of each importer, and each person who imports or offers for import these blood products.

2. When to register - Establishments must register within five days after beginning operations and must submit a list of blood products they distribute commercially. They must register annually thereafter.

3. How to register - Owners or operators of blood establishments register using the Form FDA 2830. Refer to Compliance Policy Guide (CPG) 230.110 for additional information on registration. These persons may complete and submit Form FDA 2830 on the Internet or may submit a paper form.

4. Where to mail completed paper forms - Mail completed legible forms to: Food and Drug Administration, Center for Biologics Evaluation and Research, Division of Blood Applications (HFM-370), 1401 Rockville Pike, 200N, Rockville, MD 20852-1448.

5. General Information and Questions:

   Phone: 301-827-3546

   Email: bloodregis@cber.fda.gov

   Mail: Food and Drug Administration, Center for Biologics Evaluation and Research, Division of Blood Applications, (HFM-370), 1401 Rockville Pike, 200N, Rockville, MD 20852-1448.

2.9.3.1.2 - Human Cells, Tissues, and Cellular and Tissue-Based Products (HCT/Ps)

Human Cells, Tissues, and Cellular and Tissue-Based Products (HCT/Ps):

1. Who must register - Establishment that manufacture HCT/Ps that are regulated solely under the authority of section 361 of the Publish Health Service Act (42USC264) (the PHS Act) must register and list with CBER whether or not the HCT/P enters into interstate commerce (21 CFR 1271.1). Establishments that manufacture HCT/Ps that are regulated as drugs, devices and/or biological products under section 351 of the PHS Act and/or the Federal Food, Drug and Cosmetic Act, must register and list with CBER following procedures in subpart B, 21 CFR 1271.21 thru 1271.37. Registration and listing are required if the establishment recovers, processes, stores, labels, packages, or distributes any human cell or tissue, or screens or tests the cell or tissue donor. Establishments exempted from registration are listed in 21 CFR 1271.15. Establishments that only have HCT/Ps under premarket review (IND/IDE/BLA/PMA) do not have to register and list until the HCT/P has been licensed, approved or cleared by FDA.

2. When to register - Establishments must register within five days after beginning operations and must submit a list of each HCT/P manufactured.

3. How to register - To register a Form FDA 3356 must be completed.

4. Where to mail completed forms - Mail completed legible forms to: Food and Drug Administration, Center for Biologics Evaluation and Research, (HFM-775), 1401 Rockville Pike, 200N, Rockville, MD 20852-1448, Attention: Tissue Establishment Registration Coordinator. Or it may be submitted by FAX according to form instructions. Alternatively, establishments may now submit the information electronically via the Electronic Human Cell and Tissue Establishment Registration (eHCTERs) page.

5. General Information and Questions:

   Phone: 301-827-6176 (Tissue Establishment Regis-tration Coordinator)

   Email: tissuereg@cber.fda.gov

   Mail: Food and Drug Administration, Center for Biologics Evaluation and Research, HFM-775, 1401 Rockville Pike, 200N, Rockville, MD 20852-1448.

2.9.3.2 - Biologic License

Section 351 of the Public Health Service Act requires individuals or companies who manufacture biological products for introduction into interstate commerce to hold a license for the products. Biologics licenses are issued by CBER and CDER (21 CFR 601.4).
What changes to an approved biologics license application are reportable - Applicants must inform the FDA about each change in the product, production process, quality controls, equipment, facilities, responsible personnel, or labeling established in the approved license application (21 CFR 601.12).

When to Report - Major changes require supplement submission and approval prior to distribution of products made using the change (21 CFR 601.12(b)). Certain changes require supplement submissions at least 30 days prior to distribution of the product made using the change, and other minor changes need only be described in an annual report (21 CFR 601.12(c) and (d)).

Where to send Reports - For licensed biological products regulated by CBER: Document Control Center (HFM-99), Center for Biologics Evaluation and Research, Food and Drug Administration, 1401 Rockville Pike, 200N, Rockville, MD 20852-1448. For licensed biological products regulated by CDER: CDER Therapeutic Biological Products Document Room, Center for Drug Evaluation and Research, Food and Drug Administration, 12229 Wilkins Avenue, Rockville, MD 20852. (21 CFR 600.2)

2.9.4 - Center for Veterinary Medicine (CVM)

Requirements for registration and filing of various applications by firms which manufacture animal drugs, feeds, and other veterinary products are required by the FD&C Act.

2.9.4.1 - Registration and Listing

Owners or operators of all drug establishments, not exempt under section 510(g) of the FD&C Act [21 U.S.C. 360 (g)] or subpart D of 21 CFR 207, who engage in the manufacture, preparation, propagation, compounding, or processing of a drug or drugs are required to register. Also, they must submit a list of every drug in commercial distribution, except that listing information may be submitted by the parent, subsidiary, and/or affiliate company for all establishments when operations are conducted at more than one establishment, and there exists joint ownership and control among all the establishments. Registration of animal drug firms is handled by the Center for Drug Evaluation and Research (CDER). CVM maintains its own animal drug listing database.

Who must register - Owners and operators of establishments engaged in manufacture or processing of drug products must register and list their products.

When to register - The owner or operator of an establishment must register within 5 days after beginning of the operation and submit a list of every drug in commercial distribution at that time. Owners or operators of all establishments engaged in drug activities described in 21 CFR 207.3(a)(8) shall register annually, within 30 days after receiving registration forms from the FDA.

How to register - An establishment registers the first time on the form FDA 2656 - Registration of Drug Establishment. The forms may be obtained from: Food and Drug Administration, Center for Drug Evaluation and Research, Office of Management/Division of Management and Budget, Product Information Management Branch (HFD-058), 5600 Fishers Lane, Rockville, MD 20857.

Where to mail completed forms - The completed FDA-2656 should be mailed to: Food and Drug Administration, Center for Drug Evaluation and Research, Office of Management/Division of Management and Budget, Product Information Management Branch (HFD-058), 5600 Fishers Lane, Rockville, MD 20857.

For information on registered firms - CVM's Registration Monitor is Lowell Fried (HFV-214), 7500 Standish Place, Rockville, MD 20855 301-827-0165. You may make inquiries on registration status of individual firms through Mr. Fried.

For information on animal drug listing - CVM maintains its own database for animal drug listing. You may make inquiries for information through Lowell Fried (HFV-214), 301-827-0165.

2.9.4.2 - Medicated Feed Mill License (FML)

Who must register - The manufacture of a Type B or Type C medicated feed containing a Category II drug, from a Type A medicated article, must hold an approved license (FDA 3448). The mill must be registered with the Food and Drug Administration, Information Management Team, HFD-095, to obtain an FDA Registration Number and be operating in compliance with Good Manufacturing Practices as described in 21 CFR 225 by passing an inspection conducted by FDA or a designated party.

How to obtain a license application - Form FDA 3448 is available on the Center for Veterinary Medicine's web page or from the Food and Drug Administration, Center for Veterinary Medicine, Division of Animal Feeds (HFV-220), 7500 Standish Place, Rockville, MD 20855. Where to mail completed forms - Mail completed legible form to the Division of Animal Feeds at the address above. Supplemental applications also go to the above address.

General Information and Questions:

Phone: 301-827-0170.

Mail: Food and Drug Administration, Center for Veterinary Medicine (HFV-220), 7500 Standish Place, Rockville, MD 20855.

2.9.4.3 - Abbreviated New Animal Drug Application (ANADA)

The Generic Animal Drug and Patent Term Restoration Act amended the FD&C Act to provide for the approval of generic copies of previously approved animal drug products. The generic product may be approved by providing evidence it contains the same active ingredients, in the same concentration, as the approved article, and is bioequivalent. The information is submitted to the FDA in the form of an Abbreviated New Animal Drug Application or ANADA.

How to file - An ANADA must be submitted to FDA on the form FDA 356V. The format and content of the application must be in accordance with the policies and procedures established by FDA's Center for Veterinary Medicine. The application must be filled out completely in triplicate and submitted to the address below.

Where to obtain forms - ANADA's also use the form FDA 356 which can be obtained from: Food and Drug Administration, Center for Veterinary Medicine (HFV-12), 7500 Standish Place, Rockville, MD 20855.

Where to mail completed forms - Completed legible applications should be mailed to: Food and Drug Administration, Center for Veterinary Medicine (HFV-199), 7500 Standish Place, Rockville, MD 20855.

General Information and Questions - Assistance and additional information can be obtained by writing or calling Dr. Lonnie Luther.

Phone: 301-295-8623.

Mail: Food and Drug Administration, Center for Veterinary Medicine (HFV-102), 7500 Standish Place, Rockville, MD 20855

2.9.4.4 - New Animal Drug Application (NADA)

A new animal drug is any drug intended for use in animals other than man. Manufacturers of new animal drugs must complete a New Animal Drug Application (NADA), and receive approval prior to distribution.

How to file - Applications must be submitted on a form FDA 356. The applications must be signed by the applicant or by an authorized attorney, agent, or official. The application must be filled out completely, in triplicate, and submitted to the address below.

Where to obtain forms - NADA's use form FDA 356 which can be obtained from: Food and Drug Administration, Center for Veterinary Medicine (HFV-12), 7500 Standish Place, Rockville, MD 20855.

Where to mail completed forms - Completed NADA's should be mailed to: Food and Drug Administration, Center for Veterinary Medicine (HFV-199), 7500 Standish Place, Rockville, MD 20855.

General Information and Questions - General information or questions can be answered by mail or phone by contacting Dr. Lonnie Luther.

Phone: 301-295-8623.

Mail: Food and Drug Administration, Center for Veterinary Medicine (HFV-102), 7500 Standish Place, Rockville, MD 20855

2.9.5 - Center for Food Safety and Applied Nutrition (CFSAN)

The FDA issued 21 CFR 1, an interim final regulation in FR Vol. 68 No. 197 pgs 58893-58974 on October 10, 2003 that requires affected domestic and foreign facilities that manufacture/process, pack or hold food for human or animal consumption in the United States to register with the FDA by December 12, 2003. The interim final rule implements the Public Health Security and Bioterrorism Preparedness and Response Act of 2002 (the Bioterrorism Act). For more information see the FDA/CFSAN website on food firm registration.

The FD&C Act and its regulations require certain firms to register and to file scheduled processes, while other firms are requested to do this voluntarily. CFSAN provides guidance and assistance as described below.

2.9.5.1 - Low Acid Canned Food (LACF) / Acidified Foods (AF) Food Canning Establishment (FCE) Registration

Food Canning Establishments (FCE) (foreign and domestic) engaged in the manufacture of Low Acid Canned Food/Acidified Foods (LACF/AF) offering their products for interstate commerce within the United States are required by 21 CFR Parts 108, 113, and 114 to register their facility with the FDA using form FDA 2541 and file scheduled process information for their products using forms FDA 2541a, "Food Process Filing for All Methods Except Low-Acid Acid Aseptic Systems".

Who must register - All commercial processors of LACF and AF products located in the US, and all processors in other countries who export their LACF or AF into the US must register their processing plants with the FDA. Wholesalers, importers, distributors, brokers, shippers, etc. are not required to register and file scheduled process information. However, they must ensure the processing firms they represent comply with all registration and process filing requirements.

When to register - Commercial LACF and AF processors in the US must register with FDA not later than 10 days after first engaging in the manufacture, processing, or packing of AF or LACF. Processors in other countries must register before offering any such products for import into the US.

How to register - To register with FDA, processors must complete and submit the FCE Registration Form (FDA 2541) for each processing establishment location.

The pink copy of the FCE Registration form will be returned to the firm or its authorized representative upon assigning of the five-digit FCE number to the plant. For domestic plants, a yellow and blue copy of the FCE Registration Form will be forwarded to the Investigations Branch of the FDA District Office in which the plant is located. The yellow copy is to be used for notifying the LACF Registration Coordinator of the firm's assigned CFN and the blue copy is for the District's Investigations Branch records.

FCE registration information changes - Manufacturers must notify the FDA of any changes to their FCE registration information. These notifications should be for changes in firm name, ownership, street name and number when the plant does not actually change location, preferred mailing address, or authorized representative. This can be accomplished through a letter or submission of a FCE Registration Form listing "Change of Registration Information" and the type of change requested.

Where to mail completed forms - Mail completed legible forms to: LACF Registration Coordinator (HFS-618), Center for Food Safety and Applied Nutrition, 5100 Paint Branch Parkway, College Park, MD 20740-3835.

General Information and Questions:

Phone: 301-436-2411; FAX: 301-436-2669

e-mail: LACF@fda.hhs.gov

Mail: Center for Food Safety and Applied Nutrition, (HFS-618), 5100 Paint Branch Parkway, College Park, MD 20740-3835.

Registration changes (street number, authorized representatives, etc.) can also be sent to the above address.

2.9.5.2 - FCE Process Filing of LACF/AF Processors

In addition to processors registering their establishments with the FDA, processors must also submit and file scheduled process information for their LACF/AF products with the FDA. That information must be submitted on forms FDA 2541a or FDA 2541c. Processes must be filed no later than 60 days after registration and prior to packing a new product or, in the case of firms in other countries, before importing their products into the United States.

It is the responsibility of the manufacturer and/or its authorized representative to ensure the design process used is safe from a standpoint of public health significance and will destroy or inhibit the growth of microorganisms. This is accomplished through the consultation of and recommendations by a process authority. Documentation that scheduled processes are delivered should be maintained through appropriate and accurate record keeping. Forms and documentation must be presented in English.

Process filing information consists of the following:

1. FCE number to the plant,

2. Submission Identifier (SID) number to identify a specific form submitted by the manufacturer,

3. Governing regulation (LACF - 21 CFR 108.35/113 or AF - 21 CFR 108.35/114),

4. Food name or description, which includes form or style of the product (whole, sliced, diced, etc.) and packing medium (in water, in brine, in tomato sauce, etc.),

5. Container type,

6. Process Establishment Source, and

7. Container dimensions in inches and/or capacity.

2.9.5.3 - Cosmetics

VOLUNTARY REGISTRATION OF COSMETIC PROD-UCT ESTABLISHMENTS (21 CFR 710)

Who should register - The owner or operator of a cosmetic product establishment, which is not exempt under 21 CFR 710.9, and engages in the manufacture or packaging of a cosmetic product, is asked to register each such establishment, whether or not the product enters interstate commerce. This request extends to any foreign cosmetic product establishment whose products are exported for sale in any State as defined in section 201(a)(1) of the FD&C Act [21 U.S.C. 321 (a)(1)]. No registration fee is required.

Time for registration - The owner or operator of an establishment entering into the manufacture or packaging of a cosmetic product should register the establishment within 30 days after the operation begins.

How and where to register - The FDA 2511 - Registration of Cosmetic Product Establishment is available from the FDA, CPK-2, Office of Cosmetics and Colors, Cosmetics Staff (HFS-125), 5100 Paint Branch Parkway, College Park, MD 20740-3835, or at any FDA district office. The completed form should be mailed to HFS-125. The form is also available online at http://www.cfsan.fda.gov/~dms/cos-reg2.html. Establishments can also be registered online at http://www.cfsan.fda.gov/~dms/cos-regn.html.

Information requested - The FDA 2511 requests information on the name and address of the cosmetic product establishment, including post office ZIP code; all business trading names used by the establishment; and the type of business (manufacturer and/or packer). The information requested should be given separately for each establishment.

General information and questions - Call 301-436-1257, or e-mail at http://www.cfsan.fda.gov/~ocac/vcrp-ask.html. Instructions are sent with the forms.

VOLUNTARY FILING OF COSMETIC PRODUCT IN-GREDIENT COMPOSITION STATEMENT (21 CFR 720)

Who should file - Either the manufacturer, packer, or distributor of a cosmetic product is requested to file a FDA-2512 Cosmetic Product Ingredient Statement, whether or not the product enters interstate commerce. The request extends to any foreign manufacturer, packer, or distributor of a cosmetic product exported for sale in any State as defined in section 201(a)(1) of the FD&C Act [21 U.S.C. 321 (a)(1)]. No filing fee is required.

Times for filing - The FDA 2512 should be filed for each cosmetic product being commercially distributed. The FDA-2512 should be filed within 60 days after the beginning of commercial distribution of any product.

How and where to file - The FDA 2512 and FDA 2514 - Discontinuance of Commercial Distribution of Cosmetic Product Formulation are obtainable on request from the FDA, CPK-2, Office of Cosmetics and Colors, Cosmetics Staff (HFS-125), 5100 Paint Branch Parkway, College Park, MD 20740-3835 or at any FDA district office. The forms are also available online at http://www.cfsan.fda.gov/~dms/cos-reg2.html. The completed form should be mailed or delivered according to instructions provided with the form to HFS-125. The FDA-2512 Cosmetic Product Ingredient Statement can also be filed online at http://www.cfsan.fda.gov/~dms/cos-regn.html.

General information and questions - Phone: 301-436-1257, or e-mail at http://www.cfsan.fda.gov/~ocac/vcrp-ask.html.

2.9.5.4 - Color Certification Program

Request for Certification - A request for certification of a batch of color additive (straight, repack, lake) should be submitted in duplicate. Formats for these requests are found in 21 CFR 80.21. The fee prescribed in 21 CFR 80.10 should accompany the request, unless the firm has established with the FDA an advanced deposit to be used for prepayment of such fees.

A sample accompanying a request for certification must be submitted under separate cover, and should be addressed to the Food and Drug Administration, Color Certification Branch (HFS-107), 5100 Paint Branch Parkway, College Park, MD 20740-3835.

Where to mail request - Mail or deliver the request to the Food and Drug Administration, Color Certification Branch (HFS-107), 5100 Paint Branch Parkway, College Park, MD 20740-3835.

General information and questions - Phone: 301-436-1136, or e-mail at Naomi.Richfield-Fratz@cfsan.fda.gov.

Contact the Food and Drug Administration, Color Certification Branch (HFS-107), 5100 Paint Branch Parkway, College Park, MD 20740-3835. Costs - There is a fee for services provided (analytical work) which will vary based on type (straight, repack, lake), weight, number of batches, etc. See 21 CFR 80.10.

2.9.5.5 - Infant Formula

Who should register - There are three types of notifications:

1. First Notification - All manufacturers of infant formula sold in the US, and any manufacturer of a "new infant formula", must register with FDA no less than 90 days before it is introduced into interstate commerce.

   The first notification shall include:

   a. The quantitative formulation of the infant formula,

b. A description of any reformulation of the formula or change in processing of the infant formula,

c. Assurances the infant formula meets regulations and, as demonstrated by the testing required under regulations, and

d. Assurances the processing of the infant formula complies with regulations.

2. Second notification - This notification is given to FDA after the first production of an infant formula, and before its introduction into interstate commerce. The manufacturer shall submit a written verification which summarizes test results and records demonstrating such formula comply with regulations.

3. Third notification - This notification must be sent to FDA if the manufacturer determines a change in the formulation or processing of the formula may adversely affect the article.

Where to mail notifications - Notifications should be sent to: Food and Drug Administration, Office of Nutrition, Labeling and Dietary Supplements, Infant Formula and Medical Foods Staff, HFS-850, 5100 Paint Branch Parkway, College Park, MD 20740-3835.

General information and questions phone: 301-436-1450.

2.9.5.6 - Interstate Certified Shellfish (Fresh and Frozen Oysters, Clams, and Mussels) Shippers

Persons interested in receiving general information about the National Shellfish Sanitation Program - Contact: Food and Drug Administration, Office of Seafood, HFS-400, 5100 Paint Branch Parkway, College Park, MD 20740

Phone: 301-436-2300; FAX: 301-436-2599

Persons interested in technical assistance about the National Shellfish Sanitation Program - Contact: Food and Drug Administration, Division of Cooperative Programs (HFS-628), 5100 Paint Branch Parkway, College Park, MD 20740

Phone: 301-436-2144; FAX: 301-436-2672

Persons interested in receiving the Interstate Certified Shellfish Shippers List (ICSSL) - Contact: Charlotte V. Epps. Mail: Food and Drug Administration, Division of Cooperative Programs (HFS-625), 5100 Paint Branch Parkway, College Park, MD 20740

Phone: 301-436-2154; FAX: 301-436-2672

2.9.5.7 - Interstate Milk Shippers (IMS)

Rules for inclusion in the IMS List - All Grade A milk shippers certified by State Milk Sanitation Rating authorities as having attained an acceptable sanitation compliance and enforcement rating are include in the IMS list. These ratings are based on compliance with the requirements of the "USPHS/FDA Grade A Pasteurized Milk Ordinance (PMO) and/or the Grade A Condensed and Dry Milk Products and Condensed and Dry Whey Ordinance (DMO)" and are made in accordance with the procedures set forth in "Methods of Making Sanitation Rating of Milk Shippers" and the "Procedures Governing the Cooperative State-Public Health Service/ Food and Drug Administration Program of the National Conference on Interstate Milk Shippers". The IMS List is published semi-annually and updated monthly on the FDA website.

To obtain a free copy of the IMS List contact:

Food and Drug Administration

Milk Safety Branch (HFS-626)

Division of Cooperative Programs

5100 Paint Branch Parkway

College Park, MD 20740

General Information and Questions.

Contact: Milk Safety Branch (HFS-626), Division of

Cooperative Programs, Food and Drug Administration,

5100 Paint Branch Parkway, College Park, MD 20740.

Phone: 301-436-2439; FAX: 301-436-2715.

Chapter 3: Federal and State Cooperation

CONTENT		VERSION DATE
Subchapter 3.1	Cooperative Efforts	June 11, 2009
Subchapter 3.2	Federal Agency Interaction	December 4, 2009
Subchapter 3.3	State Operational Authority	June 11, 2009
Subchapter 3.4	International Agreements	June 11, 2009
Subchapter 3.5	Non Government Agreements	June 11, 2009

3.1 - Cooperative Efforts

3.1.1 - Policy

The scope of consumer protection is extended by cooperative efforts of federal, state, and local agencies and international cooperation. Procedures to appropriately share responsibilities and cooperate with our consumer protection partners are essential.

Federal, state, and local cooperation shall be fostered whenever possible. The Agency issues the IOM as well as other FDA manuals to international regulators and conformity assessment bodies, and state and local inspectors. FDA fosters cooperation through correspon-dence, FDA testimony, press releases, reprints from the Federal Register, and distribution of all pertinent policy and regulations issued by FDA which have significance in other regulatory jurisdictions. The Agency may share FDA's non-public information as long as the sharing complies with the Agency's confidentiality laws and procedures.

Districts, headquarters' offices, and resident post person-nel in particular, should maintain liaison with federal, state and local officials.

Follow district policy regarding contacts with appropriate federal, state, county and local officials to exchange in-formation, coordinate operations, and arrange joint inspections. If an assignment calls for joint work with state or local inspectors, make every effort to accomplish this work. See IOM 3.3.1. When you travel internationally, follow policy established in the "GUIDE TO INTERNA-TIONAL INSPECTIONS AND TRAVEL."

3.1.2 - Laws, Codes, Agencies

Many states have enacted the basic Uniform Food, Drug, and Cosmetic Bill, and others have adopted at least a part of the Uniform Bill. The provisions of these laws are very similar to the 1938 provisions of the Federal Food, Drug, and Cosmetic Act. A few states have enacted the Pesticide Food and Color Additives or Kefauver-Harris type amendments. See IOM 3.3.3.

Most states without the Uniform FD&C Act, have laws based on the 1906 Food and Drug Act. Most larger cities have their own ordinances and regulations. A portion of the food supply of the United States is consumed within the state in which it is produced, and is therefore, not di-rectly under the jurisdiction of the Federal Food, Drug and Cosmetic Act as amended. Thus, the various state and local agencies are solely responsible for policing this supply.

The departments of the executive branch of the federal government operate under the laws and regulations which they are specifically responsible for enforcing. Since responsibilities may overlap and be duplicated, operating agreements and liaison between agencies is essential for smooth and efficient governmental operation. Section 702(c) of the FD&C Act [21 U.S.C. 372(c)] recognizes this by providing that the records of any department in the executive branch shall be open to inspection by authorized DHHS personnel.

District management is responsible for maintaining official liaison between FDA and other federal agencies. However, for day by day operations, personal contact between various operating federal investigators, inspectors, and agents is desirable and encouraged.

3.1.2.1 - Agreements and Memoranda of Understanding (MOU)

To provide for more efficient use of FDA and other agency manpower and resources and to prevent duplication of effort, FDA and various agencies often enter into formal or informal agreements, and/or understandings. These specify areas in which each will assume primary responsibility. Prior to disclosing FDA's information, ensure that the Agreement and MOU contains confidentiality provisions that comply with FDA's information disclosure laws and procedures (e.g., sharing with the public (FOI), federal government officials 21 CFR 20.85, state/local 21 CFR 20.88, foreign 21 CFR 20.89). Do not share information unless that sharing complies with such laws and Agency procedures even if the Agreement and MOU fails to contain proper confidentiality provisions.

Pertinent parts or paraphrasing of the Agreements and/or Memoranda of Understanding (MOU) which are of particular interest to you as operating inspectors and investigators are listed below. Copies of many of the formal Agreements and MOU are in the FDA Federal Cooperative Agreements Manual (1996 edition) and the FDA International Cooperative Agreements Manual (1996 edition). Your district and most resident posts have copies of these manuals. Refer to them as necessary. Some Agreements and MOU's are listed, for your information and reference, in this Chapter of the IOM under the appropriate agencies. For FDA personnel, the Federal Cooperative Agreements Manual is located on the FDA Gold Disk or for either the Federal or International manuals, a hardcopy can be obtained by contacting the Division of Compliance Information and Quality Assurance (HFC-240) at 301-827-0889. State and local governmental agencies may contact the Division of Federal State Relations (HFC-150) at 301-827-6906. FDA's Office of International Programs (OIP) (HFG-1) will answer your questions about international Agreements and/or MOU. If you plan to share non-public information with another federal agency, contact HFC-230; with a state agency, contact HFC-150; or with a foreign government, contact HFC-230, who will consult with OIP. The public may obtain a copy of either manual for a fee by contacting the National Technical Information Services (NTIS), U.S. Department of Commerce, 5285 Port Royal Road, Springfield, VA 22161 or by telephoning them at 800-553-6847. Partnership Agreements will be posted on the ORA Internet (See www.fda.gov/ora/partnership_agreements/default.htm.)

3.1.3 - Other Government Inspection

General procedures regarding cooperation with other federal, state, and local officials are furnished below.

During establishment inspections determine the specific type of inspection service and inspecting units, such as the name of the federal, state, county, or city health agency or department. Obtain the name and title of the inspectional official, and general method of operation. IOM 5.4.9.3 discusses coverage of grade A Dairy Plants.

3.1.3.1 - Federal

Compulsory Continuous Inspection - Do not inspect firms, or that portion of a plant, under compulsory, continuous inspection under United States Department of Agriculture's (USDA) Meat Inspection Act, Poultry Products Inspection Act, or Egg Products Inspection Act, except on specific instructions from your supervisor or assignment document.

Ingredients or manufacturing processes common to both USDA and FDA regulated products should be inspected by FDA. See IOM 3.2.1.3 for FDA/USDA Agreements in specific areas.

Provide routine FDA coverage of such firms as breweries and wineries, which may be intermittently inspected on a compulsory basis by the U.S. Treasury Department, U.S. Public Health Service, or other agencies.

Voluntary - All products inspected under the voluntary inspection service of the Agriculture Marketing Service (AMS), USDA, and the National Marine Fisheries Service (NMFS), US Department of Commerce, are subject to FDA jurisdiction and are usually given routine coverage; however, formal written Agreements or a MOU between FDA and other agencies are often executed and may govern the agreeing agencies' operations on these type of inspected plants.

3.1.3.2 - Discussion with Federal Inspector

If you are assigned to cover a federally inspected plant which is under either compulsory or voluntary inspection, check to see if an Agreement or a MOU exists between FDA and the agency involved to determine the obligations of both agencies. When you arrive at the firm:

1. Identify yourself to the inspector(s) and invite him/her to accompany you on the inspection but do not insist on their participation.

2. At the conclusion of the inspection, offer to discuss your observations and provide the in-plant inspector with a copy of your Inspectional Observations (FDA 483).

3.1.3.3 - State and Local

State and local officials usually have extensive regulatory authority over firms in their area regardless of the interstate movement or origin of the food products involved. Joint FDA-State or local inspections are occasionally conducted. These are usually arranged by district administrative or supervisory personnel. See IOM 3.3.1.

3.2 - Federal Agency Interaction

This subchapter deals with the interaction of the FDA with other federal agencies. This interaction will be discussed below. Each agency with which FDA has agreements or an MOU is listed separately. Information regarding MOU's and other interactions are discussed as appropriate. Information about the complete MOU or agreement can be found in the appropriate Cooperative Agreements Manual. Listings of all Liaison Officers are included below.

3.2.1 - U. S. Department of Agriculture (USDA)

See IOM 3.1.3 for procedures to be followed when making inspections of firms under USDA inspection or subject to inspection by USDA.

3.2.1.1 - Foods Rejected by USDA

All procurement and processing contracts administered by USDA for edible food products require compliance with FDA regulations. The USDA routinely reports to the FDA its findings on lots of flour, cereal, or other products which have been rejected for acceptance into USDA-sponsored programs, based on FDA guidelines. This notification of rejection is routinely furnished to the involved district office. When a district office receives such notification it will determine appropriate follow-up by evaluating the reason for rejection, current priority assignments, and workload.

Samples should not be routinely collected from the USDA rejected material. If a follow-up inspection is made the district will then determine the need for samples or additional action.

3.2.1.2 - USDA Complaints

Whenever a complaint is received involving any meat-containing product, including such items as soups, combination infant foods, frozen dinners, etc., evaluate the need to contact USDA. Most products containing red meat or poultry are regulated by USDA. The exceptions include:

1. Products containing meat from game animals, such as venison, rabbits, etc.

2. Meat-flavored instant noodles

3. The product "pork and beans" which contain only a small amount of pork fat and for historic reasons is regulated by FDA.

Determine from the consumer whether there is a round "shield" on the label with the USDA establishment number. Alternatively, the establishment number may be identified in the lot number. Red meat products under USDA jurisdiction will often contain the abbreviation "EST" followed by a one to four digit number; poultry products under USDA jurisdiction will contain the letter "P" followed by a number.

FDA reports suspected outbreaks to USDA and CDC. In addition, FDA and CDC have an agreement that FDA will be immediately advised whenever CDC ships botulism antitoxin anywhere in the United States or its possessions. See IOM 3.2.4.3 regarding interaction with CDC.

USDA and FDA have an agreement whereby FDA informs a designated USDA Compliance and Evaluation Area Office about any foodborne disease where a meat or poultry product is suspected. Conversely, USDA will alert the FDA district office on suspected products subject to FDA jurisdiction. In order for your district to alert USDA promptly, check with your supervisor immediately if meat or poultry products are involved in an outbreak you are investigating or which comes to your attention.

3.2.1.3 - USDA Acts

The following USDA Acts under which FDA has been delegated detention authorities for products subject to USDA inspection are:

1. Federal Meat Inspection Act (FMIA) see IOM 2.7.1.2.2

2. Poultry Products Inspection Act PPIA see IOM 2.7.1.2.3

3. Egg Products Inspection Act (EPIA) see IOM 2.7.1.2.4

See IOM 2.7.1 for additional information. See IOM Exhibit 3-1 for a chart depicting jurisdictional lines for products regulated by FDA and USDA.

3.2.1.4 - FDA-USDA Agreements & MOUs

MOU's and Agreements with USDA and its various units will be listed and in some cases described below. This first subsection covers MOU's with the USDA, USDA/other agency, and FDA. The following subsections provide information about MOU's with other USDA units.

MOU with:

1. US Department of Commerce and USDA Concerning Inspection of Industrial Fishery Products Intended For Animal 315 Feed Use (225-75-7001).

2. USDA, NIH Regarding Importation of Biological Specimens Under US/USSR Scientific Exchange Agreement (225-74-1010).

3. USDA Concerning Public Education in the Basics of Food Safety, Nutrition, and Veterinary Medicine (225-89-8000).

4. USDA Concerning Sampling and Aflatoxin Testing of Imported Pistachios or Peanuts (225-96-2003).

   Importers of pistachio nuts voluntarily offer to USDA inspectors before introducing them into U.S. commerce. USDA is responsible for sampling and testing each lot for aflatoxin, in accordance with procedures prescribed by FDA, and for issuing an analysis certificate for each lot. The Agricultural Marketing Service (AMS) will forward a copy of each certificate to the appropriate FDA District office.The FDA Liaison Officer is the Director, Office of Compliance, Center for Food Safety and Applied Nutrition, HFS-600 (301-436-2359).

   The USDA Liaison Officer is the Chief of Technologies Services Branch, Science Division, AMS (202-690-4025).

5. USDA and DHHS Regarding General War Food Inspection (225-75-8004).

   Staff units and officials of USDA and FDA shall confer on matters of joint concern. In an immediate post-attack period USDA food inspectors or designated FDA Inspectors may act to inspect and approve foods meeting emergency standards for safety. DHHS/FDA will provide appropriate guidelines for use by USDA personnel in assuring compliance for food inspection in the emergency period. The emergency liaison officers appointed by each agency may be assigned to the other agency's headquarters emergency relocation sites for the purpose of coordinating food inspection services.The FDA Liaison Officer is the Director, Office of Emergency Operations, HFA-615, (301-443-1240).

   The USDA Liaison Officer is the Director, Emergency Response Division, Food Safety and Inspection Service (202-501-7515)

6. USDA Regarding the Reduction of Salmonella enteritidis (S.E.) Infection of Humans (225-92-2000).

3.2.1.5 - Agricultural Marketing Service (AMS)/USDA (MOU's)

MOU with:

1. AMS Concerning the Inspection and Grading of Food Products (225-72-2009).

   This MOU has extensive separation of duties between AMS and FDA.

   Both agencies agree to maintain a close working relationship, in the field as well as headquarters.

   Both agencies will work with industry toward greater efficiency connected with improvement of coding methods. Each agency will designate a central contact point to which communications dealing with this agreement or other issues may be referred to for attention.

The FDA Liaison Officer is the Director, Office of Compliance, Center for Food Safety and Applied Nutrition, HFS-600 (301-436-2359).

The USDA Liaison Officer is the Chief of Technologies Services Branch, Science Division, AMS (202-690-4025).

2. AMS Regarding the Egg Products Inspection Act. FDA has exclusive jurisdiction over restaurants, institutions, food manufacturing plants, and other similar establishments, that break and serve eggs or use them in their products (225-75-4003).AMS shall notify FDA whenever it has reason to believe that shell eggs or egg products have been shipped in commerce in violation of the act to a receiver for which FDA has exclusive jurisdiction, and notify FDA when applications are made to import shell eggs into the U.S.

   FDA will notify AMS so that they can check on the seller of any restricted eggs when it is determined that more restricted eggs than are allowed in U.S. Consumer Grade B. are encountered. FDA will also notify AMS of any unwholesome egg products it encounters, including imported shell eggs which contain restricted eggs not in accordance with USDA regulations and labeling requirements.

   The FDA Liaison Officer is the Director, Office of Emergency Operations, HFA-615, (301-443-1240).

   The FDA Liaison Officer for imported shell eggs is the Branch Chief, Import Branch, Division of Enforcement, Office of Compliance, Center for Food Safety and Applied Nutrition, HFS-606 (301-436-2413).

   The USDA Liaison Officer is the Deputy Administrator, Poultry Program, Agricultural Marketing Service (202-720-4476).

3. AMS Concerning Imported Dates and Date Material (225-72-2001).

   FDA inspects samples and examines imported dates and date products intended for processing to determine whether they are in compliance with the statute.

   AMS, upon request, will provide FDA with a copy of each examination report which will contain information such as that in the FDA Technical Bulletin Number 5, Microanalytical Procedures Manual.

   The FDA Liaison Officer is the Director, Division of Natural Products, Microanalytical Branch, Center for Food Safety and Applied Nutrition, HFS-315 (301-436-2401).

   The USDA Liaison Officer is the Chief, Processed Products Branch, Fruit and Vegetable Division, Agricultural Marketing Service (202-720-4693).

4. AMS Concerning Cooperative Efforts for Inspection, Sampling, and Examination of Imported Raisins (225-73-2007).

AMS evaluates raisins for grade condition requirements and at the time and place of entry all lots of imported raisins. Upon completion of the examination, AMS promptly notifies the appropriate FDA District Office of any lots found not to meet minimum acceptance criteria because of insect infestation, filth, etc., and any questionable cases regarding the laboratory examination results. At the end of the season, the AMS provides FDA with a copy of each examination report.

FDA accepts, unless it notifies USDA to the contrary, AMS findings on any lot of raisins sampled and inspected by them. FDA will detain any lots of raisins rejected by USDA because they contain insect infestation, etc. See the cooperative agreement manual for details of responsibilities.

The FDA Liaison Officer is the Director, Division of Natural Products, Microanalytical Branch, Center for Food Safety and Applied Nutrition, HFS-315 (301-436-2401).

The USDA Liaison Officer is the Chief, Processed Products Branch, Fruit and Vegetable Division, Agricultural Marketing Service (202-720-4693).

5. AMS Regarding Aflatoxin Testing Program for In-Shell Brazil Nuts (225-96-2002).

   Importers of Brazil Nuts voluntarily offer for USDA inspections before introducing them into U.S. commerce. USDA is responsible for sampling and testing each lot for aflatoxin in accordance with procedures prescribed by FDA and for issuing an analysis certificate for each lot. The Agricultural Marketing Service (AMS) will forward a copy of each certificate to the appropriate FDA District office. FDA accepts the certificate and then allows entry of the lots into U.S. commerce provided the aflatoxin level does not exceed the current action level prescribed by FDA.

   The FDA Liaison Officer is the Director, Office of Compliance, Center for Food Safety and Applied Nutrition, HFS-600 (301-436-2359).

   The USDA Liaison Officer is the Chief of Technologies Services Branch, Science Division, AMS (202-690-4025).

6. AMS Concerning Aflatoxin in Peanuts (225-96-2001).

   AMS will use FDA administrative guidelines on objective samples to certify peanuts, recognizing that GMPs remove significant quantities of unfit peanuts and that levels of aflatoxin are reduced by heating. USDA will provide FDA with a copy of the analytical certificate and identification of the applicant on each lot found to exceed 25 ppb of aflatoxin and the analysis certificate on any lot on request. FDA will routinely confirm chemical assays in finished product at 20 ppb by bioassay procedures.

   FDA will not formally object to the offering of lots of peanuts to processors where certificates show levels of aflatoxin above 25 ppb but will examine finished products from such lots. Such lots of raw peanuts may be subject to appropriate action in cases where there is lack of assurance that the finished product will comply with current standards.

The FDA Liaison Officer is the Director, Office of Compliance, Center for Food Safety and Applied Nutrition, HFS-600 (301-436-2359).

The USDA Liaison Officer is the Chief of Technologies Services Branch, Science Division, AMS (202-690-4025).

7. AMS and FSIS and EPA re: Regulatory Activities Concerning Residues of Drugs, Pesticides, and Environmental Contaminants in Foods (225-85-8910). Parts of this MOU are discussed below. Information about the complete MOU can be found in the appropriate Cooperative Agreements Manual. The contact offices are as follows:

   The FDA Liaison Office is the Director, Division of Natural Products, Microanalytical Branch, Center for Food Safety and Applied Nutrition, HFS-315 (301-436-2401).

   The USDA Liaison Office is the Administrator, Food Safety and Inspection Service (202-720-7025).

   The EPA Liaison Office is the Office of Pesticide Programs, (703-305-7090), or Health Effects Division, (703-305-7351).

8. AMS Concerning Salmonella Inspection and Sampling Coverage of Dry Milk Plants (225-75-4002).

   Parts of this MOU are discussed below. Information about the complete MOU can be found in the appropriate Cooperative Agreements Manual.

   USDA has two types of voluntary inspection programs: Plant Inspection Program for USDA Approved for Grading Services, and their Resident Inspection and Grading Program.

   Plant Inspection Program (PIP). Under the PIP, dry milk plants are surveyed for approval every three months. This includes a salmonella surveillance testing of the plant's product and environmental material. Product inspection and grading is provided on request and dry milk products produced under this program are eligible to bear the USDA shield.

   FDA will accept the AMS Salmonella Surveillance Program results on such plants and the finished dry milk products after shipment from those plants will not be sampled by FDA for Salmonella examinations. This does not preclude FDA sampling dry milk at manufacturing plants using dry milk as an ingredient as a follow-up to consumer complaints, or where the dry milk may have become contaminated or adulterated after leaving the dry milk manufacturer's control. Neither will it preclude FDA inspections of any plant for problems other than Salmonella whether or not such plant produces dry milk products under USDA inspection, or the sampling of their products, including dry milk products, for problems other than Salmonella.

The FDA Liaison Office is the Director, Office of Emergency Operations, HFA-615, (301-443-1240).

The USDA Liaison Office is the Chief, Grading Branch, Dairy Division, Agricultural Marketing Service, (202-720-3171) or Chief, Standardization Branch, (202-720-7473).

3.2.1.6 - Animal Plant Health Inspection Service/USDA (APHIS)

MOU with APHIS Concerning Mutual Responsibilities for Regulating Biological Products (225-82-7000).

Referral and exchange information for purposes of investigation and appropriate legal action. To coordinate investigations and enforcement actions and to avoid duplication of effort, FDA and USDA agree to provide each other with any information which may be germane to either agency's enforcement functions. Information regarding pending investigations and enforcement actions shall be provided to the liaison officers noted below on a regular basis.

The FDA Liaison Office is the Director, Office of Surveillance and Compliance, Center for Veterinary Medicine, HFV-200, (240-453-6830).

The USDA Liaison Office is the Director, Center for Veterinary Biologics, Animal and Plant Health Inspection Service, (301-734-8245).

APHIS and NIH Regarding the Care and Welfare of Laboratory Animals.

3.2.1.7 - Federal Grain Inspection Service/USDA (FGIS)

MOU with FGIS Concerning Inspection of Grain, Rice, Pulses, and Food Products (225-80-2000).

During an FDA inspection of any facility that processes, packs, or holds agricultural products, the investigator and or inspector will request that the FGIS inspector or licensee stationed at a facility accompany him/her during the inspection.

The inspector/investigator will request from FGIS any information concerning quality determinations of specific lots of products against which FDA has taken or may take action.

FDA will notify FGIS of any details concerning serious objectionable conditions found by FDA to exist in processing plants, packing plants, grain elevators, or any other facility where FGIS provides official services.

General matters involving this agreement may be referred to the agencies' liaison officers.

The FDA Liaison Office is the Director, Office of Plant and Dairy Foods and Beverages, Center for Food Safety and Applied Nutrition, HFS-300, (301-436-1700) or Director, Division of Programs and Enforcement Policy, Center for Food Safety and Applied Nutrition, HFS-305, (301-436-1400).

The USDA Liaison Office is the Director, Field Management Division, Federal Grain Inspection Service, Grain Inspection, Packers and Stockyards Administration (202-720-0228).

3.2.1.8 - Food Safety and Inspection Service/USDA (FSIS)

1. FSIS Pertaining to Class I and Class II Recalls of Food Products that Contain Poultry and/or Meat Products that have been Manufactured in a FSIS Inspected Establishment (225-75-4072);

   FDA and FSIS agree that they will keep the customary records and make those related to the operation of this agreement available to the other agency. Both agencies will furnish reports of the progress of the work and such other reports as may be mutually agreed upon from time to time between cooperating parties.

   The FDA Liaison Officer is the Director, Office of Emergency Operations, HFA-615, (301-827-5660). The USDA Liaison Officer is the Director, Emergency Planning Office, Food Safety and Inspection Service (301-504-2121)

2. FSIS Concerning Inspection of Food Manufacturing Firms FDA investigators will attempt to contact any on-site FSIS inspectors when they arrive at a plant, invite them to participate in the inspection and discuss with or report any adverse findings involving meat and poultry products to that inspector prior to leaving the premises (225-99-2001).

   When report findings are classified "indicated" FDA will provide FSIS with a copy when the plant is also inspected by FSIS.

   If the FDA investigator has found unsanitary conditions or otherwise adulterated products, the appropriate FSIS office should be informed by telephone unless the FDA investigator has already reported his findings to the FSIS inspector at the plant.

   To any extent possible, consider information provided by FSIS to minimize duplication of effort.

   The FDA Liaison Office is the Director, Office of Emergency Operations, HFA-615, (301-443-1240)

   The USDA Liaison Office is the Deputy Administrator, Field Operations, Food Safety and Inspection Service (202-720-8803).

3. FSIS and AMS and EPA re: Regulatory Activities Concerning Residues of Drugs, Pesticides, and Environmental Contaminants in Foods (225-85-8400).

4. FSIS (NE and SE Regional Offices), DE Department of Agriculture, MD Department of Agriculture, PA Department of Agriculture, VA Department of Agriculture and Consumer Services, WV Department of Agriculture Regarding Regulatory Investigations Involving Drug, Pesticide, and Industrial Chemical Residues in Animal Feeds and Meat and Poultry (225-76-4002).

5. FSIS and GA Department of Agriculture Regarding Regulatory Investigations Involving Drug, Pesticide, and Toxic Chemical Residues in Animal Feeds and in Meat Tissues (225-91-4000).

3.2.1.9 - Science and Education Administration/USDA (SEA)

MOU with SEA Concerning Educational Programs in the Use of Animal Drugs (225-78-1002).

3.2.2 - U.S. Department of Commerce (DOC)

3.2.2.1 - Commerce (DOC)

MOU's with DOC and USDA Concerning Inspection of Industrial Fishery Products Intended for Animal Feed Use.

3.2.2.2 - National Oceanic and Atmospheric Administration (NOAA) - National Marine Fisheries Service (NMFS)

MOU with:

1. NOAA/NMFS Regarding Inspection Programs for Fishery Products (225-76-2001) - The National Marine Fisheries Service (NMFS) of the National Oceanic and Atmospheric Administration (NOAA), Department of Commerce, operating under the authority of the Agriculture Marketing Act and the Fish and Wildlife Act is responsible for the development and advancement of commercial grade standards for fishery products and better health and sanitation standards in the industry and for furnishing inspection, analytical, and grading services to interested parties. The major purpose is to encourage and assist industry in improving the quality and safety of its products. This MOU outlines joint responsibilities between NOAA and FDA. See IOM 3.1.3 for guidance on joint inspections when inspecting firms under the voluntary NMFS program.

   The FDA Liaison Office is the Policy Guidance Branch, Division of Programs and Enforcement Policy, Office of Seafood, Center for Food Safety and Applied Nutrition, HFS-416 (301-436-1415)

   The NMFS Liaison Office is the Seafood Inspection Program, Department of Commerce, NOAA (301-713-2355).

2. NOAA/NMFS Concerning Enforcement of Laws (225-86-2000) -Against Illegal Commerce in Molluscan Shellfish.

   FDA will support NMFS Lacey Act investigations to the extent that regulatory authority and resources allow. This may include conducting food sanitation inspections of suspect shellfish shippers, reviewing interstate shipping records and obtaining affidavits to the extent possible, collecting and analyzing shellfish samples to be used as evidence of violations, and removing adulterated shellfish from the marketplace. Refer to the appropriate Cooperative Agreements manual for further discussion of this MOU.

The FDA Liaison Office is the Policy Guidance Branch, Division of Programs and Enforcement Policy, Office of Seafood, Center for Food Safety and Applied Nutrition, HFS-416 (301-436-1415)

The NMFS Liaison Office is the Seafood Inspection Program, Department of Commerce, NOAA (301-713-2355).

3.2.2.3 - U.S. Patent and Trademark Office (USP&TO)(DOC)

MOU's with:

1. USP and TO/DOC Concerning Orphan Drugs (225-84-8000).
2. USP and TO/DOC to Establish a Product's Eligibility for Patent Term Restoration (225-86-8251).

3.2.3 - Department of Defense (DOD)

FDA has a number of MOU's with DOD and its various elements.

3.2.3.1 - DOD MOU's

1. DOD Concerning Licensure of Military Blood Banks (225-74-1017).
2. DOD Concerning FDA Responsibility for Quality Assurance of DOD Procured Drugs and Biologics (225-97-4000).

FDA also has a number of Interagency Agreements (IAG) with DOD to include IAG with:

1. DOD Concerning Investigational Use of Drugs, Antibiotics, Biologics, and Medical Devices by DOD (224-75-3003).
2. DOD Regarding FDA Quality Assurance Responsibility for DOD Contracts for Medical Devices (224-82-4001).

3.2.3.2 - U.S. Army Corps of Engineers (DOD)

MOU with U.S. Army/Corps of Engineers Concerning Consumer Protection During Natural Disasters.

3.2.3.3 - US Army Medical Research and Development Command (DOD)

MOU with U.S. Army Medical Research and Development Command Regarding Quality Assurance Support for Medical Material Having Military Application (225-99-4000).

3.2.3.4 - Defense Personnel Support Center (DPSC)

1. MOU with DPSC Concerning Exchange of Information Regarding Food and Cosmetic Recalls and Hazardous Food Situations (225-82-4003).

2. The Defense Personnel Support Center purchases vast quantities of foods and drugs for use by the Armed Forces. The products are purchased on contract and must meet standards and contract specifications to be accepted. Any products failing to meet these specifications are rejected. These are mentioned in IOM 3.2.3.1 above.

FDA, under the Government-Wide Quality Assurance Program (GWQAP), furnishes information to the military regarding the capabilities of firms bidding or desiring to bid on government contracts. Occasionally districts may be requested by the Division of Compliance Information and Quality Assurance (DCIQA) to make inspections or collect samples in support of the GWQAP. When this is necessary, DCIQA will provide the district with specific procedures and instructions. DoD depots and hospitals must notify their command centers prior to release of their stocks. For this reason, prior to visiting a U.S. Government installation to collect samples of food, drugs or medical devices, districts should contact DCIQA (HFC-240) so that visit can be expedited.

See IOM 4.1.6 for information regarding GWQAP samples and IOM 5.2.3.5 for information regarding GWQAP FDA 483.

3.2.3.5 - Department of Navy/Bureau of Medicine and Surgery

MOU with Dept. the Navy/Bureau of Medicine and Surgery Regarding the Microwave Oven Survey (225-77-1001).

3.2.4 - Department of Health and Human Services (HHS)

This Agency has a number of MOU's with the Department and other HHS units.

3.2.4.1 - HHS MOU's

MOU with USDA and HHS Regarding General War Food Inspection (225-75-8004).

3.2.4.2 - Administration for Children, Youth and Families (ACYF)

A MOU with ACYF to Assure the Feeding Programs in Head Start Centers Conform with Federal Food Safety and Sanitation Responsibilities (225-89-2000).

3.2.4.3 - Centers for Disease Control and Prevention (CDC)

MOU with:

1. CDC Concerning In-Vitro Diagnostics (225-75-5012).

2. CDC Regarding Radiation Emergencies (225-81-6000).

3. CDC Regarding Exchange of Information and Coordination of Actions(225-82-8000).

Additional information is being provided here because of the close working agreement to assure the prompt exchange of information on suspected foodborne outbreaks.

Since it is essential that any suspected outbreaks be reported promptly to CDC, communicate any information you may learn in connection with foodborne outbreaks to your supervisor as soon as possible. See FMD #64 for procedures on Epidemiological Investigations Alert Reporting Procedures.

1. Botulism Antitoxin Shipments - CDC is responsible for maintaining and shipping necessary supplies of botulinum antitoxin. When CDC makes a shipment of botulinum antitoxin, CDC will immediately, regardless of the day or time, phone the Office of Emergency Operations (OEO), HFA-615, (301-443-1240). The OEO contact will immediately phone the consignee district to advise them of the shipment.

2. Outbreaks on Foreign Flag Vessels - If an outbreak involving a foreign flag vessel or a US Flag vessel with an international itinerary comes to your attention, report it to your supervisor immediately who will then report it to OEO 301-443-1240. This situation falls under the jurisdiction of the Vessel Sanitation Program of the Centers for Disease Control and Prevention (CDC) Atlanta, Ga.

3. Outbreaks Involving Interstate Conveyances - Reports of illness attributed to travel on an interstate conveyance (plane, bus, train, or vessel) are the responsibility of FDA.

When a report of illness is received, you are encouraged to share it with state and local public health officials in case they received additional illness reports. Additionally, the procedures outlined in this Subchapter are to be followed including the following 5 items:

3.2.4.3.1 - Interviews

Interviews with the ill passenger, family members and/or physician (as applicable), should be in-depth enough to hypothesize whether the carrier may be related to the illness. Factors such as time of onset of symptoms, history of eating suspect foods, and other potential exposures should be considered. The carrier should also be contacted to determine whether other reports of illness have been received. The information developed should be evaluated to determine whether further follow-up is necessary (i.e., the carrier suspect). On those carriers where a reservation system is used, the names and phone numbers of passengers should be obtained to determine if other individuals became ill. It may be necessary to contact other passengers to determine if they consumed any food or water on the trip, and if they became ill in the time period associated with the original complaint. When a report of additional related or similar illnesses is received, immediately contact the Office of Emergency Operations, ORO, HFA-615, 301-443-1240 and relay the information. Also contact the state epidemiologist of the affected state to report the details of the illness. It may be advantageous to request assistance from them in the epidemiological investigation, particularly if patient specimens are needed to determine the cause.

3.2.4.3.2 - Information Exchange and Coordination

Recently FDA revised the MOU between FDA and CDC regarding exchange of information and coordination of actions. This MOU provides a framework for coordination and collaborative efforts between the two agencies. It also provides the principles and procedures by which information exchanges between FDA and CDC will take place. The new memorandum supersedes the MOU between CDC and FDA dated 4/1/82. When receiving a request for information from the CDC immediately notify the Director of the Office of Emergency Operations, HFA-615, 301-443-1240.

"FDA and CDC agree that the following principles and procedures will govern the exchange of nonpublic information between the two agencies. Although there is no legal requirement the FDA and CDC exchange information in all cases, FDA and CDC agree that there should be a presumption in favor of full and free sharing of information between FDA and CDC. Both agencies recognize and acknowledge however that it is essential that any confidential information that is shared between FDA and CDC must be protected from unauthorized public disclosure. See e.g., 21 USC sec. 331(j); 18 USC sec. 1905; 21 CFR Parts 20 and 21; 42 CFR Parts 5 and 5b; and, 42 USC sec. 301(d). Safeguards are important to protect the interests of, among others, owners and submitters of trade secrets and confidential commercial information; patient identities and other personal privacy information; privileged and/or pre-decisional agency records; and information protected for national security reasons. Any unauthorized disclosure of shared confidential information by the agency receiving the information shall be the responsibility of that agency.

3.2.4.3.3 - Routine Requests for Information

Routine Requests for Information:

1. The requesting agency must demonstrate, in writing, why it is necessary for it to obtain the requested information.

2. The agency receiving the request for information shall, based upon the sufficiency of the need-to-know demonstration described in section 1 above, determine whether it is appropriate to share the requested information with the requesting agency.

3. The requesting agency agrees that:
   a. It shall limit the dissemination of shared information it receives to internal agency offices and/or individuals that have been identified in its written request and/or have a need-to-know;
   b. Agree in writing not to publicly disclose any shared information in any manner including publications and public meetings without written permission of the agency that has shared the information;
   c. If the requesting agency receives a Freedom of Information Act (FOIA) request for the shared information, it will refer the request to the information-sharing agency; and,
   d. It shall promptly notify the appropriate office of the information-sharing agency when there is any attempt to obtain shared

information by compulsory process, including but not limited to a FOIA request, subpoena, discovery request, or litigation complaint or motion.

4. The agency that shares information with the requesting agency shall include a transmittal letter, along with any agency records exchanged, indicating the type of information.

3.2.4.3.4 - Emergency Requests for Confidential Information

In cases in which the requesting agency has a need to obtain certain information as soon as possible due to emergency circumstances, such as a foodborne illness outbreak, FDA and CDC may utilize the following procedures:

1. The requesting agency shall indicate orally or in writing to the agency in possession of the relevant information that it has the need to obtain certain identifiable information as soon as possible due to the existence of emergency circumstances and describe what the emergency circumstances are.

2. The requesting agency shall verbally agree to protect from unauthorized public disclosure any and all information that is shared, according to all applicable laws and regulations.

3. The existence of an actual emergency situation shall warrant, as determined by the agency in possession of the requested records, the waiver of the need-to-know demonstration and determination describedin sections 1 and 2 (Routine Requests for Information) above. However, once the requesting agency has obtained the information it seeks, it shall comply with those procedures set forth in section 3 (Routine Requests for Information) above.

3.2.4.3.5 - Liaison Officers

Liaison Officers

1. For FDA:

   Associate Commissioner for Regulatory Affairs
   Contact: Ellen Morrison, Director, Office of Emergency Operations
   Food and Drug Administration
   5600 Fishers Lane, HFA-615
   Rockville, MD 20857
   301-443-1240 or 301-827-5660

2. For CDC:

   Associate Director for Science
   Dixie E. Snyder, MD
   Centers for Disease Control
   Public Health Service

Department of Health and Human Services
Atlanta, GA 30333 404-639-7240

3.2.4.4 - Centers for Medicare and Medicaid Services (CMS)

MOU with Centers for Medicare and Medicaid Services (CMS) Concerning Blood Banking and Transfusion Programs (225-80-4000).

3.2.4.5 - Health Services Administration (HSA)

MOU with HSA Concerning Quality Assurance for Drugs, Biologics, Chemicals and Reagents Procured by HSA (225-75-8002).

3.2.4.6 - National Center for Health Statistics (NCHS)

A MOU with NCHS Regarding Exchange of Information (225-83-6000).

3.2.4.7 - National Institute of Drug Abuse (NIDA)

MOU's with:

1. NIDA Regarding Methadone Mutual Responsibilities in Implementing the Jointly Published Narcotic Addict Treatment Regulations (225-81-3000).

2. NIDA Concerning Cooperative Interaction in Expediting Domestic Scheduling of Drugs of Abuse (225-85-8251).

3.2.4.8 - National Institutes of Health (NIH)

MOU with:

1. NIH Regarding Anticancer Drugs (225-75-3001).

2. NIH and USDA Regarding Importation of Biological Specimens under US/USSR Scientific Exchange Agreement (225-74-1010).

3. NIH and APHIS Regarding the Care and Welfare of Laboratory Animals (225-83-8400).

3.2.5 - Department of Homeland Security

3.2.5.1 - U.S. Customs and Border Protection

MOU with:

1. Customs Service and the FDA Regarding Identifying Roles and Authority Concerning Electronic Products (225-74-6004).

2. Customs Service to Establish a Working Relationship for Cooperative Enforcement (225-79-4003).

3. Customs Services Regarding the Needs of the Trading Public in Expediting the Collection, Processing and the Use of Import Information (225-91-4003).

3.2.5.2 - Secret Service

The Secret Service operates under theDepartment of Homeland Securityand is charged with the responsibility of protecting the President of the United States and certain other prominent persons. They also enforce the laws and regulations relating to currency, coins, and obligations and securities of the U.S. and foreign governments.

Authority for Secret Service to request FDA assistance, and for FDA to respond, is derived from the "Presidential Protection Assistance Act of 1976", P.L. 94-524 (90 Stat. 2475-7), Sections 1-10. Section six states in part:

"Executive Departments and Executive Agencies shall assist the Secret Service in the performance of its duties by providing services, equipment, and facilities on a temporary and reimbursable basis when requested by the Director and on a permanent and reimbursable basis upon advance written request of the Director; except that the DOD and the Coast Guard shall provide such assistance on a temporary basis without reimbursement when assisting the Secret Service in its duties directly related to the protection of the President or the Vice President or other officer immediately next in order of succession to the office of the President."

Note: At the present time the Agency is not claiming reimbursement from Secret Service until a study of total costs of our support function is completed.

FDA's authority for entry and inspection is derived from Secret Service authority and its request for FDA assistance. When called upon by the Secret Service to assist with a food service function, FDA's response is that of an advisor. Authority for decisions regarding food and beverages to be consumed by protectees is retained by the Secret Service.

Note: Do Not issue a Notice of Inspection - FDA 482 unless the investigation evolves into the collection of a sample for the enforcement of the FD&C Act. You are in the firm under the Secret Service authority.

FDA may initiate action against products encountered which are suspected of being in violation of the FD&C Act or the FPLA.

3.2.5.2.1 - Liaison

The Secret Service and FDA have an arrangement whereby FDA district officials are alerted by the Secret Service when the President, Vice President or other Protectees are to visit their areas and are to consume prepared meals and Secret Service wants the food service facilities inspected. This is to assure that proper precautions are taken if any meals are to be consumed by these individuals during the stay.

If you are alerted by Secret Service Agents that the President, Vice President or other protectees will visit the area, immediately advise your supervisor in person or by telephone. Since the lead time is often short, the district must be alerted at once so proper arrangements can be made for issuance of inspectional or investigational assignments. Because of security procedures you are not to contact the Secret Service concerning protectee travel prior to notification by them even though you may hear from other sources that a protectee is to visit your area.

As part of this arrangement FDA supplies current rosters, office addresses, and telephone numbers of Regional Food and Drug Directors, District Directors, Station Chiefs, and Residents to the Secret Service Headquarters for dissemination to their field agents.

3.2.5.2.2 - Definitions

Definitions:

1. Advanced Prepared Food means food that was prepared on location at the food service establishment prior to arrival of the Lead Investigator.

2. Food Service Function means a public event where food will be provided to a protectee.

3. Lead Advance Agent means the Secret Service Agent in charge of all security arrangements. This person is responsible for all sites to be visited by the protectee, and is a representative of the Office of Protective Operations (Secret Service Headquarters).

4. Lead Investigator means the FDA person designated by the FDA district/region to coordinate the investigational activities at the site of a food service function.

5. Person-in-Charge means the available person in the food service establishment authorized to make necessary changes/decisions such as the general manager, executive chef, banquet manager, caterer's representative or other management person.

6. Pre-prepared Food means potentially hazardous food that was received at the food service establishment in a prepared form. Examples would include chicken salad, liver pate, gefilte fish, hors d'oeuvres, etc. which were prepared at another location, and then transported to the food service establishment providing food for the event.

7. Protectee means any person eligible to receive the protection authorized by law.

8. Protective Detail means a team of Secret Service agents responsible for security surrounding public events to be attended by a protectee during a trip. Protective details are assigned and coordinated by Secret Service Headquarters, but may include Secret Service field representatives.

9. District Contact means the Director, Investigations Branch.

10. Site Advance Agent means the Secret Service person responsible for security arrangements at a specific site to be visited by the protectee. This person is part of the protective detail headed by the Lead Advance Agent. Note: the term Site Advance Agent will include any agent designated by the Site Advance Agent to be the contact with the FDA Lead Investigator.

11. Support Personnel means FDA persons deemed necessary by FDA in order to properly inspect a food service function.

3.2.5.2.3 - Purpose

FDA's primary purpose in support of Secret Service is to minimize the possibility of the protectee becoming ill from a food intoxication or foodborne infection resulting from inadequate knowledge of food safety requirements by food service personnel, inadequate facilities, improper operating procedures, or carelessness. FDA is further concerned that food have no visible signs of filth, and that it is prepared in a clean environment.

FDA personnel are not trained to detect deliberate attempts to harm persons by the addition of poisonous or toxic substances to food. The Secret Service retains responsibility for matters involving criminal intent. However, FDA personnel should immediately report to the Site Advance Agent peculiar behavior or suspicious conditions observed during their investigation.

3.2.5.2.4 - Criteria for Requesting FDA Assistance

The decision to request FDA assistance is made by Secret Service Office of Protective Operations (Headquarters). FDA has provided certain criteria to aid Secret Service in determining how they might derive maximum benefit from FDA. Regardless what criteria are used, FDA should always respond to Secret Service requests for assistance. Secret Service considers factors other than the FDA supplied criteria in making its judgment regarding requests for assistance.

3.2.5.2.5 - Scope of Investigation

The focus of the FDA investigation should be on the menu items that the protectee will be served, or from which the protectee will make a selection. Food, facilities, personnel, procedures, etc. are only considered by FDA as they relate to the specific food and beverage items which may be consumed by the protectee. Do not conduct a traditional regulatory type food service inspection. The Food Service EIR (FDA 2420) will not normally be part of the report prepared following this special investigation. State/local regulatory authorities have jurisdiction over food establishments, and have a primary responsibility for public health protection of the general public or participating members or guests of the organization sponsoring the event.

3.2.5.2.6 - Interagency Cooperation

Upon contact by Secret Service and after contacting your supervisor to apprise district management of the Secret Service request, the appropriate state/local regulatory authority should be contacted and encouraged to participate prior to and during the food service function. These officials may offer invaluable assistance because of their familiarity with the establishment and because of their regulation over the establishment on a long-term basis.

3.2.5.2.7 - District Contact

The district contact should receive Secret Service requests for assistance and initiate the FDA response. If a resident post is contacted directly for assistance, immediately contact your supervisor who will notify the director investigations branch. The director investigations branch will designate the lead investigator and arrange for assignment of support personnel and equipment as required. The lead investigator could be on district or region staff according to district/region policy.

3.2.5.2.8 - Lead Investigator Qualifications

The best suited investigator (criteria optional) assigned to coordinate investigation of these food service functions should be one who:

1. Possesses OPM "Critical Sensitive" security clearance.

2. Is standardized in the use of the FDA Food Code.

3. Is experienced in Secret Service food service functions, if possible. New personnel should accompany experienced personnel before being assigned as Lead Investigator, if at all possible.

4. Is able and authorized to quickly mobilize an investigational team (FDA/State/Local).

5. Is able and authorized to make quick decisions on important food protection/sanitation questions.

6. Has a background in food microbiology.

3.2.5.2.9 - Steps for Conducting a Special Secret Service Investigation

Steps for Conducting a Special Secret Service Investiga-tion (District Contact/Lead Investigator).

Verify the call with the Secret Service and obtain from them:

1. Information about the site advance agent with whom FDA is to coordinate its activities. This should include the name(s) of agent(s) assigned, location(s) and telephone number(s).

2. Information about the firm(s) providing food for the food service function, to include:
    a. Names of persons-in-charge of food service establishment and caterers.
    b. Telephone numbers.
    c. Addresses of firm(s).
    d. Location where food service function will be held (if different).
    e. Date of function.
    f. Time of food events during function.

Obtain through means prearranged and agreed upon by FDA district/region management:

1. FDA support personnel needed.

2. Equipment required to conduct special investigation.

Contact the person-in-charge at the facility to:

1. Introduce the lead investigator.

2. Advise of purpose and scope of special investigation.

3. Arrange for personal interview to discuss menu, food preparation schedule and history (times/specific locations in establishment), and any intended use of pre- prepared foods.

4. Obtain telephone number(s) at the site(s) where FDA lead investigator may be reached while on location.

Contact state and local regulatory agencies responsible for retail food protection and sanitation. Request participation by inspectional personnel of the local office which provides routine inspectional coverage of the facility where the food service function is being held.

Meet with person-in-charge on location, in order to:

1. Be introduced to other key employees who have responsibility for the target meal or kitchen facilities, i.e. banquet manager, executive chef, maintenance supervisor, etc.

2. Inform person-in-charge of the names of other FDA, state, or local regulatory personnel to be involved.

3. Obtain the use of an area within the establishment that will become an FDA base of operations. The location should have convenient access to a telephone, but may not be necessary for small functions.

Coordinate with Secret Service command post on location, in order to:

1. Inform site advance agent of the names of other FDA, state or local regulatory personnel to be involved.

2. Determine method for final selection of specific meal(s) to be served to protectee(s).

Carry out investigation by:

1. Basing judgments on the provisions of the FDA Food Code. In consideration of food sources, food protection, personnel, food equipment/utensils, water, waste disposal, vermin control, storage and use of toxic materials, and other code items as they relate to the food items to be served to the protectee.

2. Taking the history of each item on the menu to be served the protectee. The history for each potentially hazardous food (including advance prepared and pre-prepared Food) must be detailed. Include timetables for preparation and storage, and the names of specific employees involved in its preparation. This will immediately establish parameters needed for FDA to complete a comprehensive, but well focused investigation (See IOM 3.2.5.2.3 above. Though every effort should be made by the lead investigator to help the person-in-charge and the Secret Service in their efforts to assure that preparation and arrangements for the food service function flow smoothly and efficiently, FDA personnel must be aware that their responsibility is for assuring that all prudent steps have been taken to minimize the risk of foodborne illness to the protectee.

3.2.5.2.10 - Sampling

Samples shall be collected at the discretion of the lead investigator. Two types of samples should be considered.

1. *Typical Meal* - In the unlikely event that a protectee (or others) becomes acutely or seriously ill during the hours following a food service function, it could be very helpful to have samples of meals served for analysis. Should this happen, FDA's response should be coordinated with the FDA Office of Emergency Operations at 301-443-1240.

   FDA under Secret Service authority should request that two complete meals, including beverages, be randomly selected from the meals being served to the head table. This selection should be made by the same person and at the same time head table meals are selected.

   If a reception is a planned part of the event, an example of each type of hors d'oeuvres should also be retained.

   These meals should be kept intact, covered, and retained under refrigeration by the person-in-charge for 72 hours following the event. Cost of the meals may, at the establishment's option, be invoiced to the organization sponsoring the food service function.

   Note: Examples of food items selected in this manner cannot be considered a representative sample of food offered at the function. However, such food examples could be an aid to the FBI and food regulatory personnel, should a suspected food related illness occur.

2. *Food Samples* - Occasionally, the lead investigator may elect to collect official samples of a food product because of a selected violation of the FD&C Act or for some other reason. When this is done, issue an FDA 482, Notice of Inspection. In these cases, samples should be collected in accordance with procedures outline in IOM Chapter 4.

3.2.5.2.11 - Reporting

Verbal Report - The lead investigator shall report to the site advance agent in person or by telephone.

1. Significant adverse findings should be immediately reported to the site advance agent during the investigation, if resolution of the finding has the potential for disrupting the smooth flow of the food service function.

2. At the conclusion of the investigation, and prior to leaving the location, notify the site advance agent of FDA conclusions and recommendations. One of the following responses would be normal:

   a. No restrictions recommended. Protectee should be permitted to consume any food or beverage being offered.

   b. A recommendation that the protectee be advised that one or more specifically named items available should not be selected or consumed.

   c. In unusual cases, it may be necessary to recommend that the protectee not eat food prepared for the event, or not drink the water provided.

Narrative Report - Following each special investigation conducted for the Secret Service, write a Memo of Investigation for your supervisor's endorsement. The report is for FDA's internal use and should be a chronological accounting beginning with how and when the Secret Service request was received and concluding with recommendations tendered to the Secret Service, and any F/U actions recommended to or planned by participating State/local food protection agencies. The narrative report should include time frames, contact persons, a copy of the menu, a description of the investigational process used, adverse findings, corrective steps taken, the selection and retention of typical meals, and how and why official samples (if any) were collected and submitted, and a discussion of other matters of significance in your opinion.

Each narrative report must contain:

1. Total time on location.

2. Total time of inspection including, time on location and time necessary for making arrangements in advance, and preparation and submission of required reports. It does not include travel time.

3. Total travel time and mileage.

3.2.6 - Department of Justice

3.2.6.1 - U.S. Attorney

You may be contacted by the U.S. Attorney's office to discuss possible or pending cases or other matters pertinent to FDA. Notify your supervisor of these contacts. You may be accompanied by your supervisor or a compliance officer. If you are contacted by the U.S. Attorney's Office regarding any criminal issues, this is to be referred immediately to the appropriate OCI Office.

During any discussion with the U.S. Attorney, inform him that you are qualified to report the facts of whatever case or item being discussed, but inform him that you are a fact witness only and not qualified as an "expert".

3.2.6.2 - Drug Enforcement Administration (DEA) (Formerly: Bureau of Narcotics)

You should follow the procedures outlined in the Information Disclosure manual if you receive a request to share information with another Federal agency.

3.2.6.3 - Federal Bureau of Investigation (FBI)

The FBI, USDA and FDA are authorized to investigate reported tampering of FDA regulated consumer products under the Federal Anti-Tampering Act (FATA), Title 18, USC, Section 1365. In most cases, FDA's authority for such investigations is also found in the FD&C Act.

USDA and the FBI share enforcement of the FATA with FDA as described below:

1. *FBI Responsibility* - FDA understands that the FBI's primary response in FATA matters will be to investigate particularly those cases that involve a serious threat to human life or if a death has occurred. The FBI will also investigate FATA matters involving threatened tamperings, and actual or threatened tamperings coupled with an extortion demand.

   The FBI will rely on FDA to determine if tampering with FDA products has occurred.

2. *USDA Responsibility* - The USDA will investigate and interact with the FBI on tamperings with products regulated by USDA.

For complete information regarding FBI/FDA actions under FATA, see IOM 8.8.

3.2.7 - Department of Labor: Occupational Safety and Health Administration (OSHA)

The MOU with OSHA Concerns Standards for Electronic Product Radiation (225-74-6008).

3.2.8 - Treasury Department

Many different agencies operate under the direction of this department. These include theInternal Revenue Service, and the Alcohol and Tobacco Tax and Trade Bureau . Agreements and MOU's with the Treasury Department will be discussed below.

3.2.8.1 - Alcohol and Tobacco Tax and Trade Bureau (TTB)

MOU with TTB to Delineate the Enforcement Responsibili-ties of Each Agency with Respect to Alcoholic Beverages as below (225-88-2000).

This MOU confirms that TTB is responsible for testing alcoholic beverages to determine the extent of an adulteration problem and that when FDA learns or is advised that an alcoholic beverage is or may be adulterated, FDA will contact TTB. FDA will provide laboratory assistance and health hazard evaluations, at TTB request. TTB also has responsibility for alcoholic beverage labeling, but does not have authority over wine beverages having less than 7% alcohol by volume (such as most wine coolers). "Labeling questions for wine beverages having less than 7% alcohol by volume should be directed to FDA, Director, Office of Nutritional Products, Labeling and Dietary Supplements, HFS-800, 301-436-2373" at the end of the second paragraph in this section

Based on this MOU, districts should refer all complaints involving alcoholic beverages (distilled spirits, wines, and malt beverage products except the wine beverages mentioned above) to TTB, in a manner similar to that already in effect for referring complaints about meat and poultry to USDA. When a complaint is received from a consumer, it should be entered into FACTS with the disposition "referred to other Federal agency." If the complainant is reporting a suspected tampering, it should be referred to the home district and OCI for follow-up. In all cases, a copy of the FACTS consumer complaint report should be forwarded to the FDA liaison officer with TTB at HFS-301 to facilitate appropriate follow-up between the two agencies at the headquarters level.

The FDA Liaison Officer is the Director, Office of Compliance, Center for Food Safety and Applied Nutrition, HFS-600, (301-436-2359).

The TTB Liaison Office is the Special Programs Branch, 202-927-8020.

A hard copy of the complaint should also be faxed to the closest TTB Field Office at the address listed below (as of 6/06):

TRADE INVESTIGATIONS DIVISION	
Headquarters Staff 1310 G Street, NW Suite 200 W Washington, DC 20220 202-927-9200 (Voice) 202-927-2013 (Fax)	Northwest Staff (AK; HI; WA; OR; ID; NV; UT; MT; AZ) 500 East Broadway, Suite 280 Vancouver, WA 98660 360-696-7900 (Voice) 360-696-7901 (Fax)
Northeast Staff (ME; VT; NH; NY; MA; PA; MD/DC; RI; CT; NJ; DE) Mellon Independence Center 701 Market Street, Suite 5300 Philadelphia, PA 19106 215-580-2002 (Voice) 215-580-2980 (Fax)	California Staff (CA) 650 Capitol Mall, Suite 6-700 Sacramento, CA 95814 916-930-5600 (Voice) 916-930-5610 (Fax)

TRADE INVESTIGATIONS DIVISION	
Southeast Staff (AR; LA; MS; AL; TN; GA; FL; SC; NC) 4300 West Cypress Street, Suite 340 Tampa, FL 33607 813-348-1610 (Voice) 813-348-1626 (Fax)	San Juan Alcohol and Tobacco Tax and Trade Bureau (TTB) Torre Chardon, Suite 310 350 Chardon Ave. San Juan, Puerto Rico 00918 916-766-5584 (Voice) 916-766-6426 (Fax)
Midwest Staff (WI; IN; IL; MI; OH; WV; KY; VA) 27476 Detroit Road, Suite 103 Westlake, OH 44145 440-871-6055 (Voice) 440-871-6056 (Fax)	Mayaguez Alcohol and Tobacco Tax and Trade Bureau (TTB) Suite 201 475 Hostos Avenue Mayaguez, Puerto Rico 00680-1554 787-831-3448 (Voice) 787-831-3405 (Fax)
Mountain Staff (ND; SD; WY; NE; CO; KS; NM; OK; TX; MN; IA; MO) 316 North Robert Street, Room 168 St. Paul, MN 55101 651-290-3905 (Voice) 651-290-3909 (Fax)	

A copy of the complaint should also be forwarded to the FDA liaison officer with TTB at HFS-301 to facilitate appropriate follow-up between the two agencies at the headquarters levels.

The FDA Liaison Office is the Director, Office of Compliance, Center for Food Safety and Applied Nutrition, HFS-600 (301-436-2359).

The TTB Liaison Office is the Special Programs Branch (202-927-9200).

3.2.8.2 - Internal Revenue Service (IRS)

MOU with IRS Concerning Legal Actions Taken by FDA Against Alcoholic Beverage Firms for Under filling of Containers (225-71-2006).

The FDA Liaison Office is the Division of Enforcement, Office of Compliance, Center for Food Safety and Applied Nutrition, HFS-605 (301-436-2417).

The ATF Liaison Office is the Chief, Industry Compliance Division (202-927-8100).

3.2.9 - Department of Veterans Affairs Veterans Administration (VA)

MOU with the VA are:

1. Concerning Exchange of Medical Device Experience Data (225-75-5011).

2. Concerning Communications and Cooperation Regard-ing Clinical Research with Investigational New Drugs and Devices, Including Biologicals (225-82-8400).

3. To promote cooperation and coordination between the Food and Drug Administration and the Veterans Health Administration for the purpose of enhancing food safety and sanitation in food operations serving health care facilities of the Department of Veterans Affairs (225-93-2000).

IAG's with the VA are:

1. VA Concerning FDA Responsibility for Quality Assurance for Drugs, Biologicals, Chemicals and Reagents Procured by VA (224-76-8049).

2. VA Regarding FDA Quality Assurance Responsibility for VA Contracts for Medical Devices (224-82-4002).

3. To provide mammography inspections, pursuant to Public Law 102-539 and Public Law 104-262, to Veterans Health Administration facilities.

3.2.10 - Consumer Product Safety Commission (CPSC)

MOU's with CPSC are:

1. CPSC Concerning CPSC Use of FDA Documents (225-74-8001).

2. CPSC Regarding Jurisdiction with Respect to Food, Food Containers, and Food Related Articles and Equipment (225-76-2003).

3.2.11 - Environmental Protection Agency (EPA)

The EPA administers many Acts one of them is the National Environmental Protection Act (NEPA). FDA must be guided by this Act when assisting in voluntary destructions, disposal of laboratory wastes, etc.

Do not condone the wanton pollution of waterways, uncontrolled burning, the creation of a public nuisance or other questionable disposal practices. Note that certain products should not be disposed of in a conventional manner (e.g.: sanitary landfill, flushing down the drain, etc.). In particular, certain products that have been banned in the past (chloroform, methapyrilene, hexachlorophene, PCB, etc.), are classified by EPA as hazardous and toxic substances and may require a special method of disposal by a licensed hazardous disposal facility. Any possible hazardous or toxic substance (carcinogen, mutagen, etc.) should not be disposed of without prior consultation by the firm with the U.S. Environmental Protection Agency and/or the regulating state authority. Refer to 21 CFR 25 and the National

Environmental Protection Act for guidance regarding the environmental impact of voluntary destructions.

3.2.11.1 - EPA MOU's

MOU's with:

1. EPA Regarding Matters of Mutual Responsibility Under Federal FD&C Act and Federal Insecticide, Fungicide and Rodenticide Act (225-73-8010).

2. EPA Regarding Potable Water on Interstate Conveyances (225-78-4006). The EPA administers a regulatory program in this area but FDA has the responsibility of notifying the ICC headquarters when problems are found. FDA will, if deemed appropriate include conveyances in their inspection/monitoring schedule. Both agencies will coordinate enforcement efforts, thereby avoiding duplication of efforts.

3. EPA Concerning Control of Drinking Water (225-79-2001).

   FDA has responsibility for water, and substances in water, used in food and for food processing and bottled drinking water.

   FDA will take appropriate regulatory action to control bottled drinking water and water and substances in water, used in food and for food processing.

   The FDA Liaison Office is the Division of Programs and Enforcement Policy, Office of Plant and Dairy Foods and Beverages, Center for Food Safety and Applied Nutrition, HFS-305 (301-436-1400).

   The EPA Liaison Office is the Drinking Water Technologies Branch, Drinking Water Standards Division (202-260-3022).

4. EPA and USDA (FSIS and AMS) re: Regulatory Activities Concerning Residues of Drugs, Pesticides, and Environmental Contaminants in Foods (225-85-8400).

3.2.12 - Agency for Toxic Substances and Disease Registry (ATSDR)

The ATSDR (formerly CDC Superfund) staff has been designated as the lead agency for the DHHS response to chemical emergencies. The CDC ATSDR Public Health Advisors are located at the EPA Regional Offices. These advisors would not only alert your office of chemical emergencies but would be invaluable in answering questions concerning the severity of the problem and discussing protective measures. Under no circumstances, are FDA employees to enter areas designated as hazardous.

If it is necessary to contact ATSDR employees, their addresses and phone numbers are listed below:

AGENCY FOR TOXIC SUBSTANCES AND DISEASE REGISTRY (FORMERLY KNOWN AS SUPERFUND)	
Louise A. House EPA Region I ATSDR EPA Bldg 60 Westview St. Lexington, MA 02173 617-860-4314	George Pettigrew EPA Region VI (6HE) 1445 Ross Ave. Dallas, TX 75202 214-655-8361
Arthur Black EPA Region II Rm 3137C 26 Federal Plaza New York, NY 10278 212-264-7662	Denise Jordan-Izaguirre EPA Region VII Waste Management Branch 726 Minnesota Ave Kansas City KS 66101 913-551-7692
Charles J. Walters EPA Region III 841 Chestnut Bldg Philadelphia, PA 19106 215-597-7291 303-294-1063	Glenn J. Tucker ATSDR Region VIII (8HWM-FF) Waste Management Div. Suite 500 999 18th St. Denver, CO 80202
Robert E. Safay Air & Waste Mgmt Div. Region IV 345 Courtland St. Atlanta, GA 30365 404-347-1847	William Q. Nelson ATSDR Region IX 75 Hawthorne St Rm 09261 San Francisco, CA 94105 415-744-2194
Louise A. Fabinski Emerg. & Remedial Br. EPA Region V (M-SHS-6) 77 W. Jackson Blvd Chicago, IL 60604 312-886-0840	George Thomas EPA Region X (MSHW113) 1200 6th Ave. Seattle, WA 98101 206-553-2113

Some situations where ATSDR guidance is indicated are mentioned below.

In wrecks the physical impact usually causes most damage. Toxic items in the same load, this is illegal, may rupture and add to the contamination. In train wrecks, other railcars loaded with chemicals, oils or other contaminating materials may rupture and contaminate food and drug products in otherwise undamaged cars. Removal of the wreckage may cause further physical damage or chemical contamination. Exposure to weather may also adversely affect the products.

Do not overlook the possibility that runoff of toxic chemicals from wrecked and ruptured cars may contaminate adjacent or nearby streams supplying water to downstream firms under FDA jurisdiction.

Chemical spills occurring on land or water can pose a serious threat to the environment and contaminate FDA regulated products both directly and indirectly.

Hazardous waste sites also pose a hazard to the immediate environment, as well as offsite, if runoff contaminates nearby surface waters or if leachate contaminates ground water supplies.

3.2.13 - Federal Trade Commission (FTC)

The MOU with FTC Concerns Exchange of Information (225-71-8003).

3.2.14 - U.S. Nuclear Regulatory Commission (NRC)

The U.S. Nuclear Regulatory Commission and the U.S. Department of Health and Human Services, Food and Drug Administration signed a MOU (225-03-4001) on August 26, 1993 (FR Vol. 58, No. 172, 09/08/93, 47300-47303). The purpose of the MOU is to coordinate existing NRC and FDA regulatory programs for medical devices (including utilization facilities used for medical therapy), drugs, and biological products utilizing byproduct, source, or special nuclear material regulated under the Atomic Energy Act of 1954, as amended. These regulatory programs include activities for evaluating and authorizing the manufacture, sale, distribution, licensing, and labeled intended use of such products.

Medical devices affected by this MOU include, but are not limited to: in vitro diagnostic kits (radioimmunoassay); utilization facilities licensed to perform medical therapy; and teletherapy and brachytherapy sources, systems, and accessory devices. Biologicals include, but are not limited to, licensed in vitro diagnostic kits (radioimmunoassay), and certain radiolabeled biologics for in-vivo use. Drugs include all those that contain byproduct, source, or special nuclear material.

The organizations in FDA that are principally responsible for regulating these products are CDRH, CDER, and CBER.

The FDA Liaison Offices are the Center for Devices and Radiological Health, Director, Office of Compliance, HFZ-300 (301-594-4692), Center for Drug Evaluation and Research, Director, Office of Compliance, HFD-300 (301-594-0054), and the Center for Biologic Evaluation and Research, Director, Office of Compliance and Biologics Quality, HFM-600 (301-827-6190).

The NRC Liaison Office is the Director, Office of Nuclear Material Safety and Safeguards (301-504-3352).

3.2.15 - U.S. Postal Service (USPS)

FDA cooperates with postal authorities in areas of mutual concern. If contacted by postal authorities, extend courtesy and cooperation. In any doubtful situation or incidents involving excessive expenditure of time and/or resources, check with your supervisor.

3.2.15.1 - Change of Address Information

At times during an investigation or inspection it may become necessary to visit local post offices to obtain new or forwarding addresses of individuals involved.

Procedure:

1. Introduce yourself and display your credentials to the local P.O. clerk or official.
2. State the information desired.
3. Present the clerk or official on duty the statement in writing on FDA letterhead using the wording from IOM Exhibit 3-3 which may be reproduced or typed on district letterhead.
4. If you are still refused information or delayed in any manner, contact the nearest U.S. Postal Inspector to handle the matter.
5. At this time there is no charge for providing this information to a Federal Agency. The regulation promulgating a fee has been stayed.

3.2.15.2 - Postal Box Information

At times during an investigation or inspection it will become necessary to obtain the name and address of the holder of a postal box (PO Box).

Procedure:

1. Introduce yourself and display credentials to the local P.O. clerk or official.
2. State the information you desire.
3. Present the clerk or official the statement in writing on FDA letterhead using the wording from IOM Exhibit 3-3 which may be reproduced or typed on district letterhead.
4. At this time there is no charge for providing this information to a Federal Agency. The regulation promulgating a fee has been stayed.
5. If you are still refused the information or are delayed in any manner, contact the nearest U.S. Postal Inspector to handle the matter.

3.2.15.3 - Authority

The authority for providing forwarding address information to government agencies is defined in 39 CFR 265.6(d)(4)(i) which states as follows:

(4) Exceptions. Except as otherwise provided in these regulations, names or addresses of postal customers will be furnished only as follows:

(i)To a federal, state, or local government agency upon prior written certification that the information is required for the performance of its duties.

Additionally, 39 CFR 265.6(d)(6) may apply: Address verification. The address of a postal customer will be verified at the request of a federal, state, or local government agency.

3.2.16 - Firm Locations

Many firms FDA is required to inspect are difficult to locate, including growers, farms, and other types of operations in rural areas. Directions to these firms can be obtained from many sources, including:

1. Visits to Post Offices.

2. If the envelope has a postal meter number and no return address, check with the USPS to determine the name of the firm or holder of that "PB Meter" number.

3. Visits to local health departments.

4. Visits to county extension services.

5. Visits to USDA - Agricultural Stabilization and Conservation Offices of Soil Conservation Service Offices.

Many of these offices have maps of the counties, municipalities, etc. which can be purchased or copied and used with their guidance to find the firms.

After the directions are obtained or the maps copied, copies of the maps with directions can be included in the factory jacket.

3.2.17 - Federal Food Safety Coalition

In August, 1999, FDA began an interagency Federal Food Safety Coalition with other federal agencies in an effort to focus on food protection of high-risk populations. The group's objective is to promote the development of effective public health protection systems for food safety within federal programs using the FDA Model Food Code, emphasizing foodborne illness interventions, to reduce the occurrence of the five leading illness risk factors. A formal MOU or partnership has not yet been developed. The initial participating agencies are as follows:

1. Dept. of Veterans Affairs, Veterans Health Admin.

2. United States Department of Agriculture, Food and Nutrition Service: School Lunch Program, WIC Program, and Infant Formula Program

3. Dept. of Justice, Bureau of Prisons
4. Dept. of Health and Human Services:
   a. Head Start Program
   b. Administration on Aging
   c. Indian Health Services
   d. Health Care Financing Administration
   e. Food and Drug Administration, Center for Food Safety

3.3 - State Operational Authority

3.3.1 - State Operational Authority

Establishment Inspections - All state and local officials have some type of jurisdiction over the food and drug establishments located within their state or local boundaries, regardless of the interstate movement or origin of the products involved. Some states divide the responsibility for food, drugs, etc., among the various agencies within the state. See IOM 3.3.3.

Samples - All state laws provide authority to collect samples of food, drug, and other products within the state.

Embargoes - FDA personnel, except in certain situations involving meat, poultry products, egg products and devices do not have embargo or detention powers (See IOM 3.2.1.2, 2.2.10, and 2.7.1).

State laws empower their inspectors to place an immediate embargo on products that are, or are suspected of being, adulterated or misbranded or otherwise in violation of their laws. As a cooperative measure most state agencies will have their inspectors place an embargo at the request of an FDA representative. Do not routinely request such embargo. District assignments may include instructions relative to cooperative embargoes.

In all instances, exercise care in requesting embargoes. The cooperating officials must be notified promptly of the final FDA action on the lot so that records may be updated, required releases issued, and inordinately long holding time prevented.

Embargoes should be considered not as a mere convenience to the Food and Drug Administration but as an important and effective cooperation measure to be applied only when circumstances indicate such action.

Disaster Operations - Following major disasters, FDA regional directors and district directors will arrange for close cooperation with local and state food and drug officials, Health Departments, the Public Health Service and other agencies engaged in comparable work. When requested to do so, FDA district personnel will assist local and state officials during such emergencies. At such times FDA personnel may be temporarily commissioned by local or state authorities and provided the authority to place embargoes (See IOM 8.5.5.1).

3.3.1.1 - FDA Personnel with State Authority

Certain states have designated selected FDA employees as special representatives or agents of the particular state agency. In these cases, they have furnished the FDA individuals with official state credentials. The FDA representatives given this authority will receive instructions and training, by their district, in the proper exercise of the powers conferred on them and must operate within the guidelines established by their district to monitor this authority. This is particularly important whenever state embargo powers may be used.

3.3.1.2 - Joint Inspections

Joint inspections with state or local inspectors are arranged by the district supervisory personnel. Joint inspections are conducted in the same manner as inspections by FDA alone and findings are discussed with the accompanying inspector. The cooperating inspector may wish to take action against the merchandise or the firm under pertinent local or state laws.

3.3.1.3 - FDA Commissioned State Personnel

Qualified state regulatory officials may be commissioned to conduct examinations, inspections, investigations, collect samples and to copy and verify records under the Federal Food, Drug, and Cosmetic Act. For additional information, please see Chapter 3 of the Regulatory Procedures Manual (RPM).

3.3.2 - State Memoranda of Understanding

The FDA has entered into agreements with various state and local agencies covering a variety of issues and work sharing agreements. At the present time not all the states have entered into agreements with FDA. Complete text of the MOU's is in Federal Cooperative Agreements Manual. A listing of current MOU's for states, the District of Columbia, and the Commonwealth of Puerto Rico are on OE's intranet site.

3.3.3 - State Authorities and Phone Contact Numbers

This section contains information regarding various state enforcement authorities. Some states operate under state laws patterned after the FD&C Act of 1906 or the current FD&C Act. However, most of the states operate under a "Uniform FD&C Act" which was developed by the Association of Food and Drug Officials (AFDO).

States that have adopted the Uniform FD&C Act as their legal guideline have in most cases adopted the entire act. The food authority in most cases includes among other things the adoption of the food and color additive provisions, pesticide residue amendments, enrichment guidance, etc. The Uniform FD&C Act also includes a provision for automatic adoption of changes in the FD&C Act. Some state legislatures have also included this provision in their laws. Some other provisions of the Uniform Act adopted by state include the new drug provisions, medical device laws, and cosmetic requirements.

Some states have also adopted the Association of American Feed Control Officials (AAFCO) model bill as their legal guideline for feed inspections.

In most cases the contact for "Consumer Protection Issues" would be located in the Office of the State Attorney General and would usually cover consumer fraud and other consumer protection issues. The State Attorney General's staff usually has mechanisms to deal with health fraud issues not efficiently dealt with by traditional FDA approaches. Contact your District Health Fraud Monitor for guidance in cooperative efforts with the State Attorney General's staff.

A complete listing of the personnel and programs at the state and local level may be found in the FDA Internet Directory of State and Local Officials which was prepared by the Division of Federal-State Relations (DFSR) (HFC-150) at http://www.fda.gov/ora/fed_state/default.htm. or http://www.fda.gov/ora/fed_state/directorytable.htm.

3.3.3.1 - Alabama (AL)

Alabama has adopted the FD&C Act of 1906 and the 1970 AAFCO as their legal guideline. The control agencies are Agriculture and Health. They have not adopted the new drug provisions, the medical device law, nor the automatic adoption provisions.

3.3.3.2 - Alaska (AK)

Alaska has adopted the Uniform FD&C Act without the automatic adoption provision and have not adopted either AAFCO feed bill. The controlling agencies are Health, Social Services, and Environmental Conservation. Alaska has adopted the various provisions of the Uniform bill.

3.3.3.3 - Arizona (AZ)

Arizona operates under the Uniform FD&C Act and the 1970 AAFCO Feed Bill. The controlling agencies are Health, Pharmacy and the State Chemist. They have not adopted the medical device law, cosmetics law, nor the automatic adoption provisions of the Uniform FD&C Act.

3.3.3.4 - Arkansas (AR)

Arkansas operates under the Uniform FD&C Act and the 1970 AAFCO Feed Bill. The agencies in control are Health and the Plant Board. They have not adopted the new drug provisions or the automatic adoption provision.

3.3.3.5 - California (CA)

California has adopted the Uniform FD&C Act and the 1970 AAFCO Feed Bill along with the automatic adoption provisions of the Uniform FD&C Act. The controlling agencies are Agriculture and Health.

3.3.3.6 - Colorado (CO)

Colorado has adopted the Uniform FD&C Act and the automatic adoption provisions of the Uniform FD&C Act. The controlling agencies are Agriculture and Health. They have not adopted either version of the AAFCO Feed Bill.

3.3.3.7 - Connecticut (CT)

Connecticut has adopted the FD&C Act, the Uniform FD&C Act and the 1958 AAFCO Feed Bill along with the automatic adoption provisions of the Uniform FD&C Act. The controlling agencies are Agriculture and Consumer Protection.

3.3.3.8 - Delaware (DE)

Delaware has adopted the Uniform FD&C Act and the 1970 AAFCO Feed Bill along with the automatic adoption provisions of the Uniform FD&C Act. The controlling agencies are Agriculture, Health, and Pharmacy. They have not adopted the food and color additive amendments, the pesticide residue amendment, enrichment amendment, new drug provisions, medical device law, and the cosmetics law.

3.3.3.9 - Florida (FL)

Florida has adopted the Uniform FD&C Act and the 1970 AAFCO Feed Bill along with the automatic adoption provisions of the Uniform FD&C Act. The controlling agencies are Agriculture and Health.

3.3.3.10 - Georgia (GA)

Georgia has adopted the Uniform FD&C Act and the 1970 AAFCO Feed Bill but not the automatic adoption provisions of the Uniform FD&C Act. The controlling agencies are Agriculture and Pharmacy. They have not adopted the food additive, color additive or pesticide residue amendments.

3.3.3.11 - Hawaii (HI)

Hawaii has adopted the Uniform FD&C Act and the 1970 AAFCO Feed Bill along with the automatic adoption provisions of the Uniform FD&C Act. The controlling agencies are Agriculture, Health and the Attorney General.

3.3.3.12 - Idaho (ID)

Idaho has adopted the Uniform FD&C Act and the 1958 AAFCO Feed Bill and has not adopted the automatic adoption provisions of the Uniform FD&C Act. The controlling agencies are Agriculture, Health and Pharmacy. They have not adopted the food additive, color additive or pesticide residue amendments of the Act.

3.3.3.13 - Illinois (IL)

Illinois has adopted the Uniform FD&C Act and the 1958 AAFCO Feed Bill along with the automatic adoption provisions of the Uniform FD&C Act. The controlling agencies are Agriculture and Health. They have not adopted the enrichment provisions of the Act.

3.3.3.14 - Indiana (IN)

Indiana has adopted the Uniform FD&C Act and the 1970 AAFCO Feed Bill along with the automatic adoption provisions of the Uniform FD&C Act. The controlling agencies are Health and the State Chemist.

3.3.3.15 - Iowa (IA)

Iowa has adopted the 1906 FD&C Act and the 1970 AAFCO Feed Bill along with the automatic adoption provisions of the FD&C Act. The controlling agencies are Agriculture, Health and Appeals, and Pharmacy.

3.3.3.16 - Kansas (KS)

Kansas has adopted the Uniform FD&C Act and the 1958 AAFCO Feed Bill and has not adopted the automatic adoption provisions of the Uniform FD&C Act. The controlling agencies are Agriculture and Health.

3.3.3.17 - Kentucky (KY)

Kentucky has adopted the Uniform FD&C Act and the 1970 AAFCO Feed Bill along with the automatic adoption provisions of the Uniform FD&C Act. The controlling agencies are Human Resources, Pharmacy, and the University of Kentucky Registration Services.

3.3.3.18 - Louisiana (LA)

Louisiana has adopted the Uniform FD&C Act and the 1970 AAFCO Feed Bill along with the automatic adoption provisions of the Uniform FD&C Act. The controlling agencies are Agriculture and Health. They have not adopted the provisions of the medical device law.

3.3.3.19 - Maine (ME)

Maine has adopted the Uniform FD&C Act and the 1970 AAFCO Feed Bill but not the automatic adoption provisions of the Uniform FD&C Act. The controlling agencies are Agriculture and Pharmacy. They have not adopted the food and color additive amendments nor the new drug provisions or the medical device law.

3.3.3.20 - Maryland (MD)

Maryland has adopted the Uniform FD&C Act and the 1970 AAFCO Feed Bill along with the automatic adoption provisions of the Uniform FD&C Act. The controlling agencies are Agriculture and Health. They have not adopted the enrichment provisions of the Act.

3.3.3.21 - Massachusetts (MA)

Massachusetts has adopted the Uniform FD&C Act and the 1970 AAFCO Feed Bill but not the automatic adoption provisions of the Uniform FD&C Act. The controlling agencies are Agriculture and Health. They have not adopted the new drug provisions of the Act.

3.3.3.22 - Michigan (MI)

Michigan has adopted the Uniform FD&C Act and the 1970 AAFCO Feed Bill but not the automatic adoption provisions of the Uniform FD&C Act. The controlling agencies are Agriculture, Commerce, Licensing and Registration.. They have not adopted the enrichment provisions or the cosmetics law.

3.3.3.23 - Minnesota (MN)

Minnesota has adopted the Uniform FD&C Act and the 1970 AAFCO Feed Bill but not the automatic adoption provisions of the Uniform FD&C Act. The controlling agencies are Agriculture and Pharmacy. They have not adopted the enrichment provisions, the new drug provisions, the medical device law, nor the cosmetic law.

3.3.3.24 - Mississippi (MS)

Mississippi has adopted the 1906 FD&C Act and the 1970 AAFCO Feed Bill but not the automatic adoption provisions of the Uniform FD&C Act. The controlling agencies are Agriculture, Commerce and the State Chemistry Lab. They have not adopted the food additive, color additive, and pesticide residue amendments, nor the new drug provisions or cosmetic law.

3.3.3.25 - Missouri (MO)

Missouri has adopted the Uniform FD&C Act and the 1970 AAFCO Feed Bill but not the automatic adoption provisions of the Uniform FD&C Act. The controlling agencies are Agriculture and Health. They have not adopted the enrichment provisions of the Act.

3.3.3.26 - Montana (MT)

Montana has adopted the Uniform FD&C Act and the 1970 AAFCO Feed Bill along with the automatic adoption provisions of the Uniform FD&C Act. The controlling agencies are Agriculture and Health.

3.3.3.27 - Nebraska (NE)

Nebraska has adopted the Uniform FD&C Act and the 1970 AAFCO Feed Bill but not the automatic adoption provisions of the Uniform FD&C Act. The controlling agencies are Agriculture and Health. They have not adopted the new drug provisions nor the medical device and cosmetic laws.

3.3.3.28 - Nevada (NV)

Nevada has adopted the Uniform FD&C Act but not the automatic adoption provisions of the Uniform FD&C Act. They have not adopted either version of the AAFCO Feed Bill. The controlling agencies are Agriculture and Health. They have not adopted the enrichment provisions of the Act.

3.3.3.29 - New Hampshire (NH)

New Hampshire has adopted the Uniform FD&C Act and the 1970 AAFCO Feed Bill but not the automatic adoption provisions of the Uniform FD&C Act. The controlling agencies are Agriculture and Health.

3.3.3.30 - New Jersey (NJ)

New Jersey has adopted the Uniform FD&C Act and the 1970 AAFCO Feed Bill but not automatic adoption provisions of the Uniform FD&C Act. The controlling agencies are Agriculture and Health. They have not adopted the pesticide residue amendment.

3.3.3.31 - New Mexico (NM)

New Mexico has adopted the Uniform FD&C Act and the 1958 AAFCO Feed Bill but not the automatic adoption provisions of the Uniform FD&C Act. The controlling agencies are Agriculture, Environment, Health and Pharmacy. They have not adopted the food additive or color additive amendments.

3.3.3.32 - New York (NY)

New York has adopted the Uniform FD&C Act and the 1970 AAFCO Feed Bill along with the automatic adoption provisions of the Uniform FD&C Act. The controlling agencies are Agriculture and Markets, Health, and Pharmacy. They have not adopted the cosmetics law.

3.3.3.33 - North Carolina (NC)

North Carolina has adopted the Uniform FD&C Act and both versions of the AAFCO Feed Bills along with the automatic adoption provisions of the Uniform FD&C Act. The controlling agency is Agriculture. They have not adopted the enrichment provisions of the Act.

3.3.3.34 - North Dakota (ND)

North Dakota has adopted the Uniform FD&C Act and neither version of the AAFCO Feed Bill but not the automatic adoption provisions of the Uniform FD&C Act. The controlling agencies are Consolidated Laboratories, Health and Pharmacy.

3.3.3.35 - Ohio (OH)

Ohio has adopted the Uniform FD&C Act and the 1970 AAFCO Feed Bill but not the automatic adoption provisions of the Uniform FD&C Act. The controlling agencies are Agriculture and Pharmacy.

3.3.3.36 - Oklahoma (OK)

Oklahoma has adopted the Uniform FD&C Act but neither version of the AAFCO Feed Bills nor the automatic adoption provisions of the Uniform FD&C Act. The controlling agencies are Agriculture and Health. They have not adopted the food additive or color additive amendments, the enrichment provisions nor the new drug provisions.

3.3.3.37 - Oregon (OR)

Oregon has adopted the Uniform FD&C Act and the 1958 AAFCO Feed Bill along with the automatic adoption provisions of the Uniform FD&C Act. The controlling agencies are Agriculture and Pharmacy. They have not adopted the cosmetics law.

3.3.3.38 - Pennsylvania (PA)

Pennsylvania has adopted the 1906 FD&C Act and the 1958 AAFCO Feed Bill but not the automatic adoption provisions of the Uniform FD&C Act. The controlling agencies are Agriculture and Health. They have not adopted the food additive, color additive, and pesticide residue amendments nor the enrichment provisions.

3.3.3.39 - Rhode Island (RI)

Rhode Island has adopted the Uniform FD&C Act and the 1970 AAFCO Feed Bill along with the automatic adoption provisions of the Uniform FD&C Act. The controlling agencies are Environmental Management and Health.

3.3.3.40 - South Carolina (SC)

South Carolina has adopted the Uniform FD&C Act and the 1958 AAFCO Feed Bill but not the automatic adoption provisions of the Uniform FD&C Act. The controlling agencies are Agriculture and Health.

3.3.3.41 - South Dakota (SD)

South Dakota has adopted the Uniform FD&C Act and the 1970 AAFCO Feed Bill but not the automatic adoption provisions of the Uniform FD&C Act. The controlling agencies are Agriculture, Commerce and Regulations. They have not adopted the new drug provisions, medical device law, nor the cosmetics law.

3.3.3.42 - Tennessee (TN)

Tennessee has adopted the Uniform FD&C Act and the 1970 AAFCO Feed Bill but not the automatic adoption provisions of the Uniform FD&C Act. The controlling agency is Agriculture.

3.3.3.43 - Texas (TX)

Texas has adopted the Uniform FD&C Act and the 1970 AAFCO Feed Bill along with the automatic adoption provisions of the Uniform FD&C Act. The controlling agencies are Health and the State Chemist.

3.3.3.44 - Utah (UT)

Utah has adopted the Uniform FD&C Act and the 1970 AAFCO Feed Bill along with the automatic adoption provisions of the Uniform FD&C Act. The controlling agencies are Agriculture and Health. They have not adopted the new drug provisions.

3.3.3.45 - Vermont (VT)

Vermont has adopted the Uniform FD&C Act and the 1970 AAFCO Feed Bill along with the automatic adoption provisions of the Uniform FD&C Act. The controlling agencies are Agriculture and Health. They have not adopted the enrichment provisions.

3.3.3.46 - Virginia (VA)

Virginia has adopted the Uniform FD&C Act and the 1958 AAFCO Feed Bill but not the automatic adoption provisions of the Uniform FD&C Act. The controlling agencies are Agriculture and Pharmacy.

3.3.3.47 - Washington (WA)

Washington has adopted the Uniform FD&C Act and the 1958 AAFCO Feed Bill along with the automatic adoption provisions of the Uniform FD&C Act. The controlling agencies are Agriculture and Pharmacy.

3.3.3.48 - West Virginia (WV)

West Virginia has adopted the 1906 FD&C Act and the 1970 AAFCO Feed Bill but not the automatic adoption provisions of the Uniform FD&C Act. The controlling agencies are Agriculture, Health and Pharmacy. They have not adopted the food additives or color additive amendments, the new drug provisions, the medical device law and the cosmetics law.

3.3.3.49 - Wisconsin (WI)

Wisconsin has adopted the Uniform FD&C Act and the 1958 AAFCO Feed Bill along with the automatic adoption provisions of the Uniform FD&C Act. The controlling agencies are Agriculture and Pharmacy. They have not adopted the enrichment provisions, the new drug provisions, the medical device law, and the cosmetics law.

3.3.3.50 – Wyoming

Wyoming has adopted the Uniform FD&C Act and the 1970 AAFCO Feed Bill but not the automatic adoption provisions of the Uniform FD&C Act. The controlling agency is Agriculture.

3.4 - International Agreements

3.4.1 - Memoranda of Understanding

The Agency has over the years entered into agreements with foreign governments regarding the quality of foods, drugs, and other products exported to the United States. The complete text of the agreements is in the International Cooperative Agreements Manual. The listing is by country and CPG order. Refer to FDA's website at http://www.fda.gov/oia/default.htm for additional information.

3.4.2 - Mutual Recognition Agreements

3.4.2.1 - European Community

Changes in FDAMA have required that FDA begin the process of acceptance of mutual recognition agreements relating to the regulation of FDA regulated commodities, facilitate commerce in devices between the US and foreign countries and other activities to reduce the burden of regulation and to harmonize regulatory requirements. See Section 803. Additional specific information is available at http://www.fda.gov/oia/homepage.htm.

3.4.2.2 - Pharmaceuticals and Medical Devices

The first mutual recognition agreement (MRA) to be implemented, The Joint Declaration to the Agreement on Mutual Recognition Between the United

States of America and the European Community (MRA) was signed in May 1998. It consists of the following sections:

1. Framework
2. Telecommunication Equipment
3. Electromagnetic Compatibility (EMC)
4. Electrical Safety
5. Recreational Craft
6. Pharmaceutical Good Manufacturing Practices (GMPs)
7. Medical Devices

It covers both FDA regulated and non-FDA regulated products and is an agreement between the United States and the European Union (EU) representing 15 Member States. It establishes procedures leading to FDA acceptance of inspectional work done by (EU) Regulatory or Competent Authorities (RA/CA) or Notified Bodies termed Conformity Assessment Bodies (CABs) in the MRA. The pharmaceutical annex is based on an assessment of equivalence with the Member States and the medical device annex is based on inspections by non-government firms who are recognized by the Member State regulatory authority. FDA has begun the process of implementing this agreement which has a 3 year transition period before the operational phase.

3.4.2.3 - Food Products

In July, 1999, the United States and the EC signed the "AGREEMENT BETWEEN THE UNITES STATES OF AMERICA AND THE EUROPEAN COMMUNITY ON SANITARY MEASURES TO PROTECT PUBLIC AND ANIMAL HEALTH IN TRADE IN LIVE ANIMALS AND ANIMAL PRODUCTS". This agreement is very much like a mutual recognition agreement and is based on the equivalence process. It covers a very wide range of human food products, all of animal origin, such as milk and dairy products, seafood, honey, wild game, snails, frog legs and canned pet food. For purposes of this agreement, the EC is considered one "party" and not 15 Member States. Activities to begin assessing equivalence are underway.

3.5 - Non Government Agreements

The Agency has entered agreements with various non-governmental groups to formulate various programs and guidance. The complete text of these agreements appears in the Federal Cooperative Agreements Manual. These agreements are outlined below.

3.5.1 - Association of Official Analytical Chemists (AOAC)

MOA with AOAC Concerning Analytical Methods.

3.5.2 - National Conference on Interstate Milk Shipments (NCIMS)

MOU with NCIM To Strengthen the Interstate Milk Shippers Program. See IOM 5.4.9.3 regarding inspection at dairy plants covered under the Interstate Milk Shippers Program.

3.5.3 - Interstate Shellfish Sanitation Conference (ISSC)

MOU with ISSC to Improve the Sanitation and Quality of Shellfish by Delineating Responsibilities.

3.5.4 - United States Pharmacopoeia Convention (USP)

Agreement with USP Regarding Review of Revisions to Compendial Requirements for Drugs.

3.5.5 - Conference for Food Protection (CFP)

MOU with the Conference for Food Protection (CFP) to promote input by all stakeholders toward improving food safety

Chapter 4: Sampling

CONTENT

		VERSION DATE
Subchapter 4.1	General	July 13, 2009
Subchapter 4.2	Dealer Relations	July 13, 2009
Subchapter 4.3	Collection Technique	July 13, 2009
Subchapter 4.4	Documentation & CR	July 13, 2009
Subchapter 4.5	Sampling: Preparation, Handling, Shipping	July 13, 2009

4.1 - General

4.1.1 - Authority

4.1.1.1 - Examinations and Investigations

Collecting samples is a critical part of FDA's regulatory activities. FD&C Act, Section 702(a) [21 U.S.C. 372 (a)] gives FDA authority to conduct investigations and collect samples. A Notice of Inspection is not always required for sample collections. If during a sample collection, you begin to conduct an inspection (examining storage conditions, reviewing records for compliance with laws and regulations, etc.), issue an FDA 482 and continue your activities. See IOM 5.1.1 and 5.2.2.

While inspections and investigations may precede sample collection, a sample must ultimately be obtained for a case to proceed, under the law. Proper sample collection is the keystone of effective enforcement action.

FD&C Act - See IOM section 2.2.1 for this information.

PHS Act - See IOM 2.2.3.7 for this information.

4.1.1.2 - Notice of Inspection

Samples are often collected during the course of an establishment inspection or inspection of a vehicle. See IOM 5.1.1 and IOM 5.2.2.

1. *Carriers* - Issue an FDA 482 - Use of Notice of Inspection to the driver or agent when it is necessary to inspect vehicles. See IOM 5.2.2.1.

2. *Manufacturers, etc.* - An FDA 482. A Notice of Inspection should be issued when samples are collected from lots in possession of a

manufacturer, processor, packer or repacker, whether or not regulatory action is intended toward the articles, the dealer, the manufacturer or the shipper.

4.1.1.3 - Receipt for Sample

Section 704(c) of the FD&C Act [21 U.S.C. 374 (c)] requires issuing a receipt describing any samples obtained during the course of an inspection. The receipt is to be issued to the owner, operator, or agent in charge, upon completion of the inspection and prior to leaving the premises. See IOM 5.2.4 for special situations. See IOM 4.2.5.5 for instructions on completing the form.

4.1.1.4 - Report of Analysis

Section 704(d) of the FD&C Act [21 U.S.C. 374 (d)] requires FDA furnish a report of analysis on any sample of food (including animal food and feed, medicated and non-medicated), collected during an inspection of an establishment where such food is "*** manufactured, processed, or packed ***," if the sample is examined for compliance with Section 402(a)(3) of the FD&C Act [21 U.S.C. 342 (a)(3)]. Reports of analysis are not required for non-food items examined (rodent pellets, etc.). The servicing laboratory is responsible for furnishing the report of analysis.

4.1.2 - Valid Sample

A valid sample is the starting point and keystone for most administrative and legal actions. As evidence, the sample must support the government's charge there is a violation of the law. Also, it must conform to the rules on admissibility of evidence. A properly collected and prepared sample provides:

1. A portion of the lot of goods for laboratory analysis and reserve, a 702(b) of the FD&C Act [21 U.S.C. 374 (b)] reserve portion if appropriate, and/or an exhibit demonstrating the violation represented by the lot.

2. A report of your observations of the lot.

3. Labels and labeling, or copies of such, which "accompany" the goods.

4. Documentary evidence of federal jurisdiction over the lot, information about individuals responsible for the violation, where the violation was committed, and similar data.

5. Signed statements from persons who may be called upon as witnesses, if there is a subsequent court action.

4.1.3 - Responsibility

Collect every sample as if you will be required to testify in court about everything you did concerning each and every event surrounding the sample collection. Mistakes or deficiencies, however trivial they may seem, can fatally damage the government's case. Be objective, accurate, and thorough.

4.1.4 - Official Samples (21 CFR 2.10)

A sample of a food, drug, or cosmetic is an "Official Sample" if records [see IOM 4.4.7] or other evidence obtained shows the lot from which the sample was collected was:

1. Introduced or delivered for introduction in interstate commerce, or

2. Was in or was received in interstate commerce, or

3. Was manufactured in a territory or the District of Columbia.

A sample of a device, a counterfeit drug, or any object associated with drug counterfeiting, no matter where it is collected, is also an "Official Sample". The statute permits proceeding against these articles, when violative, at any time. See Sections 304(a)(2) of the FD&C Act [21 U.S.C. 334 (a)(2)].

Import Samples are Official Samples and require the same integrity as domestic Official Samples. They must be identified with sample number, collection date and collector's handwritten initials. Interstate documentation is not required, see CPG manual section 110.200 and 110.600. Import Samples need not be sealed, unless District policy dictates, as long as the integrity of the sample is maintained.

Normally, 702(b) of the FD&C Act [21 U.S.C. 374 (b)] portions (hereby referred to as either 702(b) portion or 702(b) reserve portion) are not collected for routine Import Samples. However, in situations where a dispute arises or a potential for regulatory action exists, the 702(b) portions should be collected and the sample sealed as described in IOM 4.5.4.

4.1.4.1 - Definition - Official Sample

An Official Sample is one taken from a lot for which Federal jurisdiction can be established. If violative, the Official Sample provides a basis for administrative or legal action. Official Samples generally, but not always, consist of a physical portion of the lot sampled. To be useful, an Official Sample must be:

1. Accompanied by records establishing Federal jurisdiction, and identifying the persons having knowledge of the lot's movement and custody of the records. (Evidence of Interstate movement is not required for medical device samples, but by policy to be obtained when a seizure, injunction, prosecution or civil penalty is contemplated). See IOM 4.4.7.

2. Representative of the lot from which collected.

3. If a physical sample, large enough to permit proper laboratory examination and provide a 702(b) reserve portion when necessary.

4. Handled, identified, and sealed in such a manner as to maintain its integrity as evidence, with a clear record of its chain of custody.

4.1.4.2 - Documentary Samples

In a "Documentary" (or "DOC") sample, no actual physical sample of the product is taken. Other elements of an official sample described in 4.1.4 and 4.1.4.1 are required -- see special official sealing instructions below. This official sample consists of the article's labels (or label tracings, photocopies, or photos), accompanying labeling (leaflets, brochures, promotional materials, including Internet websites, etc.) and documentation of interstate movement (freight bills, bills of lading, affidavits, etc. See IOM 4.4.7) Photos of the product, drawings, sketches or schematics, production records, diagrams, invoices or similar items may also be part of the sample. See IOM Exhibits 4-1 and 4-2. As a rule, no FDA 484, receipt for samples is issued during collection of a DOC Sample. See subparagraph 5.2.4.1 for physical evidence exception.

A DOC samples is collected when an actual physical sample is not practical (e.g., very large, expensive, complex, permanently installed devices), in instances where the article is no longer available, or there is little need for laboratory examination. A single piece of life support equipment, which must remain in emergency service until a replacement is available, may be sampled in this manner.

Another instance where a DOC sample might be collected involves a shipment of product recommended for seizure based on misbranding charges. During availability check, the lot sampled is found to have been distributed; however, a new shipment, identically labeled, is on hand. In this instance, the new shipment may be sampled on a DOC basis since another physical sample and examination is not required. Regulatory action may proceed on the basis of the earlier examination. Thus, only labeling, transportation records, the appropriate dealer affidavits, and an inventory of product on hand need be obtained.

A variation of this procedure involves collecting one or more units and removing (stripping) the original labels/labeling from the product container. It is frequently easier and quicker to collect relatively inexpensive units to field strip than it is to photocopy or photograph all accompanying labels. The sample is handled in exactly the same manner as any other DOC sample, once original labeling has been removed and the remainder of the sample destroyed. A prominent explanation on the C/R alerts reviewers the original units collected were destroyed after the original labeling was removed. This procedure is not appropriate where complete, intact, labeled units are desired for exhibit purposes, even though there is no intention of analyzing the units obtained.

A documentary sample collected to document GMP deviations, should contain copies of records obtained to document the deviations encountered. You should explain what is being documented in the remarks section of the documents obtained screen in FACTS. Fully describe any record collected as part of the DOC sample and where possible indicate the page of the document that demonstrates the deviation.

When photos are taken as part of DOC samples, the rolls of exposed film should - unless developed by yourself - be sent to established commercial film dealers or color

processors for developing. Report identity of film processor on the FDA 525. Also see IOM 5.3.4.

See IOM 4.5.2.5 for guidance on identifying records associated with a DOC sample. Do not officially seal these records, but list them on the C/R. If any photos are taken as part of the DOC sample, the negatives or electronic media, if any, must be officially sealed per IOM 5.3.4.2 or IOM 5.3.4.3. See IOM Exhibit 4-1 and for examples of DOC samples. Attach the documents, photos and negatives along with any other records associated with the sample to the printed FACTS Collection Record. See IOM 4.4.10.5.

4.1.4.3 - In-Transit Samples

In-Transit samples are those collected from lots held on loading/receiving docks of steamships, trucklines, or other common carriers, or being transported in vehicles. The lot is considered to be in-transit if it meets any of the following characteristics:

1. A Bill of Lading (B/L) or other order to ship a lot interstate has been issued.

2. The owner/shipper or agent acknowledges, preferably by signed affidavit, he has ordered the lot to be shipped interstate.

3. The owner or operator of the common carrier acknowledges, preferably by signed affidavit, he has an order from the shipper to move the lot interstate.

4.1.4.4 - 301(k) Samples

Section 301(k) of the FD&C Act [21 U.S.C. 331 (k)] is a prohibited act, which can result in any one or more separate legal procedures. A sample collected from a lot of food, drug, device or cosmetic which became adulterated or misbranded while held for sale, whether or not the first sale, after shipment in interstate commerce is often referred to as a "301(k) Sample". The term "301(k) Sample" is misleading, but widely used within FDA to describe certain samples collected from lots which become violative after shipment in interstate commerce.

Since some act took place which resulted in the adulteration or misbranding of a previously nonviolative product, after shipment in interstate commerce, the "301(k)" documentation is incomplete without identifying the act, establishing when and how it occurred, and the person(s) responsible for causing the violation. This feature, more than any other, distinguishes a "301(k) Sample" from the other Official Samples. When you report the sample collection, the responsible party will always be the dealer. See IOM Exhibits 4-1 and 4-7, "301(k) affidavit".

For example, to document insect adulteration of a finished product, caused by a live insect population in the processing areas of a food manufacturer such as a bakery, you must document receipt of clean raw material and subsequent adulteration caused by the firm's handling or processing of the raw material. Therefore, you would need to show there was an insect infestation at the firm that either did, or may have contaminated the finished product. You would need to collect a sample of the clean incoming flour, and subsamples at points in the system to demonstrate where insect infestations exist in the system. In situations where sampling may disturb static points in the system which may result in a higher level of adulteration of the finished product than normal, you should sample in reverse.

301(k) samples can also be used to document adulteration (including noncompliance with GMPs) or misbranding of other regulated commodities, including drugs and biologics. If possible, when collecting a 301(k) sample covering a drug product, you should attempt to document 'adulteration' or 'misbranding' of the active ingredient by the firm's actions. In the case of a biologic (for example, whole blood), which has not moved in interstate commerce, document the interstate receipt of the bag, and the firm's subsequent 'adulteration' or 'misbranding' of the anti-coagulant (considered a drug) in the blood bag.

4.1.4.5 - Induced Sample

An induced sample is an Official Sample ordered or obtained by agency response to some type of advertisement or promotional activity. The sample is procured by mail, telephone, or other means without disclosing any association of the requester or the transaction with FDA. See IOM 4.3.5.4 for additional information.

4.1.4.6 - Undercover Buy

An "undercover buy" is an Official Sample, similar to and obtained in much the same manner as an "induced sample". In an "undercover buy", however, the solicitation is made in person, usually under an alias. Pre-arranged explanations or cover stories are necessary to dispel any suspicions about the requester that may surface in face-to-face discussions. "Undercover buys" are frequently used in investigating complaints of illegal activity where the information cannot be substantiated or refuted through more conventional means.

4.1.4.7 - Post Seizure (P.S.) Sample

A lot under seizure is in the custody of the U. S. Marshal. If either the claimant or the government desires a sample from the seized lot, for any reason, it may be collected only by court order. In most cases, the order will specify how the sample is to be collected, and may provide for each party to collect samples. If the order was obtained by the claimant, permit the claimant's representative to determine how his/her sample collection is made. If the method of collection is improper, make constructive suggestions, but do not argue. Report exactly how the sample was drawn. Unless the claimant objects, mark subdivisions he collects with "P.S.", your initials and date. "P.S." Samples are Official Samples.

Do not pay for Post Seizure Samples or any samples collected of a lot reconditioned under a Consent Decree. See IOM 4.2.8.1.

4.1.4.8 - Domestic Import Sample

To record information on FDA's total coverage of imported products, an additional classification of samples, "Domestic Import" or "DI" was devised. These are Official Samples of foreign products, which have passed through customs and are in domestic commerce. The FDA may have previously taken a sample of the product while in import status, or the product may have been permitted entry without being sampled. If sampled while still in import status, the samples collected are import samples, and not "DI" Samples. However, once the product leaves import status, it enters domestic commerce and any sample collected is an Official "Domestic Import" (DI) Sample. Note: When collecting DI Samples, especially if a violation is suspected, attempt to determine the port of entry and importer of record. Report this information on the CR. Include the name of the Country of Origin of the product and the Country Code if known.

A sample is classed as Domestic Import (DI), if any of the following situations apply:

1. The label declares the product to be from a foreign country.

2. The label bears the word, "Imported".

3. Records obtained or reviewed reveal the product originated in a foreign country.

4. It is known that the product is not grown or produced in the US; it is packed as a single item with few or no other ingredients added, and it is not manipulated in any major manner, which changes the product or its composition. For example, "Olive Oil" imported in bulk and merely repacked with no added ingredients and no manipulation would be a "DI" sample, while pepper which is processed, ground and packed after entry would not. However, retail packages of ground pepper processed and packaged in a foreign country would be "DI" Samples.

5. Samples of imported raw materials, which are collected before further processing or mixed with other ingredients.

DI samples are significantly different from other official samples in another important respect. Unlike domestic products, where considerable information is readily available on manufacturing and distribution channels, it is frequently difficult to identify the responsible parties for products of foreign origin once they enter domestic commerce. The most practical way is to establish a paper trail of records going back as far as possible in the distribution chain to the actual entry.

Identifying "DI" Samples - When writing the sample number on physical samples of Domestic Import products, documents related to the sample, and the seals, preface the sample number with prefix "DI" in the same manner other sample types are used, such as, "DOC", "FS", "PS", etc.

4.1.4.9 - Import Sample

Import samples are physical sample collections of products, which originate from another country, collected while the goods are in import status. Import status ends when Customs has cleared an entry for the shipment. See IOM 4.1.7.1, 4.1.7.2, and chapter 6.

4.1.4.10 - Additional Sample

This is a physical sample collected from a previously sampled lot of either a domestic or imported product.

1. *Additional Import Samples* - The sample collected must have the same sample number as the original sample collected.

2. *Additional Domestic Sample* - The sample collected may have another sample number, but it must be flagged as an "ADD" Sample and the original sample number referenced in the "Related Sample" block on the Collection Record.

4.1.5 - Food Standards Sample

Food Standards (FS) samples are collected to provide information on which to base Food Standards. Sample integrity is maintained the same as Official Samples.

Note: Samples of standardized foods are not FS Samples.

4.1.6 - GWQAP Samples

As part of the Government-Wide Quality Assurance Program (GWQAP), FDA may determine the need for testing samples of medical products procured on Government contracts in order to assure compliance with Federal specifications and the applicable requirements of the FD&C Act.

Whenever FDA determines samples are desired, Office of Enforcement's Division of Compliance Information and Quality Assurance (DCIQA) advises the home district GWQAP coordinator if a sample is to be collected, and provides written background and testing instructions. DCIQA normally arranges for DOD/VA/HRSA to ship GWQAP drug samples directly to the home district for processing and analysis. Most device samples are shipped directly to WEAC by DOD/VA/HRSA. District investigators will rarely be requested to collect GWQAP or "GQA" Samples from DOD/VA/HRSA facilities. However, they may occasionally complete a C/R and prepare a "GQA" Sample for the laboratory upon its arrival from DOD/VA/HRSA.

For more information about GWQAP Samples, contact Terry Zuch, DCIQA at 240-632-2816.

4.1.7 - Investigational Samples

These samples, referred to as "INV Samples", need not be collected from lots in interstate commerce or under federal jurisdiction. They are generally collected to document observations, support regulatory actions or provide other information. They may be used as evidence in court, and they must be sealed and their integrity and chain of custody protected. Examples of INV Samples are:

1. *Factory Samples* - Raw materials, in-process and finished products to demonstrate manufacturing conditions. Note: Photographs taken in a firm are not samples. They are exhibits except when they are part of a DOC Sample. See IOM 4.5.2.4, 5.3.3, and 5.3.4.

2. *Exhibits* - Filth exhibits and other articles taken for exhibit purposes during inspections to demonstrate manufacturing or storage conditions, employee practices, and the like. Typically filth exhibits submitted as part of an INV sample are not tied to any specific lot of product, but are meant

to illustrate the conditions at a firm. An example of an INV filth sample would be rodent excreta pellets, apparent nesting or other rodent gnawed material, and other evidence of rodent activity collected from the perimeter and at multiple locations throughout a manufacturing facility or warehouse in order to document widespread rodent infestation.

3. *Reconditioning Samples* - These are taken from lots reconditioned under a Decree or other agreement to bring the lots into compliance with the law. The sample is taken to determine if reconditioning was satisfactorily performed. These samples should be submitted as Official Samples, rather than INV.

4. *Certain Complaint Samples* - Injury and illness investigation samples from certain complaints where there is no Federal jurisdiction, or where the alleged violation offers no basis for subsequent regulatory action. Complaint samples from lots for which Federal jurisdiction is clear should be submitted as Official Samples.

When writing the sample number on sub samples, documents related to the sample, and the seals, preface the sample number with "INV" in the same manner as other sample types are used (e.g. "DOC", "DI").

4.1.7.1 - Audit/Certification Sample

A sample collected to verify analytical results provided by a certificate of analysis or private laboratory analysis that purports to show a product complies with the FD&C Act and/or regulations. This sample type will usually be used with an import sample. See IOM 4.1.4.9.

4.1.7.2 - Mail Entry Sample

A mail entry sample is a sample of an imported product that enters the U.S. through the U.S. Mail. See IOM 4.1.4.9.

4.1.7.3 - Non-Regulatory Sample

Samples collected and analyzed by FDA for other federal, state, or local agencies of products over which the FDA has no jurisdiction.

4.2 - Dealer Relations

4.2.1 - Dealer Definition and Good Will

For sample collection purposes, the dealer is the person, firm (which could include the manufacturer), institution or other party, who has possession of a particular lot of goods. The dealer does not have to be a firm or company, which is in the business of buying or selling goods. The dealer might be a housewife in her home, a physician, or a public agency; these dealers obtain products to use but not to sell. The dealer may be a party who does not own the goods, but has possession of them, such as a public storage warehouse or transportation agency.

Rapport with the dealer is important to the success of your objective. All dealers, including hostile ones, should be approached in a friendly manner and treated with fairness, honesty, courtesy and consideration. A dealer may be called as a Government witness in a court case, and a favorable attitude on his/her part is to be sought. Never use strong-arm tactics or deception, but rather be professional and demonstrate diplomacy, tact, and persuasion. Do not make unreasonable demands.

Introduce yourself to the dealer by name, title and organization; present your credentials for examination, and, if appropriate, issue an FDA 482, Notice of Inspection. See IOM 4.1.1.2, 4.2.4, 5.1.1.3 and 5.2.2. Explain the purpose of your visit. Be prepared to answer the dealer's questions and attempt to relieve any apprehensions, at the same time being careful not to reveal any confidential information. Do not disparage the product, its manufacturer, or shipper. Do not reveal the particular violation suspected unless the dealer is responsible, or unless you ask him/her to voluntarily hold the goods. The very fact we are collecting a sample is often reason enough to arouse the dealer's suspicions about the legality of the product.

4.2.2 - Dealer Objection to Sampling Procedure

If the dealer objects to your proposed sampling technique, attempt to reach a reasonable compromise on a method that will provide a satisfactory, though perhaps not ideal, sample. Assure the dealer you will make every effort to restore the lot to its original state, you are prepared to purchase a whole unit to avoid leaving broken cases, and we will reimburse him/her for additional labor costs incurred as a result of sampling. See IOM 4.2.8. If a reasonable compromise cannot be reached, proceed as a refusal to permit sampling.

4.2.3 - Refusal to Permit Sampling

A challenge of FDA authority to collect samples may be raised by a dealer who, for varied reasons, both personal and professional opposes the activities of the agency, or of governmental units in general.

Refusals to permit sample collection commonly emerge unless you can identify a section of the law which specifically authorizes it. The suggested approach for dealing with these individuals is to use patient, tactful persuasion, pointing out that the sample is a part of the investigations authorized in Section 702(b) of the FD&C Act [21 U.S.C. 372(b)]. If you have not already done so, issue an FDA 482 - Notice of Inspection as soon as it becomes apparent the dealer will continue to object. Point out and discuss the authorities provided by FD&C Act sections 702(a), 702(b), 704(a), 704(c), 704(d) [21 U.S.C. 372(a),(b), 374(a), (c), (d)] and the precedent case mentioned in IOM 2.2.1. If refusal persists, point out the criminal prohibitions of Section 301(f) of the FD&C Act [21 U.S.C. 331(f)].

If samples are still refused, leave the premises and contact your supervisor immediately. Refer to IOM section 5.2.4 and Compliance Policy Guide manual section 130.100 for further discussions on resolving the impasse.

4.2.4 - Notice of Inspection

See IOM 4.1.1.2, 5.1.1.5 and 5.2.2.

Each time you issue an FDA 482, Notice of Inspection, and subsequently collect a sample, issue the appropriate sample receipt (FDA 472 - Carriers Receipt for Samples or FDA 484 -Receipt for Samples).

4.2.4.1 - Dealer Responsible for Condition of Lot

An FDA 482 should be issued before collecting samples from firms, carriers, or individuals whom FDA can take regulatory action against for the violative condition of the lot. See IOM 4.1.1.1. When in doubt, issue a Notice of Inspection. If there is no EIR, attach a copy of the FDA 482 to the printed FACTS Collection Record. See IOM 4.4.10.5.

4.2.4.2 - Refusals

See IOM 4.2.2. An FDA 482 must be issued in all sample refusal situations to invoke the applicable provisions of the FD&C Act. The copy of the FDA 482 is to accompany the EIR; a memorandum outlining the facts of the refusal if no EIR is prepared.

4.2.4.3 - Carrier In-Transit Sampling

Caution: See IOM 4.3.4 for conditions, which must be met before collecting in-transit samples from common carriers.

When collecting samples from in-transit lots in possession of a commercial carrier, and the only regulatory sanctions possible are against the product itself or parties other than the carrier (e.g., manufacturer, shipper, etc.), furnish the carrier or his agent an FDA 482 modified to read "Notice of Inspection to Collect Samples Only...". See exhibit 5-4. Attach a copy to the printed copy of the FACTS Collection Record. See IOM 4.4.10.5.

4.2.4.4 - Dealer Requests Notice of Inspection

When inspecting a dealer, and an FDA 482 does not need to be issued, but the dealer requests a Notice of Inspection, issue an FDA 482 modified to read "Notice of Inspection to Collect Samples Only..." See Exhibit 5-4. Attach a copy to the printed FACTS Collection Record. See IOM 4.4.10.5.

4.2.5 - Receipt for Samples

Any time you collect a sample after issuing an FDA 482, Notice of Inspection, always issue the appropriate sample receipt FDA 472 - Carriers Receipt for Samples or FDA 484 Receipt for Samples.

Always issue an FDA 484 as a receipt for samples of prescription drugs, including narcotics and controlled substances. See IOM 4.2.5.3, 4.2.5.4, and 5.2.4.

4.2.5.1 - Carriers/In-Transit Lots

Caution: See IOM Exhibit 4-4. Give the original to the carrier or his agent and route a copy to the appropriate fiscal unit for your district. The fiscal clerk will notify the consignee and consignor that a sample has been collected so the owner can, if desired, bill FDA for the sample.

4.2.5.2 - Dealer Requests Receipt

When collecting physical samples of regulated products, not in connection with an EI or where no FDA 482 has been issued, do not routinely issue an FDA 484, Receipt for Samples, except for prescription drugs, narcotics, or controlled substances. See IOM 4.2.5.3 and 4.2.5.4. If any dealer specifically asks for a receipt, prepare and issue an FDA 484 and route a copy with any other records associated with the collection record. See IOM 4.4.10.5.

4.2.5.3 - Narcotic and Controlled Rx Drugs

Regulations of the Drug Enforcement Administration (DEA) impose strict controls and comprehensive record-keeping requirements on persons handling narcotics and controlled substances. As a result, an FDA 484 must be issued for all samples of such drugs collected by FDA.

Each dealer in narcotic and controlled drugs is assigned it's own unique DEA registration number. Any time you collect a sample of a narcotic or controlled drug, be sure the Dealer's DEA Registration Number is entered in the appropriate block of the FDA 484. Double-check the number for accuracy. An error may result in possible investigation for drug shortages.

The complete DEA Registration Number must be entered on the - RECEIPT FOR SAMPLES, given to the person from whom collected, by the collector when samples of narcotic or controlled drugs are collected.

Complete the FDA 484 carefully and completely. Include the trade and chemical name, strength, sample size, container size, lot, batch, or control number, manufacturer's name and address, district address and the sample number on the FDA 484 Receipt for Samples. See IOM 4.4.10.5. Use of the FDA 484 as a receipt for samples of these drugs has the approval of DEA. (See reverse of FDA 484).

4.2.5.4 - Prescription Drugs (Non-Controlled)

Issue an FDA 484, Receipt for Samples, when samples of prescription legend drugs are collected from dealers, individuals, or during inspections. Attach a copy of the FDA 484 to the printed FACTS Collection Record. See IOM 4.4.10.5.

4.2.5.5 - Preparation of FDA 484

Complete the blocks on the FDA 484 (Exhibit 4-5), Receipt for Samples, as follows:

Block 1 - Enter your District address and telephone number including area code.

Block 2 - Enter the complete name and official title of the individual to whom you issue the FDA 484.

Block 3 - Enter date on which you finished collecting the sample. If you spent more than one day on the sample collection, enter the date you completed sampling.

Block 4 - Enter complete Sample Number here. Be sure to include any prefixes such as "DI", "INV", etc.

Block 5 - Enter firm's legal name.

Block 6 - If the firm is a dealer in narcotics or control drugs, enter their DEA Number here.

Block 7 and 8 - Enter number, street, city, state, and zip code of firm.

Block 9 - Enter a brief description of the article collected, including the number and size of units collected, product name and any identifying brand and code marks.

Block 10 - In certain situations such as for large or expensive device samples, the owner of the article may not want to part with the item. In these instances, FDA may borrow the item and return it later. If the item is borrowed and to be returned, check this box on the FDA 484. Otherwise, check the purchased block even if there is "no charge".

Block 11 - Enter the amount paid for the sample (even if borrowed, the owner may ask rent for it) and check the appropriate box. If there is no charge (always offer payment except for Post Seizure Samples), enter N/C and leave boxes blank. If, as a last resort, it is necessary for you to use your personal check or credit card and this is acceptable to the person, enter amount and check "Cr. Cd." box.

NOTE: Older editions of the FDA 484 do not have a "Cr. Cd." box. If not, write in "Cr. Cd." following the amount.

Block 12 - In instances where payment is made for the Sample, whether actually purchased, borrowed or provided at no charge, and there is no Dealer's Affidavit or any other document executed to show the owner's signature for receipt of payment, obtain the signature of the person receiving payment for the sample.

If Dealer's Affidavit, regular Affidavit or other document is used, the recipient's signature will be on that document so it is not necessary for him to also sign the FDA 484. In this case insert an applicable statement such as "Dealers Affidavit signed" in this block.

Blocks 14, 15, and 17 - Enter your name and title and signature.

4.2.5.6 - Routing of FDA 484

Original - Give the signed original to the firm, preferably to the individual to whom you gave the FDA 482 and FDA 483. See IOM 4.2.5.3 regarding receipts for narcotics and controlled drug samples.

First Carbon - Accompanies the EIR. If no EIR is involved such as when collecting a sample and the dealer specifically requests a receipt, attach it to the original Collection Record. See IOM 4.2.5.2, 4.2.5.3, and 4.2.5.4.

Second Carbon - This is an extra copy for use as needed. If not filed in the factory file, or attached to the C/R or not otherwise needed, it may be destroyed.

If exact copies are used instead of carbon copies, then route one exact copy with the EIR and a second as above.

When numerous subsamples are collected, the second carbon or exact copy may be attached to the original C/R to avoid repetition of the sub descriptions. When used for this purpose, be sure the numbers you assign to the physical subsamples matches those on the FDA 484, and that the subs are adequately described. See IOM Exhibit 4-5. If errors are noted after issuance, handle the same way as instructed under IOM 5.2.3.

4.2.6 - Dealer Identification of Lot and Records

Positive identification of sampled lots and the records covering their sales and shipment are essential to legal proceedings. The dealer's identification of a sampled lot and his identification of the records covering I.S. shipment should be factual and specific. If there is a question about accurate identification of the lot or records, determine all facts and establish identification as clearly as possible. Be alert to any identifying marks, which may later be used on the witness stand for positive identification.

4.2.6.1 - Private Individuals

When collecting Official Samples from private individuals, ask the individual to initial and date the label, wrappings, promotional literature, etc. This will aid in positively identifying the product and related documents in any court proceeding that may develop months, or even years later.

4.2.6.2 - Seriously Ill Individuals

If you collect samples from a person for contemplated regulatory action, and it is obvious the person is seriously ill, you should attempt to locate and obtain a corroborating statement and identification from someone else. This corroborating witness should have personal knowledge of the facts and be available if the principle witness cannot testify in a legal proceeding.

4.2.7 - Sampling from Government Agencies

See IOM 3.2.3.4 for information.

4.2.8 - Payment for Samples

Payment for all samples, except those collected under authority of a Court Order or Decree shall be offered to the person from whom obtained regardless of the amount. See IOM 4.2.8.2.

An exception is import samples. FDA does not pay for Import samples at the time of collection. The importer should bill the District Office. FDA will not pay for violative import samples. See 21 CFR 1.91.

4.2.8.1 - Post Seizure (P.S.) and Reconditioning Samples under Court Order

Do not pay for, or offer payment for, any Post Seizure (P.S) or other samples including those from reconditioned lots, if collected under authority of a Court Order or Decree. If the dealer insists on payment before permitting sampling, show him/her the Court Order. If he/she still refuses sampling, contact your supervisor immediately for further instructions. You may be instructed to notify the U.S. Attorney.

4.2.8.2 - Determining Sample Cost

If you are collecting samples from firms or representatives of firms who have Federal Supply, Veterans Administration or other contracts with the Federal Government, the cost of the sample should be determined by the scheduled price. Inquire of the firm if they are on contract for the item. If so, pay only the scheduled price.

Some dealers may wish to charge their regular selling price. However, if the cost of the sample seems excessive, try to persuade the dealer a lower price is more fair. If asked, tell the dealer the government considers a fair price to be the dealer's invoice cost plus a nominal charge (usually 10-15%) for freight, handling and storage.

If unable, through tactful discussion, to convince the dealer to lower the sample cost, do not haggle over the price to be paid. If the cost seems exorbitant, check with your supervisor to determine if the sample size can be reduced, or for further instructions. Whenever there is a disagreement over sample cost, ask the dealer to bill the district and report the circumstances in the Collection Remarks field on your FACTS collection record.

If districts encounter requests for payment for method validation samples (either direct submission by firms to labs or during collection from responsible firms), they should contact the responsible Office of New Drug Chemistry review division, so that communication may take place with the application sponsor. If product is being collected from commercial distribution not in the control of the sponsor/manufacturer, then the district should expect to pay wholesale cost. Expenses for NDA method validation samples should be charged to a PDUFA reimbursable CAN.

4.2.8.3 - Method of Payment

There are two ways to pay for samples. The sample costs may be billed to the district or cash may be used to pay for the sample.

4.2.8.3.1 - Costs Billed to District

Billing sample costs to the district is, in many instances, the most practical method of payment. This is particularly true where substantial costs are involved due to large numbers or expensive samples, when samples are collected from third parties such as carriers and public storage warehouses, or when delivery followed by subsequent billing is the dealers normal business practice. If available, obtain the dealer's invoice and submit it to the appropriate fiscal unit for your district.

Sampling from public storage warehouses and common carriers incurs costs, which are normally billed because the owner of the product is unavailable. Determine the identity of the owner or his agent, and estimate the value of the goods sampled. Arrange with the owner or agent to bill the district.

4.2.8.3.2 - Cash Payment

If you have a government credit card and you need cash to pay for a sample, you are authorized to use your government credit card to withdraw an ATM advance to pay for your sample whether or not you are in travel status. The amount of the withdrawal should be limited to the cost of the sample. You should submit your itemized claim for samples along with the ATM fee by submitting a local voucher using Travel Manager. Include the sample number and submit to your fiscal unit for payment. Any documentation should be provided. Sample costs cannot be charged directly to your government credit card.

4.2.8.4 - Sampling - Labor Charges

Additional labor, use of forklift, or other assistance may be required to move merchandise, skids, pallets, etc., to properly sample and restore the lot. Usually assistance will be available on the premises, or arrangements can be made with management to employ outside professional help.

There is usually little need to discuss payment when requesting nominal use of labor or equipment. However, if there is an indication management expects payment, attempt to reach a clear understanding of the charges

before proceeding. If the charges to be incurred appear reasonable, and the cost is minor (about $25.00 or less), proceed with the work and add the charges to your sample cost. However, if substantial costs are involved, consult with your supervisor before making a commitment to pay.

Where the charges are substantial and have been authorized by your supervisor, arrange for the cost of labor and/or machinery to be billed to the district. Handle these charges separately from the actual cost of the sample. Determine the hourly rate and keep track of time, labor, or machinery actually used. Prepare a short memo outlining the charges and submit it to your district.

4.2.9 - Voluntary Embargo

This section deals solely with a "voluntary" hold on regulated products. See IOM 2.7.1 for specific statutory authorities for detaining meat, poultry, egg products, and medical devices.

While there is no specific authority for requesting a voluntary embargo on a lot, voluntary embargoes by a dealer shall be encouraged where the lot sampled is clearly adulterated. By voluntarily holding, the dealer prevents further distribution of suspected violative goods until seizure or other appropriate action can be accomplished.

4.2.9.1 - Perishable Goods

Except in rare instances, it is generally not practical to hold highly perishable items unless the analysis can be completed within 24 hours. You should confer with your supervisor before requesting a voluntary embargo on perishable items.

4.2.9.2 - Obtaining a Voluntary Embargo

When the lot is clearly adulterated, or when instructed to do so by your supervisor, arrange for a voluntary embargo by the dealer. If possible, direct your conversation so that the dealer suggests the embargo. Call the dealer's attention to his/her responsibility under the law, and appeal to his/her sense of public service, integrity, or the health consequences that may be involved.

Always place a time limit on voluntary embargoes using your best estimate of how long it will take to complete the analysis and reach a district decision. Consider such factors as location of the examining lab, difficulty of the analysis required, turnover rate, storage conditions and the perishable nature of the merchandise. Note: Your district's compliance branch can ask for an extension of the voluntary embargo.

Since the action is voluntary, we cannot compel the dealer to do all the things we might ask him/her to do. While requests for voluntary holds are generally granted, a dealer may act or suggest an alternative approach.

If the dealer indicates a reluctance to voluntarily hold the lot, call his/her attention to Section 301(a) of the FD&C Act [21 U.S.C. 331 (a)]. If the dealer still refuses, a state embargo may be the next action of choice. See IOM 3.3.1 and consult your supervisor.

If the dealer declines to hold the lot, but proposes returning it to the shipper, the dealer should be warned NOT to return the goods to the shipper and advised FDA does not condone shipping violative goods. Direct his/her attention to Section 301(a) of the FD&C Act [21 U.S.C. 331 (a)].

If the dealer offers to voluntarily denature or destroy the lot in lieu of voluntary embargo, provide or arrange for supervising the denaturing per IOM 2.8.1. If the dealer proposes to recondition the lot, refer him/her to your district compliance branch for approval of his/her method. See IOM 2.6 and IOM 2.6.3.

4.3 - Collection Technique

Sampling operations must be carried out using techniques that ensure the sample is representative of the lot, the sample of the product is in the same condition as it was before sampling, and that the collection technique does not compromise the compliance status of the lot.

4.3.1 - Responsibility

It is your responsibility to collect your own samples using techniques and methods which will provide the most ideal sample, yet not be objectionable to management. This subchapter and the sampling schedules that follow, contain many sampling techniques, but not all. Your training and experience will enable you to become proficient in most sampling operations. However, in new or unusual situations it is your responsibility to use imagination and ingenuity in getting the job done and, if necessary, to consult with your supervisor.

4.3.2 - Lot Restoration & Identification

4.3.2.1 - Restoring Lot(s) Sampled

Restore lots to their original condition. Do not leave partially filled shipping cases, short weight or short volume containers in the lot after sampling. Do not leave the lot in any condition, which might encourage pilferage, or make it unsalable.

When collecting from either full cases or bulk containers, replace sampled units by back filling from a container selected for that purpose. Avoid contaminating the back-filled units. If necessary, correct the contents declaration on the container(s) from which sampled to reflect the actual contents present. Refer to IOM 4.2.2 if the dealer objects to back filling because of company policy, different codes involved, or for other reasons.

As a last resort, accede to the dealer's wishes and sample intact units, but record the facts in your regulatory notes and place a brief explanation on the C/R.

Carefully re-close all containers and shipping cases. (Commercially available glues in spray cans or plastic squeeze-type bottles are an effective means of re-gluing cartons and cases without defacing with tape or other methods.) Re-cooper or reseal barrels and drums, re-sew bags, etc. If necessary, request use of the dealer's employees in helping to restore the lot, or arrange through the dealer to employ outside help. See IOM 4.2.8.4.

4.3.2.2 - Identifying Lot(s) Sampled

Identify each container from which units are taken with the date, your initials and the sample number, or you may complete and affix an FDA 2426, Examination Label, to each shipping case or bulk container sampled. For burlap or woven bags, the FDA 2426 may be glued to tags, and the tags attached to the bags.

Should the dealer object to your identification procedure, attempt to reach a compromise (e.g., placing the ID in an obscure location, etc.). If the dealer still objects, accede to his wishes, but record the facts in your regulatory notes.

Positive identification of the containers sampled is important if it becomes necessary to resample the lot(s), or if an embargo, seizure, or other action ensues. It also aids the dealer to differentiate between containers that have been opened by FDA as opposed to those opened by pilferage or torn opened by rough handling. It may be necessary to mark more containers than sampled to assure proper identification of the lot. This can be done by using the Examination Label, a handwritten ID or by using a rubber stamp.

Do not use industrial or permanent type markers on sample containers which allow penetration by ink. Many inks will penetrate to the product and act as a contaminant, interfering with the analysis. Water base markers will run when damp and must be covered with tape. See IOM 4.5.2.3 for identification techniques.

Do not permanently identify articles that are borrowed and will be returned to the dealer.

4.3.3 - Sample Size

To determine sample size, first consult your assignment. If the assignment doesn't specify the sample size, follow the guidance in the applicable Compliance Program. The IOM SAMPLE SCHEDULE, should be used if the Compliance Program doesn't state the sample size. If none of these furnish the sample size, consult with your supervisor or the laboratory. Collect sufficient sample to allow for the FDA reserve portion and the 702(b) portion. See IOM 4.3.3.2 and IOM 4.3.3.3.

4.3.3.1 - Medical Device Samples

The following table represents the devices for which there are sampling instructions in Compliance Policy Guides:

Device	CPG Reference
Clinical Thermometers	See CPG 335.800
Condoms	See CPG 345.100
Surgeons and Patient Exam Gloves	See CPG 335.700

In addition to providing instructions on sample size, these compliance policy guides provide guidance on criteria to determine adulteration and whether or not regulatory action should be recommended.

4.3.3.2 - 702(b) Requirement

When the sample schedule, assignment or other instruction does not specifically provide for the 702(b) portion, collect a sufficient amount to provide this required portion. You are not required to obtain a 702(b) portion in the following instances exempted by statute or by regulation 21 CFR 2.10(b):

1. Devices are not included in the statutory requirement of Section 702(b).
2. The amount available for sampling is less than twice the quantity estimated to be sufficient for analysis, in which case, collect all that is available.
3. The cost of twice the quantity estimated to be sufficient for analysis exceeds $150.00. (Currently 21 CFR 2.10 uses $50.00 as the amount. However, ORA policy sets a limit of $150.00. If the sample is critical, and the cost exceeds $150.00, check with your supervisor.
4. Import samples, collected from a shipment being imported or offered for entry into the United States.
5. The sample is collected from a person named on the label of the article or his agent, and such person is also owner of the article. For example, it is not necessary to obtain a 702(b) portion if the sample is collected from a lot owned by and in the possession of the manufacturer whose name appears on the label.
6. The sample is collected from the owner of the article or his agent, and the article bears no label, or if it bears a label, no person is named thereon.

Note: *Regardless of the exemptions under 21 CFR 2.10(b) listed above, a good rule of thumb to follow for most filth samples, is to collect the 702(b) portion.*

4.3.3.3 - Collecting the 702(b) Portion

Whenever possible, collect separate subdivisions in order to provide the firm a portion as required by Section 702(b). Each duplicate subdivision should be collected from the same bag, box, case, or container. The total sample should be at least twice the quantity estimated to be sufficient for analysis, including a reserve portion for FDA's laboratory. If unable to collect separate subdivisions, assure that the total amount collected for each sample subdivision, or the total amount collected from an undivided sample, is at least twice the amount estimated to be sufficient for analysis. See IOM 4.3.7.4.

4.3.4 - In-Transit Samples

The exterior of any domestic package thought to contain an article subject to FDA regulation and in the possession, control, or custody of a common carrier may be examined (photographed, information on the outside copied, etc.) and records of the shipment may be obtained. Such package may not be opened either by an FDA employee or by an employee of the common carrier at the request of an FDA employee except as provided below.

4.3.4.1- Examination without a Warrant

The Office of Chief Counsel has advised FDA employees may, without a warrant, open, examine the contents and/or sample a package which is part of a domestic commercial interstate shipment in the possession, control, or custody of a common carrier only if:

1. The consignor or consignee affirmatively consents to examination and/or sampling of the contents; or

2. The Agency has reliable information the carrier regularly carries FDA regulated articles, and the facility where the sampling is contemplated is subject to FDA inspection. Reliable information may come from agency files, the carrier itself, other customers of the carrier, etc. and

3. The Agency has reliable information a particular package sought to be examined is destined for, or received from another state, and contains an FDA regulated article. [Such information may be found on the exterior of the package and/or shipping documents in specific terms. Information may also come from reliable sources, which establish the consignor is in the business of manufacturing and/or shipping FDA regulated articles using a distinctive type of package (shipping container); and the package in question meets such description and shows the consignor to be such firm.]

4.3.4.2 - Examination with a Warrant

Confer with your supervisor on any question concerning the need for a warrant. However, headquarters approval must be obtained because such inspection and sampling may require a search warrant. Contact the Division of Field Investigations (DFI) (HFC-130) at 301-827-5653 to discuss the matter. They will coordinate as necessary with Office of Enforcement (HFC-200) and Chief Counsel (GCF-1) and provide further nstructions.

If a decision has already been made by the district office to obtain a warrant, follow the procedures outlined in the Regulatory Procedures Manual, Chapter 6-3.

If a common carrier reports a violative article which it discovers under its own package opening procedures, independent of any request by an FDA employee or any standing FDA cooperative program with the carrier, FDA may still need a warrant to examine the material. Unless all the conditions for independent sampling in 1 or 2 above exist, you must consult with your supervisor, who will arrange for headquarters consultation as outlined above.

Note: *Where the identity of an Interstate product is known by virtue of it being visible in bulk, or being in labeled containers or packages which are verified as to contents by shipping records, and where such product is under FDA jurisdiction at a given location, it may be sampled according to established IOM procedures.*

4.3.4.3 - Resealing Conveyances

If it is necessary to break the commercial seal to enter a railcar or other conveyance, reseal the door with a numbered self-locking "U.S. Food and Drug" metal seal. Record in your regulatory notes (and on C/R if sample taken) the number of the car or conveyance, the identifying number on any car seals removed, and the number of the FDA metal seals applied.

4.3.5 - Special Sampling Situations

Do not collect human or animal biological materials (urine, feces, sputum, blood, blood products, organs, tissue etc.) unless arrangements for special handling and special treatment have been made in advance. Most ORA servicing laboratories are not prepared or certified to handle these materials. In addition to guidance for special sampling situations provided below, sampling guidance may also be found in these areas of the IOM:

IOM 1.5. - Safety

IOM 1.5.3 - Sampling

Sampling Containers for Lemon Oil or Other essential Oils - Plastic or paraffin-coated liners in caps of containers used to hold samples of this type product are not satisfactory in that the plastic or paraffin is soluble in the oils and interferes with the analysis. Use glass, cork, foil covered, or non-plastic, non-paraffin closures.

Sampling medicinal and other gasses - Gasses represent a special sampling situation. Please contact your servicing lab to determine an appropriate sampling container and sample size.

4.3.5.1 - Complaints, Counterfeiting / Tampering, Foodborne Disease, Injury Illness

Detailed instructions for investigating and sampling products in connection with consumer complaints, tampering, foodborne outbreaks, injury and adverse reactions, etc. appear in the following sections of the IOM:

IOM 8.2 - Complaints

IOM 8.2.7 - Sample Collection

IOM 8.3 - Investigation of Foodborne Outbreaks

IOM 8.3.3 - Sampling Procedure

IOM 8.4 - Investigation - Injury and Illness Reactions

IOM 8.8 - Counterfeiting/Tampering

IOM 8.8.5.3 - Sampling

Be cognizant of conserving scarce resources when investigating consumer complaints that do not involve injury, illness, or product counterfeiting / tampering. Unnecessary samples waste both operational and administrative resources. Use judgment as to whether or not it is necessary to collect the consumer's portion in situations that do not involve injury, illness, or product tampering. For example, there is little need to collect a physical sample of an insect infested box of cereal from the complainant. Both you and the consumer can readily see it is insect infested. The laboratory would find it insect infested, and the district would merely report the same thing back to the complainant. No practical purpose would be served by either collecting or examining such a sample.

4.3.5.2 - Recalls

See IOM 7.1 and IOM 7.1.1.7.

4.3.5.3 - Natural Disasters

See IOM 8.5.

4.3.5.4 - Induced Samples

If this type sample is desired your supervisor will provide specific instructions and procedures to be followed. This may involve:

1. Whether to use your correct name or an alias. Caution: if you use an alias, do not use a similar name or a name with initials the same as yours (e.g., Sidney H. Rogers should not use Samuel H. Right). In addition, do not use a district office or resident post as a return address when ordering products or literature.

2. Do not telephone your order in from the office or your home phone because the firm may have "Caller ID" and be able to identify your location by the phone number.

3. Whether to use order blanks contained in the promotional package, advertisement, or promotional activity; or whether false ones will be used.

4. Whether money orders, your charge plate numbers, bank checks, or your personal checks should be used for payment. It depends on the situation, but money orders are preferred since these do not involve personal accounts.

5. Where the requested items are to be sent: rented P.O. Box, home address, General Delivery, or other address.

6. How the address and/or your name is to be recorded on the order blank. A code may be used either in your name or address so any follow-up

promotional material sent to that name and address can be keyed to your original order.

When it has been decided to induce a sample and you have discussed the procedures with your supervisor, prepare the order and obtain the money order, or payment document. When all documents for ordering the item(s) are prepared, photocopy all the material, including the addressed envelope, for your record and submit the order.

When the order is received, identify the sample item, all accompanying material such as pamphlets, brochures, etc. (including all wrappings containing any type of printing, identification, numbers, post marks, addresses, etc.), and submit the item and exhibits in the same manner as any other official sample. If payment of the item was by personal check or credit card number, attach a photocopy of the canceled check or credit card receipt if available. You may do this later, after clearance of the check or charge slip.

4.3.5.5 - Undercover Buy

See IOM 4.1.4.6.

4.3.6 - Aseptic Sample

Aseptic sampling is a technique used to prevent contamination by your sampling method. Aseptic sampling involves the use of sterile sampling implements and containers. Your sampling technique is where the lot or sample are contacted only by the sampling implements or the container. Samples collected using aseptic technique, will permit testimony that the bacteriological findings accurately reflect the condition of the lot at the time of sampling and, ideally, at the time of the original shipment. Whenever possible collect intact, unopened containers. Aseptic sampling is often used in the collection of in-line samples, environmental samples, product samples from bulk containers and collection of unpack-aged product that is being collected for microbial analysis.

Note: *Products in 55 gallon drums, or similar large containers, either aseptically filled or heat processed, should not be sampled while the shipment is en route unless the owner accepts responsibility for the portion remaining after sampling. Try to arrange sampling of these products at the consignee (user) so the opened containers can be immediately used or stored under refrigerated conditions. Use ASEPTIC TECHNIQUE when sampling these products.*

For more guidance on aseptic technique, you may consult the course Food Microbiological Control 10: Aseptic Sampling, which is available to FDA employees through the ORA U intranet site.

4.3.6.1 - General Procedures

If it is necessary to open containers, draw the sample and submit it under conditions, which will prevent multiplication or undue reduction of the bacterial population. Follow the basic principles of aseptic sampling technique. Take steps to minimize exposure of product, sampling equipment, and the interior of sampling containers to the environment.

4.3.6.1.1 - Sterilized Equipment

Use only sterilized equipment and containers. These should be obtained from the servicing laboratory or in emergency, at local cooperating health agencies. Pre-sterilized plastic or metal tools should be used. However, if unavailable, the metal tools can be sterilized immediately before use with a propane torch. Permit the tool to cool in the air or inside a sterile container before using. Soaking with 70% alcohol and flaming off is an acceptable method of field sterilization, and may be used as a last resort.

If it is necessary to drill, saw, or cut the item being sampled (such as large frozen fish, cheese wheels, frozen fruit, etc.), if at all possible, use stainless steel bits, blades, knives, etc. Wooden handled sampling instruments are particularly susceptible to bacterial contamination, are difficult to sterilize, and should be avoided.

4.3.6.1.2 - Cautions

Be extremely careful when using a propane torch or other flame when sterilizing tools and equipment. Evaluate the conditions pertaining to explosive vapors, dusty air, flame-restricted areas, firm's policy or management's wishes. The use of supportive devices should be considered when torch is not being hand held. Also be sure all flammable liquids, such as alcohol, in your filth kit are in metal safety cans and not in breakable containers.

If it is necessary to handle the items being sampled, use sterile disposable type gloves (rubber, vinyl, plastic, etc. - surgeon's gloves are good). Use a fresh glove for each sub and submit an unopened pair of gloves as a control. See IOM 4.3.6.5.

4.3.6.1.3 - Opening Sterile Sampling Containers

Opening Sterile Sampling Containers - Work rapidly. Open sterile sampling containers only to admit the sample and close it immediately. Do not touch the inside of the sterile container, lip, or lid. Submit one empty sterile container similarly opened and closed as a control. See IOM 4.3.6.5.

4.3.6.1.4 - Dusty Areas

Do not collect samples in areas where dust or atmospheric conditions may cause contamination of the sample, unless such contamination may be considered a part of the sample.

4.3.6.2 - Sampling Dried Powders

Cautions - The proper aseptic sampling of dried milk powder, dried eggs, dried yeast, and similar type products is difficult because they are generally packed in multilayer poly-lined paper bags. These may be stitched across the entire top, may have filler spouts, or the top of the poly-liner may be closed or sealed with some type of "twists".

The practice of cutting an "X" or "V" or slitting the bag and folding the cut part back to expose the contents for sampling should not be used because it creates a resealing problem; the opening cannot be properly repaired.

The following procedures have been approved by the scientific units in Headquarters and should be used when sampling this type product.

4.3.6.2.1 - Bag and Poly-Liner Stitched Together Across Top Seam

1. Remove as much dust as possible from the seam end by brushing and then wiping with a cloth dampened with alcohol. Note: This does not sterilize the bag as porous paper cannot be sterilized.

2. Remove the seam stitching carefully (and dust cover, if any) and spread the walls of the bag and the poly-liner open enough to permit sampling being careful that no extraneous material such as dust, bits of twine, paper, etc., drops into the product.

3. Carefully scrape off the surface of the product with a sterile device and aseptically draw the sample from the material below.

4. Carefully reclose the bag and restitch by hand, or by machine if firm or FDA portable sewing machine is available.

4.3.6.2.2 - Bag Stitched Across Top and Poly-Liner Twist-Closed and Sealed with "Twist" Device - Wire, Plastic, Etc

1. Brush, alcohol wipe, and remove stitching as described.

2. Remove "twist" seal and carefully open poly-liner using caution that no extraneous material drops into the product.

3. Draw aseptic sample in same manner as in 3. above.

4. Carefully close the poly-liner with a twisting motion and reseal with "twist" seal arranging it so it will not puncture the poly-liner, and resew bag as in 4. above.

4.3.6.2.3 - BAGS WITH FILLING SPOUTS

1. The filling spout will be located at one side of the top stitching and will either pull out to form a top or side spout.

2. Brush and alcohol wipe the area around the spout and carefully pull it out to reveal the opening. It is better to have the bag on its side while pulling the spout so any dust in the opening falls outside the bag.

3. Carefully spread the sides of the spout apart and aseptically draw the sample. A trier or long handled device is usually better for this type opening because of the limited opening.

4. Carefully close the spout with a firm twisting motion and be sure the opening is closed prior to pushing back into the bag.

4.3.6.3 - Collecting Water Samples

When it is necessary to collect water samples for bacteriological examination, use the following procedures:

1. Use sterile bottles. If dechlorination of sample is necessary, sodium thiosulfate sufficient to provide 100 mg/l should be placed in the clean bottles prior to sterilization. The sodium thiosulfate will prevent the chlorine from acting on the bacteria and assures, when the sample is analyzed, the bacterial load is the same as when collected.

2. Carefully inspect the outside of the faucet from which the sample will be drawn. Do not collect sample from a faucet with leaks around handle.

3. Clean and dry outside of faucet.

4. Let the water run from the fully open faucet for at least 1/2 minute or for 2 or 3 minutes if the faucet is on a long service line.

5. Partially close faucet to permit collecting sample without splashing. Carefully open sample bottle to prevent contamination, as for any other aseptic sampling operation.

6. Fill bottle carefully without splashing and be sure no water from your hands or other objects enters the bottle. Do not over fill, but leave a small air bubble at top.

7. Unless otherwise instructed, minimum sample size for bacteriological examination is 100 ml.

8. Deliver sample to lab promptly. If sample is not examined within 24 hours after collection, the results may be inaccurate.

Note: When documenting specific situations in a plant, you may need to vary this procedure to mimic the actual conditions used by the firm.

4.3.6.4 - Sample Handling

For frozen samples, pre-chill sterile containers before use and keep frozen with dry ice. Use ordinary ice or ice packs for holding and transporting unfrozen samples that require refrigeration. See IOM 4.5.3.5 and IOM 8.3.3.3. Under normal circumstances dried products may be shipped unrefrigerated except in cases where they would be exposed to high temperatures, i.e., above 37.8oC (100oF).

Submit samples subject to rapid spoilage (specimens of foods involved in poisoning cases, etc.) by immediate personal delivery to the bacteriologist where feasible.

4.3.6.5 - Controls

When collecting samples using aseptic technique and the subs are collected using presterilized containers and equipment, submit a number of control subs. If the sampling covers a long period of time you should submit controls which show environmental conditions during the time of sampling. The controls should be collected at the start, during, and at the end of the sampling period. List control subs on your C/R.

Examples of various control subs are:

1. *Sterile Containers* - Where sterile containers are used to collect aseptic samples, submit one unopened container, which was sterilized in the same manner as containers used for sampling. Also submit at least one empty sterile container which has been opened and closed in the sampling area.

2. *Sterile Disposable Gloves* - If sterile disposable gloves are used to handle the product, submit one unopened pair of gloves as a control.

3. *Sterile Sampling Equipment* - Where presterilized sampling tools are used (e.g., spoons, spatulas, triers, etc.), submit at least one unopened sampling tool as a control.

4.3.7 - Adulteration Violations

Since adulteration samples are collected to confirm the presence of filth or other deleterious material, they are generally either larger or more selective than samples collected for economic or misbranding purposes.

When widespread evidence of filth or other adulteration is present, 402(a)(4) conditions can be documented by selective sampling. See IOM 4.3.7.3. You will need to field examine (See IOM 4.3.7.1) a number of lots of product to determine the extent of the adulteration and can collect an investigational (INV) sample of filth exhibits and take photographs to document the widespread nature of the evidence. See IOM 4.1.7. Collect separate sub samples of filth from various areas of the firm to illustrate the extent of adulteration within the firm. Field examine various lots of regulated products and collect official selective samples to document filth or other adulteration. Filth found on the exterior of containers, on pallets containing regulated product, or on the floor adjacent to lots of regulated product you are selectively sampling can be considered subsamples of that official sample. Consult with your supervisor and be guided by the criteria in Compliance Policy Guide (CPG) 580.100 Food Storage and Warehousing - Adulteration - Filth (Domestic and Import). The criteria in the Compliance Policy Guide can be used to determine if a particular lot meets the minimum criteria for direct reference seizure. Documenting a number of lots which meet the criteria helps establish the widespread nature of the adulteration.

When lots appear actionable, determine recent sales from the lot in question. Follow up may be necessary as directed by your supervisor.

4.3.7.1 - Field Examination

Some field examinations are also referred to as bag-by-bag exams or unit by unit exams. When you conduct such exams take care to describe observations of each unit of product examined, any physical subsamples collected which reflect the violative nature of the lot, and exhibits which corroborate your report of observations.

Record in your regulatory notes, subsequently in C/R Collection Remarks field or Continuation Form, or on Analyst Worksheet FDA 431, the results of your unit by unit examination of the lot. Observations should be specific. Report the general storage conditions, the violative condition of the lot, the physical relationship of the violative lot to other lots in the area, how you conducted the examination and how many units you examined. Wherever possible, record quantitative observations.

Report the number and location of live and dead insects, rodent pellets, or other adulteration discovered inside the containers as well as on their exterior surface. Provide graphic measurements of areas of urine/chemical stains on each container and the extent of penetration. Correlate findings of the unit by unit examination with any photographs and physical subsamples collected.

Where the field examination is carefully described and documented, the sample collected from obviously violative lots may be reduced to carefully selected exhibits. The field examination and the report of findings will serve as the analysis.

4.3.7.2 - Random Sampling

The concept of random "blind" sampling is to yield information about the average composition of the lot. It is employed when you have no information or method of determining which units are violative. Usually the violation is concealed and must be found by laboratory methods.

Sample size is usually described in your assignment, IOM Sample Schedule, Compliance Program Guidance Manual, or the applicable schedules. If none of these furnish the sample size, a general rule is to collect samples from the square root of the number of cases or shipping containers but not less than 12 or more than 36 subs in duplicate. If there are less than 12 containers, all should be sampled. Discuss sample size and 702(b) requirements with your supervisor. See IOM 4.3.3.2.

4.3.7.3 - Selective Sampling

In some situations, random sampling is unnecessary or even undesirable. Under these conditions, examine the lot and select the portions which will demonstrate the violative nature of the lot.

In addition to the selective samples collected, exhibits should include diagrams and photographs to demonstrate the violative conditions reported, and which containers were sampled and photographed.

4.3.7.4 - Sample Criteria

The Agency has defined minimum direct reference seizure criteria to assist in assessing filth of individual lots. Criteria for rodent, insect, and bird filth are defined in Compliance Policy Guide (CPG) 580.100, Food Storage and Warehousing - Adulteration - Filth (Domestic and Import) for human foods, and reiterated in IOM sections 4.3.7.2 - 4.3.7.4. When collecting selective samples of products to show adulteration by filth, be guided by this criteria.

When evidence of rodent, insect, bird, or other animal activity is encountered during an inspection it is your responsibility to assess the evidence you observe and determine and document whether the activity is:

1. Current or old
2. Isolated to one lot (possible FD&C 402(a)(3) charges - contain in whole or in part filth or is otherwise unfit for food).
3. Widespread, which requires evidence and documentation to illustrate all of the firm's susceptible products are potentially adulterated because they are being prepared, packed, or held under conditions whereby they may be contaminated. (possible FD&C 402(a)(4) charges)

Your assessment, and documentation of the evidence you observe by diagrams, photos and sample collections will determine what actions may be required by either the establishment, the Agency, the Court, or all three to correct the problem. The evidence and documentation you collect and develop will be used to show by a preponderance of evidence that conditions at the firm have resulted, or could result in adulteration.

Your sample collection should be sufficient to document the extent of the violative conditions and not be limited to this minimum. Even where these minimum prerequisites are not met, you should collect samples as exhibits and evidence, particularly where adulteration under section 402(a)(4) of the FD&C Act [21 U.S.C. 342 (a)(4)] may be a factor. Your evidence may be used in a subsequent action against the firm, if corrections are not made.

Consult with your supervisor as soon as possible when you find evidence which meets the criteria set forth in CPG 580.100. If you are collecting several samples, the lab should be notified in advance that samples are on their way and should be analyzed expeditiously to facilitate regulatory action. Your supervisor may also want to notify your compliance branch so evaluation of evidence for a possible mass seizure can commence.

4.3.7.4.1 - General

When Selective Sampling consists of an actual sample of a product, however small, as distinguished from bag cuttings, rodent pellets, insects, etc., a 702(b) portion must be obtained. In such cases, collect duplicate subs of the product to provide the 702(b) portion. This 702(b) portion is usually not an exact duplicate of the product collected for the Selective Sample, but should be collected from the same bag, box, or other container of product sampled. Whether collected from a container or bulk, the 702(b) portion should be taken as close as possible to that portion selectively sampled for analysis. Specify for each sub and duplicate collected, the origin, manner in which taken, and the examination to be made on your C/R.

Submit each portion of bagging or container portion, rodent pellets, material from beneath sampled area, control etc., in separate vial or subsample container.

It's important when collecting a selective sample for adulteration violations that you:

1. Use a coherent numbering/identification system for subsamples to avoid unnecessary confusion for the lab.
2. Provide a detailed listing of individual sub descriptions on the C/R.

3. If possible, provide a copy of any maps, photos or other additional documentation to the laboratory.

4. Be sure to obtain product labeling. Since samples of lots which are sampled selectively are official samples, complete labeling must be collected. See FD &C Act Section 704(d) applies and the CR should be marked as such.

5. *Note:* Whenever a portion of food is collected as part of a selective sample FD &C Act Section 704(d) applies and the CR should be marked as such.

4.3.7.4.2 - RODENT CONTAMINATION

The minimum direct reference seizure criteria to assist in assessing rodent adulteration of individual lots, as defined in Compliance Policy Guide (CPG) 580.100, are summarized as follows:

1. Three or more of the bags in the lot are rodent gnawed; or

2. At least five of the bags in the lot bear either rodent urine stains at least 1/4" in diameter, or two or more rodent pellets; or

3. The food in at least one container in the lot contains rodent gnawed material, or rodent excreta or urine.

Whether or not the warehouse is rodent infested; IF:

1. At least three bags bear rodent urine stains of at least 1/4" in diameter which penetrates to the product even though the product cannot be demonstrated to have been contaminated; or:

2. At least two bags are rodent-gnawed and at least five bags bear either rodent urine stains at least 1/4" in diameter, with or without penetration to the product, or two or more rodent pellets; or:

3. The food in at least one bag in the lot contains rodent-gnawed material or rodent excreta or rodent urine, and at least five bags bear either rodent stains at least 1/4" in diameter or two or more rodent pellets.

Additional regulatory guidance concerning rodent adulteration of pet foods can be found in CPG, 690.600 Rodent Contaminated Pet Foods.

4.3.7.4.2.1 - Examination and Documentation of Rodent Contamination

Examine the exterior of the containers looking for rodent hairs, urine stains, excreta pellets, gnaw marks, holes, nesting material and live rodents. Make a diagram of the entire lot and note your findings as you examine the individual containers. You will need to include these descriptions on your C/R.

Describe excreta pellets as carefully as possible, Note whether they appear dusty or shiny; soft or hard.

Examine suspected urine stains with ultra-violet light in as near total darkness as possible. A minimum of 15 minutes is normally required for the eyes to become properly adjusted to accurately differentiate between rodent stain fluorescence and normal fluorescence of rice and certain other commodities.

Wet, fresh or continually wetted runs may fluoresce poorly, but the odor of urine will usually be present and should be described on the C/R. Fresh dry urine stains will fluoresce blue-white, while older stains may be more yellowish/white. Rodent hairs will look like blue/white streaks. Look for the typical droplet pattern because rodents commonly urinate while in motion. Report the presence of droplet patterns on your C/R.

Urine stained areas may be photographed under ultra-violet light conditions. Check with your supervisor about the technical aspects of this procedure. Do not mark container surfaces to outline the stained areas when taking either ultra violet or normal photographs. This may contaminate the product by migration through the containers.

A number of things can interfere with the visual identification of urine stains. Many types of bagging and threading materials will fluoresce under U.V. light, however, the characteristic rodent stain fluorescence can be identified by its yellowish color and characteristic pattern. In addition a number of products exhibit a natural fluorescence. The following products may be difficult to evaluate because of either natural fluorescence or "quenching" of UV rays, even if contaminated. ("Quenching" refers to a covering up or a decrease in the ability of a product to fluoresce.)

FOODS

High Gluten Flour (Natural)

Nut Meats (Natural)

Bean Flours (Natural)

Brans (Natural)

Pop & Field Corn (Natural)

Wheat (Natural)

Starch (Natural)

Spices (Natural or Quenching)

NON-FOOD ITEMS

Burlap Bags (Quenching)

Bleached Sacks (Natural-White Glow)

Lubricants (Oils & Greases)

(Natural-Blue/White to yellow/brown glow)

Pitches & Tars (Natural-Yellow)

Detergents & Bleaches (Natural-White)

Sulfide Waste Matter (Natural-Blue/White)

Note clearly on your C/R if the product or package contains or is directly associated with any of the following:

1. Dried milk products (contain urea).

2. Whole grain wheat (contains urea and allantoin).

3. Animal feeds (urea is usually intentionally added).

4.3.7.4.2.2 - Collecting Exhibits or Subsamples

When sampling lots for rodent contamination follow the safety precautions in IOM 1.5.5.4. Wear gloves and handle the exhibits with tweezers or forceps.

Collect a representative number of rodent pellets for laboratory confirmation. Place the pellets in a vial or other rigid container to prevent crushing. One of the identifying characteristics the lab looks for is the presence of rodent hairs in the pellets. The more pellets examined increases the possibility of a good identification. However, do not collect all the evidence you see as this would recondition the lot.

Collect portions of urine stains or gnawed holes from containers using small scissors or a sharp knife. Leave a portion of the stain or gnawed hole intact, but take a cutting large enough to provide good identification. Usually ½ inch around the stain is sufficient to allow manipulation during the lab exam. *Note:* The bag cutting should not be so large as to remove the entire contaminated portion, since this would recondition the product. For multilayer bags, be sure you cut through all layers of the bag and identify the layers with pencil. (Do not use ink as it often contains urea.) If possible, take stained cuttings from areas which have not been exposed for extended periods of time to light, in particular, ultraviolet light sources or to intense heat. If you have no alternative or cannot determine the stained areas' history, note the conditions on the C/R. Place cuttings and gnawed holes between 2 pieces of white paper, and then fold, roll, or leave flat and place into a glass container or other suitable container. This will hold the evidence in place and prevent possible loss of hairs or parasites due to static charges. Do not separate a multilayer cutting. Avoid the use of polyethylene containers as rodent hairs may adhere to containers made from this material. Put the cuttings in a large enough container to avoid excessive folding of the cutting.

Collect a minimal amount of product from under the stained area or hole, preferably just clumped product as a separate subsample. This prevents dilution of the contaminated product with uncontaminated product. Whenever you collect product, regardless of amount, collect a separate subsample to provide a 702(b) portion. See IOM 4.3.7.4.1.

In addition, you need to collect product controls, in duplicate, to provide for the 702(b) portion. These subsamples should be collected from beneath unstained portions of the container. Collect control samples from 3 different containers.

Identify the 702b subsamples as such on subsample identification (See IOM 4.5.2.1.) and note on your C/R which subsamples are the 702(b) portions.

Collect a portion of unstained container, which does not fluoresce, as a separate subsample for a control. As a general guide, collect the controls from the opposite side of the bag or make the cutting large enough to separate the control area and the stain. Separate the controls from the stains and submit in separate containers. Collect at least 3 container controls for each sample. If the lot consists of different containers or bags of different manufacturers, collect controls to represent each type or manufacturer of the containers.

Collect nesting material with minimal handling. A half cup is enough for analysis. Do not collect any live rodents.

Where you separate, count, or identify the various elements of an exhibit, (e.g.: sieve and find X number of rodent pellets), maintain the counted portions separate from the other subs. Note on the C/R those subs that were counted, separated, etc.

Handle exhibits carefully to prevent loss of microscopic evidence.

Submit each portion of bagging or container portion, pellets, material from beneath sampled area, control, etc., in separate vial or subsample container. Place the subsamples in a dark container, such as a cardboard box to protect them from light and protect the exhibits from being crushed.

4.3.7.4.2.3 - Summary of Sample for Rodent Evidence

The complete official sample will consist of:

1. Subsamples of rodent excreta pellets
2. Subsamples of stained bagging, or portions of the containers, and any adhering pellets.
3. Subsamples of unstained bagging, or portions of the containers, which do not fluoresce, for controls (minimum three required).
4. Subsamples of small portions of the product from directly beneath the stained areas. Do not dilute the contaminated product beneath the stain with the non-contaminated product.
5. Subsamples of small portions of product to serve as 702(b) portions
6. Subsamples of uncontaminated product from beneath the unstained bagging, or other container. These serve as controls, and should be collected in duplicate to provide 702(b) portions. Collect control samples from 3 different containers.
7. Subsamples of cuttings from gnawed holes
8. Subsamples of small amounts of product collected from beneath the gnawed holes.
9. Subsamples of small portions of product to serve as 702(b) portions.
10. Product labeling.

11. Interstate documentation.

4.3.7.4.3 - Insect Contamination

The criteria from CPG 580.100 below, involving dead insects only, will not be used for action against any food intended to undergo further processing that effectively removes all the dead insects, e.g. processing of cocoa beans.

The product contains:

1. One live insect in each of two or more immediate containers; or, one dead insect in each of three or more immediate containers; or, three live or dead insects in one immediate container; plus
   - Similar live or dead insect infestation present on, or in the immediate proximity of, the lot to show a 402(a)(4) [21 U.S.C. 342 (a)(4)]violation.
   - The product contains one or more live insects in each of three or more immediate containers.
2. The product contains two or more dead whole insects in at least five of the immediate containers. Note: a situation such as this may follow fumigation of the lot and vacuuming of the exteriors of the bags.
3. The product is in cloth or burlap bags and two or more live or dead insects are present on at least five of the containers. Note: Some live insects must be present. Product need not be shown to have become contaminated.

4.3.7.4.3.1 - Examination and Documentation of Insect Contamination

Examine the exterior of the containers (especially along seams or creases) looking for insects, larvae, webbing, nesting material, entrance or exit holes, and cast skins. Make a diagram of the entire lot and note your findings as you examine the individual containers. Describe insects or larvae carefully, noting if they are dead or alive. You will need to include these descriptions on your C/R.

4.3.7.4.3.2 - Collecting Exhibits or Subsamples

Collect a representative number of insects for laboratory confirmation. Place the specimens in a vial or other rigid container to prevent crushing. Collect all forms of insects you see, however do not collect all the evidence from the lot or you might recondition the product. If you collect live insects, be sure to note that on your C/R. However, you should not send live insects to the lab. Freeze the subsamples prior to shipment to ensure they are not alive when you ship them. Note the fact that the subsamples were frozen on the C/R.

Cut portions of bags or containers containing suspected insect entrance or exit holes from containers using small scissors. Usually ½ inch around the holes is sufficient to allow manipulation during the lab exam. Note: The bag cutting should not be so large as to remove the entire contaminated portion, since this would recondition the product. For multilayer bags, be sure you cut through all layers of the bag and identify the layers with pencil. (Do not use ink as it often contains urea.) Place cuttings between 2 pieces of white paper, and then fold, roll, or leave flat and place into a glass container or other suitable container. This will hold the evidence in place and prevent possible loss microscopic evidence due to static charges. Do not separate a multilayer cutting. Avoid the use of polyethylene containers as insect fragments may adhere to containers made from this material. Put the cuttings in a large enough container to avoid excessive folding of the cutting

Collect product from beneath holes which penetrate the packaging as a separate subsample. Whenever you collect product, regardless of amount, collect a separate subsample to provide a 702(b) portion. Note on the subsample itself and on your C/R which subsamples are the 702(b) portions.

4.3.7.4.3.3 - Summary of Sample for Insect Evidence

The complete official sample will consist of:

1. Subsamples of insects, larvae, webbing, etc.

2. Subsamples of portions of the containers with entrance or exit holes.

3. Subsamples of small portions of the product from directly beneath holes.

4. Subsamples of small portions of product serve as 702(b) portions See IOM 4.3.7.4.1.

5. Product labeling.

6. Interstate documentation.

4.3.7.4.4 - Bird Contamination

Per the criteria from CPG 580.100, if the product is in permeable containers (paper, cloth, burlap, etc.), and

1. The product contains bird excreta in one or more containers, and you feel the insanitary storage conditions will clearly support a 402(a)(4) [21 U.S.C. 342 (a)(4)] violation.

2. Bird excreta is present on the exteriors of at least five of the containers, and the product contains bird excreta in one.

3. At least 30% of the number of bags examined, but at least five bags, are contaminated with bird excreta; and at least three of the bags bear excreta stains which penetrate to the product, even though the product may not be contaminated.

   Note: In all instances of bird excreta contamination the excreta must be confirmed by positive test for uric acid.

4.3.7.4.4.1 - Examination and Documentation of Bird Contamination

Examine the exterior of the containers looking for bird excreta. Make a diagram of the entire lot and note your findings as you examine the individual containers. You will need to include these descriptions on your C/R.

4.3.7.4.4.2 - Collecting Exhibits and Subsamples

Remove portions of bird excreta stains from containers using small scissors. Leave a portion of the stain intact, but take a cutting large enough to provide good identification. Usually ½ inch around the stain is sufficient to allow manipulation during the lab exam. Note: The bag cutting should not be so large as to remove the entire contaminated portion, since this would recondition the product. For multilayer bags, be sure you cut through all layers of the bag and identify the layers with pencil. (Do not use ink as it often contains urea.) If possible, take stained cuttings from areas which have not been exposed for extended periods of time to light, in particular, ultraviolet light sources or to intense heat. If you have no alternative or cannot determine the stained areas' history, note the conditions on the C/R. Place cuttings between 2 pieces of white paper, and then fold, roll, or leave flat and place into a glass container or other suitable container. This will hold the evidence in place and prevent possible loss of microscopic evidence due to static charges. Do not separate a multilayer cutting. Avoid the use of polyethylene containers as rodent hairs may adhere to containers made from this material. Put the cuttings in a large enough container to avoid excessive folding of the cutting.

Collect a minimal amount of product from under the stained area, preferably just the clumped product as a separate subsample. This prevents dilution of the contaminated product with uncontaminated product. Collect a separate subsample to provide a 702(b) portion (See IOM 4.3.7.4.1).

In addition, you need to collect product controls, in duplicate, to provide for the 702(b) portion. These subsamples should be collected from beneath unstained portions of the container. Collect control samples from 3 different containers.

Identify the 702b subsamples, as such on subsample identification (See IOM 4.5.2.1.) Note on the subsample itself and on your C/R which subsamples are the 702(b) portions.

Collect a portion of unstained container as a separate subsample for a control. As a general guide, collect the controls from the opposite side of the bag or make the cutting large enough to separate the control area and the stain. Separate the controls from the stains and submit in separate containers. Collect at least 3 container controls for each sample. If the lot consists of different containers or bags of different manufacturers, collect controls to represent each type or manufacturer of the containers.

4.3.7.4.4.3 - Summary of Sample for Bird Evidence

The complete official sample will consist of:

1. Subsamples of stained bagging, or portions of the containers.

2. Subsamples of unstained bagging, or portions of the containers for controls (minimum three required).

3. Subsamples of small portions of the product from directly beneath the stained areas. Do not dilute the contaminated product beneath the stain with the non-contaminated product.

4. Subsamples of small portions of product to serve as 702(b) portions.

5. Subsamples of uncontaminated product from beneath the unstained bagging, or other container. These serve as controls, and should be collected in duplicate to provide 702(b) portions. Collect control samples from 3 different containers.

   Submit each portion of bagging or container portion, pellets, material from beneath sampled area, control, etc., in separate vial or subsample container.

6. Product labeling.

7. Interstate documentation.

4.3.7.4.5 - Chemical Contamination

Collect samples from lots suspected of dry chemical contamination in much the same manner as described for rodent urine. After collecting a sample of the contents from immediately beneath the suspected area, collect residues from the surface of the bag or container. In the case of infiltration of loosely woven bags, shake or tumble the bag over a large sheet of clean paper to collect the siftings as a sample.

4.3.7.4.6 - Mold Contamination

The USDA/FGIS has approved a number of commercial screening tests for detecting aflatoxin contaminated corn. However, these tests usually require a chemical extraction process and are therefore not amenable to FDA field examination procedures.

The blacklight test (also referred to as the bright greenish-yellow Fluorescence (BGYF) test) is a presumptive test used to screen and identify corn lots that should be tested further for aflatoxins. The test is based on BGYF observed under long wave (366 nm) ultraviolet (UV) light produced by the molds Aspergillus parasiticus and A. flavus on "living" corn (i.e. corn that has been stored less than 3 months). The growth of these fungi may result in aflatoxin production. Aflatoxins per se do not produce BGYF under long wave UV light. It is thought the BGYF is produced by the reaction of kojic acid formed by the fungi and a peroxidase enzyme from living corn. Corn that has been in storage for a lengthy period of time (3 months or more) may give false positive BGYF. Therefore, determine how long the corn being sampled has been in storage. If it has been in storage over three months, do not use the following field screening procedure.

Essential steps for this blacklight procedure are:

1. A 10 lb. sample representative of the corn lot must be obtained by probing, or by continuously sampling a grain stream.

2. Examine using a 366 nm UV light (portable black-lights meet this criteria).

3. Wear goggles or use a viewer that screens out UV light. Shine the light on the corn sample which has been spread in a single layer on a flat surface in a darkened room.

4. Use a 2 lb. Portion, and carefully observe the entire corn surface one kernel at a time. Examine the entire sample using this procedure.

5. Count all BGYF glowers (kernels or particles that "glow" bright greenish-yellow). Compare the BGYF color with a fluorescent standard, if one is available. Remember normal corn, if it fluoresces, will fluoresce a bluish white.

6. If four (4) or more BGYF particles are detected in the 10 lb screening sample, collect a sample for laboratory analysis.

4.3.7.5 - Abnormal Containers

See IOM SAMPLE SCHEDULE CHART 2 - LACF for listing can defects.

4.3.7.6 - In-Line Samples

Mold Samples - During inspections of manufacturers such as canneries, bottling plants, milling operations, etc., it may be necessary to collect scrapings or swabs of slime or other material to verify the presence of mold. The sample should represent the conditions observed at the time of collection and consist of sufficient material to confirm and identify mold growth on the equipment. If possible, take photographs and obtain scrapings or bits of suspect material. Describe the area scraped or swabbed, e.g., material was scraped or swabbed from a 2" x 12" area.

Suspected filth, collected from ceilings, walls, and equipment, for mold examination must be kept moist by placing it in a container with a small amount of a 3% formalin solution. Large amounts of slime may be placed in a wide mouth glass jar with either a 1% formaldehyde solution or a 3% formalin. *Note:* Formalin is normally sold as a standard stock solution of 37%. To obtain the required 3-4% formalin solution, mix 5 ml of the 37% stock solution with 95 ml of distilled water. This will furnish the solution necessary to fix the mold.

Although formaldehyde or formalin are the preservatives of choice you may preserve the subs in either a 50% alcohol solution or in acetic acid (vinegar).

The above instructions apply to the collection of raw material, in-line and finished product samples for mold. However, in-line and finished product subs such as doughs, etc., which may be harmed by the formaldehyde, may be frozen. Check with your laboratory for its recommendation regarding preserving mold samples.

Bacteriological Samples - During inspections of firms producing products susceptible to microbial contamination (e.g., frozen precooked; ready to eat seafood, creme filled goods, breaded items, egg rolls, prepared salads, etc.), proof of adulteration, with fecal organisms, or elevated levels of non-pathogenic microorganisms, must be established. Sampling of raw materials, in-line and finished product is warranted. Follow instructions under IOM 4.3.7.7 - Products Susceptible to Contamination with Pathogenic Microorganisms, Sampling During Inspection.

4.3.7.7 - Products Susceptible to Contamination with Pathogenic Microorganisms

A top priority of the agency and CFSAN is to decrease foodborne illness caused by microbial contamination. With the rise of foodborne outbreaks detailed guidance was developed for sample collections and inspections dealing with microbial contamination.

Note: *This guidance is intended to augment guidance found in the Compliance Programs listed below. Instructions in current compliance programs and ongoing assignments supersede this guidance. Before conducting inspections under these programs, investigator/analyst teams should be thoroughly familiar with the guidance provided in the appropriate Compliance Program.*

For the following Compliance Programs collect samples for microbiological analyses only if:

1. Directed to do so in the current compliance program or ongoing assignments.

2. The firm has a previous history of microbiological contamination (e.g., follow up to illness or injury complaint, recalled/seized product, previous inspectional history, etc.) or

3. Sampling is conducted 'for cause' during an inspection (e.g., inspectional observations warrants collection for microbiological analyses):
    - Domestic and Imported Cheese and Cheese Products (7303.037)
    - Domestic Food Safety (7303.803)
    - Domestic Acidified and Low-Acid Canned Foods (7303.803A)
    - Domestic Fish and Fishery Products (7303.842) and
    - Juice HACCP Inspection Program (7303.847). Except as directed by the compliance program, you should not conduct any in-line, environmental, or finished product sampling, for microbiological concerns, during the inspection. Instead, fully document the lack of HACCP control(s) without physical sampling. If in the investigator's judgment the firm's HACCP plan is extremely inadequate and therefore sampling is warranted, contact CFSAN/OC/Division of Enforcement/Domestic Branch HFS-607 to determine what in-line sampling will be performed and the type of regulatory action that may be warranted for the situation at hand.

During inspections of these types of firms, or where inspectional observations indicate there may be a microbial contamination problem, whenever possible an investigator/ microbiologist team approach should be used.

A bacteriological inspection requires a thorough understanding of critical factors associated with the production of the specific product being inspected. To prove the establishment is being operated in an insanitary manner it is necessary to show the manufacturing operation or conditions at the facility are likely to, or have contributed, to the bacterial load of the product. When feasible, inspections should cover equipment condition before a day's production begins, and the clean-up at the end of the day's production.

For all inspections at firms meeting the criteria previously referenced, environmental swabs, in-line and finished product samples must be collected to document possible or actual routes of contamination of the finished product. Other environmental swabs (e.g., floor drains, walls, etc.) will be collected based upon the investigator's observations of extensive insanitary conditions.

4.3.7.7.1 - In-Line Sampling

In-Line Sampling During Inspection:

Sampling Areas (this is not a comprehensive listing of areas to collect in-line samples, since each firm will be different, depending on processing/packaging techniques and the finished product produced).

Each in-line subsample will consist of approximately 114 g (4 oz), in duplicate (702b portion), if that amount is available (Also see IOM 4.3.3.2 - 702(b) Requirement). All in-line samples must be collected aseptically.

"Raw" ingredients used in the manufacturing of finished foods (including those conveyed by bulk tankers) should be considered for sampling to determine the effect of subsequent processing on bacterial content. Of particular concern are raw materials, which can support microbial growth, are not normally cooked or prepared in a manner lethal to pathogenic microorganisms (such as dairy, soy, corn or sugar syrup based products), and adequate controls to ensure the safety of the finished product are not in effect. Since the major portion of some finished food products are not homogeneously contaminated, it may be necessary to collect multiple subsamples of the raw material(s) to establish a reliable microbial base line.

Obtain sequential subsamples with the view of bracketing each step of the processing operation, in particular those steps suspected as routes of product contamination. A series of in-line samples should be collected during the first part of a shift, and a duplicate series during the latter part.

If products or components are heated (e.g., blanched, boiled, etc.) take subsamples immediately before and immediately after heating, before possible insanitary equipment and processing delays contribute to bacterial increases. Particular attention should be given to determine routes of cross-contamination from the raw product to the "heated" product, especially if this heating step is critical to the destruction of pathogenic organisms.

If a product is capable of supporting microbial growth and is not being handled expeditiously, sample before and after this particular processing step.

Take time and temperature measurements of cooking, freezing and cooling procedures. Sample when appropriate to demonstrate possible microbial growth. Large masses of ingredients may cool or warm slowly enough to permit microbial growth.

Improperly cleaned equipment may contaminate the product with bacteria. This may result in either a uniform or a spotty increase in bacterial numbers. If possible, scrapings of questionable material should be in sufficient quantity to be easily weighed and quantitatively diluted, if collected for analysis.

4.3.7.7.2 - Environmental Sampling

"Environmental" swab sampling does not give quantitative results. Because a swab takes a very small sample, microorganisms of significance are often missed. It is important to keep in mind a negative result on a swab will often negate an inspectional observation unless the observation is fully documented. A positive finding will give more support to a fully documented observation.

Environmental swabs from food contact surfaces are to be collected initially (See IOM 4.3.7.6). Other environmental swabs (e.g., floor drains, walls, etc.) will be collected based upon the investigator's observations of extensive insanitary conditions.

Document the possible link between the source of an environmental sample and contamination of the food product. For example, if a swab was taken from:

A floor drain - Did cleaning procedures provide "back splash" to the food contact surfaces or product? Were employees observed walking through the area of the floor drain and back to the processing area (how many and when)? Was product dropped on the floor and placed back on the processing line (how many times and when)?

A wall - Did insects (e.g., flies and number) land on the wall and have subsequent contact on the food contact surface or product (how many and when)?

The ceiling area - Is condensate, flaking paint, etc., located over the processing area? Did you observe the condensate dripping on the food surfaces of the processing equipment and/or product?

4.3.7.7.3 - Finished Product Sampling

Collect finished product from production on the day of the inspection and from the previous day's run. Sampling multiple lots should be considered depending on the type of product and process used. The subsamples should consist of ten (10) retail size containers at least 114g (4 oz) each, in duplicate (702b portion).

If the finished product is also to be analyzed for Salmonella, the number of finished product subs should be 15, 30 or 60, depending upon product classification. See Salmonella Sampling Plan, Schedule Chart 1.

See IOM 5.4.7.2 for inspectional guidance for firms producing products susceptible to contamination with pathogenic/non-pathogenic microorganisms.

4.3.7.8 - Samples for Viral Analysis

Sample instructions will be issued by the appropriate Center on a case by case basis.

4.3.8 - Economic Violations

4.3.8.1 - Net Weight

Field weighing for net weight is primarily to determine the likelihood of short weight units. The laboratory will confirm both tare and net weights.

Use either a Gurley, Troemner, or equivalent balance. Check the accuracy of the balance before and after use. If this equipment is not available, or the units exceed their capacities, use commercial scales. If possible, have the commercial scales checked in your presence by the local Sealer of Weights and Measures. If this is not possible, report the name, type of scale, style and capacity, minimum graduations, apparent sensitivity, and date of last sealing and by whom.

4.3.8.1.1 - Tare Determination

Whenever possible, determine a minimum of six tares selected at random. If empty containers are readily available, or if tares vary widely (e.g.; glass jars), determine at least 12 tares.

4.3.8.1.2 - Field Examination

Weigh 48 units, if that number is available, selected at random from the square root of the number of cases in the lot with a minimum of 6 and a maximum of 12. Where units are selected from the production line, do so in representative manner. Report the code weighed and if short weight, the quantity in the code. Unless otherwise instructed, do not weigh leaking containers. Identify each unit with the corresponding sub number on the Field Weight Sheet (FDA 485).

Submit the units indicated by the asterisks on the FDA 485 plus twelve additional weighed units for reserve if the average net is below that declared on the label.

4.3.8.1.3 - Field Weight Sheet

Record weights on Form FDA 485, Field Weight Sheet. See IOM Exhibit 4-6. Submit Field Weight Sheet with the printed FACTS Collection Record.

Individual Captions:

Block 1 Date - Enter the date weighed.

Block 2 Sample No.- Enter the sample number of the C/R.

Bloch 3 Product - Enter the specific name of the product, i.e., macaroni in cellophane, print butter in aluminum wrappers, olive oil in glass, etc. Quote significant portions of the label including the declared net weight.

Block 4 Type of Balance - Enter the type of balance used i.e., Gurley, Troemner, etc. If balance used is not FDA equipment, give style, capacity, minimum graduations, etc.

Block 5 Responsible Firm and Address - Enter the name and address of the firm most likely responsible for the short weight violation.

Block 6 Address Where Weighed - Enter the name and address or location where weighed.

Block 7 Warehouse - Enter the type of warehouse where product is stored, i.e., cold storage, truck dock, production line, etc. Enter the temperature and estimate the humidity where possible.

Block 8 No. Of - Enter the number of cases, and number and size of units per case in the lot. Enter the number of cases from which subs were weighed and the number of subs weighed from each case. If the units are collected from a production line, estimate the number of units produced of the code weighed.

Block 9 Gross Weight - Arbitrarily assign and record the shipping case number from which each sub was weighed. Number each unit submitted to correspond with the sub number on the Field Weight Sheet. Record weights to second decimal place.

Block 10 Preliminary Tare - Determine and record tare weights as provided in IOM 4.3.8.1.1. Obtain the preliminary average tare by totaling preliminary tares and dividing by the number of tares weighed.

Block 11 Weighing Results - Determine the average gross weight by totaling gross weights and dividing by the number weighed; enter preliminary average tare from caption 10 in block 11b; determine average net weight by subtracting block 11b from 11a; enter the declared net weight as stated on the package weighed; determine the shortage by subtracting block 11c from 11d.

Block 12 Preliminary % Short - Enter the preliminary percent short, which is determined by dividing e by d.

Block 13 Remarks - Record any observations on the condition of the lot or storage facilities which might affect net weights, (faulty machine sealing of packages, extreme high temperature, extended length of storage, etc.)

Block 14 District - Enter the name of the collecting district.

Block 15 Employee Signature

Block 16 Employee Title

4.3.8.2 - Volume Determination

Field determination of volume is a screening procedure to determine the likelihood of short volume units in the lot. The laboratory will confirm both tare and net volume.

4.3.8.2.1 - Free Flowing Liquids

The approximate volume of small containers of free flowing liquids may be obtained by direct measurement. Standardized graduated cylinders calibrated to "contain" a given volume can be obtained from the laboratory. Use the smallest graduate that will hold the volume to be measured. Under no circumstances use a graduate to measure a volume less than 25% of the maximum capacity of the graduate. Proceed as follows:

1. Select 8 units at random; one from each of 8 cases or otherwise representative of the lot.

2. Empty contents into calibrated graduate holding the container in a nearly vertical position, but tipping so that the bottom of the container will drain. Allow to drain one minute after stream breaks into drops. Obtain an anti-foaming agent from the laboratory if beer or other product likely to foam are measured.

3. Hold the graduate vertically with the surface of the liquid level with the eye. Place a shade of some dark material immediately below the meniscus and read volume from the lowest point of the meniscus. A convenient device for this purpose is a collar-shaped section of thick black rubber tubing cut open at one side and of such size as to clasp the graduate firmly.

4. If no units containing less than declared volume are found, no further determinations are required.

5. If one or more units containing less than declared volume are found, measure 4 additional units selected as above.

6. If the total of twelve determinations contains only one short volume unit, be guided by the significance of the average shortage as related to the individual program guideline.

7. If the total of twelve determinations contains more than one short volume unit, an Official Sample of 48 units should be collected regardless of the average shortage figure.

4.3.8.2.2 - Viscous Liquids

Direct measurement of viscous liquids or large containers is not practical. Field weigh 48 units as specified in IOM 4.3.8.1.3.

4.3.8.3 - Labeling

See the document "Guide to Nutritional Labeling and Education Act (NLEA) Requirements" for guidance. See Office Nutrition, Labeling, and Dietary Supplements (ONLDS) website (http://www.cfsan.fda.gov/~dms/lab-hlth.html) for the most up-to-date information regarding claims in labeling.

Also, see CPGM 7321.005 to determine enforcement priorities for food labeling violations, including those related to the Food Allergen Labeling and

Consumer Protection Act (FALCPA) http://www.cfsan.fda.gov/~dms/alrgact.html.

4.3.9 - Organoleptic Examinations

Examination of many products may be conducted on the spot without fixed laboratory equipment. These examinations vary from simple visual observations for gross filth, such as rodent pellets in wheat, to the detection of odors of decomposition in seafood. Organoleptic examinations for regulatory purposes shall be made only by those individuals qualified by training or experience to conduct such examinations.

If it is necessary to collect physical subsamples for organoleptic examination and they are collected from bulk, the subs must be packed in glass jars to prevent the product from picking up foreign odors.

Review your Compliance Program Guidance Manual and IOM 4.3.7.1 and IOM 6.3.1 for field examination techniques which may be applicable to specific products or industry.

4.3.9.1 - Whole-Bag Screening

When making filth examination by screening shelled peanuts, dried bean, peas and similar products, packed in large containers (i.e., 50-125 lb. bags) use the portable folding whole-bag screens available in your district.

Conduct the examination in a well lighted area. Set up screen and adjust height to permit opening the bags directly onto the high side of the screen. Place another bag or container on the screen's low side to catch the screened product.

Place a sheet of clean butcher or similar paper in screen body to catch screenings and insert screen wire over paper.

Open stitches of bag being examined to permit approximately ten to twenty pound portions to enter onto high side of screen. Gradually work the product across the sieve to the low side and into the receiving container. Do not push large quantities rapidly across screen because insects, eggs, stones, excreta pellets, etc., will be carried along with the product and will not sift through the sieve openings.

Examine the screening from each bag and subjectively report live or dead insects, rodent excreta pellets, or other obvious filth. Submit screenings as separate subs if actionable.

4.4 - Documentation & CR

4.4.1 - Authority

Section 703 of the FD&C Act [21 U.S.C. 373] describes FDA's authority to access and copy records of interstate shipment.

4.4.2 - Objective

For FDA to initiate formal legal action, interstate jurisdiction must be established. Most often, this is done by documenting interstate movement of a product by copying records ("getting the records") of a shipment represented by an Official Sample. However, on occasion, jurisdiction can be fixed on a limited list of articles, e.g., counterfeit drugs, medical devices, oleomargarine, through other means.

4.4.3 - Policy

Fully document every Official Sample at the time of collection unless instructed otherwise by the program, the assignment or your supervisor. Current agency policy does not require the collection of records of interstate movement for the issuance of a Warning Letter. Also, the FDA Modernization Act expanded the (rebuttable) presumption of interstate commerce for medical devices to all commodities regulated by FDA. Nevertheless, in any situations where you think a formal legal action may occur, make sure you collect copies of interstate records.

The decision to collect copies of records of interstate commerce in situations involving warning letters may be further covered by District policies or situations. As an example, in cases where the records are readily available and the site is located a long distance from an FDA office, it may be better to collect copies of the records at the time the sample is collected. This will ensure FDA has the records in the event a different action is chosen and you will have saved resources in their collection.

4.4.3.1 - Collection Records

Sample Collections are recorded in the Field Accomplishments and Compliance Tracking System (FACTS). Individuals who may be assigned to collect samples should routinely obtain in advance, a supply of FACTS sample numbers, to be used by the collector to identify samples in the field, prior to accessing FACTS to prepare a sample collection record.

4.4.4 - Responsibility

Document samples in accordance with procedures in this Subchapter being certain the copies of records obtained cover the product sampled.

Do not remove the dealer's only copy of records. Whenever possible, photocopy or mechanically copy records, if duplicates are not available. Reproductions should be reviewed to ensure all relevant information is readable.

It is possible to enhance the clarity of photocopies from poor originals (e.g., second or third carbon copies, copies in blue ink, etc.) by overlaying the "original" document with one or two clear yellow plastic sheets. These clear yellow plastic sheets are available at most stationary stores.

If the above procedure does not enhance the copied document, pen and ink additions should be made. Records copied on FDA forms must be accurate and legible.

If you are documenting a shipper violation at a dealer, it is your responsibility to show the storage conditions did not contribute to the violation. Obtain an affidavit describing handling of the goods after receipt, and any other information which supports the violation.

In cases where the product does not move Interstate but is formulated from I.S. raw materials, government jurisdiction may be established by documenting the I.S. nature of the major raw materials. This is done by linking copies of records for the I.S. raw material with the production of the final product, by affidavit from a knowledgeable and responsible firm official. See IOM Exhibit 4-7.

Note: In the case of imported products which have been released to commerce, documentation of the sample should also include the port of entry and the importer of record to facilitate investigation by the home district if necessary.

4.4.5 - Sample Records Identification

Identify copies of all records obtained and attached to the collection report (except FDA forms) with the sample number (including the prefix if appropriate), collection date, and collector's handwritten name or initials. See IOM 4.5.2.5. If a document is more than one page in length, it must be numbered or attached in a manner that will always allow further reviewers to determine if any pages are missing.

If the firm maintains their records on film or electronically, see IOM 5.3.8.3.1 and 5.3.8.3.2.

4.4.6 - Evidence Required

When documenting violative situations, consider whether you have established FDA's jurisdiction, documented interstate commerce, shown a violation, and determined responsibility for the violation. The contemplated legal action determines the extent of documentation. A preponderance of evidence is required to prevail in a civil action, such as a contested seizure, as opposed to a criminal prosecution, which requires evidence establishing guilt beyond a reasonable doubt.

4.4.6.1 - Seizure

For a seizure action, FDA must establish jurisdiction over the product, show its interstate movement and document a violation.

Obtain copies of any document proving the article was introduced into or in interstate commerce, or held for sale after shipment in interstate commerce. Collect copies of the best records available, without extensive search or travel. See section 304(a)(1) of the FD&C Act [21 U.S.C. 334].

4.4.6.2 - Injunction or Criminal Prosecution

The proof required depends on the violation of Section 301 of the FD&C Act [21 U.S.C. 331].

4.4.6.2.1 - Introduction into I.S.

Proof is required showing introduction into interstate commerce on or about a certain day by a specific person of a specific consignment of the article. In addition, delivery for introduction into I.S. requires proof the seller had knowledge the purchaser intended to introduce the article into interstate commerce. See Section 301(a) or (d) of the FD&C Act [21 U.S.C. 331 (a) or (d)].

4.4.6.2.2 - Adulteration or Misbranding in Interstate Commerce

Proof is required showing that a specific consignment was in interstate commerce and was rendered violative by a specific person on or about a certain date while therein. See Section 301(b) of the FD&C Act [21 U.S.C. 331 (b)].

4.4.6.2.3 - Receipt in I.S.

Proof is required showing receipt of a violative consignment in interstate commerce on or about a certain date, along with evidence to show specific delivery thereafter by a specific person. It is essential to show the violative condition of the shipment was known to the consignee before the delivery or proffered delivery. Whether it was sold or given away is immaterial. See Section 301(c) of the FD&C Act [21 U.S.C. 331 (c)].

4.4.6.2.4 - Manufacture within a Territory

Proof is required of manufacture within any territory by a specific person on or about a certain date. See Section 301(g) of the FD&C Act [21 U.S.C. 331 (g)].

4.4.6.2.5 - False Guaranty

Proof of the giving on or about a certain date of a specific guaranty and proof of its falsity; usually a specific sale (and delivery) on or about a definite date to the holder of the guaranty. Interstate commerce is not required, except evidence the consignee normally engages in some interstate business. See Section 301(h) of the FD&C Act [21 U.S.C. 331(h)] and 21 CFR 7.13, 201.150 and 701.9.

4.4.6.2.6 - Dealer Violation

Proof of interstate origin of the article, and proof of a specific manipulation which adulterates or misbrands the article, on or about a certain date by a specific person. See FD&C Act Section 301(k) [21 U.S.C. 331 (k)].

4.4.6.3 - Complaint or Injury Samples

Generally samples collected from complainants during investigation of injuries or foodborne out-breaks are investigational in nature and not documented. However, if the nature of the contamination or adulteration is such that regulatory action may be warranted, the interstate nature of the sample should be documented. Affidavits from the consumer, retailer, and wholesaler should be obtained.

At times even though you may not be able to obtain physical portions of the involved item, a Documentary Sample can be collected by photographing the container, contents, labels, codes, etc., and obtaining necessary affidavits and interstate records. See IOM 4.1.7 for sample criteria on complaint samples.

During investigations of alleged tampering incidents, complainants must be advised of the provisions of the Federal Anti-Tampering Act (FATA). A general discussion of the FATA, its provisions for investigation, filing of false reports, and tampering can be useful and informative to those individuals.

Prior to concluding your interview of the complainant, obtain a signed affidavit attesting to the circumstances of the complaint. See IOM 8.8.5.4.

4.4.7 - Documenting Interstate Shipments

The minimum set of records ordinarily submitted with a sample will consist of a copy of the invoice covering the sale of the lot to the dealer, the transportation record showing interstate commerce, and an affidavit signed by the dealer, which identifies both the lot sampled and the applicable records. See IOM 4.3.3 and 4.4.5.

4.4.7.1 - Sales Records

An invoice does not establish interstate commerce and thus federal jurisdiction. It does not prove actual movement. However, it may provide information as to the value of the goods, carrier, date of shipment, etc. and bear a Food and Drug type guarantee. Collect copies of the invoice to show the owner's intent to sell the product and tie other records to the sample. If the invoice covers numerous items, copy entries covering items sampled and indicate omissions by asterisks. Copy the invoice on the FDA 1662. See IOM Exhibit 4-8. If the invoice bears a Food and Drug guarantee, copy the guarantee on the back of the FDA 1662. Other records which may be substituted in the absence of an invoice are copies of purchase orders, receiving records, canceled checks, correspondence, etc.

Invoices covering in-transit shipments usually are not available. Document any available transportation record that establishes the lot to be in interstate commerce. Be sure to name the shipper and consignee if known. Where positive identification of a shipment cannot be made by personal observation, obtain a statement from the carrier's agent identifying the shipment sampled as having been delivered by the consignor on a certain day for delivery to the consignee. Include in this statement reference to the particular transportation record covering the shipment. The transportation record will generally be available after the shipment is delivered.

Where the sample is taken from a vehicle or dock as the vehicle is loaded, and there are no unusual circumstances which must be explained in a regular affidavit, use the FDA 1664b, Affidavit (In-Transit Sampling).

See IOM Exhibit 4-3.

4.4.7.2 - Transportation Records for Common Carrier Shipments

Section 703 of the FD&C Act [21 USC 373] provides for mandatory access to and copying of all records showing interstate movement of commodities subject to the Act. This is provided the request is in writing, and the records are in the possession of common carriers, or persons receiving or holding such commodities.

Section 704(a) of the FD&C Act [21 USC 374(a)] provides mandatory access, upon presenting your credentials and issuing a written notice of inspection, to documents covering the interstate movement of, nonprescription drugs for human use, prescription drugs and restricted devices. The authority applies to inspection of any factory, warehouse, establishment, or consulting laboratory in which prescription drugs, nonprescription drugs for human use, or restricted devices are manufactured, processed, packed or held.

Note: *At times, you may have only the name of the carrier (trucking company), with no address or phone number. If you are unable to locate the trucking company, contact the local office of the Office of Motor Carrier Safety, Federal Highway Administration, Department of Transportation. If you furnish this office the name of the trucking company, they will be able to provide the address and phone number. The DIB has the phone number of the local offices of the OMCS as part of a MOU between DOT and FDA.*

4.4.7.2.1 - Refusal to Permit Access to Records in Possession of Common Carriers

Refusal to permit access to and copying of all records showing interstate movement of articles subject to FDA jurisdiction is unlawful provided the request for such permission is issued in writing. You cannot state that the law requires the records be furnished to FDA unless you also explain it is required only after a written request is issued. If refused, after providing a written request, politely explain the law requires the records to be furnished. You are more likely to get the records through courteous persuasion and tact than through stressing the force of law.

4.4.7.2.2 - Written Request for Records

If a carrier, consignee, or any other person refuses to supply I.S. records, and it is apparent he will not do so without a written request, report the facts to your supervisor. Do not routinely issue a written request for I.S. records since evidence so obtained may not be used in the criminal prosecution of the person from whom obtained.

If the request is being made of a carrier who has no responsibility for the violation, issue a written request only after approval by District Management. When authorized by your supervisor to issue a written request, prepare a statement, using the following guidance, or as otherwise directed by your supervisor:

"Pursuant to Section 703 of the Federal Food, Drug, and Cosmetic Act (21 U.S.C. 373) permission is hereby requested for access to and copying of all records showing quantity, shipper, and consignee, showing movement in interstate commerce and/ or the holding after interstate movement of___________."

Clearly identify the specific lots which are the subject of the request, the firm and the individual to whom the request is given.

4.4.7.2.3 - Bill of Lading

The shipper who delivers the goods to the carrier for shipment, prepares The Bill of Lading. It is an order for the carrier to move the goods. When the carrier's agent signs the Bill of Lading he acknowledges receipt for the shipment. The carrier's office in city of origin of shipment maintains a copy of the Bill of Lading. Information normally included is the name and address of shipper, name and address of consignee, date of shipment, name of carrier, vehicle number, and a description of the goods. Copy Bill of Lading on Section II of the FDA 1662. See IOM Exhibit 4-8.

4.4.7.2.4 - Freight Bill

This record is prepared by the transportation company for the purpose of collecting freight charges. It includes the same information found on the Bill of Lading, plus additional data about the carrier's handling of the shipment and cost involved. Railroads prepare Freight Bills at their destination offices, where copies can be made. Steamship and airlines combine the Bill of Lading and Freight Bill into one form. Copies are filed at both origin and destination offices of these carriers. Truck lines prepare Freight Bills at the origin office and both origin and destination offices should have copies. The dealer should have a Freight Bill if he received the goods directly in interstate commerce.

Copy Freight Bills on Section II of the FDA 1662. Enter the type of shipping record in block 21. Section I and II may be executed together on one sheet. If only one section is used, leave the other section blank, and submit the entire page.

4.4.7.2.5 - Waybill

The transportation company uses the Waybill in its own operations, and it accompanies the shipment during transit. Copies are not given to the shipper or consignee, but can be obtained from the carrier. Other transportation records are generally more readily available than Waybills. Air Freight Waybill numbers are designed so that the originating line and point of origin are encoded in the Waybill number itself. Each airline has a numerical code description, indicated by the first two digits of the number. The three letters, which next follow indicate the point of origin. For example, Waybill No. 01LGA, designates American Airlines (01) as the carrier, and La Guardia Field (LGA) as the point of origin. Most airline offices have a copy of "Official Air Freight Transmittal Manual", which lists the codes. Other express shipping companies, such as Federal Express, and United Parcel Service have their own codes.

4.4.7.3 - Mail or Parcel Service Shipments.

Always attempt to collect the original wrappings showing cancellation of origin office and address sticker. Record the facts obtained from the dealer on the FDA 463, Affidavit (Parcel Post/Service). Before the individual signs the statement he should be asked to affirm the affidavit is true and accurate. A statement to that effect can also be added at the conclusion of the affidavit. See IOM Exhibit 4-9.

Note: Shipments made by "Express Mail" do have a shipping record maintained. These are:

1. Express Mail - Form A - used for Post Office to Post Office service.
2. Express Mail - Form B - used for Post Office to Addressee service.

3. Express Mail - Form C - used for Airport to Airport service.

Obtain copies of the Postal Service record from the consignee, if possible, or from the Post Office to document shipments using Express Mail Service.

4.4.7.4 - Shipment by Privately-Owned Conveyance

Obtain on the FDA 463a, Affidavit, a dealer's statement setting forth the facts, including the date and manner of receipt. The affidavit by the dealer may not be evidence, since the dealer lacks personal knowledge of the point of origin. Ascertain the name and home address of the driver of the conveyance, vehicle license number, the name and address of the driver's employer or the owner of the conveyance and the driver's license number. Obtain an Affidavit, from the driver setting forth the facts of the shipment. See IOM Exhibit 4-10.

4.4.7.5 - In-Transit Sampling Affidavit

See IOM 4.1.4.3 and 4.3.4.3 for definition and sampling procedures. When obtaining samples from in-transit lots, if it is a straightforward uncomplicated sample requiring no unusual explanations, use the FDA 1664b, Affidavit (In-Transit Sampling). See IOM Exhibit 4-3. Otherwise, use the regular Affidavit, FDA 463a.

4.4.8 - Affidavits

Statements on various affidavit forms may be obtained from persons who have dealt somehow with the goods sampled, know material facts relating to the movement of the goods, and/or to events affecting their condition. Such facts, recorded in writing and signed by the person who can testify in court to those facts, can be used either to establish federal jurisdiction or fix the responsibility for a violation. The statement may identify documents proving I.S. movement of goods sampled; it may name the person who could testify to the identity of the goods sampled, and it may certify the sample collected is from the lot of goods covered by the records.

4.4.8.1 - General Considerations for all Affidavits

You should have the affiant read the statement and make necessary corrections before signing the affidavit. Mistakes, corrected and initialed by the affiant are an indication he/she has read and understood the statement. A handwritten statement by the affiant, declaring he/she read and understood the statement is a valuable tool to counter the possibility the affiant might later claim ignorance of what was signed.

Before the individual signs the statement, ask him/her to affirm the affidavit is true and accurate. A statement to that effect can also be added at the conclusion of the affidavit. See IOM Exhibit 4-11.

You should only sign the affidavit AFTER the affiant has signed it. The wording above your signature is, "Subscribed and sworn to before me at ***" Subscribed, in this context means to attest by signing. Thus, your signature is attesting to the fact that the affiant has read and understood the statement and has confirmed that the statement is the truth. You MUST NOT sign an affidavit until after the affiant swears (affirms) to you the written statement he/she has signed is true. If you provide a copy of the affidavit to the affiant, you should keep the original affidavit since the original is an official FDA document.

4.4.8.2 - Refusal to Sign the Affidavit

Prepare the statement as described above even if it is apparent the affiant will refuse to sign the affidavit. Have the affiant read the affidavit. If they decline, read it to them. Request the affiant correct and initial any errors in his/her own handwriting. Ask the affiant if the statement is true and correct. Ask him/her to write at the bottom of the statement "I have read this statement and it is true, but I am not signing it because..." in his/her own handwriting.

If the affiant still does not sign the affidavit, you should write a statement noting the refusal situation. Write this near the bottom and within the body of the affidavit. Include the actual situation, such as, you recorded the above facts as the affiant revealed them, the affiant read or refused to read the statement and avowed the statement to be true, and the affiant's reason for refusing to sign (e.g., "upon advice of corporate counsel", "per corporate policy", etc.). Sign and date this statement in the body of the document; only sign in the signature block if the affiant signs the affidavit.

4.4.8.3 - Confidential Informants

You should take special precautions when obtaining an affidavit from a confidential informant. The affiant may be reluctant to sign a statement, which reveals his or her identity. See IOM 5.2.9 for guidance on interviewing confidential informants.

4.4.8.4 - Affidavit (Dealer/Warehouseman)

The Affidavit (Dealer/Warehouseman), FDA 1664, is used to document the dealer or warehouseman identification of the lot and related records. See IOM Exhibit 4-12.

Fill in all blanks on the form as applicable. There are sufficient blanks for listing up to three invoices and up to three shipping records covering the lot in question. Any unused blanks should be lined out, and strike out the words or letters in parentheses which are not applicable.

Be certain the dealer knows what he is signing. Before the individual signs the statement, he/she should be asked to affirm the affidavit is true and accurate.

You should only sign the affidavit AFTER the affiant has signed it. The wording above your signature is, "Subscribed and sworn to before me at ***" Subscribed, in this context means to attest by signing. Thus, your signature is attesting to the fact the affiant has read and understood the statement and has confirmed that the statement is the truth. You MUST NOT sign an affidavit until after the affiant swears (affirms) to you the written statement he/she has signed is true. Also see IOM 4.4.8.5 for conditions not amenable to use of the FDA 1664.

4.4.8.5 - Affidavit (FDA 463a)

Unusual sampling situations may present circumstances that do not lend themselves to presentation on the FDA 1664 or 1664b. In these situations, record the facts on an FDA 463a, Affidavit.

There is no prescribed format for composing the statement. However, you should positively identify the affiant by name, title, and address at the beginning of the statement and show why he/she is qualified to make the statement. The facts should be arranged in an order roughly paralleling that of the FDA 1664. The most manageable narrative describes the events and circumstances chronologically. Whatever format is used, the recorded facts must be intelligible to the reader unfamiliar with the transaction. See IOM Exhibit 4-7, 4-11, and 4-13.

Ascertain all the facts and record those which are material, relevant, and to which the affiant can affirm.

Narrate the facts in the words of the affiant, using the first person singular. Do not use stilted terms such as, "that" as in the expression "that I am the president of..." If the statement is long and complex, break it down into logical paragraphs.

Have the affiant read the statement and make necessary corrections before signing the affidavit. Mistakes that have been corrected and initialed affiant are an indication he/she has read and understood the statement. A handwritten statement by the affiant declaring he/she read and understood the statement is a tool to counter the possibility the affiant might later claim ignorance of what was signed.

Before the individual signs the statement, he/she should be asked to affirm the affidavit is true and accurate. A statement to that effect can also be added at the conclusion of the affidavit. Only sign in the signature block if the affiant signs the affidavit. See IOM Exhibit 4-11.

You should only sign the affidavit AFTER the affiant has signed it. The wording above your signature is, "Sub-scribed and sworn to before me at ***" Subscribed, in this context means to attest by signing. Thus, your signature is attesting to the fact that the affiant has read and understood the statement and has confirmed that the statement is the truth. You MUST NOT sign an affidavit until after the affiant swears (affirms) to you the written statement he/she has signed is true. You and the affiant should sign all pages of a multi-page affidavit.

4.4.8.6 - Affidavit (Jobber)

Form FDA 1664a is used to document movement of goods from a jobber to a dealer. See IOM Exhibit 4-14. Complete all blanks as applicable. There are sufficient blanks to list up to three invoices and three shipping records. Line out any unused blanks and strike out all words and letters in parentheses, which are not applicable.

Be sure the jobber knows what he/she is signing. Before the individual signs, he/she should be asked to affirm the affidavit is true and accurate. A statement to that effect can also be added at the conclusion of the affidavit. Only sign in the signature block if the affiant signs the affidavit. See IOM Exhibit 4-11.

You should only sign the affidavit AFTER the affiant has signed it. The wording above your signature is, "Subscribed and sworn to before me at ***" Subscribed, in this context means to attest by signing. Thus, your signature is attesting to the fact that the affiant has read and understood the statement and has confirmed that the statement is the truth. You MUST NOT sign an affidavit until after the affiant swears (affirms) to you the written statement he/she has signed is true. The dealer may be provided a copy of an affidavit if he/she requests it and it has been signed.

See >IOM Exhibit 4-14.

4.4.9 - Labels and Labeling

No sample documentation is complete without copies of the label and labeling. No special effort is needed to obtain copies of the label when it is on the individual units collected. However, the goods may be accompanied by labeling which is not affixed to the product. In this case, you must obtain copies of all labeling. Although your sample assignment may not specifically request the collection of accompanying labeling, determine if such labeling exists, and if it is present, collect it.

Collect at least three copies of all labeling. When you are collecting labeling specifically to document labeling violations, the Compliance Program Guidance Manual may require the collection of additional copies so that various offices can review the labeling simultaneously (for example, CPGM 7321.005 requires the investigator collect 4 copies). Be sure to review the CPGM to ensure you collect enough original copies of labeling. Mount individual copies or sets of labeling so they can be reviewed by various individuals located in separate offices. Do not collect the actual labeling if only one copy is available. To do so may remove the offending literature and thus correct the misbranding or you may misbrand the product yourself, by removing legally mandated information. Photographs or other copies must be made in this case.

4.4.9.1 - Labels & Accompanying Labeling

These are defined as:

1. *Label* - A display of written, printed, or graphic matter upon the immediate container of an article.

2. *Labeling* - All labels and other written, printed, or graphic matter upon any article or any of its containers or wrappers, or accompanying such article. Labeling includes such material as circulars, booklets, placards, displays, window streamers, books, article reprints, etc., that supplement or explain a product and /or are part of an integrated distribution system for the product. If the labeling and the product are in functional proximity at a point of sale, provide diagrams or photographs of this relationship. If the labeling and the product are found at a manufacturer or distributor, document the role that the labeling will play in the distribution of the product (e.g. to whom will it be sent and when).

Dealer Identification - Request the dealer (Note: a manufacturer may be considered a dealer if the product being sampled is located at the manufacturer) identify collected copies of accompanying labeling with his initials and the date. This will identify these copies of labeling if they are introduced in court later. Prepare a dealer's affidavit on the FDA 463a, covering the relationship of the labeling to the goods. This affidavit should include the following information.

1. *Description of Labeling* - Describe briefly each piece of literature by name of identifiable quote, i.e., Leaflet, "Do You Have Tired Blood" or Window Streamer, "Amazing New Tranquilizer". State the quantity of such labeling on hand.

2. *Location of Labeling* - Report the location of each different piece of literature and how much of each is at that location.

3. *Method of Distribution* - Determine how the labeling is made available to the public. Describe how it is displayed such as: for voluntary pick-up; mailed to prospective customers; distributed without being displayed, etc.

4. *Source of Labeling* - Describe whether the labeling was sent to the dealer by the shipper of the goods or if the dealer prepared the labeling himself or if it originated from another source. It is important to document this point to fix responsibility in the event the agency wishes to pursue action against that individual. It is not necessary to determine or fix responsibility in order to seize the goods. Document the shipment of the labeling if a source other than the dealer supplied the labeling.

5. *Instructions to Dealer* - The manufacturer or shipper often provide sales promotion instructions to the dealer. Obtain copies of such instructions if available.

4.4.9.2 - Bulk Shipments

Do not remove the label from bulk containers such as drums, barrels, and large bags, if this results in misbranding the article. Remove and submit an identical label from an empty container if available. Photograph or trace the label if none other is available.

Note: Besides using tracing paper, it is possible to trace a label on a piece of plastic, similar to a document protector, using either a ball point pen or stylus. If it is difficult to read, filling in the tracing with a marker, may highlight the tracing.

4.4.9.3 - Unlabeled or Partially Labeled Lot

The regulations provide for controlled shipment in IS commerce of unlabeled goods. It is a violation to ship unlabeled goods unless:

1. The shipper operates the establishment where the article is to be processed, labeled or repacked, or

2. If the shipper is not the operator of the establishment, he must first obtain from the owner a written agreement signed by the operator. The agreement must contain the post office addresses of both parties and describe the specifications and the processing, labeling, or repacking procedures, in sufficient detail to insure that the article will not be

adulterated or misbranded within the meaning of the Act, upon completion of the processing, labeling or repacking.

Determine if there is a labeling agreement and obtain copies of pertinent correspondence. See 21 CFR 101.100, 201.150, and 701.9.

4.4.9.3.1 - Documentation

Collect both unlabeled and relabeled units or specimens of the label to be affixed. Collect specimens of any shipping case labels and any labeling which accompanied the original shipment.

Obtain evidence showing how the lot was labeled at the time of receipt; how the misbranding occurred, and who was responsible. Use photographs and diagrams if necessary to portray the present condition of the lot. If any of the lot has been resold, collect documentary evidence of the resale.

4.4.10 - Reporting Sample Collections

See IOM 1.1 English language requirement. For each sample collected prepare a FACTS Sample Collection Record. Remember the collection report is the basis for most administrative and regulatory actions. The data entered into specific fields of the report are intended to provide information for the compliance officer to prepare documents for legal proceedings. While there may be more than one right way to describe the specific circumstances you are documenting, it is important to keep in mind the subsequent readers of your collection report. See IOM Exhibits 4-1, 4-2, 4-15, and 4-16 for examples. Sample collection data may be entered either from an FDA office or from a remote location in the field using a laptop computer and modem. If change is needed to the data in the FACTS Firms table relating to the sample collection, e.g., the firm's name or address has changed; you (the collector) should notify your district's OEI coordinator, so the information can be updated in the FACTS firm table.

After collection data is entered into the FACTS system, you (the collector) must check the record for accuracy and completeness, send it to a supervisor for review, if appropriate, and then sign it electronically. The original data will be stored and permanently associated with this record. Any future changes to the FACTS database reference tables, such as the firm files, employee name, data codes, etc., will not alter the original data in the electronically-signed sample collection record.

Only you (the collector) have editing privileges for the signed original sample collection record. You may modify the original record but must electronically sign each revision. All modifications of the original record are permanently retained as part of the original record. A permanent electronic record trail is created, capturing and retaining every change to original and subsequent records. If retrieval of the sample collection data is needed, the original record and all changes to the original record can be retrieved.

4.4.10.1 - Flag

The following situations require an entry in the Sample Flags screen in FACTS See IOM Exhibit 4-15.

See the Other Codes Section of the Data Codes Manual for an explanation of the flags.

4.4.10.1.1 - 301(K) Sample

"301(k) Sample " - See IOM 4.1.4.4.

4.4.10.1.2 - Complaint Sample

Use this flag for any sample collected from a complainant during follow-up investigation.

4.4.10.1.3 - Dealer Voluntarily Holding

This flag alerts the reviewer the lot is being voluntarily held. Enter how long in the Flag Remarks field. This information will be important for the compliance officer to know when preparing a seizure or other regulatory action.

4.4.10.1.4 - Exhibit Sample

When sample is to be used exclusively for court exhibit without analysis.

4.4.10.1.5 - Factory Food Sample

Flag as "Factory Food Sample" when sample(s) of any item, used in the production of any food product, are taken during the EI. See IOM 4.1.7.

4.4.10.1.6 - Fumigated

Enter name of fumigant in Flag Remarks field.

4.4.10.1.7 - Inv. Samples of Filth Exhibits

Enter the product code of the filth exhibits (obtained from the Data Codes Manual) in the Product Code field of the FACTS Sample Collection Screen. Note the product code for exhibits consists of the Industry Code followed by "YY-99" or "Y--99" as below.

Example: Filth Exhibits of gnawings, pellets, wood splinters, etc.

In a food plant = 52YY-99

52 = Misc. food related items

Y = Exhibits

Y = Sub class - None

- = Dash

99 = Evidence exhibits n.e.c.

In a drug plant = 66Y--99

66 = Misc. drug related

Y = Exhibits

- = Dash

- = Dash

99 = Evidence exhibits n.e.c.

Other industries: Handled in same manner using applicable industry code from the Data Codes Manual.

4.4.10.1.8 - Pesticide Sample

After flagging a pesticide sample, the basis for sampling must be entered in the Flag Remarks field as either "Pesticide Compliance" or "Pesticide Surveillance". Additionally, the name of the county and state, or country where grown must be entered in the appropriate fields in the Collection Record.

Pesticide Episode - An "episode" is defined as a violative pesticide (or other chemical contaminant) finding and all samples collected in follow-up to that finding. All samples must be associated with one responsible firm (grower, pesticide applicator, etc.) and one specific time period (e.g. growing season). The following examples are provided for clarification of this definition:

1. Samples of cantaloupes from Mexico reveal violative residues. Any destination point samples or subsequent compliance samples from the same shipper or grower would along with the original sample be considered an episode.

2. Grower Jones has violative residues of chlorothalonil on collards for which there is no tolerance. Field samples, I.S. samples, and packing shed or warehouse samples of these collards would all be part of the same episode.

3. Grower Jones also has violative residues of omethoate on kohlrabi about two months later. This is a separate episode.

4. Along with the omethoate on kohlrabi, Grower Jones has violative residues of omethoate on beets. Normally this would be considered a separate episode from the previous episode. However, if information were available showing that both residues resulted from the same application of the pesticide or the residues were closely related in some other way, the beets might be considered as part of the kohlrabi episode.

5. Grower Smith has violative residues of disulfon and permethrin on kale. This would be considered as one episode because only one commodity is involved.

Note: *The detention without physical examination procedures provide for recommending detention based on a single violative pesticide finding. See RPM Chapter 9-6. Under these procedures we may anticipate that the number of compliance samples collected in follow-up to a violative finding may diminish appreciably and, in most cases, will be limited to occasional audit samples. These samples should also be linked to the sample number (episode number) of the original violative sample that prompted the automatic detention. This episode number will be indicated in the applicable*

Import Alert.

The Episode Number will be the sample number of the first violative sample collected in a series of samples and is used to identify the other related samples within an episode. The district must assure that the Episode Number is used within the district and any other districts which follow-up to the original violative sample. This number must appear in the Episode Number field of the FACTS CR.

4.4.10.1.9 - Reconditioned

When collected in connection with a reconditioning operation in accordance with a court order.

4.4.10.1.10 - Sampled in Transit

Use when the sample is collected from a carrier or while in transit. Indicate this flag in the Collection Remarks field. See IOM 4.1.4.3 and 4.3.4.

4.4.10.1.11 - Split Sample

Use this flag when a sample is divided between two or more laboratories.

4.4.10.1.12 - Survey Sample

Use this flag for any sample collected under a Compliance Program, which directs samples be collected as part of a survey, or if an assignment to collect the sample(s) indicates the sample(s) are "Survey" sample(s). Use this flag for any sample collected under the Drug Surveillance Program (CPGM 7356.008); enter the survey number in the flag remarks section.

4.4.10.1.13 - Under State Embargo

This flag alerts the compliance officer that the lot is being held under state embargo. Enter how long in the Flag Remarks field.

4.4.10.2 - Type Identification

When applicable, using the list of values, choose one of the following to complete the Sample Type field in FACTS. Identify any documents associated with the sample, and the sample itself, with the corresponding prefix, if noted followed by the FACTS sample number.

4.4.10.2.1 - Additional (ADD)

To identify a physical sample collected from a previously sampled lot. Do not report or document as an "ADD Sample" those instances when only additional records or documentation are obtained for the sample.

4.4.10.2.2 - Audit/Certification

To identify a physical sample collected to verify analytical results provided by a certificate of analysis or private laboratory analysis that purports to show the product complies with the Food, Drug and Cosmetic Act.

4.4.10.2.3 - Documentary (DOC)

To identify an official sample comprised of documents and photographs, collected without a physical portion. Do not use this designation to identify a physical sample for which you wish to delay analysis. See IOM 4.1.4.2 and Exhibits 4-1 and 4-2.

4.4.10.2.4 - Domestic Import (DI)

To identify samples collected of foreign products, which have passed through Customs and entered domestic commerce. The country of origin must be reported on the C/R. See IOM 4.1.4.8.

4.4.10.2.5 - Food Standards (FS)

To identify samples collected to provide information on which to base Food Standards. See IOM 4.1.5.

4.4.10.2.6 - Investigational (INV)

To identify samples collected to document observations and/or where interstate commerce does not exist or is not necessary. See IOM 4.1.7.

4.4.10.2.7 - Mail Entry

To identify a sample of an imported product that entered the United States through the U.S. Mail.

4.4.10.2.8 - Non-Regulatory

To identify a sample collected and analyzed by FDA for other federal, state or local agencies of products over which FDA has no jurisdiction.

4.4.10.2.9 - Official

To identify a sample which is representative of a lot of any product covered by the Food, Drug and Cosmetic Act for which interstate commerce can be documented.

4.4.10.2.10 - Post Award (GQA)

To identify samples collected as part of the Government Wide Quality Assurance Program administered by ORA/OE/Division of Compliance Information and Quality Assurance. See IOM 4.1.6.

4.4.10.2.11 - Post Seizure (PS)

To identify samples collected pursuant to a court order from a lot under seizure. See IOM 4.1.4.7.

4.4.10.2.12 - Regulatory

A sample collected or analyzed by non-FDA personnel, including samples submitted by industry.

4.4.10.3 - Preparation

The collection record (C/R) is the starting point and the basic reference for all actions and considerations based on the sample. It contains or bears direct reference to every important point about the sample and the lot from which it was collected. See IOM Exhibits 4-1, 4-2, 4-15, and 4-16 for examples.

Individual Fields - Complete the individual fields on the FACTS Sample Collection Screen as indicated. The following fields must be completed to save the sample information; Sample Class; Sampling District; Collector; Collection Date; Sample Basis; Sample Type; FIS Sample Number; Sample Description; Product Code; Product Description; Resp. Firm Type; Resp. Firm FEI Number; PAC; Sample Origin; and CR and Records Sent To. The fields described below are listed in alphabetical order to facilitate locating the instructions. Please note, when a collection report is generated, the field names may change on the report.

Any information that needs to be included regarding the sample and cannot be documented via FACTS, should be documented on the C/R Continuation Sheet, FDA 464a. For example, pictorial descriptions of a field exam for a filth sample; or a description of relative documents and what they demonstrate regarding the subject lot of a documentary sample; etc.

4.4.10.3.1 - Accomplishment Hours

Enter the accomplishment data for every sample collected, by clicking on the "clock" icon at the FACTS task bar. In the Accomplishment hours screen, enter the PAC by selecting from the list of values and type in the number of hours spent collecting the sample. Also enter all PACs that were entered in the Collections PACs field on page 2 of the collection record. If another person is involved in the collection, add their time by clicking on the "Add" button. See IOM exhibit 4-16 page 2.

4.4.10.3.2 - Analytical Assignment

After saving a collection record, the system will prompt you for analytical assignment data. Enter lab analysis data (PAC and PAF) for your sample. The analytical PAC and PAF (Problem Area Flag) may be different from the collection PAC and PAF. Enter split sample data on separate lines. For DOC samples leave this field blank. Do not enter any data in this form if the sample is being delivered to a non-FACTS lab.

4.4.10.3.3 - Brand Name

Enter the Brand Name of the product. This is found on the labeling of the product. It is important to identify the product completely so the compliance officer can communicate accurate information to the court and the U.S. Marshall in the event of a seizure.

4.4.10.3.4 - Carrier Name

Enter name of the transportation company who transported the goods in interstate commerce if known at the time of preparation of the CR. You may need to obtain this later to fully document interstate commerce. In the case of a 301(k) sample, this is the transportation company who moved the component you are documenting across state lines. For a 301(a) sample documenting the shipment of a violative product in interstate commerce, enter the name of the carrier utilized by the manufacturer or distributor to carry the goods across state lines.

4.4.10.3.5 - Collection Date

Enter the date using the format - mm/dd/yyyy. Note: the default date is today's date. Be careful not to use the default date if the sample was not collected on the date the CR is created. Only one date can be entered; if the sample collection was accomplished over several days, use one date. Be consistent. This date should be used to identify the physical sample and any records attached to the CR. This field is critical; be certain to verify the date.

4.4.10.3.6 - Collection Method

Describe how you collected the sample and which subs are the 702(b) portion. Relate the number and size of the sampled units and subsamples to show how each was taken, e.g., "Two cans of product randomly collected from each of 12 previously unopened cases selected at random." Note any special sampling techniques used, e.g.: "Subs collected using aseptic technique and placed in sterile glass jars or whirl-packs" or "Subs 1-10 consist of approx. 1# of product. Subsamples 1-10 collected from bulk storage Bin #1 composited in unused, brown, paper bag." Completely describe the collection method of each sub of selective samples with multiple subsamples, including your observations of the conditions, e.g.: "Two live insects collected from seam of bag #2. Live insects were observed exiting bag and two were collected upon exit." You will normally need to use a continuation sheet to describe collection of all subsamples and your description of the lot "bag-by-bag" examination. See IOM 4.5.2.1 regarding sub identification.

4.4.10.3.7 - Collection PACs

Enter the Program Assignment Code (PAC), which is most correct, from the list of values. If the PAC on your assignment is not listed, discuss with your supervisor or FACTS Lead User.

4.4.10.3.8 - Collection Reason

Enter the complete reason for collection giving the suspected violation, compliance program guidance manual, and analysis desired. Identify any interdistrict, regional, headquarters initiated, assignment document(s) in sufficient detail so the document can be located, if necessary. If the sample was collected during an inspection to document violations found, state that and indicate the date of inspection. See IOM exhibits 4-1 and 4-16.

4.4.10.3.9 - Collection Remarks

Enter any remarks you feel are necessary. Describe any special circumstances. If a 704(d) [21 U.S.C. 374(d)] letter is indicated, include the name and title of the most responsible person at the firm to which the letter should be addressed. If the sample is an in-transit sample, state the sample was collected in-transit, from whom sampled (e.g. driver and carrier firm), and where sampled. If the dealer firm is a consumer, the name and address of the consumer should be entered in the Collection Remarks field, and the consumer's state in the State field. You may use a "CR Continuation Sheet", FDA 464a if you need more space.

4.4.10.3.10 - Collector

Your name should appear here by default.

4.4.10.3.11 - Collector's ID on Package/Document

As the Sample Collector, quote your identification placed on the packages, labels, etc., e.g., "55563 12/5/05 SAR". See IOM 4.5.2.3. When multiple units are collected, all or at least a portion should be labeled as subsamples. Subsample numbers need to be included on the C/R and in the EIR. You may include the sub numbers used in this block outside of the quotes, e.g., "55563 12/5/05 SAR" subs 1-30.

4.4.10.3.12 - Collector's Id On Seal

Quote your identification used on the Official Seal applied to the sample, e.g., "55563 12/5/05 Sylvia A. Rogers". See IOM 4.5.4.1 and exhibit 4-17. If you use the FDA metal seal, enter the words "Metal Seal" followed by the seal identification and number, e.g., "U.S. Food and Drug 233", entering the actual number of the seal used. Samples need to be kept under lock or in your possession, until sealed. The Collection Remarks field needs to describe any discrepancy between the date sealed and the date collected. Normally, the sample should be sealed on the same day as collected.

4.4.10.3.13 - Consumer Complaint Number

If the sample relates to a consumer complaint, enter the complaint number. This will allow your CR to be linked to the complaint and viewed by the Consumer Complaint Coordinator and other District and Center personnel.

4.4.10.3.14 - Country Of Origin

Select the Country of Origin, if known. This field is of particular need when the sample is a Domestic Import Sample.

4.4.10.3.15 - County

Select the County where the sample was collected (or grown if appropriate, i.e. a pesticide sample of an agricultural product.) This field is not needed for many samples. Use for pesticide samples to aid in later communication with State officials in the event of a violative result.

4.4.10.3.16 - CR & Records Sent To

Enter the division or district office to which you will send the CR and records. This should be the office which is most likely to initiate any regulatory action. This field requires some thought on the part of the collector and communication with the supervisor. For a 301(k) sample, where the dealer is responsible, this is the district where the sample was collected. Do not assume the address on the label is the location where follow-up to a violative sample will be initiated. Do not send the records to another district unless you know it is the district of the actual responsible firm. Per Staff Manual Guide f 2460.2, Field Office Filing System (or f:3291.2 as listed on the FDA intranet site), field survey samples will be filed by the collecting district.

4.4.10.3.17 - CRX/DEA Schedule

Choose the appropriate schedule from the list of values, if applicable.

4.4.10.3.18 - Dairy Permit Number

Enter if applicable. If you are collecting samples from a dairy, obtain this number from the firm.

4.4.10.3.19 - Date Collected

See Collection Date IOM 4.4.10.3.5.

4.4.10.3.20 - Date Shipped

Enter date in the format, mm/dd/yyyy. This is the date of interstate shipment. Obtain it from the documentation you collected to document interstate movement of the product. Identify the document you used to determine this date in the "Documents Obtained" section.

4.4.10.3.21 - Documents Obtained

Click on the "Documents" Obtained button to enter Document Type, Document Number, Document Date and Remarks for any records collected to support a violation or show interstate movement of the product sampled. Enter an identifying number and date for invoices, freight bills, bills of lading, etc. Include the name and title of person signing any affidavits in the Remarks field. Be sure to describe the reason each document attached to the collection record was obtained. For example, when referring to a bill of lading, indicate it was collected to document the interstate movement of the product. Also indicate which documents were collected to document specific violations encountered during inspections. State the number of pages for each document if it contains more than one page and refer the reader to the appropriate section of the document which shows the deviation you are documenting. Indicate the number of photographs attached. Depending on the sample and what you are trying to document, you may use the document number to record the actual number of the document (i.e., invoice number or bill of lading number) or to order the documents attached. You should order your documents in a manner that allows easy review (be guided by your supervisor or Compliance Branch) and attach the documents to the printed C/R in the order they were entered into FACTS. This section may also be used to list C/R attachments including FDA generated forms. See IOM exhibit 4-1.

4.4.10.3.22 - Episode Number

Enter an episode number if applicable. See IOM 4.4.10.1.8.

4.4.10.3.23 - Estimated Value

Enter the estimated wholesale value of the lot remaining after sampling. Obtain this information from invoice or other records. (This is not the value to be used for seizure bond purposes; however, it may be used by the district to evaluate whether seizure is an appropriate action.) Estimate value if you have no documentary reference. For DOC samples (see Exhibits 4-1 and 4-2,), indicate the estimated value of the lot. If the DOC sample is collected to document a lot that has already been shipped, estimate the value, or obtain a figure from your documentation, which represents what was shipped. Many times a DOC sample is collected merely to establish interstate commerce, in those situations, the value of the goods that traveled, or will travel, in interstate commerce is what is needed.

4.4.10.3.24 - FEI Number

The FEI number is a 10-digit unique identifier, which is used to identify firms associated with FDA regulated products. Use the Build button to query the database and find an FEI for firms associated with your sample. If one does not exist, FACTS will assign one to the firm. Take care in entering search criteria to avoid creating unnecessary FEI numbers. You must enter an FEI for a dealer on every CR, unless you check the box indicating the dealer is a consumer.

4.4.10.3.25 - Firm Name

This will be filled in by FACTS when you select an FEI.

4.4.10.3.26 - Firm Type

Using the list of values, select one of the following with for each FEI entered, with respect to the product sampled:

4.4.10.3.26.1 - Dealer

This is always the firm from which the sample was collected. There must be a dealer entered on every CR, unless you check the box indicating the dealer is a consumer. *Note:* this is not the same as the establishment type of the firm identified by the FEI. There are circumstances where you may identify the same firm as the dealer and another establishment type, such as when collecting a plant in-line sample.

Note: *If the dealer firm is a consumer, the name and address of the consumer should be entered in the Collection Remarks field, and the consumer's state in the State field. When the sample is an in-transit sample (see IOM 4.1.4.3), enter the consignee of the lot as the dealer and state in collection remarks the sample was collected in-transit, from whom sampled (e.g. driver and carrier firm), and where sampled.*

4.4.10.3.26.2 - Grower

Select "Grower" if the FEI identifies a producer of a raw agricultural commodity.

4.4.10.3.26.3 - Harvester

Use "Harvester" for an FEI identifying the harvester of the product sampled.

4.4.10.3.26.4 - Ingredient Supplier

"Ingredient Supplier" should be used to identify a firm which supplied a raw material or component. For example, when documenting a 301(k) [21 U.S.C. 331(k)] situation.

4.4.10.3.26.5 - Manufacturer

Use "Manufacturer" with an FEI, which identifies the manufacturer of the product sampled. Note: this may be the same as the dealer when a product is sampled at a manufacturer. In that case, you can enter the FEI twice and identify it as both the manufacturer and the dealer.

4.4.10.3.26.6 - Shipper

The shipper is the firm responsible for causing the interstate movement of the product.

4.4.10.3.27 - FIS Sample Number

Enter the last two digits of the fiscal year. The remainder of the number will be assigned by FACTS. Note: FIS sample numbers will no longer be required when the FIS is turned off.

4.4.10.3.28 - Food Canning Establishment

Enter "Food Canning Establishment" if applicable.

4.4.10.3.29 - Hours

See Accomplishment Hours in IOM 4.4.10.3.1.

4.4.10.3.30 - How Prepared

Explain how the sample was prepared prior to submission to the laboratory; how you identified some or all the units; and how you wrapped and sealed the sample. Note any special preparation methods such as fumigation, frozen, kept under refrigeration, etc, and the form in which the sample was delivered to the laboratory, e.g. in paper bags, original carton, etc. If coolants or dry ice were used, indicate so here. It is important to be specific as to how you protected the integrity of the sample and the chain of custody, e.g.,

"Subs identified as noted (describe how 702(b) portion was prepared/handled- see IOM 4.5.2.1), placed in unused, brown paper bag; bag taped shut and FDA seal completed (as noted) and applied, bag ID'd as noted in pen/ink. FDA 525 attached to sealed bag, placed in brown, cardboard box and prepared for shipment, then delivered to district security guard desk for FEDEX pick-up".

4.4.10.3.31 - Lot Size

Enter the amount of goods on hand before sampling as determined by your inventory of the lot. Include the number of shipping cases and the size of the components, e.g., 75 (48/12 oz.) cases, 250/100 lb. burlap bags, 4/100,000 tab drums, 24 cases containing 48/12/3 oz. tins. If accompanying literature is involved, describe and state the amount on hand. For DOC samples (see Exhibit 4-1 and 4-2), also indicate the lot size, e.g. "one x-ray machine" or "50000 syringes and 1000 promotional brochures."

4.4.10.3.32 - Manufacturing Codes

Click on the "Manufacturing Codes" button to enter and identify all codes, lot numbers, batch control codes, etc., and how they are displayed on labels, cartons and shipping containers. Enclose the code in quotes, e.g. "code". For example, code embossed on can cover, "87657888" or code applied in ink on side of carton, "0987878". Also indicate the manufacturing codes used on products for which a DOC sample was collected, for example, "serial number "ABC" stamped on metal ID plate." See IOM Exhibit 4-2.

Enter any expiration dates in the Exp Date field.

4.4.10.3.33 - Method of Collection

See Collection Method in IOM 4.4.10.3.6.

4.4.10.3.34 - National Drug Code

Enter if applicable

4.4.10.3.35 - Orig CR & Records To

See CR and Records Sent To in IOM 4.4.10.3.16.

4.4.10.3.36 - Payment Method

Select one of the following from the from the list of values: "Billed"; "Borrowed"; "Cash"; "Credit Card"; "No Charge"; "Voucher". The "Credit Card" option means you used your personal credit card as a last resort.

4.4.10.3.37 - Permit Number

See Dairy Permit Number in IOM 4.4.10.3.18.

4.4.10.3.38 - Product Code

Enter the 7-digit product code. Use the product code build feature or your data codes manual. When 301(k) samples are collected, the full product code of the finished product must be entered. See IOM exhibit 4-1. See IOM 4.4.10.1.7 for product codes for filth or evidence exhibits.

4.4.10.3.39 - Product Description

Enter a complete description of the product including the common or usual name and the product packaging/container system. For example, aspirin tablets packed in clear, non-flexible plastic bottle with white screw on top with yellow stick-on label and black printing. Bottles packed in white, paperboard boxes with black printing. Paperboard boxes packed in brown cardboard boxes with black printing. If you need additional space, continue the description in remarks. See IOM exhibit 4-1.

4.4.10.3.40 - Product Label

Quote pertinent portions of the label such as brand name, generic name, quantity of contents, name and address of manufacturer or distributor, code, etc. In the case of drugs, quote the potency, active ingredients and indicate whether Rx or non-Rx. Quote sufficiently from accompanying literature to identify. In the case of a Documentary Sample, sufficiently describe the article to identify what is sampled.

When the product sampled is packaged in a carton, shipping case or similar container, quote the pertinent labeling from the container.

When quoting from a label, or labeling, use exact spelling, capitalization, punctuation, arrangement, etc., as found on the original label(ing). Use asterisks to indicate any omissions.

4.4.10.3.41 - Product Name

Product Name field is completed by FACTS when you select the product code.

4.4.10.3.42 - Reason for Collection

See Collection Reason in IOM 4.4.10.3.8.

4.4.10.3.43 - Recall Number

If the sample was collected as part of a recall investigation where the recall number is already known, enter the recall number.

4.4.10.3.44 - Receipt Issued

Select "FDA472", "FDA484", or "None" from the list of values.

4.4.10.3.45 - Receipt Type

See Receipt Issued in IOM 4.4.10.3.44.

4.4.10.3.46 - Related Samples

This field is used to identify a sample number to which other sample information can be linked. When you collect more than one sample from a single shipment or there is more than one sample relating to a possible regulatory action, designate one sample as the "lead" sample. Enter that sample number in this field of the collection record for each related sample. Other related sample numbers should be listed in the Collection Remarks field.

4.4.10.3.47 - Resp. Firm Type

Choose the appropriate type from the list of values for the firm most likely to be responsible for a violation. For a 301(k) [21 U.S.C. 331(k)] sample the responsible firm should be "Dealer". You should only enter one firm with the firm type you designate as the responsible firm type.

4.4.10.3.48 - Sample Basis

Choose "Compliance" if the sample was collected on a selective basis as the result of an inspection, complaint or other evidence there may be a problem with the product. Select "Surveillance" if the sample was collected on an objective basis where there is no inspectional or other evidence of a problem with the product. Please note official samples can be either compliance or surveillance, and INV samples can also be either. See IOM Exhibit 4-15.

4.4.10.3.49 - Sample Class

Make a selection from the following list of values: "Collaborative Study"; "Criminal Investigation"; "District Use Sample"; "Normal Everyday Sample"; "Petition Validation"; "Quality Assurance"; "State Partnership"; "Total Diet".

4.4.10.3.50 - Sample Cost

Enter the cost of the sample. If no charge, enter 0. If, as a last resort, you use your personal credit card to pay for the sample, enter the amount paid in this field and select "Credit. Card" in the Payment Method field. If you are unable to determine the cost of the sample and the firm states they will bill you later, enter the estimated cost in this field and state that it is an estimate in the Collection Remarks field.

4.4.10.3.51 - Sample Delivered Date

Enter the date on which the sample was delivered to the laboratory or for shipment. For DOC samples, you must leave this field blank. If you make an entry, you must enter a laboratory.

4.4.10.3.52 - Sample Delivered To

Enter to whom you delivered the physical sample. If delivered to your own sample custodian under seal, show delivery to servicing laboratory or sample custodian. If delivered to an analyst, report e.g., "In person to Analyst Richard R. Doe." If you shipped the sample, enter the name of the carrier to whom the sampled was delivered. Enter the Government Bill of Lading

Number, if used. If the sample is shipped by air, enter the air waybill number. If shipment is by parcel post, give the location of the post office, e.g., "P.P., Austin, TX." For a DOC sample, leave this field blank. If the sample is being sent to a non-FACTS laboratory, enter the laboratory here.

4.4.10.3.53 - Sample Description

Briefly describe what the sample consists of, i.e., three unopened, 200 tablet bottles; 20 lb case of iceberg lettuce; or documentary sample consisting of records, literature and photographs, etc.

4.4.10.3.54 - Sample Flags

Click on the "Sample Flags" button to choose an appropriate flag using the list of values. See IOM 4.4.10.1 and exhibit 4-15.

4.4.10.3.55 - Sample Number

Select a pre-assigned sample number, using the list of values button, or the system will enter a sample number when the record is saved.

4.4.10.3.56 - Sample Origin

Choose "Domestic" or "Domestic/Import" from the list of values.

4.4.10.3.57 - Sample Sent To

Choose appropriate lab from the list of values. Select the laboratory to which you are sending the sample. If you are splitting the sample among multiple laboratories for various analyses, enter each laboratory separately. Generally, in that case you will have more than one PAC code. If, because of your assignment, you are aware the sample should be forwarded to a second laboratory after the first analysis is complete, include that information in the Collection Remarks field. However, you should only enter a laboratory in this field if you are sending the sample there, not if the laboratory will be expected to forward it. For a DOC sample, leave this blank. If the sample is to be sent to a non-FACTS lab, leave this field blank, enter the lab in the Sample Delivered To field, print a copy of the collection record and enclose it in the FDA 525 attached to the sample.

4.4.10.3.58 - Sample Type

Make a selection from the list of values. You can enter only one value. If more than one type applies, choose one and indicate the other in remarks. If the sample is a domestic import, be sure to enter "DI", so that you can enter the foreign manufacturer. See IOM 4.4.10.2.4.

4.4.10.3.59 - Sampling District

Make a selection from the list of values. This is the district that actually collects the sample.

4.4.10.3.60 - State

Select the State where the sample was collected. This field is optional for many samples. Always use it for pesticide samples.

4.4.10.3.61 - Status

This field is pre-filled by the system as "In-Progress". Select "Ready for Review", from the list of values, when you are ready to send the record to your supervisor for review, if you are required to do so. After supervisory review, if appropriate, change the status to "Complete". This will cause the electronic signature form to be activated.

4.4.10.3.62 - Storage Requirements

Select from the following list of values: Ambient; Frozen; Refrigerated.

4.4.10.3.63 - 702(B) Portion Collected

Check this box if you collected the duplicate portion of food, drug or cosmetic to be held by FDA for release to the owner or person named on the label for their own analysis. Note: for routine surveillance samples, collected per a sample schedule, the sample size already includes the 702(b) portion.

4.4.10.3.64 - 704(D) Sample

Check this box if the sample is collected during an inspection, i.e., a FDA 482 has been issued, from a food manufacturer, processor or packer, the firm is entitled to a copy of the analytical results. Include in Collection Remarks name and title of the individual to receive at the firm. This only pertains to when you collect the sample at the manufacturing/processing/packing firm.

4.4.10.4 - National Sample Distributor (NSD)

The NSD system was implemented in October 2007. NSD automates the FACTS lab selection function, directing the flow of samples to ORA laboratories which can best conduct sample analysis work at specific times. NSD will identify/suggest an appropriate lab for the Problem Area Flag (PAF), PAC, and district information provided in FACTS. The suggested lab information will then be transmitted back to FACTS for further processing. NSD consists of three modules: Routing module, Lab Capacity module and Lab Contacts module.

The Routing module automatically determines the appropriate lab(s) that can best handle the work for the PAC/PAF combination provided by the user. The NSD Routing module consists of three screens: Questionnaire Screen, Confirm/Override Selections Screen and Print Laboratory Information Screen. The NSD questionnaire screen allows the user to enter additional information that is used to determine the routing of the sample.

The Lab Capacity module allows the users to view/update the capacity of the lab for the upcoming week(s) depending on the user role and affiliation. The NSD Lab Capacity screen allows the Sample Manager to set the capacity for laboratory work by PAF and track the number of samples assigned by NSD to a given laboratory on a weekly basis.

The Lab Contacts modules allow the PAF manager to enter any number of contacts for each PAF, as well as any number of sample custodians. The NSD Lab Contact screen allows the PAF manager to enter contact information for the laboratory, names and phone numbers for a number of Sample Monitors and Sample Custodians for each PAF for which the lab has capacity. This information can be accessed by the collectors from the Confirm/Override Selections screen.

4.4.10.4.1 - NSD and Assignments

Existing Import Alert and Domestic Assignments issued before NSD - use NSD to choose the servicing laboratory and disregard the servicing laboratories referenced in the assignments. Be alert for specific guidance issued in which NSD is manually overridden.

Assignments and alerts issued after 10/15/07 will have a NSD section with instructions when to override the system.

4.4.10.4.2 - Overriding NSD

Do not override NSD unless specific guidance is distributed. Examples of when NSD may be overridden are:

1. Follow-up samples - send these samples to the original lab which analyzed the initial sample.

2. For-Cause Samples - when collected as part of a violative inspection should go to the servicing lab, especially when the lab is co-located with the responsible Compliance branch.

3. Sample Shipping Cost Prohibitive - the collecting district makes this decision.

Communication - when you override the NSD lab selection, contact the servicing lab prior to shipping the sample. The servicing lab will determine if adequate resources and capacity are available to conduct the analysis in a timely manner.

4.4.10.4.3 - Other Information

The Division of Field Science intranet website maintains current documents related to the Laboratory PAF managers Contact List and the District Compliance Contacts.

Sample collectors should complete NSD training on the ORA intranet; this site includes the National Sample distributor tutorial and user manual.

Questions on sample analyses, assignments, laboratory capability, or otherwise can be directed to the Division of Field Science the Scientific Compliance and Regulatory Review branch manager (George Salem 301-827-1031) or Laboratory Operations Branch manager (Todd Bozicevich 301-827-9552).

4.4.10.5 - Routing

Anyone who has user access to the FACTS system has access to the electronic records contained therein, including sample collection records. Individuals requiring sample collection data can query the system and retrieve data, based on the query parameters. In those cases where an individual needs to receive immediate notification of a sample collection, the collector may communicate the sample number via E-mail, telephone, or another means to a user, and the user may then query the system and obtain the desired data. It is not always necessary to print paper copies of FACTS sample collection records for those who have access to FACTS.

Routing Records Accompanying Sample Collection Record - Print a copy of the Collection Record in FACTS. Attach original records to the printed FACTS Collection Record and route, through your supervisor, to the district office compliance unit most likely to take regulatory action. When requested, additional copies should be routed, attached to a routing slip, marked "records to accompany CR _________(number), as requested." Include a copy of the printed FACTS Collection Record in the FDA 525 if it is available at the time of sample shipment.

When a sample is to be billed, route a copy of the FDA 484, if issued, annotated with the FACTS sample number to the appropriate fiscal unit for your district. If possible at the time of collection, provide the FACTS sample number to the firm and request that this number be placed on the billing invoice. If no sample number is available, ask the firm to identify the bill with your name as the collector to help the fiscal unit match the bill to the sample record in FACTS. The fiscal unit will have access to the sample collection record in FACTS to obtain detailed sample information.

4.5 - Sampling: Preparation, Handling, Shipping

4.5.1 - Objective

The preparation, handling, and shipping of samples is your responsibility, and must be carried out in a manner which assures the sample's integrity and supports testimony that the sample examined was the same sample you collected from the shipment you documented.

As few persons as possible should handle the sample to reduce the likelihood of compromising sample integrity. See the Laboratory Procedures Manual (LPM), Chapter 4 , 4.1 for information about relinquishing samples.

4.5.2 - Identifying Marks

4.5.2.1 - Subsamples

Identify a representative number of subsamples (subs) with the sample number (including prefix, if appropriate), collection date and your handwritten initials. If individual sub identity must be maintained, assign and mark each sub with a separate Arabic numeral. In some comprehensive inspections or investigations it may be important to correlate the manufacturing control code with the sub number.

When a variety of articles are included under one sample number, fully identify each sub and describe them on the C/R. Factory exhibits should be fully identified and, where appropriate, correlated with inspectional observations, manufacturing procedures, and/or routes of contamination. See IOM 4.2.5.6 for using the FDA 484 - Receipt for Samples as a memo to accompany C/R to describe subs collected.

When multiple subs are taken from cases, bales, boxes, etc. in the lot, Arabic numerals and letters in combination may be used for identification. For example: if two cans are taken from each case in the lot, the cans may be marked as subs 1a, 1b, 2a, 2b, etc. to identify the subs as coming from case #1, case #2, etc. If the second can or container taken from each case is the 702(b) [21 U.S.C. 372(b)] portion, it is desirable that all duplicate portions be sealed separately from the FDA portion. This fact should be so noted on the cases and C/R.

If multiple subsamples are to be collected, it may be advantageous to place identifying information such as sub number, sample number, and collection date on peel-off labels, tape, etc. in advance of sampling to save valuable time. Your initials must be in your own handwriting.

4.5.2.2 - Borrowed Samples

Although most samples are purchased, some may be borrowed, non-destructively examined, and returned to the owner. These samples must be handled carefully to avoid defacing or damaging the product.

Identify borrowed samples so the identification can be removed with no damage to the product, i.e. a sticker label that can be peeled off.

4.5.2.3 - Identification Techniques

Mark a representative number of subsamples with the sample number, collection date and your written initials. Similarly identify any outer packaging, labels or circulars. If more than one person is involved in collecting the sample, the person preparing and signing the C/R initials the subs. Reinsert circulars removed from packages. See IOM 4.2.9.2 for procedures on identifying lots from which sampled.

Transparent tape such as Scotch Magic Transparent tape accepts ball point ink and may be used on glossy items such as glass, plastic, tin, etc. Glass, such as bottles, vials and ampoules, may be identified by using a very fine pointed felt or nylon marking pen and covering the identification with transparent tape for protection.

Do not use tape on very small containers such as ampoules, which must be snapped or broken to remove the contents for analysis. Tape wrapped around the container may interfere with assay.

Do not use permanent type markers when identifying subs in absorbent containers if the ink may penetrate into the product thus contaminating the sample.

Diamond or carbide tipped stylus pencils may be used to mark tin, glass, etc. Do not use diamond or carbide tipped stylus to mark products in glass under pressure (i.e., carbonated beverages).

4.5.2.4 - Photographs

Unless they are part of a DOC Sample, photographs are exhibits, to an EIR, report of investigation, or complaint. They are not samples. Photos taken during inspections and investigations are not described on a C/R, but are submitted as exhibits with the EIR. Photographs related to DOC Samples, i.e., labeling, records, product, etc. are identified with the sample number, collection date, and handwritten initials on the border or backside. See IOM 5.3.4.2.1 Attach the photos to the printed FACTS Collection Record. See IOM 4.4.10.5.

In describing photographs, do not mark the face of the print. Narrative descriptions may be placed on the mounting paper next to the print or, if explanatory graphics are required, use a plastic overlay. See IOM 5.3.4.2.3 for negative identification and submission procedures.

4.5.2.5 - Records - Accompanying Literature and Exhibits

Identify all copies of sample records, accompanying literature, and attached documents with the sample number (including prefix, if applicable), collection date and your handwritten initials as described in IOM 4.5.2.1. If an attached document is more than one page in length, it must be numbered or attached in a manner that will always allow further reviewers to determine if any pages are missing.

4.5.3 - Sample Handling

All samples must be handled, packaged, and shipped to prevent compromising the identity or integrity of the sample. Samples must be packed with shock absorbing materials to protect against breakage of containers or damage to Official Seals. Frozen samples must remain frozen; perishable products may be frozen, if freezing doesn't interfere with the planned analysis, products requiring refrigeration (e.g., fresh crabmeat for bacteriological analysis) should be shipped in ice. Use your experience and knowledge (and that of your supervisor, if necessary) to determine the most appropriate packing and shipping method.

4.5.3.1 - Fumigation

See IOM 1.5.3.1 for safety precautions.

General - As soon as possible, freeze any sample containing, or suspected to contain live insects, as long as freezing will not change or damage the product or break the container. If freezing is inappropriate to maintaining the integrity of the sample, fumigation may be carried out using air tight containers (such as a mason-type jar with inner ring, or a polypropylene container with air tight lid), with sufficient fumigant to kill the insect infestation. Contact your servicing laboratory for alternative fumigants.

Moth crystals, containing paradichlorobenzene (PDB), is an alternative fumigant. Do not use mothballs or moth flakes containing naphtha or naphthalene. Do not use moth crystals in or near plastics, particularly Styrofoam/ polystyrenes as crazing or melting may occur. Other alternative fumigants include: liquid household ammonia or ethyl acetate, either of which can be used to dampen a cotton ball and placed in an appropriate container; or cut small portions of commercial pesticide strips.

4.5.3.1.1 - Fumigation Safety Precautions

Follow safety precautions when fumigating samples. Contact your local servicing laboratory or MSDS for the appropriate protective gear and handling of fumigants. Guidance is as follows:

1. Carry all alcohols, fumigants, and other hazardous liquids in approved safety containers.

2. When fumigants or preservatives are used, limit your exposure to these chemicals. Minimize transfer and exposure time. Avoid getting chemicals on hands or clothing. DO NOT MIX CHEMICALS.

3. Insure DOT guidelines are followed when mailing or shipping samples containing fumigant or preservative. Exceptions for small quantities are listed in 49 CFR 173.4. If the samples are sent via Federal Express, the International Air Transport Association (IATA) dangerous goods regulations must be met. (Call 1-800-238-5355, extension 922-1666 for specific instructions for shipment.)

4. The sample identification data on your packaging, the FDA-525 and C/R, must always identify the fumigant and method of fumigation, and/or preservative used.

5. Material Safety Data Sheets (MSDS) for each chemical fumigant or preservative used must be available at each duty site and enclosed with the shipped sample. Read and follow all instructions and precautions listed on the MSDS.

4.5.3.1.2 - Procedures for Fumigation

Place a small amount of fumigant, in an airtight container. Separate the fumigant from the sample with a piece of paper, paper napkin, or unscented facial tissue. Put specimen or product into container and seal tightly. Do not re-open container unless absolutely necessary. If possible, use a glass container with a lined screw lid. A mason-type jar with inner ring is also acceptable.

4.5.3.1.3 - Exceptions to Fumigation

When submitting samples or exhibits to show live infestation, do not fumigate. Consult with your supervisor or your servicing laboratory PRIOR to sending or bringing a live infestation into the laboratory to permit preparation for proper handling and storage. Do not fumigate sample when submitting samples for pesticide residue analysis.

4.5.3.1.4 - Preservation Liquids

Insects may be killed and preserved in 70% ethyl alcohol or a 1:1 mixture of 70% ethyl alcohol and glycerin (may be labeled glycerol). These chemicals can be obtained from your servicing laboratory. Do not collect rodents or animal tissues unless specifically instructed. Insure all vials or bottles of preservation liquids are tightly sealed to avoid leakage. Identification labels may be placed in containers, but must be written in India ink or 2H pencil only. Keep all preservation liquids away from excessive heat or open flame.

Identify preservative used on FDA 525, C/R, and on sample container. Enclose a copy of the MSDS with the shipped sample. Follow DOT and IATA guidelines when shipping or mailing samples with preservatives as stated under fumigants.

4.5.3.2 - Labeling

Samples collected for label review only should be officially sealed in clear plastic bags. This will permit cursory review and, if necessary, photocopying of the container label and reduce the need to break the seal each time the label is examined.

4.5.3.3 - Samples for Pathological Examination

Tissue samples are not routinely collected for microscopic or pathological examination. Authorization must be obtained from the appropriate Center before collecting samples of this material.

When assigned to collect tissue samples, unless directed otherwise by the program, the assignment, or your supervisor, cut the tissue into 1/4 inch pieces and preserve in 10% buffered formalin, or in other suitable preservatives as directed. Do not freeze the sample since frozen tissue is not suitable for pathological studies.

4.5.3.4 - Small Sample Items

Samples in small vials, bottles, boxes and similar type containers may be placed inside the FDA 525 envelope after identification. When the envelope is used as the sample package, place the official seal across the glued flap and the blank face of the form.

If the sample container (vial, bottle, etc.) is officially sealed, it may be placed in the same FDA 525 together with copies of the assignment.

4.5.3.5 - Frozen Samples

Containers - Pre-chill sterile containers before collecting frozen samples. Transfer liquids in glass to expandable containers before freezing. If the liquid must be frozen in glass, leave sufficient headspace to allow expansion. If freezer facilities are not available or if the sample is to be shipped, pack with dry ice in insulated cartons.

Dry ice and insulated cartons may be obtained from ice cream or dry ice dealers, and economical polystyrene (Styrofoam) containers are available at most variety stores. However, while Styrofoam containers have excellent insulating qualities, they will not withstand shipping abuse unless protected by sturdy outer cartons.

Note: If your district desires the return of Styrofoam freezer chests or ice packs used in shipping samples, note this fact on the C/R and FDA 525.

Dry Ice - Caution: Dry ice is potentially dangerous and requires caution in handling and shipping. Do not handle with unprotected hands; transport in your car without adequate ventilation; or place inside tightly closed metal, glass, plastic, or similar type containers that do not breathe. If it is necessary to use this type container, adequately vent to prevent pressure build up.

Note: *If a sample is to be analyzed for ammonia contamination, it must not be shipped frozen in dry ice. Use other methods of freezing, if frozen shipment is necessary.*

4.5.3.5.1 - Shipping Frozen Samples

If using a U.S. Government Bill of Lading, it is important to give a full and accurate description of the sample for rate purposes. If more than one commodity is in the shipment, describe and enter each separately.

In all packages where dry ice is used, distribute the dry ice equally on all sides of the sample package using pieces as large as possible. Be sure the container is insulated on all six sides and tape all edges securely to assist in insulating the carton. Do not place dry ice inside officially sealed packages.

Freezing by dry ice is not effective for more than forty-eight hours. For overnight shipments, use at least one pound of dry ice per pound of sample. Increase the amount for longer hauls or unusually warm weather. (Note: When samples are in plastic type containers, the dry ice must be wrapped in paper to prevent direct contact with the plastic. The extreme cold generated by the dry ice may cause plastic to become brittle and rupture.)

Shipments made via FedEx Corporation, Priority I, Purolator, Airborne or by other fast air express carriers, will be delivered to consignees early the next business day. Tests have shown the following amounts of dry ice will be adequate when this method is used:

For samples already in frozen state: five to ten pounds of dry ice depending on sample size is normally sufficient. For samples requiring only to be refrigerated: A minimum of ten pounds of dry ice is sufficient.

Note: The dry ice may freeze the edges of the product, so if it is imperative no part of the sample becomes frozen, use coolants other than dry ice. Mark the FDA 525 that dry ice was used.

See IOM 4.5.5.8.6 when shipping sample packages containing hazardous or toxic items, including dry ice, by air.

4.5.3.5.2 - Control

To prove the shipment did not thaw in transit, place a jar or leak proof plastic bag of chipped ice in the shipment adjacent to the sample package, but not within the officially sealed package.

4.5.3.6 - Refrigerated (Not Frozen) Samples

Maintain refrigerated (not frozen) samples in a refrigerator at 4.4oC (40oF) or below. Use either wet ice or some type of "Ice Pak", "Liquid Ice", "Sno-Gel", "Kool-It", or similar products to maintain the required temperature range.

Place Ice Paks, etc., in sealed plastic bags to protect samples from possible contamination should the container break, the ice melt, or the refrigerant penetrate the sample. Use Styrofoam insulated shipping cartons for shipping samples to the laboratory.

4.5.3.6.1 - Control

If it is necessary to show the sample temperature did not go above the desired or specified temperature, you can use one of several methods, such as including a pre-chilled, shaken down, maximum reading thermometer or commercially available indicators. Take care to place the thermometer outside of the sealed sample package and attempt to place in an area anticipated to be likely to reach the highest temperature. Describe the method used on your C/R.

4.5.4 - Official Seals

Domestic samples, regardless of type, shall be sealed with form FDA 415a, Official Seal, or, in some situations with the FDA "metal Seal". See IOM 4.5.4.6 for use of metal seals. See also IOM 4.1.4.2.

Note: With the approval of your supervisor and laboratory, it is not necessary to affix an official seal to a sample that will be in the sample collector's continuous personal custody until it is submitted personally to an analyst. This procedure should be reserved for emergencies and high priority situations. The sample should be submitted the same day it is collected with the subs properly identified. The C/R must state you personally delivered the sample to "Analyst ______"or other appropriate staff member.

Make every effort to prepare and submit your samples on the date collected so the C/R, sub identification, and the final official seal bear the same date, and thus enhance sample integrity. However, if you cannot finish the sample preparation on the same day collected, you must explain in the C/R Collection Remarks field what steps you took to protect the integrity of the sample, e.g., officially sealed and locked in supply cabinet, locked in safe, etc.

Never place more than one sample in the same officially sealed package.

4.5.4.1 - Preparation

Inscribe FDA 415a, official seal, with the district office name, sample number (with the appropriate prefix), the date applied, your signature, printed name and title. See IOM Exhibit 4-17. The seal must bear only one signature. If more than one person is involved in collecting the sample, the person preparing and signing the collection record must sign the seal.

4.5.4.2 - Application

Seal the sample package so that it cannot be opened at any point without evidence of tampering. If the surface of the sample container is of such construction or condition that the FDA-415a, official seal, will not adhere (e.g., waxed carton, frosted over, sweating, etc.), wrap or place sample in a container to which the official seal will hold. See IOM 4.5.4.6.

When using the self-adhering seals, the surface on which the seal is to be placed must be clean and dry. The seal must be rubbed when affixed to generate heat and help it bond.

4.5.4.3 - Sealing Method

There are many acceptable methods of officially sealing samples. Because of the wide variety of shapes and sizes of samples, and the ingenuity you may have to apply to package and packaging situations, explicit methodology will not be detailed here. Your supervisor, your on-the-job training, and your developing experience will familiarize you with the most effective methods.

4.5.4.4 - Protecting the Official Seal

Protect the sealed surface by wrapping the package securely with heavy wrapping paper for mailing or shipment. If your officially sealed package is not further wrapped for shipping and the tape(s) and official seal are thus exposed, you must protect the Official Seal from damage during shipment by:

1. Covering the official seal with a sheet of heavy wrapping paper or heavy clear plastic (e.g. from a document protector) of sufficient size to cover the surface of the official seal.

2. Tape the protective paper or heavy clear plastic securely around the edges so it cannot come loose and expose the official seal. Do not paste or glue the paper or plastic to the face of the official seal since this will obliterate the official seal when removed.

3. When you protect the official seal by heavy paper, write "FDA Seal Underneath", or similar wording across the protective paper. This alerts the receiving custodian the official seal is underneath, and to take care when removing the protective paper. If you cover and protect the seal with heavy clear plastic, the sample custodian will be able to copy the necessary information off the seal without removing the protective cover.

4.5.4.5 - Broken Official Seals and "Temporary Seals"

Reseal the sample whenever you break the official seal. Each seal used on the sample will be submitted with the records associated with the collection record, properly initialed and dated, to provide a continuous history.

There is only one class of seal: an "official seal". Anytime a sample is sealed with the FDA 415a, or with the FDA Metal Seal, the item is "officially sealed". An officially sealed sample must sometimes be reopened to prepare it for submission to the laboratory, or for some other legitimate reason. In that situation, the original seal must show the date it was broken. When the sample is ready to be resealed the new seal must show the date it is applied. This procedure must be followed each time the official seal on a sample is broken. Each seal will show the history of the date it was applied and broken. See instructions in Exhibit 4-17. Indicate in the collection remarks field of the FACTS C/R the fact that the seal was broken and reapplied and attach the broken seal to the printed FACTS C/R. This provides an unbroken, documented chain of custody.

4.5.4.6 - Metal Seals

Where it is impossible to use the paper official seal, the numbered self-locking "U.S. Food and Drug" metal seal may be used. This seal is effective for use on wooden crates, drums, baskets, etc., where the FDA 415a cannot be used. Record the number of the metal seal used on the CR. See IOM 4.3.4.3 for instructions on the use of the metal seal to reseal railroad cars or conveyances. When a supply of these seals are needed by your district, contact the Division of Field Investigations (DFI) (HFC-130) at 301-827-5653.

4.5.4.7 - Sealing Non-Sample Items

Although the primary purpose of the official seal is for sealing samples, there are times when the official seal may be used to officially seal items other than samples. The FDA metal seal is often used to seal rail cars or vehicles as indicated in IOM 4.3.4.3.

When directed by your supervisor, you may use an official seal to seal questionable or suspicious bioresearch records encountered during an inspection or investigation to prevent tampering or to preserve their integrity. As explained in the applicable compliance program, the procedure must have the approval of the bioresearch monitoring staff (HFC-230) prior to implementation.

4.5.5 - Sample Shipment

When you cannot personally deliver a sample to the examining laboratory, ship it by the most economical means commensurate with the need for rapid handling. See IOM 4.5.5.2 and 4.5.5.6 for special information on shipments to FDA Headquarters' laboratories.

FDA collects a wide variety of samples, many of which are unstable, toxic or hazardous material, e.g., etiological agents, radiation products, chemical, hard swells, etc. Use safety precautions in handling and shipping commensurate with the hazard. See IOM 4.5.5.8.7.

4.5.5.1 - Sample Package Identification

Form FDA 525 - Place the FDA 525, sample package identification, near the official seal. For small containers or surfaces that will not accommodate the FDA 525, you can tie it to the sample package by using twine through the eyelet. Do not affix the FDA 525 on the outside of the shipping carton or under the official seal. Enclose a copy of the assignment document in the FDA 525 envelope and provide the following information on the FDA 525:

1. District or Headquarters' laboratory to which the sample is directed, City, State, and unit symbol (e.g., SRL, HFD-400, HFS-300, etc.).
2. Date.
3. Your district and symbol.
4. Sample Number.
5. Name of dealer.

6. Product Identification.

7. Address of dealer.

8. Enter the reason for collection. (Copy from C/R.) Provide reference to any sampling assignment.

9. Provide information as to the analysis to be made.

10. Enter any pertinent remarks. Note if your district desires the return of any freezer chests, ice packs, or maximum/minimum thermometers used.

11. Provide any special storage instructions. Mark appropriate block and enter suggested refrigeration temperature if necessary. Elaborate in Remarks if necessary.

12. Print your name.

See IOM 4.5.3.4 when using the FDA 525 as a sample package. See IOM 4.5.5.3.6 for information to include with the FDA 525 for medical device samples.

Outer Wrapper - Always place the words, "SAMPLE NO. ________" followed by the actual FACTS or OASIS sample number(s)(with appropriate prefix) on the outside of the package near the address label. This alerts the receiving mail room that the package contains a sample and must go to the sample custodian.

4.5.5.2 - Routing of Samples

In general, samples will be submitted to your district's designated servicing laboratory, except as directed by the Compliance Program Guidance Manual, assignment or your supervisor. The following provides general guidance for sample submission.

1. Vitamin and Nutritional Labeling - Submit to FDA, Science Branch (HFR-SE680), 60 Eighth St. N.E., Atlanta, GA 30309.

2. Radiopharmaceuticals for Sterility - Submit samples to WEAC.

3. Tissue Residues - Submit to the Denver District Tissue Residue Lab.

A complete, current listing of designated servicing laboratories can be found in the current ORA Field Workplan as Appendix III. This appendix is comprised of a table designating the servicing laboratories for each collecting district and for each compliance program or subpart.

4.5.5.3 - Samples to Administration Laboratories

When shipping samples to headquarters or other special laboratories follow the procedures for each laboratory.

4.5.5.3.1 - Split Samples

Where the sample examination is split between a Headquarter's Division, the National Center for Drug Analysis, and a district lab:

1. Follow the above procedures on the portion sent to a Headquarter's laboratory or NCDA.

2. Submit Original C/R and records to the servicing laboratory, whether or not the home district.

4.5.5.3.2 - National Center for Drug Analysis or Headquarters' Division

National Center for Drug Analysis or Headquarters' Division analysis alone.

1. Do not forward original C/R and records.

2. Enclose a copy of the assignment memorandum in the FDA 525 envelope.

3. Affix the FDA 525 to the officially sealed sample package.

4. Submit the Original C/R and records to the home district, or forward to the home district if other than the collecting district.

4.5.5.3.3 - Center for Food Safety and Applied Nutrition (CFSAN)

Unless specifically directed by a Compliance Program or an assignment, do not submit samples to the CFSAN without approval of the Office of Compliance, Division of Field Programs, Compliance Programs Branch, HFS-636 at 301-436-2061. Send samples to CFSAN at the following address:

Food and Drug Administration
5100 Paint Branch Parkway
College Park, Maryland 20740

CFSAN Laboratories are as follows:

1. Office of Cosmetics and Colors
   a. Division of Cosmetics and Compliance (HFS-125) - Conducts chemical and/or toxicological analyses of all cosmetic complaint samples needed for medical evaluation.
   b. Division of Colors Certification and Technology (HFS-105) - Conducts color analysis of foods/drugs/ cosmetics.

2. Office of Nutritional Products, Labeling, and Dietary Supplements

   Division of Research and Applied Technology (HFS-840) - Conducts examinations related to food standards and food technology. Analyzes conventional foods for requirements of nutritional properties where special skills and expertise are not available in the field.

3. Office of Applied Research and Safety Assessment

   Division of Molecular Biology (HFS-025) - Analyses foods when the chemical methodology is under development or unusual equipment or skills are required, such as radioactivity analysis/migration of food additives from blood packaging materials. Microbiologically examines samples for potential food pathogens by rapid molecular biological testing using DNA probes, PCR and DNA fingerprint analysis.

4. Office of Plant and Dairy Foods

   a. Division of Natural Products, Microanalytical Branch (HFS-315) - Examines foods for bacterial contamination if field laboratory facilities are not available.

   b. Division of Natural Products (HFS-345) - Analyzes foods for non-nutritive components, including toxins.

   c. Division of Pesticides and Industrial Chemicals -(HFS-335) - Conducts examinations related to industrial chemicals contamination, including pesticides, toxic elements and radionuclides.

   d. Division of Microbiological Studies (HFS-515) - Conducts examinations related to Food Standards and food technology investigations, including the intended effect of food additives and the integrity of packaging.

5. Office of Seafood

   Division of Science and Applied Technology (HFS-425) Conducts decomposition, toxicity and parasite analysis of seafood where special skills or equipment required for analysis are not available in the field.

6. Office of Food Additive Safety

   Division of Chemistry Research and Environmental Review (HFS-245) - Analyses foods and food packaging materials for direct and indirect food additives where special skills and expertise are not available in the field.

4.5.5.3.4 - Center for Drug Evaluation and Research Division of Pharmaceutical Analysis (DPA)

Center for Drug Evaluation and Research Division of Pharmaceutical Analysis (DPA)

Center for Drug Analysis (HFH-300)

Division of Pharmaceutical Analysis (DPA)

US Courthouse and Customhouse Bldg.

1114 Market Street, Room 1002

St. Louis, MO 63101

Examines surveillance drug samples collected and shipped under current program directives. Analyzes all heparin and insulin samples.

4.5.5.3.5 - Center for Biologics Evaluation and Research

Center for Biologics Evaluation and Research

Sample Custodian (ATTN: HFM-672)

Building NLRC, Room 113

Kensington, MD 20895

Examines and reviews biological products not covered by a Compliance Program. Prior to shipping a sample, the district should notify either the Sample Custodian, 301-594-6517, or the Surveillance and Policy Branch, 301-594-1070, who in turn will notify the Sample Custodian.

4.5.5.3.6 - Center for Devices and Radiological Health (CDRH)

WEAC (see 1. below) is the primary laboratory for devices and radiation-emitting products. The CDRH OST laboratory accepts medical devices and radiation-emitting products for testing, but only after assignment or approval from CDRH, Office of Compliance. Note: Include in the FDA 525 envelope a copy of the manufacturers finished device specifications test methods and acceptance/rejection criteria.

1. Send samples for sterility analysis to:

   Winchester Engineering and Analytical Center (WEAC)
   109 Holton Street (HFR-NE400)
   Winchester, MA 01890-1197
   Pamela MacKill Director, Analytical
   Telephone: 781-729-5700 ext. 748
   FAX: 781-729-3593

2. Send bioburden analysis samples to WEAC.

3. Send bioindicator analysis samples to WEAC.

4. Send device and GWQAP device samples for physical and engineering analysis to WEAC.

5. Send in-vitro diagnostic device samples to WEAC.

6. Send devices used for antibiotic susceptibility testing (including discs) requiring performance testing to WEAC.

7. Send Southwest and Pacific Region condom and glove samples to the Pacific Regional Laboratory (PRS)

8. Send all other condom and glove samples to WEAC.

9. Send radiological health samples to:

   CDRH/OST Sample Custodian HFZ-105
   12725 Twinbrook Parkway, Room 210
   Rockville, MD 20852

Telephone: 301-827-4723
FAX: 301-827-4731

Note: Contact Electronic Products Branch, HFZ-342, 301-594-4654 prior to collection and shipment of any radiological product sample.

4.5.5.3.7 - Center for Veterinary Medicine

Center for Veterinary Medicine

Division of Compliance (HFV-230)

7500 Standish Place (MPN II)

Rockville, MD 20855

301-827-1168

Samples of veterinary products, not specifically covered by one or more of the CVM Compliance Programs, can be sent to the above address for review, evaluation, and comment. This includes documentary samples, and labels/ labeling and advertising materials. There are no laboratory facilities at MPN II. If you have questions about sampling or sample destinations, contact HFV-230 and/or the applicable program contact.

4.5.5.4 - Sample Shipment to Outside Agencies

Do not ship any samples outside FDA unless your assignment, applicable program, or your supervisor specifically instructs you to do so.

4.5.5.5 - Notifying Receiving Laboratories

When frozen, perishable, or high priority items are shipped, notify the receiving district or lab by telephone, or e-mail, that you have shipped the sample. Provide the following information:

1. Sample Number
2. Name of Product
3. Number of Parcels in Shipment
4. Carrier's Name
5. Carrier's Waybill Number
6. Carrier's Train, Truck, Bus, or Flight Number
7. Estimated Time and Date of Arrival
8. Relevant Remarks, i.e., "Sufficient Dry Ice to maintain frozen until 8:00 AM, (date)"
9. Place the name and telephone number of the person that is to receive the sample on the outer shipping carton near the address with

instructions to the carrier to contact the above named individual upon arrival of the package.

4.5.5.6 - Method of Shipment

Note: If samples are shipped to headquarters laboratories by bus lines, delivery of the sample must be specified on the bus bill. Use the most economical method of shipment consistent with the need for special handling. Shipping costs may be reduced by packing samples addressed to the same consignee into a larger carton or by "piggy-backing" (taping a number of larger boxes together and shipping them as one package). Make sure the total package is within the carrier's weight and size limits.

4.5.5.7 - Parcel Post

When samples are shipped by parcel post, do not exceed the parcel post limits as to size and weight.

1. Package Limits
    a. From a first class post office to a first class post office:

       Weight - 40 lbs.

       Size - 84 in. length and girth combined.

    b. Mailed at or addressed to a second or lower class post office:

       Weight - 70 lbs.

       Size - 100 in. length and girth combined.

2. *Address Labels* - The use of franked labels and envelopes is no longer allowed. Affix proper postage to envelope or address label after using district or resident post postal scale and meter. If no postal meter is available, use the resident post postage scale to weigh the envelope or package and add the proper postage using postage stamps. If no stamps are available purchase them from the post office and claim reimbursement on your voucher. Obtain a receipt for the stamps or postage, if required by your District Office.

If the package is addressed to an FDA unit, show the FDA routing symbol following the name of the FDA unit.

Note: Wrap parcels shipped "Registered Mail" in kraft paper because the postal service must affix an ink stamp seal to each closure point. Do not wrap the outer package with tape that has a shiny or glossy surface (e.g., masking tape, filament tape, scotch type tape, etc.).

4.5.5.8 - Common Carrier

Certain Department of Transportation (DOT) regulations exist pertaining to carrier inspection of packages. Instruct the carrier to contact the shipper (FDA) prior to any package inspection requires breaking the official seal. Carriers have broken FDA official seals for package inspection during transit, thereby compromising the sample integrity.

If an FDA 3082 - Shippers Declaration for Dangerous Goods is executed for shipments of restricted items, place a statement in the special handling section that breaking an FDA official seal is not authorized, and to contact the shipper (FDA) if there are any questions regarding the shipment. See IOM Exhibit 4-18.

4.5.5.8.1 - Shipment

You must decide how your samples are shipped. The judgment must be based on your knowledge of the practices and performance of the transportation firms in your area. As a general rule, Parcel Post, United Parcel Service, or current GSA contract carrier should be used for small packages and other express or comparable carriers for packages too large for PP, UPS, or current GSA contract carrier. Before using motor express lines and passenger bus lines determine that their schedules and delivery practices are satisfactory and reliable. Bus lines must not be used for shipments to Washington, DC offices unless delivery at the destination address is specified.

Air express or air freight shall be used only for samples requiring extremely rapid handling or where more economical means of shipment are not available or feasible.

Air freight service is offered by the individual air lines and, although usually not as convenient as express, is more economical and should be used especially for shipments of 50 lbs. or more.

4.5.5.8.2 - Designated Carriers

You may ship by any carrier you wish with the objective of obtaining the best possible service at the most economical rate.

Always indicate on the carrier's shipping document that the shipment is a U.S. Government shipment.

4.5.5.8.3 - Government Bill of Lading

Prepare Form SF-1103, Government Bill of Lading (GBL), for shipments made by common carrier except as described below. Distribute GBL as follows:

Give the Carrier:

1. Original (White) Form SF-1103
2. Shipping Order (Pink) Form SF-1104
3. Freight Waybill Original (White) Form SF-1105
4. Freight Waybill Carriers Copy (White) Form SF-1106

   Submit the remaining 4 copies "Memoranda Copy" (Yellow), Form SF-1103a, and the "Memorandum Copy" (Blue), Form SF-1103b, to your district.

If available, obtain the transportation costs or the rate from the carrier and enter it in pencil on the copies submitted to the district.

4.5.5.8.4 - Commercial Bill of Lading

The use of commercial forms (in lieu of GBL's) and procedures for small shipments is subject to the limitations and instructions set forth in the following paragraphs. The use of commercial forms shall be limited to those carriers that have a letter of agreement with FDA or GSA.

The use of commercial forms is to be applied only to the following types of shipments:

1. Shipments for which the transportation charges ordinarily do not exceed $100.00 per shipment and the occasional exception does not exceed that monetary limitation by an unreasonable amount.

2. Single-parcel shipments via express, courier, small package, or similar carriers, without regard to shipping cost, if the parcel shipped weighs 70 lbs. or less and does not exceed 108 inches in length and girth combined.

3. Multi-parcel shipments via express, courier, small package or similar carriers for which transportation charges do not exceed $250.00 per shipment.

4.5.5.8.5 - Address Labels

Affix a completed address label, form HHS-409, U.S. Government shipment to each shipping carton. Use the street address of the consignee, do not use the post office box numbers, since carriers usually will not deliver to PO box numbers. If the package is going to an FDA unit, include the FDA routing symbol in the consignee address. If shipment is made under the GSA-Carrier Agreement, strike out the information on GBLS in the lower left corner of the form since a GBL is not used.

4.5.5.8.6 - Shipment of Hazardous or Toxic Items

The Department of Transportation (DOT) regulations require certain packaging, forms, certifications, declarations, and/or statements covering shipment of hazardous or toxic items. Except for dry ice, most of the samples of hazardous or toxic materials we ship are classified as "ORM-D, Consumer commodity". Both dry ice classified as "9", and ORM-D classifications require a certification/declaration for shipment by air but not for shipment by surface transportation.

Shipments containing dry ice - use the dedicated Dry Ice Sticker (available from the carrier - for an example see IOM Exhibit 4-19). Complete the bottom portion of the sticker and note the amount of dry ice in kilograms. In addition to the label, the package itself must be clearly marked in 1" block letters: "DRY ICE; 9; UN1845".

Contact the carrier involved to execute the necessary forms, certification/declarations, packaging, marking, etc. required for the particular shipment or hazardous or toxic items.

4.5.5.8.7 - PRECAUTIONS

The following precautions should be observed when shipping samples:

1. Always pack liquid products in sufficient cushioning and absorbent material to absorb any breakage which might occur. Check with the Post Office or other carriers regarding shipment of liquids.

2. Hard swells may explode. Wrap them heavily in paper and cushioning material for shipment and submit promptly.

3. Observe special precautions when shipping products in pressurized containers to avoid exposure to excessive heat. Air shippers who ship in non-pressurized planes may also have special requirements for this type container. Check Post Office and carrier for regulations, precautions, or restrictions before shipping products in this type container.

4. Special precautions for both packaging and shipping radioactive substances must be observed. If necessary, consult your supervisor, the regional radiological health representative, WEAC or the applicable program.

Note: *The compliance program for radioactive drugs directs the manufacturer to ship samples via their normal mode of transportation to WEAC. The Nuclear Regulatory Commission (NRC) requires that firms manufacturing radioactive drugs ship only to NRC licensed consignees. WEAC's NRC license number is 20-08361-01 Exp. Date 2-28-2006. This license number should be used for any shipments of radioactive products to WEAC.*

4.5.5.9 - Certified and First Class Mail

Where speed is essential and a record of receipt of the sample is desired, small samples may be sent by express mail or certified air mail, or, in situations where speed is a factor but the receipt is not necessary, by first class air mail. Where other methods of shipment do not suffice, larger samples may be shipped certified or first class as a last resort. Normally do not use certified or first class for routine samples.

4.5.6 - Payment of Shipping Charges

1. Cash Payment - Agencies have authority to use imprest funds (pay cash) for Cash On Delivery (COD) payment of transportation charges. See IOM 4.5.5.8.1 and IOM 4.5.5.8.2.

   a. Shipments between districts may be shipped COD when the conditions cited above are met.

   b. Shipments to headquarters may be shipped COD but you must enter on the firm's commercial bill of lading that the FDA billing unit is as follows:

      Food and Drug Administration
      Accounting Branch (HFA-120)
      5600 Fishers Lane
      Rockville, MD 20857

2. Other Means of Payment - If you do not pay cash or the shipping cost exceeds those circumstances in IOM 4.5.5.8.4, you must use one of the following payment methods:

   a. Postal meter or postage stamps - You can use these for shipments under 70 lbs/ when it is cost effective.

   b. Billed shipments - Those shipments meeting the criteria in IOM 4.5.5.8.1 and IOM 4.5.5.8.4 and are billed by an invoice from the carrier.

   c. Government Bill of Lading (GBL) - If the other methods discussed above are not appropriate, a GBL must be issued at the time of the shipment.

   d. In an emergency, if you are without a GBL or the carrier refuses to accept a GBL at the time of shipment, you can convert the carrier's invoice to a GBL after the completion of the shipment. Avoid this procedure if at all possible.

Chapter 5: Establishment Inspections

CONTENT		VERSION DATE
Subchapter 5.1	Inspection Information	June 11, 2009
Subchapter 5.2	Inspection Procedures	June 11, 2009
Subchapter 5.3	Evidence Development	June 11, 2009
Subchapter 5.4	Food	June 11, 2009
Subchapter 5.5	Drugs	June 11, 2009
Subchapter 5.6	Devices	August 27, 2009
Subchapter 5.7	Biologics	June 11, 2009
Subchapter 5.8	Pesticides	June 11, 2009
Subchapter 5.9	Veterinary Medicine	June 11, 2009
Subchapter 5.10	Reporting	June 11, 2009

5.1 - Inspection Information

5.1.1 - Authority to Enter and Inspect

See IOM 2.2 for discussion of statutory authority.

It is your obligation to fulfill the following requirements because failure to do so may prevent use of evidence and information obtained during the inspection.

There may be occasions where you may be accompanied on your inspection or investigation by other officials. These officials may be state or local officials who have their own inspectional authority or other officials who do not have authority to enter the firm. You should obtain permission from the firm's most responsible person if officials without inspection authority wish to accompany you during your inspection/investigation. You should document in your EIR when other non-FDA officials accompany you during your inspection, and whether they entered under their own authority or the responsible individual at the firm gave permission (identify, by name and title, the responsible individual giving permission). See IOM 5.2.2 and 5.10.4.3.2.

5.1.1.1 - FDA Investigator's Responsibility

Your authority to enter and inspect establishments is predicated upon specific obligations to the firm as described below. It is your responsibility to conduct all inspections at reasonable times and within reasonable limits and in a reasonable manner. Proceed with diplomacy, tact and persuasiveness.

5.1.1.2 - Credentials

Display your credentials to the top management official be it the owner, operator, or agent in charge. See IOM 5.2.2.

NOTE: Although management may examine your credentials and record the number and your name, do not permit your credentials to be photocopied. Federal Law (Title 18, U.S.C. 701) prohibits photographing, counterfeiting, or misuse of official credentials.

5.1.1.3 - Written Notice

After showing the firm's representative your credentials, issue the original, properly executed, and signed FDA 482, Notice of Inspection, to the top management official. Keep the carbon copy for submission with your report.

5.1.1.4 - Written Observations

Upon completing the inspection and before leaving the premises, provide the highest management official available your inspectional findings on an FDA 483 - Inspectional Observations. See Section 704(b) of the FD&C Act [21 U.S.C. 374 (b)] and IOM 5.2.3 and 5.2.7.

5.1.1.5 - Receipts

Furnish the top management official the original of the FDA-484 - Receipt for Samples describing any samples obtained during the inspection. See IOM 5.2.4.

5.1.1.6 - Written Demand for Records

In low-acid canned food and acidified food EI's, an FDA 482a - Demand for Records (exhibit 5-2) is required under 21 CFR 108.35(h) and 21 CFR 108.25(g) to obtain records required by 21 CFR 113 and 114.

5.1.1.7 - Written Requests for Information

There are several methods of requesting records. These may include a request for information under LACF or AF inspections, 703 written requests, and requests for records under the BT Act (IOM 5.4.1.3).

5.1.1.7.1 - LACF / AF Food Inspections

In low-acid canned foods and acidified foods EIs, an FDA 482b, Request for Information (exhibit 5-3), is required under 21 CFR 108.35(c)(3)(ii) and 21 CFR 108.25(c)(3)(ii) to obtain information concerning processes and procedures required under 21 CFR 113 and 114.

5.1.1.7.2 - Requests for Records Under Section 703 of the FD&C Act

Per CPG Sec. 160.300, Requests for Records under Section 703 [21 U.S.C. 373], evidence obtained in response to a specific written request under Section 703 cannot be used in a criminal prosecution of the person from whom obtained. With Supervisory approval, in certain circumstances, you may decide to issue a 703 written request when the importance of the evidence is crucial to protecting the public health.

Procedure: All 703 written requests must comply with IOM 4.4.7.2.2. Consider obtaining the evidence from other sources before using the 703 written request. In the case of foods and feeds, if there is a risk or threat of serious adverse health consequences, the district should invoke the BT Act records access authority. All BT Act records requests must comply with IOM 5.4.1.3.

5.1.1.8 - Business Premises

Authority to inspect firms operating at a business location is described in IOM 5.1.1 and requires issuing management an FDA 482, Notice of Inspection, and presenting your credentials. A warrant for inspection is not necessary unless a refusal or partial refusal is encountered or anticipated.

5.1.1.9 - Premises Used for Living Quarters

All inspections where the premises are also used for living quarters must be conducted with a warrant for inspection unless:

Owner Agreeable - The owner or operator is fully agreeable and offers no resistance or objection whatsoever or;

Physically Separated - The actual business operations to be inspected are physically separated from the living quarters by doors or other building construction. These would provide a distinct division of the premises into two physical areas, one for living quarters and the other for business operations, and you do not enter the living area.

In both the latter cases, proceed as any other inspection with the appropriate presentation of credentials and issuance of a Notice of Inspection.

5.1.1.10 - Facilities where Electronic Products are Used or Held

Section 537(a) of the FD&C Act provides the FDA with the authority to inspect the facilities of manufacturers in certain circumstances. The electronic product radiation control provisions were originally enacted as the Radiation Control for Health and Safety Act of 1968 (P.L. 90-602)

It is lawful for FDA personnel to enter the facilities of an electronic product distributor, dealer, assembler or user for the purpose of testing an electronic product for radiation safety when the entry is voluntarily permitted. Congress has not specifically prohibited FDA from conducting such voluntary examinations and such examinations would clearly agree with the congressional declaration of purpose expressed in section 532(a) of the RCH&S Act.

Under the Medical Device Authority, electronic products utilized in human and/or veterinary medicine, e.g., x-ray, laser, ultra-sound, diathermy, etc. can be considered prescription devices. In these cases the authority of Section

704 of the FD&C Act [21 U.S.C. 374] can be used to obtain entry to inspect the user facility. If the Medical Device Authority is utilized, credentials must be displayed and a FDA 482, Notice of Inspection, must be issued.

5.1.1.11 - Multiple Occupancy Inspections

You are required per FD&C Act 704(a)(1) [21 U.S.C. 374(a)(1)] to issue a Notice of Inspection, FDA 482, to each firm inspected. When firms have operations located in different sites or buildings, you should use judgment to determine when multiple FDA 482 forms need to be issued. For sites located a distance apart, it is preferable to issue a FDA 482 to the most responsible person at each site. One rule of thumb which can be used is if the sites or buildings are within walking distance, your original Notice of Inspection can be considered sufficient to cover both. During your initial interview with management, after you issue the FDA 482, make sure you clearly indicate the facility and sites you intend to inspect. The Act requires the issuance of a Notice of Inspection, but does not prohibit issuing multiple notices if management so requests. As with all of our work, good judgment, and knowledge of the OEI and the FD&C Act are necessary in deciding what legally must be done.

5.1.1.12 - Authority for Examinations and Investigations

Section 702(a) of the FD&C Act [21 U.S.C. 372 (a)] authorizes examinations and investigations for the purpose of enforcing the Act.

5.1.1.13 - Authority to Implement Section 702(e)(5) of the FD&C Act

Section 702(e) of the FD&C Act [21 U.S.C. 372 (e)] contains certain authorities relating to counterfeit drugs including the authority to seize ("confiscate") counterfeit drugs and containers, counterfeiting equipment, and all other items used or designed for use in making counterfeit drugs prior to the initiation of libel proceedings. This authority has been delegated, with certain restrictions, to holders of official credentials consistent with their authority to conduct enforcement activities. Additional authority in 702(e) to make arrests, to execute and serve arrest warrants, to carry firearms, or to execute seizure by process under Section 304 of the FD&C Act [21 U.S.C. 334] have not been delegated.

The agency does intend to utilize the authority contained in Section 702(e) to execute and serve search warrants, but such use does not require delegation from the ACRA.

Section 702(e)(5) contains authority for such delegated persons to confiscate all items which are, or which the investigator has reasonable grounds to believe are, subject to seizure under Section 304(a)(2). Items subject to seizure, and thus to confiscation under Section 702(e)(5), includes most things associated with counterfeit drugs. Confiscation authority does not, however, extend to vehicles, records, or items (i.e., the profits) obtained as a result of counterfeiting.

5.1.1.13.1 - Scope

Under this delegation, with supervisory concurrence and prior to the initiation of libel proceedings, investigators and inspectors are authorized to confiscate:

1. Any counterfeit drug
2. Any container used to hold a counterfeit drug,
3. Any raw material used in making a counterfeit drug
4. Any labeling used for counterfeit drug
5. Any equipment used to make a counterfeit drug including punches, dies, plates, stones, tableting machines, etc.
6. Any other thing which you have reasonable grounds to believe is designed or used in making a counterfeit drug.

NOTE: You and your supervisor must be constantly aware of the potential dangers involved in confiscating property from individuals. Special care should be taken to ensure your safety. Arranging for teams of investigators to conduct the investigation, or arranging for assistance by local police, or other agencies with police powers, should be considered in planning the confiscation of counterfeit materials.

5.1.1.13.2 - Inspectional Guidance

Guidance provided for implementing the authority to confiscate drug counterfeits is as follows:

1. The authority is not to be utilized unless there has been an agency determination the drug to be confiscated is a counterfeit and it is a drug which "without authorization, bears a trademark, *** or any likeness" of a legitimate product. The determination usually is based upon evidence supplied by the firm whose product is being counterfeited. A written agency determination will issue to the District Director from the Office of Enforcement, in conjunction with the Office of Regional Operations, and the Center for Drug Evaluation and Research.
2. When engaged in counterfeit investigations, you should proceed as follows upon encountering items to be confiscated.
   a. Evaluate safety needs and check the location to ensure it is safe to proceed. Do not attempt to remove an item by force. If it appears there will be resistance, contact the local police, or other agencies with police powers for backup, if not already done in advance.
   b. Inventory the items to be confiscated.
   c. Prepare a written receipt and offer it to the person in charge.
   d. Remove the items, if possible, from the premises (if they cannot be removed, secure them under seal).

e. Place all items removed under lock at a secure location. In most cases, confiscated items will be stored at the district or resident post office until they are seized.

5.1.1.13.3 - Follow up Guidance

After items are confiscated, certain actions must be taken to bring confiscated items under the control of the court. Proceed as follows:

1. After an item is confiscated, immediately notify your supervisor.

2. Supervisors must then notify the appropriate compliance units of the items confiscated.

3. Compliance units should initiate seizure proceedings against any items confiscated.

4. ORO/DFI should be advised of any action utilizing this authority.

5.1.1.13.4 - Search Warrants

Section 702(e)(2) contains authority to execute and serve search warrants. Proceed as instructed by your district after a search warrant has been obtained.

5.1.1.14 - Products Imported Under the Provisions of Section 801(d)(3) of the FD&C Act

The FDA Export Reform and Enhancement Act of 1996 (PL 104-134 and 104-180) amended the FD&C Act by adding Section 801(d)(3) ("Import for Export") which permits the importation of unapproved drug and medical device components, food additives, color additives, and dietary supplements intended for further incorporation or processing into products destined for export from the United States. Section 801(d)(3) was subsequently amended by Section 322 of the Public Health Security and Bioterrorism Preparedness and Response Act of 2002 (Bioterrorism Act), Public Law 107-188, which specified certain requirements an importer has to satisfy in order to import a product under this Section. See IOM 6.2.3.4.

5.1.1.14.1 - Requirements for BT Act

These requirements include:

1. A statement confirming the intent to further process such article or incorporate such article into a product to be exported,

2. The identification of all entities in the chain of possession of the imported article,

3. A certificate of analysis "as necessary to identify the article" (unless the article is a device), and

4. Executing a bond providing for liquidated damages in the event of default, in accordance with U.S. Customs. This bond remains in effect until the final product is exported and destroyed.

In addition, the initial owner or consignee must keep records showing the use of the imported articles, and must be able to provide upon request a report showing the disposition or export of the imported articles. An article imported under this section, and not incorporated or further processed, must be destroyed or exported by the owner or consignee. Failure to keep records or to make them available to FDA, making false statements in such records, failure to export or destroy imported articles not further incorporated into finished products, and introduction of the imported article or final product into domestic commerce are Prohibited Acts under Section 301(w).

Filers making entry under the Import for Export provisions must either identify entry submissions with the OASIS Affirmation of Compliance "IFE" (Import for Export), or supply FDA with written documentation stating the product is entered under the Import for Export provisions. A Certificate of Analysis (as necessary) and identification of all involved entities must be submitted in writing to the import district. The import district will forward all written documentation to the home district of the initial owner or consignee for incorporation into the appropriate Establishment File.

5.1.1.14.2 - Inspectional Preparation

Before conducting an Establishment Inspection, contact your district's designated individual with access to OASIS/EEPS Reports to obtain a printout of any import entries made by the establishment under the Import for Export provisions through OASIS. In addition, check the district factory file for copies of any Import for Export documents forwarded from the district where entry was filed. During the inspection examine the firm's records to determine the disposition of any items identified at time of entry as intended for incorporation into products for export. Document any instances in which such products were introduced into domestic commerce or cannot be accounted for (see IOM 6.2.3.4.3).

5.1.2 - Inspectional Approach

An establishment inspection is a careful, critical, official examination of a facility to determine its compliance with laws administered by FDA. Inspections may be used to obtain evidence to support legal action when violations are found, or they may be directed to obtaining specific information on new technologies, good commercial practices, or data for establishing food standards or other regulations. In order to facilitate on-the-job training, multiple points of view, and perspectives of firms being inspected whenever practical, those with assignment authority, should consider assigning different Investigator/s or different Lead Investigators at different times. This is recommended particularly when there have been multiple sequential NAI inspections or when the firm's management has been uncooperative.

The kind and type of inspection you conduct will normally be defined by the program, assignment, or your supervisor; according to the following definitions:

Comprehensive Inspection - directs coverage to everything in the firm subject to FDA jurisdiction to determine the firms compliance status; or

Directed Inspection - directs coverage to specific areas to the depth described in the program, assignment, or as instructed by your supervisor.

See IOM Subchapter 1.5 for information on safety, use of protective gear, dealing with potential hazards and other safety issues.

5.1.2.1 - Depth of Inspection

The degree and depth of attention given various operations in a firm depends upon information desired, or upon the violations suspected or likely to be encountered. In determining the amount of attention to be given in specific cases, consider:

1. The current Compliance Program,
2. Nature of the assignment,
3. General knowledge of the industry and its problems,
4. Firm history, and
5. Conditions found as the inspection progresses.

5.1.2.2 - Inspection Walk Through

A preliminary tour of the premises should be conducted early in an establishment inspection to become familiar with the operation and to plan the inspection strategy. A walk through visual inspection of the manufacturing site is helpful in establishing the depth of the inspection, learning about products and processes, identifying sources of manufacturing records and identifying potential areas of concern. The size of the facility, the number of employees, employee practices, environmental conditions inside and outside the plant, raw materials, manual and automated processes, sources of contamination, manufacturing flow, method of data collection including computer terminals, are some of the areas to be taken into consideration in establishing the depth of the inspection. A visual inspection of a manufacturing site should also be used to check obvious potential problem areas such as: general housekeeping, state of operation for processes and processing equipment, and people dependent operations. Visual inspections of areas used for failure investigation, product sampling and testing, product reworks, return goods, and product quarantine areas should be inspected for obvious potential product problems.

Depending on the product is being inspected, some of the general inspectional equipment an investigator should have available, may include, eye and ear protection, boots and protective clothing. Some specialized equipment may include radiation or EO monitoring devices, magnifiers, and timing devices as needed. For some domestic and foreign plant sites, investigators may be required to be inoculated prior to the inspection for protection from potential environmental concerns such as hepatitis, yellow fever, malaria and live biological products which may be encountered in vaccine products. See subchapter IOM 1.5.

5.1.2.3 - Signing Non-FDA Documents

Occasionally a firm will request you sign various documents including:

1. A waiver which will exempt the firm from any responsibility or liability should an accident occur and you are injured on the firm's premises,

2. Form letters concerning access to confidential information the firm does not want released,

3. Information/data you request during the inspection be put into writing, etc.

If you receive such a request, inform the firm you are not authorized to sign such documents, letters, requests, waivers, etc., but will report the firm's request in your EIR. The use of common sense is expected with this procedure. All FDA employees are authorized to sign-in and sign-out at a firm and to comply with security measures employed by the firm, including documenting the removal/replacement of seals to inspect vehicles and containers. See IOM 4.3.4.3 and 4.5.4.6. Obviously, the key issue is you are not authorized to waive, without supervisory approval, any of FDA's rights to inspect, sample, photograph, copy, etc. or to sign any interstate shipping record document which could infer the firm could not be prosecuted under the Act.

5.1.2.4 - Technical Assistance

If you determine specialized technical assistance is necessary in conducting inspections of new technologies, products or manufacturing procedures, it may be available through Regional or National experts, other ORA components or Center scientists and engineers. If specialized skills are necessary and are not available locally or through your Region, contact the Division of Field Investigations (DFI), (HFC-130) at 301-827-5653. See FMD 142 and IOM 1.9.2.2.1 for additional information.

5.1.2.5 - Team Inspections

The use of teams to conduct inspections may be beneficial. Very often individuals well versed in an analytical or inspectional technique or technology can provide assistance and advice.

When inspection teams are involved in an inspection, one investigator will be designated as the team leader by the inspecting district or by the Division of Field Investigations (DFI/HFC-130) if a headquarters directed special inspection is involved. The team leader is in charge of the inspection and bears the overall responsibility for the inspection and the EIR. A team may consist of multiple investigators, laboratory personnel and other FDA employees, and your supervisor/coach, who may participate as part of the ORA Quality Assurance program.

5.1.2.5.1 - Team Member Responsibilities

Each team member is responsible for preparing those portions of the report pertaining to his/her activities. Team members shall identify their portion of the report so they can later identify that portion as the part he/she performed and reported. Since reports should be written in the first person, one system might be to head each portion with a statement "The following operation(s) was/were observed and reported by Investigator ___________", who can then report in the first person.

All team members must sign the original EIR. Ideally, all team members should sign the FDA 483, if one is issued. However, issuance of the FDA 483 should not be delayed, in the absence of a team member's signature. See IOM 5.2.3 for instructions for signing a multi-page FDA 483.

5.1.2.5.2 - Team Leader Responsibilities

The Team Leader shall be responsible for:

1. Issuing unused notebooks for taking regulatory notes during the EI or investigation to headquarters personnel on the team. He/she is also responsible for instructions on their use, if necessary, and when the report is finished, for obtaining the headquarters individual's signature on the original EIR and completed and properly identified regulatory notes and submitting them to the supervisor for filing. See IOM 2.1.3.

2. Directing the overall inspection to accomplish the objectives of the assignment including;

    a. Planning the inspection,

    b. Scheduling and coordinating team members' pre-inspection preparations,

    c. Determining, to the extent possible, the firm will be open and operating,

    d. Planning for needs of visiting scientists if applicable. When the team leader is not familiar with all the processes or technology involved in the inspection, provide for primary coverage of selected areas by other team members,

    e. Determining an orderly, efficient, and effective approach and sequence to be used and discussing the inspection plan with the team,

    f. Modifying the inspection plan as necessary during the EI, to permit following leads, documenting evidence, etc.,

    g. Setting team policy on how communications with the firm are to be handled,

    h. Discussing personal conduct in dealing with headquarters personnel as necessary,

    i. Assuring an early understanding by team members of their roles in note taking and reporting,

    j. Assuring communications are open among team members, especially if the team is allowed to separate and work independently,

    k. Reviewing inspection progress at least daily, discussing remaining objectives with the team members, and setting objectives for the following day,

l. Continually assessing the progress of the inspection to evaluate how the inspectional approach is working and to keep the district supervisor advised of the inspection's progress,

m. Providing guidance and direction to team members as necessary,

n. Advising each team member of reporting responsibilities and dates when drafts are to be provided,

o. Following up promptly on any delays or failures to report as required, and

p. Assisting the supervisor with further follow up, as indicated.

3. Making sure any person who joins the team after the inspection has started presents credentials and issues a Notice of Inspection, FDA 482, to the firm prior to actually taking part in the EI;
4. Completing and/or correcting the computer generated coversheet;
5. Preparing the Summary of Findings;
6. Completing all headings of an administrative nature in the narrative report;
7. Compiling and submitting the complete final report; and
8. Resolving any disputes or differences of opinion among the team members, including items, which may be listed on the FDA 483.

5.1.3 - Inspection of Foreign Firms

Inspectional requirements apply to all inspections, including foreign inspections. However, there are some exceptions. For instance the FDA 482 is not required, unless the firm is a US Military facility. Be guided by relevant Compliance Programs and the Guide to International Inspections and Travel Manual for other differences. See IOM 1.2.1.2.

5.1.4 - Inspectional Precautions

Our concern over microbiological contamination emphasizes the need for you to be alert to criticism or allegations that you may have contributed to or caused contamination at a firm. This is especially important in drug firms and high-risk food firms, among others. You must adhere to good sanitation practices to refute any such criticisms. You could also unknowingly introduce or spread disease during inspections of or visits to animal production or sale facilities, conducting environmental investigations at poultry layer facilities, conducting dairy farm inspections or audits of state activities, investigating tissue residue reports or working in the veterinary bioresearch area. See IOM 5.2.10 for information outlining precautions for you to follow.

Exercise caution in all activities in the firm. Follow the firm's sanitation program for employees and wash and sanitize hands, shoes, vehicles and equipment as indicated. Restrict unnecessary movement between various areas in plants and when possible, complete your activities in one area before moving to the next.

When inspecting areas where sterility is maintained or sterile rooms are located (especially in pharmaceutical or device firms), follow the sterile program required of the firm's employees. In general it is unnecessary to enter sterile rooms except in the most extraordinary circumstances. These areas are usually constructed to provide visual monitoring. Take no unsterile items with you (notebook, pencils, etc.). In this type of situation you can enter your observations in your regulatory notes immediately after leaving the sterile area.

Always use aseptic techniques, including hand sanitizing, when collecting in-line and raw material samples, as well as finished product samples for microbiological examination. See IOM 4.3.6.

Do not use or consume a firm's products at any of a firm's facilities. This could be interpreted as accepting a product as being satisfactory and could possibly embarrass you and the Agency, both during the inspection and in the future. In general, consuming food products in a manufacturing area is considered an objectionable practice.

When conducting inspections of firm's using chemicals, pesticides, etc., ask to review the Material Safety Data Sheets (MSDS) for the products involved to determine what, if any, safety precautions you must take. This could include the use of respirators or other safety equipment.

5.1.4.1 - Clothing

Wear clean coveralls or other protective clothing for each inspection and if circumstances dictate, use a clean pair when returning from lunch, or upon entering certain machinery or critical areas.

Remove and secure all jewelry, pens, pencils, notebook, etc., so they cannot fall into the product or machinery. Do not depend on clips on pens, etc., to hold these items in your outer pockets.

Clean protective clothing should be either individually wrapped or placed in clean plastic bags and taped to protect from contamination. If the package has been sterilized, protect the package from possible contamination or puncture. The package should not be opened until you are ready to use the clothing. After use, clothing should be turned inside out as it is removed, and immediately placed in clean paper or plastic bags to prevent spread of contamination until washed and/or sterilized.

Use disposable hair and head coverings throughout the inspection and disposable hand and foot coverings in areas where floor tracking or cross contamination may be a factor. Use hard hats and other protective devices where the situation dictates.

If reusable protective boots are used, wash and sanitize before each use. Always use sterile disposable boot covers when entering machinery such as dryers or where unavoidable contact with product is a factor.

When discarding contaminated disposable head and boot coverings, it is suggested they be placed with used clothing for proper disposal after leaving the plant area.

See IOM 5.2.10.1 for protective clothing and equipment necessary when visiting livestock or poultry producing areas.

5.1.4.2 - PHS Recommendations - Basic Sanitary Practices

FDA personnel are not required by law to have health certificates, take physical exams or submit to requirements, which ensures their compliance with sanitary procedures in the performance of their official duties. However, it is critical you adhere to basic sanitation practices. See IOM 1.5.1.5.

The Food Code is available electronically form the FDA CFSAN web page at http://www.cfsan.fda.gov under Federal/State Programs-Retail Food Safety References. Printed copies may be ordered from the National Technical Information Service, NTIS, www.ntis.gov.

5.1.4.3 - Representatives Invited by the Firm to View the Inspection

While conducting an inspection, you may find the firm's management has invited individuals who are not directly employed by the firm to view the inspectional process (e.g., representatives from the press, trade associations, consumer groups, congressional staff, other company officials).

Regardless of whom the firm invites to observe the progress of an inspection, the presence of outside representatives should not disrupt the inspectional process. You should continue to conduct the inspection in a reasonable fashion. The presence of these individuals should have no impact on the manner in which the inspection progresses except you should take precautions to preserve the confidentially of any information you may have obtained as a result of the Agency's statutory authority. This is especially true when the inspection is recorded via videotaping, other photography, and/or audio recordings. Where applicable, refer to IOM 5.3.5 for procedures on how to prepare your own recording in parallel with the firm's recording.

It is the Agency's position that while the investigator must protect privileged information provided to him/her during the inspection, it is the firm's responsibility to protect privileged/confidential information observed or recorded by those individuals invited by the firm.

5.1.5 - General Procedures & Techniques

The procedures and techniques applicable to specific inspections and investigations for foods, drugs, devices, cosmetics, radiological health, or other FDA operations are found in part in the IOM (inspectional and investigational policy/procedure), various Guides to Inspections of... (a "how to" guidance series), and the Compliance Program Guidance Manual (program specific instructions). Some procedures and techniques which may be applicable to overlapping areas or operations are as follows:

5.1.5.1 - Candling

Candling is defined as: "to examine by holding between the eye and a light, especially to test eggs in this way for staleness, blood clots, fertility and growth." Like most techniques learned through the food inspection programs, there are uses for this technique in other program areas such as looking for mold in bottled liquids which could be drugs, devices or biologics. Candling can also be useful in the examination of original documents to see below white-out or to look for over-writing.

Many types of products lend themselves to inspection by some type of candling. For these products, firms generally have candling equipment which may be built into the production lines or may be a separate operation.

Where checking products by candling, it may be possible to utilize the firm's candling equipment. Various other light sources for candling are also available including overhead projectors. Exercise care when using overhead projectors and protect the glass surface and the lens from scratches and damage. All candling is best accomplished when light outside the item being candled is masked so the light passes through the object rather than being diffused around it. A heavy paper or cardboard template can be quickly prepared at the time candling is done.

5.1.5.2 - Label Review

Do not undertake a critical review of labels unless instructed by the assignment, program, or your supervisor. Limit your comments to the mandatory label requirements required by the Acts. However, if after review of the formula, it is obvious an active ingredient or an otherwise mandatory ingredient statement does not appear on the label, such discrepancy may be called to management's attention. See also IOM 5.2.3.2 regarding labeling for blood and blood products.

If asked for other label comments, refer the firm to the appropriate Center to obtain a label review.

When the labeling is suspect or when you are requested to collect labels/labeling, collect three copies of all labels and accompanying literature for further review. For medical devices, if there is a question regarding the need for a new 510(k) or PMA supplement, it is essential the label and labeling be collected.

5.1.5.3 - Field Exams

A field examination is an on-site examination of a domestic product (or a foreign product in domestic channels of trade) sufficient in itself to determine if the product is in compliance with the Acts enforced by FDA.. A field exam can be conducted of any commodity in any location. If the examination does not reveal a violation or the appearance of a violation, a sample of the lot is usually not collected. If your exam reveals a violation or potential violation, you should collect an official sample. With the implementation of FACTS, your time spent conducting the field exam is reported even if you do collect a sample. Only the actual time spent in the collection of the sample would be reported as sample time.

Instructions on how to conduct a field exam are contained in "Guides To The Inspection of ***" and Compliance Programs. The Sample Schedules in Chapter 4 also provide guidance on lot examinations for special situations.

5.2 - Inspection Procedures

5.2.1 - Pre-Inspectional Activities

Prior to the start of any inspection or investigation, you should conduct a number of activities. These will differ based on whether this is an inspection or an investigation. You should a review of the establishment's factory jacket (if one exists), and registration and listing (if applicable) information. The purpose of this review is to determine the location of the establishment and obtain an overview of the establishment's operations and products as well as an understanding of their compliance history. You should also evaluate the establishment factory jacket to determine if there were any prior safety issues noted, e.g. documented Investigator safety incidents or whether any specific personal protective equipment is needed prior to the start of the inspection. If there has been a past personal safety incident, you should discuss with your supervisor and develop a Situational Plan prior to the start of the inspection. See IOM 5.2.1.4 – Personal Safety Plan.

Prior to initiating any inspection you should become familiar with the reporting requirements for the specific assignment, as well as the requirements of IOM Subchapter 5.10.

If the inspection or investigation is a directed assignment from a Center, ORA headquarters or another district, read it and attached materials to assure you understand the assignment. If the inspection or investigation is being conducted in part or solely as a recall follow-up or complaint, refer to Chapter 7 (Recalls) or Chapter 8 (Investigations) of the IOM for additional guidance.

You should review the applicable FACTS assignment to determine if the Personal Safety Alert indicator is checked for this specific firm. The reason for the Personal Safety Alert should be listed in Endorsement and should be accompanied by a Memo to the Establishment File Jacket or documented in a prior EIR. See IOM 5.2.1.3 Personal Safety Alert.

You should also review the applicable Compliance Program Guidance Manual(s) prior to the start of your inspection or investigation. ORA's Division of Field Investigations (DFI) has written numerous Inspection Guides to assist you in conducting inspections of various types of establishments, products or processes. You should become familiar with the appropriate guides prior to the start of the inspection and utilize them as needed throughout the inspection. The Centers have issued numerous guidance documents for industry. These documents are normally posted to the appropriate Center's Internet and Intranet web sites.

Subchapters 5.4-5.9 of the IOM contain additional, program specific pre-inspectional activities, which you should follow.

Imported products cross all program areas and our regulation of them does not stop at the border. Determine if there are any "import for export" follow-up assignments and be prepared to cover them during your inspection. See IOM 6.2.3.4 for guidance. Please be alert to imported products whenever you make an inspection. During inspections of domestic firms, if you encounter imported products that appear adulterated, misbranded, counterfeit, tampered with or otherwise suspect, attempt to fully identify the product and the source of the imported products. Contact your supervisor and DIOP (HFC-170) if necessary.

5.2.1.1 - Pre-Announcements

Pre-announcements are mandatory for all medical device inspections in accordance with the criteria and instructions below and BIMO sponsor/monitor inspections. In all other program areas, pre-announcements may be made at the discretion of the district. If you are going to visit facilities where livestock (including poultry) or wild animals are housed or processed, review IOM 5.2.10. In general, it may be inappropriate to pre-announce inspections of food establishments, blood banks, source plasma establishments and some BIMO inspections, but this too is subject to district discretion. If a district believes pre-announcing an inspection of an establishment will facilitate the inspection process then the procedures below for doing pre-announcements for medical device inspections should be followed. ORA's primary purpose for pre-announcing is to assure the appropriate records and personnel will be available during the inspection. It is not to make an appointment for the inspection. It should not be referred to as an appointment to inspect. When doing a pre-announcement, it is important you communicate to the establishment the purpose of the inspection and a general idea of the records you may wish to review. If you find neither the appropriate personnel nor records available, note this in your Establishment Inspection Report (EIR). The District may use this data in the future when considering whether this establishment should be eligible for pre-announced inspections.

The following is the general outline for pre-announcement of medical device inspections. You are advising the establishment's management of the date and time you will be arriving at the establishment to conduct the inspection. The establishment has no authority to negotiate this. If you, as the investigator, feel the need to accommodate the establishment's request, be sure there are sound reasons for doing so and report them in your inspection report.

5.2.1.1.1 - Basic Premises

Pre-announcement of inspections is to be applied only to establishments that meet specific criteria. Pre-announcement may be considered for establishments that manufacture both drugs and devices or biologics and devices. The eligibility of an individual establishment for pre-announced inspection is at the discretion of the inspecting office using clearly described criteria. (See Criteria for Consideration) The district does not have the discretion to decide the types of medical device establishments eligible for pre-announcement, but may decide the specific establishments' eligibility because they meet the criteria.

The pre-announcement should generally be no less than 5 calendar days in advance of the inspection. Should a postponement be necessary, the decision as to rescheduling rests with the investigator/team, but the new inspection date should not be later than 5 calendar days from the original date. Inspections may be conducted sooner than 5 calendar days if requested by or acceptable to the establishment and if this date is acceptable to the investigator/team.

To participate in the pre-announcement portion of the program, establishments are expected to meet the commitment to have appropriate records and personnel available during the inspection.

Pre-announced inspections will not limit an investigator's authority to conduct the inspection. Inspections will be as thorough as necessary.

5.2.1.1.2 - Criteria for Consideration

When deciding whether an establishment qualifies for a pre-announced inspection, you must consider whether both the type of inspection and the establishment's status meet the following specific criteria.

5.2.1.1.2.1 - Type of Inspection

Only the following types of inspections are appropriate:

1. Pre-market inspections (PMA, 510(k))
2. Foreign inspections
3. Quality System/Good Manufacturing Practice (QS/GMP) inspections:
    a. Biennial routine inspections
    b. Initial inspections of new facilities or newly registered establishments
    c. Initial inspections under new management and/or ownership.

5.2.1.1.2.2 - Eligibility Criteria

Establishment's eligible for pre-notification should meet the following requirements:

1. Non-violative QS/GMP inspection histories (inspections classified as no action indicated (NAI) or voluntary action indicated (VAI)). For VAI, adequate corrections of conditions observed and listed on FDA 483 during the previous inspection were verified and did not lead to any further agency action.
2. To remain eligible for pre-announced inspections, establishments must have a history of having individuals and/or documents identified in previous pre-announced inspections reasonably available at the time of the inspection.

5.2.1.1.3 - Procedures

Procedures:

1. The investigator designated to conduct the inspection will contact the most responsible individual at the facility. You should leave a message requesting a return call if the most responsible person at the facility is

unavailable at the time the call is made. The district should use good judgment as to what is a reasonable time frame to await the return call.

2. Changes in dates should be kept to a minimum. If a change is made, a new date should be provided as soon as possible, which will facilitate the inspection and accommodate the investigator's schedule. The establishment should provide a valid reason for requesting a change in the start date. A valid reason should be the same as you would accept if presented with the information during an unannounced inspection.

3. Inform the establishment as to the purpose, estimated duration, and the number of agency personnel expected to take part in the inspection. The products or processes to be covered should be described if this will facilitate and be consistent with the objectives of the inspection.

4. When known, specific records/personnel will be requested at the time the inspection is pre-announced.

5. The notification should be as specific as reasonably possible and specify the date for the start of the inspection.

Include in your EIR whether or not the inspection was pre-announced and include information on any difficulties experienced in notification or accessing records or personnel, which should have been available as a result of pre-announcing the inspection. For medical device establishment inspections, if not pre-announced, describe briefly in the EIR why not. If an establishment should become ineligible for pre-announcement, the endorsement of the EIR should include this statement. This information will be necessary for making a determination regarding future pre-announced inspections of the establishment. In addition, it is advisable to inform the establishment during the current and subsequent inspections of the action(s), which may have caused them to be ineligible for pre-announcement.

Subchapters 5.4-5.9 of the IOM contain additional, program specific pre-inspectional activities, which you should follow.

5.2.1.2 - Personal Safety

ORA considers the safety of Investigators, Inspectors and all those who meet with regulated industry to be of the utmost importance. Personal safety concerns are defined as those factors FDA employees should maintain awareness of which potentially affect their safety during an inspection, such a threatening situation; or where specific personal protective safety equipment is warranted; or where a particular inspection may be medically contraindicated for specific FDA personnel. When these conditions are noted during an inspection, the Investigator should discuss the situation with their Supervisor and ensure that the Personal Safety Alert is checked in FACTS and a Memo to the File is generated– see IOM 5.2.1.3 For information concerning personal protective equipment, see IOM Subchapter 1.5.

Physical resistance to FDA inspections and threats to, or assaults on, FDA employees engaged in their work are extremely rare. However, there will be times you are confronted by unfriendly or hostile persons. ORA has offered various conflict resolution training courses to assist and prepare you for how to diffuse a situation. In most instances, conducting your activities with tact, honesty, diplomacy, and persuasiveness will be enough to diffuse the situation. While at times, you may have to adopt a firm posture, you should not resort to threats, intimidation, or strong-arm tactics. Refer to IOM 5.2.5.4 for Hostile and Uncooperative Interviewees.

Safety is the responsibility of all FDA employees, including you, your supervisor and other Agency management. When you receive an assignment, it is important to evaluate the assignment not only in accordance with IOM Section 5.2.1, but also with respect to your personal safety. If you determine there is the possibility of a threat to your personal safety, consult with your supervisor. You and your supervisor should consider developing a Situational Plan in preparation for the inspection.

5.2.1.2.1 - Preparation

Below are some suggested items the District may consider when preparing for your next assignment to assess if there are potential personal safety issues. This list is not meant to be all inclusive.

1. Does the assignment involve working with other Federal Agencies such as U.S. Marshals, Federal Bureau of Investigations, US Customs in executing search warrants, seizures etc?

2. Does the assignment involve working with or contacting FDA's Office of Criminal Investigation?

3. Does the assignment involve a firm where there is a suspicion and/or knowledge of questionable or illegal activities?

4. Does the assignment involve a suspected tampering and/or a visit to an individual's residence?

5. What is the past history from a personal safety standpoint with the prior interactions with representatives of this firm? Have the FDA's State counterparts or other Federal and/or local agencies indicated a concern for personal safety? What does the firm's establishment file indicate about personal safety over the past inspections?

6. What is the location of the firm or the operation? Is it in an area which may be unsafe? Have the inspected firm or any of it's employees been uncooperative with government officials?

7. Is the firm known to the Agency? Has the Agency any additional information which would assist in your evaluation?

If these questions and/or others result in a concern for your personal safety, then a Personal Safety Plan should be developed and approved by District management before conducting the assignment. See IOM 5.2.1.4 - Situational Plan.

Due to the unlimited variability of potential safety situations, it is not feasible to prescribe in the IOM what to do in every instance. The decision of what to do in each individual circumstance rests with the Investigator and their District management. Your district management is most familiar with the specific firm in question, the regulated industry, as well as other local Federal, State and Local officials who may be able to provide you additional information and assistance. In addition, the experience of your District management combined with the various training courses on conflict resolution may also be consulted. Districts should notify Division of Field Investigations to inform headquarters of any potential safety concern, so that DFI may track personal safety issues. DFI will also maintain a library of Personal Safety Plans which may also be of use to your District. DFI may be contacted at 301-827-5653 or at the following personal safety e-mail address: ORAHQDFICSOSAF@FDA.HHS.GOV

5.2.1.2.2 - Physical Resistance/Threats/Assaults

If you receive physical resistance or threats, or if you sense the real possibility of an assault, disengage from the confrontation, get to safety, and call your supervisor immediately. Make careful and exact notes later of who said what to whom, who did what, and whether someone tried or succeeded in threatening, assaulting or taking information or equipment or samples from you. Be careful in any descriptions you give or write of such events, just as you are in recording other evidence that may result in a court case. Your safety is more important to the United States than the inspection or the sample. FDA will work with law enforcement government officials, e.g. FDA's Office of Criminal Investigations' (OCI) Special Agents, local police, or United States Marshals to assist an inspection team if there is a reasonable fear of danger to the investigator.

If you are assaulted (either physically or put in fear by threats of physical violence), your supervisor can summon local police, United States Marshals, FBI or contact OCI headquarters for assistance (301-294-4030). While OCI does not normally provide physical security in these cases, they will assist in threat evaluation based on specific facts and available criminal databases. OCI can also make contacts with local police and federal agencies based on previous established liaisons. If you have been assaulted or threatened and you are unable to reach your supervisor or other District management, you should contact the local police in the area where the assault or threat occurred. Be careful in any descriptions you give or write of such events, just as you are in recording other evidence that may result in a court case. Make sure that any inspected facility where weapons are observed, or where threats or assaults occur, is identified on that facility's Endorsement page of the inspection report for that facility and to your supervisor, so that Investigators or Agents who follow you into that facility will be alert to those possibilities. Your supervisor would also be responsible for checking the Personal Safety Alert box in FACTS and for beginning the notification process to alert other Federal or State agencies that also inspect the facility of the possible danger. For more information see IOM 5.2.1.3 Personal Safety Alert. For specific safety guidance related to inspections and interviews, see IOM 5.2.5.4.2 Hostile and Uncooperative Interviewees.

In addition, in any instance where you have perceived a threat to your personal safety during an inspection, investigation or sample collection, you should exit the situation immediately and report it to your supervisor. You should then write a memorandum of the event in a factual manner including information pertaining to the who, what, when, where, and how of the event. Be careful in any descriptions you give or write of such events, just as you are in recording other evidence that may result in a court case. This memo will be filed in the official establishment file jacket and copies be sent to any and all resident posts and import offices who may interact with this firm. The memo will be filed on the opposite side of the folder from all other documents and will be a printed on eye-catching color paper in order for the document to be visible to the next Investigator. The memo should be retained and maintained within the District. A copy of the Memo documenting the personal safety situation should also be sent to Division of Field Investigations, HFC-130.

5.2.1.3 - FACTS Personal Safety Alert

Within the Maintain Firms Option in the FACTS system, there is Personal Safety Alert option that allows the Supervisor (FACTS Supervisor Role) to check the appropriate box to advise the FDA Investigator that there is a personal safety issue. Only the FACTS Supervisor Role will allow for updating the Maintain Firms screen. This personal safety alert may be selected when there is a potential hazard identified:

1. Where specific personal protective equipment is needed (respirators etc)

2. Where a previous threat/assault or physical resistance occurred

3. Where there are specific medical considerations for a population of Investigators (e.g. the firm manufactures a drug hazardous to women of child-bearing years or those with allergies to peanuts, penicillin, or other products.)

In any example listed where there is a Personal Safety Alert, the specific safety alert should be documented both in the Endorsement and in a Memo to the File. The memo should be flagged "MEMO TO FILE — PERSONAL SAFETY ALERT" and should provide the factual information to support why the Investigator should be alerted to the safety issue. Be careful in any descriptions you give or write of such events, just as you are in recording other factual evidence that may result in a court case. The memo should be filed in the official establishment file jacket and copies sent to any and all Resident Posts and Import Offices who may interact with the firm. The memo will be filed on the opposite side of the folder from all other documents and will be a printed on eye-catching color paper in order for the document to be visible to the next Investigator. The memo should be retained and maintained at the District Office. A copy of the Memo documenting the personal safety situation should also be sent to Division of Field Investigations, HFC-130. The Supervisor and/or other District management will be responsible for evaluating any corrective actions taken by the firm or individual to remove or stop the potentially dangerous situation or condition. If the situation remains potentially dangerous, the Personal Safety Alert should be maintained in FACTS. Follow-up inspections at the facility should continue to document whether or not the safety situation continues exists. If the situation has been resolved (new management, dismissal of an employee, cessation of penicillin in a facility, etc), the Personal Safety Alert should be removed from FACTS by the supervisor.

5.2.1.4 - Personal Safety

A Personal Safety plan is an investigative tool developed to assist in managing and preparing for a potentially dangerous situation. Districts should consider developing a Personal Safety Plan when the conditions surrounding the specific inspection, investigation or sample collection indicate a plan is needed. The plan allows all those involved to carefully evaluate the specific inspection in order to prepare for a successful conclusion. Utilizing Personal Safety Planning concepts prior to a potentially dangerous situation is supported by the Federal Law Enforcement Training Center and is part of the training programs of many other Federal Agencies. The plan should document what specific roles and responsibilities are needed to conduct the inspection/investigation or sample collection. The plan should also answer the questions: Who, What, Why, When and Where concerning the potential danger.

There are seven principles to a Personal Safety Plan. These are:

1. *Summary of Potential Hazards:* This section of the personal safety plan includes all of the potential hazards, in a detailed description, that prompted the need for a personal safety plan. Be sure to answer the questions: Who, What, Where, When, and Why. Also include any specific hazards that require personal protective equipment or situations at the facility that may cause allergic reactions for CSOs/Analyst. Include in the section information from past inspection reports, discussions with past FDS, State or local investigators, as well as any environmental or plant/facility specific information that would negatively impact a successful personal safety plan when initiated.

2. *Sources of Information:* This section of the personal safety plan includes all the sources from where your potential hazards were collected. For instance, document which CSO or State inspector supplied their factual statements; state which documents/databases the information was from that assisted in your hazard summary. This section is important, as it documents factual evidence, similar to all of you other FDA factual inspection gathering information.

3. *Response Alternatives:* In this section, provide a list of factual, practical responses or options to consider. This will also allow your supervisor to see all the possible ways to handle the situation.

4. *Response Plan:* This section will be the most important part of your plan because it includes all of the details of what will be done to mitigate the hazards

   A. The response plan should also include all of the tools that your possess to assist you in handling the situation carefully. This should include training, experience, and other tools/procedures you have at your disposal. Roles and Responsibilities of all involved in the plan will be identified include those intended to be on-site, and those who will be off-site, and participating in the plan.

   B. *Communication:* provide all information about how communication will occur between on/off site; amongst those present on-site, and any emergency, law enforcement or medical responders. Also consider types of communication code words for emergency.

C. *Transportation:* Provide information in the plan as to how travel to the facility will happen. Is there a coordination point? Do you intend to use Government marked or unmarked cars? Who will ride in each car. What route will be taken going to and leaving the facility. Consider where you will park the car when you arrive at the facility. Consider what modes of communication will be used to communicate if multiple vehicles are used.

D. *Equipment:* Include in this section all equipment needed to initiate this plan. Is personal protective equipment needed? Is there any special sampling equipment or other equipment needed? Include in this section, equipment such as communication tools, FDA forms, etc. Assure that the equipment needed is in full functioning mode.

E. *Emergency Exit Strategy:* Describe in this section what the exit strategy will be in the event of an emergency. Consider emergency strategies for safety (issues), as well as any medical emergency. How will the emergency be communicated on-site and off-site? How do you exit the facility and return to your vehicle? Is there a scheduled meeting point to assure all are safe? Remember, we do not want to leave any one behind.

Remember to contact your supervisor when you return to safety.

5. *Evaluation:* Once the plan has been completed, a debriefing of the situation should occur with all who were involved in the plan development. Evaluate what went well, what needed improvement, what would we do next time. Evaluate whether the plan was successful and document lessons learned for the next time.

The Personal Safety Plan should be developed by the Investigator, Supervisor, other CSO's who may be familiar with the facility, Compliance Officer, if needed, and any other individuals (District, Region, or HQ experts, etc.) who may be able to assist in the depth, scope, and specifics of the firm in question. The decision of who should be involved in the development and approval of the plan is left to the Districts' discretion.

District management and all involved in writing the Personal Safety plan should meet when necessary in order to assure a well developed, and understood personal safety plan. You and your supervisor should maintain contact during the execution of the personal safety plan. The Supervisor should contact the employee during these personal safety situations at a predetermined frequency outlined in your plan. A debriefing session should be held following the execution of the plan. Discussions should include what actions worked well and where there are areas of improvement.

For foreign inspections where a Personal Safety Plan is warranted, DFI will assist the inspection team. The inspection team's management may also wish to participate so that there is clear understanding of what actions will be taken for the foreign inspection.

The Personal Safety Plan should be placed in the official establishment file jacket separately from any EIRs in the same location as any Personal Safety Alert memos. A copy of completed and executed Personal Safety Plans must be sent to DFI (HFC-130) in order for DFI to maintain a reference library of all Personal Safety Plans.

5.2.2 - Notice of Inspection

Upon arrival at the firm locate the owner, operator or agent in charge of the establishment. This should be the top Management Official on site. Be certain of this individual's status. Introduce yourself by name, title and organization. Show your credentials to this person and present a properly signed, completed, original of the FDA 482, Notice of Inspection.

If additional Agency personnel accompany you during the inspection, they must show their credentials to the top Management Official upon arrival at the site. A new FDA 482, Notice of Inspection must be issued. Submit the carbon copy of the FDA 482(s) with your EIR. Explain the purpose of your visit. Readily accept any management offer to have a representative accompany you on the inspection.

If non-FDA officials accompany you during your inspection and do not have authority to enter and inspect, you should obtain permission (preferably in advance) from the most responsible individual at the firm. Non-FDA officials and those who do not hold FDA credentials do not sign the FDA 482. See IOM 5.1.1 and 5.10.4.3.3.

For multiple occupancy inspections in drug establishments, refer to IOM 5.1.1.11. Inspections of multiple firms, which are separate legal entities, should be reported under separate EIRs.

If faced with a refusal, or partial refusal of inspection proceed as outlined in IOM 5.2.5.4.

Any time a FDA 482 is issued, also issue FDA 484, Receipt for Samples, if you collect any samples at the firm. See IOM 5.2.4. See IOM 4.1.1.1 and 4.1.1.2 for instructions for issuance of the FDA 482 in certain sampling situations.

See IOM 4.2.4.3 and 4.2.4.4 for situations where you would issue an amended FDA 482 for sample collections only. The FDA 482 may be amended "To Collect Samples Only" as shown in IOM Exhibit 5-4.

If you have concerns of when to or when not to issue the FDA 482, discuss with your supervisor.

5.2.2.1 - Multiple Date Inspections

If your inspection covers more than one day, advise management at the close of each day you have not finished the inspection and when you will return. Do this each day until you finish the inspection. A FDA 482 is not required for each day of an inspection or when different individuals are interviewed. If there will be an extended period of time (i.e., a week or longer) before you can return to the firm to complete the inspection, be sure management is aware of the delay and discuss with your supervisor whether or not you need to issue another FDA 482.

5.2.2.2 - Inspection of Vehicles

If vehicles are present which are owned or leased by the firm being inspected and it is necessary to inspect the vehicles, the inspection of these is covered by the FDA 482, Notice of Inspection, you issued to the firm.

If vehicles (trucks, trailers, RR cars, etc.) which are not owned or leased by the firm are present and inspection is necessary, a separate FDA 482, Notice of Inspection, is required:

1. Issue the FDA 482 to the driver of the vehicle.

2. If the driver is not present and if, after a diligent search, he cannot be located, issue a separate FDA 482 jointly to the firm being inspected and to the firm whose name appears on the cab. Enter the license number of the vehicle on the FDA 482. Give the original FDA 482 to the firm and leave a copy in the cab of the vehicle.

3. If there is no cab present, prepare a separate FDA 482 modified to read "*** to inspect unattended vehicle ***" and issue it to the firm being inspected as the "agent in charge" of the vehicle. Enter the license number of the vehicle, trailer or RR car number, etc., on the FDA 482. Should the firm being inspected refuse to accept the Notice, leave it in a conspicuous place in the vehicle. Describe the circumstances in your EIR.

5.2.2.3 - Follow-Up Inspections by Court Order

At times you may be instructed to conduct inspections of firms by authority of an injunction or other court order. This situation provides separate and distinct inspectional authority involving both the authority of the court order and the authority of Section 704 of the FD&C Act [21 U.S.C. 374], each providing independent courses of action.

When assigned to conduct inspections under these situations, obtain a copy of the injunction or other court order bearing the filing stamp and all relevant signatures. Prior to starting the inspection study the order thoroughly for any special instructions of the court. Your supervisor will assist you in determining the depth of the inspection necessary to cover all of the court requirements.

Take a clearly legible copy of the court decree (not necessarily a certified copy) with you to the firm to be inspected.

Present your credentials in the same manner as for any other EI. Issue the FDA 482, Notice of Inspection, modified to read, "Notice of Inspection is hereby given under authority of injunction (provide here the injunction number and/or other identification) against the firm and pursuant to Section 704 ***". Show the person to whom the FDA 482 was issued a copy of the Order, and, read the following statement to that person.

"This inspection is being conducted under the authority of injunction (add the injunction number and/or other identification) (or other court order) granted by the United States District Court against this firm on (date). The inspection will cover all items specified in the decree. In addition to the inspection authority granted in the court decree, I am issuing you a Notice of Inspection under the authority of Section 704 of the Federal Food, Drug and Cosmetic Act which authorizes inspections of firms subject to that Act."

If, the firm refuses access to records, facilities, or information for which the decree provides inspectional authority, read the pertinent section(s) or portion of the order to the person refusing so there will be no misunderstanding as to the requirements of the decree. If the person still refuses, report the facts to your supervisor as soon as possible so the court can be promptly advised of the situation. See IOM 5.2.5 for information on handling refusals.

At the conclusion of the inspection and a FDA 483 is to be issued and you are using Turbo EIR, follow the Turbo instructions to get injunction specific cites on the FDA 483.

When you prepare your EIR, describe the sequence of events in detail including exactly what happened and how you handled the situation. This documentation will help support any charge of violating the court order and/or Section 704 of the FD&C Act [21 U.S.C. 374].

The court order may require a report to the court. Discuss this with your supervisor since the district will normally handle this part of the requirement.

5.2.2.4 - Conducting Regulatory Inspections When the Agency is Contemplating Taking, or is Taking, Criminal Action

You should not issue a Notice of Inspection if the agency is contemplating taking, or is taking, criminal action against a firm without first discussing the matter with your Supervisory Investigator. Federal Rules of Evidence may not permit using evidence in a criminal matter if it is knowingly obtained under administrative authorities such as Section 704 of the FD&C Act [21 U.S.C. 374]. It is the responsibility of the office generating the inspection assignment to inform the District if a criminal action is ongoing or contemplated. Once alerted, the Supervisory Investigator will then obtain advice from the Office of Chief Counsel and, once obtained, will assign the inspection to the Investigator(s).

Decisions to inspect under such circumstances should be based on considerations of whether or not the request is consistent with FDA's responsibility to assure articles are not produced or distributed in violation of the Federal Food, Drug, and Cosmetic Act or other Federal law within FDA's jurisdiction. It would be lawful to conduct an inspection to identify such violative products and to determine if corrective action was necessary to bring such products into compliance. However, it would be an abuse of the regulatory inspection authority for FDA to conduct a regulatory inspection under that authority for the sole purpose of gathering evidence of criminal violations. Such an abuse is unlawful, and could have significant consequences.

This is because, in general, the Fourth Amendment to the United States Constitution prohibits searches without a warrant. One exception to the warrant requirement includes the inspection of industries long subject to close supervision and inspection, which are conducted under a statute that dispenses with the need for a warrant. Because such inspections are not subject to advance scrutiny for probable cause, as would be an inspection conducted pursuant to a criminal warrant, the Supreme Court has warned government entities not to use administrative inspections to search for criminal violations in an effort to sidestep the Fourth Amendment. So long as the Agency conducts the administrative inspection in good faith for a valid, non-criminal purpose, evidence gathered in such inspections generally may be used in a criminal prosecution. However, the facts of each case are unique, and employees involved must carefully document the Agency's purpose in conducting the inspection.

Because the Agency's underlying purpose in conducting an inspection ultimately will determine whether the inspection was conducted in good faith to pursue a valid, non-criminal purpose it is important to document the non-criminal purpose for an inspection undertaken under these circumstances. The need for and extent of such documentation is at a minimum when the non-criminal purpose of the inspection is evident and compelling, for example, when the purpose is to determine articles are being produced in conformity with the Food, Drug, and Cosmetic Act. The need to document the non-criminal purpose of the regulatory inspection increases as the likelihood of criminal prosecution increases. For example, there would be an increased need to document the regulatory purpose of an inspection if the matter has been referred to the Department of Justice for grand jury investigation.

There may be occasions when neither the office generating the inspection assignment nor the District conducting the inspection is aware the Office of Criminal Investigations is conducting a criminal investigation of a firm that is the subject of a regulatory inspection. The Office of Criminal Investigations may determine it is not in the interest of the agency to disclose to other components of FDA the existence of its investigation, as long as the Office of Criminal Investigations is not involved in the agency decision to conduct a regulatory inspection. However, the Office of Criminal Investigations and other components of FDA may also share information as set out below.

5.2.2.5 - When Evidence of a Criminal Violation is Discovered in the Course of a Regulatory Inspection

There may also be occasions where you are conducting a regulatory inspection at a facility, and, in the course of that inspection, you discover evidence of a criminal violation. If this occurs, you should continue the regulatory inspection as you would under normal circumstances. Document the observation and notify your supervisor. Evidence of the observation could be used in a criminal investigation, and the evidence could legally be disclosed to criminal investigators.

If you know criminal investigators are conducting a criminal investigation, your supervisor should notify the criminal investigators of any such observations. If you do not know of any ongoing criminal investigation, your supervisor should refer the information for review by the Office of Criminal Investigations. See the current Regulatory Procedures Manual (RPM). If the regulatory inspection is Center-directed (such as a bio-research monitoring inspection, a pre-approval inspection, or an inspection related to data integrity issues) your supervisor should immediately notify the Center involved of the referral to the Office of Criminal Investigations.

The discovery of evidence of a criminal violation may also be relevant to FDA's responsibility to assure articles are being produced in conformity with the Food, Drug, and Cosmetic Act. Additional inspections may be warranted. Such inspections should be planned and documented in accordance with the preceding section, "Conducting Regulatory Inspections When the Agency is Contemplating Taking, or is Taking, Criminal Action."

5.2.2.6 - Use of Evidence Gathered in the Course of a Criminal Investigation

The extent to which information gathered in the course of a criminal investigation may be shared with other components of FDA will vary with each case. Investigators should determine the extent of information sharing in accordance with the following guidelines.

Information and evidence gathered in the course of a criminal investigation may be shared with regulatory personnel, subject to two reservations:

1. Information obtained pursuant to grand jury subpoena or testimony may not be shared. Disclosure of such information to anyone other than individuals identified by the Department of Justice attorney involved could subject the individual making the improper disclosure to sanctions for contempt by the court. Only the court can authorize disclosure beyond these parameters. Information obtained by other means (search warrant, cooperative witnesses, surveillance, etc.) may be shared, subject to the following paragraph.

2. There may be a need to protect the confidentiality of the criminal investigation. For example, disclosure to regulatory investigators might prematurely disclose the existence of the criminal investigation or the identity of confidential informants. However, whenever you are calculating the need to protect the confidentiality of information gathered in the course of a criminal investigation through means other than the grand jury, you must consider whether it will be in the interest of public health to protect the confidentiality of that information.

Criminal investigators should consult their supervisors to determine whether disclosure should be made to regulatory investigators.

5.2.2.7 - Use of Evidence Voluntarily Provided to the Agency

Criminal and regulatory investigators may share information and evidence voluntarily provided to FDA, without use of the regulatory inspection authority, search warrant, or subpoena. If criminal investigators decide not to share such information because of a need to protect the confidentiality of the criminal investigation, they should consider the potential impact on the public health of protecting the confidentiality of that information.

5.2.2.8 - Concurrent Administrative, Civil, and Criminal Actions

It may be appropriate to seek administrative and/or civil remedies against a firm or individual under investigation for criminal violations. There are many issues involved in determining whether such actions may proceed concurrently, or whether certain actions should proceed first. Each situation must be evaluated on an individual basis. If administrative and/or civil remedies are under consideration against a firm or individual also under investigation for criminal violations, representatives from the Center responsible for evaluating the administrative and/or regulatory action should meet with the Office of Criminal Investigations Headquarters staff to issues related to the timing of administrative, civil, and criminal actions. The Office of Criminal Investigations and other components of FDA may share information subject to the reservations set out earlier.

5.2.2.9 - Working with a Grand Jury

Finally, if you are assigned to work with a grand jury, you should not participate in a regulatory inspection or other regulatory matter involving the same firm or individual(s). Such participation is contrary to long standing agency policy, might be unlawful, and could result in sanctions against the investigator and the agency. You should not participate in any regulatory matters that could result in improper disclosure of grand jury information, even after the grand jury investigation is closed. Grand jury proceedings remain secret even after they are concluded. Under no circumstances should you undertake such participation without first obtaining clearance from the Department of Justice attorney or the Office of Chief Counsel attorney assigned to the grand jury case. See IOM 2.2.7.3 for additional information on Grand Jury proceedings.

5.2.3 - Reports of Observations

The FORM FDA 483 INSPECTIONAL OBSERVATIONS (see Exhibit 5-5) is intended for use in notifying the inspected establishment's top management in writing of significant objectionable conditions, relating to products and/or processes, or other violations of the FD&C Act and related Acts (see IOM 5.2.3.2) which were observed during the inspection. These observations are made when in the Investigator's "judgment" conditions or practices observed, indicate that any food, drug, device, or cosmetic have been adulterated or are being prepared, packed, or held under conditions whereby they may become adulterated or rendered injurious to health. The issuance of written inspectional observations is mandated by law and ORA policy.

Be alert for specific guidance in assignments or Compliance Programs which may supplement the following general instructions.

All FDA-483s should adhere to the following general principles:

1. Observations which are listed should be significant and correlate to regulated products or processes being inspected.

2. Observations of questionable significance should not be listed on the FDA-483, but will be discussed with the firm's management so that they understand how uncorrected problems could become a violation. This discussion will be detailed in the EIR.

All FDA-483s should have the following characteristics to be useful and credible documents:

1. Each observation should be clear and specific.

2. Each should be significant. Length is not necessarily synonymous with significance.

3. Observations should not be repetitious.

4. The observations should be ranked in order of significance.

5. All copies of the FDA-483 should be legible.

If an observation made during a prior inspection has not been corrected or is a recurring observation, it is appropriate to note this on the FDA 483.

As of 1997, ORA established a FDA 483 annotation policy for medical device inspections. See IOM 5.2.3.4. Regardless of whether an establishment's FDA 483 is annotated, investigators and analysts should make every reasonable effort to discuss all observations with the management of the establishment as they are observed, or on a daily basis, to minimize surprises, errors, and misunderstandings when the FDA 483 is issued. This discussion should include those observations, which may be written on the FDA 483 and those that will only be discussed with management during the closeout meeting. Industry may use this opportunity to ask questions about the observations, request clarification, and inform the inspection team what corrections have been or will be made during the inspection process. Investigators are encouraged to verify the establishment's completed corrective actions as long as the verification does not unreasonably extend the duration of the inspection.

There may be instances where same day discussion of observations may not be possible due to the volume of documents collected and document review reveals observations on a different day than the documents were collected or in other circumstances. When these instances occur immediately prior to the conclusion of the inspection the lack of a daily discussion of observations does not preclude listing of significant observations which were not previously discussed on the FDA 483.

Turbo EIR

Turbo EIR is an automated FDA 483 and EIR reporting system. Use Turbo EIR to generate the FDA 483 where applicable cite modules exist. Turbo EIR should not be used to create a FDA 483 during an inspection of a firm involving multiple commodity areas when FDA 483 cites do not exist for ALL of the commodity areas for which observations need to be included on the FDA 483. You should be able to write the entire FDA 483 using Turbo EIR.

Use Turbo EIR for all EIRs whether or not your FDA 483 was generated using Turbo and when no FDA 483 was issued. See IOM 5.10.4.

5.2.3.1 - Preparation Of Form FDA 483

It is not necessary to complete all headings of the FDA 483, when multiple page 483s are issued. Complete all headings on the first page and, on subsequent pages, only those necessary to identify the firm and dates inspected. FDA 483s should be issued at the conclusion of the inspection and prior to leaving the premises. However, in preparing some complex FDA 483s, it may be necessary to leave the premises and return at a later time to issue and discuss your inspectional observations. In this case, you should advise the firm's management your inspection has not been completed and you will return to issue the FDA 483 and discuss inspectional findings. There should be no unreasonable or unwarranted delays in issuing and discussing the FDA 483. During the inspection, do not show the firm's management a draft, unsigned copy of the FDA 483 or an electronic copy of the FDA 483 on your computer screen. You should issue only a signed FDA 483 at the closeout discussion with management.

5.2.3.1.1 - Individual Headings

District Office address and phone number - Legibly print the district address. Include the District Office commercial telephone number and area code.

Insert this language in the address block of the form FDA 483 Inspectional Observations referencing the Information for FDA - Regulated Industry website:

"Industry information: www.fda.gov/oc/industry".

1. Turbo EIR users - Turbo has been modified to automatically add the text and web address.

2. Adobe PDF or hardcopy FDA 483 forms – add or print the text and website address above below or beside the District Office Phone number.

See IOM 1.6.5.1 – Professional Stature for situations where firms express a concern during routine enforcement activities where an FDA 483 was not issued or the activity is not an inspection.

Name and Title of individual to whom report is issued - Enter legal first name, middle initial and last name and full title of the person to whom the form is issued.

Firm name - Enter full, legal name of the firm, including any abbreviations, quotation marks, dashes, commas, etc.

Street address, city, state and Zip Code - Enter street address, city, state and Zip Code. (Not P.O. Box unless P.O. Box is part of the address such as on a Rural Route).

Date(s) of inspection - Enter actual or inclusive date(s) of inspection.

FEI Number - If the FDA Establishment Identifier is on the assignment, enter it here. If not readily available, leave blank.

Type of establishment inspected - Enter the types of the establishment, such as bakery, cannery, wholesale warehouse, drug repackager, salvage warehouse, etc.

Employee(s) signature and Employee(s) name and title - The names of everyone who participated in the inspection with the issuance of a FDA 482 should be listed on the FDA 483 even if they are not available to sign the FDA 483. Each member of an inspection team should sign the FDA 483. However, absence of a team member at the conclusion of an inspection need not prevent issuance of the FDA 483. See IOM 5.1.2.5.1. If you use an electronically generated FDA 483, assure you have a copy for the District files -- an unsigned photocopy or printed duplicate is unacceptable. See IOM 5.2.3.6.2.

5.2.3.1.2 - Signature Policy

Everyone present at issuance signs the first and last pages of the FDA 483 and initials each intervening page in the signature block.

Note: if you are not using the official multi-part FDA 483 form and a copier is not available, insert carbon paper to reproduce a signed copy of the FDA 483.

See IOM 5.2.3.6 – Distribution of the FDA 483.

5.2.3.1.3 - Date issued

Enter date the form is actually issued to the firm's management.

5.2.3.1.4 - Observations

"During an inspection of your firm (I) (We) observed" - Where applicable, when formulating each FDA 483 observation, answer Who (using titles or initials when necessary), What, When, Where, How, and challenge each observation by asking So What? (regarding its significance)

Enter your reportable observations succinctly and clearly. Conditions listed should be significant and relate to an observed or potential problem with the facility, equipment, processes, controls, products, employee practices, or records. "Potential problems" should have a reasonable likelihood of occurring based upon observed conditions or events. Do not cite deviations from policy or guidance documents on your FDA 483.

As appropriate, FDA 483 observations should include relationship of observations to a given population, for example, "Two out of 50 records examined were * * *" or "4 out of 12 bags examined were ***." When appropriate, a FDA 483 observation may refer to inadequate situations as long as you provide supporting facts (examples) or explanation as to why the condition, practice or procedure observed is inadequate.

You should not identify individuals or firms by name on the FDA 483. Where appropriate to support the FDA 483 observation, identify the individual(s) or firm(s) by substituting other non-specific identifying information as below. Document your evidence in your EIR, fully explaining the relationship(s).

1. The lot number for a component received from or shipped to firm "A".
2. The invoice number for a shipment from or to firm "A".
3. A patient #, record #. See IOM 5.2.3.3 item 7.
4. The study number for a particular Clinical Investigator site.
5. Other necessary but non-specific identifying information to show the observation's relationship to a particular firm and/or individual.

FDA 483 Statements:

The following statement should be included on each FDA 483: "This document lists observations made by the FDA representative(s) during the inspection of your facility. They are inspectional observations, and do not represent a final Agency determination regarding your compliance. If you have an objection regarding an observation, or have implemented, or plan to implement, corrective action in response to an observation, you may discuss the objection or action with the FDA representative(s) during the inspection or submit this information to FDA at the address above. If you have any questions, please contact FDA at the phone number and address above."

Presently there are three ways to issue a FDA 483. Use the following guidance as it applies to the specific type of FDA 483 you are issuing.

1. Traditional hard copy FDA 483: This language is to be written or typed on the form until additional hardcopy forms are ordered. Note: it is only necessary to write or type this statement on the first page of a multi page FDA 483.

2. Electronic (non-turbo EIR) version of the FDA 483: Use the updated FDA 483 on the official forms web site to replace previous versions of the electronic version of the document in use.

3. Turbo EIR Field Agent incorporates this language in the FDA 483.

5.2.3.1.5 - Medical Device inspections

The following language should be inserted on the FDA 483 in addition to the above statement: "The observations noted in this form FDA 483 are not an exhaustive listing of objectionable conditions. Under the law, your firm is responsible for conducting internal self audits to identify and correct any and all violations of the quality system requirements."

5.2.3.1.6 - Correction of FDA 483 Errors

These procedures do not pertain to adverse conditions noted and then corrected during the inspection. Observations of this type stand and should remain on the FDA 483.

The Inspectional Observations (FDA 483) is of critical importance to both the Agency and regulated industry. Individual FDA 483s may become public through publishing in industry trade press, FOI inquiries, Headquarters postings and other means. Therefore, complete and accurate documentation of corrections to this official document is critical.

5.2.3.1.6.1 - Errors discovered prior to leaving the establishment

Non-Turbo, FDA 483s:

1. Make handwritten changes to correct the error/s on the original FDA 483 and initial the changes. Correct errors by striking through the erroneous text and entering the correct information (if any). When possible retrieve and destroy all uncorrected copies of the FDA 483 either provided to or produced by the establishment.

2. If the establishment has photocopying equipment available and will provide you with a copy of the corrected original FDA 483 then obtain a

copy of the corrected original document from the establishment. If the establishment has no such equipment or refuses to provide you with you a copy of the original corrected FDA 483 then make the corrections and initial the changes using carbon paper and retain the carbon copy of the corrected FDA 483 for your District's official establishment file.

Turbo FDA 483s - All corrections/deletions should be made in Turbo.

1. Changes made to correct errors in the text of the observation will show on the face of the final printed FDA 483. Changed Text deletions will remain visible as strike through and correction made. For example, "lot 1234 5678" – (select text, right click, select font and select strike-through) or from "lot 1234" to "lots 1234 and 5678" and bold the changes "lots 1234 and 5678"

2. If an entire observation is removed, incidental text will be used to add the statement "An observation concerning *** was removed based on discussion with management."

3. Addition of a new item

5.2.3.1.6.2 - Errors discovered after leaving the establishment

Normally, you should not use addenda/amendments to issue additional FDA 483 items after the inspection has been closed out and you have left the premises.

1. Non-Turbo, FDA 483s (addenda): Discuss any errors with your supervisor. If necessary, an FDA 483 addendum limited to the corrected item(s) will be prepared.

2. Turbo FDA 483s (amendments): Discuss any errors with your supervisor. Make all corrections/deletions in Turbo. Changes made to correct errors in the text of the observation will show on the face of the final printed FDA 483. Changed Text deletions will remain visible as strike through and additions added.

3. Issuing FDA 483s (addenda/amendments): Personally deliver the FDA 483 addendum/amendment to the firm for discussion. If personal delivery is not practical, mail the addendum/amendment to the firm with a full explanation cover letter. Include a copy of the original FDA 483, FDA 483 addendum/amendment, and a copy of the letter in the EIR. In addition, you should call the person to whom the original FDA 483 was issued, to discuss the change(s). Document your discussion in your EIR.

5.2.3.2 - Reportable Observations

You should cite factual observations of significant deviations from the FD&C Act [21 U.S.C. 301], PHS Act, 21 CFR, and other acts where FDA has enforcement authority unless these cites require concurrence or are specifically prohibited – see IOM 5.2.3.3 Non-Reportable Observations. Examples of these observations generally fall into two categories.

5.2.3.2.1 - Adulteration Observations

Review Sections 402, 501, 505(K), 601, and 704 of the FD&C Act [21 U.S.C. 342, 351, 355(K), 361, and 374]. Include specific factual observations of:

1. Foods, drugs, devices, or cosmetics consisting in whole or in part of filthy, putrid, or decomposed substances.
2. Undesirable conditions or practices, bearing on filth or decomposition, which may reasonably result in the food, drug, device, or cosmetic becoming contaminated with filth.
3. Insanitary conditions or practices which may reasonably render the food, drug, device, or cosmetic injurious to health.
4. Careless handling of rodenticides or pesticides.
5. Results of field tests (organoleptic examination of fish, crackout of nuts, etc.) if the results revealed adulteration.
6. Observations of faulty manufacturing, processing, packaging, or holding, of food, drug, or device products as related to current good manufacturing practice regulations including inadequate or faulty record keeping.
7. Observations of faulty can closures and/or deviations from recommended processing times and temperatures.
8. Deviations from the animal proteins prohibited in ruminant feeds requirements (21 CFR 589.2000).

5.2.3.2.2 - Other Observations

You may include other factual observations of significant deviations from the FD&C Act [21 U.S.C. 301], 21 CFR, Government Wide Quality Assurance Program (GWQAP) requirements, and other Acts as directed by CPGMs and other agency directives. In some cases, you may cite labeling deviations as directed below. This list is not all inclusive.

1. Observations indicating non-conformity with commitments made in a New Drug Application (or NADA) or in am antibiotic certification or certification exemption form. See Section 505 FD&C Act, [21 U.S.C. 355].
2. Observations, forming the basis for product non-acceptance under the Government Wide Quality Assurance Program (GWQAP). See IOM 5.2.3.5.
3. Deviations from blood and blood products labeling requirements as specified in 21 CFR 606.121 and 21 CFR 640.
4. Animal protein products, and feeds containing such products, that are not in compliance with the labeling requirements of paragraphs (c)

through (f) of 21 CFR 589.2000. See Section 403(a)(1) or 403(f) of the FD&C Act [21 U.S.C. 343(a)(1) or 343(f)].

5. Deviations from the applicable labeling regulations for human cells, tissue, and cellular and tissue-based products (HCT/Ps) as specified in 21 CFR 1271 and CPGM 7341.002.

6. Observations indicating drug misuse, failure to maintain proper drug use records, and/or poor animal husbandry practices during tissue residue investigations. See the applicable Compliance Program(s) for guidance.

7. Observations indicating non-conformity with the postmarketing adverse drug experience reporting requirements as specified in 21 CFR 310.305, 314.80, 314.98, 314.540, or 600.80 or other postmarketing requirements as specified in 21 CFR 314.81 or 600.14. See Sections 505 and 760 of the FD&C Act [21 U.S.C. 355(k) and 379aa].

8. Observations indicating non-conformity with the Medical Device Reporting requirements as specified in 21 CFR 803

   {See Section 519(a) of the FD&C Act [21 U.S.C. 360i]}; the Medical Devices Reports of Corrections and Removals requirements as specified in 21 CFR 806 {See Section 519(f) of the FD&C Act [21 U.S.C. 360i(f)]}; and the Medical Device Tracking requirements as specified in 21 CFR 821 {See Section 519(e) of the FD&C Act [21 U.S.C. 360i(e)]}.

9. Observations indicating noncompliance with medical device pre-market notification requirements and pre-market approval requirement under FD&C Act sections 510(k) and 515 [21 U.S.C. 360 (k) and 360e] respectively, should only be made with the prior confirmation of CDRH and/or CBER.

10. 21 CFR PART 200.10 does allow reporting observations noted at a contract facility to the contracting facility. Before doing this, check with your supervisor to determine if this is appropriate.

11. Observations indicating non-compliance with LACF/Acidified food registration and failure to file scheduled processes. Before doing this, verify lack of such, as covered in CPGM 7303.803A.

5.2.3.3 - Non-Reportable Observations

Do not report opinions, conclusions, or characterize conditions as "violative." The determination of whether any condition is violative is an agency decision made after considering all circumstances, facts and evidence. See IOM 5.2.7 involving discussions with management at which time opinions may be discussed.

Do not quote Regulations (e.g., specific CFR sections) when listing items.

Do not report observations pertaining to:

1. Label and labeling content, except per IOM 5.2.3.2.2, items 2, 3, 4 and 5 above.

2. Promotional materials.

3. The classification of a cosmetic or device as a drug.

4. The classification of a drug as a new drug.

5. Non-conformance with the New Drug Regulations, 21 CFR 312.1 (New Drugs for Investigational Use in Human Beings: Exemptions from Section 505(a)) unless instructed by the particular program or assignment.

6. The lack of registration required by Section 415 and 510 of the FD&C Act. The lack of registration per 21 CFR 1271 Subpart B Procedures for Registration and Listing, promulgated under Section 361 of the PHS Act.

7. Patient names, donor names, etc. If such identification is necessary, use initials, code numbers, record numbers, etc.

8. Corrective actions. Specific actions taken by the firm in response to observations noted on the FDA 483 or during the inspection are not listed on the FDA 483, but are reported in the EIR. Except as described in IOM 5.2.3.4.

9. The use of an unsafe food additive or color additive in a food product.

Use Turbo EIR to document in the "General Discussion with Management" section Non-Reportable Observations, which you discussed with management. These objectionable conditions fall into three basic categories:

1. Observations of significant deviations from specific Laws and/or regulations, non-reportable items 1-9 above.

2. Observations of deviations from specific Laws and/or regulations, which in your judgment, are of "questionable significance" and "deemed not to merit inclusion on the FDA 483," but do warrant discussion with management.

3. Observations which in your judgment deviate from official published guidance, not regulations, but warrant discussion with management.

The reporting of observations in these 3 categories is as follows:

Category 1: You should select the appropriate Turbo cite, verify or set the "Print type" to "Do Not Print," and save the observation in the Turbo database. This should be done even if there are no other reportable observations. For example, Lack of Food Registration as covered in IOM 5.4.1.5.3 is not reportable.

Category 2 or 3: You should always report these two categories of observations which were discussed with management under the "General Discussion with Management" heading in the EIR as specified by IOM 5.10.4.3.15. You have options in choosing how observations in category 2 are reported. You may select the appropriate cite in Turbo, enter the "specifically" text regarding the observation, and discussion with management, set it to "Do not print", save, and it will be automatically entered into the Turbo EIR when it is generated.

The second option which is also true for category 3 (i.e., there are no Turbo cites for official guidance, only regulations) is the observation/s discussed with management may be entered directly into the Turbo EIR under the "General Discussion with Management."

5.2.3.4 - Annotation of the FDA 483

Offer to annotate the FDA 483 for all medical device inspections. The district has discretion to annotate the FDA 483s in other program areas. BIMO inspections are generally excluded from annotations. Annotations of FDA 483s for inspections in other program areas may be done if both the establishment and the investigator/team believe annotation will facilitate the inspection process. When a FDA 483 is annotated it should be done in accordance with the guidance that follows.

Inform the establishment of the annotation program at some point prior to the final discussion with management. Determine from management whether they wish to have their FDA 483 observations annotated. It is voluntary on the part of the establishment. If the establishment does not want one or more observations annotated, you must honor the request.

The actual annotation of the FDA 483 should occur during the final discussion with management. The annotations are succinct comments about the status of the FDA 483 item. It is not permissible to pre-print or pre-format the annotations onto the FDA 483 form. The annotations can be made after each observation, at the end of each page of the FDA 483 or at the bottom of the last page of the FDA 483 prior to the investigator's signature. The establishment should review the annotations on the issued FDA 483 to ensure there are no misunderstandings about promised corrective actions. See IOM 5.2.3 for discussions of FDA 483 observations with management.

If the establishment has promised and/or completed a corrective action to an FDA 483 observation prior to the completion of the inspection, the FDA 483 should be annotated with one or more of the following comments, as appropriate:

1. Reported corrected, not verified.
2. Corrected and verified.
3. Promised to correct.
4. Under consideration.

   The term "verified" means "to confirm; to establish the truth or accuracy". In this case, you must do the verification. In some situations, you will not be able to verify the corrective action unless there is further district or Center review or until there is another inspection of the establishment.

The establishment's stated objections to any given observation or to the FDA 483, as a whole should not be annotated on the FDA 483. If they would prefer no annotation, do not annotate it. The EIR should include the establishment's objections to the observation and the fact the establishment declined to have the observation annotated.

When an establishment has promised corrections and furnishes a date or timeframe (without a specific date) for completion, then you may add "by xxx date" or "within xxxx days or months" in the annotation. Where the investigator and the establishment have "agreed to disagree" about the validity of an observation, you may annotate this observation with "Under consideration" or with no annotation based on the establishment's desire.

All corrective actions taken by the establishment and verified by FDA should be discussed in detail in the Establishment Inspection Report (EIR) and reported using the Compliance Achievement Reporting Systems (CARS).

5.2.3.5 - Government Wide Quality Assurance Program (GWQAP)

When performing product acceptance examinations under the GWQAP, you must discuss all deficiencies with management and report these deficiencies in writing on the FDA 483. This includes all deficiencies related to the FD&C Act as well as deficiencies in complying with contract requirements, which result in non-acceptance. There must be a clear differentiation on the FDA 483 between these two types of deficiencies.

Enter the FD&C type deficiencies (GMP deviations, etc.) first on the FDA 483. If there are deficiencies in contract provisions, draw a line across the sheet and add a heading "The Following Additional Contract Non-Conformances Were Observed." Enter each deficiency, which forms a basis for non-acceptance, followed by the reference to the applicable contract requirement or specification.

5.2.3.6 - Distribution of the FDA 483

Be sure all copies of the original FDA 483 are legible and distribute as follows.

5.2.3.6.1 - Original

The FDA 483 issued to the firm signed in pen and ink.

Before leaving the premises at the end of the EI present the original to the individual who received the FDA 482, Notice of Inspection, if the person is present and qualifies as "most responsible." If the person is not available or is outranked by someone else, present it to the individual who meets the definition of owner, operator, or agent in charge.

5.2.3.6.2 - Copies

Replicas of the "original".

Attach one copy of all FDA 483s issued to the firm to the EIR. This includes turbo or non-turbo copies of any signed, modified, and/or amended FDA 483, or 483 addenda. See IOM 5.2.3.1.6 (Correction of FDA 483 Errors). A copy may be sent to the top management of the firm including foreign management, unless the individual to whom you gave the original is the top official of the firm.

If the inspection covered vehicles as described in IOM 5.2.2.2, leave an exact copy of the list of observations with the firm being inspected. The original will be sent by your district to the firm owning or leasing the vehicle. You must make every effort to obtain the name and address of the vehicle owner. Usually the firm name is on the vehicle; however, it may require a trace of the vehicle license number. Discuss with your supervisor before taking this step. See IOM 4.4.7.2.

5.2.4 - Receipt - Factory Samples

You must issue an FDA 484, Receipt for Samples, if you collect any physical sample during an inspection. At the end of the EI and prior to leaving the premises, issue the original FDA 484 to the same individual who received the FDA 482. (See IOM 4.2.5) If this person is not available, give it to someone else who meets the definition of owner, operator, or agent in charge. Submit an exact copy with the EIR. Do not comment on type of examination expected or promise a report of analysis.

5.2.4.1 - Items Requiring Receipt

Issue FDA 484 for any item of food, drug, device, or cosmetic actually removed from the establishment.

NOTE: A receipt must always be issued to anyone from whom you obtain Rx drugs. This includes individuals as well as firms. See IOM 4.2.5.4 and IOM 4.4.10.3.44.

The following are examples of exhibit materials also requiring a Receipt for Samples:

1. Air filter pads,
2. Rodent pellets, and
3. Any other physical evidence actually removed from the plant.

5.2.4.2 - Items Not Requiring Receipt

Do not issue a FDA 484 for:

1. Items or materials examined during the inspection but not removed from the establishment (report adverse results of analysis of materials on FDA 483 as indicated in IOM 5.2.3.2),
2. Labels or promotional material, or
3. Photographs taken during the inspection.
4. Record(s): including production, quality control, shipping and interstate records.

Firm's management may request copies of documents or records you obtain from their firm. There is no objection to supplying them.

See IOM 5.3.8.5 for procedures when a firm requests a receipt for records copied during an inspection or investigation.

5.2.5 - Inspection Refusal

Refusal as used in your IOM means refusing to permit an inspection or prohibiting you from obtaining information to which FDA is entitled under the law. See IOM 4.2.3 for information regarding refusal to permit sampling.

In the case of a refusal you must show your conduct was reasonable, fair, and you exercised reasonable precaution to avoid refusal. You must have shown your credentials and given the responsible individual a properly prepared and signed Notice of Inspection, FDA 482.

Inspection refusals may take several forms. All refusals to permit inspection must be reported in your EIR under the "Refusals" heading.

5.2.5.1 - Refusal of Entry

When you are faced with a refusal of entry, call the person's attention to the pertinent sections of the Acts (Sections 301(f) and 704 of the FD&C Act [21 U.S.C. 331 (f) and 374] and Section 351(c), 360A(a), (b) and (f); 360B(a); and 361(a) of the Public Health Service Act. Portions of these are listed on the front and back of the FDA 482. If entry is still refused, leave the completed FDA 482, leave the premises and telephone your supervisor immediately for instructions.

5.2.5.2 - Refusal to Permit Access to or Copying of Records

If management objects to the manner of the inspection or coverage of specific areas or processes, do not argue the matter but proceed with the inspection. However, if management refuses to permit access to or copying of any record which you are entitled under law, call attention to Section 301(e) of the FD&C Act [21 U.S.C. 331] or applicable sections of the PHS Act. If management still refuses, proceed with the inspection until finished. It is not an inspection "refusal" when management refuses to provide formula information, lists of shipments, codes, etc., except where specifically required by the law. If the refusal is such you cannot conduct a satisfactory inspection, discuss with your supervisor if a Warrant for Inspection should be requested.

5.2.5.3 - Refusal after Serving Warrant

If you have been refused entry, obtained a warrant, tried to serve or execute it and are refused entry under the warrant, inform the person, the warrant is a court order and such refusal may constitute contempt of court. If the warrant is not then immediately honored (entry and inspection permitted), leave the premises and promptly telephone the facts to your supervisor.

If you have served the warrant and during the inspection you encounter partial refusal or resistance in obtaining access to anything FDA is authorized to inspect by the warrant, inform the firm that aspect of the inspection is part of a court order and refusal may constitute contempt of court. If the warrant is not then immediately honored, leave the premises and promptly telephone the facts to your supervisor.

5.2.5.4 - Hostile and Uncooperative Interviewees

More often than not, investigations or inspections are conducted in a reasonable atmosphere. Nonetheless, there will be times you are confronted by unfriendly or hostile persons.

Your activities must always be conducted with tact, honesty, diplomacy, and persuasiveness. Even though you must at times adopt a firm posture, do not resort to threats, intimidation, or strong-arm tactics.

Many times a hostile or uncooperative attitude on the part of individuals being interviewed results from fear, timidity, or previously distasteful encounters with law enforcement personnel. In most cases a calm, patient, understanding and persuasive attitude on your part will overcome the person's reluctance or hostility. Often the mere fact you patiently listen while individuals share their views will make them receptive to your quest.

5.2.5.4.1 - Indicators

Normally you have no way to predict the nature of the individuals you meet. However, there are often indicators, which can alert you, such as:

1. Establishment inspection reports, endorsements or memorandums may show situations where investigators encountered belligerent or hostile individuals. These reports may be FDA reports and/or State contract reports, if available.

2. Discussions and conversations with FDA, federal, state and local inspectors and investigators may reveal instances where uncooperative individuals and problem situations were encountered.

3. The nature of the assignment, program or information requested may indicate some degree of caution is needed.

4. A firm located in an area with a reputation for unfriendliness to law enforcement personnel should alert you some employees of the firm may be less than cooperative during the investigation.

If you find yourself in a situation which, in your judgment, indicates violence is imminent, stop the operation and make an exit as soon as possible. Immediately report the facts to your supervisor.

5.2.5.4.2 - Safety Precautions

The FDA recognizes there are situations where it is advisable to take precautions for your personal safety. In those, consult your supervisor. Some procedures, which may be utilized to minimize the danger, include:

1. Inspections or investigations carried out by a team of two or more persons.

2. Consider whether or not the use of an unmarked government car would be more beneficial to assist you in your inspection in lieu of a marked government car.

3. Request additional information from your State and/or Local Agencies who also regulate and inspect the facilities in question. In many instances, your State counterparts may have more information regarding the facility. This may be especially helpful for those firms that FDA has not yet inspected but were inspected by your State counterparts.

4. Each government car or inspection team should be assigned one FDA cell phone or alternate communication device. While we recognize that some Investigators carry a personal cell phone, FDA strongly suggests that your personal cell phone not be utilized to contact the firm or firm's management. In some instances, such uses in the past have resulted in later inappropriate contacts from the firm to the individual FDA Investigator.

5. Request assistance from local law enforcement agencies prior to or during investigations. This assistance may include information about the facility you are to inspect, assistance with communication devices, or police protection, if the police jurisdiction allows for such an action.

6. In potentially hazardous investigations such as methadone or schedule II Class Drugs, two investigators may be used and personnel from the U.S. Drug Enforcement Administration, State, or local law enforcement agencies may be requested to accompany you.

5.2.5.4.3 - Procedures when Threatened or Assaulted

In instances when you are actually assaulted or threatened, you should immediately notify your supervisor. Your supervisor can summon local police, United States Marshals, or contact OCI headquarters for assistance (301-294-4030). OCI can make contacts with local police and federal agencies based on previous liaison. Also, the District should notify Division of Field Investigations, HFC-130 at 301-827-5653 FAX 301-443-3757 or via e-mail ORAHQDFICSOSAF@FDA.HHS.GOV.

If you are physically attacked, you have the same recourse as any other citizen as well as the benefit of federal laws protecting government officials while in the performance of their official duties. If you are physically attacked, you should get to safety, call your supervisor, report the incident and seek medical attention if needed. Remember that the medical attention you receive may be used as documentation for the Agency in support of any legal action taken against the firm or the individual.

5.2.5.4.4 - Notification of FBI and US Attorney

It is a federal crime for anyone to kill, assault, resist, oppose, impede, intimidate, or interfere with, a federal official in the performance of their official duties.

In case of assault or threat against you, notify your supervisor immediately, so the facts can be submitted to the Federal Bureau of Investigations and the U.S. Attorney's office for immediate action.

The referenced sections in Title 18 of the U.S. Code are:

1. Title 18 U.S.C.A. Section 111, which provides:

   "111. Assaulting, resisting, or impeding certain officers or employees.

   Whoever forcibly assaults, resists, opposes, impedes, intimidates, or interferes with any person designated in Section 1114 of this title while engaged in or on account of the performance of his official duties, shall be fined not more than $5,000 or imprisoned not more than three years, or both.

   Whoever, in the commission of any such acts uses a deadly or dangerous weapon, shall be fined not more than $10,000 or imprisoned not more than ten years, or both. **** ".

2. Title 18 U.S.C.A. Section 1114, which provides:

   "1114. Protection of officers and employees of the United States.

   Whoever kills ***** or any officer or employee of the Department of Health and Human Services or of the Department of Labor assigned to perform investigative, inspection, or law enforcement functions while engaged in the performance of his official duties, shall be punished as provided under sections 1111 and 1112 of this title. ****".

   See Title 18 of the US Code Sections 111 and 1114 for the complete text. See also IOM 1.5.

5.2.6 - Inspection Warrant

A refusal to permit inspection invokes a criminal provision of section 301(f) of the FD&C Act [21 U.S.C. 331(f)]. Depending on the individual situation, instances of refusal may be met by judicious use of inspection warrants.

Instructions for obtaining warrants are contained in the Regulatory Procedures Manual, Chapter 6-3. See your supervisor for information and instructions.

You are operating as an agent of the court when you serve an inspection warrant and it must be executed expeditiously once served. See IOM 5.2.5.3 for guidance on how to handle any refusal after obtaining a warrant.

In situations where a potential problem is anticipated with the service of a warrant, the District should consider sending a Supervisory Consumer Safety Officer or Compliance Officer and a U.S. Marshal with the Investigator to assist and supervise the serving of the warrant.

After obtaining an Inspection Warrant, return to the firm and:

1. Show your credentials to the owner, operator, or agent in charge,

2. Issue the person a written Notice of Inspection (FDA 482),
3. Show that individual the original signed Inspection Warrant,
4. Give him/her a copy (not the original) of the warrant.

The copy you provide need not be signed by the issuing judge, but the judge's name should be typed on the copy.

Follow the procedures of the court or U.S. Attorney involved, if their methods differ from the above.

When an inspection is made pursuant to a warrant, a Return showing the inspection was completed must be made to the Judge (or U.S. Commissioner or Magistrate) who issued the warrant. The Return, executed on the original warrant, should be made promptly and usually no later than 10 days following its execution.

5.2.7 - Discussions with Management

After completion of the inspection, meet with the highest ranking management official possible to discuss your findings and observations. The FDA 483 is not a substitute for such discussion since there may be additional questionable practices or areas not appropriate for listing on this form.

During the discussion be frank, courteous and responsive with management. Point out the observations listed on the FDA 483, are your observations of objectionable conditions found during the inspection, and explain the significance of each. Try to relate each listed condition to the applicable sections of the laws and regulations administered by the FDA. You should inform management during the closeout discussion the conditions listed may, after further review by the Agency, be considered to be violations of the Food, Drug and Cosmetic Act or other statutes. Legal sanctions available to FDA may include seizure, injunction, civil money penalties and prosecution, if establishments do not voluntarily correct serious conditions. Do not be overbearing or arbitrary in your attitude or actions. Do not argue if management voices a different view of the FDA 483 observations, or of your opinions. Explain, in your judgment the conditions you observed MAY be determined by the FDA, after review of all the facts, to be violations. Make clear the prime purpose of the discussion is to call attention to objectionable practices or conditions, which should be corrected.

Obtain management's intentions regarding correcting objectionable conditions. They may propose corrections or procedural changes and ask you if this is satisfactory. If this involves areas where your knowledge, skill, and experience are such that you know it will be satisfactory, you can so advise management. Do not assume the role of an authoritative consultant. In areas where there is any doubt, you must explain to management you cannot endorse the proposed corrections. Advise the individuals FDA will supply comments (see RPM 4-1-3 #4) if the establishment will submit its request and its proposed corrections or procedures in writing to the district office.

Concentrate on what needs to be done rather than how to do it. Do not recommend the product or services of a particular establishment. If asked to suggest a product or consulting laboratory, refer the inquirer to a classified directory or trade publications and or organizations.

Report in your EIR all significant conversations with management or management representatives. In most instances it is not necessary to quote management's response verbatim. Paraphrasing the replies is sufficient. However, if the situation is such that quoting the reply or replies is necessary, enclose them in quotation marks.

5.2.7.1 - Protection of Privileged Information

You have certain responsibilities under the FD&C Act, Section 301(j); Sections 359(d) and 306(e) of the Public Health Service Act; and Section 1905 of the Federal Confidential Statute (18 U.S.C. 1905) regarding protection of confidential material obtained during your official duties. See IOM 1.4.

Do not volunteer information about other firms or their practices. Ignore casual exploratory questions or remarks from management about competitors or their processes. Your casual and seemingly innocuous remarks may reveal privileged information. Therefore, be alert and avoid voluntarily or unknowingly divulging information, which may be privileged or confidential and possibly compromise FDA's and your own integrity.

Management often request copies of any documents or records you obtain from their firm. There is no objection to your supplying these. When management requests copies of photos taken by you in a plant, follow IOM 5.3.4.5.

You may encounter situations when management invites outside individuals to observe the inspectional process (e.g., representatives from the press, trade associations, congressional staff, other company officials). As discussed in Section 5.1.4.3 of the IOM, the presence of representatives invited by the firm should not disrupt the inspectional process. You are to continue the inspection in a reasonable manner.

If the firm allows invited individuals to photograph, videotape, or prepare audio recordings during the inspection, you should make every effort to protect privileged information in your possession. However, it is the Agency's position that it is the firm's responsibility to protect confidential and/or proprietary information observed or recorded by those individuals invited by the firm. Where applicable, refer to IOM 5.3.5 for additional procedures on how to prepare your own recording in parallel with the firm's recording.

5.2.7.2 - Refusals of Requested Information

Should management refuse to provide any reasonable request for information, which is not specifically required by the law, determine the reasons for the denial and report the details in the EIR. Types of refusals of interest to FDA and refusal codes to be entered in FACTS are listed in the FDA Data Codes Manual. Refusal codes' data are used when reporting to Congress. See IOM 5.2.5.4 for instructions in dealing with hostile and/or uncooperative interviewees.

5.2.8 - Consumer Complaints

Prior to conducting any inspection, you should review the FACTS system and the factory jacket becoming familiar with all FDA Complaint/Injury forms. Be especially alert for ones marked "Follow-Up Next Inspection" and make sure you investigate these during your inspection.

During the inspection, discuss these complaints with management without revealing the complainant's name(s). Determine if the firm has had similar complaints on the same product. Determine what action the firm has taken to identify the root cause of the problem and to prevent a recurrence in the future. See IOM 5.10.4.3.11 for reporting instructions.

5.2.9 - Interviewing Confidential Informants

When you are faced with a situation involving sources of information who want to remain anonymous, please contact your supervisor and follow the procedures here. In addition, refer to IOM 5.2.1.2 regarding your personal safety. If your management concurs with the decision to utilize a confidential source, it is particularly important you take the necessary steps to keep the identity of the source, and any information which could lead to the identity, confidential. For purposes of this subchapter, a confidential source is a person who provides information that may be of assistance to FDA without necessarily becoming a party to the actual FDA investigation. If you believe the information provided by the source could lead to a criminal investigation, please contact the Office of Criminal Investigations (OCI).

5.2.9.1 - How to handle the first contact

When you interview a person who may become a confidential source use the following procedures:

1. *Type of meeting.* Try to schedule a personal interview with the person rather than a telephone interview. At a face-to-face interview you can assess the person's demeanor, body language, overall presentation, and truthfulness.

2. *Meeting location.* The place and time of the interview should be the choice of the person, unless there is a concern with personal safety. If the person's suggested location is unsuitable, the investigator should suggest the location. When you conduct the interview off FDA premises, notify your supervisor of your destination, purpose, and estimated time of return. When an off-site interview has been completed, check-in with your supervisor.

5.2.9.1.1 - Interviewing methods/techniques

It is strongly recommended you have two investigators conduct interviews of a confidential source. The lead investigator conducts the interview, while the second investigator takes notes and acts as a witness to the interview. You should:

1. Prepare carefully for the interview. The investigators should develop the questions they intend to ask the person during the interview, e.g.,

"establish motivation," and record and number the questions to be asked in their diaries prior to the interview. This preparation assists in documenting the interview process and reduces the amount of note taking needed during the interview. The investigators also should discuss their interviewing strategy, and determine the method by which they will consult with each other during the interview and (during extensive interviews) share the interviewing and note-taking responsibilities;

2. Have the person tell the story chronologically, placing complex situations into logical order; and

3. If the person makes allegations, ask him or her how he or she knows the allegations are true.

    a. How were they in a position to know?

    b. Did they personally see, hear, or write about the information/incident?

    c. Can they provide proof of the allegations?

5.2.9.1.2 - Establish motivation

At the end of the interview ask the person why he or she is divulging this information. This may reveal their motive(s):

1. Is the person a disgruntled current or former employee who harbors a grudge?

2. Is the person looking for some type of whistle-blower reward or notoriety?

3. Does the person just want to do the right thing?

4. Is the person involved in actual or prospective litigation about or related to the information?

5.2.9.1.3 - Anonymity

If the person is requesting anonymity, inform him or her FDA:

1. Will not divulge his or her identity, the occurrence of the interview, or the sensitive information provided to FDA if the information could lead to the identity of the person, unless FDA is required to disclose the information by law, e.g., the investigation leads to a hearing or trial and he or she is required to testify, and

2. Will try to corroborate all information provided by the person, minimizing the chances he or she must later testify. However, testifying remains a possibility.

Ask the person for names of other persons who might be willing to speak with you about the allegations and corroborate their story.

5.2.9.2 - Protect the identity of the source

Collection of information. Obtain sufficient personal information necessary to enable you to contact the person for follow up if needed. However, to maintain the confidentiality of the person, do not include the person's identifier information such as gender, name, address, and phone number in the memorandum of interview. You should assign the confidential source a code name or number and use the identifier in memoranda and other communications relating to the confidential source (see IOM 5.2.9.2.2 item 2).

5.2.9.2.1 - Access

Know who is authorized by District procedure to access the information, and restrict access by others accordingly. Share the minimum amount of information necessary to meet the purpose of the disclosure.

5.2.9.2.2 - Storage Requirements

Each District should establish procedures, in addition to those listed below, to properly store confidential information. The following list contains information related to storage procedures.

1. Use security measures necessary to protect the confidentiality of personal information, whether it is in hard copy or electronic form, on FDA premises, in an FDA home-based computer, or in any other form. Use whatever means necessary and appropriate to physically safeguard the information, such as storing in a safe, or locked file cabinets, or password-coded computers, etc.

2. When referring to the source in any manner (orally, in writing, electronically, etc.), consider using code to identify the source. For example, use a number rather than the individual's name, to identify the source. Personal privacy information should be safeguarded. Use discreet subject headers in the file labels as appropriate.

3. Remove personal information from a file only after you have noted in the file your name, date, etc. Promptly return that information to the file.

5.2.9.2.3 - Disclosure

Do not disclose information from or about the source, unless the disclosure complies with the law and FDA's procedures. Do not share non-public information outside of the Freedom of Information (FOI) process, unless the sharing is done according to our regulations and procedures. Refer FOI requests to your FOI officer (see item 3 below). See also IOM Subchapter 1.4. The following information relates to disclosures of information from or about a confidential source.

1. Make duplicates of the personal information only to the extent necessary for authorized disclosure (inside or outside of FDA). Do not leave the copy machine unattended.

2. Make only authorized disclosures of the information, regardless of the manner of disclosing (oral, written, etc.). Do not use mobile telephones or leave voice mails with the information. Avoid transmitting the non-public information by facsimile or e-mail.

3. If you receive a FOI request for information from or about a source consult with your supervisor immediately Disclosure to a non-FDA government official of information from or about a source may be disclosed only if permitted by law and FDA procedures, and after consulting your supervisor and, if needed, OCI.

4. Immediately retrieve information from or about a source is inadvertently disclosed.

5.2.9.2.4 - Destruction

Destroy personal information by shredding or similar means which physically destroys the record and/or, if the information is in electronic form, makes it unreadable.

Office of Chief Counsel. After a matter has been referred to the Office of Chief Counsel (OCC) for litigation or enforcement action, consult with OCC if you are interested in contacting the source.

5.2.10 - Routine Biosecurity Procedures for Visits to Facilities Housing or Transporting Domestic or Wild Animals

This section is FDA's guidance when you visit any type of facility where any domestic or wild animals are housed or transported. If a firm has more restrictive controls, follow those in addition to the controls cited below as long as they do not interfere with your assignment needs. The controls and procedures are intended to prevent you from becoming a vector or carrier of animal diseases, to prevent the spread of animal disease, and to set a good example for stockmen, growers and industry servicemen. A number of chronic diseases, such as Johne's Disease, bovine virus diarrhea (BVD) and others exist in domestic animals which you can unknowingly spread. Any inspectional contact with herds of livestock (including poultry) or non-domesticated animals exposes you to potential claims of introducing or spreading disease. This could occur between sections of a single site, such as poultry houses, or between different sites or farms. The potential also exists for the introduction of disease from an animal processing plant, such as a slaughterhouse or renderer to a live animal facility. You can prevent this by following appropriate cleaning and disinfection steps between facilities. Generally, a break of 5 days or more between sites is sufficient to eliminate concern about transmission of infectious agents.

These precautions, biosecurity measures, are necessary in two types of situations. The first is when there is no known disease present and your actions are precautionary. This section primarily addresses those kinds of activities. The other situation involves known or suspected disease outbreaks or more notorious disease conditions such as salmonella in eggs, infectious Laryngotracheitis, foot and mouth disease, vesicular stomatitis, and blackhead which can be highly contagious and spread from one group of animals to another by movement of people and objects between infected and non-infected groups. In these cases, special precautions must be taken to make sure you are not an unknowing vector for the spread of disease. See IOM 5.2.10.3.

If you will only be inspecting an office or house away from areas where animals are housed or kept, clean and suitable street attire may be sufficient. Be aware if you visit any area of a facility where animals have been, you should always sanitize, clean or change footwear and it may be necessary to change outerwear before visiting another animal site to prevent any possibility of transmission of disease.

Your vehicle may also transport infection if you drive through contaminated areas.

5.2.10.1 - Pre-Inspection Activities

When you know you are going to visit or inspect any animal production or holding facility, consider contacting the State Veterinarian and/or the Regional APHIS office to determine if there are any areas in the state under quarantine or special measures to control animal diseases. APHIS office locations can be found on their website. The State Veterinarian will be listed under Government Listings in your phone book and is listed at this website. Regional Milk Specialists frequently working with State counterparts in the Interstate Milk Shippers program should contact these sources at least quarterly for updates. Ask for any special controls or procedures they recommend. Follow any guidance they offer in addition to the precautions in this section. You should also consider pre-notification of the facility following guidance in IOM 5.2.1.1, Pre-Announcement, unless your assignment does not allow pre-notification. If you elect to pre-announce the inspection, in addition to the normal contact, ask to speak with the person at the facility responsible for their biosecurity measures and find out what they require of employees and visitors. If their requests do not interfere with your ability to do your job, follow their requests as we do when inspecting sterile manufacturing facilities.

Make sure your vehicle is clean and has been recently washed. Commercial car washes are adequate as long as you check to make sure any dirt, manure or other debris, which may be present from a previous site, has been removed. Some facilities may require additional disinfection of tires upon entry to the premises. Ensure tires and floor mats are clean. Consider designating places in your vehicle for storage of clean, unused supplies and dirty or used supplies.

In addition to your normal inspectional tools, obtain the following equipment and supplies from your district:

1. Laundered or disposable coveralls or smocks (coveralls are suggested because they give better coverage). If you are going to visit multiple facilities in one day or trip, obtain sufficient quantities so you can change into clean or unused clothing between each site.

2. Disposable plastic gloves, rubber boots, which can be sanitized, and disposable shoe/boot covers. Rubber boots over which you place disposable shoe/boot covers are preferred.

3. Reusable cloth or plastic laundry bag(s) for clothing to be laundered. (Disposable bags can be used.)

4. Soap, water and disposable or freshly laundered individual hand (or paper) towels.

5. Sanitizing solution(s) and equipment (brushes, bucket, tray, measuring devices, etc.) to permit you to properly sanitizing hands, boots, equipment and your vehicle. Most disinfectants will require removing organic matter before use and good brushes are essential to remove dirt from boots and other objects.

Make sure any equipment you take with you has been thoroughly cleaned and sanitized as necessary. Clip boards, briefcases, flashlights, inspectional sampling tools, coolers, brushes, buckets and other objects should be cleaned between uses as necessary and between visits to any suspected infected facilities. Disposable equipment should be used to the fullest extent possible.

Maintain copies of any applicable Material Safety Data Sheets (MSDS) for disinfectants with you in your vehicle. If the firm's management requests information on the disinfectants you are using, they may read or copy these MSDS. Be familiar with the instructions and precautions concerning use of disinfectants. Any disinfectant should be effective against known or suspected microbiological agents.

In the event of a foreign animal disease, contact the USDA, APHIS Veterinary Services area Veterinarian in Charge for additional precautions and procedures to follow. (See 5.2.10.3)

5.2.10.2 - General Inspection Procedures

Always begin each day with a clean vehicle free from any visible dirt or debris. During the day, take precautions to minimize contamination of your vehicle. If your vehicle becomes obviously dirty with adhering mud or manure, clean it before visiting another animal facility. When you arrive at a facility where animals are located, check to see if there are designated parking spots or pads for visitors. If so, park your vehicle there unless directed otherwise by the firm. If there is no guidance, park well away from all areas housing animals. When you arrive, inquire about or reconfirm any biosecurity measures the firm employs. Confirm your actions are suitable and follow expectations of the facility when this does not interfere with your inspection ability. Follow steps requested by the firm to remove contamination from vehicles, which may include troughs or pools of disinfectants for tires or other control measures. Avoid driving through manure, mud or wastewater at these sites.

In general, entry to animal housing or feeding areas, corrals, calf pens, hospital pens or special treatment facilities should be avoided unless the assignment requires their inspection or there are specific reasons requiring entry. If you must visit the feeding area occupied by livestock or birds, first determine if any groups are infected with disease. Arrange to visit the known non-disease areas first. Do not handle any animals unless official duty requires such contact. Before leaving the area where you parked your car, put on protective clothing as described and proceed with the purpose of your visit; sanitizing hands (and gloves if worn) and boots as necessary during the visit or inspection.

General procedures:

1. Wear rubber boots or other suitable footwear, which you disinfect upon arriving at the site and prior to departure. It is preferable to also place disposable foot coverings over your footwear, regardless of the type, after you have disinfected them. If the firm has footbaths, use them. Boots and footwear should be disinfected with any of the agents identified at the end of this subsection using a good brush. Clean and disinfect the brush(es) and bucket you use for these activities.

2. Wash your hands with soap and water. If you are visiting a facility where a known animal disease is present or the firm's biosecurity protocol requires, wear disposable gloves.

3. Wear disposable or freshly laundered coveralls, when appropriate. Some facilities may provide disposable coveralls and require visitors to shower in and shower out at their facilities. If requested by the firm and facilities are provided, you should follow those requests.

4. Wear appropriate head coverings, as necessary. If you wear a head covering, clean and disinfect between facilities or use disposable head coverings.

5. Minimize any materials you carry with you such as notebooks, flashlights, etc. to what is required. Consider keeping these things in clean plastic bags or containers between uses. Disinfect any of these types of items as best you can between visits to facilities or between different animal-housing areas.

6. If you are visiting production units with animals of multiple ages, always try to work from the youngest to the oldest.

7. Avoid direct contact with livestock or wild animals, bodily fluids or animal byproducts when visiting facilities.

8. Regional Milk Specialists, Milk Safety Branch and State Training Team staff frequently working with State counterparts in the Interstate Milk Shippers program shall follow any biosecurity measures the firm employs, any biosecurity measures the State employs, and as a minimum shall follow the coded memoranda issued by CFSAN Milk Safety Branch on this subject.

Upon completing your assignment in a given animal area, return to the same area where you donned protective clothing. Remove disposable shoe/boot covers and gloves, if applicable, and place them in a disposable paper or plastic laundry bag. Clean and sanitize boots/footwear. Remove the protective clothing, if applicable, by peeling it off inside out. (This keeps the surfaces exposed to contamination on the inside.) Place all disposable items in a disposable laundry bag for disposal back at your office. If the firm has special containers for disposing of such articles, it is preferable to leave them there rather than transport them back to the office. Place reusable coveralls or other reusable protective clothing in a separate laundry bag for disposition at the office.

Follow guidance on biosecurity provided in the applicable Compliance Program or "Guide to the Inspection of "***" in addition to precautions in this Section.

Repeat these procedures for each separate location visited or inspected.

Purchase commercially available solutions for disinfecting objects or consult with your servicing laboratory. Commercial products such as Nolvosan, Efersan, One Stroke Environ or Virkon-S may be used as long as they are registered by EPA for the intended purpose. Lye or chlorine based cleaners and disinfectants may also be used.

The following formula for household bleach may be used. Mix 3/4 cup (6 oz) of liquid bleach (5.25%) in one gallon of water (128 oz). This solution will be approximately 1:20 dilution. Formulations of household bleach, which are more concentrated than 5.25% are commercially available. Dilute accordingly to these directions. A more concentrated 1:10 solution (1-oz bleach to 9-oz water) may be used with decreased contact time required. Dilutions should be prepared fresh daily and protected from light.

You should read the label and be familiar with directions and precautions, such as removing any organic matter from objects to be disinfected, for any disinfectant you use. In the absence of directions or for chlorine solutions you prepare: 1. Remove visible dirt from the object (boots, tools, tires, etc.). 2. Wipe, brush or scrub surfaces with the solution and keep wet for 2 minutes. 3. Allow to air dry or dry with previously sterilized toweling.

5.2.10.3 - Special Situation Precautions

If you are required to inspect or visit a facility known or suspected to be involved in a contagious animal disease an outbreak or otherwise identified as having diseased animals, contact the Center for Veterinary Medicine and/or Center for Food Safety and Applied Nutrition for additional precautions which may be necessary before you visits these sites. Your activities may be limited to visiting a single site in a day, taking extra-ordinary decontamination steps, ensuring you do not visit or inspect another facility for 5 or more days following the visit to the contaminated site or other steps. APHIS may have special restrictions or precautions for you to follow. The State Veterinarian may also request you follow additional requirements. During inspections of poultry operations where salmonella contamination is known or suspected, you should make sure you contact CFSAN directly for specific procedures to follow. Additional decontamination steps will be required.

5.3 - Evidence Development

5.3.1 - Techniques

The recognition, collection, and effective presentation of admissible evidence is essential to successful litigation. Tangible evidence is required to support your observations and reports of violative conditions.

Although the inspectional procedures to detect adulteration and contamination, etc., are described under specific headings in the IOM, the same procedures and/or techniques may also apply to other areas. For instance, the procedures to detect contamination from filth, insects, rodents, birds, etc., described in IOM section 5.4.7 may also apply to drugs or other products. Your experience and training assists you in making this transition and enables you to detect possible violative conditions.

Keep in mind the policy annunciated in the 4/23/1991 memorandum from the Director, Office of Compliance: The lack of a violative physical sample is not a bar to pursuing regulatory and/or administrative action providing the CGMP deficiencies have been well documented. Likewise, physical samples found to be in compliance are not a bar to pursuing action under CGMP charges.

5.3.2 - Factory Samples

Samples of raw materials or finished products collected during inspections provide the necessary key to establish routes of contamination. They also document the character of products packed prior to the inspection. Collect Factory Samples for laboratory examination only when they contribute to confirming the suspected violation. Be selective since negative reports of analysis of food samples are required under Section 704(d) of the FD&C Act [21 U.S.C. 374 (d)] and might give management a false picture of the firm's operation.

When possible collect duplicate subsamples to provide for the 702(b) portion of the sample. See IOM 4.3.2.1 and 4.3.7.4.1 for additional guidance and 21 CFR 2.10 for exemptions regarding the collection of duplicate portions.

5.3.3 - Exhibits

Impressive exhibits are extremely effective and important forms of evidence to establish existence of violative conditions or products. They should relate to insanitary conditions contributing or likely to contribute, filth to the finished product, or to practices likely to render the product injurious or otherwise violative. Diagrams of the establishment, floor plans, flow charts, and schematics are useful in preparing a clear concise report and in later presentation of testimony. A small compass is useful in describing exact locations of objectionable conditions in the plant, in your diagrams, and locations from which samples were taken, etc. See IOM Exhibit 4-5.

Describe and submit under one INV Sample Number all exhibits (except photographs) collected during the inspection or investigation. Identify and number individual subs and officially seal all samples collected.

Examples of exhibits include:

1. Live and dead insects.

2. Insect frass, webbing, and insect chewed materials; nesting material of rodents and/or other animals; and other behavioral evidence of the presence of insects, rodents and other animals.

3. Samples of components or ingredients, in-process materials and finished products or dosage forms.

4. Manufacturing and control devices or aids.

5. Physical samples if possible and practical or, photographs with descriptions of scoops, stop-gap expediencies, other unorthodox manufacturing equipment or makeshift procedures. If photos are taken, follow the procedures described in IOM 5.3.4.

6. Evidence showing the presence of prohibited pesticide residues. A method of swabbing for prohibited pesticide residues was published in Laboratory Information Bulletin # 1622. Excerpts are quoted as follows:

   a. *Apparatus* - Four dram size glass vials, 95% ethanol, and cotton swabs preformed on 6" long wooden handles. Keep uncontaminated in a clean plastic bag.

   b. *Procedure* - Blow away loose dirt or debris from approximately a 3" x 3" selected area. Measure approximately 2 cm of 95% ethanol in vial, dip swab into ethanol, press out excess on inside of vial and roll moist swab back and forth firmly across the selected area. Return swab to vial, swirl in alcohol, press out excess on inside of vial and again roll moist swab across the same area 90° to the previous swabbing. Re-insert swab into vial, break off swab handle and cap the vial with the swab inside.

   c. When swab subsamples are submitted, also submit a blank control sub consisting of an unused swab placed in a capped vial containing 2 cm of the same alcohol that was used for the other swabs.

   d. Describe the type of material swabbed (cardboard carton, metal table top, rubber inspection belt, etc.) and the area covered. A reasonable area is approximately 10 sq. inches. Always try to establish a definite link in the chain of subsamples leading towards the highest level of contamination. If possible, identify the pesticide suspected. Be sure to include a floor plan with the areas sampled identified.

5.3.4 - Photographs

Photos taken during EI's are not classified as INV Samples. They are exhibits. No C/R is used for photos taken unless the photos are part of an Official Sample. See IOM 4.1.4 for information on Official Samples.

Since photographs are one of the most effective and useful forms of evidence, every one should be taken with a purpose. Photographs should be related to insanitary conditions contributing or likely to contribute filth to the finished product, or to practices likely to render it injurious or otherwise violative.

CAUTION: Evaluate the area where flash photography is contemplated. Do not use flash where there is a potentially explosive condition; e.g. very dusty areas or possible presence of explosive or flammable vapors. In these situations use extremely fast film and/or long exposure time instead of flash.

Examples of conditions or practices effectively documented by photographs include:

1. Evidence of rodents or insect infestation and faulty construction or maintenance, which contributes to these conditions.

2. Routes of, as well as, actual contamination of raw materials or finished products.

3. Condition of raw materials or finished products.

4. Employee practices contributing to contamination or to violative conditions.

5. Manufacturing processes.

6. Manufacturing and various control records showing errors, substitutions, penciled changes in procedure, faulty practices, deviations from GMP's, NDA's, or other protocols, altered or inadequate assays or other control procedures and any variation from stated procedure. See IOM 5.3.8.1 for identification of records.

7. Effluent contamination of water systems. See IOM 5.4.3 for techniques in photographing this type of contamination.

When photographing labels, make sure your picture will result in a legible label with printing large enough to be read by an unaided eye. Photograph whited out documents by holding a flashlight against the whited out side and taking a close up photo of the reverse using high-speed film. This will produce a photo with a mirror image of the whited out side.

If you use a Polaroid camera or color slide film, explain the facts in your EIR or on the C/R to alert reviewers that there are no negatives.

5.3.4.1 - In-Plant Photographs

Do not request permission from management to take photographs during an inspection. Take your camera into the firm and use it as necessary just as you use other inspectional equipment.

If management objects to taking photographs, explain that photos are an integral part of an inspection and present an accurate picture of plant conditions. Advise management the U. S. Courts have held that photographs may lawfully be taken as part of an inspection.

If management continues to refuse, provide them with the following references:

1. "Dow Chemical v. United States", 476 U.S. 227 (1986) This Supreme Court Decision dealt with aerial photographs by EPA, but the Court's language seems to address the right to take photographs by any regulatory agency. The decision reads in part, "** When Congress invests an agency with enforcement and investigatory authority, it is not necessary to identify explicitly each and every technique that may be used in the course of executing the statutory mission. ***"

2. "United States of America v. Acri Wholesale Grocery Company, A Corporation, and JOSEPH D. ACRI and ANTHONY ACRI, Individuals",

U.S. District Court for Southern District of Iowa. 409 F. Supp. 529. Decided February 24, 1976.

If management refuses, advise your supervisor so legal remedies may be sought to allow you to take photographs, if appropriate. If you have already taken some photos do not surrender film to management. Advise the firm it can obtain copies of the photos under the Freedom of Information Act. See IOM 5.3.4.5.

5.3.4.2 - Photo Identification and Submission

One of the most critical aspects about photographs or videotapes is the ability for the agency to provide testimony clearly verifying the authenticity of the conditions depicted in the photograph or video. It makes no difference if the photo is a 35 mm print from acetate negatives, a Polaroid photo, a digital photo or video taken with a video recorder. You must create a trail, starting with the taking of the photo, confirming its original accuracy and establishing a record describing the chain of custody. To do this, you must make sure each photograph is described in your regulatory notes in sufficient detail to assure positive correlation of the photo or video with your inspection findings. One way you can do this is to photograph a card with your name, district address and phone number as the first frame or picture on a roll of film or in the digital record. This will help identify the film or file and assist in tracking if it is lost or becomes separated from its identification envelope during processing or storage. Proper procedures will also allow the agency to provide evidence confirming the authenticity of the photographs or video recording in the event you are not able to testify personally.

5.3.4.2.1 - Prints

Identify each print on the margin with exhibit number, firm name (or DOC Sample Nos., if DOC Sample), date taken or inclusive dates of inspection, and your initials. Do not place any identifying marks on the picture area of the print. (Some photo developing firms are supplying borderless prints. For this type print, place identification along the back bottom edge of the print and mount the print so the identification can be read without removing the print from the mounting paper. Place a narrative description on the mounting paper next to the print and attach as exhibits to the EIR and/or route with other records associated with a DOC Sample.)

5.3.4.2.2 - Color Slide Identification

If color slides are used, identify each slide, in the same manner as for prints. Districts may have special mounting frames for color slides, so the narrative description of each slide must be in the body of the report with proper reference to exhibits, or, each description may be placed on sheets of paper following the mounting frames and properly referenced.

5.3.4.2.3 - Negative Identification

Identify the edge of at least two negative strips, with the same information as for prints using a 3/16" strip of pressure sensitive tape. Place all negatives in a FDA-525 envelope. Complete blocks 2, 3, (4 if DOC Sample), 5, 7, and 12 and seal with an Official Seal, FDA-415a. If negatives are not part of a DOC Sample, enter firm name in the Sample Number block.

As applicable, submit the sealed FDA-525 or envelope as an exhibit to the EIR, with the Investigative Report as an attachment, or with the other associated records/documents with a DOC Sample.

5.3.4.2.4 - Video Recordings

Handle and protect the original video record just as if it were a photograph negative. Unused videotapes should generally be used to capture the video and, for subsequent copies of the original recording. Write-protect and identify the original videotape with a label with the firm name (or Sample number if it is being submitted as part of an official sample), date taken, and your initials. Officially seal the original videotape in a FDA-525 envelope or similar envelope. If you use a larger, unfranked envelope, identify the envelope with your name, title, home district, date, firm name, firm address (include zip code), description of the contents of the envelope, and marked in large, bolded letters "STORE AWAY AND PROTECT FROM MAGNETIC FIELDS." You may place more than one videotape in a single FDA-525 as long as you state on the envelope how many videotapes are in the envelope. If the original envelope is opened, document the chain of custody and use new seal(s) after each entry to the envelope.

If you perform any editing of the recording, you should only perform this on a copy of the original video recording to prevent possible damage to the original. Document in your regulatory notes you made a copy of the original and verified the copy is an accurate copy of the original video you took. This "original copy" should be treated just as if it is the original. When you sign the report, memorandum or other agency document, your signature certifies you are saying the content of the document, including any video recordings, is true and accurate to the best of your ability.

As applicable, submit the officially sealed FDA-525 or envelope as an exhibit to the EIR, with the Investigative Report as an attachment, or with the other associated records/ documents with a DOC Sample.

5.3.4.2.5 - Digital Photographs or Video Recordings

Prior to the year 2000, FDA investigators have traditionally worked with silver acetate photographic film or used analog video tapes. Early digital cameras recorded photographic images directly to floppy disks or mini CD-Rs in which the evidence could be handled like photographic negatives.

The important difference today is digital cameras are capable of recording high resolution images on the order of ten megapixels. The corresponding image file sizes can be over ten megabytes when using uncompressed file formats. To cope with the increased file sizes, digital camera manufacturers have introduced non-volatile flash memory cards which can record digital images, delete images, and be recorded over and over again. This presents a new issue since the original digital images, which are captured at the moment when the images are recorded on the memory card, will be copied at a later time to a CD-R or other permanent storage media. Due to the cost of flash memory cards and the large file sizes, it is not feasible to purchase new memory cards for each inspection/investigation as you did using photographic film. You will be working with a "original copy" of the images which have to be copied in the exact format to a CD-R as they were originally recorded on the flash memory card to preserve the chain of custody.

In the same manner, digital video recordings may involve the use of different media types such as tapes, CD-Rs or DVD-Rs, or built-in hard drives. If you cannot handle the original video recording as in IOM 5.3.4.2.4, you will need to create an "original copy" of the video recording.

Despite the differences in photographic film and digital technology, you are responsible for collection, handling, documenting the chain of custody, storage, and submission of your evidence in a manner where you can testify to its authenticity in a court of law. See IOM 5.3.4.2 and 5.3.4.3.

5.3.4.2.6 - GLOSSARY OF DIGITAL TERMINOLOGY

Some basic terminology is used when referring to digital devices in IOM 5.3.4.2.4, 5.3.4.2.5, 5.3.4.3.

5.3.4.2.6.1 – Digital Data

Electronic data in binary form consisting in its simplest form as "1"s and "0"s. A computer interprets data by whether the state is on ("1") or off ("0").

5.3.4.2.6.2 – Analog Data

Information captured in a directly measurable signal versus an analog signal converted and stored in binary.

5.3.4.2.6.3 – Memory Card

Any non-volatile memory media that can be removed and which retains data without the need for electrical power. Examples of current memory cards are: Compact Flash (CF), Secure Digital (SD), Memory Stick (Sony), and Extreme Digital (xD).

5.3.4.2.6.4 - Original

The file recorded by a digital device on digital storage media at the moment in time when the user takes a picture or makes a recording. This concept is similar to a film camera where the photographic film records the image when exposed by light. The film image negatives produced when the film is developed are considered the originals and prints are considered copies. See IOM 5.3.4.2.1 and 5.3.4.2.3.

5.3.4.2.6.5 – Original Copy

An exact copy of the original file recorded by the digital device (camera, video recorder, etc.). The original copy will retain all the characteristics of the original and is indistinguishable from the original.

5.3.4.2.6.6 - Permanent Storage Media

A media format in which the digital files cannot be altered once written. Examples are CD-Rs and DVD-Rs.

5.3.4.2.6.7 - Time/Date Stamp

The internal clock within the camera which records the time/date information on the image file. Set the time/date stamp for the location where the photographs or videos are being taken. In this usage, the time/date stamp does not refer to imprinting the time/date stamp within the photographic image although the time/date stamp can also be imprinted on the photograph as some film cameras could do.

5.3.4.2.6.8 - Working Copy

A copy of the original copy used when you need to make additional copies for your report, sample C/R. Creating a working copy decreases the chance the original copy is damaged.

5.3.4.3 - Preparing and Maintaining Digital Photographs as Regulatory Evidence

Assure and protect a digital photo's chain of custody (and authenticity) following this procedure:

1. Prior to using the digital camera, verify the date and time stamp is correct and there are no images stored on the memory card. Reformat the memory card using your camera's reformat command to delete any images not related to your current assignment. Depending on your inspection/investigation, camera, and memory card capacity you should consider bringing more than one memory card if possible.

2. Handle your camera and the memory cards in a manner to protect your evidence and maintain the trail of the "chain of custody" for the evidence you have collected. For example, keep the camera and memory cards in your personal possession at all times or held under lock/key in a secure storage area. Also, keep any additional memory cards containing images in your personal possession until transferred to permanent storage media. Where necessary, document these facts in your regulatory notes or written report (EIR, CR etc).

3. As soon as practical, create an original copy of the digital photos. Some older FDA cameras will capture images directly to a (Write-once Compact Disk Recordable (CD-R)); in this case, the CD-R from these cameras becomes the original CD-R. Identify, date and initial the CD-R as an original image record. If a CD-R/W was used, copy the images to a CD-R to create an original copy with files that can not be altered. Follow additional instructions for creating and finishing a CD-R in step 4 below.

4. If the camera requires downloading of images to a CD-R, download all the images from the digital camera to an unused CD-R or other electronic storage media to create an original copy. If there was more than one memory card used, use a separate CD-R for each memory

card. The storage capacity of a CD-R is about 650 mb; thus, more than one CD-R may be needed to create an original copy of your memory card depending on your camera's resolution, the storage capacity of your memory card, and the number of pictures taken. The images should be transferred in a file format maintaining the image resolution at the time the image was captured. If possible, avoid the use of any file compression in transferring the images to the CD-R. Prior to preparing the CD-R or transferring image files, verify that the computer you are using is set to the correct date and time. Make the CD-R permanent in a format readable by any CD-R reader. Prior to making the working copy from the original copy, identify the original copy with the same information as in IOM 5.3.4.2.1. It is important to identify the original copy as soon as possible to prevent possible mix up of the original copy with any working copies.

5. Use a permanent CD safe marker to identify the original copy CD-R. Do not use ball point pens or similar tipped markers since the CD-R may be damaged. See www.itl.nist.gov/iad/894.05/docs/CDandDVDCareandHandlingGuide.pdf. This NIST document, "Care and Handling of CDs and DVDs - A Guide for Librarians and Archivists" figure 12, page 23 shows where to identify the CD-R.

6. Where applicable, document in your regulatory notes the verification and identification of each photographic image comparing them to your regulatory notes, which were recorded at the time the photographs were taken.

7. Make only one working copy from each original copy and make any additional working copies using the initial working copy. No more than one copy should be made from the original copy in order to preserve the original copy a pristine set. After making the initial working copy, place the original copy in a suitable package, officially seal and store the original copy (CD-R or other electronic storage media) until submitted with the written report (EIR, CR etc). If the images are captured or transferred to diskettes, refer to IOM 5.3.8.3 for the handling of diskettes. If possible, the investigator (who took the photos and will authenticate them at trial) should store the sealed CD-R or other electronic storage media until it is submitted with the written report. If you break the seal for any reason, document this on the broken seal, in your regulatory notes or written report, and reseal the package with a new official seal.

8. Working copies should be used to print photos, insertion into an EIR, cropped, otherwise edited or to be included in a referral.

9. Document in your regulatory notes or written report (EIR, CR, etc.) any steps taken for any unusual editing of original photo images. For example: Superimposing over a important area of the image, image enhancement, composite images, etc.

5.3.4.4 - Preparing Digital Photos for Insertion in a Turbo Establishment Inspection Report (EIR)

Digital photos taken during an inspection can be inserted into the body of a report in Turbo EIR or can be printed and attached to the EIR as an exhibit. Inserting digital photos can dramatically increase the file size of the Turbo EIR document. To maintain a minimum Turbo EIR document file size, the following is recommended: Do not open a digital picture/photo and use copy and paste to insert the picture/photo into the Turbo EIR document. Instead, save pictures/photos in a JPEG image format (.jpg file name extension) in a separate folder in preparation for inserting into Turbo EIR. Then resize all the JPEG pictures to a reasonable image file size. To do this,

1. Open the folder with all the pictures that may be inserted into the Turbo EIR document.

2. Hold the control key down and left click to select each image file to be resized.

3. Right click, choose resize pictures. See exhibit 5-6.

4. Select a size-- click on Small (fits a 640 x 480 screen), and click OK. Selecting one of the other screen sizes will also work with the exception of "Handheld PC (fits a 240 x 320 screen)"

5. New resized files will be created within the same folder. Each original file will be maintained. Each new resized file will be renamed as original file name (Small).jpg to differentiate it from the original file.

6. The resized pictures/photos are now ready for insertion into the Turbo EIR document. Remember to maintain the original image files and not the resized digital image files for submission with your hard copy report, forms, and exhibits to the official establishment file.

To insert a picture into the Turbo EIR document:

1. Open the Turbo EIR document Position cursor to where you want to insert the picture.

2. From the menu bar, click on Insert, choose Picture, click on From File, find and select folder with resized pictures to be inserted. See exhibit 5-7.

3. Double click on the resized picture to be inserted.

4. Picture inserted into the Turbo EIR document can be made larger or smaller by clicking on the picture and grabbing the corner of the picture frame and dragging to achieve the desired size.

Captions can be added outside the borders of the picture or can be inserted within picture using more advanced photo editing techniques.

Alternative method: The Microsoft Office 2003 Tools folder contains a program called Office Picture Manager which can be used to resize pictures. See exhibit 5-8 which shows the "resize" menu option.

NOTE: *When any digital photos are used in an EIR, submit the original or original copy of the camera images following procedures as outlined in IOM 5.3.4.3 – Preparing and Maintaining Digital Photographs as Regulatory Evidence.*

5.3.4.5 - Photograph Requests

Do not routinely advise firms they may have copies of photos. However, if management of the firm initiates the request, advise them it is possible to obtain copies of photographs taken in their plant under the Freedom of Information Act. Any request should be sent to The Food and Drug Administration, at the address listed on the FDA 482 or FDA 483. The firm must bear the cost of duplicating the photographs.

Since photographs are records in an investigative file, they are not available under the Freedom of Information Act until the file is closed.

Do not discourage firms from taking their own photographs at the same time and of the same scenes as you.

5.3.5 - Recordings

Under normal circumstances recording devices will not be used while conducting inspections and investigations. However, some firms are now recording and/or video taping, the inspection and/or the discussion with management portion of the inspection. These firms should be advised we do not object to this procedure, but we will also record the discussion to assure the accuracy of our records. Occasionally a firm's management may record the serving of an inspection warrant or, in a hostile situation, may want to record everything. In such cases, depending on the circumstances, you may prepare your own recording in parallel with the firm's recording. Do not depend on the firm to provide a duplicate of their recordings.

Use a clear tape cassette and identify the tape verbally as follows:

"This is Investigator ____________ of the U.S. Food and Drug Administration speaking in the (state location) of (firm name), (address), (city), (state), and (zip code). It is now a.m./p.m. on (date). Present are (list individuals present with title). This discussion is being recorded by both the representative of (firm name) and by me. We are going to discuss the inspectional findings of an inspection conducted at this firm on (inclusive dates)."

At the close of the discussion and prior to leaving the firm, the recording will be verbally identified as follows:

"This is Investigator ____________ speaking. It is now _______ a.m./p.m. on (date). This was a recording of the discussion with management at the conclusion of an inspection of (firm name and address) conducted on (dates)."

If the recording covers a different situation, the identification should be modified accordingly. If the representative of the firm refuses permission to record the discussion, continue with your discussion and report the facts in your EIR.

The tape cassette must be identified with the firm name, date of the inspection, and investigator's name. Districts have the option of transcribing the tape and making the transcription an exhibit for the EIR. However, the tape itself must be made a permanent part of the EIR as an exhibit.

5.3.6 - Responsible Individuals

The identification of those responsible for violations is a critical part of the inspection, and as important as determining and documenting the violations themselves. Responsibility must be determined to identify those persons to hold accountable for violations, and with whom the agency must deal to seek lasting corrections.

Document and fully report individual responsibility whenever;

1. It is required by the assignment,
2. Inspectional findings suggest the possibility of regulatory action, or
3. Background information suggests the possibility of regulatory action.

Under the Medical Device Quality System regulation (21 CFR 820.20), if the management at the firm is not exercising the controls required by the regulation, the deviations may be cited on your FDA 483.

5.3.6.1 - Discussion on Duty, Power, Responsibility

Duty - An obligation required by one's position; a moral or legal obligation.

Power - Possession of the right or ability to wield force or influence to produce an effect.

Responsibility - An individual who has the duty and power to act is a responsible person.

Three key points to consider are:

1. Who had the duty and power to detect the violation?
2. Who had the duty and power to prevent the violation?
3. Who had the duty and power to correct the violation?

5.3.6.2 - Inspection Techniques How to Document Responsibility

Always determine and report the full legal name and title of persons interviewed, who supplied relevant facts and the name/title/address of top management officials to whom FDA correspondence should be directed.

Obtain the correct name and correct title of all corporate officers or company officials. Obtain pertinent educational and experience backgrounds, and the duties and powers of the officers and employees in key managerial, production, control, and sanitation positions. Ascertain the experience and training of supervisory personnel, in terms that will describe their qualifications to carry out their responsibilities.

There are numerous ways to establish and document responsibility. Evidence may be obtained during interviews and record review specifically intended to determine responsibility. Cover and report items such as:

1. Organizational charts,

2. Statements by individuals admitting their responsibility or attributing responsibility to others,

3. Company publications, letters, memos and instructions to employees, and

4. The presence or absence of individuals in specific areas at specific, significant times, and their observed activities directing, approving, etc.

In order to establish relationships between violative conditions and responsible individuals, the following types of information, would be useful:

1. Who knew of conditions?

2. Who should have known of the conditions because of their specific or overall duties and positions?

3. Who had the duty and power to prevent or detect the conditions, or to see they were prevented or detected?

4. Who had the duty and power to correct the conditions, or to see they were corrected? What was done after person(s) learned of the conditions? Upon whose authority and instructions (be specific)?

5. What orders were issued (When, by whom, to whom, on whose authority and instructions)?

6. What follow-up was done to see if orders were carried out (when; by whom; on whose authority and instructions)?

7. Who decided corrections were or were not complete and satisfactory?

8. What funding, new equipment, new procedures were requested, authorized or denied in relation to the conditions; who made the requests, authorizations, or denials.

Duties and power related to general operations should be established to supplement the specific relationships to violations. Examples of operational decisions that indicate responsibility are:

1. What processing equipment to buy.

2. What raw materials to purchase.

3. What products to produce and what procedures to follow in production?
4. Production schedules - how much to produce, what to make, when to stop or alter production?
5. What production controls to be used?
6. What standards are set for products, raw materials, processes?
7. How to correct or prevent adverse conditions; how much to spend and whom to hire to correct or prevent adverse conditions; when to clean up?
8. How products will be labeled; what products to ship; label approval?
9. When to reject raw materials or products; when to initiate a recall; acceptable quality levels for products?
10. When to hire or fire personnel?
11. Who will accept FDA 482, Notice of Inspection; refuses inspection; accept Inspectional Observations, FDA 483?
12. Who designed and implemented the quality assurance plan; who receives reports of Q.A.; who acts or should act upon the reports?
13. Who is responsible for auditing other facilities, contractors, vendors, GLP sites, etc.?
14. In the firm's business relationships, who signs major contracts, purchase orders, etc?

In some circumstances, documenting of individual responsibility requires investigative techniques that lead to sources outside the firm. These sources may include contractors, consultants, pest control or sanitation services, local health officials and others. Copies of documents between the firm and outside parties may help establish responsibilities. Do not overlook state officials as another possible source of information in selected cases.

During the course of the inspection you may observe persons who hold responsible positions and/or influence in the firm whose abilities or judgment may be affected by an obvious infirmity, handicap, or disability. If it is obvious the infirmity adversely affects the person's responsibilities or duties that are under FDA oversight, describe in your EIR the extent of the infirmity and how it relates to the purported problem or adverse condition.

5.3.7 - Guarantees and Labeling Agreements

Review the Code of Federal Regulations, 21 CFR 7.12, 7.13, 101.100(d), 201.150, and 701.9, for information concerning guarantees and labeling agreements.

5.3.7.1 - Guaranty

Certain exemptions from the criminal provisions of the FD&C Act are provided where a valid guarantee exists as specified in Section 303(c) of the FD&C Act [21 U.S.C. 333 (c)]. Obtain a copy of any Food and Drug guarantee, which the firm claims to use relating to a violation noted during your inspection. No person may rely upon any guaranty unless he has acted merely as a conduit through which the merchandise reached the consumer.

5.3.7.2 - Labeling Agreement

Products regulated by FDA are normally expected to be completely labeled when introduced into or while in interstate commerce. Under certain conditions exemptions are allowed when such articles are, in accordance with trade practices, to be processed, labeled, or repacked in substantial quantity at an establishment other than where originally processed or packed. Sections 405, 503(a) and 603 of the FD&C Act [21 U.S.C. 345, 353(a), and 363] also provide exemptions from complete labeling for products.

5.3.7.3 - Exemption Requirements

To enjoy this exemption, the shipment must meet one of the following:

1. The shipper must operate the establishment where the article is to be processed, labeled or repacked; or

2. If the shipper is not the operator of the establishment, he must first obtain from the owner a written agreement signed by and containing the post office addresses of such persons and such operator and containing such specifications for the processing, labeling or repacking of such articles as will insure that such article will not be adulterated or misbranded within the meaning of the Act, upon completion of the processing, labeling or repacking.

Submit copies and dates of labeling agreements where unlabeled articles are shipped in interstate commerce.

5.3.8 - Records Obtained

Many types of inspections and investigations require collection of copies of records to document evidence of deviations. In some cases, this may involve voluminous copies of Good Manufacturing Practice (GMP) records, commitments made in the Pre-Approval process, adherence to the requirements of the Low Acid Canned Food regulations or other areas. Copies of records are also obtained to document interstate commerce, product labeling and promotion, and to identify the party or parties responsible for a variety of actions. All documents become part of the government's case should it go to litigation.

Normally, during litigation proceedings, the best evidence rule prevails in court, whereby the copy of the record in the custody of the government can be authenticated, if the original record is not produced by the custodian of the record.

It is imperative the government witness [usually the collector of the record(s)] be able to testify where, when and from whom the copies were obtained, and that the copy is a true copy of the source document, based on their review of the source document.

5.3.8.1 - Identification of Records

Articles used as evidence in court cases must be marked to assure positive identification. This includes all records as noted in IOM 5.3.8, and any others for evidence in administrative or judiciary proceedings. When identifying and filing records, you must assure the record is complete and no identification method or filing mechanism covers, defaces or obliterates any data on the record/document.

It is imperative you identify the records used as evidence so you can later testify the documents entered as evidence are the very ones you obtained. See IOM 5.3.8.2. You should always review source documents to assure the records you obtained are an accurate representation (copy) of the source document. Record in your Regulatory Notes the when, where, and from who copies are obtained so you can properly prepare for testimony as needed.

5.3.8.2 - Identifying Original Paper Records

NOTE: Policy Changes - In keeping with other regulatory and enforcement agencies' policies, the mandatory identification of the original or source document copied during an inspection or investigation is no longer routinely required. IOM 4.5.2.5 covers identification of records collected and submitted as part of a sample collection.

When you collect an Official or Documentary (or "DOC") Sample, each page of the copied records will become part of the collection report and should be identified as noted in this section and as in IOM 4.4.5. This includes records of interstate commerce, manufacturing deviations, label and labeling violations, or any other record copied which may become "evidence.

While it is no longer routinely required for you to identify the original or source record(s), you must verify the copy of the record(s) you received is an accurate reproduction of the original or source record(s). You must be able to testify your copy is an exact duplicate of the original or source record. You should record in your regulatory notes you authenticated copies of records you obtain so you can provide this testimony during any trial proceedings.

To ensure you are able to positively identify the specific copies you received during your inspection or investigation and to avoid any filing mix-up, you must identify the copies you obtained. This identification will cover records submitted in support of the inspection or investigation, and include all those submitted whether it is an Establishment Inspection Report (EIR) or a narrative memorandum.

You should identify records/exhibits submitted with an EIR using at least the Exhibit number, firm name, date(s) of the inspection, and your initials. This should be done in such a way that you will be able to clearly identify the copy of specific record(s) you obtained. If some type of label is used, it must be permanently applied so any removal will be obvious. Records submitted with a Collection Report will be similarly identified with the sample number, date of collection, but with your handwritten initials. Records submitted with a memorandum will include a phrase or firm or subject name to tie them to the investigation, the date(s) of the investigation and your initials.

There are occasions when a single record may include hundreds of sheets of bound paper. Abbreviated methods of identification may be used for bound documents by fully identifying the first and last few pages. In some cases, firm's clearly mark each page with the sequential and total pages number (e.g., page 6 of 10, 7 of 10, etc.) and this allows you to fully mark only a few pages in the beginning and end of the exhibit.

All pages must be identifiable if not in bound documents. One example of a shortened method of identifying individual exhibits containing a large number of pages (usually more than 25) is to fully identify the first few and last few pages with at least the exhibit number, date and your initials. Then identify the remaining pages with the page number of the total page numbers, and your initials, e.g., "5 of 95 SHR". This may not be acceptable if you have more than one exhibit consisting of exactly 95 pages.

Whatever method is used, you must assure the document is complete and is always identifiable. This is so you can testify as to the "where", "when" and "from whom" the copies were obtained, and that the copy is a true copy of the source document based on your review of the source document. The identification method should allow any reviewer to determine if the document is complete or pages or parts are missing.

5.3.8.3 - Filmed or Electronic Records

When attempting to obtain records, you may find they are stored on microfilm, microfiche, or some form of a computerized management information system as electronic records.

5.3.8.3.1 - Microfilm/Microfiche and Electronic Information

You may encounter records stored on microfilm/microfiche or as electronic records on a computer system. Hard copy records obtained during the course of the inspection from these sources are handled the same as any hard copied records following procedures outline in IOM 5.3.8, 5.3.7.1 and 5.3.8.2.

NOTE: *See CPG Section 130.400 for Agency Policy concerning microfilm and/or microfiche records. 21 CFR Part 11 contains information concerning Electronic Records and Electronic Signatures and may be of value to you.*

5.3.8.3.2 - Electronic Information Received on CD-R, or other Electronic Storage Media

You may obtain electronic information, databases, or summary data from a firm's databases during an establishment inspection. The methods used must maintain the integrity of the electronic data and prevent unauthorized changes. Do not personally access a firm's electronic records, databases, or source/raw data during the course of an inspection.

When it is necessary to access a firm's data during an inspection:

1. Oversee the firm's personnel accessing their system and have them answer your questions.

2. Request the firm run queries specific to the information of interest.

3. Have the firm generate reports/data to be copied to a CD or other electronic storage media, which you can subsequently analyze, or have the data printed in hardcopy.

Electronic data, such as blood bank databases, drug production records, medical device complaints, service records, returned products and other records are often dynamic data files with real time updating. Information from these files is generally provided at the time of the inspection. Your request may require the firm to develop one or more custom queries to provide the requested information. You must assume the query logic is not validated and take appropriate action to ensure the data is accurate and no data has been accidentally omitted due to a programming logic error occurring at the firm.

When appropriate, a copy of electronic data can be obtained on one or more CD-R, or other electronic storage media. If you provide the diskettes to the firm, use only new, previously unused and preformatted diskettes. An additional safeguard is to request the firm reformat the disk on their own computer to assure it is usable and "clean".

Any request for electronic information on a CD-R, or other electronic storage media must be made with a computer application in mind and the data obtained must be useful. Request for electronic information should be in a format compatible with software applications knowledgeable to you and available from the Agency. Converting files into different file formats is difficult and should not be attempted without the necessary knowledge and availability of conversion type programs where applicable. If help is needed for file conversion, assistance may be available within the district, region or from DFI HFC-130.

Any CD-R or other electronic storage media containing electronic information received during the course of an inspection should be considered and handled as master CD-Rs. The firm may or may not retain a copy of the information provided during the course of an inspection. Ask the individual providing the copy(s) to provide actual CD-R or other electronic storage media labeling information, such as filename(s), date and other information to facilitate their later identification of the CD-R or other electronic storage media and the data provided on the CD-R or other electronic storage media. The name of the appropriate software and version used to ensure readability of the information should also be maintained with the copy of the electronic information.

You should perform a virus scan of the master CD-R or other electronic storage media according to Agency requirements. Each master diskette should be write-protected, labeled and identified as you would any hard copy document.

There are no guarantees the files provided on CD-R or other electronic storage media will be useable data. It is your responsibility to make a working copy of each master CD-R or other electronic storage media. Before making any working copies from the master CD-R or other electronic storage media, confirmation should be made that the write-protection has been activated on each master diskette. You will need to use a computer to view the copied files and verify each file contains the information requested and the information is useable to you. Some electronic data files may be too large to open from a CD-R or other electronic storage media and must be loaded on a hard disk before opening. If this is the case, the file should be put on a subdirectory before opening and viewing.

As a general practice, any findings developed from electronic information provided by the firm should be requested in a hard copy format. The hard copy provided by the firm should then be used as an exhibit to support the investigator's observation. This will preclude or limit any errors that may have occurred from the investigator querying of the electronic information.

The master CD-R, diskettes or other electronic storage media, should be secured to assure the integrity of the data when used in a subsequent enforcement action. Identify the master CD-R as an exhibit, write-protect diskettes, and place in a suitable container, e.g., FDA-525, and officially seal. Mark the FDA-525 or other container as containing diskettes and to "Protect from magnetic fields." The diskette(s) should be stored as part of the exhibits with the original EIR. See IOM 5.10.5.1.

5.3.8.4 - Requesting and Working with Computerized Complaint and Failure Data

The auditing of FDA regulated firms has found that an increasing number of firms are developing and maintaining computerized complaint and failure data to meet GMP record requirements. Records, hardcopy and electronic, are becoming increasingly voluminous. The auditing of information contained in computerized databases is generally most effectively accomplished with the use of a computer.

Computer auditing of computerized complaints and failure data may require the transfer of electronic data to CD-R or other electronic storage media for you to use in your computer. You should use a computer and application software familiar to you to query information obtained in electronic format. You should not use the audited firm's equipment or personnel to perform repetitive queries or manipulation of the audited firm's own computerized data.

5.3.8.4.1 - Computerized Complaint and Failure Data

Requesting and obtaining electronic data on CD-R or other electronic storage media is becoming more common during the course of routine inspections. Providing computerized data on electronic media is advantageous to both you and the firm and can result in shorter inspection time. These types of databases contain large numbers of records, which can be easily and quickly queried if they are in electronic format. Inspection time would be lengthened if all such information was only provided in hardcopy format. It may result in you reentering all of the hardcopy data into a new database or reviewing volumes of documents. Be aware if the firm should generate custom software to provide requested electronic records, it would be difficult for you to validate or verify the firm's algorithm used to extract the requested data and ensure that records were not accidentally or deliberately omitted due to programming logic errors, data entry errors, etc.

5.3.8.4.2 - Requesting Computerized Data

Before requesting a copy of computerized data, you should determine several things including information about the size and contents of the database, the program used by the firm, and the program you will use, among others. The following steps are useful in preparing for an electronic record request.

1. Determine the firm's application program used to maintain the data of interest. This may be in a DOS compatible application program such as Access, Excel, Dbase, Paradox, Lotus 123 or others. It is best to obtain data files in a format compatible with application programs you will be using. Large data files with record counts in excess of 10,000 records are best converted to file formats that can be used by programs designed to handle such large databases. There are spreadsheet record limits in some commercial programs that would not allow these application programs to handle much over 5,000 records. Check the program you plan to use to ensure it can handle the file size you will be using.

2. Most large and real-time data files reside in mainframe or network systems requiring programming and downloading to a PC using an [Structured Query Language (SQL)] SQL format. Although data may be captured and downloaded in an SQL format, not all spreadsheet or database application software can load an SQL file. In addition, it may be difficult or impossible to manipulate data in that format. Problems can also be encountered downloading data from Apple computers to an IBM format. Successful conversions are possible if the firm selects the proper conversion format or you have conversion software designed to convert from an Apple to an IBM platform.

3. You may need to request an ASCII (American Standard Code for Information Interchange) text/flat file format. ASCII format is an industry standard, which assigns a unique code to every printable, keyboard, and screen character. An ASCII file should be stripped of all non [-] standard codes that are used by specific application programs for fonts, underlining, tabs, etc. The ASCII text file can be imported by all application programs, and once imported, can be restructured for the specific application program. ASCII delimited is the format of choice, with ASCII fixed length as an alternative. Care must be exercised in specifying a hard carriage return at the end of each line to be DOS compatible, or additional conversion may be necessary before the file is useable.

4. You should determine what fields of information are routinely captured by the firm. This can be accomplished by requesting a printout of the data structure of the data file or observing the inputting of data at a computer terminal or workstation. It is common for databases to contain numbers or other coded information requiring translations from look up tables to give meaningful text. You should determine if information fields contain coded data, and if so, a code breakdown should be obtained. Information about code breakdowns should be located in the SOPs for that computerized system. Also be aware in relational databases, there may

be linking data fields that exist in other tables that should also be considered in the overall data request.

5. If the files are too large to fit on a disk, file compression must be used. If possible, ask that the firm prepare the data in a compression format that is self-extracting. Self-extracting files are executable files and should be virus scanned before and after executing. All CD-R, diskettes or other electronic storage media should be scanned prior to being used on any FDA computer. Whatever compression utility is used, make sure you have the software to manipulate the files as needed.

6. You should always get the total record count of the data file provided by the firm. This count should be verified any time the file is loaded, converted, manipulated, or queried.

5.3.8.4.3 - Identification and Security of CD-R, Diskettes or Other Electronic Storage Media

You should follow these steps to ensure proper identification and security of CD-R or other electronic storage media:

1. Label each CD-R or other electronic storage media
   a. Firm name
   b. Date and your initials
   c. Initials by a representative of the firm (optional) If you provide the diskettes to be used, use only new and preformatted diskettes from an unopened box.
   d. The name of the appropriate software and version to ensure readability of the information

2. Make a working copy of CD-R or other electronic storage media
   a. Write protect the original diskette
   b. Virus scan the original diskette
   c. Copy the original CD-R or other electronic storage media

The original CD-R or other electronic storage media should not be used for manipulating data so as to maintain the integrity of the CD-R or other electronic storage media and data. NOTE: If a virus is detected, do not remove the virus from the source diskette provided by the firm. This may become evidence if it is suspected that the firm intentionally transferred the virus. Attempt to obtain another, uninfected copy of the data file from the firm.

Create a subdirectory on the computer hard drive:

1. Transfer data from the virus-free, working copy of the CD-R or other electronic storage media to your hard drive.

2. Virus scan any decompressed files before and after decompression. (Some virus scan software will scan compressed files but it is safer to scan all foreign files

3. You have now transferred confidential information to the hard drive and that information must be protected.

4. Upon completion of the use of the data, the file must be deleted and totally overwritten with a utility to wipe the data from the hard drive. A delete file operation is not adequate to totally remove the data from the hard drive.

5. Do not leave confidential files in any shared directories or e-mail.

5.3.8.4.4 - Data Integrity of Records Provided by Firm

Many manufacturers are using computers to store records concerning complaints, failure data, returned goods, servicing, testing results and others. Record traceability and data integrity are always concerns when you copy or use computerized data.

1. It is difficult to determine what records are to be designated as originals or copies of original records. It is important, when obtaining hardcopy or copy of computerized data, for you to capture some method of dating. The date of an electronic file can be captured by recording the date and time from a file listing in DOS or with File Manager in Windows. This may not always be possible, but some attempt should be made to date and time stamp electronic data.

2. Requests for most information from manufacturers will require the use of some custom software routine to generate the Investigator's requested information. Any data generated at the request of an Investigator should always be considered custom data. The firm will seldom validate or verify software routines used to generate data in response to your request. You should request a copy of any software program or scripts used to generate the computerized data provided. The request for the software program is not a request for a copy of the application program but a request for the special commands or programs created within the application program for the querying and extraction of data into a new data file. You should review the command structure to ensure it includes all data related to your request.

5.3.8.4.5 - Electronic Information for Official Documentation

During your use of queried data, if you find a violative situation, you should request the firm prepare a hardcopy report of the specific data that depicts the situation. (Do not request an entire copy of the data base and do not rely on the digital database or your extractions from the data to serve as official documentation.) Any records of interest, such as complaints, failure information, etc., noted from querying the computerized data should be copied from original hardcopy documents to support the findings in the database. You should also maintain the procedures or commands you used to find the violative situations in the data base. Follow procedures in IOM 5.3.8.4.3 for maintaining and identifying original disks.

5.3.8.5 - Listing of Records

If management requests a list of the copies of records you obtain, prepare it in duplicate and leave the original with the firm. Many firms prepare duplicate copies of documents requested during our inspections. In the interests of conserving inspectional time, you may ask the firm to prepare the list of copies concurrently with the photocopying and you then verify the accuracy. Do not use form FDA-484, Receipt for Samples. Describe the circumstances in your report including the name and title of the individual to whom you gave the list. Submit the duplicate list with your report as an Exhibit.

5.3.8.6 - Patient and/or Consumer Identification on Records

During the course of many types of inspections and investigations you will review and collect records which specifically identify (by name) patients or consumers. Under most state Privacy Laws this information is confidential. Some firms we inspect may mistakenly believe this information is not releasable to the federal government. However, Federal laws preempt State laws; with few exceptions we are entitled to review and copy the complete record, including the identifying patient/consumer names. The Agency is then required to maintain the confidentiality of the records/files, as with any confidential record you collect. Any disclosure of the information contained in the record(s) can only be by Law, i.e., judge's order, disclosure, Congressional order, etc.

General, routine guidance is as follows:

1. For records copied as a result of injury or complaint investigation, where you obtain patient identification, the identification should remain intact and stored in the official FDA files. Frequently, medical releases must be obtained from a complainant, consumer or "next-of-kin". At least one or two extra should be obtained and stored in the files.

2. For methadone inspections, continue the Agency policy of deleting patient identification specific to the patient (name, SSN, Driver License #, etc.).

3. For any inspection/investigation involving a regulation required Informed Consent, such as clinical investigations, IRBs, bioequivalence testing, etc., patient identification should remain intact and stored in the official FDA files.

4. For most others, such as MQSA, plasmapheresis, blood donations, etc., only the patient initials and unique identifier supplied by the firm (such as donor number, donation number, etc.) need be routinely retained in the FDA files.

It is not uncommon for a firm to voluntarily purge the documents of the pertinent identifiers as they are copied. You must verify (by direct comparison to the original document) you received an accurate reproduction of the original, minus the agreed to purging, prior to accepting the copy.

As with any inspection there are times when the specific identifiers must be obtained, copied and retained, such as if/when further interview of the patient/consumer could be necessary. If in doubt, obtain the data. It is always easier to delete later than to return to obtain the information, especially in the few cases where questionable practices may result in the loss of the information.

All documents obtained containing confidential identifiers will be maintained as all documents obtained by FDA containing confidential information, i.e., in the official FDA files. Confidential identifiers may be flagged in the official FDA files for reference by reviewers to assure no confidential data are released under FOIA.

5.3.9 - Request for Sample Collection

There are times one district will request another district to collect surveillance or compliance samples for it. The requesting district should provide as much of the following information as is available on specific shipments, using the FACTS Create Assignment Screen. See IOM Exhibit 5-9.

The following fields must be completed in order to save the assignment: Requesting Organization, Priority, Subject, POC Name, Op Code, Accomp Org, Num of Ops, and PAC. When you create a sample collection assignment, which will require laboratory analysis, you should also create an assignment for the laboratory, using operation 41.

The screen is organized in sections.

5.3.9.1 - FACTS Assignment Section

The Assignment section has the following fields:

Compliance Number: Enter the Compliance Number if known. This will make it easier to tie all associated activities together if the District is considering a compliance action. You can generate a compliance number after completing the mandatory fields on the Maintain Inspection Results screen.

ORA reqd: This field only applies to assignments generated by Centers or other organizations outside of ORA. It will indicate whether or not ORA concurrence is required for the assignment.

ORA Cncrnc Num: This field is for the requesting organization (other than an ORA component) to indicate ORA concurrence for the assignment.

POC Name: This field Indicates the point of contact in the requesting organization for the assignment.

Priority: Choose High or Routine

Remarks: This is a free form field, which should briefly describe the assignment.

Reporting Method: Indicate how the other district should notify the contact of problems with or status of the assignment. For example: e-mail, phone, etc.

Requesting Organization: Enter your District Office, if you are requesting a sample from another district or other appropriate FACTS organization.

Requestor Completion Date: Enter the completion date desired, using the format, MM/DD/YYYY.

Subject: Enter a subject for the assignment. It may be helpful to create a subject others will recognize as related to a specific action, for example a firm or product name.

5.3.9.2 - FACTS Operations Section

The Operations section has the following fields:

Estmtd Hours: Enter the number of hours you believe the assignment should take. This is done to assist the collecting district in planning their work.

Estmtd Smpl Cost: Enter the estimated sample cost, if known.

Op Code: Enter the operation code for the assignment. If you are requesting a sample collection, it is 31.

Requester Remarks: Enter as many details about the sample collection as you can. Include: date of shipment, number and size of units or amount, codes, carrier (routing and freight bill number), invoice number, and name of responsible firm with date of inspection (if one occurred).

Rqstr Prty: Enter High or Routine. This will default to the same data entered in the Assignment section if it was prepared first.

Subject: This will default to the same data entered in the Subject field in the Assignment section if it was prepared first.

5.3.9.3 - FACTS Organizations Section

The Organizations section contains the following fields.

Accomp Org: Enter the District or other FACTS organization you are requesting collect the assignment. If you are completing the sample analysis assignment, be sure to enter a laboratory.

Num of Ops: Enter the number of sample collections or analyses you are requesting from the organization identified in the previous field.

Perf Org (Adhoc Work): If the performing organization is part of the accomplishing organization you are in, you may enter the performing organization here. If you are requesting the sample of another District, you will probably leave this blank.

The PACS and Products section of the form contains fields for entering the assignment PAC and Product code.

Enter the FEI number(s)/CFN(s) of the firm or firms from which the sample is to be collected in the Firms and Cross References section. See IOM 4.4.10.3.24.

5.3.10 - Post-Inspection Notification Letters

Issuance of Post-inspection notification letters have been discontinued in all program areas. See FMD 145.

5.4 - Food

5.4.1 - Food Inspections

Food plant inspections are conducted to evaluate the methods, facilities, and controls used in manufacturing, storage and distribution of foods.

See CFSAN Office of Compliance's intranet website for the most current guidance (e.g., compliance programs, field assignments, field guidance).

5.4.1.1 - Preparation and References

Before undertaking an inspection:

1. Review the district files of the firm to be inspected and acquaint yourself with the firm's history, related firms, trade marks, practices and products. The review will identify products difficult to manufacture, require special handling, special processes or techniques, and hours of operation, which is especially important in bacteriological inspections. Remove, for subsequent investigations and discussion with management, Complaint/Injury Reports, which are marked for follow-up during the next inspection. See IOM 5.2.8.

2. Become familiar with current programs relating to the particular food or industry involved and relevant DFI inspection guides. Become familiar with any applicable Compliance Policy Guide (CPG Chap 5).

3. Understand the nature of the assignment and whether it entails certain problems, e.g., Salmonella or other bacteriological aspects.

4. Review the FD&C Act Chapter IV - Food.

5. Review and become familiar with the appropriate parts of 21 CFR pertaining to foods, for example:

    a. 21 CFR Part 110 - GMP's on foods

    b. 21 CFR Parts 108 and 113 - Thermally Processed Low-Acid Foods Packaged in Hermetically Sealed Containers

    c. 21 CFR Part 114 - Acidified Foods are of particular importance

    d. 21 CFR Part 120 - HACCP Systems (covers Juice Processors)

    e. 21 CFR Part 123 - Fish and Fishery Products

    f. 21 CFR Part 129 - Processing and Bottling of Bottled Drinking Water

    g. 21 CFR Part 130, et al - Food Standards

    h. 21 CFR Part 1240 - Control of Communicable Disease

    i. 21 CFR Part 1250 - Interstate Conveyance Sanitation

6. Review reference materials on food technology and other subjects available in the District Inspectional Reference Library.

7. If you are assigned to inspect food-service establishments under the FDA - Secret Service Agreement, you should use the most current copy of the "Food Code" and be standardized in its use. All Regional Food Service Specialists and most Interstate Travel Sanitation Specialists are standardized in use of the code.

8. Be familiar with the "Food Chemicals Codex". See IOM 5.4.4.3.

5.4.1.2 - Inspectional Authority

See IOM subchapter 2.2 for broader information on this topic.

Authority to Obtain Records and Information in LACF and Acidified Foods Plants:

FDA's regulation in 21 CFR 113 requires commercial processors of low-acid foods packaged in hermetically sealed containers to maintain complete records of processing, production and initial distribution. 21 CFR 114 requires the same of commercial processors of acidified foods. 21 CFR 108.25(g) and 21 CFR 108.35(h) provide that a commercial processor shall permit the inspection and copying of the records required by 21 CFR 113 and 21 CFR 114 by duly authorized employees of FDA. The demand for these records must be in writing on an FDA 482a, Demand for Records, signed by you and must identify the records demanded.

5.4.1.2.1 - Written Demand for Records

To obtain the records:

1. Prepare a FDA 482a, "Demand for Records", listing the records demanded. Describe the processing records to be reviewed and/or copied as accurately as you can, e.g., "All thermal process and production records mandated by 21 CFR 113 (or 114 if applicable) for the foods (state name of food) processed at this plant on (specific date or period of time)". If only a specific record is desired list it specifically as follows: e.g., "Fill Weight Records for #2 Filling Machine for the period 4-15-87 through 6-7-87."

2. Sign the form.

3. Issue the original to the same person to whom the FDA 482, "Notice of Inspection", was issued.

4. Submit the carbon copy with your EIR.

5.4.1.2.2 - Written Request for Information

21 CFR 108.35(c)(3)(ii) states commercial processors engaged in thermal processing of low-acid foods packaged in hermetically sealed containers shall provide FDA with any information concerning processes and procedures necessary by FDA to determine the adequacy of the process. 21 CFR 108.25(c)(3)(ii) requires the same of commercial processors of acidified foods. The information in this regulation is the data on which the processes are based. Many processors will not have this information and in fact 21 CFR

113.83 requires only that the person or organization establishing the process permanently retain all records covering all aspects of establishing the process. The processor should, however, have in his files a letter or other written documentation from a processing authority delineating the recommended scheduled process and associated critical factors.

You may encounter situations where you believe control of certain factors is critical to the process and there is no evidence to document these factors were considered when the process was established (e.g., a change in formulation which could effect consistency). It is appropriate to issue a written request for a letter or other written documentation from a processing authority, which delineates the recommended scheduled process and associated critical factors. This represents the processing authority's conclusions and should correlate with the filed process.

If you believe control of certain factors are critical to the process and are not delineated in the process authority's recommendation or the filed process, obtain all available information about the situation. Include the name of the person or organization who established the process and the specific practices of the firm. This information should be included in your report and forwarded by your District to the Center for Food Safety and Applied Nutrition, Division of Enforcement (HFS-605) for review, as soon as possible. If the process establishment data and information is deemed necessary by the center, they will either request it directly from the processor or will direct the district to request it. If requested to obtain the information:

1. Prepare a FDA 482b - Request for Information listing the specific information requested. Specify each product involved by food product name and form, container size and processing method.

2. Sign the form.

3. Issue the original to the same person to whom the FDA 482, "Notice of Inspection", was issued.

4. Submit the carbon copy with your EIR.

5.4.1.3 - Records Access Under BT Authority

The following guidance should be used to demand records under the Agency's Bioterrorism (BT) authority when the following conditions are met:

1. The Secretary has a reasonable belief that an article of food is adulterated and presents a threat of serious adverse health consequences or death to humans or animals.

2. The records are necessary to assist the Secretary in making such a determination. When these conditions are met, the following guidance should be followed: http://www.cfsan.fda.gov/~dms/secgui13.html.

FDA will not invoke this authority during routine inspections unless the requirements for record access under the BT Act are satisfied. Note: FDA will continue to request that food records be voluntarily provided by the owner, operator, or agent in charge in a variety of circumstances of routine inspections. The procedures and the guidance above will be followed only if records are requested under the Agency's BT Act authority.

Procedure: Upon the determination that a food presents a threat of serious adverse health consequences or death to humans or animals, and after concurrence by the individuals listed in the guidance above, a FDA 482c (Exhibit 5-10) will be issued to the most responsible individual.

5.4.1.4 - Food and Cosmetic Defense Inspectional Activities

Food and cosmetics security inspectional activities should be conducted during all routine food and cosmetics safety inspections. During the normal course of the inspection be alert to opportunities for improvement or enhancement of the firm's food and cosmetics security preventive measures, as compared to those recommended in the guidance documents described below. You should not perform a comprehensive food and cosmetics security audit of the firm or conduct an extensive interview of management or employees in an attempt to determine the level of adoption of preventive measures listed in the guidance. The goal is to facilitate an exchange of information to heighten awareness on the subject of food and cosmetics security.

5.4.1.4.1 - Food and Cosmetic Security

Inspectional activities relative to food and cosmetic security for routine food and cosmetic establishment inspections should include:

1. Discussion with firm management of relevant FDA guidance documents including:

    a. Food Producers, Processors, and Transporters: Food Security Preventive Measures Guidance

    b. Importers and Filers: Food Security Preventive Measures Guidance

    c. Cosmetics Processors and Transporters: Cosmetics Security Preventive Measures Guidance

    d. Retail Food Stores and Food Service Establishments: Food Security Preventive Measures Guidance

    e. Dairy Farms, Bulk Milk Transporters, Bulk Milk Transfer Stations, and Fluid Milk Processors: Food Security Preventive Measures Guidance.

    These documents should be used as references during inspections, as appropriate. Copies may be obtained at: http://www.fda.gov/oc/factsheets/foodsecurity.html. If firm management does not already have a copy of the relevant guidance documents provide them with hard copies or information on how to obtain the guidance from FDA's web site.

2. Identification of opportunities for improvement or enhancement of the firm's food and cosmetic security preventive measures, as compared to those recommended in the guidance documents, and encouragement of management to make such improvements or enhancements to their security system.

Keep in mind that: the guidance does not represent mandatory conditions or practices; some of the recommended food and cosmetics security preventive measures may not be appropriate or practical to the specific operation; and other means of achieving the goals of the preventive measures listed in the guidance may be more suitable for the specific operation than those cited as examples. The important message for management is to consider the goals of the food and cosmetics security preventive measures; evaluate the goals relative to the specifics of their operation; and address those that are relevant to the extent practical.

Food and cosmetics security observations should not be listed on form FDA-483, Inspectional Observations, unless they likewise constitute deviations from Current Good Manufacturing Practice. Security discussions should be handled discretely and should only involve management of the firm.

The fact that the discussion took place and, if applicable, that a copy of the guidance document(s) was provided should be recorded in the Summary section of the EIR. For example, under a section heading titled "Food and Cosmetics Security" you should only state, "A copy of the Food and Cosmetics Security Guidance documents were provided to and food and cosmetics security issues were discussed with (name of firm official)." The details of inspectional findings regarding security should NOT be recorded. You should also minimize the quantity and detail of notes taken relative to the firm's food and cosmetics security program, taking only those needed to serve as a "memory jog" during the discussion with management.

5.4.1.4.2 - Reconciliation Examinations

During routine food and cosmetic inspections, conduct one reconciliation examination during each food and cosmetic establishment inspection. The examinations are to be conducted on raw materials used in the manufacture of foods or cosmetics, or finished products received by the firm for further distribution. Preference should be given to products of foreign origin. Where possible, these examinations should be performed on products as they are received by the firm.

Consult the factory jacket for any information on special conditions in the facility that may affect selection of personal protective equipment; consult your supervisor for any recommendations on personal protective equipment; and have available all necessary personal protective equipment to conduct the activity.

As Part of an Import Field Examination and Entry Review - See IOM 6.3.1 and 6.4.3. For imported food and cosmetics, a reconciliation examination should be conducted:

Per Part A [IOM 5.4.1.4.3] during all routine import field exams. You should only report time under the Counter Terrorism PAC at the direction of your supervisor or if there is a for cause assignment.

1. In instances where review of entry information raises suspicion (resulting in a detailed reconciliation exam per Part B [IOM 5.4.1.4.4]).

2. A detailed reconciliation exam should be conducted when there are anomalies in entry declaration information. These may include new, unusual, or unfamiliar commodities, manufacturers, importers; suspicious

trans-shipments; or credibility issues such as those between the product and declared country of origin.

If anomalies are found, entry documents should be requested and reviewed for discrepancies between the information declared through electronic filer submissions and that found in entry documents. Entry documents may include invoices, bills of lading, export certifications, and other relevant documents obtained from the importer, filer, or manufacturer/processor of the product. Fields in which discrepancies are found that may raise concern include country of origin, manufacturer, product description, product code, and quantity.

Avoid duplication of examination of the same foreign manufacturer, unless a prior reconciliation examination disclosed an unexplained discrepancy.

Follow guidance in IOM 5.4.1.4.3 to IOM 5.4.1.4.4 below for domestic and import reconciliation exams.

5.4.1.4.3 - Reconciliation Examination Guidance Part A

Reconciliation examinations are performed to ensure that:

1. The food or cosmetic is what it purports to be

2. There are not unexplained differences in the quantity of product ordered, shipped, and received, and

3. There are no signs of tampering or counterfeiting.

Before initiating the exam make a general assessment of the appearance of the lot. Look for packaging that: appears to have been opened and resealed; appears wet, stained, punctured, or powdered. Also be alert to abnormal chemical odors. If any of these conditions are detected stop the exam and contact your supervisor for guidance. If the lot appears normal proceed with the examination. To the extent possible the exam should be performed in a well-ventilated, well-lit area.

Determine, to the extent possible, whether:

1. The actual goods in a lot are the same as those that are declared in the shipping documents

2. There is consistency in the manufacturer declared on the product labeling, bulk product packaging, and shipping documents; and

3. There is no (unexplainable) inconsistency in actual quantity of goods in the lot, and the quantity ordered and declared in the shipping documents.

If no unexplained inconsistencies are detected, no further action is indicated.

If unexplainable inconsistencies are detected, document the occurrence, including photographs of the labeling and packaging, and an accurate count of the lot. Contact your supervisor, who should, in the case of imported products, contact the U.S. Customs and Border Protection for appropriate action. If the examination discloses evidence that inaccurate product identification data was submitted to the OASIS entry screening system, the District should evaluate the need for follow-up with a compliance filer evaluation and consider providing the information to the U.S. Customs and Border Protection for appropriate action.

In addition, if unexplained inconsistencies are detected, follow part B [IOM 5.4.1.4.4] of this guidance while conducting a detailed reconciliation exam.

5.4.1.4.4 - Reconciliation Examination Guidance Part B

Open the shipping packaging of a quantity of product approximating the square root of the number of shipping cartons/packages in the lot, and examine the contents. Look for the following:

1. Product identity on the package that does not match the identity declared on the shipping documents
2. Mixed product sizes within a carton or within the lot;
3. Product sizes that do not match the sizes declared on the shipping documents
4. Differences in product configuration or package type (e.g. plastic containers mixed with glass jars or aluminum or steel cans)
5. Easily apparent variations in weight
6. Product labels that display crude, unprofessional, or inconsistent styles of print, color or use of language
7. Unusual placement of labels (e.g. off-center)
8. Variations in lot coding ink color, appearance of embossing, or format (e.g., two line vs. three line, use of letters, numbers and symbols). unusually excessive use of a single code in a very large lot
9. Differences between the actual can codes in the lot and those listed on the shipping documents
10. The existence of a tamper-evident notice on the labeling when the packaging does not contain a tamper-evident feature
11. Product that is beyond its expiration date
12. Inconsistencies in expiration dates within a lot

If no unexplainable discrepancies are noted select at least 1 package at random from the entire shipment and examine their contents. For those products that the contents are visible through the package it is not necessary to open the package. For other products, open the package and examine and field destroy the contents. Look for the following:

1. Differences between the product and that which is declared on the label

2. Color differences in the product between containers of the same lot

3. Style differences in the product between containers of the same lot or between the actual product and the label and document declaration (e.g., sliced vs. whole, colorless noodles vs. egg noodles)

4. Readily detectable abnormal odors (e.g. strong decomposition, bitter almond, petroleum odor, garlic, chlorine, sulfur). Note: specific sensory examination is not expected.

Verification that the product is consistent with the product ordered may require that you obtain information from the owner of the goods, importer, filer, or custom house broker. Review of the following types of documentation may be necessary to accomplish the above instructions, to the extent that they are available: authentic label supplied by the owner of the goods, importer, filer, or custom house broker; purchase order; invoice; shipping records (bill of lading, weigh bill, manifest). Depending on the findings of the exam and record review, you may wish to request that the importer assist in an evaluation of the authenticity of the product, based on the importer's experience with the product.

Every effort should be made to document any discrepancies through use of photographs, and additional records that may be available from the filer, importer, owner, or customs house broker.

5.4.1.4.5 - Special Safety Precautions

See IOM Subchapters 1.5 Safety, subsections including 1.5.1.1 thru 1.5.1.4, and Section 1.5.3 on sampling hazards.

When performing an establishment inspection or reconciliation examination, follow these instructions:

1. If there are no signs of tampering or counterfeiting, use level I protection, which consists of: work gloves; coveralls; work boots; and in a dusty situation, a dust mask.

2. If there are signs of tampering or counterfeiting, use level II protection and consult your supervisor for any additional safety precautions needed. Level II protection consists of: work gloves worn over surgical gloves; full face respirator with appropriate cartridges; disposable coveralls; and work boots.

5.4.1.5 - Food Registration

The Public Health Security and Bioterrorism Preparedness and Response Act of 2002 (the Bioterrorism Act) requires most domestic and foreign facilities that manufacture/process, pack, or hold food for human or animal consumption in the United States to register with FDA by December 12, 2003. The Bioterrorism Act covers both interstate and intrastate firms. FDA published a final rule on October 3, 2005 (70 FR 57505) to implement this requirement. The regulations are codified at 21 CFR 1 Subpart H - Registration of Food Facilities. The agency has also issued a guidance to industry document, "Questions and Answers Regarding Registration of Food Facilities." Facilities may register electronically at http://www.access.fda.gov, by mail or fax, or by CD-ROM for multiple submissions. Registrations will be maintained in the FDA Unified Registration and Listing System (FURLS). Facilities are not considered to be registered until their information is entered into FURLS.

The owner, operator, or agent in charge of a facility must register the name and address of each facility at which, and all trade names under which, the registrant conducts business. If applicable, they must register the same information for their parent companies. Foreign facilities must also provide information about their U.S. Agent.

The purpose of registration is to provide sufficient and reliable information about food facilities. When used with the detention, recordkeeping, and prior notice provisions of the Bioterrorism Act, registration will help to provide information on the origin and distribution of food and feed products to allow for detection and quick reaction to real and potential threats to these products. In the event of a potential threat or an outbreak of foodborne illness, such information will help FDA and other authorities to notify food facility representatives and investigate the event, source, and/or cause of the outbreak. Also, it will enable FDA to notify quickly the facilities that might be affected by the outbreak.

For both domestic and foreign facilities, the Bioterrorism Act makes failure to register a prohibited act. In addition, food from an unregistered foreign facility may be held at the port of entry. Failure to register under the BT Act, does not make the food product(s) violative.

FDA estimates that the total number of food facilities that must register could exceed 400,000, including both domestic and foreign facilities.

5.4.1.5.1 - Facilities Exempted from Registration

The Bioterrorism Act, as implemented by the interim final rule for registration of food facilities exempts the following from registration:

1. A foreign facility, if food from such facility undergoes further manufacturing/processing (including packaging) by another facility outside the U.S. (Note: A facility is not exempt under this provision if the further manufacturing/processing (including packaging) conducted by the subsequent facility consists of adding labeling or any similar activity of a de minimis nature. The facility conducting the de minimis activity also must register;

2. Farms that are devoted to the growing and harvesting of crops, the raising of animals (including seafood), or both. Washing, trimming of outer leaves of, and cooling produce are considered part of harvesting. The term "farm" includes:

    a. Facilities that pack or hold food, provided that all food used in such activities is grown, raised, or consumed on that farm or another farm under the same ownership; and

b. Facilities that manufacture/process food, provided that all food used in such activities is consumed on that farm or another farm under the same ownership.

3. Retail food establishments whose sales to consumers exceed their sales to non-consumers (businesses are considered non-consumers);

4. Restaurants that prepare and serve food directly to consumers for immediate consumption;

5. Nonprofit food establishments in which food is prepared for, or served directly to, the consumer;

6. Fishing vessels, including those that not only harvest and transport fish but also engage in practices such as heading, eviscerating, or freezing intended solely to prepare fish for holding on board a harvest vessel. However, those fishing vessels that otherwise engage in processing fish are required to register. For the purposes of this section, "processing" means handling, storing, preparing, shucking, changing into different market forms, manufacturing, preserving, packing, labeling, dockside unloading, holding, or heading, eviscerating, or freezing other than solely to prepare fish for holding on board a harvest vessel;

7. Facilities that are regulated exclusively, throughout the entire facility, by the U.S. Department of Agriculture under the Federal Meat Inspection Act (21 U.S.C. 601 et seq.), the Poultry Products Inspection Act (21 U.S.C. 451 et seq.), or the Egg Products Inspection Act (21 U.S.C. 1031 et seq.)

Other exemptions from registration in the interim final rule are based on the definition of food included within the scope of the registration regulation. Facilities that manufacture/process, pack, or hold food contact substances (including packaging materials) or pesticides are exempt from registration.

5.4.1.5.2 - Agency Website Link

More specific information regarding the Bioterrorism Act and food registration may be obtained at the following website: http://www.cfsan.fda.gov/~dms/fsbtact.html.

5.4.1.5.3 - Inspectional Guidance

See Compliance Policy Guide Sec. 110.300: Registration of Food Facilities Under the Public Health Security and Bioterrorism Preparedness and Response Act of 2002. During inspections of domestic and foreign facilities subject to the rule, make sure that firm management is aware of the registration requirements. Inform the firm's management that information regarding food security, the BT Act, facility registration, required and optional information, definitions, exemptions, and penalties for failure to register, etc., is available at the following website: http://www.cfsan.fda.gov/~dms/fsbtact.html. For facilities that are required to register, but have not yet done so, encourage electronic registration (see http://www.fda.gov/oc/bioterrorism/bioact.html), and refer them to a copy of the blank registration form (see http://www.cfsan.fda.gov/~furls/helpol.html)

and the web site address (http://www.access.fda.gov) for electronic registration. Also encourage submission of the optional information on the form to assist and facilitate future communication with the facility as intended by the BT Act.

Document the registration status of the firm, and registration discussions with firm management, in the "Summary of Findings and Discussion with Management" sections of the EIR. Per CPG 110.300, do not report the FURLS Registration number. Observations about failure to register are NOT to be placed on the FDA 483.

5.4.1.6 - CFSAN Bio-research Monitoring

Bio-research monitoring (BIMO) assignments for foods will generally be issued by the Center for Food Safety and Applied Nutrition (CFSAN) (see IOM 5.5.6).

5.4.2 - Personnel

5.4.2.1 - Management

Follow the guidance described in IOM 5.3.6 when documenting individual responsibility including obtaining the full name and titles of the following individuals:

1. Owners, partners, or officers.
2. Other management officials or individuals supplying information.
3. Individuals to whom credentials were shown and FDA 482, Notice of Inspection, and other inspectional forms issued.
4. Individuals refusing to supply information or permit inspection.

Individuals with whom inspectional findings were discussed or recommendations made.

Regulations require plant management take all reasonable measures and precautions to assure control of communicable disease, employee cleanliness, appropriate training of key personnel, and compliance by all personnel with all requirements of 21 CFR 110.10, 113.10, and 114.10.

Determine if adequate supervision is provided for critical operations where violations are likely to occur if tasks are improperly performed.

5.4.2.2 - Employees

Improper employee habits may contribute to violative practices in an otherwise satisfactory plant. Observe the attitude and actions of employees during all phases of the inspection. Observe employees at their work stations and determine their duties or work functions. Note whether employees are neatly and cleanly dressed and whether they wear head coverings which properly cover their hair.

Determine if employees working with the product have obvious colds, or infected sores, cuts, etc. Under no circumstance should you swab a sore, touch or remove a bandage from an employee in an attempt to obtain bacteriological data. To do so is a violation of personal privacy, possibly hazardous to you and/or the employee, and usually provides little useful data.

Note whether employees eat while on duty.

Observe and record insanitary employee practices or actions showing employees handling or touching unsanitized or dirty surfaces and then contacting food products or direct food contact surfaces. Such practices might include employees spitting, handling garbage, placing their hands in or near their mouths, cleaning drains, handling dirty containers, etc. and then handling food product without washing and sanitizing their hands. Observe whether employees comply with plant rules such as, "No smoking", "Keep doors closed", "Wash hands before returning to work", etc. See IOM 5.4.7.2.2.

Be alert to employees handling insanitary objects, then quickly dipping their hands in sanitizing solutions without first washing them. Depending upon the amount and type of filth deposited on the hands during the handling of insanitary objects, such attempts at sanitizing are questionable at best. Sanitizers work most effectively on hands, which have been first cleaned by washing with soap and water.

Conversations with employees doing the work may provide information on both current and past objectionable practices, conditions and circumstances. These should be recorded in your notes.

Where appropriate, determine employee education and training. Also determine type, duration, and adequacy of firm's training programs, if any, to prepare employees for their positions and to maintain their skills. See IOM 5.10.4.1.

5.4.3 - Plants and Grounds

Observe the general nature of the neighborhood in which the firm is located. Environmental factors such as proximity to swamps, rivers, wharves, city dumps, etc., may contribute to rodent, bird, insect or other sanitation problems.

5.4.3.1 - Plant Construction, Design and Maintenance

Determine the approximate size and type of building housing the firm and if suitable in size, construction, and design to facilitate maintenance and sanitary operations. Check placement of equipment, storage of materials, lighting, ventilation, and placement of partitions and screening to eliminate product contamination by bacteria, birds, vermin, etc. Determine any construction defects or other conditions such as broken windows, cracked floor boards, sagging doors, etc. which may permit animal entry or harborage.

Inspect toilet facilities for cleanliness, adequate supplies of toilet paper, soap, towels, hot and cold water, and hand washing signs. Check if hand washing facilities are hidden, or if located where supervisory personnel can police hand washing.

Determine who is responsible for buildings and grounds maintenance. Many facilities such as docks, wharves, or other premises are owned and maintained by other firms, municipalities, or individuals for lease for manufacturing operations. Determine who is legally responsible for repairs, maintenance, rodent proofing, screening, etc. Evaluate the firm's attitude toward maintenance and cleaning operations.

5.4.3.2 - Waste Disposal

Waste and garbage disposal poses a problem in all food plants depending upon plant location and municipal facilities available.

Check the effectiveness of waste disposal on the premises and ensure it does not cause violative conditions or contribute toward contamination of the finished products. Check for in-plant contamination of equipment and/or product, if its water is supplied from nearby streams, springs, lakes or wells.

Suspected dumping of sewage effluent into nearby streams, lakes, or bay waters near water intakes can be documented by color photographs and water soluble fluorescein sodium dye. Place approximately two ounces dye, which yields a yellowish red color, into the firm's waste system and/or toilets, as applicable, and flush the system. The discharge area of the effluent becomes readily visible by a yellowish-red color on the surface of the water as the dye reaches it. Color photographs should be taken.

Determine collecting or flushing methods used to remove waste from operating areas. If water is used, determine if it is recirculated and thus may contaminate equipment or materials.

Determine the disposition of waste materials that should not be used as human food such as rancid nuts, juice from decomposed tomatoes, etc.

Determine the disposition of waste, garbage, etc., which contain pesticide residues. Determine how this is segregated from waste material which contains no residues and which may be used for animal feed.

5.4.3.3 - Plant Services

If applicable, check steam generators for capacity and demand. Demand may reach or exceed the rated capacity, which could effect adequacy of the process. Check boiler water additives if steam comes in direct contact with foods.

Check central compressed air supply for effective removal of moisture (condensate) and oil. Determine if any undrained loops in the supply line exist where condensate can accumulate and become contaminated with foreign material or microorganisms.

5.4.4 - Raw Materials

List in a general way the nature of raw materials on hand. Itemize and describe those, which are unusual to you, or involved in a suspected violation (copy quantity of contents and ingredient statements, codes, name of manufacturer or distributor, etc.). Be alert for additives and preservatives. Evaluate the storage of materials. Determine the general storage pattern, stock rotation and general housekeeping. Materials should be stored so they are accessible for inspection. Thoroughly check ceilings, walls, ledges, and floors in raw material storage areas for evidence or rodent or insect infestation, water dripping or other adverse conditions.

5.4.4.1 - Handling Procedure

Determine if growing conditions relative to disease, insects, and weather are affecting the raw material. Check measures taken for protection against insect or rodent damage. Raw materials may be susceptible to decomposition, bruising or damage, e.g., soft vegetables and fruits delivered in truckload lots. Determine the holding times of materials subject to progressive decomposition.

5.4.4.2 - Condition

Evaluate the firm's acceptance examination and inspection practices including washing and disposition of rejected lots. Where indicated, examine rejected lots and collect appropriate samples and report consignees.

Determine the general acceptability of raw materials for their intended use and their effect on the finished product. Raw stocks of fruits or vegetables may contribute decomposed or filthy material to the finished product. Be alert for use of low quality or salvage raw materials. Check bags, bales, cases and other types of raw material containers to determine signs of abnormal conditions, indicating presence of filthy, putrid or decomposed items. Check any indication of gnawed or otherwise damaged containers, to ascertain if material is violative. Be alert to contamination of raw materials by infested or contaminated railroad cars or other carriers.

Document by photographs, exhibits or sketches any instances where insanitary storage or handling conditions exist.

5.4.4.3 - Food Chemicals Codex

Any substance used in foods must be food-grade quality. FDA regards the applicable specifications in the current edition of the publication "Food Chemicals Codex" as establishing food-grade unless FDA publishes other specifications in the Federal Register.

Determine whether firm is aware of this publication and whether or not they comply.

5.4.5 - Equipment and Utensils

By arriving before processing begins, you are able to evaluate conditions and practices not otherwise observable before plant start-up. This includes adequacy of clean-up, where and how equipment is stored while not in use, how hand sanitizing solutions and food batches are prepared and if personnel sanitize their hands and equipment before beginning work.

Dirty or improperly cleaned equipment and utensils may be the focal point for filth or bacterial contamination of the finished product. Examine all equipment for suitability and accessibility for cleaning. Determine if equipment is constructed or covered to protect contents from dust and environmental contamination. Open inspection ports to check inside only when this can be done safely. Notice whether inspection ports have been painted over or permanently sealed.

5.4.5.1 - Filtering Systems

Observe the firm's filtering systems and evaluate the cleaning methods (or replacement intervals of disposable filters) and schedules. Check types of filters used. There have been instances where firms have relied on household furnace type filters.

5.4.5.2 - Sanitation of Machinery

Check the sanitary condition of all machinery. Determine if equipment is cleaned prior to each use and the method of cleaning. If the firm rents or leases equipment on a short-term basis, report prior cleaning procedures. Equipment may have been used for pesticides, chemicals, drugs, etc., prior to being installed and could therefore be a source of cross-contamination.

5.4.5.3 - Conveyor Belt Conditions

Inspect conveyor belts for build-up of residual materials and pockets of residue in corners and under belts. Look in inspection ports and hard-to-reach places inside, around, underneath, and behind equipment and machinery for evidence of filth, insects, and/or rodent contamination. Chutes and conveyor ducts may appear satisfactory, but a rap on them with the heel of your hand or a rubber mallet may dislodge static material, which can be examined. See IOM 4.3.7.6 for procedure on taking In-line Sample Subs.

5.4.5.4 - Utensils

Determine how brushes, scrapers, brooms, and other items used during processing or on product contact surfaces are cleaned, sanitized and stored. Evaluate the effectiveness of the practices observed.

5.4.5.5 - Mercury and Glass Contamination

Be alert for improper placement or inadequately protected mercury switches, mercury thermometers, or electric bulbs. Breakage of these could spray mercury and glass particles onto materials or into processing machinery.

5.4.5.6 - UV Lamps

If firm is using ultra violet (UV) lamps for bacteria control, check if it has and uses any method or meters to check the strength of UV emissions. If so, obtain methods, procedures, type equipment used, and schedule for replacement of weak UV bulbs.

5.4.5.7 - Chlorine Solution Pipes

In plants where chlorine solution is piped, check on type of pipe used. Fiberglass reinforced epoxy pipe has been observed to erode inside through the action of the chlorine solution. This poses a threat of contamination from exposed glass fibers. Pipes made with polyester resin do not deteriorate from this solution.

5.4.5.8 - Sanitation Practices

Observe sanitizing practices throughout the plant and evaluate their effectiveness, degree of supervision exercised, strength, time, and methods of use of sanitizing agents. Determine the use, or absence of, sanitizing solutions both for sanitizing equipment and utensils as well as for hand dipping. If chlorine is used, 50 ppm - 200 ppm should be used for equipment and utensils, while a 100 ppm will suffice for hand dipping solutions. Sanitizing solutions rapidly lose strength with the addition of organic material. The strength of the solution should be checked several times during the inspection.

5.4.6 - Manufacturing Process

Where helpful to describe equipment and processes, draw flow plans or diagrams to show movement of materials through the plant. Generally a brief description of each step in the process is sufficient. List all quality control activities for each step in the process and identify Critical Control Points. Provide a full description when necessary to describe and document objectionable conditions, or where the assignment specifically requests it.

Observe whether hands and equipment are washed or sanitized after contact with unsanitized surfaces. For example:

1. Workers do general work, then handle the product;
2. Containers contact the floor, then are nested or otherwise contact product or table surfaces;
3. Workers use common or dirty cloths or clothing for wiping hands;
4. Product falls on a dirty floor or a floor subject to outside foot traffic and is returned to the production line.

Be alert for optimum moisture, time and temperature conditions conducive to bacterial growth.

In industries where scrap portions of the product are re-used or re-worked into the process (e.g., candy and macaroni products), observe the methods used in the re-working and evaluate from a bacteriological standpoint. Re-working procedures such as soaking of macaroni or noodle scrap to soften or hand kneading of scrap material offers an excellent seeding medium for bacteria.

When a product is processed in a manner which destroys micro-organisms, note whether there are any routes of recontamination from the "raw" to the processed product (e.g. dusts, common equipment, hands, flies, etc.).

5.4.6.1 - Ingredient Handling

Observe the method of adding ingredients to the process. Filth may be added into the process stream from dust, rodent excreta pellets, debris, etc. adhering to the surface of ingredient containers. Evaluate the effectiveness of cleaning and inspectional operations performed on the materials prior to or while adding to the process. Determine specific trimming or sorting operations on low quality or questionable material. Observe and report any significant lags during the process or between completion of final process and final shipping. For example, excessive delay between packing and freezing may be a factor in production of a violative product.

5.4.6.2 - Formulas

The Act does not specifically require management to furnish formula information except for human drugs, restricted devices and infant formulas. Nonetheless, they should be requested especially when necessary to document violations of standards, labeling, or color and food additives. Management may provide the qualitative formula but refuse the quantitative formula.

If formula information is refused, attempt to reconstruct formula by observing:

1. Product in production,
2. Batch cards or formula sheets,
3. Raw materials and their location.

Any refusal to furnish requested information is reported in your EIR under the refusal heading.

5.4.6.3 - Food Additives

Refer to the food additives programs in CPGM (Chapter 9) for instructions on conducting establishment inspections of firms manufacturing food additive chemicals. Information is also available in DFI's "Guide to the Inspection of Manufacturers of Miscellaneous Food Products - Volume 2.

When making food plant inspections direct your evaluation of food additives only to those instances of significant violation or gross misuse.

Routine inspectional coverage will be directed primarily to the following two types of additives:

1. Unauthorized and illegal as listed in the Food Additive Status List (safrole, thiourea, et al), and
2. Restricted as to amount in finished food.

Because of special problems, exclude the following additives from coverage during routine inspections:

1. Packaging materials,
2. Waxes and chemicals applied to fresh fruit and vegetables,
3. Synthetic flavors and flavoring components except those banned by regulations or policy statements (these products will be covered under other programs), and
4. Food additives in feeds (these products will be covered under other programs).

The Food Additives Status List (FASL) found on the CFSAN website contains an alphabetical listing of substances, which may be added directly to foods or feeds and their status under the Food Additives Amendment and

Food Standards. In addition, a few unauthorized or illegal substances are included.

You may encounter substances not included in the Food Additives Status List (FASL). Such substances will include:

1. Obviously safe substances not on the list of items generally recognized as safe (GRAS), which are not published in the regulations, i.e., salt, cane sugar, corn syrup, vinegar, etc.;

2. Synthetic flavoring substances because of their indefinite status;

3. Substances pending administrative determination,

4. Substances granted prior sanction for specific use prior to enactment of the Food Additives Amendment.

Give primary attention to unauthorized substances. Document and calculate levels of restricted-use additives in finished food only where gross misuse or program violations are suspected as follows:

1. List ingredients, which may be restricted substances or food additives, and determine their status by referring to the current FASL. Report complete labeling on containers of these substances.

2. Obtain the quantitative formula for the finished product in question.

3. Determine the total batch weight by converting all ingredients to common units.

4. Calculate the theoretical levels in the final product of all restricted or unauthorized ingredients from the formula by using the Food Additives Nomographs. See IOM Exhibit 5-11.

5. Determine probable level of restricted ingredients by observing the weight of each ingredient actually put into the batch.

5.4.6.4 - Color Additives

Evaluate the status of color additives observed during each establishment inspection by using the Color Additive Status List and the Summary of Color Additives Listed in the United States in Food, Drugs, Cosmetics, and Medical Devices. Both of these links can be found on the CFSAN website. These lists provide the current status and use limitations of most color additives likely to be found in food, drug, device, or cosmetic establishments.

Stocks of delisted and uncertified colors may be found in the possession of manufacturers where there is no evidence of misuse. Advise the firm of the status of these colors. If management wishes to voluntarily destroy such colors, witness the destruction and include the facts in your EIR. If the firm declines to destroy the colors, determine what disposition is planned, i.e., use in non-food, non-drug, non-cosmetic or non-medical device products. The validity of certification information can be checked by accessing the online Color Certification Database system maintained by the Office of Cosmetics and Colors or contact Ray Decker, Director, Division of Color

Certification and Technology, HFS-105, by e-mail at raymond.decker@fda.hhs.gov to be granted user privilege.

Where decertified or restricted-use colors are used in manufacturing food, drug, device, or cosmetics products, proceed as follows:

1. Collect an Official Sample consisting of the color and the article in which it is being used. Make every effort to collect interstate shipments of the adulterated product before attempting to develop a 301(k) or 301(a) case. When regulatory action is an alternative, obtain sufficient interstate records to cover both the color and the basic ingredients of the manufactured product. Refer to IOM Sample Schedule, Chart 9 - Sampling Schedule for Color Containing Products for guidance.

2. Document the use of decertified colors after the decertifying date. Documentation should include batch formula cards, employee statements, code marks indicating date of manufacture, color certification number, etc. The presence of color in the finished product will be confirmed by your servicing laboratory.

5.4.6.5 - Quality Control

The objective of quality control is to ensure the maintenance of proper standards in manufactured goods, especially by periodic random inspection of the product. Your inspection should determine if the firm's quality control system accomplishes its intended purpose. Establish responsibility for specific operations in the control system. Determine which controls are critical for the safety of the finished product.

5.4.6.5.1 - Inspection System

Determine what inspectional control is exercised over both raw materials and the processing steps. Such inspection may vary from simple visual or other organoleptic examination to elaborate mechanical manipulation. Determine what inspection equipment is used, i.e., inspection belts, sorting belts, grading tables, ultraviolet lights, etc. Ascertain its effectiveness, maintenance or adjustment schedules. Where indicated, determine the name of the manufacturer of any mechanical inspection device and the principles of its operation.

Evaluate the effectiveness of the personnel assigned to inspection operations. Determine if the inspection belts or pick-out stations are adequately staffed and supervised.

Determine the disposition of waste materials, which are unfit for food or feed purposes.

5.4.6.5.2 - Laboratory Tests

Describe routine tests or examinations performed by the firm's laboratory and the records maintained by the firm. Determine what equipment is available in the laboratory and if it is adequate for the purpose intended. If the firm uses a consulting laboratory, determine what tests are performed and how often. Review laboratory records for the period immediately preceding the inspection.

5.4.6.5.3 - Manufacturing Code System

Obtain a complete description of the coding system with any necessary keys for interpretation. Provide an example by illustrating the code being used at the time of the inspection. (See 21 CFR 113.60(c) and 114.80(b)). Report coding systems, which require the use of ultra-violet light for visibility. Hermetically sealed containers of low acid processed food must be coded in a manner clearly visible. (See 21 CFR 113.60). Check 21 CFR 113 and 114 for regulations on coding for the type plant you are inspecting.

5.4.6.6 - Packaging and Labeling

Evaluate storage of packaging materials including protection from contamination by rodents, insects, toxic chemicals or other materials. Appraise the manner in which containers are handled and delivered to the filling areas. Determine if there is likelihood of chipping of glass or denting, puncturing, tearing, etc., of packaging materials. Observe the preparation of containers prior to filling. Consider any washing, steaming, or other cleaning process for effectiveness. Determine, in detail, the use of air pressure or other cleaning devices.

5.4.6.6.1 - Quantity of Contents

If slack fill is suspected, weigh a representative number of finished packages. See IOM 4.3.8 for net weight procedure. Sets of official weights are available in the district servicing laboratory. These may be used to check the accuracy of firm's weighing equipment.

5.4.6.6.2 - Labeling

Check the sanitary condition of labelers and equipment feeding cans to, and away from, the labeler. Determine if old product is present on any equipment which touches the can end seams, in the presence of moisture carry-over from the can cooling operation. Check availability of floor drains in the labeling area. Absence of floor drains could indicate infrequent cleaning of the equipment unless it is physically moved to another area for cleaning.

Determine what labels are used and what labeling is prepared or used to accompany or promote the product. Obtain specimens of representative labels and labeling including pamphlets, booklets, and other promotional material. Obtain 3 copies of labels and labeling believed to be violative.

5.4.6.6.3 – Nutritional and Allergen Labeling

See document "Guide to Nutritional Labeling and Education Act (NLEA) Requirements" for guidance. See http://www.cfsan.fda.gov/~dms/wh-alrgy.html for guidance on Food Allergen Labeling and Consumer Protection Act of 2004 (FALCPA) requirements.

5.4.7 - Sanitation

Documented observation of the conditions under which food products are processed, packed, or stored is essential to the proper evaluation of the firm's compliance with the law. This involves the determination of whether or not insanitary conditions contribute to the product being adulterated with filth, rendered injurious to health, or whether it consists in whole or in part of a filthy, putrid or decomposed substance.

Observations that dirt, decomposed materials, feces or other filthy materials are present in the facility and there is a reasonable possibility these filthy materials will be incorporated in the food are also ways of determining products may have become contaminated.

5.4.7.1 - Routes of Contamination

It is not sufficient to document only the existence of insanitary or filthy conditions. You must also demonstrate how these conditions contribute or may contribute to contaminating the finished product. Investigate and trace potential routes of contamination and observe all means by which filth or hazardous substance may be incorporated into the finished product. For example, defiled molding starch in a candy plant may contribute filth to candy passing through it, or filth in insect or rodent contaminated raw materials may carry over into the finished product. IOM Section 4.3.7 contains instructions on sample collection techniques for adulteration violations, including instructions for field exams and sample collections to document evidence of rodent, insect, etc., contaminated lots, and instructions for in-line sampling, including bacteriological samples. Finished product sample sizes for filth and micro collections can be found in the applicable Compliance Program (CPGM) or DFI "Guide to Inspections of ***."

5.4.7.1.1 - Insects

Insect contamination of the finished product may result from insect infested raw material, infested processing equipment or insanitary practices, and by insanitary handling of the finished product. When routes of contamination with insect filth are encountered, identify the insects generally, e.g., weevils, beetles, moths, etc. If qualified, identify as to species. You must be correct in your identification. See IOM Appendix A.

5.4.7.1.2 - Rodents

Rodent contamination of the finished product may result from using rodent defiled raw materials, exposure to rodents during processing, and by rodent depredation of the finished product. When evidence of rodents are discovered, you should thoroughly describe its composition, quantity, estimated age and location. Explain its significance and potential for product contamination.

5.4.7.1.3 - Pesticides

Pesticide contamination of the finished product may be the result of mishandling of food products at any stage in manufacturing or storage. The use of toxic rodenticides or insecticides in a manner, which may result in contamination, constitutes an insanitary condition. Where careless use of these toxic chemicals is observed, take photographs and provide other documentation showing its significance in relation the food products.

Additional guidance can be found in 21 CFR as follows:

1. Part 110.20(b) - Plant Construction and Design,
2. Part 110.40(a) - Equipment and Utensils,
3. Part 110.35(c) - Pest Control,
4. Part 110.10(b) - Personnel Cleanliness.

Additional guidance can be found in 40 CFR Part 180 - Tolerances and Exemptions From Tolerances For Pesticides in Food Administered by The Environmental Protection Agency as follows:

1. Part 180.521 - Fumigants for grain-mill machinery; tolerances for residues, and
2. Part 180.522 - Fumigants for processed grains used in production of fermented malt beverages; tolerances for residues.

Be alert for:

1. Possible PCB contamination. Articles containing PCBs (e.g., transformers, PCB containers stored for disposal, electrical capacitors) must be marked with prescribed labeling to show they contain PCBs. No PCB-containing heat exchange fluids, hydraulic fluids or lubricants are allowed used in food plants. All PCB storage areas must be marked to show the presence of PCBs. Observe food plant transformers for possible leakage. If observed, determine if food items are stored in the area, and sample for PCB contamination. If PCBs are encountered in a food establishment, immediately advise management this is an objectionable condition and advise your supervisor.
2. Possible mix-up of pesticides or industrial chemicals with food raw materials.
3. Improperly stored pesticides or industrial chemicals (lids open, torn bags in close proximity to foods, signs of spillage on floors, pallets, shelves, etc.).
4. Incorrect application methods including excessive use. Many pesticide labels give instructions for use and precautions on the container.
5. Improper disposal or reuse of pesticide or industrial chemical containers.
6. Evidence of tracking powder or improper use of bait stations or baited traps.
7. Improper handling of equipment. Movable or motorized equipment used for handling possible chemical contaminants should not be used for handling food products unless they are thoroughly decontaminated. For example, fork-lifts moving pallets of pesticides should not also be used to move pallets of flour, etc.
8. Use of unauthorized pesticides.

9. Use of foods treated with pesticides and marked "Not For Human Consumption" (e.g., Treated seed wheat, etc.).

10. Noticeable odor of pesticides.

11. Careless use of machinery lubricants and cleaning compounds.

12. Chemical contaminants in incoming water supply.

When inspecting products with a known potential for metals contamination, determine whether the firm tests for such contamination in raw materials.

Determine who administers the firm's rodent and insect control program. Determine responsibility for the careless use of toxic materials.

If pesticide misuse is suspected, obtain the following information;

1. Name of exterminator and contract status,

2. Name of pesticide,

3. Name of pesticide manufacturer,

4. EPA registration number,

5. Active ingredients, and

6. Any significant markings on pesticide containers.

Fully document the exact nature of any pesticide or industrial chemical contamination noted or suspected. If samples are collected to document misuse, exercise caution to prevent contamination of the immediate area of use, product or yourself.

5.4.7.1.4 - Other

Contamination of food products by bats, birds and/or other animals is possible in facilities where food and roosting facilities are available. Examine storage tanks, bins, and warehousing areas to determine condition and history of use. There have been instances where empty non-food use containers were used for food products.

5.4.7.2 - Microbiological Concerns

During the inspection, you must fully identify likely sources and possible routes of contamination of the product. See IOM 4.3.7.7 for instructions on sampling for pathogens. Before and during processing, become completely familiar with the flow of the process and determine the potential trouble spots, which may be built into the operation. To document the establishment is operating in an insanitary manner, it is necessary to show the manufacturer has contributed to the bacterial load of the product. If there are several products being prepared at once, do not try to cover the entire operation during one inspection. Select the product which has the greatest potential for bacterial abuse or which poses the greatest risk for the consumer.

It is extremely important each EIR contain complete, precise, and detailed descriptions of the entire operation. The EIR must be able to stand alone without the analytical results, which serve to support the observations.

Observations made during the inspection must be written in clear and concise language. The EIR will be reviewed in conjunction with analytical results of in-line, environmental and finished product samples. Based on this review and other information, which may be available, the district must then decide if the total package will support a recommendation for regulatory action.

Each inspection/process will be different, but the techniques for gathering the evidence will be the same. However, the critical points in the operation should always be defined and special attention given to these areas.

Depending on the type of product being produced and the process being used, it may be useful to record the time each critical step takes from beginning to end of the entire processing period with correlating temperature measurements. This should be done especially for products, which would support the growth of microbial pathogens. During the entire inspection, be aware of and document delays in the processing of the product (e.g., temperature of product prior to, during and after the particular processing step, and the length of time the product has been delayed prior to the next step).

Some products receive a thermal process at the end of production, which may reduce bacterial counts to or near zero. Include detailed observations of heating step, temperature, length of time, controls and documentation used/not used by the firm. Even in the presence of end-product thermal processing, there is a regulatory significance to insanitary conditions prior to cooking, coupled with increases in bacterial levels demonstrated through in-line sampling.

5.4.7.2.1 - Processing Equipment

Document the addition, or possible addition of pathogenic microorganisms from accumulated material due to poorly cleaned and/or sanitized processing equipment

Observe and report the firm's clean up procedures and the condition and cleanliness of food contact surfaces before production starts, between production runs and at the end of the day. Document any residue on food contact surfaces of equipment, especially inside complex equipment not easily cleaned and sanitized. Report firms clean-up procedures in depth, since it may lend significance to insanitary conditions of residues on the plant machinery which are left to decompose overnight or between shifts. Where possible, observe equipment both before and after cleaning to assess it adequacy. Observations of residues on plant machinery can dramatically document the addition of pathogenic microorganisms, if present, into the product.

Identify any vectors of contamination (e.g. birds, rodents, insects, foot traffic, etc.), and describe sources and the routes of contamination from them to the product. Support this with your actual observations.

5.4.7.2.2 - Employee practices

Document any poor employee practice and how they have or would provide a route for contaminating the product. For example, did employees (number/time of day) fail to wash and sanitize their hands at the beginning of processing, after breaks, meals, or after handling materials likely contaminated with a microbial pathogen, etc.; and then handle the finished product. Did employees handle product in an insanitary manner (cross contaminating raw product with cooked product, etc., how many, how often).

5.4.7.3 - Storage

Evaluate the storage of finished products in the same manner as for raw materials. Determine if products are stored to minimize container abuse, facilitate proper rotation, and adherence to the storage requirements. This includes refrigeration temperatures, critical temperature tolerance, aging of products, and proper disposition of distressed stock.

5.4.7.3.1 - Food Transport Vehicles

During food sanitation inspections, (See IOM 5.2.2.2 regarding issuance of FDA 482, Notice of Inspection while inspecting vehicles.), conduct inspections of food transport vehicles to include:

1. Evidence of insanitary conditions,
2. Conditions which might lead to food adulteration,
3. Physical defects in the vehicle,
4. Poor industry handling practices.

The following types of transport vehicles should be covered:

1. Railroad boxcars, both refrigerated and non-refrigerated, and hopper cars.
2. Any type of truck used to transport foods; both refrigerated and non-refrigerated.
3. Use extreme caution, if it is necessary to inspect tank railcars or tank trucks. Usually this coverage will be limited to determining what was transported in the tank previously and was the tank cleaned and/or sanitized as necessary between loads.
4. Vessels used to transport food in I/S commerce. Direct coverage primarily to intercoastal type vessels, including barges.

Coverage should be limited to food transport vehicles used for long haul (I/S) operations. Long haul vehicles are defined as those which travel at least 150 miles between loading and unloading or which do not return to the point of loading at the end of the day.

Regulatory actions are possible if unfit cars are loaded and, as a result of loading, adulteration occurs. Fully document any violations noted with appropriate samples and photographs. When vehicle insanitation is observed, it is imperative the carrier's and shipper's responsibility for the food adulteration be documented by appropriate evidence development, such as:

1. The nature and extent of the conditions or practices, and

2. The mechanical or construction defects associated with the food transport vehicle.

3. Individual responsibility for vehicle or trailer cleaning, vehicle assignments, load assignments, etc.

If gathering evidence about a single carrier, seek a series of occurrences at numerous locations involving as many different shippers as possible.

Basically two types of vehicles will be covered.

5.4.7.3.2 - Vehicles at Receivers

When inspecting receivers of food products, examine the food transport vehicle prior to or during unloading. Make a preliminary assessment of food product condition, then inspect the vehicle after unloading to determine its condition and whether the unloaded food may have been contaminated during shipment. If the food appears to have been adulterated, collect a sample(s) for regulatory consideration. Samples collected from vehicles, which have moved the product in interstate commerce are official samples. You may also collect Documentary (DOC) Samples from the vehicle to substantiate the route of contamination.

5.4.7.3.3 - Vehicles at Shippers

When inspecting shippers of food products, examine the food transport vehicle just prior to loading to determine its sanitary/structural conditions. If the vehicle has significant sanitation or structural deficiencies, notify the shipper of these conditions and of the possibility of product adulteration. If the shipper loads food aboard the vehicle, alert your supervisor so he/she can contact the FDA District where the consignee is located for possible follow-up. You may also collect samples from the load. These samples will become official when the Bill of Lading is issued.

5.4.8 - Distribution

Report the general distribution pattern of the firm. Review interstate shipping records or invoices to report shipment of specific lots. If access to invoices or shipping records is not possible, observe shipping cartons, loading areas, order rooms, address stencils, railroad cars on sidings, etc., to determine customer names, addresses and destination of shipments. If no products are suspect, obtain a listing of the firm's larger consignees.

5.4.8.1 - Promotion and Advertising

Determine the methods used to promote products and how the products reach the ultimate consumer. Determine what printed promotional materials are used and whether they accompany the products or are distributed under a separate promotional scheme. Check on the possibility of oral representations, i.e., door-to-door salesmen, spieler, etc. and obtain copies of brochures, pamphlets, tearsheets, instructions to salespersons, etc. Where indicated, obtain the lecture schedule of any promotional lecture program. If applicable, determine the general pattern of the media used for promotion and advertising.

5.4.8.2 - Recall Procedure

Determine the firm's recall procedure. Audit enough records to determine the effectiveness of established procedures. Report if there is no recall procedure.

5.4.8.3 - Complaint Files

Review the firm's complaint files. Where possible, copy the names and addresses of representative complainants; include a brief summary of each significant complaint in the EIR.

Identify who reviews complaints and their qualifications. Describe the criteria used by the firm in evaluating the significance of complaints and how they are investigated. Determine if records are kept of oral and telephone complaints. See IOM 5.2.8 for discussion of complaints with management and IOM 5.10.4.3.11 for reporting of complaints in the EIR.

Complaints may not be filed in one specific file, but may be scattered throughout various files under other subject titles including Product name; Customer name; Injured party name; Adjustment File; Customer Relations; Repair orders, etc.

During the inspection investigate all complaints contained on FDA-2516 and FDA-2516a forms in the firm's district factory jacket. See IOM 5.2.8, 5.4.1.1 and 5.10.4.3.11.

5.4.9 - Other Government Inspection

See IOM 3.1 for general procedures on cooperating with other Federal, State, and local officials.

During Establishment Inspections determine the specific type of inspection service and inspecting units, which cover the firm, such as the name of the federal, state, county, or city health agency or department. Obtain the name and title of the inspectional official, and general method of operation.

5.4.9.1 - Federal

Do not inspect firms, or those portions of the plant, subject to compulsory, continuous inspection under USDA's Meat Inspection Act, Poultry Products Inspection Act, or Egg Products Inspection Act, except on specific instructions from your supervisor or assignment document.

Ingredients or manufacturing processes common to both USDA and FDA regulated products should be inspected by FDA. See IOM 3.2.1.3 for FDA-USDA Agreements in specific areas.

Provide routine FDA coverage of such firms as breweries and wineries, which may be intermittently inspected on a compulsory basis by the U.S. Treasury Department, U.S. Public Health Service, or other agencies.

All products inspected under the voluntary inspection service of the Agriculture Marketing Service (AMS), USDA, and the National Marine Fisheries Service (NMFS), US Department of Commerce, are subject to FDA jurisdiction and are usually given routine coverage. However, formal written Agreements or Memoranda of Understanding between FDA and other agencies are often executed and may govern the agreeing agencies' operations on this type of inspected plants. When assigned this type of plant for inspection, always check to see if an Agreement or a Memorandum of Understanding exists between FDA and the agency involved to determine the obligations of both agencies. See IOM 3.1.2.1 and 3.2.

If you are assigned to cover a Federally Inspected plant which is under either compulsory or voluntary inspection, present your credentials and an FDA 482 "Notice of Inspection" to management and:

1. Identify yourself to the inspector(s) and invite him/her to accompany you on the inspection but do not insist on their participation.

2. At the conclusion of the inspection, offer to discuss your observations and provide the in-plant inspector with a copy of your Inspectional Observations (FDA 483).

5.4.9.2 - State and Local

State and local officials usually have extensive regulatory authority over firms in their area regardless of the interstate movement or origin of the food products involved. Joint FDA-State or local inspections are frequently conducted. These are usually arranged by district administrative or supervisory personnel. See IOM 3.1.2 and 3.3.

5.4.9.3 - Grade A Dairy Plant Inspections

If you are assigned to do an inspection or sample collection at a dairy firm in the Grade A program or a firm which has products labeled and sold as Grade A, you should verify the need to complete the assignment with your supervisor and the Regional Milk Specialist. Grade A plants and most products labeled as Grade A are inspected by state inspectors or FDA's Regional Milk Specialists and you should not inspect these products. Firms in the Grade A program and covered by the Interstate Milk Shippers (IMS) program are identified in the Interstate Milk Shippers List of Sanitation Compliance and Enforcement Ratings book published every year by the Milk Safety Branch, HFS-626. The reference lists the specific plant and each product covered under the IMS program. These products are covered by a MOU between the FDA and the states, which places primary inspectional responsibility with the state.

There are situations where you will need to conduct an inspection in a Grade A plant and cover products they manufacture which do not carry the "Grade A" designation (such as juices). If the plant is an IMS shipper and has fluid or other products rated as acceptable they may also manufacture optional products and label them as Grade A, without having those product lines covered in the IMS program. Fluid products, sour cream, cultured milk products and yogurt are not optional products. Optional products include cottage cheese, condensed milk/whey and dry milk/whey and may be labeled as Grade A. As an example, some firms are listed in the IMS Sanitation Compliance and Enforcement Ratings book who manufacture cottage cheese and label it as Grade A, but is not specifically covered under the Grade A inspection program. As long as the plant is listed and has one or more products rated as acceptable in the Grade A program, they can manufacture a product and label it as Grade A without having the particular product line covered in the IMS program. In those situations, the product will not be shown in the Enforcement Ratings book and you should cover its production, labeling, etc.

5.4.10 - Food Standards

The Federal Food, Drug, and Cosmetic Act requires the Secretary of Health and Human Services to promulgate reasonable definitions and Standards for food to promote honesty and fair dealing in the interest of consumers. When a Standard becomes effective, it establishes the common or usual name for the article, defines the article and fixes its standard of identity. It is then the official specification for the food. The food industry actively participates in the development of a Standard, and supplies much of the data upon which the regulation is based.

The Food Standards (FS) Inspection is made to obtain data for use, together with information from other sources in developing a Food Standard. Food Standard inspections are also made to determine a firm's compliance with food standards regulations, when manufacturing a standardized food.

5.4.10.1 - Food Establishment Inspection

Food Standard (FS) inspection assignments usually originate from CFSAN. When an inspection is planned for the purpose of collecting data to support a proposed food standard regulation, the district may elect to advise the firm, if the CFSAN has not already done so. If the firm selected does not choose to cooperate, it may be necessary to visit additional plants in order to obtain the desired information. Selection of additional firms should be done in consultation with the CFSAN.

Some firms often contend their entire process and formulas are "trade secrets". Attempt to persuade management the term "trade secret" should only be used to cover the process and/or quantitative-qualitative formulation which is truly unique to the firm. In instances where the firm is reluctant to release any of the information requested, point out FDA will, within the limits of the Freedom of Information Act, make every effort to preserve the confidentiality of the composition, make-up, and production levels of the product through the use of codes, which cannot be traced back to the firm. Include as much of the compositional and processing information as you can in the body of the report, without violating the firm's confidence.

5.4.10.2 - Food Inspection Report

FS EIR's may be used as exhibits at public hearings and are subject to review by any interested party.

Three copies of the report are prepared. The original and one copy will be submitted to the CFSAN and one copy kept for the district file. Sign the original and duplicates of the first and last pages of each report sent to the Center.

Divide the report into three sections.

5.4.10.2.1 - Establishment Inspection Record (EI Record)

In order to relate the sections of the report to each other and to any assignments, and to assure any parts of the reports made public will not be identified as to the name of the firm or individuals therein, each district will set up a master list of numbers. One number will be assigned to each establishment covered, e.g., "BLT FS-3". For each FS Inspection place the assigned number next to the firm name on the EI Record. All other pages of the report shall be identified only by this number, the name of the commodity, and date. Example: "EIR Frozen Fish Sticks 10-3-87 BLT FS-3". This indicates a FS EI of frozen fish sticks conducted by Baltimore District on 10-3-87 in a plant designated as #3.

Where a producer may be reluctant to release any of the information requested, point out the FDA will, within the limits of the FOIA, make every effort to preserve the confidentiality of the composition, make-up, and production levels of his product through the use of codes, which cannot be traced back to the firm.

5.4.10.2.2 - Body of Report

Prepare the body of the report following the narrative outline as for any other food EIR except for the restrictions below.

The body of the FS report should also contain information in regard to the approximate annual value and volume as well as the percent of interstate business for each product covered. This is necessary because the coversheet, which contains this information, identifies the firm and will not be made public. Processes and the listing of raw materials used by the firm, which are not restricted by the term "trade secret" should be included. Any opinions, recommendations, or other information obtained or offered by individuals interviewed should be reported. Any suggestions made by individuals interviewed regarding what should be placed in the Standards for the products covered should be included. All individuals interviewed, firm name, etc. should have an identifying code assigned.

The body of the report should not include names and titles of individuals, (including USDA, USDI, or other inspectors), trade secret information, labeling, trade names, formulas, sample numbers, firm name or location of plant (other than by state or region), shipments, or other distribution information, legal status, or regulatory history. This information will be placed in the "Special Information" section of the report.

5.4.10.2.3 - Special Information Section

This is a separate attachment to the EIR which lists the names and titles of individuals (including other government inspectors) and firms with a reference code for each. The EIR should refer only to "Mr. A.," "Mr. B.," "Firm

X," "Firm Y", etc. Do not use the firm or individual's actual initials in the body of the report. Include all information excluded from the body of the report and mount all labels obtained during the EI Labels may be quoted in the body of the report, but do not identify the firm. List the "Special Information Sheet" in the FACTS endorsement section as an enclosure.

Supplemental Reports - If, because of an additional visit or visits to the same firm on the same project, it is necessary to prepare another EIR, flag the report with the same number as assigned to the original report. For example, mark the EI Record "BLT FS-3 Supplemental Report", and the remaining pages, "EIR Frozen Fish Sticks 10-25-87 BLT FS-3 Supplemental Report."

5.4.10.3 - Violative Inspections

When an inspection made in connection with the Food Standards project shows insanitary or other conditions which are not germane to the assignment or in the District's opinion suggests regulatory action, an appropriate narrative of the violative conditions should be prepared as a Regulatory Addendum.

5.5 - Drugs

5.5.1 - Drug Inspections

Authority for inspection is discussed in IOM 2.2. FD&C Act Sections 501(a)-(d) [21 U.S.C. 351(a)-(d)] describe the ways in which a drug may be or may become adulterated. Section 502 of the FD&C Act [21 U.S.C. 352] does the same, with respect to misbranding. Section 505 of the FD&C Act [21U.S.C. 355] requires that new drugs be approved by FDA. Therefore, the purposes of a drug inspection are:

1. To determine whether a firm is distributing drugs that lack required FDA approval including counterfeit or diverted drugs;

2. To determine and evaluate a firm's adherence to the concepts of sanitation and good manufacturing practice;

3. To assure production and control procedures include all reasonable precautions to ensure the identity, strength, quality, and purity of the finished products;

4. To identify deficiencies that could lead to the manufacturing and distribution of products in violation of the Act, e.g., non-conformance with Official Compendia, super/sub potency, substitution;

5. To obtain correction of those deficiencies;

6. To determine if new drugs are manufactured by the same procedures and formulations as specified in the New Drug Application documents;

7. To determine the drug labeling and promotional practices of the firm;

8. To assure the firm is reporting NDA field alerts as required by 21 CFR 314.81 and Biological Product Deviation Reports (BPDRs) for therapeutic biological products as required by 21 CFR 600.14;

9. To determine if the firm is complying with the requirements of the Prescription Drug Marketing Act (PDMA) and regulations; and

10. To determine the disposition of Drug Quality Reports (DQRS) received from the Division of Compliance Risk Management and Surveillance/CDER; and

11. To determine if the firm is complying with postmarket Adverse Drug Experience reporting requirements as required by 21 CFR sections 310.305 (prescription drugs without approved NDA/ANDA), 314.80, 314.98, and 314.540 (application drug products), and 600.80 (therapeutic biological products), and Section 760 of the FD&C Act (non-application nonprescription products) [21 U.S.C. 379aa].

5.5.1.1 - Preparation and References

Become familiar with current programs related to drugs. Determine the nature of the assignment, i.e., a specific drug problem or a routine inspection, and if necessary, consult other district personnel, such as chemists, microbiologists, etc., or center personnel, such as office of compliance staff. Review the district files of the firm to be inspected including:

1. Establishment Inspection Reports,

2. District Profiles,

3. Drug Applications (New, Abbreviated and Investigational),

4. Therapeutic Biologics License Applications,

5. Sample results,

6. Complaints and recalls,

7. Regulatory files,

8. Drug Quality Reports (DQRs), NDA Field Alert Reports (FARs), and Biological Product Deviation Reports (BPDRs),

9. Drug Registration and Listing

During this review identify products which:

1. Are difficult to manufacture,

2. Require special tests or assays, or can not be assayed,

3. Require special processes or equipment, and

4. Are new drugs and/or potent low dosage drugs.

Review the factory jacket, FACTS OEI and registration/listing data, and all complaint reports which are marked follow-up next inspection. These complaints are to be investigated during the inspection and discussed with management. See IOM 5.2.7.

Become familiar with current regulations and programs relating to drugs, CPGM 7356.002, et al. When making GMP inspections, discuss with your supervisor the advisability of using a microbiologist, analyst, engineer, or other technical personnel to aid in evaluating those areas of the firm germane to their expertise. Review the FD&C Act, Chapter V, Drugs and Devices. Review parts of 21 CFR 210/211 applicable to the inspection involved and Bioavailability (21 CFR 320). In the case of APIs, review FD&C Act section 501(a)(2)(B) [21 U.S.C 351(a)(2)(b)] and the ICH industry guideline entitled "Q7A Good Manufacturing Practice Guidance for Active Pharmaceutical Ingredients."

Review the current editions of the United States Pharmacopeia (USP), and Remington's Pharmaceutical Sciences for information on specific products or dosage forms. Also IOM 1.10.3 provides a link to a consolidated list of pertinent guides and guidelines which may be applicable during drug inspections.

Review 21 CFR 203 "Prescription Drug Marketing", 21 CFR 205 "Guidelines for State Licensing of Rx Drug Distributors", and CPGM 7356.022, Enforcement of the Prescription Drug Marketing Act (PDMA).

Before conducting an inspection that may involve postmarketing adverse drug experience reporting, you should review 21 CFR Sections 310.305, 314.80, 314.98, 314.540, and 600.80, Section 760 of the FD&C Act [21 U.S.C. 379aa], CPGM 7353.001, and the training video, 'Field Investigators: Adverse Drug Effects (ADE) Detectives,' available online at http://www.fda.gov/ cder/learn/ADE/ADE_Pagex.htm.

The Division of Manufacturing and Product Quality (DMPQ) in CDER has established two mechanisms for you to obtain technical assistance before, during, or after an inspection:

1. Division of Manufacturing and Product Quality (DMPQ) Subject Contacts (http://www.fda.gov/cder/dmpq/ subjcontacts.htm#subjects). This list contains the names and phone numbers of DMPQ individuals identified as technical specialists in various areas.

2. Questions and Answers on Current Good Manufacturing Practices for Drugs (http://www.fda.gov/cder/20guidance/cGMPs/default.htm). This forum is intended to provide timely answers to questions about the meaning and application of CGMPs for human, animal, and biological drugs, and to share these widely. These questions and answers generally clarify statements of existing requirements or policy.

5.5.1.2 - Inspectional Approach

Follow Compliance Program Guidance Manual (CPGM) 7356.002 and others as appropriate when conducting CGMP inspections. In-depth inspection of all manufacturing and control operations is usually not feasible or practical. A risk-based systems audit approach is recommended in which higher risk, therapeutically significant, medically necessary, and difficult to manufacture drugs are covered in greater detail during an inspection. The latter group includes, but is not limited to, time release and low dose products, metered dose aerosols, aseptically processed drugs, and formulations with components that are not freely soluble.

CPGM 7356.002 incorporates the systems-based approach to conducting an inspection and identifies six (6) systems in a drug establishment for inspection: Quality, Facilities and Equipment, Materials, Production, Packaging and Labeling and Laboratory Control Systems. The full inspection option includes coverage of at least four (4) of the systems; the abbreviated inspection option covers of at least two (2) systems. In both cases, CPGM 7356.002, indicates the Quality System be selected as one of the systems being covered. During the evaluation of the Quality System it is important to determine if top management makes science-based decisions and acts promptly to identify, investigate, correct, and prevent manufacturing problems likely to, or have led to, product quality problems.

When inspecting drug manufacturers marketing a number of drugs meeting the risk criteria, the following may help you identify suspect products:

1. Reviewing the firm's complaint files early in the inspection to determine relative numbers of complaints per product.

2. Inspecting the quarantine, returned, reprocessed, and/or rejected product storage areas to identify rejected product.

3. Identifying those products which have process control problems and batch rejections via review of processing trends and examining annual reviews performed under 21 CFR 211.180(e).

4. Reviewing summaries of laboratory data (e.g., laboratory workbooks), OOS investigations, and laboratory deviation reports.

5.5.1.3 - CDER Bio-research Monitoring

Bio-research monitoring (BIMO) assignments for drugs will generally be issued by the Center for Drug Evaluation and Research (CDER) (see IOM 5.5.6).

5.5.2 - Drug Registration & Listing

Registration and listing is required whether or not interstate commerce is involved. See Exhibit 5-12 and IOM 2.9.1.1 for additional information.

Two or more companies occupying the same premises and having interlocking management are considered one establishment and usually will be assigned a single registration number. See IOM 5.1.1.11 - Multiple Occupancy Inspections for additional information.

Independent laboratories providing analytical or other laboratory control services on commercially marketed drugs must register.

FACTS will indicate if the establishment is registered for the current year. If you determine registration and listing is required, advise your supervisor.

After checking for past registration, cancellation, etc., the district will provide the firm with the proper forms and instructions.

Each establishment is required to list with FDA every drug in commercial distribution, whether or not the output of such establishment or any particular drug so listed enters interstate commerce. During the establishment inspection, you should remind the firm of its responsibilities for ensuring its drug listing accurately reflects the current product line and updating its listing as necessary to include all product changes, NDC changes, and discontinuations in accordance with 21 CFR 207. If registration and listing deficiencies are found, document it in your EIR, collect a documentary sample and/or contact your supervisor.

5.5.3 - Promotion and Advertising

21 CFR 202.1 which pertains only to prescription drugs, covers advertisements in published journals, magazines, other periodicals, and newspapers, and advertisements broadcast through media such as radio, television, and telephone communication systems. Determine what department or individual is responsible for promotion and advertising and how this responsibility is demonstrated. Ascertain what media (radio, television, newspapers, trade journals, etc.) are utilized to promote products.

Do not routinely collect examples of current advertising. Advertising should be collected only on assignment, or if, in your opinion, it is clearly in violation of Section 502(n) of the FD&C Act [21 U.S.C. 352 (n)] or 21 CFR 202.1.

5.5.4 - Guarantees and Labeling Agreements

Determine the firm's policies relative to receiving guarantees for raw materials, and issuing guarantees on their products. Also determine firm's practices regarding shipment of unlabeled drugs under labeling agreements. See IOM 5.3.7.2.

5.5.5 - Other Inspectional Issues

5.5.5.1 - Intended Use

Please see the discussion of jurisdiction in section IOM 5.10.4.3.6.

5.5.5.2 - Drug Approval Status

The investigator should ascertain whether the drugs manufactured by the firm are covered by an NDA, ANDA, OTC monograph, or marketed under a claim of DESI or "grandfather" status.

5.5.5.3 - Drug Status Questions

If you have questions about misbranding, new drug status, drug/cosmetic, or drug/food (dietary supplement) status, call the Division of New Drugs and Labeling Compliance in the CDER Office of Compliance (301-796-3110).

In rare cases, a drug may be unapproved and inappropriate for marketing under any circumstances (i.e., it cannot be reconditioned or reformulated into a product appropriate for marketing). If you encounter products in this category, contact your supervisor to determine if a CGMP inspection is warranted.

5.5.5.4 - Drug/Dietary Supplement Status

In instances where the drug/dietary supplement status of a product is unclear, the investigator should collect all related labeling and promotional materials including pertinent Internet web sites. This labeling and promotional material is often useful in determining the intended use of a product (See 21 CFR 201.128). Labeling, promotional materials and Internet web sites often contain information, for example, disease claims, that can be used to determine the intended use of a product and thereby if it is a dietary supplement or a drug and an unapproved new drug.

5.5.5.5 - Approved Drugs

Check the current programs in your CPGM, Section 505 of the FD&C Act [21 U.S.C. 355] and 21 CFR part 314 for required information. You may take the District's copy of the NDA into the plant as a reference during the inspection. Document and report all deviations from representations in the NDA even though they may appear to be minor.

5.5.5.6 - Investigational Drugs

Follow the instructions in pertinent programs in your CPGM or as indicated in the specific assignment received.

5.5.5.7 - Clinical Investigators and/or Clinical Pharmacologists

Inspections in this area will be on specific assignment previously cleared by the Administration. Follow guidance in the CPGM or assignment.

5.5.6 - CDER BIO-RESEARCH MONITORING

Inspectional activities in the bio-research monitoring (BIMO) programs involve all product areas and Centers, including In Vivo Bio-equivalence, Good Laboratory Practice (GLP) for Non-Clinical Laboratories, Institutional Review Boards (IRB), Sponsors, Monitors, Contract Research Organizations, and Clinical Investigators (CI). In most instances, inspections conducted under this program will be done on assignment from the respective Center and occasionally with the participation of Center personnel as part of the inspection team.

During team inspections with Center personnel, the Field Investigator is the team leader. See IOM 5.1.2.5. The Compliance Program Guidance Manual (CPGM) for each program provides a description of the program and detailed instruction for conducting inspections.

Districts will make the initial classification of inspections and the Center issuing the assignment will make the final decision after review.

5.5.7 - ADVERSE EVENT REPORTING

FD&C Act section 760 [21 U.S.C. 379aa] and 21 CFR sections 310.305, 314.80, 314.98, and 314.540 require reporting of adverse events associated with the use of human drug products and section 600.80 requires reporting of adverse events associated with the use of biological products (including therapeutic biological products). Responsible firms include holders of NDAs and ANDAs, and manufacturers, packers and distributors that are named on the labels of all FDA approved drug products and all prescription drug products. Firms are required to develop written procedures and to maintain records related to adverse events, both foreign and domestic. Firms must evaluate adverse event data to determine if the event has had a serious outcome such as death, disability, hospitalization, or was a life threatening event, and if the event was expected (labeled) or unexpected (unlabeled) for the product. Responsible firms must submit adverse event information to FDA in expedited or periodic reports, as described in the regulations.

Refer to the Compliance Program Guidance Manual (CPGM) (section 7353.001) for the description of the program and for detailed instructions for conducting inspections.

5.5.8 - DRUG INSPECTION REPORT

See IOM 1.1 English language requirement. The requirements in IOM 5.10.4.3, and any applicable Compliance Program Guidance Manuals can be used to help you prepare your report.

This does not cover the reporting requirements for a directed inspection with a narrow focus, such as a complaint follow-up or investigation into a recall. In those cases, use your judgment and guidance in IOM 5.10.4 about the depth of reporting required. Follow the instructions and format for a human drug inspection report as contained in IOM 5.10.4.2 and 5.10.4.3.

This human drug inspection report does not require full and detailed narratives for every area for every inspection. The firm's state of compliance, the previous inspectional report and information, complexity of operations and other aspects all are determinants in how much reporting will be necessary. In many cases, brief summaries addressing the format areas will be sufficient.

5.6 - Devices

5.6.1 - Device Inspections

See IOM 2.2 for discussion of statutory authority.

The term "device" is defined in Sec. 201(h) of the FD&C Act [21 U.S.C. 321 (h)]. In-vitro diagnostics (21 CFR 809) are devices, as defined in 201(h) of the Act [21 U.S.C. 321 (h)], and may also be biological products subject to Section 351 of the PHS Act.

Inspections involving devices should be made only by those individuals qualified by training and experience in the device area. Electronic product radiation is defined in 21 CFR 1000. Because of the specific nature of inspections and investigations involving radiation, only personnel who have special training in this field should be assigned such work. However, others may participate for training purposes. Specific Compliance Program Guidance Manuals designate the type of individual and special training required for work in these areas.

CAUTION: Radiation-emitting devices and substances present a unique hazard and risk potential. Every effort should be taken to prevent any undue exposure or contamination. Monitoring devices must be used whenever radiation exposure is possible. Investigators should also be on the alert for, and avoid contact with, manufacturing materials and hazards associated with the manufacturing of many types of devices, which may present a threat to health, e.g., ethylene oxide, high voltage, pathogenic biomaterials, etc. See IOM 1.5 for additional safety information.

5.6.1.1 - Technical Assistance

Each region and some districts have engineers and radiological health personnel available for technical assistance and consultation. Do not hesitate to make use of their services.

Engineers, quality assurance specialists, and expert investigators in ORA/ORO/Division of Field Investigations (DFI), HFC-130, 301-827-5653, are available for on-site consultation and assistance in problem areas. The division's subject matter experts are also available by telephone for consultation and to answer questions regarding regulation and program interpretation and QS/GMP application. Additionally, the CDRH Office of Compliance enforcement divisions (organized by device product) can be contacted as necessary.

WEAC has various personnel (biomedical, sterility, electronic, materials, mechanical, nuclear and plastics engineers) available for telephone consultation and on-site assistance. They can be reached at 617-729-5700.

5.6.1.2 - Sample Collection During Inspection

Because of the limited funds available for samples and the relatively high cost of device samples, it is essential you consider, in consultation with your supervisor, the following factors before collecting a physical sample of a device:

1. If follow-up to a QS/GMP deviation, will sampling demonstrate the deviation and/or a defective product? Documentary Samples may be more suitable for QS/GMP purposes.

2. Likelihood of the analysis showing the device is unfit for its intended use.

3. Samples costing over $250.00.

4. Laboratory capability to analyze the sample. See IOM 4.5.5.3.6 for sample routing information.

If you are still uncertain, discuss with your supervisor and contact the CDRH Laboratory or WEAC 781-729-5700 for assistance.

Contact CDRH for assistance as follows:

1. In-vitro Diagnostic Devices - Office of Science and Technology (HFZ-113).

NOTE: Device samples do not require 702(b) portions. Include in the FDA 525 and with the C/R, if destined for different locations, a copy of the firm's finished device specifications, test methods and acceptance and/or rejection criteria.

5.6.1.3 - Types of Inspections

General device inspections will be conducted under various Compliance Programs found in the Compliance Program Guidance Manual. The majority of these will be QS/GMP inspections, but often the reason for the inspection will vary. For example, inspections may be conducted to assist the pre-market clearance process (PMA or Class III 510(k)), to specifically address MDR concerns, or to assure in-depth coverage of an aspect of manufacturing (sterility). The following describes some of these inspections.

5.6.1.4 - CDRH Bio-research Monitoring

Bio-research monitoring (BIMO) assignments for medical devices will generally be issued by the Center for Devices and Radiological Health (CDRH) (see IOM 5.5.6).

5.6.2 - Medical Device Quality System/Good Manufacturing Practices

Section 520(f) of the FD&C Act [21 U.S.C. 360j(f)] provides the Agency with authority to prescribe regulations requiring that the methods used in, and the facilities and controls used for, the manufacture, packing, storage, and installation of medical devices conform to good manufacturing practices. The medical device Quality System/Good Manufacturing Practices Regulation (QS/GMP)(21 CFR 820) became effective on June 1, 1997.

21 CFR 820 is established and promulgated under the authority of Sections 501, 502, 510, 513, 514, 515, 518, 519, 520, 522, 701, 704, 801 and 803 of the FD&C Act (21 U.S.C. 351, 352, 360, 360c, 360d, 360e, 360h, 360i, 360j, 360l, 371, 374, 381 and 383). Failure to comply with the provisions of 21 CFR 820 renders a device adulterated under Section 501(h) of the FD&C Act [21 U.S.C. 351(h)].

The regulations promulgated under 21 CFR 820 establish minimum requirements applicable to finished devices, as defined in 820.1(a). This regulation is not intended to apply to manufacturers of components or parts of finished devices, but instead recommended to them as a guide. In some special cases, components have been classified as finished devices (dental resins, alloys, etc.) and are subject to the QS/GMP. Manufacturers of human blood and blood components are not subject to this part, but are subject to 21 CFR 606.

The QS/GMP includes regulations regarding Purchasing Controls, 21 CFR 820.50, Receiving, In-process and Finished Device Acceptance, 21 CFR 820.80, and Traceability, 21 CFR 820.65, that require finished device manufacturers exercise more control over the components they use in their devices. The preamble of the QS/GMP states: "Since FDA is not regulating component suppliers, FDA believes that the explicit addition to the CGMP requirements of the purchasing controls...is necessary to provide the additional assurance that only acceptable components are used." And "...inspections and tests, and other verification tools, are also an important part of ensuring that components and finished devices conform to approved specifications." It further states, "...traceability of components must be maintained so potential and actual problem components can be traced back to the supplier."

The medical device QS/GMP is an umbrella GMP that specifies general objectives rather than methods. It is left to the manufacturer to develop the best methods to meet these objectives. You must use good judgment in determining compliance with the QS/GMP, keeping in mind that it is an umbrella GMP and all requirements may not apply or be necessary. The purpose of the QS/GMP is to assure conformance to specifications and to ensure that all requirements that will contribute to assuring the finished device meets specifications are implemented. You should not insist that a manufacturer meet non-applicable requirements. Refer to IOM Exhibit 5-13 for types of establishments that are required to comply with the QS/GMP.

5.6.2.1 - Pre-Inspectional Activities

Prior to the start of any medical device inspection, the factory jacket or establishment history of the establishment should be reviewed. You should review the previous inspectional findings and subsequent correspondence between the establishment and FDA; any MDR or consumer complaints where it was determined follow-up would occur at the next inspection; and any notifications of recalls since the last inspection.

The following on-line databases should be queried through the CDRH Information Retrieval System (CIRS):

1. For Medical Device Reporting (MDR) data (MAUDE)

2. Registration and Listing data, and 510(k)

3. PMA summary data (OSCAR);

These databases are accessible to users with individual accounts. Accounts can be requested through the district or regional CIRS liaisons to DFI/Alan Gion 301-827-5649.

MDR data most useful in preparing for an inspection includes specific MDRs for the manufacturer (i.e., query by establishment's short name) for the time frame since the last inspection, or MDRs for the generic devices manufactured by that establishment (i.e., query by product code) for some reasonable time frame. This data assists you in determining potential problem areas in the manufacture or design of the device, or lot or batch specific issues.

The establishment's reported registration and listing data should be verified during any GMP inspection to assure there have been no changes and the registration and listing data was accurately reported. Changes or inaccuracies should be immediately reported to the district medical device registration and listing monitor. See also Field Management Directive (FMD) 92.

510(k) and PMA data assists you in determining what devices the establishment is manufacturing and whether any new devices have been designed or changed since the last inspection. This data is useful in focusing the inspection on new or changed devices as well as devices that are higher risk devices, i.e., Class II or III versus Class I.

IOM 5.2 should be followed in regards to pre-announcement of medical device inspections.

5.6.2.2 - Quality Audit

The inspectional approach for identifying inadequate auditing of a quality assurance program is limited by the agency's policy, which prohibits access to audit results. The policy is stated in CPG section 130.300 (7151.02). Under the QS/GMP regulation (21 CFR 820.180 (c)) this prohibition extends to evaluations or audits of suppliers, 21 CFR 820.50(a), and Management Reviews conducted per 21 CFR 820.20. Evidence of inadequate auditing may be discovered without gaining access to the written audit reports. See the Guide to Inspections of Medical Device Manufacturers or Guide to Inspections of Quality Systems for inspectional guidance.

The preamble to the QS/GMP specifically states, "FDA will review the corrective and preventive action procedures and activities performed in conformance with those procedures without reviewing the internal audit reports. FDA wants to make it clear that corrective and preventive actions, to include the documentation of these activities, which result from internal audits and management reviews are not covered under the exemption at 820.180(c)." Therefore, these corrective and preventive actions and documentation are not excepted from inspectional scrutiny.

The QS/GMP regulation (21 CFR 820.180(c)) requires a manufacturer to certify in writing that audits and reaudits have been conducted whenever requested to do so by an investigator. Investigators through their supervisors should consult with CDRH (HFZ-306) prior to requesting such certification.

5.6.2.3 - Records

FDA has distinct authority under section 704(e) of the FD&C Act [21 U.S.C. 374 (e)] to inspect and copy records required under section 519 or 520(g) of the FD&C Act [21 U.S.C. 360i or 360j (g)]. Investigators should only collect copies of documents as necessary to support observations or to satisfy assignments. Manufacturers who have petitioned for and obtained exemption from the QS/GMP are not exempted from FDA authority to review and copy complaints and records associated with investigation of device failures and complaints.

You may advise manufacturers they may mark as confidential those records they deem proprietary to aid FDA in determining which information may be disclosed under Freedom of Information.

Records must be maintained for as long as necessary to facilitate evaluation of any report of adverse performance, but not less than two years from the date the device is released for distribution. Records required by the Radiation Control for Health and Safety Act must be maintained for five years. It is permissible to retain records in photocopy form, providing the copies are true and accurate reproductions.

5.6.2.4 - Complaint Files

Complaints are written or oral expressions of dissatisfaction with finished device identity, quality, durability, reliability, safety, effectiveness or performance. Routine requests for service would not normally be considered complaints. However, service requests should be reviewed to detect complaints, and as part of any trend analysis system, and to comply with 820.20(a)(3).

FDA has the authority to require a device firm to open its complaint files, and review and copy documents from the file.

Provisions in the FD&C Act pertaining to FDA review of records are:

1. For restricted devices the FD&C Act in Section 704(a)(1)(B) [21 U.S.C. 374 (a)(1)(B)] extends inspection authority to records, files, papers, processes, controls and facilities bearing on restricted medical devices. See FD&C Act Sec. 704 [21 U.S.C. 374] for a full explanation and for a list of the items, e.g., financial data, which are exempt from disclosure to FDA.

2. For all devices, including restricted devices, refer to Section 704(e) of the FD&C Act [21 U.S.C. 374 (e)], which provides for access to, copying and verification of certain records.

3. Section 519 of the FD&C Act [21 U.S.C. 360i] requires manufacturers, importers, or distributors of devices intended for human use to maintain such records, and provide information as the Secretary may by Regulation reasonably require.

4. Section 520(g) of the FD&C Act [21 U.S.C. 360j (g)] covers the establishment of exemptions for devices for investigational use and the records which must be maintained and open for inspection.

QS/GMP requirements for complaint files are found in 21 CFR 820.198. GMP requirements for complaint files first became effective on December 18, 1978. The Quality System Regulation, which went into effect on June 1, 1997, added to and modified the requirements for complaint handling. The regulation contains a provision that records maintained in compliance with the QS/GMP must be available for review and copying by FDA (21 CFR 820.180). Complaint files are QS/GMP required records; therefore, the manufacturer must make all complaints received on or after December 18, 1978 and the records of their investigation available for FDA review and copying. EIRs should contain enough information to allow cross-referencing between complaints and MDRs.

21 CFR Part 803 requires medical device manufacturers to report deaths, serious illnesses, and serious injuries to FDA for which a device has or may have caused or contributed, and manufacturers must also report certain device malfunctions. The MDR reportable events must be maintained in a separate portion of the complaint files or otherwise clearly identified. These complaints must be investigated to determine whether the device failed to meet specifications; whether the device was being used for treatment or diagnosis; and the relationship, if any, of the device to the reported incident or adverse event.

When a firm determines complaint handling will be conducted at a place other than the manufacturing site, copies of the record of investigation of complaints must be reasonably accessible at the actual manufacturing site.

5.6.3 - Sterile Devices

Inspections of sterile device manufacturers are conducted per Compliance Program Guidance Manual 7382.845, as a production process under the Production and Process Control Subsystem. See the Guide to Inspections of Quality Systems for further guidance.

5.6.4 - Labeling

Specific labeling requirements for in vitro diagnostics (IVDs) are contained in 21 CFR 809.10.

Part 809.10(a) contains explicit labeling requirements for the individual IVD containers, and for the outer package labeling and/or kit labeling. Part 809.10(b) contains special labeling requirements for the product insert, which must be included with all IVD products. These two sections also contain the requirements for: lot numbers, allowing traceability to components (for reagents) or subassemblies (for IVD instruments); stability studies for all forms of the product; an expiration date, or other indication to assure the product meets appropriate standards; and, the requirements for establishing accuracy, precision, specificity and sensitivity (as applicable).

Part 809.10(c) lists the labeling statements required for IVDs which are being sold for investigational and research use. Determine whether the firm is limiting the sale of IVDs, labeled as such, to investigators or researchers. Document any questionable products, and submit to CDRH for review.

Warning and caution statements recommended for certain devices, along with certain restrictions for use, are described in 21 CFR 801. This same section also contains the general labeling regulations, which apply to all medical devices.

5.6.5 - Government-Wide Quality Assurance Program (GWQAP)

Inspections under the GWQAP are conducted upon request by OE, Division of Compliance & Information Quality Assurance (HFC-240). Each assignment is specific and may involve more than a single compliance program. These inspections should be completed within 6 days from the date of the receipt from HFC-240. Specific questions arising during or as a result of these inspections should be directed to HFC-240.

5.6.6 - Contract Facilities

Device manufacturers may employ the services of outside laboratories, sterilization facilities, or other manufacturers (i.e., injection molders, packagers, etc). The finished device manufacturer is responsible for assuring these contractors comply with the QS/GMP and that the product or service provided is adequate. These contractors are subject to FDA inspection and some are subject to the QS/GMP regulation. This "...includes but is not limited to those who perform the functions of contract sterilization, installation, relabeling, remanufacturing, repacking, or specification development, and initial distributors of foreign entities performing these functions," per 21 CFR 820.3(o). Whether under contract or not if a firm manufactures a finished device by the definition found in 21 CFR 820.3(l) "Finished device means any device or accessory to any device that is suitable for use or capable of functioning, whether or not it is packaged, labeled, or sterilized they are subject to QS/GMP. NOTE: if the product manufactured by the contractor also meets the definition of a component and a finished device, the contractor is subject to the QS/GMP regulation.

Determine how a manufacturer evaluates and selects potential contractors for their ability to meet the manufacturer's requirements, as required by 820.50, Purchasing Controls. Conducting audits can be an effective method for assessment. However, not all contractors allow audits. Audits may not be feasible in some instances. In other instances the activity the contractor is conducting may not have a significant impact on the device safety or function; therefore, expending the resources necessary to audit the contractor may not be warranted.

Evaluations may be accomplished by other means such as requesting that the potential contractor fill out a questionnaire about their quality system, asking other customers of the contractor about their experiences with the firm, or basing assessments on past performance. Evaluations must be documented. The extent to which a manufacturer has evaluated a contractor, as well as the results of the evaluation, should govern the degree of oversight exercised over products and services supplied by the contractor.

5.6.7 - Small Manufacturers

When inspecting one-person or very small manufacturers for compliance with the QS/GMP master record and written procedure requirements, the investigator should realize that detailed written assembly, process, and other instructional procedures required for larger firms may not be needed. In a small firm, division of work is at a minimum, with one person often assembling and testing the finished device. In many cases, blueprints or engineering drawings could be adequate procedures. The QS regulation requires that certain activities be defined, documented and implemented. The regulation does not require separate procedures for each requirement and often several requirements can be met with a single procedure. The complexity of the procedures should be proportional to the complexity of the manufacturer's quality system, the complexity of the organizational structure and the complexity/risk of the finished device being produced. In assessing the need for detailed or lengthy written procedures, the investigator should make judgments based on training and experience of the individuals doing the work and the complexity of the manufacturing process. However, this does not mean small manufacturers have any less responsibility for complying with the QS regulation or assuring safe and effective devices are produced.

5.6.8 - Banned Devices

Section 516 of the FD&C Act [21 U.S.C. 360f] provides a device for human use may be banned by regulation (21 CFR 895) if it presents substantial deception or an unreasonable and substantial risk of illness or injury. Investigators should become familiar with this regulation. When you determine, during an inspection or investigation, that banned devices are being distributed, the distribution, manufacture, etc., should be documented as for any other violative product.

5.6.9 - Device Inspection Reports

See IOM 1.1. English language requirement. You should write your EIR following the guidance in IOM 5.10.4, 5.10.4.1, 5.10.4.2, 5.10.4.3. Section headings can be added to address the needs of other Compliance Program Guidance Manuals such as 7383.001 for pre-market and post-market PMA inspections. Include in your report the systems, processes, products, and product classification covered during the current inspection.

5.7 - Biologics

5.7.1 - Definition

A "biological product" means a virus, therapeutic serum, toxin, antitoxin, vaccine, blood, blood component or derivative, allergenic product, or analogous product, or arsphenamine or derivative of arsphenamine (or any other trivalent organic arsenic compound), applicable to the prevention, treatment, or cure of a disease or condition of human beings (Public Health Service Act Sec. 351(i)). Additional interpretation of the statutory language is found in 21 CFR 600.3. Biological products also meet the definition of either a drug or device under Sections 201(g) and (h) of the Federal Food, Drug, and Cosmetic Act (FD&C Act).

Veterinary biologicals are subject to the animal Virus, Serum, and Toxin Act which is enforced by USDA (21 U.S.C. 151-158).

5.7.2 - Biologics Inspections

FDA has developed a strategy known as "Team Biologics", a reinvention of the agency's approach to inspectional coverage of certain biological products. The periodic cGMP inspections and compliance operations of plasma fractionated products, allergenic products, vaccines, and biological in vitro diagnostic devices are now led by investigators and compliance officers in the Core Team. The Core Team investigators report to ORO headquarters; Core Team compliance officers report to OE. Inspections of certain CBER-regulated medical devices are not covered by the Core Team (e.g., blood establishment software) are conducted by District investigators who may or may not be part of the Biologics Cadre. See IOM 2.2 for a discussion of statutory authority. CBER maintains the lead for pre-licensing and pre-approval inspections of biological products, while ORA customarily leads PMA/510(k) inspections.

5.7.2.1 - Authority

Biological products are regulated under the authority of Section 351 of the Public Health Service Act and under the Food, Drug, and Cosmetic Act, as drugs or devices, with the exception of certain human cells, tissues, and cellular and tissue-based products (HCT/Ps) regulated solely under Section 361 of the Public Health Service Act (see 21 CFR 1271.10). Blood and blood products for transfusion are prescription drugs under the FD&C Act. Under the FD&C Act, source plasma and recovered plasma may have the legal identity of either a drug or device depending on its intended use. Section 351(a) of the PHS Act provides for licensure of biological products and inspection of the products covered is per 351(d). Most biological drugs are licensed. The investigational new drug application regulations (21 CFR 312) also apply to biological products subject to the licensing provisions of the PHS Act. However, investigations of blood grouping serum, reagent red blood cells, and anti-human globulin in-vitro diagnostic products may be exempted (21 CFR 312.2(b)).

5.7.2.1.1 - Blood and Source Plasma Inspections

The investigators in the Biologics Cadre perform inspections of blood and plasma establishments. For blood bank and source plasma establishment inspections (CP 7342.001 and 7342.002) use the CGMPs for Blood and Blood Components (21 CFR 606) as well as the general requirements for biological products (21 CFR Part 600), the general biological product standards (21 CFR Part 610), and the additional standards for human blood and blood products (21 CFR Part 640.) The drug GMPs (21 CFR 210/211) also apply to biological drugs. In the event it is impossible to comply with both sets of regulations, the regulation specifically applicable to the product applies. This would generally be Parts 606 and 640 of the regulations in the case of blood banks and source plasma establishments.

5.7.2.1.2 - Human Tissue Inspections

In February 1997, FDA proposed a new, comprehensive approach to the regulation of human cellular and tissue-based products (now called human cells, tissues, and cellular and tissue-based products or HCT/Ps). The agency announced its plans in two documents entitled, "Reinventing the Regulation of Human Tissue" and "A Proposed Approach to the Regulation of Cellular and Tissue-based Products" (62 FR 9721, March 4, 1997).

Since that time, the agency has published three final rules and one interim final rule to fully implement the proposed approach. On January 19, 2001, FDA finalized regulations to create a new, unified system for registering HCT/P establishments and for listing their HCT/Ps (registration final rule, 66 FR 5447). Part of the definition of "human cells, tissues, or cellular or tissue-based products" became effective on January 21, 2004. On January 27, 2004 (69 FR 3823), we issued an interim final rule to except human dura mater and human heart valve allografts from the scope of that definition until all of the tissue rules became final. On May 25, 2004, FDA finalized regulations requiring most cell and tissue donors to be tested and screened for relevant communicable diseases (donor-eligibility final rule, 69 FR 29786). On November 21, 2004, FDA finalized regulations requiring HCT/P establishments to follow current good tissue practice (CGTP), which governs the methods used in, and the facilities and controls used for, the manufacture of HCT/Ps; recordkeeping; and the establishment of a quality program. The new CGTP regulations also contain certain labeling and reporting requirements, as well as inspection and enforcement provisions (GTP final rule, 69 FR 68612). The donor eligibility and CGTP rules became effective May 25, 2005.

Part 1271 contains six subparts:

1. Subpart A of part 1271 - general provisions
2. Subpart B of part 1271 - registration
3. Subpart C of part 1271 - screening and testing of donors to determine eligibility
4. Subpart D of part 1271 - provisions on CGTP
5. Subpart E of part 1271 - certain labeling and reporting requirements
6. Subpart F of part 1271 - inspection and enforcement provisions.

The subparts apply as follows:

Subparts A through D apply to all HCT/Ps, i.e., to those HCT/Ps described in Sec. 1271.10 and regulated solely under section 361 of the PHS Act, and to those regulated as drugs, devices, and/or biological products. Subparts E and F, which pertain to labeling, reporting, inspection, and enforcement, apply only to those HCT/Ps described in Sec. 1271.10 and regulated solely under section 361 of the PHS Act. However, with the exception of two provisions (Sec. 1271.150(c) and 1271.155) subparts D and E are not being implemented for reproductive HCT/Ps described in 21 CFR 1271.10 and regulated solely under section 361 of the PHS Act.

HCT/Ps subject to the provisions of 21 CFR Part 1271 include, but are not limited to, bone, ligaments, skin, dura mater, heart valve, cornea, hematopoietic stem/progenitor cells derived from peripheral and cord blood, manipulated autologous chondrocytes, epithelial cells on a synthetic matrix, and semen or other reproductive tissue.

For HCT/P inspections, use the CPGM 7341.002, "Inspections of Human Cells, Tissues, and Cellular and Tissue-Based Products."

5.7.2.2 - Donor Confidentiality

Blood bank, source plasma, and human tissue establishments are sensitive to maintaining confidentiality of donor names. The mere reluctance to provide records is not a refusal. However, FDA has the authority under both the PHS and the FD&C Acts to make inspections and 21 CFR 600.22(g) and 1271.400(d) provides for copying records during a blood establishment inspection. For prescription drugs, section 704 of the FD&C Act specifically identifies records, files, papers, processes, controls, and facilities as being subject to inspection.

If you encounter problems accessing records, explain FDA's authority to copy these records. IOM 5.2.5 should be followed if a refusal is encountered. When donor names or other identifiers are necessary, they may be copied, but the information must be protected from inappropriate release. See IOM 5.3.8.6.

5.7.2.3 - Inspectional Objectives

The inspectional objective for biological products is to assure the products are safe, effective, and contain the quality and purity they purport to possess, and are properly labeled. The inspectional objective for HCT/Ps is to assure that HCT/Ps are recovered, processed, stored, labeled, packaged and distributed, and the donors are screened and tested, in a way that prevents the introduction, transmission, or spread of communicable diseases. Facilities will be inspected for conformance with:

1. Provisions of the PHS Act and FD&C Act,

2. Applicable regulations in 21 CFR 210-211, 600-680, and 820.

3. HCT/P regulations in 21 CFR 1270 and 1271.

4. FDA Policies, which include guidance to the industry, and the Compliance Policy Guides Chapter 2.

5.7.2.4 - Preparation

Review the district files of the facility to be inspected and familiarize yourself with its operation and compliance history. Review:

1. Appropriate Compliance Programs and related Compliance Policy Guides (CPG), Chapter 2.

   NOTE: Federal Cooperative Agreements Manual; MOU with the Department of Defense, and MOU with the Centers for Medicare and Medicaid Services (CMS) on transfusion services;

2. Correspondence from the firm depicting any changes since the last inspection;

3. Firm's registration and product listing information;

4. DFI's Guide to Inspections of Source Plasma Establishments, Guide to Inspections of Blood Banks, and Guide to Inspections of Infectious Disease Marker Testing Facilities.

5. Biological Product Deviation Reports, Adverse Reaction Reports, complaints, and recalls;

6. Guideline for Quality Assurance in Blood Establishments, (July 14, 1995).

Through guidance documents, CBER sets forth its inspection policy and regulatory approach. A list of these documents is attached to the current Compliance Program Guidance Manuals (CPGM) available on the CBER internet site at (http://www.fda.gov/cber/cpg/cpg.htm).

The OSHA regulation 29 CFR 1910.1030 dated December 6, 1991, was intended to protect health care workers from blood borne pathogens, including those involved in the collection and processing of blood products. The regulation defines expectations for the use of gloves, hand washing facilities, decontamination of work areas, waste containers, labeling and training of employees and exemptions for volunteer blood donor centers. FDA Investigators should adhere to these safety guidelines during inspections or related activities in establishments that process biologically hazardous materials.

Become familiar with the OSHA regulations and their applicability to 21 CFR 606.40(d)(1) and (2), which require the safe and sanitary disposal for trash, items used in the collection and processing of blood and for blood products not suitable for use. Consult your district biologics monitor for copies of the above references. Additional copies may be obtained from ORO, Division of Field Investigations (DFI), Biologics Group, HFC-130, 301-827-5653 or see CBER's web site at http://www.fda.gov/cber.

5.7.2.5 - Inspectional Approach

Use the Compliance Program Guidance Manuals (CPGM) and Guides to Inspection of Blood Banks, Source Plasma Centers and Infectious Disease Marker Testing Facilities for inspectional instructions. The EIR must clearly identify the areas covered. The report should include a summary of the inspection, the FDA 482, the FDA 483, if issued, and the required FACTS EI Record.

Particular attention should be given to biological products deviation reports indicative of problematic areas or processes, adverse reactions, transfusion associated AIDS (TAA), transfusion or donation associated fatalities and hepatitis and HIV lookback procedures. For additional information regarding TAA, see CP 7342.001. The follow-up investigations to such reports should also be covered.

Complaints, in particular those involving criminal activity, must be promptly investigated and coordinated with other agency components as needed.

For blood banks and source plasma establishments, refer to CPGM 7342.001 and 7342.002 for a discussion of the systems approach to inspection. The CPGM incorporates a systems-based approach to conducting an inspection and identifies five (5) systems in a blood bank and source plasma establishment operation for inspection. Each system may not be in a particular establishment operation; therefore, the inspection should focus on the systems present. The CPGM directs an in-depth audit of the critical areas in each system. A multi-layered system of safeguards has been built into the blood collection, manufacturing and distribution system to assure a safe blood supply.

For HCT/P establishments, refer to CPGM 7341.002.

For Biological Drug Products, refer to CPGM 7345.848.

For Licensed Viral Marker Test Kits, refer to CPGM 7342.008.

If Investigators encounter products not specifically referenced in the regulations, they should contact CBER/OCBQ/ Division of Inspections and Surveillance for guidance.

5.7.2.6 - Regulations, Guidelines, Recommendations

Guidance documents for industry are made available to the public in accordance with good guidance practice regulations at 21 CFR 10.115. The contents of most of these documents are incorporated into the establishment's SOPs and/or license applications or supplements. Also, DFI has issued Blood Bank, Source Plasma Establishment and Infectious

Disease Marker Testing Facility Inspectional Guides to be used by investigators during inspections.

Deviations from guidance documents must not be referenced on a FDA 483. However, since these documents are often related to specific GMP requirements, in most cases deviations can be referenced back to the GMP. If a deviation is observed during an inspection and the investigator relates it to the regulations or law, then the item may be reported on the FDA 483. During the discussion with management, the relationship of the deviation to the regulation or law, or accepted standard of industry, should be clearly explained.

If an establishment indicates it is not aware of any of these documents, provide the web site and the telephone number of CBER's Office of Communication, Training, and Manufacturers Assistance, 301-827-2000.

If a firm claims approval for an alternative procedure, verify by reviewing the firm's written approval letter. Approved alternative procedures may be verified by contacting CBER/Division of Blood Applications or the appropriate CBER product office.

5.7.2.7 - Technical Assistance

Several FDA regions and districts have biologics specialists who are available for technical assistance and consultation. Do not hesitate to avail yourself of their services.

The services of expert investigators in ORA/ORO/ Division of Field Investigations (DFI), Biologics Group, HFC-130, 301-827-5653, are available for telephone or on-site consultation and assistance in problem areas.

CBER/OCBQ, Division of Inspections and Surveillance (HFM-650), 301-827-6220, can provide technical assistance, and can coordinate assistance with other CBER offices.

5.7.2.8 - CBER Bio-research Monitoring

Bio-research monitoring (BIMO) assignments for biological products will generally be issued by the Center for Biologics Evaluation and Research (CBER) (see IOM 5.5.6).

5.7.3 - Registration, Listing And Licensing

5.7.3.1 - Registration and Listing

See IOM 2.9.3.1.

5.7.3.1.1 - Transfusion Services

Most transfusion services are exempt from registration under 21 CFR 607. This includes facilities that are certified under the Clinical Laboratory Improvement Amendments of 1988 (42 U.S.C. 263a) and 42 CFR Part 493 to perform the FDA-required tests on blood or has met equivalent requirements as determined by the Centers for Medicare and Medicaid Services, and are engaged in the compatibility testing and transfusion of blood and blood components, but which neither routinely collect nor process blood and blood components. Such facilities include establishments:

1. Collecting, processing and shipping blood and blood components under documented emergency situations,

2. Performing therapeutic phlebotomy and therapeutic plasma exchange after which the product is discarded,

3. Preparing recovered human plasma and red blood cells,

4. Pooling products/platelets for in-house transfusion,

5. Thawing frozen plasma or cryoprecipitate for transfusion.

5.7.3.1.2 - HCT/Ps

Establishments manufacturing HCT/Ps (human cells, tissues, or cellular or tissue-based products) as defined in 21 CFR 1271.3(d) must register and list using form FDA 3356. Examples of HCT/Ps include, but are not limited to, bone, ligament, skin, cornea, hematopoietic stem cells derived from peripheral and cord blood, manipulated autologous chondrocytes, and semen or other reproductive tissue. Establishments manufacturing HCT/Ps regulated as medical devices, drugs or biological drugs must also register and list with the FDA pursuant to 21 CFR 1271 using form FDA 3356.

5.7.3.1.3 - Laboratories

Laboratories performing infectious disease testing of donors of blood or blood components or HCT/P are an FDA obligation and required to register. Clinical laboratories were previously exempted from registration by 21 CFR 607.65(g), but FDA revoked this regulation. Your inspections should focus on activities relevant to blood product and HCT/P testing operations.

5.7.3.1.4 - Military Blood Banks

Inspection of military blood banks is an ORA responsibility. These facilities are required to meet the same standards as other blood banks although military emergencies may require deviations from the standards. A separate license is held by each branch of the service; although each individual establishment may be licensed or unlicensed, all are required to register. Districts should notify the appropriate military liaisons 30 days before inspection of a military facility. For additional information on inspection of government establishments, see Compliance Program Guidance Manual 7342.001, the Federal Cooperative Agreements Manual, and the MOU with Department of Defense Regarding Licensure of Military Blood Banks.

Field Management Directive 92, Agency Establishment Registration and Control Procedures, details the registration process within the agency. Refer to FDA Compliance Policy Guides (CPG), Chapter 2, Subchapter 230 (230.110), for additional information on registration.

Ensure the firm's current registration forms reflect actual operations.

5.7.3.2 - MOUs

Under the 1983 Memorandum of Understanding (MOU) between the FDA and the Centers for Medicare and Medicaid Services (CMS, formerly Health Care Financing Administration - HCFA), CMS agreed to survey these facilities that engage in minimal manufacturing in order to minimize duplication of effort and reduce the burden on the affected facilities while continuing to protect transfusion recipients. However, no transfer of statutory functions or authority is made under the MOU and the FDA retains legal authority to inspect these unregistered transfusion services whenever warranted. When appropriate, Districts should conduct inspections jointly with the CMS regional liaison. If you determine during a routine inspection an establishment is a CMS obligation under the MOU, you should terminate the inspection and report as such. See Federal Cooperative Agreements Manual - FDA/HCFA Memorandum of Understanding.

5.7.3.3 - Biologic License

See IOM 2.9.3.2. A biologics license application (BLA) shall be approved only after inspection of the establishment(s) listed in the application and upon a determination that the establishment complies with the standards established in the BLA and the requirements prescribed in applicable regulations (21 CFR 601.20(d)). CBER is responsible for conducting all pre-license (PLI) and pre-approval (PAI) inspections of CBER-regulated products. These inspections are part of the review of a BLA or BLA supplement. CBER identifies the scope of the inspection and invites ORA to participate in the inspections. Copies of CBER's PLI and PAI inspection reports are forwarded to the districts and should be part of the firm's file.

5.7.3.4 - Approval of Biological Devices

There must be a pre-approval inspection (PAI) of the establishment for compliance with the QS/GMP regulation and the firm's PMA. For licensed devices, CBER conducts the pre-license inspection (PLI). Devices used in the collection and testing of blood for transfusion are approved/cleared through the PMA/510(k) authorities. ORA Investigators customarily inspect the CBER regulated devices, which are subject to PMA/510(k) applications.

5.7.4 - Responsible Individuals

In licensed establishments, the applicant or license holder may designate an authorized official(s) to represent the applicant to the FDA in matters of compliance. The FDA 482 and any 483 should be issued to the most responsible person on the premises at the time of inspection. An exact copy of the FDA 483 should also be forwarded to the top official of the firm if that person did not receive the FDA 483. The designation as authorized official does not necessarily mean that individual is the most responsible for any non-compliance of the firm. In licensed or unlicensed facilities, establish and document all individuals responsible for violations and their reporting structure in the organization.

5.7.5 - Testing Laboratories

Blood bank, source plasma, and HCT/P establishments may use outside testing laboratories to perform required testing.

Laboratories conducting testing for licensed blood banks are usually licensed. CBER may approve the use of a non-licensed laboratory to do required testing, provided the lab is capable of performing the tests and the lab registers with CBER prior to CBER approving the licensing arrangement.

Laboratories performing required testing for source plasma manufacturers must either be:

1. Licensed or

2. Certified to perform such testing on human specimens under the Clinical Laboratory Improvement Amendments of 1988 (42 U.S.C. 263a) and 42 CFR part 493, or has met equivalent requirements as determined by CMS.

Laboratories performing required testing for HCT/Ps must:

1. Test using approved FDA-licensed, approved or cleared donor screening tests according to the manufacturers instructions, and

2. be either certified to perform such testing on human specimens under the Clinical Laboratory Improvement Amendments of 1988 (42 U.S.C. 263a) and 42 CFR part 493, or has met equivalent requirements as determined by CMS.

Instructions for inspecting testing laboratories are included in the appropriate Compliance Program Guidance Manuals. Coordinate the inspection of non-registered laboratories with CMS regional office contacts. If a testing laboratory is located outside of the district, request an inspection by the appropriate district office, where appropriate.

5.7.6 - Brokers

Blood establishments may use brokers to locate buyers for products such as recovered plasma or expired red blood cells. These articles are used for further manufacture into products such as clinical chemistry controls and in-vitro diagnostic products not subject to licensure. Fractionators also use brokers to locate suppliers of plasma under the short supply provisions (21 CFR 601.22). During inspections, determine if the facility is selling products to any brokers. If brokers are used, determine if the brokered products are shipped to a facility operated by the broker or directly to the consignee.

Brokers who take physical possession of blood products and engage in activities considered manufacturing or labeling are required to register and are included in the OEI for routine inspection under the blood bank compliance program. Brokers who only arrange sales of or store blood and blood components, but do not engage in manufacturing activities are not required to register.

5.8 - Pesticides

5.8.1 - Pesticide Inspections

The objective of a Pesticide Inspection is to determine the likelihood of excessive residues of significant pesticides in or on products in consumer channels, and to develop sources of information for uncovering improper use of pesticide chemicals.

This requires directing coverage to two major areas:

1. Pesticide practices in the production and processing of field crops.

2. Application of pesticide chemicals in establishments storing and processing raw agricultural products.

Pesticide coverage must be provided during all food establishment inspections. Coverage of raw agricultural products will generally be on a growing-area basis.

Problem areas include:

1. *Improper use of pesticides around animals* - gross misuse of sprays and dips in animal husbandry may result in pesticide residues in foods.

2. *Use of contaminated animal feeds* - waste and spent materials from processing operations may contain heavy concentrations of pesticide residues, which were present in the original commodity. See Compliance Policy Guide 575.100.

3. *Past pesticide usage* - past pesticide practices on growing fields. Past use of persistent pesticides may result in excessive residues in the current food crop. You may need to check on pesticide usage for several years prior to an incident to ensure you gather enough information. Some pesticides last for many years in the environment.

5.8.2 - Current Practices

Cooperative Activities - important sources of information relative to evaluating the "Pesticide Environment" include:

1. At the start of the growing season, spray schedules recommended for each crop by county agents, state experiment stations, large pesticide dealers, farmers cooperatives, et al should be obtained.

2. Visits to agricultural advisors may provide information relative to heavy infestation of insect pests and fungal infections on specific crops in specific areas.

3. Daily radio broadcasts in most agricultural areas may provide information on spray schedules, insect pests, harvesting and shipping locations, etc.

4. Field employees of fruit and vegetable canning and freezing plants usually recommend spray schedules, pesticides, and harvesting schedules for products produced by contract growers.

5. United States Weather Bureau Offices and their reports will provide data on weather conditions, which may effect insect growth and their development, size of fruit or leaf growth, and dissipation of pesticide chemicals.

6. USDA Market News Service daily price quotations, and weekly quotations in trade magazines provide information regarding harvesting schedules since market prices are indicators of how quickly a crop will be harvested in a given area. Growers who have the opportunity to obtain high prices may harvest their crops without regard to recommended pre-harvest intervals.

7. State Colleges of Agriculture seminars or short courses on food and vegetable production may alert you to significant departures from usual agricultural practices. Prior approval to attend such meetings should be secured from your supervisor.

8. Pesticide suppliers and distributors may provide information on spray practices, schedules, and the name and address of growers, etc.

NOTE: The U.S. Department of Agriculture has a Pesticide Data Program (PDP), which provides data on pesticide use and residue detection. This program helps form the basis for conducting realistic dietary risk assessments and evaluating pesticide tolerances. Coordination of this program is multi-departmental, involving USDA, EPA and FDA, covered by a MOU (Federal Cooperative Agreements Manual). As a part of this program USDA collects data on agricultural chemical usage, and factors influencing chemical use, and collects pesticide residue data through cooperation with nine participating states. USDA provides this data to EPA, FDA and the public. Several USDA publications are listed below as reference material.

The contact point at USDA for pesticide residue matters is:

Martha Lamont, Chief
Residue Branch, Science Division
Agricultural Marketing Service, USDA
8700 Centreville Road, Suite 200
Manassas, VA 221110
703-330-2300

Reference materials - the following reference materials provide background and data necessary or helpful in evaluating current practices. This material should be available at the District office.

1. Pesticide Chemicals - Regulations under the Federal Food, Drug and Cosmetic Act on tolerances for pesticides in food administered by the Environmental Protection Agency (EPA). (See 40 CFR 185)

2. EPA's Pesticide Regulations - Tolerances for Raw Agriculture Products. (See 40 CFR 180)

3. EPA's Rebuttable Presumption Against Registration (RPAR) List.

4. Pesticide Index. - By William J. Wiswesser. A publication containing information on trade names, composition and uses of commercial pesticide formulations.

5. The Daily Summary or Weekly Summary. News releases and reports from USDA.

6. USDA's Weekly Summary Shipments-Unloads.

7. Agricultural Economic Report No. 717 Pesticide and Fertilizer Use and Trends in U.S Agriculture (May 1995)

8. Annual Pesticide Data Summary

9. Reports from USDA's Crop Reporting Board.

10. USDA's Pesticide Assessment Reports.

5.8.3 - Growers

Preliminary investigation of growing areas at the start of the season will provide data necessary for district work planning including production schedules, types and acreage of crops, pesticides used and the names and addresses of growers and shippers.

Growing Dates - The significant growing dates relative to pesticide usage are as follows:

1. Planting date,

2. Date of full bloom, and

3. Date of edible parts formation.

Harvest Dates - The dates of the anticipated harvest season will provide planning information relative to pre-harvest application and shipping.

Acreage - This will provide volume information for work planning.

5.8.3.1 - Pesticide Application

Ascertain the actual pesticide application pattern for each crop. Look for objective evidence to document actual grower practice. Check the grower's supply of pesticide chemicals, look for used pesticide containers, visit his source of supply, etc. Check spraying and dusting practices. Establish if pesticide chemicals are used in such a manner that excessive residues might result.

The following information provides a basis for evaluating pesticide usage:

1. *Pesticide Chemical Applied* - List the common name if there is no doubt as to the chemical identity of the pesticide. Include labeling indications and instructions.

2. *Method of Application* - Describe the method of application i.e., ground rig, airplane, greenhouse aerosol, hand, etc.

3. *Formulation* - Describe the formulation i.e., wettable powder, emulsifiable concentrate, dust, granules, aerosol, etc. Express as pounds of active ingredient per gallon or percent wettable powder.

4. Number of Applications and Dates.

5. *Rate of Last Application* - Calculate the amount of active ingredient per acre.

6. *Pre-Harvest Interval (PHI)* - Calculate the number of days between the day of the last application of pesticide and the harvest date or anticipated harvest date. Compare to the PHI.

7. Visible residue on grower's crop.

8. *Summary of Usage* - Determine the USDA Summary Limitations and evaluate the responsible usage.

5.8.3.2 - Pesticide Misuse/Drift/Soil Contamination

Pesticide residues, which exceed established tolerances, action levels, or "regulatory analytical limits" may be caused by pesticide misuse which can include:

1. Excessive application of a chemical on a permitted crop.

2. Failure to follow labeled time intervals between the last pesticide application and harvest.

3. Use of a non-approved pesticide on a crop.

4. Failure to wash a crop when pesticide labeling requires it (e.g., for certain EBDC's).

Other conditions, which may cause illegal residues, include spray drift and soil contamination.

Drift may be documented by determining which crops and pesticides have been grown/used in fields adjacent to those sampled. Determine direction of prevailing winds and wind condition on the day of spraying. Selective sampling will aid in determining if drift occurred. Compliance Samples collected to document pesticide drift should be Flagged and noted in block 16 of the CR as "Drift Sample - Maintain as Individual Subs".

Soil contamination by compounds, which are relatively stable in the environment, may cause systemic uptake of the compounds by growing crops. Follow-up investigations to violative samples may, in some limited cases, include soil samples as an attempt to determine the source of the contaminant. Do not routinely collect soil samples.

5.8.4 - Packers and Shippers

Follow the same general procedure as in IOM 5.8.3. Observe and report the following:

1. *Treatment Before Shipping* - This may include stripping of leaves, washing, vacuum cooling, application of post-harvest preservative chemicals, use of cartons with mold-inhibiting chemicals, waxes, colors, fumigation, etc.

2. *Identification of Growers' Lots* - Determine procedure or methods used to maintain the identity of each grower's lot. Provide the code and key if any.

3. *Labeling* - Quote labeling or brand names.

4. *Responsibility* - Determine whether the packer or shipper knows what sprays have been used on the products shipped.

5.8.5 - Pesticide Suppliers

Pesticide suppliers should be visited routinely during growing-area coverage. They may provide valuable information about pesticides being used on various crops in the growing area. Some suppliers may suggest spray schedules or advise growers about pesticide usage.

Determine what representations were made by the manufacturer of pesticide chemicals for which there is only a temporary tolerance or experimental permit. Get copies of any correspondence relating to sale and use of these products. Obtain names of growers to whom sales are made if such sale was not for use on acreage assigned under the experimental permit. Collect Official Samples of any crops treated with the pesticide.

5.8.6 - Pesticide Applicators

Pesticide applicators may provide valuable information about pesticides being used on various crops in the growing area. Interview several pesticide applicators, particularly those using airborne equipment. Determine the pesticide chemicals, their formulation, and on what crops they are currently being applied. Determine who supplies the pesticides and how they are prepared to assure proper concentration. If state law requires the applicator to keep a record of each spray application, request permission to review such records. Determine what steps are taken to assure drift on adjoining crops does not result in violative residues. Where there is likelihood of drift, collect Selective Samples from adjoining fields.

5.8.7 - Sample Collections

See IOM Sample Schedule Chart 3 - Pesticides.

5.9 - Veterinary Medicine

5.9.1 - CVM Website

The Center for Veterinary Medicine has its own website. The website contains an alphabetical listing of topics under "Index"; a listing of current and planned Guidance Documents; and on line access to the "Green Book" database listing animal drug approvals. There is a "search" feature allowing you to search for documents containing various words or phrases. The website also contains organizational information for the Center and an explanation of the various laws and regulations which the Center enforces. Information on the website can provide guidance for inspectional efforts related to CVM obligations.

5.9.2 - Veterinary Drug Activities

CVM is responsible for inspections of therapeutic and production drugs, and Active Pharmaceutical Ingredients (APIs). Therapeutic drugs are used in the diagnosis, cure, mitigation, treatment or prevention of disease. Production drugs are used for economic enhancement of animal productivity. Examples include: growth promotion, feed efficiency and increased milk production.

Preapproval inspections are conducted pursuant to pending NADA or ANADA applications.

Post approval inspections of veterinary drugs are conducted to determine compliance with the Current Good Manufacturing Practices (CGMPs) for Finished Pharmaceuticals under 21 CFR Part 211. These cGMPs apply to both human and veterinary drugs. Information on veterinary drugs approved can be found in the "Green Book" database accessed through CVM's website.

APIs are active pharmaceutical ingredients. Many of the APIs used to manufacture dosage form drugs are imported from foreign countries. The intended source for an API must be indicated in NADA/ANADA submissions for new animal drug approvals. Any change in a source for an API would require a supplement to the application.

Extra label drug use refers to the regulations in 21 CFR Part 530 codified as a result of the Animal Medicinal Drug Use Clarification Act (AMDUCA) of 1994. These regulations set forth the requirements for veterinarians to prescribe extra label uses of certain approved animal and human drugs and the requirements for the existence of a valid veterinarian/client/patient relationship (VCPR). The regulations under 21 CFR Part 530 address issues regarding extra label use in non-food as well as food producing animals. 21 CFR 530.41 contains a list of drugs that cannot be used in an extra label fashion in food-producing animals. During an inspection or investigation if you encounter any situations on extra label use of the listed drugs, you should contact CVM's Division of Compliance (HFV-230) (240-276-9200).

The regulations under 21 CFR Part 530 also address compounding of products from approved animal or human drugs by a pharmacist or veterinarian. The regulations clearly state compounding is not permitted from bulk drugs. This would include APIs. CVM has an existing CPG on Compounding of Drugs for Use in Animals (CPG 608.400). A copy can be found on CVM's website. The Division of Compliance (HFV-230) has issued assignments to conduct inspections of firms, including internet pharmacies, who may be engaged in the practice of manufacturing under the guise of pharmacy compounding. You should contact the Division of Compliance (HFV-230) at 240-276-9200 to report instances of compounding or to seek guidance on inspectional issues, or regulatory and enforcement policies.

5.9.3 - Medicated Feeds and Type A Articles

Animal feed is defined under section 201(w) of the FD&C Act [21 U.S.C. 321 (w)]. CVM is responsible for control of medicated and non-medicated animal feeds, Type A medicated articles and pet foods.

The regulations for animal food labeling are in 21 CFR Part 501. The regulations for medicated feed mill licensure are in 21 CFR Part 515. The cGMPs for Medicated Feeds are in 21 CFR Part 225. The cGMPs for Type A Articles are in 21 CFR Part 226.

Inspections are routinely conducted of medicated feed mills and manufacturers of Type A Medicated Articles.

If you have questions related to cGMPs and enforcement policies and strategies concerning Medicated Feeds and Type A Articles you should contact the CVM/Division of Compliance (240-276-9200).

Guidance on pet food labeling requirements can be found on CVM's website.

5.9.4 - BSE Activities

CVM is responsible for FDA's educational and regulatory activities involving BSE. BSE is "Bovine Spongiform Encephalopathy" and is often referred to as "mad cow disease." BSE information can be found on the CVM website. CVM has four Guidance Documents in place dealing with BSE (67-70, dated February 1998). The Guidance Documents address renderers, protein blenders, feed manufacturers, distributors and on farm feeders.

Questions on inspectional assignments and regulatory activities in the BSE area should be addressed to the CVM/Division of Compliance (HFV-230) at 240-276-9200.

5.9.5 - Tissue Residues

The presence of violative drug residues in food from slaughtered animals is a human health concern. Tissue residue investigations/inspections are performed in response to reports of violative drug residue levels found in tissue sampled at slaughter by the USDA.

Tissue residues are commonly caused by the medication of animals prior to marketing and failure to follow the withdrawal times. When a new animal drug is approved the manufacturer must conduct studies to accurately determine withdrawal times. Allowable tolerances for residues of new animal drugs in food can be found in 21 CFR Part 556.

Tissue residue inspections and investigations are unique in comparison to other fieldwork. Although your investigation may begin at the establishment or person named on the USDA/FSIS "Warning letter," you may inspect and/or visit more sites as part of your overall investigation. You may have to visit an auction barn, dealer, trucker, veterinarian, drug supplier, slaughter facility (USDA firm management or State personnel), etc. One or more of these establishments may have caused or allowed the tissue residue to occur. Thus, each establishment's activities may warrant a recommendation for regulatory action such as Warning Letter, Injunction, etc. should the establishment's involvement with residue violations continue.

Upon receipt of a FACTS assignment from CVM to conduct a tissue residue follow-up investigation, the district may create a second assignment, linked to the original CVM assignment, which will include all operations required to complete the assignment. This could include multiple inspections, sample collections and/or investigations. You may not be aware of all the establishments prior to beginning your investigation. Appropriate operations should be added to or deleted from the district assignment.

Each site visit is unique and each produces its own set of unique documents and evidence requiring individual reporting by establishment. You should use good judgment during case development to assure you document your investigation thoroughly. Explain the chain of events and evidence, from the initial tissue residue report, and how other establishments were involved. Collect samples (usually DOC samples) as appropriate. Consultation with your supervisor and/or compliance branch during these operations is essential to assure all evidence necessary to develop a quality case is obtained and submitted in an appropriate format.

Following completion of all operations, you should prepare a Memo of Investigation referencing the FACTS assignments for your supervisor's endorsement to the district Compliance Branch, with a copy to the originating CVM office. This Memo will summarize each site visit (EI or Investigation), sample(s) collected and relevance to the overall CVM assignment. A copy of the memo will be routed to each appropriate factory file.

The individual operations will then stand alone and/or may be used together to build one or multiple cases.

For example, a site visit to a slaughter facility may obtain information on the animal from the USDA inspection personnel on site; and obtain verification from management the establishment ships in interstate commerce. Information obtained at the slaughter facility or other establishments may be documented in an affidavit from each individual providing salient information. A site visit to a veterinarian may be important to establish whether the drugs which caused the tissue residue(s) were prescribed and, if so, how they were prescribed. When there is reason to believe off-label use or other activities have occurred which may warrant a recommendation for regulatory action, an establishment inspection should be conducted and your evidence included with your report.

For information on tissue residue violations and activities you should contact the CVM/Division of Compliance (HFV-230, 240-276-9200).

5.9.6 - Veterinary Devices

Medical devices for animal/veterinary use are not subject to the premarket approval requirements like human medical devices. Once an animal use device is marketed the Center is concerned with safety and efficacy of the veterinary device. CVM often recommends firms use the human device GMPs in controlling the manufacturing of animal use devices. CVM also suggests labeling be sent in for review by the Division of Compliance (HFV-230) to avoid misbranding. Regulatory questions for veterinary/animal use devices should be directed to the CVM/Division of Compliance (HFV-230).

5.9.7 - Animal Grooming Aids

Grooming aids for animals formulated and labeled only to cleanse or beautify the animal are not cosmetics within the meaning of Section 201(i) and not subject to the Federal Food, Drug, and Cosmetic Act. Where animal grooming aids are labeled to contain an active drug ingredient or otherwise suggest or imply therapeutic benefit, they may be considered to be drugs and/or new animal drugs as defined by Section 201(v) of the Act (see CPG 7125.21).

Questions on labeling and regulatory concerns should be directed to the Division of Compliance (HFV-230) at 240-276-9200.

5.9.8 - CVM Bio-Research Monitoring

CVM issues assignments to the field to conduct BIMO inspections of animal drug studies, including both therapeutic and production drugs. Currently, there is no requirement for animal drug studies to be controlled by any sort of institutional review board (IRB). See IOM 5.5.6.

5.10 - Reporting

5.10.1 - Establishment Inspection Report (EIR)

See IOM 1.1 English language requirement. The EIR consists of the following in this order: a printed copy of the FACTS Establishment Inspection Record (EI Record) including, at least, the endorsement with the EIR distribution printed at the bottom of the "endorsement" section of the EI Record; carbon or other copies of FDA forms issued during the inspection such as the FDA 482, FDA 483, and FDA 484; investigator's narrative report; copy of assignment if available; exhibits; and/or any additional material attached and referred to in the narrative report. Regarding the use of checklists (such as the BSE Checklist), the original raw data completed checklist should be submitted with the EIR. If you maintain the data in your regulatory notes, rather than entering directly on the form, then enter on the electronic copy. A printed copy from FACTS becomes the data to include with the EIR.

No copies of inspection reports will be maintained other than in headquarters, district, and resident post files. The signed original report is maintained in the district office or in the case of foreign inspections in the appropriate Center HQ office.

5.10.2 - Endorsement

The endorsement of the establishment inspection is prepared by the supervisor. Some supervisors may have the investigator prepare proposed endorsements. Endorsements should fit in the available space provided in FACTS. If the endorsement exceeds the 2000 character space provided in FACTS, a separate endorsement should be prepared, fully identifying the firm with a Summary of the Endorsement included in FACTS. The FACTS EI Record will be printed and used as the endorsement and routing document to accompany the EIR. See also IOM 5.10.4.1.

Normally the endorsement consists of:

1. The reason for the EI, i.e., workplan, or assignments from headquarters. State the subject of the assignment and reference. If the assignment was issued hard copy (i.e. not through FACTS), it should be attached to the EIR following the narrative. Include the FACTS assignment number and compliance tracking number if applicable.

2. A brief history of previous findings including classification of previous EI, any action taken by the district and/or corrective action taken by the firm in response to inspectional observations from the previous inspection.

3. A concise summary and evaluation of current findings and samples collected.

4. Refusals, voluntary corrections or promises made by the firm's management.

5. Classification and follow-up consistent with inspectional findings and Agency policy including notification of other districts and headquarters as warranted.

6. Distribution consistent with District policy and the requirements of the specific Compliance Program Guidance Manual(s).

7. *Note:* route a copy of the FACTS Establishment Inspection Record and the EIR to DIOP (HFC-170) when any violative, imported products are identified.

8. Per CPG section 110.300, do not report the FURLS Registration number.

The existence of Personal Safety Alerts (IOM 5.2.1.3) or Situational Plans (IOM 5.2.1.4) pertaining to the firm should be included in the endorsement section only and not in the EIR. The signed endorsement should be updated to indicate if an addendum to the EIR (IOM 5.10.6) or an amended FDA 483 (IOM 5.2.3.1.6.2) has occurred.

PROFILES: Updating the Field Accomplishments and Compliance Tracking System (FACTS) database with a Compliance Status for each profile class code associated with the firm's operations and/or products, is the responsibility of Field and Center Investigators, Supervisors and Compliance Officers.

For Domestic inspections, hardcopy or e-mail notification of Potential OAIs are not necessary. FACTS automatically sends OAI Notifications to DCIQA (HFC-240) electronically.

For foreign inspections, the instructions in Exhibit 5-14, Updating Profile Data in FACTS-Guidance, states "When a potential OAI Notification cannot immediately be entered in the FACTS firm profile record, the investigator should notify the Division of Field Investigations (DFI) of the potential OAI situation via FAX (301-827-6685 or 301-443-6919) as soon as the potential OAI situation is known and during the investigation. DFI will notify the appropriate Center and Division of Compliance Information and Quality Assurance (DCIQA) at 240-632-6824 or by e-mail to ORA HQ DCIQA Employees."

See Exhibit 5-14. The COMSTAT Guidance to Field and Centers document can be accessed from the DCIQA web site.

5.10.2.1 - Compliance Achievement Reporting System (CARS)

FACTS is used to report achieved and verified compliance actions, which are not the result of a legal action. A compliance achievement is the observed repair, modification, or adjustment of a violative condition, or the repair, modification, adjustment, relabeling, or destruction of a violative product when either the product or condition does not comply with the Acts enforced by the FDA.

5.10.2.1.1 - Reporting Criteria

There are three criteria for reporting into the CARS system:

1. The detection or identification of the problem. A problem may be observed by FDA, other federal officials, or by state or local authorities and referred to FDA; and as a result of an inspection, investigation, sample analysis, or detention accomplished by ORA or states under contract to ORA.

2. The correction of the problem. The correction is directly attributable to the efforts of ORA or state officials under contract to ORA (involving contract products only); and is unrelated to the filing of a legal action, i.e., seizure, prosecution, injunction.

3. The verification of the correction of the problem. The correction is verified by the FDA, other federal officials or state or local authorities and reported in writing to the FDA; and is based on an inspection, investigation, sample analysis, or letter from a firm to FDA certifying the problem has been corrected.

5.10.2.1.2 - Data Elements

Only when the corrective action(s) has been verified should a CARS be reported. The data elements are those entered/coded in FACTS (See IOM Exhibit 5-15):

1. *PAC.* See the Data Codes Manual. Should there be insufficient space to code all corrections verified on an occasion, record the most significant corrections.

2. *PROBLEM TYPE.* The problem type is the problem(s) identified during the operation(s). Use the List of Values (LOV) found in this field on the Compliance Achievement Reporting Screen. If "Other" is chosen, you should include an explanation in the 'Remarks" field.

3. *CORRECTIVE ACTION.* The action the establishment took to correct the identified problem. Use the LOVs found in this field on the CARS screen. If "Other" is selected, you should include an explanation in the "Remarks" field.

4. *VERIFICATION DATE.* Use the date the corrective action(s) is verified, either through an establishment inspection, an investigation, or a letter from the establishment certifying the corrections have been made. Include documentation to verify the action such as repair receipts/plans.

5. *CORRECTING ORGANIZATION.* The FDA, other federal agency, or state or local authority, which observed the verified correction. Use the LOVs found in this field on the CARS screen.

6. *REPORTING DISTRICT.* The FDA, other federal agency, or state or local authority, which is actually inputting the verified correction. Use the LOVs found in this field on the CARS screen.

7. *REASON FOR CORRECTION.* The action the FDA took to make the correction happen. Use the LOVs found in this field on the CARS screen. If "Other" is chosen, you should include an explanation in the "Remarks" field.

5.10.3 - Facts Establishment Inspection Record (EI Record)

Per FMD-130, each ORA District is responsible to ensure all investigators verify, correct, and enter changes to the OEI (including Profile data for profilable firms) on the firm's maintenance screens in FACTS during each inspection, investigation and during any OEI update. Consult with your supervisor and District OEI Coordinator to assure data is accurately updated. See IOM Exhibits 5-15 and 5-16. The FACTS Profile Data instructions and FACTS generated assignment are attached as IOM Exhibits 5-9 and 5-14.

Inspectional accountable time in FACTS consists of the hours devoted to file reviews (operational preparation), actual inspectional, investigational, audit, etc. time (onsite), document (exhibit) preparation and EIR (report) write-up. Accountable time does not include travel time. One occasional exception could be when more than one participant in an inspection/investigation travel together and discuss/prepare while in route.

5.10.4 - Narrative Report

See IOM 1.1 English language requirement. You should use Turbo EIR for all EIRs. The narrative report is the written portion of the EIR, which accurately describes the investigator's inspectional findings. The narrative report may be prepared in two formats depending on the type of inspection, inspection classification, and program area. A Summary of Findings narrative report is used for non-violative, non-initial inspections - see IOM 5.10.4.1. The full Standard narrative report is used for human drug and medical device inspections, initial and potential Official Action Indicated (OAI) classified inspections in other program areas - see IOM 5.10.4.3. The "Summary of Findings" report format may be used for some Voluntary Action Indicated (VAI) classified inspections as directed by your supervisor. Additional requirements for human drug and medical device reports are described in IOM 5.5.8 and 5.6.9. For all reporting formats, include additional information as directed by your assignment, Compliance Program Guidance Manual, or your Supervisor.

All reports should be prepared as stand-alone documents outside of FACTS. Your Establishment Inspection Report (EIR) should:

1. Be factual, objective, and free of unsupportable conclusions.

2. Be concise while covering the necessary aspects of the inspection.
3. Not include opinions about administrative or regulatory follow-up.
4. Be written in the first person.
5. Be signed by all FDA and commissioned personnel participating in the inspection. See IOM section 5.1.2.5.1 when more than one FDA or commissioned person participated in the inspection.

5.10.4.1 - Non-Violative Establishments

Investigators should use "Summary of Findings", stand-alone, narrative reports for non-violative establishments, unless otherwise directed by your supervisor, the assignment or the Compliance Program Guidance Manual involved.

Exception: human drug and medical device GMP inspection reports, which have additional reporting requirements should be written in the Standard Narrative report format as in 5.10.4.3.

The Summary of Findings Report may not be written solely in the FACTS provided "Inspection Summary" heading. The Summary of Findings report should include:

1. The reason for the inspection;
2. The date, classification and findings of the previous inspection;
3. The actual inclusive dates of the inspection (these may be included as part of a header or in the body of the EIR.)
4. The name of the person to whom credentials were shown and the Notice of Inspection was issued and the person's authority to receive the Notice. Explain if you were unable to show credentials or issue forms to top management;
5. The scope of the inspection; i.e., comprehensive or directed; and a brief description of the products, processes or systems covered during the inspection; the manufacturing codes and if necessary their interpretation.
6. The significant findings if any;
7. Management's response or corrections;
8. Warnings given to management; and
9. The investigator's handwritten signature.

5.10.4.2 - Violative Establishments

For domestic inspections where regulatory action is being recommended and when the District has final classification responsibility, the inspection report should normally be submitted within 10 days to the District or Center

Compliance Branch as per established procedures. Please note, that depending on the type and severity of the regulatory action, it may be necessary to submit the EIR in less than 10 days. You should consult with your supervisory investigator in these instances. Refer to FMD-86 and the Regulatory Procedures Manual regarding other timeframes associated with non-violative inspections.

All violative EIR's should in addition to the information required for non-violative reports contain the following:

1. The objectionable conditions or practices described in sufficient detail so someone reading the report will clearly understand the observation(s) and significance.

2. The objectionable conditions or practices cross-referenced to FDA 483 citations, samples collected, photographs, or other documentation including exhibits attached to the EIR.

3. Information as to when the objectionable conditions or practices occurred, why they occurred, and who is or was responsible, developed to the highest level in the firm.

5.10.4.3 - Individual Narrative Headings

There are many acceptable ways of organizing a narrative report. The key is to cover the required information in IOM 5.10.4 and 5.10.4.2, or as required by the assignment, Compliance Program Guidance Manual, or your supervisor. The appropriate use of headings should not result in repetition of the same information in different sections. You are encouraged to create headings as necessary to present the inspectional findings in the most concise manner. For non-violative and some VAI reports, a single heading such as "Summary of Findings" is sufficient (for exceptions, see IOM 5.10.4.1). Turbo EIR should be used to generate the FDA 483. In certain instances, if you experience computer problems, do not delay the issuance of the FDA 483. See IOM 5.2.3. You should use Turbo EIR for all EIRs.

5.10.4.3.1 - STANDARD NARRATIVE REPORT

STANDARD NARRATIVE REPORT: HEADINGS, CONTENT AND ARRANGEMENT OF YOUR REPORT

Use the Standard narrative report format for all program areas. The Standard narrative format contains sections within specific headings. Reporting requirements under these headings fall into two categories: those which should be reported every time (if applicable) and those which only need to be reported if an element has changed.

Initial or potential OAI classified inspections: complete a full standard narrative report for all program areas. You should include a Table of Contents for all complex or full standard narrative reports.

Note: *All human drug and medical device inspection reports should be full narrative Reports. You should add the supplemental information listed under the subheadings for human drug and medical device inspection reports as appropriate. Human drug inspection reports do not need full and detailed narratives for every heading. In many cases, brief summaries addressing the format areas will be sufficient.*

5.10.4.3.2 - Summary

Summary:

1. Provide the reason for the inspection (e.g., compliance program, by assignment, etc.);

2. The scope of the inspection (comprehensive, directed, sample collection only, QSIT level, etc.).

3. Provide a summary of the findings, date, and classification of the previous inspection and the firm's response/corrective actions.

4. List the products, systems and processes covered during the current inspection, and the types of records and documents reviewed. For human drug reports, list the systems not covered.

5. Provide a summary of the current findings, refusals, samples collected, warnings given to management, and a summary of management's response or voluntary corrections.

6. Per CPG section 110.300, do not report the FURLS Registration number.

5.10.4.3.3 - Administrative Data

Administrative Data:

1. The firm name, address, phone, FAX and e-mail address.

2. Report the names and titles of the Investigator(s), Analyst(s), non-FDA officials, etc. Report the name of the firm's responsible official who gave permission to non-FDA officials without inspection authority to accompany you during your inspection. See IOM 5.1.1 and 5.2.2.

3. The inclusive date(s) of the current inspection, i.e., list the actual dates in the plant.

4. If a team inspection and some individuals were not present during the entire inspection, indicate dates in plant for each team member.

Report Full Names and Titles of:

1. To whom FDA Official Credentials were shown,

2. To whom any FDA forms were issued to or signed by during the inspection (FDA 482, 483, 484, 463, etc.); where appropriate, explain the reason a form(s) was not issued to or signed by the most responsible individual (this may be reported in the Individual Responsibility and Persons Interviewed heading below),

3. Who wrote which section of the EIR, if this was a team inspection report, and

4. In-plant inspectors or other government agencies (IOM 5.4.9).

5.10.4.3.4 - History

History:

1. Report the legal status of the firm (corporation, partnership, limited liability corporation, etc.). If a corporation, list in which state and when the firm was incorporated.

2. List the parent corporation, corporate address and any subsidiaries.

3. Provide a summary of any regulatory actions and prior warnings (do not cite any action only recommended but not approved). You should also report any significant/relevant inspectional history pertinent to the current EI or recommendation.

4. Include any relevant recalls, etc. since the last inspection.

5. Report the hours of operation and any changes from past inspections (include seasonal variations).

6. Report the current registration(s) status or any changes to registration status. Per CPG section 110.300, do not report the FURLS Registration number.

7. If directions to the firm would be helpful in future visits, include the information.

8. Provide the names, titles and addresses of top management official(s) to whom correspondence should be addressed (FMD 145, W/L, etc.).

9. For foreign inspections, list U.S. consignees to whom the firm's products are shipped.

10. For Human Drugs - domestic firms, identify the general types of customers and provide the names and addresses for several regular customers of a few of the firm's products.

5.10.4.3.5 - Interstate (I.S.) Commerce

Interstate (I.S.) Commerce:

1. Report changes in the previous estimate of the percentage of products shipped outside of the state (or exported to the U.S.) and the basis of the estimate.

2. Report the firm's general promotion and distribution patterns.

3. If there is an apparent violative product, provide examples of I.S. shipments of violative product(s); or

4. If no such shipments, provide examples of I.S. shipments of major components of apparent violative products - with complete I.S. documentation in either case.

5.10.4.3.6 - Jurisdiction (Products Manufactured and/or Distributed)

Jurisdiction (Products Manufactured and/or Distributed):

1. Include a list of a representative number of currently marketed products subject to FD&C Act or other statute enforced by FDA or counterpart state agency, including any believed violative.

2. Collect appropriate labeling (product and case labels, inserts, brochures, manuals, promotional materials of any type) for those products believed violative or representing any significant new or unusual operation, industry or technology; or as directed by your supervisor.

3. Document any applicable labeling agreements (and obtain a copy) and statutory guaranty given or received per Sections 301(h) and 303(c)(2) of the FD&C Act [21 U.S.C. 321 (h) and 333 (c)(2)] (IOM 5.3.7.2)

In addition, the label, labeling and promotional materials are a critical part of determining a product's intended use.

1. In instances where a regulatory action is being considered based on product labels, labeling, and/or other promotional materials, including any Internet websites, you should collect all available documentation. This includes all written, printed or graphic matter on the immediate container of an article or accompanying the article (the product's label and labeling, see FD&C Act, 201(k) and (m) [21 U.S.C. 321(k) and (m)] and IOM 4.4.9.1). Accompanying labeling could include brochures, pamphlets, circulars, and flyers, as well as audio and video tapes.

2. In cases where there may be a dispute about whether a product is a drug or a dietary supplement, you should collect all materials which claim a product can be used for the treatment of any disease.

5.10.4.3.7 - Individual Responsibility and Persons Interviewed

Report with whom you dealt, and in what regard (both during and prior to the start of the inspection):

1. Who provided relevant information,

2. Who accompanied you during the inspection,

3. Who refused access to required records or any other refusal of information (Note: a separate heading for Refusals may be needed if refusals are significant, extensive or an Inspection Warrant is anticipated),

4. Who refused to permit inspection (IOM 5.2.5.1) and

5. For Human Drug inspection reports, also include the name, title, physical mailing address, phone, and fax number and e-mail address for any U.S. Agent or broker who represents the company when dealing with the FDA.

Describe roles and authorities of responsible individuals, including the full names and titles of individuals providing you with information.

Report changes to the following:

1. Who is the most responsible individual at the inspected firm? Who is the responsible head or designated correspondent? Refer to IOM 5.3.6, 5.3.6.1, and 5.3.6.2.

2. Report full names and titles of owners, partners, and corporate officers. Who has the duty, power and responsibility, and authority to prevent, detect, and correct violation(s), and how is this demonstrated and/or documented? See IOM 5.3.6.2.

3. Report the chain of command; include an organizational chart (create if necessary).

4. Obtain a copy of public annual report, if any.

5. List the names and titles of key operating personnel.

5.10.4.3.8 - Firm's Training Program

The firm's training programs are of particular significance where inspectional findings find people may not be adequately trained.

5.10.4.3.9 - Manufacturing/Design Operations

Manufacturing/Design Operations:

1. Report only changes to the firm's general overall operations, including significant changes in equipment, processes, or products since the previous inspection. Include schematics, flow plans, photographs, formulations and diagrams, if useful.

2. List names and sources of new or unusual components or raw materials.

3. Report equipment considered new or unusual unless otherwise directed.

4. Submit pertinent formulas (especially those being manufactured during your inspection) and processing instructions with labeling of suspect products.

For human drug inspection reports:

This section of the EIR should be organized by system covered during the EI as outlined in CPGM 7356.002. In each section, include a brief summary of what you reviewed in order to meet the key system element outlined in the CPGM. You should add more detail for the system elements found to be deficient, or the subject of a FDA 483 observation.

For medical device inspection reports:

1. Describe manufacturing operations by sub system covered in your inspection (Management Controls, Design Controls, Production and Process Controls, Corrective and Preventive Action Controls, Material Controls, Facility and Equipment Controls, and Records/Documents/Change Controls). For ALL Level 2, 3, and "for cause" inspections: for production and process controls - indicate which production processes were covered/reviewed. If a subsystem was not specifically covered during your EI, you do not need to separately describe the general operations of that subsystem.

2. For all inspections covering CAPA - indicate which data sources were available for review and which were actually reviewed; include a brief statement regarding coverage or non-coverage of applicable tracking requirements, MDRs, sterilization, and reports of corrections and removals.

3. If the Design Control system was covered, indicate the design project(s) covered during the inspection. Where design activities occur at a location other than the manufacturing site, list the name, address of the design location and responsibilities of those performing the design activities.

4. If applicable, identify the name and address of the specification developer if different from either the manufacturing site or where design activities occur.

5.10.4.3.10 - Manufacturing Codes

Manufacturing Codes

1. If the manufacturing codes are unchanged, include a statement in the EIR the system is the same as described in reports on file at the District. Indicate the date of the EIR in which the codes are fully explained.

2. If the manufacturing codes have changed, describe the manufacturing coding system (lot, batch, product, etc.), and a key to interpretation of codes.

3. For medical device inspections reports: where appropriate, include a description of the system used to identify and maintain control of components during the manufacturing process, as well as, the codes used for traceability (for applicable finished devices).

5.10.4.3.11 - Complaints

Note: These complaints include those reported to the FDA by consumers, health care professionals, industry, etc.; and all complaints received by the firm.

1. Report your review of the firm's complaint file(s).

2. In addition, if returned goods and/or documents for returned goods are examined, describe findings. If not examined, so indicate.

3. Report your follow-up of consumer/trade complaints, Adverse Event Reports, MDR's, MedWatch reports or recalls identified in the district factory jacket for coverage. Correlate consumer/trade complaints, Adverse Event Reports, MDR's, MedWatch reports to specific objectionable conditions observed.

5.10.4.3.12 - Recall Procedures

Describe plans and procedures for removing products from marketing channels if necessary. If these procedures are in written SOP-type format, you may reference any copies obtained to aid in your explanation.

5.10.4.3.13 - Objectionable Conditions and Management's Response

If any observations were provided to management in writing (FDA 483) at the conclusion of the inspection list each observation and report each observation providing information organized under the two headings Supporting Evidence and Relevance, and Discussion with Management below.

NOTE: Observations of a verbal nature should be reported in sufficient detail under the General Discussion with Management (correlate any Exhibits, samples, etc. to any "verbal" observations).

5.10.4.3.13.1 - Supporting Evidence and Relevance

Sufficiently describe the observation as necessary to relate the facts as you found them.

1. Identify specific pages of exhibits and/or samples (e.g., procedure title, section, paragraph, sentence), labeling text, interstate shipping records which in your judgment document violations so supervisors, compliance officers, and other reviewers can readily evaluate your evidence.

2. Describe verbal statements (verbatim if possible) by firm officials having knowledge, duty, power, and responsibility to detect, prevent, or correct the apparent violation.

3. Identify the responsible party for each apparent violation (i.e., if known.)

4. Identify which team member (if applicable) was responsible for the observation.

5. When appropriate explain how this observation relates to the overall situation; i.e., impact on the product, batches, or lots involved, and any relationship to other products, processes, or other FDA 483 observations.

6. The duration of the problem.

5.10.4.3.13.2 - Discussion with management

Discussion with management:

1. Report management's response to each specific observation, time frames given for corrections and/or corrective action.

2. Report any disagreements with or refusals to correct the observation.

For medical device inspection reports:

1. For each observation based on sampling of records, indicate which Sample Table and level of confidence was used and the actual number of records sampled.

2. If the number sampled is different than the actual number reviewed, so indicate.

5.10.4.3.14 - Refusals

Provide full details of all refusals of/for requested information, statutory information, photography, entry, etc. received during the inspection, including who made the refusal and, if available, why the refusal was given.

5.10.4.3.15 - General Discussion with Management

General Discussion with Management:

1. Report the names and titles of all present, including those present via electronic media (describe).

2. Include the name and title to whom the FDA 483 was issued.

3. Provide additional discussion items not provided in writing at the conclusion of the inspection, such as: questionable labels, labeling and/or labeling practices, commercialization of products covered by IDE or IND, fraudulent health claims, registration/listing deviations, lack of approved PMA, 510(k), NDA, ANDA, etc. These include all verbal observations deemed not to merit inclusion on the FDA 483 (IOM 5.2.3)

4. A description of each warning, recommendation, or suggestion given to the firm, and to whom given.

5. Management's general responses to the inspection and/or to groups of items listed on the report of observations or discussed at the conclusion of the inspection.

5.10.4.3.16 - Additional Information

Report changes as appropriate.

1. Describe contractors used and for what purpose. For Medical Device inspection reports: also include names and addresses of all applicable third party installers or servicing organizations used by the manufacturer. Include their responsibilities.

2. Describe suppliers (major raw material, active ingredient, etc.) used and for what.

3. During inspections, when violative products imported into the U.S., or intended to be imported into the U.S. are encountered, document the product and foreign manufacturer in the EIR. Violative products could be rejected APIs due to non-conformance with the USP, foods without appropriate labeling, etc. Send a copy of the EIR to DIOP (HFC-170). See IOM 5.2.1 and 5.10.2.

4. For initial inspections, verify distribution patterns for the firm's products, raw materials, and components to firms which warehouse or further process products which may be subject to FDA regulations. Districts should incorporate information obtained into their Official Establishment Inventory improvement activities and complete form FDA 457, Product/Establishment Surveillance Report as appropriate. See IOM 8.6.2.

5. Report pertinent facts, which do not fit another section of the EIR. (For firms located in foreign countries, include information relative to lodging and travel; for domestic firms, include information relative to location of firm if difficult to find; etc.).

For human drug inspection reports - PDMA Coverage:

1. Describe what sample loss, theft, or diversion reports were covered during the inspection.

2. Describe the firm's sample audit and security systems, including a review of the firm's SOP's. Significant problems which may contribute to the firm's inability to adequately monitor sample distribution via sales representative, mail or common carrier should be addressed under objectionable conditions.

5.10.4.3.17 - Samples Collected

List and describe samples collected during the inspection.

5.10.4.3.18 - Voluntary Corrections

Voluntary Corrections:

1. Provide a brief description of improvements initiated by the firm in response to a previous inspection, report of observations and/or a warning letter.

2. Report voluntary destructions, recalls, and similar actions since the prior inspection or during this inspection.

3. Report any follow-up to recalls identified during the inspection (may be by referencing Attachment B recall report).

4. Include recalls to specific objectionable conditions observed.

5. Provide the identity of person(s) responsible for the corrections.

6. Report any appropriate voluntary corrections in FACTS CARS.

5.10.4.3.19 - Exhibits Collected

List all exhibits attached. See IOM 5.10.5, Exhibits.

Briefly, describe or title each exhibit and sample number attached. You should include in your description the number of pages for each Exhibit listing.

NOTE: For complex inspections a cross-reference from the FDA 483 and verbal observations to applicable exhibits and samples can be useful during further review.

5.10.4.3.20 - Attachments

Attachments as referred to here are any material attached to and referred to in the EIR, which are not evidentiary in nature; such as assignments, Center provided protocols, etc. See IOM 5.3.8.2 for identification of non-evidentiary material attached to the EIR. Documents attached to the EIR may be referred to in the EIR and listed here, such as the FDA 482, FDA 483, copy of the FDA 463a, etc. (in form number order); but such documents/forms may not be numbered, altered from their issued state, bear adhesive identification labels, etc. See the opening sentence of IOM 5.10.5. List and attach copies of associated reports (Recall Attachment B Report, etc.).

5.10.4.3.21 - Signature

All participants will sign the final narrative portion of the EIR. The prescribed format is to type each persons name, title, and district (or other affiliation) below the signature. In some cases immediate signature by all participants is not possible. An example as to how this can be accomplished is to forward an electronic "draft" copy of the EIR for all to read and approve, then followed or accompanied by the original signature sheet. When signed, return to the lead investigator for proper filing and routing. When using this method, a photocopy of the original signature page is made with the lead investigator's signature and temporarily attached to the EIR.

5.10.5 - Exhibits

Exhibits are materials collected from the firm and do not include FDA forms or copies of assignments. Exhibits should contribute to the objective of the assignment and the clarity of the report. They may include flow-plans, schematics, layouts, etc. If the materials collected from the firm are not needed as exhibits, they should be destroyed in accordance with district policy. Submit at least three copies of new or suspect labeling or other material collected as exhibits for labeling purposes. See IOM 4.4.9 for exceptions. These should be mounted in a manner so complete sets are submitted that can be reviewed by individuals in separate offices, i.e., labels 1-10 in each of three sets. You should identify records/exhibits submitted with an EIR using at least the Exhibits' number, firm name, date(s) of the inspection, and your initials. See IOM 5.3.8.2.

5.10.5.1 - Electronic information

Electronic information, databases or summary data from databases may be obtained from firms and evaluated during the course of an EI. This data may form the basis for observations or information included in the EIR. It is preferable to include a printed version and/or a summary of the data as an exhibit. When it is included as an exhibit to the EIR, it should be stored so as to protect the integrity of the data. See IOM 5.3.8.3.2 for procedures for collecting and identifying electronic data. Electronic media should be protected from extreme temperatures and most magnetic fields. Additional precautions may be necessary and you should be guided by your district procedures for storage of electronic data.

5.10.6 - Addendum To EIR

If your EIR requires correcting or clarification after it has been finalized, signed and distributed, you should prepare an addendum, with your supervisor's approval. The addendum should clearly identify itself with the EIR being added to, explain the necessity for the addendum, and clearly define what section(s) and page(s) are being revised. The addendum will be signed by the preparer.

Chapter 6: Imports

CONTENT		VERSION DATE
Subchapter 6.1	Imports	July 13, 2009
Subchapter 6.2	Import Procedures	July 13, 2009
Subchapter 6.3	Review of Records	July 13, 2009
Subchapter 6.4	Field Examination	July 13, 2009
Subchapter 6.5	Import Sample Collection	July 13, 2009
Subchapter 6.6	Filer Evaluations	June 11, 2009
Subchapter 6.7	Glossary of Import Terms	July 13, 2009

6.1 - Imports

6.1.1 - Authority

Section 801 of the FD&C Act [21 U.S.C. 381] authorizes FDA examination of foods, drugs, cosmetics and devices offered for entry into the United States. Section 536 of the FD&C Act [21 U.S.C. 360mm] authorizes refusal of radiation emitting products which fail to comply with the requirements of Section 534 (h) of the FD&C Act [21 U.S.C. 360kk (h)]. 19 CFR 151.4 of the U.S. Customs regulations authorizes employees of FDA to examine or take samples of entry merchandise released under immediate delivery.

The procedures outlined in this chapter cover imported merchandise subject to, but not limited to, the following Acts/Regulations:

1. Federal Food, Drug, and Cosmetic Act
2. Fair Packaging and Labeling Act
3. Nutrition Labeling and Education Act (NLEA)
4. Import Milk Act/Filled Milk Act
5. Federal Caustic Poison Act
6. Bioterrorism Act

7. Public Health Service Act, Part F, Subpart 1, Biologic Products

8. Title 21 CFR Subpart E - Imports and Exports (1.83), etc.

9. Title 19 CFR Customs Duties (authority to sample delegated by Custom Regulations, etc.)

6.1.2 - Import Investigations

Import operations, normally focus on entry review, field examinations, and sample collections. However, investigations are an essential tool in uncovering and developing evidence documenting violations such as entry misdeclaration, product substitutions, and "port shopping." Invaluable sources of information include: Import Alerts, assignments from headquarters or other districts, interagency cooperation and local intelligence.

When documenting these situations, your supervisor may request a memo of investigation or an EIR to be sent to the compliance branch. Follow your district procedures, IOM Chapter 5 for preparation of the EIR and IOM Subchapter 8.10 for preparation of memorandums.

When examining, sampling, or following up on refused imported products you may use an affidavit to document the facts surrounding the situation. Refer to IOM 4.4.8 and Exhibit 6-5 for guidance on preparation of an affidavit.

6.2 - Import Procedures

6.2.1 - Scope

These procedures in this section cover imported merchandise. Your personal safety during any import procedures outlined in this subchapter is important. For more information concerning personal safety, see IOM 5.2.1.2.

6.2.2 - Division of Authority

FDA determines if an article is in compliance with the Acts enforced by FDA. It also determines whether or not the article can be brought into compliance with the appropriate statute and authorizes reconditioning for that purpose.

Supervision over the reconditioning is exercised by either FDA or Customs as mutually arranged. At ports in reasonably close proximity to an FDA office, supervision is ordinarily exercised by FDA. At remote ports supervision may be exercised by Customs.

The refusal of admission, exportation, or destruction of merchandise is carried out under the direction of Customs. However, at some ports the actual supervision of the destruction of violative merchandise may be conducted by FDA pursuant to a local FDA/Customs agreement.

6.2.3 - Entries

6.2.3.1 - Formal Entries

All articles offered for entry into the U.S. and subject to the Acts enforced by FDA, with a value greater than $2000 (current), are considered formal entries. They are subject to bond requirements, which include a condition for the redelivery of the merchandise, or any part of it, upon demand by Customs at any time, as prescribed for in the Custom's regulations in force on the date of entry. (See section 801(b) of the FD&C Act [21 U.S.C. 381(b)], 19 CFR Part 113). The bond is filed with Customs which, in case of default, takes appropriate action to effect the collection of liquidated damages provided for in the bond after consultation with FDA. (See 19 CFR Section 113.62(l) and 21 CFR Section 1.97).

Notification of the Customs entry is generally accomplished by electronic submission through the Customs Automated Commercial System (ACS). Non-electronic entries are submitted directly to FDA. Electronic entries received by FDA may be reviewed on screen (OSR) to determine if further action is needed, or if full documentation must be submitted. For entries requiring further review, FDA will be provided the appropriate Customs Entry documents (CF 3461/3461ALT, commercial invoice, bill of lading and any other relevant documents to aid in making an admissibility decision), and which also document interstate commerce. If an entry is not filed electronically, these documents will be submitted to FDA at the time Customs entry is made, in accordance with local port operations.

6.2.3.2 - Informal Entries

Normally, informal entries (value less than $2000 currently) do not require posting a redelivery bond. All informal entries of articles subject to FDA jurisdiction, entered electronically, are forwarded to FDA through the Customs/FDA ACS interface. When FDA takes action on an informal entry not filed electronically by the filer, FDA personnel will input the informal entry into OASIS as a manual entry. When taking FDA action with an informal entry, Customs will be requested to convert it into a formal consumption entry.

6.2.3.3 - Mail/Personal Baggage

In the case of imports by mail or personal baggage, FDA districts should arrange for coverage with their local Customs International Mail Office or border crossing office. This should include agreements designating who is responsible for coverage, when (how often), etc. Customs is responsible for examination of personal baggage. If an article subject to FDA review is encountered, the Customs officer will determine if it should be brought to the attention of the local FDA office. Personal importations meeting the criteria of a formal entry will be processed in accordance with normal non-electronic entries. Generally, since most personal importations are small in size and value, guidance has been developed for evaluating these importations. (See RPM Chapter 9-2 "Coverage of Personal Importations".)

"Section 321 entries" for Customs are those entries with a value of $200 or less. Generally, this form of entry applies to articles which pass free of duty and tax, as defined in 19 C.F.R. 101.1(o), and imported by one person.

Customs and FDA may conduct periodic "blitzes" to determine the volume and type of FDA-regulated merchandise admitted under "Section 321 entries." The use of the 321 entry process should not apply to multiple shipments covered by a single order or contract, sent separately for the express purpose of securing free entry and avoiding compliance with pertinent law or regulation.

6.2.3.4 - Import for Export (IFE) Entries

PRODUCTS IMPORTED UNDER THE PROVISIONS OF SECTION 801(d)(3) OF THE FD&C Act [21 U.S.C. 381 (d)(3)]: Import For Export (IFE) Processing and Follow-Up

PURPOSE: To establish procedures facilitating the uniform review of Import for Export (IFE) at the time of entry and domestic follow up to insure articles entered as Import for Export are either exported or destroyed but not distributed domestically.

REFERENCES: Regulatory Procedures Manual Chapter 9-15, Federal Food, Drug, and Cosmetic Act

BACKGROUND: Section 801(d)(3) of the FD&C Act [21 U.S.C. 381 (d)(3)] allows the importation of certain violative FDA-regulated articles into the U.S. on a conditional basis that they are not for domestic distribution. Those articles include human and veterinary drugs (or their components); device components or accessories, or other devices requiring further processing for health-related purposes; and food additives, color additives and dietary supplements including in bulk form. They must be explicitly intended for further processing or incorporation into other products and subsequent export.

Documentation required at the time of importation under section 801(d)(3) of the Act [21 U.S.C. 381 (d)(3)] includes:

A statement the article is intended to be further processed or incorporated into a drug, biologics product, device, food, food additive, color additive or dietary supplement that will be exported under sections 801(e) or 802 of the FD&C Act [21 U.S.C. 381 (e) or 382] or section 351(h) of the Public Health Service Act (PHSA);

Information to identify the manufacturer of the article and each processor, packer, distributor, or other entity in chain of possession from manufacturer to importer;

Such certificates of analysis as necessary to identify the article, unless it is a device or falls under section 801 (d)(4) of the FD&C Act [21 U.S.C. 381 (d)(4)] - blood and blood components;

In addition, a bond must be executed providing for payment of liquidated damages in accordance with the Bureau of Customs and Border Protection's (CBP) requirements.

6.2.3.4.1 - IFE Entry Review

Import for Export entry procedures are as follows:

1. If electronic submission is made, it is unlikely all of the information required under section 801(d)(3) FD&C Act [21 U.S.C. 381 (d)(3)] will be provided electronically. Districts should request the supporting documents (if not already received from the broker or importer) by setting an entry option of Documents Requested (DRQ) and/or Entry Incomplete (DEF) on all entries with IFE in the Affirmation of Compliance (AOC) field in OASIS, or those suspected to be IFE, which lack complete supporting documents.

2. If the entry is indeed an IFE entry and the AOC was not included in the original entry, the entry reviewer should modify the AOC field in OASIS to indicate "IFE".

   If the required documentation is not provided after a DRQ, entry reviewers should take the appropriate compliance follow-up, under the basis the required IFE documentation was not provided to FDA at the time of initial importation.

   Districts should determine the appropriate time frame for receiving the required IFE documents in particular circumstances. It is anticipated three (3) days from the DRQ or DEF notice will usually be adequate for the required IFE documentation to be submitted. This is because the broker may need to communicate FDA's requirement for documents to an importer. If all required documentation is provided, the entry should be given a "May Proceed". NOTE: All documentation supporting the IFE entry should be processed in accordance with step 4 below.

   If documentation is not adequate, the district should issue a detention after review of the documentation, in accordance with normal procedures outlined in the RPM Chapter 9 .

3. If the entry is marked IFE, but review of the entry information or supporting documents indicates the AOC was entered inappropriately, the entry reviewer should note this in the entry remarks section.

4. Copy and attach all entry documentation and forward to the FDA home district of the initial owner or consignee, identifying the following:

   a. FOREIGN MANUFACTURER/SHIPPER
   b. ENTRY NO.
   c. U.S.IMPORTER OF RECORD
   d. INITIAL OWNER/CONSIGNEE
   e. ARTICLE/PRODUCT

6.2.3.4.2 - Domestic Follow-up

The FDA home district of the initial owner or consignee should:

1. Ensure the IFE Entry is copied from the IFE shipments for the last 30 days list which is generated by the Division of Import Operations and Policy (DIOP).

2. Ensure supporting documents are sent to the establishment file of the initial owner or consignee.

3. Ensure follow-up inspections are conducted within 6 - 9 months of the initial notification the firm is receiving an IFE entry. All existing IFE entries for the firm should be investigated during the initial IFE inspection. If the product has not been "further processed" or "incorporated" into product for export, the home district should monitor the firm's practices to ensure there is no violation of the IFE provisions of the Act.

6.2.3.4.3 - Inspection Guidance

When a firm is scheduled for inspection, you should:

1. Review the IFE entry documentation and/or follow-up inspection information from the establishment file prior to conducting the inspection.

2. Verify during the inspection the IFE article:
   a. Was used to produce an exported product,
   b. Was destroyed, or
   c. Still under the firm's control pending disposition. If the article is pending disposition, verify a current and valid Customs bond covering the article exists, and the article is the same article that was offered for entry.

If the article was exported or destroyed, you should request the manufacturer's import, export, and/or destruction records to verify the imported article was further processed or incorporated into another product and was exported in accordance with sections 801 (e) or 802 of the FD&C Act [21 U.S.C. 381 (e) or 382] or section 351(h) of the PHSA , or destroyed. Please note, for drug products, an initial owner or consignee may be allowed to retain a sample of the imported article in order to comply with good manufacturing process (GMP) regulations concerning sample retention.

Include in the Establishment Inspection Report or a memo the status of the IFE product and if further follow-up is required.

Following review and determination of the necessity of further follow-up, forward the completed EIR or memo and supporting documents to the District which initiated the IFE follow-up.

Upon receipt of the completed IFE Follow-up, ensure the following actions are taken:

1. Verify if further follow-up is needed. If so, schedule a follow-up inspection. If further follow-up is NOT need-ed, document the completed follow-up.

2. Any inspections identifying a prohibited act under section 301(w) of the FD&C Act [21 U.S.C. 331 (w)] should be forwarded immediately to the district compli-ance branch for regulatory action. See RPM Chapter 9 . In

addition, a copy of the violative inspection findings should be forwarded to DIOP immediately.

6.2.3.5 - Prior Notice of Importation of Food and Animal Feed

The Public Health Security and Bioterrorism Preparedness and Response Act of 2002 (the Bioterrorism Act) requires that FDA receive prior notice of food imported into the United States. Most of the prior notice information required by the interim final rule is data usually provided by importers or brokers to Customs and Border Protection (CBP) when foods arrive in the United States. The Bioterrorism Act requires that this information also be provided to FDA in advance of an imported article of food's arrival to the United States. FDA uses this information in advance of the arrival to review and assess the information, and determine whether to inspect the imported food. Prior notices can be submitted either through ABI/ACS or FDA's Prior Notice System Interface (PNSI).

6.2.3.5.1 - Prior Notice Reception

Prior notice for food articles subject to the rule must be received and confirmed electronically by FDA no more than 5 days before arrival and, as specified by the mode of transportation below, no fewer than:

1. 2 hours before arrival by land by road

2. 4 hours before arrival by air or by land by rail

3. 8 hours before arrival by water

In addition, prior notice must be received and confirmed electronically by FDA before food is mailed by international mail. (The parcel must be accompanied by confirmation of FDA receipt of prior notice.)

6.2.3.5.2 - Products Requiring Prior Notice

Prior notice applies to food for humans and other animals that is imported or offered for import into the United States. For purposes of prior notice requirements, "food" is defined by reference to section 201(f) of the Federal Food, Drug, and Cosmetic Act. Section 201(f) defines "food" as articles used for food or drink for man or other animals, chewing gum, and articles used for components of any such articles.

Examples of "food" include:

1. Dietary supplements and dietary ingredients

2. Infant formula

3. Beverages (including alcoholic beverages and bottled water)

4. Fruits and vegetables

5. Fish and seafood

6. Dairy products and shell eggs

7. Raw agricultural commodities for use as food or components of food

8. Canned and frozen foods

9. Bakery goods, snack food, and candy (including chewing gum)

10. Live food animals

11. Animal feeds and pet food

6.2.3.5.3 - Products Excluded from Prior Notice

Foods that are excluded from the prior notice requirement are:

1. Food carried by or otherwise accompanying an individual arriving in the United States for that individual's personal use (i.e., for consumption by themselves, family, or friends, and not for sale or other distribution);

2. Food that is exported without leaving the port of arrival until export;

3. Meat food products, poultry products and egg products that are subject to the exclusive jurisdiction of the U.S. Department of Agriculture (USDA) under the Federal Meat Inspection Act, the Poultry Products Inspection Act, or the Egg Products Inspection Act;

4. Food that was made by an individual in his/her personal residence and sent by that individual as a personal gift (i.e., for non-business reasons) to an individual in the United States; and

5. Food in diplomatic pouches.

6.2.3.5.4 - PRIOR NOTICE SUBMISSION

The prior notice must be submitted electronically and contain the following information in accordance with 21 CFR 1.281:

1. Identification of the submitter, including name, telephone and fax numbers, email address, and firm name and address

2. Identification of the transmitter (if different from the submitter), including name, telephone and fax numbers, email address, and firm name and address

3. Entry type and CBP identifier

4. The identification of the article of food, including complete FDA product code, the common or usual name or market name, the estimated quantity described from the smallest package size to the largest container, and the lot or code numbers or other identifier (if applicable)

Imports

5. If the food is no longer in its natural state (21 CFR 1.276(b)(8)), the manufacturer's name and address, and registration number, if applicable

6. If the food is in its natural state, the name of grower, if known, and growing location

7. The FDA Country of Production

8. The identification of the shipper (or sender's if the food is mailed), including the registration number if applicable

9. The country from which the article of food is shipped or, if the food is imported by international mail, the anticipated date of mailing and country from which the food is mailed

10. The anticipated arrival information (location, date, and time) or, if the food is imported by international mail, the U.S. recipient (name and address)

11. The identification of the importer, owner, and ultimate consignee, except for food imported by international mail or transshipped through the United States

12. The identification of the carrier and mode of transportation, except for food imported by international mail

13. Planned shipment information, except for food imported by international mail

6.2.3.5.5 - Inadequate Prior Notice Submission

Food that is imported or offered for import with inadequate prior notice is subject to refusal and holding at the port or in secure storage. FDA provided guidance to its stakeholders and U.S. Customs and Border Protection staff on enforcing the prior notice requirements in a Compliance Policy Guide, Prior Notice of Imported Food Under the Public Health Security and Bioterrorism Preparedness and Response Act of 2002 at http://www.cfsan.fda.gov/~pn/cpgpn6.html. This guidance, however, does not affect FDA's ability to take actions that may be necessary, including conducting inspections for food safety and security concerns or taking any other action under the Federal Food, Drug, and Cosmetic Act. This policy will also not affect the ability of Customs to assess penalties under 19 U.S.C. 1595a(b) or to take enforcement action under any other authority.

6.2.3.5.6 - Prior Notice Process

This prior notice process begins with an automated screening process. If additional evaluation of the prior notice information is necessary, all review of prior notice information is performed by the Prior Notice Center (PNC); FDA headquarters staff, operating 24 hours a day, 7 days a week. The review process is a manual review by the PNC. It is designed to identify food products that may pose serious risks to public health so that appropriate action can be taken upon arrival in the United States. The review process is not impacted by the method of electronic submission. The results of this process will be transmitted to CBP.

The PNC reviews and assesses the prior notice information and may initiate an examination or other action by FDA or CBP of the article of food at the port of arrival or elsewhere, or in the case of rail shipments, within the confines of the closest appropriate examination site. The PNC will advise the FDA field offices and/or Customs of the inspection requirements. The PNC is also responsible for communication with submitters regarding the compliance of prior notice, the initiation of refusal due to inadequate prior notices, the response to requests for review of refusals, and the completion of the prior notice process.

In addition, the OASIS system review will determine if further staff evaluation of the article of food is necessary for admissibility determinations under section 801(a) of the FD&C Act (e.g., subject to the guidance in an import alert). If the food meets the prior notice requirements; the food will be subject to further review by FDA staff for determination of admissibility under section 801(a) of the FD&C Act.

This admissibility examination may take place at the border but may also take place at an examination site, a public warehouse, or other appropriate locations. If FDA determines that refusal under section 801(a) of the FD&C Act is appropriate, the appropriate admissibility procedures will be used.

6.2.3.6 - Entry Processing

FDA district offices generally receive notification of all formal and informal entries subject to FDA's jurisdiction at ports of entry located in its territory. However, through the use of Custom's Automated Commercial System and FDA's Operational and Administrative System for Import Support (ACS/OASIS) some electronic entries may be forwarded to off-site districts for processing during certain periods of time, i.e., late night coverage of air carrier hubs. The means of receiving notification for non-ABI/OASIS entries can be arranged through local Customs/FDA District agreements.

The most satisfactory and efficient means of getting notification is through FDA's OASIS system. Electronic entries processed through this system are electronically screened against criteria established by FDA for coverage. Automated Broker Interface (ABI) filers using the Customs ACS for cargo release are required to provide FDA information on entries subject to its jurisdiction submitted through ACS.

6.2.3.6.1 - U. S. CUSTOMS

Customs' ACS uses guides established by each Federal agency to identify which commodities are subject to their jurisdiction. These guides are known as Other Government Agency (OGA) flags. FDA flags are identified as FD0, FD1 and FD2. FD0 indicates the article, even though subject to FDA regulation, may be released without further presentation of entry information to FDA. For entries flagged FD1, the commodity may or may not be subject to FDA regulation. The filer may, based on information received from the importer regarding the intended use of the commodity, specify the entry is not subject to FDA regulation and "Disclaim" the entry. Otherwise, FDA required information must be submitted. FDA review of "Disclaimed" entries is performed periodically to confirm the accuracy of the declaration. Entries covered by an FD2 flag must include FDA required information.

Electronic entries for Customs review includes all mandatory Customs entry required information, i.e., entry number, entry date, importer identification, port of entry, vessel/voyage information, filer identification, Harmonized Tariff System (HTS) code for product description, information on foreign shipper, country of origin, etc. Through the screening process in ACS, Customs determines if the article is subject to FDA examination (see OGA flag identifications above).

6.2.3.6.2 - FDA

FDA's electronic screening of the Customs ABI/ACS entry requires the filer to provide the following information.

1. FDA product code. (FDA's product code is not the same as the HTS codes used for Customs screening purposes.)

2. The "Manufacturer's Identification" (MID) code (a Customs designation) of the foreign manufacturer. The MID consists, at a minimum, of the 2 letter identification of the foreign country, the name of the foreign firm, generally made up of the first three letters of the first and second names of the firm, where applicable. Up to 4 numbers, if present in the address, and the first three letters of the city where the firm is located. This code is subsequently transmitted to FDA's screen as the un-coded identified firm.

3. The MID information of the foreign shipper, including city and country. (Which may or may not be the same as the foreign manufacturer.) and

4. The country of origin. (Which may be different from the country of origin identified for Customs purposes.)

FDA has also established Affirmation of Compliance (A of C) codes which are designed to provide FDA reviewers with information concerning the imported article (example: medical device listing number). Use of the A of C is voluntary, and may or may not provide for a more expeditious screening of the entry.

In OASIS, the FDA forms identified as: "Notice of Sampling," "Release Notice," "Notice of Detention and Hearing," and "Notice of Refusal of Admission," are no longer issued as specific forms. OASIS generates a "Notice of FDA Action" providing information on the actions taken regarding a particular entry line. The notice identifies the specific line(s) of the entry, where appropriate, with the description of the sample collected or intended for sampling, specific line(s) identified as detained, and/or the specific line(s) identified as released, refused, etc. As the status changes for a particular line, a new "Notice of FDA Action" is issued to advise the appropriate individuals of the changes. The use of the designation "Product Collected by FDA," "Detained," "Released," "Refused," etc., or similar wording on the "Notice of FDA Action," meet the requirements of the wording of the law and regulation when applied to "giving notice thereof to the owner or consignee." See Exhibit 6-1.

OASIS notices are designed to be mailed to the addressees. A copy of each notice is produced with the filer, importer of record, and consignee on the addressee line. (If the same firm acts in one or more of those functions, only one copy is produced for the firm.) Notices are official documents which provide FDA decisions on entries. The distribution of the notices is made by FDA, not the filer, to ensure proper notification to the parties involved (i.e., FAX, express pick-up services, postal service, etc.). The intention is for FDA to distribute to the responsible firm without an intermediary.

6.2.4 - Sampling

6.2.4.1 - Ports Covered by FDA

For electronic entry submissions, if the filer receives a message indicating FDA review, the filer will provide appropriate entry information to the FDA office having jurisdiction over the port of entry. For those entries submitted by paper, all appropriate entry documents should be included with the package sent to the local FDA office.

After evaluating the entry, if FDA decides to collect a sample, the appropriate individuals/firms will be provided with a Notice for Sampling and advised:

1. If the entry is to be held intact for FDA examination or sampling;

2. Only those designated items need be held; etc.

6.2.4.2 - Ports not Covered by FDA

For those ports where Customs does not maintain its ACS electronic entry process, and FDA does not generally cover the port under its normal operating schedule, the responsible FDA district office will coordinate coverage with the responsible Customs Port manager to assure FDA notification. If FDA decides to examine or sample articles being entered through such a port, Customs, the importer, and broker will notified.

Generally, for these entries, examination and/or sampling can take place at the point of destination. Under certain conditions, however, FDA may ask Customs to collect a sample at the point of entry for forwarding to the FDA servicing laboratory. Appropriate information on the entry, sample requirement, and requirements for holding the entry will be provided to the Customs officials and importer by the responsible district.

6.2.4.3 - Entry Sampling

If no examination or sample is requested, FDA will notify Customs and the filer (who is responsible for notifying the importer, or other designated parties). This electronic notification is called a "May Proceed Notice," and indicates the shipment may proceed without further FDA examination. In the ACS/OASIS process, this may occur as a result of the initial FDA/OASIS screening, or after the district performs an "On-Screen-Review". (NOTE: Since the article is allowed entry without FDA examination, should the article, at a later time, be found in violation of the law, the Agency is not prevented from taking legal action because the article was allowed admission by FDA without examination at the time of importation. (See section 304(d) of the FD&C Act [21 USC 334(d)]).

If an examination or sample is requested, FDA notifies Customs, broker or filer, importer, or other designated parties, either through the electronic entry system or other form of notification, (Notice of FDA Action) to hold the entry, and will identify the specific product(s) to be sampled, etc.

6.2.4.4 - Notice of Sampling

When a sample is collected by FDA, a Notice of FDA Action is issued to the importer of record, consignee, and filer. If Customs collects the sample for FDA, the district will enter the entry information into OASIS and issue the Notice of FDA Action.

For those entries where specific lines (items) of an entry are not sampled or examined, the Notice of FDA Action will be amended to indicate which lines (items) "May Proceed." (See RPM Chapter 9-19 "Notice of Sampling" for detailed guidance.)

6.2.4.5 - Payment for Samples

The FDA will pay for all physical samples found in compliance or collected as an audit of private laboratory reports of analysis submitted to FDA in response to detention (See 21 CFR 1.91). (NOTE: This does not apply in the case of an audit sample collected to document reconditioning). See IOM 4.2.8.2 for guidance on sample costs.

Billing for reimbursement should be made to the FDA district office in whose territory the shipment was offered for import. FDA will not pay for a sample if the article is

initially found to be in violation, even though it is subsequently released. For this reason, do not pay for samples at the time of collection.

Samples taken in connection with the supervision of a reconditioning are not paid for by FDA.

6.2.5 - Procedure when Products Cannot be Sampled or Examined

If the entry is still under control of the district inspection operations, and the sample collection can not be completed, the district may annotate the notice to the filer and importer no product was collected, and return the entry to the flier designating the entry "May Proceed." If the designated product was part of a multi-line entry where other products were collected, the notice issued for the other items sampled will be appropriately updated with the release of the product not sampled.

In the OASIS system, when a notice is issued for the collection or examination of a product, and neither operation is accomplished, the filer will be advised through a revised Notice indicating the article is given a "May Proceed" status. The system will print a status of "May Proceeded" in the Line Summary and also print a detail section "Lines Which May Proceed."

In OASIS, the following are definitions used to describe "May Proceed" or "Release" actions:

May Proceed: "Product may proceed without FDA examination. FDA has made no determination the product complies with all provisions of the Food,

Drug, and Cosmetic Act, or other related acts. This message does not preclude action should the products later be found violative." (No compliance decision has been made.)

Release: "The product is released after FDA examination. This message does not constitute assurance the product complies with all provisions of the Food, Drug and Cosmetic Act, or other related Acts, and does not preclude action should the product later be found violative." (A compliance decision has been made.)

Districts will follow the appropriate guidance under each of the above procedures, according to their import operations.

6.2.6 - Procedure when No Violation is Found

If the shipment is found in compliance after examination, the importer of record, consignee (where applicable), filer, and Customs are notified with a Notice of Release. The shipment may be admitted. (See RPM Chapter 9-5 "Release Notices" for detailed guidance).

6.2.7 - Procedure when Violation is Found

6.2.7.1 - "Notice of Detention & Hearing"

If examination of the sample or other evidence indicates the article appears to be in violation, and detention is the course of action chosen by the district, the filer, owner and consignee, where applicable, are advised of such action by "Notice of Detention and Hearing." The Notice will specify the nature of the violation charged and designate a site for the owner or consignee (or authorized representative) to appear at a hearing. These hearings are informal meetings with the district, designed to provide the respondents an opportunity to present evidence supporting admissibility of the article. Ordinarily the respondents are allowed 10 working days to appear. However, if for some compelling reason the district determines ten (10) working days are insufficient, this time period may be extended. On the OASIS generated "Notice of FDA Action", this date is identified under the caption "Respond By". A copy of this Notice is also sent to Customs. (See RPM Chapter 9-7 "Notice of Detention and Hearing".)

6.2.7.2 - Response to "Notice of Detention & Hearing"

Response to the Notice of Detention and Hearing may be made personally, by representative or by mail. The importer may present evidence supporting the admissibility of the article, request refusal of admission, propose an effective manner of reconditioning, or a method to remove the product from the authority of the Act.

6.2.7.3 - Request for Authorization to Relabel or Perform Other Acts

FDA may authorize relabeling or other remedial action upon the timely submission of an "Application for Authorization to Relabel or To Perform Other Action," (FD Form 766 - See Exhibit 6-2). This form is also available in fillable formats online at http://www.fda.gov/opacom/more choices/fdaforms/FDA-766.pdf.

Application may also be made by letter and the execution of a good and sufficient bond by the owner or consignee (See section 801(b) of the FD&C Act [21 U.S.C. 381(b)]). The redelivery bond on file with the District Director of Customs for the particular importation applies to any re-labeling or other action authorized, and a new bond will not have to be filed.

After review of the application, FDA will notify the importer of its approval or disapproval. If approved the original application will be returned outlining the conditions to be fulfilled and the time limit within which to fulfill them will be noted. Notification to other parties will be made where appropriate. A copy will be retained in the district files. (See RPM Chapter 9-8 "Response (Hearing) to Notice of Detention and Hearing", and RPM Chapter 9-10 "Reconditioning" for detailed guidance).

6.2.7.4 - Inspection after Completion of Authorization to Bring Article into Compliance

After the re-labeling or reconditioning operation has been completed, the applicant will submit the "Importer's Certificate" (the reverse side of Form FDA 766, Exhibit 6-2) or advise the district reconditioning is complete. At this point, FDA may conduct a follow-up inspection and/or sampling to determine compliance with the terms of the authorization, or it may accept the statement from the importer with no further follow-up. The follow-up inspection and/or sampling may be made by FDA or Customs, depending on agreements between the district and the local Customs. The "Report of Inspector" (reverse side of FDA 766, Exhibit 6-2), or other appropriately completed summary of reconditioning, should be forwarded to the appropriate FDA office.

6.2.7.5 - Procedure when Conditions of Authorization Have Been Fulfilled

If the conditions of the authorization have been fulfilled, the district will notify the owner or consignee by Notice of Release. This notice is usually identified as "Originally Detained and Now Released." A copy is also sent to Customs and filer. Where there is a non-admissible portion (rejects), they must be destroyed or re-exported under FDA or Customs supervision. A Notice of Refusal of Admission should be issued for the rejected portion. FDA may include in its approval of the reconditioning a provision for the non-admissible portions (rejects) of the reconditioning to be destroyed and not exported.

6.2.7.6 - Procedure when Conditions of Reconditioning Have Not Been Fulfilled

If the initial attempt at reconditioning is unsuccessful, a second attempt should not be considered unless a revised method of restoration shows reasonable assurance of success.

If the conditions of the authorization have not been fulfilled, a "Notice of Refusal of Admission" is issued to the importer, consignee, where applicable, to the filer, and to Customs.

6.2.7.7 - Procedure after Hearing - "Notice of Release"

If, after presentation of testimony, the district determines the article should be released, the importer of record and consignee are issued a "Notice of Release". The Notice will declare the detained goods may be admitted. The Notice will also be identified "Originally Detained and Now Released" and, where appropriate, explain the reason for the change of action. A copy of the Notice is sent to Customs, and all parties receiving the Notice of Sampling/Notice of Detention. (See RPM Chapter 9-5 "Release Notices" for detailed guidance.)

6.2.7.8 - Procedure after Hearing - "Refusal of Admission"

When the importer requests the district issue a notice of refusal of admission, or the district decides the shipment still appears to be in violation, the importer, owner, and consignee where applicable, are issued a "Notice of Refusal of Admission." On this Notice, the charge(s) is stated exactly as shown on the original (or amended) Notice of Detention and Hearing. A copy of the Notice is also sent to Customs. (See RPM Chapter 9-9 "Notice of Refusal of Admission" for detailed guidance.)

The Notice of Refusal provides for the exportation or destruction of the shipment, under Customs supervision, within 90 days of the date of the notice, or within such additional time as specified by Customs Regulation. Under OASIS, the Notice will also contain language which includes reference to the requirement for redelivery, and contain all the above required information concerning the product and charge(s). The FDA file remains open until the district receives notification indicating the merchandise was either destroyed or exported.

FDA is responsible for the protection of the U.S. public regarding foods, drugs, cosmetics, etc. until the violative article is either destroyed or exported.

6.2.7.9 - Payment of Costs of Supervision of Relabeling and/or Other Action

After completion of the authorized relabeling or other action, FDA will submit a detailed statement of expenses incurred, including travel, per diem or subsistence, and supervisory charges, on an FDA 790 (See Exhibit 6-3, Charges for Supervision) of officers of employees of the FDA regarding the supervision of the authorized relabeling or other action to Customs National Finance Center. The expenses shall be computed on the following basis:

1. Inspector's time
2. Analyst's time
3. Per diem allowance
4. Travel other than by auto - actual cost of such travel
5. Travel by auto (mileage, toll fees, etc.)
6. Administrative support

Future enhancements to FDA import system may result in electronic processing of the supervisory charges submitted to Customs, in which case the FDA 790 will no longer be used. (See RPM Chapter 9-11 "Supervisory Charges" for detailed guidance.)

Customs, upon receipt of the charges for supervision, will send a notice for payment to the identified importer of record. The expenses shall include charges of supervision of destruction of the article or rejects. The remittance by the owner or consignee shall be to Customs. Payment of supervisory charges should not be accepted by FDA district offices.

6.2.7.10 - Exportation of Merchandise Refused Admission

Exportation of refused merchandise is done under Customs supervision. However, if after a reasonable time, FDA has not received notification of exportation or destruction, the district should investigate the status of disposition. Districts should also consider, under certain conditions, verifying the refused goods have been held intact pending exportation or destruction, or that re-export actually occurred. Guidance on refusals to be verified may change, based on the reason for detention.

6.2.7.11 - Bond Action

Under the provisions of the FD&C Act (section 801(b) of the FD&C Act [21 U.S.C. 381(b)]) and Customs regulations (19 CFR 113.62) a bond is required for all conditionally released articles offered for importation. This bond provides relief to the government on the default of the conditions of the bond and the payment of liquidated damages in the amount specified in Customs notice of assessment of liquidated damages for failure to redeliver such merchandise.

Bond actions are taken when an entry is distributed prior to FDA release and can not be redelivered, or when an article has been detained and refused and the article is not destroyed or exported in accordance with the requirements of the law.

If district has evidence the entry, or any portion of an entry subject to FDA jurisdiction, was disposed of in violation of the terms of the appropriate Act, or its regulations, or of the terms of the bond, (see 19 CFR Section 113.62(l)(1)) they should immediately contact the appropriate Customs office.

The district, upon receiving evidence the refused article was not exported or destroyed should immediately investigate the matter. Send a detailed statement showing the importer's liability under the redelivery bond or other applicable customs bond to the responsible Customs office. If the facts warrant, and the article was under detention, and the Notice of Refusal of Admission has not been issued, immediately issue a Notice of Refusal to the owner or consignee, with a copy to Customs.

Upon the receipt of an application for relief (appeal for Mitigation or Cancellation of Assessed Liquidated Damages) Customs may agree to mitigate the amount of damages. However, in cases involving FDA merchandise, Customs does not usually mitigate unless FDA is in full agreement with the action [see 21 CFR section 1.97(b)]. (See RPM Chapter 9-12 "Bond Actions" for detailed guidance.)

6.3 - Review of Records

6.3.1 - General

"Records review" is the initial examination provided the importer's documentation (including any electronic entry filing information.) Also, see IOM 5.4.1.4 for Food and Cosmetics Defense Inspection Activities. This operation is performed on every entry of regulated product to determine if additional action, such as sampling, is necessary. (Review of electronic filings follows the same decision-making criteria applied to hard-copy entry filings.) At this point, one of four decisions is made:

1. Release the lot, or
2. Detain the lot, or
3. Examine the lot by Field Examination, or Sampling, or
4. Verify registration, listing, declarations, certifications, etc. where applicable.

The decision will be supported by:

1. Electronic screening on entry information,
2. Computerized information (FIARS, local/regional data systems),
3. Import Alerts,
4. Monthly Refusals List,
5. Past history,
6. Compliance Program Guidance Manual,
7. Assignments, and
8. Local assignments and programs (e.g., Regional Pesticide Sampling Plan).

See Regulatory Procedure Manual (RPM) Chapter 9 for additional guidance concerning the review/processing of entries of specific types of commodities, including products under detention without physical examination.

Record reviews are reported into PODS as Entry Reviews.

6.4 - Field Examination

6.4.1 - General

A field examination is simply an on-the-spot examination or field test performed on a product to support a specific decision. It may be conducted on products discharged from vessels on to the wharves (piers), pier sheds, and other locations; products in trucks, trains, freezers, and containers, etc., at border entry points; or on products set aside for FDA examination. Some compliance program guidance manuals do not address field examinations. Nevertheless, field examinations are appropriate for certain problems and/or commodities and should be conducted.

A field examination involves actual physical examination of the product for such things as storage or intransit damage, inadequate refrigeration, rodent or insect activity, lead in dinnerware (Quick Color Test - QCT), odor and label compliance

A field examination does not have the same level of confidence as a laboratory examination. Consequently, more rigorous standards of acceptance are applied than those used for formal regulatory levels. For example, if the formal action guideline for whole insects is 10 per 100 gm in product X, you may sample product X when your field examination shows only one or two insects per 100 gm. The decision to sample is, to some degree, left to your discretion. In most instances, it should be based on findings significantly lower than specified by the formal guideline.

A field examination begins when the physical examination is started. Do not include, as reported Field Examination time, the time to locate the lot or travel time. Time spent in locating the lot is reported as import investigation.

See IOM 5.1.4.3 for suggestions on what to do when conducting a field examination and the firm responsible for the products invites individuals who are not directly employed by the firm to observe the examination.

6.4.2 - Field Examination Schedule

A Field Examination should include a physical examination of a minimum of five containers (cases, cans, bags, etc.) of a product, or as directed by Compliance Program Guidance Manuals, specific product examination schedules (e.g., LACF), or other guidance.

When you conduct any field examination of a product's label or labeling, in addition to the specific items discussed in the following sections, be alert for any overlabeling where a product name or identify may have been changed; products without mandatory English labeling; changes in expiration date or lot numbers or similar questionable practices. If you encounter any of these items, collect an example and discuss the appropriate action with your supervisor.

6.4.3 - Field Examinations - Foods

See IOM 5.4.1.4.2 for guidance on performing reconciliation examinations during import field examinations.

6.4.3.1 - Food Sanitation

Microbiological - field examinations can not be used for suspected microbiological contamination.

Filth and Foreign Objects - field examine only those product/container combinations in which you can physically view and examine the product, e.g., products which can be probed, products in see-through containers, etc. See 5.1.5, et al for some specific guidance on performing field examinations.

Low acid and other Canned Foods - See IOM SAMPLE SCHEDULE CHART 2.

Decomposition in Non-sealed Foods - This can include organoleptic examination for fish, seafood, frozen eggs, etc.

6.4.3.2 - Pesticides, Industrial Chemicals, Aflatoxins, " Toxic Elements

Field examinations can not be performed for most of these materials, except for metals in dinnerware and the side -seam solders of cans.

NOTE: *Districts should use commercial versions of the Quick Color Test (QCT) and the Rapid Abrasion Test for lead, e.g. Lead Check Swabs, for the field examination of dinnerware and food cans to determine if follow-up sampling is required. The testing scheme for dinnerware can be found in CPGM 7304.019B. Specific information regarding the techniques of testing dinnerware and can side-seam solder can be found in Lab Information Bulletin (LIB) 4127 and LIB 4041, respectively on the DFS intranet site.*

6.4.3.3 - Food and Color Additives

Perform a visual examination of the container and a label review for the mandatory labeling requirements."nbsp; For example, determine if a color additive is declared for a product which appears coloring has been added. Determine if a preservative declaration includes its function; for example, "Sodium Benzoate as a preservative."

The use of a color additive must conform with the requirements stated in the color additive's listing regulation. These requirements are outlined in the "Color Additive Status List" and the "Summary of Color Additives Listed for Use in the United States in Food, Drugs, Cosmetics, and Medical Devices." These lists provide the current status and use limitations of color additives permitted in food, drug, cosmetic, and medical device products.

Requirements for declaring color additives on food labels are given in 21 CFR 101.22(k)."nbsp; Color additives subject to certification may be declared by the names listed in 21 CFR parts 74 and 82 or by abbreviated names that omit "FD"C" and "No." The term "Lake" must be included in the names of color additive lakes. FD"C Yellow No. 5 is specifically required to be declared on food labels under 21 CFR 101.22(k) and 21 CFR 74.705. Color additives not subject to certification may be declared by the names listed in 21 CFR part 73 or in general terms such as "Artificial Color," "Artificial Color Added," or "Color Added."

NOTE: *Label examinations of products to determine whether there is a declaration of certain food and/or color additives are reported as import investigations.*

6.4.3.4 - Nutrition and Food Allergen Labeling and Consumer Protection Act (FALCPA)

The only valid field examination which can be performed for this type of problem is a label examination for the mandatory labeling requirements. See the "Guide to Nutritional Labeling and Education Act (NLEA) Requirements" document. Also"nbsp;see the Office of Nutrition, Labeling and Dietary

Supplements, ONLDS, website (http://www.cfsan.fda.gov/~dms/lab-hlth.html) for the most up-to-date information regarding claims in labeling. Also, see CPGM 7321.005 to determine enforcement priorities for food labeling violations.

6.4.3.5 - Food Economics (On Consumer Size Containers only)

Label Examination - Review labels for all aspects of the labeling requirements.

Net weight - See IOM 4.3.8.1

Food Standards - The only valid field examination which can be performed for Food Standards is a label examination for the mandatory labeling requirements of a particular Food Standard.

NOTE: *Label examinations of products to determine if the labeling meets the mandatory labeling requirements for a particular Food Standard must be reported as an Import Investigation.*

6.4.3.6 - Cosmetics

Valid cosmetic field examinations include a reconciliation examination for security purposes and/or a label examination for the mandatory labeling requirements. The most important labeling considerations are:

1. Ingredient Labeling (21 CFR 701.3),
2. Prohibited ingredients (21 CFR 700.11 through 700.27 and 250.250),
3. Non-permitted color additives"nbsp; (see Color Additives Status Lists at http://www.cfsan.fda.gov/~dms/opa-appa.html#col),
4. Warning Statements (21 CFR 740.11, 740.12, 740.17, and 740.19),
5. Cautionary/Other Required Statements (Coal tar hair dyes not displaying the caution statement can be considered adulterated - FD"C Act sec. 601(a), caution statement for the color additive lead acetate -"nbsp;21 CFR 73.2396, required label information for the color additive bismuth citrate - 73.2110, and required label information for the color additive henna - 73.2190)
6. Tamper Resistant Packaging Requirements (21 CFR 700.25)

For further questions contact the Office of Cosmetics and Colors, (301) 436-1130.

NOTE: *Label examinations of products to determine whether their labeling declares certain ingredients must be reported as an Import Investigation.*

6.4.4 - Field Examination - Drugs

When you conduct field examinations of drugs (bulk drugs and finished dosage forms) ensure you check:

1. Labeling compliance (e.g., Reye Syndrome warning)

2. Probable contamination

3. Tamper Resistant Packaging Requirements

6.4.4.1 - Labeling

Bulk drugs and finished dosage forms should be evaluated for compliance with the Drug Listing Act, 21 CFR 207.40. Refer to the Drug Listing Compliance Program Guidance Manual.

6.4.4.2 - Contamination

Drugs should be examined for container integrity, e.g.: cracked vials, ampoules, bottles, etc.

6.4.4.3 - Samples

A decision to collect samples for Drug Listing Act compliance evaluation should be made in accordance with the drug listing CPGM. The nature of samples to be taken from lots where the drug substance or finished product has been subjected to actual or suspected contamination, should be decided on a case-by-case basis.

6.4.4.4 - Special Instructions

Field examinations may be made of drug lots to obtain information in determining the new drug status of a given shipment. Districts should contact the Division of New Drugs and Labeling Compliance, Import/Export International Drug Team, (HFD-319) for guidance.

6.4.5 - Field Examinations - Devices

Medical device field exams include electrode lead wires, patient cables, labeling, and physical damage. Lead wires and patient cable exams should conform to applicable standards set forth in 21CFR Part 898.

6.4.6 - Field Examinations - Biologics

Review RPM Chapter 9-3 "Importation of Biologics" and the Import Alert regarding biologics prior to conducting any field examinations of biological products.

In general, products controlled by Center for Biologics Evaluation and Research (CBER) do not require field examination, because they are licensed under Section 351 of the PHS Act. In addition, lot release procedures pursuant to 21 CFR 610.2 apply to many products, such as vaccines.

Products imported under IND Applications are also monitored, but due to the small volumes involved, no specific guidance is necessary.

Shipments of biologics which are not licensed, or are not directly related to an active IND should be examined for:

1. Labeling

2. Consignee

3. Manufacturer

4. Intended use

Contact CBER/OC/Division of Case Management (HFM-610) for guidance.

6.4.7 - Field Examinations - Veterinary Products

Contact the CVM Division of Compliance (HFV-230), the Enforcement and Regulatory Policy Team, with general questions on the importation of veterinary products. You should be aware of various Import Alerts, Compliance Policy Guides or Guidance Documents as they affect individual import situations. See the CVM website for additional information or notifications on current import situations

6.4.7.1 - Drugs

Field examinations of veterinary drugs are visual examinations to determine potential misbranding or adulteration. This may include examination for:

1. Container Integrity

2. Labeling Compliance

3. Product adulteration

Dosage form drugs must be examined to determine if they are new animal drugs. If the products are new animal drugs, you need to determine if an approved NADA/ANADA exists or if there is a valid INAD exemption in place. You should consult with CVM's Division of Compliance (HFV-230) regarding the status of imported veterinary products (240-276-9200).

Bulk New Animal Drug substances and Active Pharmaceutical Ingredients (APIs) may be legally imported only if destined to the holder of an approved NADA or INAD exemption. You will need to consult with the Center for the status of particular drugs.

Entries of prescription animal drugs for use by the consumers (laymen) must be examined for labeling content, consignee (name and address) and to determine if a valid prescription/order exists from an appropriately licensed veterinarian. The Center (240-276-9200) should have records of any exemptions or permission granted for personal imports.

6.4.7.2 - Devices

Devices intended for animal do not require premarket approval. However, they are still subject to examinations for misbranding violations. Animal devices must bear adequate directions for use and label claims must not be false or misleading. You should consult with CVM for guidance (240-276-9200).

6.4.7.3 - Animal Feed

Animal feeds and feed components, including pet foods should be examined for conformance with all applicable and appropriate food labeling requirements, drug claims, food additive violations and use of banned or objectionable ingredients as well as filth and foreign objects. You should consult with CVM on individual issues and to determine specific requirements (240-276-9200).

6.4.7.4 - Animal Grooming Aids

'Cosmetics' for animals are referred to as "animal grooming aids". While the Center does not actively pursue enforcement actions with animal grooming aids, the products are expected to be safe, effective and properly labeled. The labels and labeling of any incoming animal grooming aids are subject to examination and review for potential instances of misbranding. Consult with the Center for appropriate guidance. The Division of Compliance (240-276-9200) can answer regulatory and enforcement questions.

6.4.7.5 - Biologicals

CVM does regulate animal biologic products. They are considered as drugs. However, the Center does not regulate animal vaccines. The vaccines are regulated by USDA/APHIS.

6.4.8 - Field Examinations Radiological Health

Field Examinations for imported electronic products consist of reviewing the Entry Documents and FDA-2877, Declaration for Products Subject to Radiation Control Standards, to determine if they are properly completed and accurate. This applies to each shipment of electronic products for which performance standards exist. Performance standards, covering ionizing, optical, microwave and acoustic radiation-emitting products, are specified in 21 CFR 1020 through 1050.

For electronic products, physical samples may only be collected on specific assignment. DTR/DER recommendations are to be submitted when the Field Examination indicates the product may not be in compliance and detention is recommended.

Import coverage for radiation emitting products is provided for in a CDRH Compliance Program Guidance Manual. Do not collect physical samples except on specific assignment, or with concurrence of CDRH.

6.5 - Import Sample Collection

6.5.1 - General

In general, the difference between Official Domestic and Import Samples is that import samples do not require official seals or collection of a 702(b) reserve portion. However, these are district options. See Chapter 4 for sampling instructions and guidelines. There will be instances when the collection of a reserve portion and an official seal is warranted, i.e., when enforcement action (e.g., seizure, injunction, prosecution) is contemplated. Many sample sizes are provided in the Sample Schedule Section (Chapter

4). When using the sample sizes furnished elsewhere in this manual, do not collect the duplicate portion of the sample unless directed by your district. In addition, when preparing to collect import samples, you should be aware of your personal safety. Refer to IOM 5.2.1.2.

FDA does not pay for import samples at the time of collection. The Importer should be told to bill the responsible district. FDA will not pay for violative import samples, per 21 CFR Part 1.91 See IOM 6.2.4.5.

When collecting IMPORT "ADDITIONAL Samples", the original Import C.R. Number should be used. Under OASIS, this will be the entry number with appropriate line information, etc.

Import Samples are compliance samples, except for those collected for pesticide analysis. These MUST BE FLAGGED either "Pesticide Surveillance" or "Pesticide Compliance" depending on the basis for sampling. See IOM Sample Schedule Chart 3 (Chapter 4) for guidance.

6.5.2 - Procedures

Review the submitted entry (electronic or hard copy documentation) to assure the location of the product(s) is known and the lots are available for FDA examination/ sampling before initiating action. The general description of the shipment in the entry documentation submitted to FDA should match the description of the product(s) in the invoice from the broker.

6.5.3 - Techniques

Follow guidance furnished in IOM Subchapter 4.3 - Collection Technique.

6.5.4 - Import Forms Procedures

Because forms are now generated electronically by OASIS, individuals performing field examination or sample collections should follow guidance provided in the OASIS Training Manual, or consult their lead OASIS personnel.

6.5.5 - Sample Collection Reports

See IOM 1.1 English language requirement. For every sample collected, a corresponding electronic collection report must be completed in OASIS. (See IOM Exhibit 6-4.) You are responsible for making sure the date collected, quantity collected, unit of weight, and description of text fields are completed accurately. The following are instructions for completing an OASIS Collection Report:

1. Highlight the line sampled in your available work personal in box in OASIS or self assign the sample request.

2. Prior to entering any data, double check all entered data for accuracy.

3. Double click the work type, i.e. "SAM" and click the "line Details" button. The line details screen is the only place you can make corrections to the entered data.

4. Verify all data is correct, i.e., product code matches actual product, manufacturer, country of origin, quantity and value are correct. If there is a build button on the line you need to correct, you must use the build function to make corrections. Once data has been changed, click on save button; enter brief description in pop up box of corrections made.

5. Click on "Rescreen" in the Application Tool bar to see if changing any data caused the line to hit on any other criteria or alerts.

6. Highlight the line sampled and click on "Wk Detail" in the Application Toolbar.

7. Click to highlight the appropriate PAFs in the bottom area of the screen. If you are sending the sample to more than one laboratory, highlight the PAF for each laboratory individually and complete a separate collection report for each lab.

8. Click "Work Result" button near the top right of the screen.

OASIS completes the following fields for you. Entry number, Investigator initials, Date Collected, Product Code, Product Code Description, Importers Corrected Description, Location of Goods, default laboratory in Submitted To and the FACTS Lab Number. The Date Collected, Location Of Goods and Submitted To fields can be corrected on this screen.

Enter data in the following fields:

6.5.5.1 - Collection Date

Collection Date: Make sure the date reflects the date the sample was actually collected, not the date you are entering the sample in OASIS.

6.5.5.2 - Episode

An "episode" is defined as a violative pesticide (or other chemical contaminant) finding and all samples collected in follow-up to that finding. All samples must be associated with one responsible firm (grower, pesticide applicator, etc.) and one specific time period (e.g. growing season). For example, samples of cantaloupes from Mexico reveal violative residues. Any destination point samples or subsequent compliance samples from the same shipper or grower would along with the original sample be considered an episode. Enter the episode number.

6.5.5.3 - Submitted To

Select the appropriate lab from the pull-down menu. The default will be your district servicing laboratory for the type of analysis. It can be changed if necessary.

6.5.5.4 - Quantity Collected

Enter the number of sampled units you collected.

6.5.5.5 - Units

Select the appropriate units from the pull-down menu. If the appropriate unit does not appear on the menu, go back to the line detail screen and correct the units before you complete the collection report. Note: at this point a new lab number will be assigned when you return to your collection report screen.

6.5.5.6 - DescText

Enter a description of the sample. Be guided by your District policy on how you enter the description. Any text you enter in this field will be printed on the Notice of FDA Action. Describe how you collected the sample. Relate the number and size of the sampled units to show how each was taken and note any special sampling techniques used.

6.5.5.7 - Hand Ship

This field does not transfer to FACTS for the laboratory to view. If special handling instructions are needed, enter them in Remarks. Enter the method of shipping, collecting district, country of origin, collector's name and phone number.

6.5.5.8 - Remarks

Enter any information your District, Laboratory, or the compliance program requires. Make sure you review the entire screen before you click "OK". The sample will be transferred immediately in FACTS to the respective lab once the OK button is clicked. (Unless your supervisor has set up a supervisory review of your work)

6.5.5.9 - Record Time Screen

The Record Time Screen will appear. Enter your time. If more than one person worked on the sample, click on "add" button to the right. A box will come up; enter the person's initials and the tab key. Highlight the person's name, click on OK. Enter other person's time. Repeat for each person that worked on the sample. Click on OK Note: time is entered in decimal format for OASIS.

6.6 - Filer Evaluations

6.6.1 - General

Since we now handle the majority of entries utilizing the OASIS system, evaluation of the data submitted by the electronic filers is done on a periodic basis. These audits of submitted data are done on a periodic basis depending on the number of entries, quality of the data and other factors. You should follow DIOP policy in the conduct of these evaluations.

6.7 - Glossary of Import Terms

Refer to the Regulatory Procedures Manual Chapter 11 "Glossary" for a more complete listing of import terms. Below is some common import language:

6.7.1 - American Goods Returned

Goods produced in the U.S. which are exported, and then returned to the U.S. They are considered imports. (See Sec. 801(d)(1)of the FD&C Act.[21 U.S.C. 381])

6.7.2 - Bonded Warehouse

One of several classes of Customs Warehouses authorized to receive merchandise that has not been entered into the commerce of the US. Merchandise is entered into a Customs Bonded Warehouse (CBW) by a "formal entry" or "warehouse entry" requiring complete documentation for the entry, and payment of a fee, but not payment of duty and taxes. Merchandise in the warehouse can be held for up to 5 years. After 5 years the merchandise must be entered, exported, or destroyed. Merchandise in a CWB can be manipulated, but except in certain smelting operations, cannot be manufactured into something else. If the CBW is located in the US, the merchandise is in interstate commerce and subject to the FD&C Act.

6.7.3 - Break-Bulk Cargo

Cargo transported in individual units, such as bags or cartons, which are not containerized.

6.7.4 - Consumption Entry (CE)

"Entered for Consumption" means an entry summary for consumption has been filed with CBP in proper form, with estimated duties attached. The duty can be submitted electronically at the same time as the entry is transmitted or on a 15 day schedule when approved by CBP.

6.7.5 - Container Freight Station (CFS)

Another location authorized to receive merchandise under Customs Bond for the purpose of breaking bulk and redelivery of cargo. Containerized cargo can be moved from the place of unlading to a designated container station, or may be received directly at the container station from a bonded carrier after transportation in-bond, before the filing of an entry of merchandise.

6.7.6 - Date Collected

The date an import sample is collected.

6.7.7 - Date of Arrival

The date a carrier transporting imported cargo arrives in the U.S.

6.7.8 - Date of Availability

The date imported cargo is available/accessible for sampling by FDA. Goods may not be available for sampling as soon as they arrive in the U.S., due to the way the items were shipped/stored.

6.7.9 - Detention

A temporary administrative action taken by FDA against articles offered for entry which are not or appears not to be in-compliance with the laws FDA administers. Detained articles can be released if brought into compliance, refused entry, or seized if not brought into compliance.

6.7.10 - Detention Without Physical Examination (DWPE)

An action directed against specific products manufactured or shipped by specific foreign firms. "Import Alerts" list products which may be detained without physical examination due to their violative history or potential.

6.7.11 - Domestic Import (DI) Sample

A sample of an imported article collected after it has been released from import status. See IOM 4.1.4.8.

6.7.12 - Entry

"Entry" means documentation required by CBP to be filed with the appropriate Customs Officer to secure the release of imported merchandise from CBP custody, or the act of filing the documentation.

6.7.13 - Entry Admissibility File

The file, hard copy and/or electronic, as appropriate, maintained by the District, which contains relevant documentation to support the District's admissibility decision.

6.7.14 - Entry Documents (Entry Package)

Information submitted to CBP to determine the merchandise quantity, its contents, and the parties of interest. Actual documentation for an individual entry can vary greatly, but it generally, consists of a CBP Form CF-3461, and an invoice. Entry documents can be submitted by paper, or through an electronic transmission in CBP's Automated Commercial System (ACS), or a combination of both.

6.7.15 - Failure To Hold

Failure to hold means that the goods have been distributed by the importer/consignee without an FDA release from import status. Such goods are usually subject to CBP's redelivery provisions. See IOM 6.7.31 - REDELIVERY BOND.

6.7.16 - Filer

A `CBP term used to identify the individual or firm responsible for filing an entry.

6.7.17 - Formal Entry

The entry type required for shipments valued over $2000 or for shipments containing specific commodities designated by CBP. Formal entry is usually a three-step process, "Entry" - which gains the release of the merchandise from CBP control, "Entry Summary" - which includes determination of the classification and collection of the duty/taxes owed, and "Liquidation" - which is the finalization of the entry process and the completion of an CBP changes to classification and monies owed.

6.7.18 - Foreign Trade Zones

Foreign Trade Zones are established under the Foreign Trade Zones Act. Merchandise properly admitted into an FTZ is considered outside the territory of the US for the purposed of duty and taxes. Several classes of merchandise are present in an FTZ at any one time. Some of these classes provide duty advantages when the merchandise is eventually entered into the commerce of the US. Other classes of merchandise are prohibited by law from entering the commerce and must be exported or destroyed. There is no time limit on how long merchandise can remain in a FTZ without entry or export. If the FTZ is located in the US, the merchandise is in interstate commerce and subject to the FD&C Act.

6.7.19 - Immediate Delivery (ID) / Conditional Release

Entry/Immediate Delivery (CF 3461) must be filed within 15 calendar days of arrival of merchandise in the U.S. Merchandise may be released for immediate delivery if it is arriving by land from Canada and Mexico. Products may be released for immediate delivery pending entry process completion. Even though CBP has allowed the immediate delivery, FDA regulated products are conditionally released until FDA makes an admissibility decision. The conditional release period ends when FDA May Proceeds the entry or issues a refusal.

6.7.20 - Import Alerts

Import Alerts are guidance documents concerning significant re-occurring, new or unusual problems affecting import coverage. They are available on the internet at www.fda.gov/ora/fiars/ora_import_alerts.html.

6.7.21 - Importer of Record

The party in whose name the entry is made. For example, a Customs House Broker might make an entry and become the "importer of record" by using his importer ID and bond on behalf of his client, the true "importer" of the merchandise. For FDA purposes, the "importer of record" is the person or company filing the redelivery bond under Sections 802(b) and 536(b) of the FD&C Act [21 U.S.C. 382(b) and 360mm(b)].

6.7.22 - Import Sections

Import Sections (536, 801 and 802) are those sections of the Federal Food, Drug, and Cosmetic Act containing the Import/Export Provisions

6.7.23 - Import Status

The standing of an article in the import system which is not yet released.

6.7.24 - IMPORTER MISDECLARATION

Importer misdeclaration refers to the importer's providing incorrect and/or incomplete information to FDA and CBP, usually via the filer. This may include incorrect product codes and/or product descriptions; incorrect/incomplete manufacturer/shipper name/address; incorrect quantity and value. May occur as an attempt to avoid FDA and/or CBP actions/regulations such as DWPE, sampling, duties, etc.

6.7.25 - Informal Entry

A simplified import entry procedure accepted at the option of CBP for any shipment not exceeding a specified value. Informal entries are filed with complete paperwork and any duties and taxes are paid at the time of filing. The entry liquidates at time of filing.

6.7.26 - Immediate Transportation (IT)

An entry document filed with Customs by the importer. It allows the immediate transport of merchandise without a determination of admissibility, from the port of unlading under Customs bond. In general, the importer must file a consumption entry within 6 months of the date of importation or export the merchandise. FDA typically examines this merchandise at inland port of entry.

6.7.27 - Line (Line Item)

Each portion of an entry which is listed as a separate item on an entry document. An importer may identify merchandise in an entry in as many portions as he chooses, except each item in the entry having a different tariff description and rate must be listed separately.

6.7.28 - Lot

An entry, group of entries, or a portion of an entry of merchandise which can clearly be defined as appropriate for FDA sampling and examination purposes.

6.7.29 - Marks

Words or symbols, usually including the country of origin, marked on cartons, bags, and other containers of imported merchandise for identification purposes. A Customs requirement.

6.7.30 - Port (Point) of Entry

The Customs location where the Consumption Entry is made. This may or may not be at the Port of Unloading (the point of physical entry into the U.S.)

6.7.31 - Redelivery Bond (AKA Entry Bond)

A bond posted by the importer of record with Customs. For FDA regulated products, this is currently in the amount of three times the value of the imported product, to insure redelivery of the product for examination, reconditioning, export, or destruction.

6.7.32 - Stripping (Of Containers)

The removal of articles from a transportation "Container" for examination or sampling.

6.7.33 - Substitution

Substitution is an attempt by the importer/consignee to present goods to the FDA as corresponding to a particular entry when they are in fact not the goods from that entry. May occur as an attempt to hide distribution without an FDA release and avoid CBP bond actions. See 6.7.15 FAILURE TO HOLD.

6.7.34 - Supervisory Charges

The charges for FDA supervision of the reconditioning and examination of articles after detention. (See 21 CFR 1.99).

6.7.35 - Warehouse Entry (WE)

An entry document filed with Customs by the importer which allows the goods to go immediately into a bonded warehouse.

Chapter 7: Recall Activities

7.1 - Recalls

7.1.1 - Definitions

7.1.1.1 - Recall

A Recall is a firm's removal or correction of a marketed product that FDA considers to be in violation of the laws it administers, and against which the Agency would initiate legal action (e.g., seizure). Recall does not include a market withdrawal or a stock recovery. See the Agency recall policy outlined in 21 CFR 7.1/7.59 - Enforcement Policy - General Provisions, Recalls (Including Product Corrections) - Guidance on Policy, Procedures, and Industry Responsibilities.

7.1.1.2 - Recall Classification

Means the numerical designation, i.e., I, II, or III, assigned by the FDA to a particular product recall to indicate the relative degree of health hazard presented by the product being recalled.

7.1.1.2.1 - Class I Recall

A situation in which there is a reasonable probability that the use of, or exposure to, a violative product will cause serious adverse health consequences or death.

7.1.1.2.2 - Class II Recall

A situation in which use of, or exposure to, a violative product may cause temporary or medically reversible adverse health consequences or where the probability of serious adverse health consequences is remote.

7.1.1.2.3 - Class III Recall

A situation in which use of, or exposure to, a violative product is not likely to cause adverse health consequences.

7.1.1.3 - Recall Type

A designation based on whether the recall is Voluntary, FDA Requested (at the request of the Commissioner or his designee), or ordered under section 518(e) of the FD & C Act [21 U.S.C 360h (e)].

7.1.1.4 - Recall Strategy

A planned specific course of action to be taken in conducting a specific recall, which addresses the depth of recall, need for public warnings, and extent of effectiveness checks for the recall.

7.1.1.5 - Depth of Recall

Depending on the product's degree of hazard and extent of distribution, the recall strategy will specify the level in the distribution chain to which the recall is to extend, i.e., wholesaler, retailer, user/consumer.

7.1.1.6 - Recall Number

Number assigned by a responsible Center for each re-called product they initiate. This number consists first of a letter designating the responsible Center (see letter Codes below), a 3-digit sequential number indicating the number of recalls initiated by that Center during the fiscal year, and a 1-digit number (the Center for Devices and Radiological Health (CDRH) uses 2-digit numbers) indicating the fiscal year the recall was initiated. For example: F-100-2 identifies the 100th recall initiated by the Center for Food Safety and Applied Nutrition (CFSAN) in FY-2002. The following letters are used to identify the Centers.

Letter Center/Office

F Foods - CFSAN

D Drugs - Center for Drug Evaluation and Research (CDER)

Z Medical Devices & Radiological Health - CDRH

V Veterinary Medicine - Center for Veterinary Medicine (CVM)

B Biologics - Center for Biologics Evaluation and Research (CBER)

N Medical Devices (Voluntary Safety Alerts and Notifications)

A Audit Numbers issued by the District performing the recall, the Centers, Office of Enforcement (Di-vision of Compliance Management and Operations [DCMO], or the Division of Field Investigations (DFI) to monitor recalls requiring audit checks.

7.1.1.7 - Medical Device Notification Order

An order issued by FDA requiring notification under section 518(a) of the FD & C Act [21 U.S.C. 360h (a)]. The directive issues when FDA determines a device in commercial distribution, and intended for human use, presents an unreasonable risk of substantial harm to the public health. The notification is necessary to eliminate the unreasonable risk of such harm, and no more practicable means is available under the provisions of the Act to eliminate such risk.

7.1.1.8 - Medical Device Notification

A communication issued by the manufacturer, distributor, or other responsible person in compliance with a Notification Order. It notifies health professionals and other appropriate persons of an unreasonable risk of substantial harm to the public health presented by a device in commercial distribution.

7.1.1.9 - Medical Device Safety Alert

This is a communication voluntarily issued by a

manufacturer, distributor, or other responsible person (including FDA). It informs health professionals and other appropriate persons of a situation which may present an unreasonable risk to the public health by a device in commercial distribution.

NOTE: *Medical Device Notifications and Safety Alerts as described in IOM 7.1.1.7, 7.1.1.8, and 7.1.1.9 are to be handled by the Districts as recalls. They will go through the stages of alert, recommendation, classification, field notification, firm notification letter, firm effectiveness checks and status reports, FDA audit checks, and termination recommendations.*

7.2 - Recall Notification/Inspection

If FDA learns of a potentially violative product which may lead/has lead to a class I or significant class II recall, an inspection should be made to determine the root cause(s) of the problem(s). If the firm has failed to take appropriate preventive action, violations should be documented for possible regulatory action.

NOTE: In all discussions of violative or potentially violative products with the responsible firm, make it clear FDA is not requesting recall action. FDA requested recalls are authorized only by ORA, or by delegation of authority such as Drug Efficacy Study Implementation (DESI) recall requests.

When an investigation determines there is no evidence of manufacturing or distribution problems, but a firm has removed products from the market as a result of actual or alleged tampering with individual units, the action will be considered a Market Withdrawal. A market withdrawal means a firm's removal or correction of a distributed product which involves a minor violation that would not be subject to legal action by the FDA or which involves no violation, e.g., normal stock rotation practices, routine equipment adjustments and repairs, etc.

7.2.1 - Inspection Procedures

An important part of your job is to identify the root cause for the recall and assure the firm has implemented procedures to prevent it from reoccurring. In some cases, management will have conducted its own analysis and reached conclusions about the problem and its cause. The initial judgments about the problem are not always correct nor discriminating enough to identify the underlying causes. You need to verify the steps taken were sufficient in depth and scope and reflect the correct conclusions about both the problem and correction.

Determine if the firm conducted a failure analysis using techniques such as fault tree analysis or failure mode analyses. Did it consider things such as the length of time the product has been manufactured and sold, complaints or returns for the same or similar problems, any reworking of product prior to release or distribution which may have been due to the same or similar problems and, process or personnel changes which occurred about the time the problem appeared.

For all recall inspections, in addition to verifying the identification of the root cause:

1. Issue a Notice of Inspection (FDA 482)

2. Discuss the suspected problem with management and review the firm's complaint file.

3. Investigate all areas, control points and/or circumstances which may have a bearing on the product's deficiency.

4. Fully develop individual responsibility for the problem.

5. Review batch records, processing logs and/or other types of records for violative lots and associated lots.

6. Review and obtain copies of the firm's quality control/analytical data.

7. Determine any actions the firm has taken, is taking, or has planned to take to prevent similar occurrences. If corrective action is not underway, determine the firm's timetable for achieving correction.

8. Determine what action the firm has taken or plans to take, and the time frames involved, regarding questionable product(s) remaining in commerce.

7.2.1.1 - Recall Decision Follow-up

If the firm has decided to recall, do the following:

1. Request that management obtain their FDA District's review of recall correspondence and any press releases before they are issued to prevent misunderstandings between the firm, its customers, and the FDA. This suggestion is voluntary on the part of the firm and is not required.

2. If the firm requests guidance in preparing recall communications, provide it in accordance with your District policy. See Chapter 7 of the RPM and IOM Exhibit 7-1 for an example of recall communications.

3. See RPM Chapter 7-10, Attachment B "Recommendation for Recall Classification" and 21 CFR 7.46a(1)-(9) for information to be obtained.

4. Obtain an Official Sample of the recalled product. (See IOM 7.2.6 for the collection of samples for electronic products or medical devices.)

5. Obtain a complete distribution list of all shipments of the suspect lot(s), including foreign distribution.

6. Obtain specimens or copies of all labels and labeling associated with the recalled product.

7. Obtain complete copies of all recall communications issued or planned including the text of phone conversations, and submit them to your District's recall coordinator. Look in the Blue Pages for a list of District Recall Coordinators.

8. Advise the firm on how the returned products should be handled. FDA must witness or otherwise verify the reconditioning or destruction of the products returned under the recall.

9. Take any other steps necessary in your judgment, or that your District requires.

NOTE: At this early stage there usually has not been a recall evaluation by the appropriate Center. In the absence of such an evaluation, avoid suggesting the firm extend its recall efforts.

7.2.2 - Food Recalls

Experience with food recalls dictates specific information be obtained from firms which have used recalled material in the production of another product. This is necessary to decide if the recall must be extended to a new product(s). In those instances, the following are some areas to be covered:

1. Incoming ingredient quality control procedures.

2. Quality control over ingredients at the time of use, and the products in which the ingredients are used.

3. A detailed description of the methods used in preparation and packaging of the processed product.

4. How the finished product is stored and shipped.

5. Labeling of product, and any cooking instructions for consumer or purchaser.

6. Quality control testing of the finished product. Detail any test(s) performed by firm.

7. For products produced in USDA plants, determine if the USDA was notified of the suspect incoming ingredient? Did USDA determine what testing was done by the firm?

This information must be evaluated by CFSAN (HFS-607) prior to the initiation of any sub-recall.

7.2.2.1 - Interstate Milk Shippers

The FDA will not ordinarily be involved in the classification and auditing of Interstate Milk Shippers (IMS) product recalls where such actions have been, or are being, handled expeditiously and appropriately by the State(s). However, the FDA district office in which the recalling firm is located must be assured that all States involved in an IMS plant's recall are participating in ensuring removal of the product from commerce and that, when appropriate, States issue warnings to protect the public health.

In the event that FDA determines that the States are unable to effect the recall actions necessary, the Agency will classify, publish, and audit the recall, including issuance of a public warning when indicated.

7.2.3 - Medical Device Recalls

Medical device recalls may result from manufacturing defects, labeling deficiencies, failure to meet premarketing requirements [PMA, 510(k)], packaging defects or other nonconformance problems. How firms identify the causes of medical device recalls and corrective action activities is essential to the analysis of medical device failures and the determination of the effectiveness of the medical device GMP program. It is also useful in evaluating the medical device program, and for directing attention to problem areas during inspections. 21 CFR Part 806.1 requires device manufacturers and importers to report certain actions concerning device corrections and removals. They must also maintain records of all corrections and removals regardless of whether such corrections and removals are required to be reported to FDA. (See 21 CFR Part 806.20). Failure to report as required by 21 CFR 806.10 is a violation and should be listed on the FDA-483, "Inspectional Observations." This may be included in a direct reference Warning Letter.

Each device manufacturer or importer must submit a written report to FDA of any correction or removal of a device initiated by such manufacturer or importer, if one was initiated:

1. To reduce a risk to health posed by the device; or

2. To remedy a violation of the Act caused by the device which may present a risk to health, unless the informa-tion has been provided according to

21 CFR 806.10 (f), or the correction or removal action is exempt from the reporting requirements under 21 CFR 806.1(b).

Collection of complaint, PMA and 510(k) related information is necessary to determine compliance with the GMP requirements. During recall follow-up inspections, answers should be obtained to the questions below, in addition to routine recall information. For firms where it has been established a manufacturing defect led to the recall, conduct a complete GMP evaluation of the manufacturing operations. Report such inspections into FACTS as "qualifying" GMP inspections.

7.2.3.1 - Problem Identification

1. How did the firm identify the nonconformance which led to the recall, e.g., complaint, in-house data, etc.

2. If the recall was due to a device defect, did the firm conduct a documented failure analysis of the device, using such techniques as fault tree or failure mode analyses? If so, report whether these results were provided for review.

   a. Did the firm determine the failure mechanism, e.g., shorted component, incomplete weld, etc.?

   b. If not, how did firm determine the cause of the nonconformance?

   c. If not, what rationale does the firm have for not conducting a failure analysis?

3. Did the firm determine at what phase of the device life cycle the nonconformance occurred, i.e., design, manufacturing, storage, use, etc., and the actual cause of the nonconformance, for example, software design error, process out of specifications, employee error, user misuse, etc.? What evidence does the firm have to support the determination?

4. Did the firm determine if the nonconformance resulted in an injury or death?

5. If a component was responsible for the defect, determine if the same component was used in other devices manufactured by the firm. If so, has the firm conducted an analysis to assure the defect in the component will not have a deleterious effect on the operation of the other device(s)?

6. If a component was responsible for the device defect, what other device manufacturers use the same component (and especially the same lot number of the component)? Has the manufacturer of the recalled device notified the component manufacturer? Has the component manufacturer contacted its other customers about the problem?

7. Why was the component defective? Did the manufacturer of the component change the specifications without notifying the finished device manufacturer? Did the component fail to meet its release specifications?

NOTE: A visit to the component manufacturer may be needed to adequately answer questions 5, 6 and 7. Before doing so, confirm with CDRH and your supervisor that the matter is egregious enough to warrant this "next step."

8. Did the finished device manufacturer have an incoming component/raw material sampling and testing procedure? If not, why not?

9. If the manufacturer recalled the device because the labeling was inaccurate, or the wrong labeling was applied to the device (label mix-up) determine the following:

    a. What quality system procedures should have been established to prevent the problem?

    b. If the label or instructions for use were inaccurate, was the inaccuracy introduced in the design stage, or was it due to a printing problem?

10. If the device has been on the market for a year or more, and the manufacturer claims the problem is the result of design:

    a. Why is the problem just now showing up? How many reports concerning the problem did the firm receive before deciding a recall was necessary? Does the firm have a procedure established for determining if a recall is necessary, and if so, did it follow the procedure? Obtain a copy of the procedure.

    b. If the firm doesn't provide rational answers to the above questions, determine if they explored other possible causes for the problem.

    c. Was the design feature which caused the problem included in the design of the device that was the subject of a premarket submission?

    d. If the design feature which caused the problem is part of the original design, did the manufacturer recall all products manufactured since the device was introduced to the market? If not, why not?

    e. If the problem was introduced via a design change, did the manufacturer follow established design change or change control procedures? If yes, are the procedures adequate? Was the nature of the problem such that it should have been anticipated, and the design verification/ validation study fashioned to detect the problem?

    f. Has the manufacturer recalled all products distributed since the design change was introduced? If not, why not?

7.2.3.2 - Corrective Action

1. Describe the corrective action taken to correct the immediate problem, e.g., redesign, modify SOP, process validation, etc.

2. Did the firm qualify/validate the corrective action?

3. Did the firm establish responsibility to assure that the corrective action would be implemented and satisfactorily completed?

4. What action did the firm take to prevent recurrence of the nonconformance, e.g., training, increased process monitoring, etc.

5. Was the nonconformance information provided to those responsible for the areas in which the nonconformance occurred?

6. Did the firm determine if the nonconformance extended to other devices?

7. Did the firm determine if changes were needed in procedures and, if so, did it validate and implement the changes?

8. Has the manufacturer taken appropriate corrective action?

7.2.3.3 - Complaint and Medical Device Reporting (MDR) Reporting

Determine if adequate complaint investigations were performed as required by 21 CFR 820.198(b). Also, determine if the investigation verified the complaint was a failure of the device to meet any or all of its specifications.

For complaints related to the recall, the firm should have made a determination whether the events are MDR reportable. Any event associated with a death or serious injury must be reported under MDR. Malfunctions likely to cause or contribute to a death or a serious injury are also reportable under MDR. Document the firm's explanations for the events they believe are nonreportable. Failure to submit required MDR reports are violations, and should be listed on the FDA-483 at the completion of the inspection.

Provide adequate documentation with the EIR to cross-reference complaints with associated MDRs.

Device Information - Obtain the 510(k) or PMA number for each device under recall. If there is no 510(k) or PMA, determine if the device is a pre-enactment device (i.e., in commercial distribution prior to May 26, 1976). If multiple devices are being recalled, obtain this information for each device model or catalog number under recall.

7.2.4 - Drug Recalls

7.2.4.1 - Recalls of Human Drug Products

If the recalled product is covered by a New Drug Application (NDA) or Abbreviated New Drug Application (ANDA), determine if the defective product involves the type of problems shown under CFR 314.81(b)(1)(i) and (ii). Also note whether or not the firm reported the problem to the FDA district office that is responsible for the firm within 3 working days of its receipt of the information, as required by that section.

7.2.4.2 - Recalls of Veterinary Drug Products

Veterinary Drug Products Recalls are classified by and health hazard evaluations are obtained through CVM's Division of Compliance (HFV-230), Neal Bataller, Director. To inquire about specific veterinary drug product recalls or to obtain information on how to proceed, contact the Division at 240-276-9200 or contact Kathy Hemming-Thompson at 240-276-9216.

7.2.5 - Human Cells, Tissues, And Cellular and Tissue Based Products (HCT/Ps) for Implantation, Trans-Plantation, Infusion, or Transfer

The agency may consider an order of retention, recall, destruction, or cessation of manufacturing when any of the conditions specified in 21 CFR 1271.440(a)(1) to (3) exist. The conditions include an agency finding that:

1. The HCT/P is infected or contaminated so as to be a source of dangerous infection to humans; or

2. An establishment is in violation of the regulations in this part and, therefore does not provide adequate protections against the risks of communicable disease transmission."

In addition to the conditions noted above, the agency may issue an order of cessation of manufacturing until compliance with the regulations has been achieved, as stated in 21 CFR 1271.440(a)(3), when the FDA determines there are reasonable grounds to believe there is a danger to health. An order to cease manufacturing would be issued where violations create an urgent situation involving a communicable disease, because an establishment is in violation of the regulations in Part 1271 and, therefore, does not provide adequate protections against the risks of communicable disease transmission. An order to cease manufacturing is a remedial action taken to put important protections in place to prevent communicable disease transmission.

NOTE: FDA will not issue an order for the destruction of reproductive HCT/Ps, nor will FDA carry out such destruction itself (21 CFR 1271.440(f)).

7.2.6 - Sample Collection

Collection of samples for regulatory consideration is at the discretion of District management. Consult your supervisor and/or compliance branch for guidance. If a sample is indicated, only collect documentary samples for electronic products or medical devices, unless otherwise instructed.

If, after consulting with the Centers, it is determined that a product must be examined physically for health hazard evaluation, ship an appropriate sample to the designated Center office by the most expeditious and practical means available. Notify the Center of the time and method you sent the product and its estimated time of arrival.

7.2.7 - Recall Alert

When a District learns of or confirms a recall situation exists or is planned, they will give the appropriate Center Recall Office and OE/DCMO (HFC-210) a twenty-four hour alert. See RPM Chapter 7-10, Attachment A "Recall Alert Information."

7.2.8 - Recommendation for Recall Number

A memorandum should be prepared as soon as the recall number is available, and transmitted to your District's R&E Coordinator through your

Supervisor. Do not wait for writing, typing and submission of the EIR. A copy of the memo may be attached to your EIR so the information need not be repeated in the body of the report. From the time the recall alert is sent to the appropriate Center, the district has five days to submit the Recall Recommendation (ten days if the recall is completed). See RPM Chapter 7-10, Attachment B "Recommendation for Recall Classification."

7.2.8.1 - Product

For each recalled product, provide: its name; type (e.g. tablet, sugar coated); strength; sizes; form; route of administration; shipping or unit package; and a brief description of the product and its use. If it is a drug product, indicate whether it is a prescription (Rx) or Over-the-Counter (OTC) product. If product labeling does not indicate how the product is to be used, and the health hazard is dependent on use, consult the firm's catalog, the Red Book, or similar sources for that information.

For each recalled product also provide: the brand name; name, address, and type of responsible firm on label; number and description of private labels. Complete copy of all labeling (including product inserts or information sheets). These must be sent to the appropriate Center by an expeditious method.

7.2.8.2 - Code

List all lot and/or serial numbers, catalog numbers, product numbers, packer or manufacturer numbers, etc., which appears on the product or its labeling.

7.2.8.3 - Recalling Firm/Manufacturer

Provide complete name and address of the recalling firm, and identify the type of firm, i.e., manufacturer, importer, broker, repacker, own label distributor. Provide complete name and address of the manufacturer, if different from the recalling firm. Also identify firms which processed or handled the product, or supplied components which might have been responsible for the problem. Indicate which firm(s) appear(s) responsible for the violation.

7.2.8.4 - Reason for Recall Recommendation

Provide detailed information as to how the product is defective and violates the FD&C Act or related statutes.

1. Include any analytical findings in qualitative and/or quantitative terms, whether from the firm or FDA analysis, and which laboratory was involved.

2. Provide inspectional (e.g., GMP) or other evidence, where appropriate.

3. List in chronological order any complaints, injuries, or associated problems with the product. Include any MDR's that have been submitted.

4. If firm management was advised of FDA findings, and the problem was discussed with them, report their reactions and plans. If the firm advised

FDA of the problem, report and explain firm's own analytical results and how it learned of the need for a recall.

Explain all State involvement in the recall, including sample collection or analysis, recall agreement or initiation, recall monitoring, and product disposition.

For DESI related recalls, use the following terminology: "Federal Register Publication (date), Drug Efficacy Study Implementation."

In cases where a veterinary drug product is recalled due to subpotency prior to labeled expiration date provide the following information:

1. The firm's stability testing plan (including the analytical methodology) which established the labeled expiration date.

2. Specific batch numbers in the stability studies, and assay values that are the basis of the firm's recall.

3. Potency specifications which the firm uses for recall purposes.

4. Final assay values for the active ingredients which were the basis of the initial release of the batch.

Note if information regarding stability data on file with the firm, and the Quality Control (QC) procedures used by the firm to determine the potency of the active ingredients, is available in the EIR.

7.2.8.5 - Volume of Product in Commerce

Provide total volume of product(s) distributed. Provide estimate of amount and availability of stocks remaining on market, at all levels. (Indicate whether this is the firm's or FDA's estimates.) Include product expiration dates or shelf life expectancy.

NOTE: If recommendation is for an FDA Requested Recall, assure there is, in fact, product remaining in commerce.

7.2.8.6 - Distribution Pattern

Report the areas of distribution, the number of direct accounts, the approximate percentage of each type consignee, and the percentage of product sent to each type of consignee. List foreign countries and U.S. Government military and/or civil units/agencies to which product(s) were distributed. If various labels are involved, describe any differences in distribution pattern.

Where there were any Defense Personnel Support Center (DPSC), Department of Veterans Affairs (DVA), or other government agency sales/distribution, the consignee list should be submitted separately through your District's R&E Coordinator to OE/DCMO. Show if these were direct or contract sales. If contract sales, report the contract number, contract date, and implementation date.

7.2.8.7 - Firm's Recall Strategy

Describe the firm's planned recall strategy. Comment on the adequacy of this strategy from your District's viewpoint, and evaluate the firm's ability to accomplish an effective recall. See Sections 7.42 and 7.46 of 21 CFR, Part 7, which set forth information to be obtained from the firm which will be evaluated by the Center. The firm's strategy should include the intended course of action when an account which distributed the recalled product is found out of business. Include the date the recall was initiated, if already underway.

7.2.8.8 - Firm Official

Report the name, title, location, and telephone number of the firm official who should be contacted concerning the recall. In case of potential Class I or FDA requested recalls, also provide this information for the firm's chief executive officer (CEO).

7.2.8.9 - District Audit Program

Report what actions have already been taken (FDA inspections, sample collections, etc.). Provide specific recommendations for the appropriate Center's action, where appropriate.

Provide details of any publicity issued or planned by FDA, the firm, the State, or local government.

Provide your District's proposed program for monitoring the recall. Include time table for reviewing the recall status and the level and type of audit checks which will verify the recall's effectiveness.

7.2.8.10 - Recommending Official

Name and title of your District's recommending official.

7.3 - Monitoring Recalls

7.3.1 - Inspections to Monitor Recall Progress

It may be necessary to re-inspect the firm between the initiation and closeout of a recall to monitor its progress and verify the recalled product's disposition. These visits are limited inspections; issue an FDA-482, Notice of Inspection, at each one. Request recalling firms to submit periodic status reports to FDA. See 21 CFR 7.53.

7.3.2 - FDA Recall Audit Checks

7.3.2.1 - Definition

A recall audit check is a personal visit, telephone call, letter, or a combination thereof, to a consignee of a recalling firm, or a user or consumer in the chain of distribution. It is made to verify all consignees at the recall depth specified by the strategy have received notification about the recall and have taken appropriate action.

7.3.2.2 - Level of Audit Checks

Level A - 100% of the total number of consignees to be contacted.

Level B - Greater than 10% but less than 100% of the total number of consignees to be contacted.

Level C - 10% of the total number of consignees to be contacted.

Level D - 2% of the total number of consignees to be contacted.

Level E - No effectiveness checks.

NOTE: A statistical audit plan may be directed by the Center involved.

7.3.2.3 - Sub-Account Checks

If a recall strategy includes sub-recall by a firm's direct accounts, sub-recall checks will be made following the above levels, as instructed by the Center and your supervisor.

7.3.2.4 - Conducting the Check

Your assignment contains the necessary details of the recall, recall strategy, and a list of accounts to be checked. The Center will indicate how checks will be made, i.e., visit, phone calls, record checks, etc. Obtain at least the following information, plus any additional information requested by the monitoring district or your home District:

1. Name and title of person interviewed.
2. Was notification received, understood, and followed?
3. Date and method of notification.
4. Amount of recalled product on hand at time of notification.
5. Amount returned and the method of return.
6. Amount destroyed and method of destruction.
7. Amount presently on hand and its status (held for sale, awaiting return, etc.).
8. Date of anticipated return or destruction, and planned method (if applicable).
9. Was sub-recall conducted? (If so, obtain a list of consignees from which to select your sub-recall check locations).
10. Have injury reports or complaints been received? If so, report details.

When you conduct an audit check by visit, you should visit the storage sites for the recalled product and check the shelf stock to ensure all recalled product has been identified, removed from areas of use and properly quarantined. In firms where products are stored in multiple locations, a sufficient number should be checked to verify the consignee properly found and removed all product subject to the recall. This is especially important in Class I recalls and you should check each storage site.

7.3.2.5 - Audit Check Reporting

The narrative results of your audit check should be reported on an FDA 3177, "Recall Audit Check Report" form. See IOM Exhibit 7-2. Districts have the option of using computer generated audit check forms or hard copies. The FDA 3177 is a three-part form, which is basically self-explanatory. If necessary, instructions for completing it may be found in RPM, Chapter 7, Exhibit 7-12. It is distributed as follows:

Original - Monitoring district.

Yellow Copy - Accomplishing district files.

Pink Copy - District Use

Version 2 of FACTS allows you to enter the amount of time and other data information. When you complete Recall Audits, you should report your time using the "Miscellaneous Operations Accomplishment Hours" screen. You do not need to report the information on the 3177 unless your District SOP requires this. Until some other reporting procedure is developed, continue to report audit checks using the FD-3177 form or memorandum.

7.3.2.6 - Ineffective Recalls

If your audit check discloses recalled product being held for sale, or a requested sub-recall has not been initiated, document the responsibility for failure to follow recall instructions. This is particularly important if the account received the recall notice and ignored it. An Official Sample should be collected from these remaining products. If in doubt, contact your supervisor or R&E Coordinator. Encourage the consignee to follow the recalling firm's instructions. If a sub-recall is justified, obtain a commitment and details of the firm's sub-recall effort. Get distribution information for follow-up sub-account audit checks.

7.3.3 - Recall Terminated/Recall Completed

7.3.3.1 - Definitions

Recall Terminated - A recall will be terminated when the FDA determines that all reasonable efforts have been made to remove or correct the violative product in accordance with the recall strategy, and when it is reasonable to assume that the product subject to the recall has been removed and proper disposition or correction has been made commensurate with the degree of hazard of the recalled product. Written notification that a recall is terminated will be issued by the appropriate District office to the recalling firm.

Recall Completed - For monitoring purposes, the FDA classifies a recall action "Completed" when all outstanding product, which could reasonably be expected is recovered, impounded, or corrected.

7.3.3.2 - Closeout Inspection

The final monitoring step is a limited inspection made to verify recall closeout by the recalling firm. A memorandum or limited EIR should be prepared. See RPM Chapter 7, Attachments B1 , "Recommendation for Recall Classification and Termination" and Attachment C , "Recall Termination or Recommendation for Termination" for the format. Portions of this format (i.e., Section II and certain items in Section III) will be completed by your supervisor, R&E Coordinator, or compliance officer, depending upon your District's policy.

During the closeout inspection, you should witness destruction or reconditioning of the recalled product when possible. If you are unable to witness the destruction or reconditioning, obtain written documentation from the firm and/or any state or local government agencies which may have witnessed or otherwise verified product disposition. The disposal of large amounts of contaminated or hazardous items may require the firm to file an Environmental Impact Statement (EIS), or pre-disposal processing to render the goods harmless. Do not agree to witness destruction without resolution of these issues. Obtain a "Letter of Voluntary Destruction" from the firm whenever you witness this operation. See IOM 2.6.4.1.

7.4 - Special Recall Situations

7.4.1 - General

There are several special recall situations which may require you to deviate from the normal recall procedures. Seek your supervisor's or R&E Coordinator's guidance on these. Examples include:

1. Products in the possession of U.S. Defense Installations.
2. NDA and NADA withdrawals.
3. National Academy of Science (NAS)/Nuclear Regulatory Commission (NRC) (DESI) recalls of drugs judged ineffective.
4. Recalls involving jurisdiction of more than one Federal Agency (e.g., FDA/EPA, FDA/Consumer Product Safety Commission (CPSC), etc.).

Chapter 8: Investigations

CONTENT		VERSION DATE
Subchapter 8.1	Investigations	June 11, 2009
Subchapter 8.2	Complaints	August 27, 2009
Subchapter 8.3	Investigation of Foodborne Outbreaks	June 11, 2009
Subchapter 8.4	Investigation - Injury & Adverse Reaction	June 11, 2009
Subchapter 8.5	Disaster Procedures	June 11, 2009
Subchapter 8.6	Surveillance	June 11, 2009
Subchapter 8.7	Investigational Research	October 13, 2009
Subchapter 8.8	Counterfeiting/Tampering	June 11, 2009
Subchapter 8.9	Office of Criminal Investigations (OCI)	June 11, 2009
Subchapter 8.10	General Investigation Report	June 11, 2009

8.1 - Investigations

This Chapter contains specific information on many types of investigations and each section provides additional guidance for you on how to investigate particular issues, special reporting requirements and where additional assistance can be obtained. Recall work, a special type of investigation, is covered in Chapter 7. There is an on-line training course in Investigations which covers many types of investigations and provides additional information.

An investigation is an information gathering activity you conduct for many different reasons. The purpose of any investigation is to determine and document facts concerning a particular issue so the Agency can make informed and sound decisions. Investigation is a general term and can apply to a very general activity or a specific type of information gathering process. Some specific types of investigations include a complaint investigation, a disaster investigation, a health fraud investigation and a product tampering investigation. Investigations can be distinguished from inspections because usually you will not need to issue an FDA 482, you will be working somewhere other than a manufacturing plant, you may be visiting retail establishments, consumers, or other government agencies. On rare occasions, you may be conducting an investigation without advising individuals you are a FDA employee. Keep in mind that investigations can not all be categorized and there will be times when you do issue an FDA 482, such as when you are at a manufacturing site or doing work similar to an inspection. Experience gained on the job will help you determine the proper course of action for these special situations.

Reporting an investigation is almost always done using a memorandum. The format is not as defined in sections as an inspection report. A good rule of thumb to follow is to first summarize what you did, why or give the reason for the investigation and briefly state the findings. After this, you can go into detail about how you conducted the investigation and what you found. Reporting the course of your investigation and your findings chronologically works in many situations. For long narratives, using headings will make it easier for the reader to follow your reporting. Some types of investigations have forms that need to be completed in addition to the narrative. Your report will be in English, see IOM 1.1.

8.2 - Complaints

A complaint is notification that a product in commercial distribution may be in violation of the laws and regulations administered by FDA.

Complaints are received from various sources, including consumers, other government agencies, Congress on behalf of their constituents, trade associations, etc. Enter complaints into the FACTS Consumer Complaint System. Complaints should be promptly acknowledged in written format, by telephone or visit. See Field Management Directive FMD-119.

Consumers contacting field offices with complaints of injury or illness should receive a prompt, courteous response and assurance their complaints will receive appropriate consideration. An immediate follow-up may be warranted when there is an indication of a serious illness or injury. Unless a visit to the complainant is assigned, any and all information should be obtained during a telephone call with the consumer. Do not rely on the consumer to freely offer all pertinent information. Use critical thinking skills and ask pertinent questions to aid in identifying the problem and where it may have occurred. Record information on the consumer complaint form in FACTS.

Obtain sufficient information to enable evaluation of the complaint, determination of appropriate follow-up, and, if possible, enough facts to permit further FDA evaluation and response without subsequent contact with the complainant. If a complaint cannot be resolved immediately, determine if the complainant expects further contact. If so, report the best time to reach the complainant. For complaints involving special nutritional products, i.e., infant formula, medical foods and dietary supplements, complete the FACTS Adverse Event Questionnaire, See Exhibit 8-1. See IOM 8.4.5.2.2 for additional instructions regarding special nutritional complaints.

The FDA Office of Crisis Management/Office of Emergency Operations (OCM/OEO) HFA-615, 301-443-1240 must be notified immediately of all significant injury, illness and suspected tampering complaints. OCM/OEO must also be notified of all complaints regarding infant formula/baby food.

Significant injury/illness includes, but is not limited to, any life threatening event; seizures; severe respiratory distress syndrome including broncho-constriction or bronchospasm; acute asthmatic attacks, anaphylactic or hypotensive episodes; unconsciousness or coma, or any event requiring medical treatment. Also to be included are behavioral or mood disorders of sufficient intensity to alter the daily activities of the consumer. These complaints require immediate and thorough follow-up, unless specifically directed otherwise by OCM/OEO. OCM/OEO is also to be kept advised of the status of all such follow-up investigations. Information about complaints nationwide is available in FACTS and from OCM/OEO and may be helpful in determining appropriate follow-up.

Complaints concerning products which do not present a hazard to health may be investigated by the home district during the next planned inspection of the responsible firm.

If the complaint concerns a matter not under FDA jurisdiction, or one which would more properly be handled by another agency, refer the complainant to the appropriate organization whenever possible.

8.2.1 - Complaint Categories

Complaints can be divided into two categories.

8.2.1.1 - Injury/Illness Complaints

A complaint indicating a serious injury, illness, hospitalization, or death requires immediate reaction. It will, in all likelihood, require immediate investigation. It may include the accumulation of epidemiological data and prompt liaison with other appropriate federal, state and local agencies.

A complaint that clearly indicates an illness resulting from consuming a FDA regulated product, and manifested by symptoms such as nausea, vomiting, fever, or diarrhea, should receive prompt follow-up by FDA or cooperating officials.

Conversely, some illnesses are considered psychological in nature, e.g., a consumer finds a foreign object in a product and becomes ill because it is revolting. For purposes of conducting follow-up and reporting to headquarters, these should be handled as non-injury/illness complaints and do not need to be reported to the OCM/OEO.

8.2.1.2 - Non-Injury/Illness Complaints

These do not require immediate follow-up at the consumer level. Follow-up may include examining the parent lot, referral to another FDA district, state, or local agency, or deferral until the next regularly scheduled inspection. Examples include mold in beverages, obvious filth or insects in canned goods, etc. It may be possible that adequate investigation would be contacting the dealer, advising them of the nature of the complaint and requesting notification of any action taken. Non-injury/illness complaints do not need to be reported to the OCM/OEO unless product tampering is suspected or the product is a baby food or infant formula.

8.2.2 - Infant Formula and Baby Food

There is a continued sensitivity to all reported incidents involving infant formula or baby food. All complaints involving either infant formula or baby food are to be thoroughly investigated on a high-priority basis. This will include follow-up at the doctor or hospital (if an injury/illness is involved), with the collection and analysis of appropriate samples. Complaints involving baby food that is regulated by USDA should be referred to USDA for appropriate follow-up. See IOM 8.3.1.3 and IOM 3.2.1.2.

There are two exceptions for collecting samples as part of the follow-up to infant formula/baby food complaints:

1. Complaints involving outdated product in the marketplace, with no associated injury or illness. These do require investigation to assure all outdated product has been removed from the identified retail and/or wholesale source.

2. Complaints involving an illness associated with normal appearing product, but follow-up investigation discloses a physician's diagnosis that the event does not appear to be product related, or that the event was an allergic response to a properly labeled product.

Also see the following:

1. IOM 8.4.5.2- Dietary Supplements

2. IOM 8.3.1- Foodborne Outbreaks

8.2.3 - Complaints Involving Alcoholic Beverages

All tampering complaints involving alcoholic beverages should be entered as a consumer complaint in FACTS. OCM/OEO and OCI should be notified immediately. For all other complaints involving alcoholic beverages, please see IOM 3.2.8.1 for guidance.

8.2.4 - Office of Emergency Operations Guidance

The FDA Office of Crisis Management/Office of Emergency Operations& (OCM/OEO) HFA-615, 301-443-1240 must be notified immediately of all serious injury/illness and suspected tampering complaints. The OCM/OEO is also to be kept advised of the status of all such follow-up investigations. Information about complaints nationwide is available in FACTS and from the OCM/OEO and may be helpful in determining appropriate follow-up.

As unique situations arise, OEO provides guidance concerning the type of follow-up to be made. This guidance should be kept on file by the district consumer complaint coordinator.

8.2.5 - Interviews

The key to thorough consumer complaint investigation is complete interviews with the complainant and/or others knowledgeable about the incident (other family members, health professionals, law enforcement officials, etc.). In addition, in preparation for any consumer complaint interviews, you should take your personal safety into consideration. Refer to IOM 5.2.1.2 for more information.

8.2.5.1 - Basic Information to Obtain

The basic information to be obtained is in the FACTS Consumer Complaint Report which replaces the 2516 and the Consumer Complaint Follow-Up Report which replaces the 2516a. See IOM Exhibits 8-2 and 8-3. Obtain an accurate and complete description of the product to include brand name, product name, flavor or variety, how packaged, and storage conditions required (i.e. refrigerated or shelf stable). Enter this description in the Brand Name and Product Name sections of the FACTS complaint form.

It is important to accurately determine the sequence of events leading up to the complaint. This includes a 72-hour food history (for food related illness); whether the complainant used the product before (cosmetic or drug products); condition of the product when purchased or consumed (tampering complaints, mold in foods, possible mishandling, product abuse in the home, etc.); and storage of the products (if filth is the subject of the complaint).

8.2.5.2 - Injury/Illness Complaints

There are additional considerations with injury/illness complaints. The prior medical history of the complainant may provide indications regarding allergies, drug side effects or drug-food/drug-drug interactions which may be responsible for the illness or injury. Medical verification should be sought in these situations. Food illnesses are frequently associated with the most recent food consumed, food that didn't appear or smell right, or a food consumed only by the ill person. Additional interviews may be required to identify other suspect foods, especially if the food implicated is not a likely vehicle for illness. Familiarity with items previously associated with illness or injuries is helpful in pursuing the investigation; such as pet turtles or occupational sources for Salmonella; incompatibility of soft contact lenses with lens solution or other eye products not specifically approved for use with them; production of acetic acid by aspirin as it decomposes; and the bitter or burning taste of calcium chloride-contaminated frozen ice cream novelties. Consider that individuals differ in sensitivity to bacterial levels or toxins, and not everyone using or consuming a contaminated product will show symptoms.

8.2.5.3 - Additional Information to Obtain

Additional information to be obtained for adverse events involving foods, dietary supplements, botanicals and cosmetics is contained in the FACTS Adverse Event Questionnaire and the Cosmetic Questionnaire, IOM Exhibits 8-1 and 8-4. This information should be entered into FACTS by the District receiving the complaint prior to forwarding the complaint to the home district of the manufacturer.

8.2.5.4 - Complainant Access to Report/Results

The complainant may request a copy of your investigative report or sample results. Inform the complainant that they can receive the results of any sample collected from them, in accordance with the Freedom of Information Act (FOIA), after the Agency has determined that there is no consideration of criminal prosecution or such consideration has occurred and the matter is closed. Also inform them there may be a slight charge for the investigatory report as required by the FOI Regulations. See IOM 1.4.4.

8.2.6 - Medical Records

In investigating complaints where a health professional was seen by the complainant, contact the health professional concerning the nature of the alleged illness/injury, and the relationship to the product. You may occasionally find the complainant has not mentioned the product as a potential cause of the illness or injury to the health professional. Use judgment as to the usefulness of collecting medical records. Examples of medical records to collect include: Admission History and Physical; Emergency Room/Clinic Record of the event if patient not admitted; Discharge Summary; Autopsy Report; and, Death Certificate. See also IOM 5.3.8.6.

If collection of medical records is necessary, use the FDA 461, Authorization for Medical Records Disclosure, signed by the patient or someone authorized to act for the patient. See IOM Exhibit 8-5. It may be necessary to use multiple forms if medical records are at different locations. Have at least three FDA 461 forms available for patient signature. The FDA 461 is not required to obtain records from the Department of Defense (DOD) medical facilities. Identify yourself to the Commanding Officer of the facility or representative and request authorization to examine and copy records. DOD Directive 6040.2, Release of Information from Medical Records, authorizes release of medical information to government agencies.

NOTE: *Many states require statements concerning other subjects besides those covered on the FDA 461. If the hospital does not accept the FDA version of the Authorization for Medical Records Disclosure, obtain and complete one of their forms for use at their facility.*

Collect all medical records pertinent to the investigation.

8.2.7 - Sample Collection

Sample collection authority, definitions and procedures are discussed in detail in IOM Chapter 4.

Prior to initiating sampling collection, you may consider contacting the home district of the manufacturing plant. They may be aware of an existing issue related to the product and problem.

A thorough investigation will provide information to form a hypothesis as to the cause of the illness, injury, or product problem and will assist in determining what sample(s) to collect. Adequate samples should be collected immediately, while they are available. Do not overlook sampling any product which may be remotely implicated in the incident. Consult with your servicing laboratory for guidance on specific sample sizes. See IOM 8.4.5.2 for guidance on sampling dietary supplements.

In addition to the consumer portion, intact containers of products of the same lot should be collected from the retail and wholesale levels. These samples provide more useful information regarding the product in consumer channels, and may prove useful in any future legal action. Refer to IOM 4.3.5.1 for information concerning collection of consumer portions.

8.2.8 - Recording Complaints/Follow-ups

The FACTS Consumer Complaint Report and Follow-Up Report are used for recording and investigating all complaints (except drug reactions - see IOM 8.4.2.1), unless previously reported through one of FDA's other post-marketing surveillance systems. See IOM Exhibits 8-2 and 8-3.

8.3 - Investigation of Foodborne Outbreaks

8.3.1 - Foodborne Outbreaks

If you become aware of a foodborne outbreak, contact the OCM/OEO 301-443-1240 immediately. Generally, epidemiological investigations are conducted by state and local public health authorities. Epidemiological investigative techniques have been established to assist in determining the cause of a foodborne outbreak or illness. The information presented describes the standard methods for gathering and evaluating data. In fact, these techniques are useful in investigating all types of complaints.

8.3.1.1 - Outbreaks on Foreign Flag Vessels

If a suspect outbreak involving a foreign flag vessel or a US flag vessel with an international itinerary comes to your attention, report it to your supervisor and OCM/OEO 301-443-1240 immediately. The Centers for Disease Control and Prevention (CDC) assumes primary jurisdiction for foreign flag (non-US registry) and US flag vessels with international itineraries entering the US and traveling in US waters. See IOM 3.2.4.3.

8.3.1.2 - Outbreaks Involving Interstate Conveyances

Reports of illness attributed to travel on an interstate conveyance (plane, bus, train, or vessel) are a shared responsibility of FDA and CDC. When a report of illness is received, notify OCM/OEO at 301-443-1240 and you are encouraged to share the report with state and local public health officials. The following procedures are to be coordinated with local/state public health officials:

Interviews with the ill passenger, family members (well and ill), caregivers, and/or health professional (as appropriate) should be sufficiently probative to hypothesize if the food, water or an environmental transmission is related to the illness. Transmission of illnesses, particularly viral diseases, by ill employees and contaminated environmental surfaces can result in illness carryover between successive trips and should be considered. Factors such as time of onset of symptoms, symptoms, food history for the 72 hours prior to onset of the first symptom, any clinical laboratory results, and other potential exposures should be documented. The carrier should also be contacted to determine if other reports of illness have been received (passengers and employees). Obtain any illness logs from the carrier. The information developed should be evaluated to determine if further follow-up is necessary. On those carriers where a reservation system is used, obtain the names and phone numbers of passengers. It may be necessary for the state/local health authorities, CDC or FDA to contact other passengers to determine if they became ill.

If additional cases are uncovered during these contacts, immediately notify the OCM/OEO and the state and local public health authorities in all of the affected states. FDA will work cooperatively with these authorities and request their assistance in conducting an epidemiological investigation and collecting patient specimens. Note: If at any time the local/state public health officials are unable to assist with an investigation, notify the OCM/OEO, who will contact CDC and request assistance in the epidemiological investigation.

8.3.1.3 - Cooperation with Other Agencies

One of FDA's functions is to assist local, State, and other Federal agencies in conducting investigations, collecting samples, and conducting plant inspections if warranted.

In addition to state and local health departments, the following federal agencies may also become involved in investigating foodborne disease outbreaks:

1. U.S. Department of Agriculture (USDA)
2. Centers for Disease Control and Prevention (CDC)
3. Environmental Protection Agency (EPA)

Whenever a complaint is received involving any meat-containing product, including such items as soups, combination infant foods, frozen dinners, etc., evaluate the need to contact USDA. Most products containing red meat or poultry are regulated by USDA. The exceptions include:

1. Products containing meat from game animals, such as venison, rabbits, etc.;
2. Meat-flavored instant noodles;
3. The product "pork and beans" (which contain only a small amount of pork fat and is regulated by FDA); and
4. Closed face sandwiches.

Determine from the consumer if there is a round "shield" on the label with the USDA Establishment Number. Alternatively, the establishment number may be identified in the lot number. Red meat products under USDA jurisdiction will often contain the abbreviation "EST" followed by a one to four digit number; poultry products under USDA jurisdiction will contain the letter "P" followed by a number.

IOM 3.2.1 and IOM 3.2.4.3 provide information for reporting suspected outbreaks to USDA and CDC. In addition, FDA and CDC have an agreement that FDA will be immediately advised whenever CDC ships botulism antitoxin anywhere in the United States or its possessions.

Whenever the source water is suspected as a likely origin of the agent of an illness outbreak, Environmental Protection Agency (EPA) should be notified. For example, when investigating a foodborne outbreak on a vessel passenger conveyance, you may find the water used in food preparation to be from a land-based source or from an on-board water treatment plant. Both of these sources would fall under EPA jurisdiction. See IOM 3.2.11.

8.3.1.4 - Outbreaks Associated with Salmonella Enteritidis (SE) in Eggs

All reports regarding SE outbreaks, including any epidemiological and environmental data associated with whole shell eggs are to be referred to the OCM/OEO, 301-443-1240, (emergency.operations@fda.gov). The OEO will notify CFSAN Outbreak Coordination Staff immediately, who will serve as the lead CFSAN contact.

8.3.2 - Follow-Up Guidance

8.3.2.1 - Preparation

Investigator kits with proper equipment should be maintained in the district to facilitate immediate investigation of foodborne outbreaks. The kits should be re-stocked on a schedule recommended by FDA laboratory personnel to ensure continued sterility of sampling equipment. A supply of commercially available environmental sampling swabs containing transport media should be readily available as part of the investigation kit. These tubes provide a transport medium that will help preserve the environmental and food swabs.

If an alert or complaint indicates a large outbreak, inform your servicing laboratory immediately that samples will probably be collected and give the approximate time they are expected to arrive at the laboratory. This will assist laboratory managers planning work schedules, equipment and supplies.

Each district may have individuals specifically trained in epidemiological investigations who can provide advice on investigations. If not, consult with OCM/OEO at 301-443-1240 and the state and local public health authorities.

8.3.2.2 - Interviews

Health professionals, hospital personnel, or consumers may report suspected cases of foodborne illness. Regardless of the source of the report, the diagnosis must be verified by a thorough case history and, if possible, by examination of appropriate food samples and clinical specimens. This verification is done by public health professionals.

8.3.2.2.1 - Contacting the Complainant

Upon contacting the affected person, identify yourself and explain the purpose of the visit or call. Neat attire, pleasant manner of speech, professional attitude and confidence in discussing epidemiology and control of foodborne illnesses are important in developing rapport with an affected person or family. Exhibit a genuine concern for persons affected, and be sincere when requesting personal and confidential information. Communicate a sense of urgency, and emphasize the positive contribution already made by the complainant toward the control and prevention of foodborne illness.

8.3.2.2.2 - Setting Communication Level

Set your level of communication based on the person being interviewed. Tact is essential. Phrase your questions so the person(s) interviewed will describe their illness, and the foods and events which they feel were associated with it, in their own way. Use open ended questions. Never suggest answers by the way you phrase your questions.

Ask specific questions to clarify the affected person's comments. Realize people are sometimes sensitive to questions about age, gender, special dietary habits, ethnic group, excreta disposal and housing conditions. Phrase questions thoughtfully. Some information may usually be deduced from observations, but if doubt remains, confirm your hypothesis by asking questions. Information on recent travel, gatherings, or visitors may indicate common sources or events.

8.3.2.2.3 - Information to Gather

Gather information about all meals and snacks eaten seventy-two hours before onset of illness. The food, even the meal, which precipitated the illness, might not be obvious. The type of illness will sometimes give a clue.

If the first and predominant symptoms are nausea and vomiting, concentrate questions on foods eaten recently.

If the first and predominant symptoms are diarrhea and abdominal cramps, foods eaten six to twenty hours before onset of illness are suspect.

If diarrhea, chills and fever predominate, foods eaten twelve to seventy-two hours before onset of illness are suspect.

Remember that these suggestions relate to common foodborne illnesses. The more unusual illnesses often present different clinical patterns. For instance, some illnesses such as Typhoid Fever and Hepatitis A, have incubation periods greater than 72 hours. Refer to IOM Exhibit 8-6.

Use this detailed interview approach with every person identified in the initial complaint or alert, even though some may not have been ill, until you have sufficient information to determine if there is a foodborne disease outbreak.

8.3.2.3 - Medical Records

Physicians' and hospitals' records can be useful in verifying reported signs, symptoms and other clinical data and can sometimes rule out the possibility of foodborne illness. See IOM 8.2.6 and IOM Exhibit 8-5.

8.3.3 - Sampling Procedures

CAUTION: Never taste any of the food products, and handle all samples with caution to prevent accidental ingestion of even minute amounts of the contaminated or suspect product.

8.3.3.1 - Sample Collection

During investigations of foodborne diseases, cooperate with other health officials in collecting samples of items that may be associated with the outbreak.

Use a menu or data from an attack-rate table to determine which of the foods from the implicated meal are most suspect, and collect samples of them. Check storage areas for items that may have been overlooked. Check garbage for discarded foods or containers. Suspect foods often are discarded by an operator if he thinks someone may have become ill as a result of eating in his establishment. Because one of the primary tasks of the investigator is to prevent further illness, take appropriate action to prevent distribution or serving of any suspect food until it has been proven safe. If no foods remain from the suspect meal or lot, try to collect samples of items prepared subsequently to the suspect lot, but in a similar manner. Collect ingredients or raw items used in the suspect food. Determine supplier, distribution, and code information on ingredients and packaged foods to aid any investigation of the same lot in distribution channels.

Collect samples aseptically. If foods are to be examined for organophosphate pesticides or heavy metals, do not use plastic containers. Use glass jars with foil lined lids because substances from the plastic can leach into the food and interfere with analysis.

The following are examples of articles normally collected:

1. Remaining portions of all suspect foods;
2. Parent stocks of suspect foods;
3. Insecticides, rodenticides, or other poisons which may be involved.
4. Suspect food containers such as cans, bottles, etc.;
5. Utensils or materials used in the preparation and storage of the suspect food;
6. Table scrapings and food residues from equipment such as slicing machines, cutting boards, etc.

NOTE: Clinical specimens such as vomitus, stools, swabs of nasal and throat passages or open sores or lesions of food workers are collected by local, state, or CDC health officials or private physicians.

8.3.3.2 - Sample Size

In general, follow the IOM SAMPLE SCHEDULE in Charts 1, 2, and 3 (IOM, Chapter 4). Where only small amounts of items remain, such as bits of left-overs, empty containers with adhering particles, etc., collect all or as much as possible by scraping from utensils, equipment or containers. It may also be necessary to collect the empty container(s). See IOM 8.3.4.6.

8.3.3.3 - Sample Handling

Record the temperature of the room, refrigerator, or warmer in which the food was stored, and record the temperature of the food that remains after a sample is collected.

Inform the laboratory of the type and number of samples, and discuss methods to preserve and transport samples, time of arrival, and the person who will receive the shipment.

Samples of products frozen at the time of collection should be maintained frozen until analyzed. Samples of perishable foods, which are not frozen at the time of collection, should be cooled rapidly to a temperature of 4.4oC (40oF) and maintained at this temperature if they can be analyzed within eight hours. If analysis cannot be started within eight hours, and you suspect microbial contamination, contact your servicing microbiology laboratory for proper handling procedures.

Transport refrigerated or frozen samples to the laboratory in insulated containers, packed with an appropriate refrigerant to maintain the desired temperature during transit. Send samples to the laboratory by the most expeditious means. Clearly mark: "PERISHABLE FOOD SAMPLE FOR MICROBIAL EXAMINATION - RUSH," "PRIORITY." Label specimens according to applicable regulations governing transport of hazardous material. See IOM 4.5.5.8.6.

If the suspect food is a commercial product, examine the original package or container for coding information to identify the place and time of processing. Your district may notify all agencies responsible for regulating the products alleged or suspected to have caused the illness. Collect additional packages bearing the same code number for analyses for microorganisms, toxins, seam defects, vacuum, leaks, or other conditions. Be specific as possible in requesting the type of analysis.

8.3.4 - Epidemiological Associations

Conduct a preliminary evaluation of your epidemiological data as soon as possible. If your data suggests an outbreak has occurred, develop a hypothesis about the causal factors. Test your hypothesis by obtaining additional information to prove or disprove its validity.

8.3.4.1 - Outbreak Determination

An outbreak is an incident in which two or more individuals have the same disease, have similar symptoms, or excrete the same pathogens; and there is a time, place, and/or person association between these individuals. A foodborne disease outbreak results from ingestion of a common food by such individuals. However, a single case of suspected botulism, mushroom poisoning, paralytic shellfish poisoning, rare disease, or a disease which can be definitely related to ingestion of a food, may be considered as an incident of foodborne illness which warrants investigation.

Sometimes it will be obvious from an initial report that a foodborne disease outbreak has occurred, simply because of the number of individuals displaying certain symptoms at or near the same time. Many complaints, however, involve illness in only one or two individuals, and determining a particular food was responsible, or its consumption and the onset of illness was only coincidental, is often difficult. Certain diseases that are highly communicable from person to person, such as epidemic viral gastroenteritis, or those associated with a common place, such as carbon monoxide poisoning, may simulate a foodborne illness.

If additional complaints connected with the same food or eating establishment are received, food is almost certainly involved. A food-related or enteric disease alert/complaint log assists in determining if similar complaints have been received.

Time associations primarily refer to onset of similar illnesses within a few hours or days of each other. Place associations deal with buying foods from the same place, eating at the same establishment, residing at the same place, or attending the same event. Person associations have to do with common experiences, such as eating the same foods or being of the same age, gender, ethnic group, occupation, social club, or religion. Once some of these associations become obvious, verify the outbreak by identifying and interviewing other individuals who were at risk by virtue of their association with the ill persons.

8.3.4.2 - Assistance

If the outbreak affects a large number of individuals or food establishments, consult with your supervisor regarding the need to seek assistance from other health professionals. A team consisting of an epidemiologist, microbiologist or chemist, sanitarian, and others may be required to make a sufficiently detailed foodborne illness investigation. Such personnel may be provided by local, state or provincial, or national agencies concerned with health, food and drug, environment, fish or agriculture.

8.3.4.3 - Additional Case History Interviews

Seek and interview additional individuals both ill and well, who had time, place, or person associations with the identified cases. If the suspect meal was served during a particular occasion, determine the name of the person in charge. That person may have a list of names, addresses, and telephone numbers of persons who attended. Obtain menus of suspect meals as soon as possible. Additional cases may be identified by checking reservation books and credit card receipts. Review the districts food-related, enteric disease alert/complaint log for recently received complaints which may be related to the outbreak. Consult with your supervisor as to further contact with other health agencies, hospital emergency rooms, poison control centers, and local physicians to find additional cases. At this stage of the investigation, interviews can be accelerated by reviewing the event itself to stimulate each individual's memory. Inquire about specific symptoms known to be common to the suspected syndrome, and mention each food served at the event or meal.

The number of individuals to be interviewed depends on the proportion of attendees who are probably affected. As a rule of thumb, if no more than 100 people attended the meal, an effort should be made to interview everyone. If several hundred were present, a random, representative number should be interviewed.

Prepare a separate FDA 3042, Food Illness Investigation Report, for each person interviewed. See IOM Exhibit 8-7. The FDA 3042 is intended as a guide to supplement a complete narrative report. Do not be restricted to this form in obtaining details during investigations. Information can be extracted from this form to compile an Attack Rate Table to pinpoint the suspect food. See IOM Exhibit 8-8.

8.3.4.4 - Establishment Investigation

When a botulism or other foodborne outbreak is reported, and an establishment is inspected, the initial impact of the incident can create confusion at the plant, and conflicting instructions if too many individuals become involved.

To reduce the confusion, one investigator should be designated as the team leader. A supervisor should be the coordinator for overall district activities, and the district contact for headquarters personnel. All communications from FDA field or other offices to the firm's management should be channeled through the supervisor. The lead investigator should be responsible for all phases of the physical inspection of the facilities, and briefing the supervisor as to his progress. See IOM 5.1.2.5.2.

Upon arrival at the establishment where the suspect food was processed or prepared, the implicated meal was served, identify yourself to the person in charge and state your purpose. Emphasize the purpose of the investigation is to determine what contributed to the outbreak, so preventive measures can be taken. Attempt to create a spirit of cooperation. Consider the position, feelings, and concerns of the manager and his staff; defensive reactions are common.

Many factors could have contributed to contamination before foods came under the control of the manager. Assure him these possibilities will also be investigated. Inform the manager of the activities proposed and benefits which may be gained for educating his workers.

Review of distribution records and examination of warehouse stock are two important aspects of a botulism follow-up inspection. Each of these operations should be monitored by an investigator reporting directly to the team leader. These two monitoring investigators are responsible for all reports from their assigned areas, regardless of the number of investigators assisting them. Field examination should also include an inventory by code of all stock on hand. When conducting field examinations follow instructions in IOM Sample Schedule Chart 2 (IOM, Chapter 4).

When preparing the report, follow instructions in IOM 5.1.2.5.1.

8.3.4.5 - Food Handlers Interviews

If a food is already suspect, interview separately all persons who were directly involved in processing, preparing, or storing of the food and others who could have observed preparation and storage. Ask questions in a sequence that discloses the flow of food from the time it was received until it was served or distributed. Especially inquire about foods that were prepared several hours or days before being served with the suspect meal. Ask similar questions, suitably modified, of the managers or workers who were involved in producing, transporting, processing, preparing, or storing food at other levels of the food chain, as well as individuals who prepared the food at home.

Food workers who fear criticism or punitive action because of their possible role in the outbreak do not always accurately describe the food handling as it actually happened. Their descriptions should be plausible, account for possible sources of contamination, and indicate possibilities of survival and potentials for growth of pathogens. If the description does not contain all the information desired, rephrase the questions and continue the inquiry. Seek confirmation of one person's story by talking to others who have knowledge of the food operation, or by watching the food preparation or processing practices. Be alert for inconsistencies among the accounts, as told by different individuals.

8.3.4.6 - Possible Contamination Source

It is important to have an understanding of the pathogen and the factors that contribute to the contamination that resulted in the foodborne illness. Some pathogens, such as Shigella, are associated with human fecal contamination, while other pathogens, may be more commonly associated with a particular food source (e.g. raw meat and E. coli O157:H7). Exhibit 8-6 and microbiologists can help provide useful information on sources and contributing factors.

8.3.4.6.1 - Pests

Pests are a possible contamination source and can be an indication of poor hygiene, sanitation, food storage, handling and preparation practices. These pests include certain rodents, flies, cockroaches or other pests that:

1. Occur around human settlements.

2. Occur indoors as well as outdoors.

3. Are attracted to potential sources of pathogens (garbage, drains, excrement, etc.) and to human food.

4. Travel back and forth between possible sources of pathogens and food or food contact surfaces.

Evaluate whether a pest is a potential contributing factor to the outbreak by comparing your direct observations of pest activity combined with other evidence of pest activity (excreta, urine, gnawing, etc.) to the above criteria. A pest species that appears to meet all four of the above criteria is a possible source of pathogen contamination. It is helpful to collect specimens of any insect pest that meets these criteria for identification to determine if the pest species is one that is known to carry foodborne pathogens. See Appendix A.

8.3.4.6.2 - Raw Meat

Raw poultry, pork, and other meats are often contaminated when they come into kitchens. If any of these agents are suspected in an outbreak, samples of meat and poultry, meat scraps, drippings on refrigerator floors, and deposits on saws or other equipment can sometimes be helpful in tracing the primary source. Swabbing food contact surfaces of equipment (as tables, cutting boards, slicing machines) which had contact with the suspect food may establish links in the transmission of contamination. This is especially true if a common utensil or piece of equipment is used for raw and cooked foods. Swab these surfaces with sterile swabs, moistened with a sterile solution (such as sterilized 0.1% peptone water or buffered distilled water). Break off the tip of the swab into a tube containing 5 to 10 ml of this solution or into a tube of enrichment broth for specific pathogens. Samples or swabs from air filters, drains, vacuum sweepings, food scrap piles, dried deposits on equipment, and dead ends of pipe lines may reflect the presence of organisms previously in the establishment.

8.3.4.6.3 - Poor Sanitation

Evaluate the cleanliness, manner, and frequency of cleaning equipment. Seek possible routes of cross-contamination between raw and cooked foods. As ingredients may be the initial source of pathogens, determine which were added before, and which were added after any cooking or heat processing.

8.3.4.6.4 - Workers

Workers can be a source of foodborne pathogens. Enterotoxigenic Staphylococcus aureus strains are carried in the nostrils of a large percentage of healthy persons. They are also found on the skin and occasionally in feces. Clostridium perfringens can be recovered from the feces of most healthy persons. Workers are sometimes infected with other enteric pathogens. Employee food safety training and knowledge should be investigated. Poor hygiene practices among food workers (e.g. not washing their hands) continues to be a major contributing factor to foodborne illnesses. See IOM Exhibit 8-6. If the same type of pathogenic organism is recovered from a fecal specimen of a worker and the suspect food, do not immediately conclude the worker was the source. A worker who ate some of the implicated food could be one of the victims. A history that includes a skin infection (boil or carbuncle) or a gastrointestinal or respiratory disturbance preceding the preparation of the suspect food would be more incriminating. Employee attendance and sick leave records may provide additional information.

Look for pimples, minor skin inflammation, boils and infected cuts and burns on unclothed areas of the body; ask if there are any infections in other areas.

8.3.4.7 - Pathogen Growth Factors

In addition to tracing sources of contamination, the circumstances which permitted survival and growth of foodborne pathogens in the implicated foods must be identified. This information is vital to develop preventive measures. Factors usually contributing to outbreaks of specific foodborne illnesses are cited in IOM Exhibit 8-6. Identify these factors by careful and diligent interviews of food workers; close observation of employees' food handling practices; checking temperatures of foods during processing and equipment in which the foods were held; and by conducting studies to determine time-temperatures relationships during processing and storage. Consider times and temperatures which were involved in freezing, thawing, cooking or thermal processing, hot and cold holding, chilling, reheating, and any other steps in the processing operations. It is important to know the survival and growth characteristics of the pathogen that caused the illness outbreak. For example, viruses do not replicate outside of the body and therefore will not "grow" regardless of the temperature. However, their survival characteristics should be considered. You should consult with a microbiologist or OCM/OEO prior to your investigation in order to understand the characteristics of the pathogen and focus on the relevant contributing factors.

8.3.5 - Analyzing Data/Hypothesis Formulation

Organize and group the data obtained from the interviews of both ill or well individuals. From appropriate calculations and analyses, the illness can be classified, the hypothesis tested as to whether the outbreak was associated with a common source, a vehicle can be determined, and the necessity for further field or laboratory investigation can be decided.

8.3.5.1 - Epidemic Curve

An epidemic curve is a graph which depicts the distribution of onset times for the initial symptoms of all cases that occurred in a disease outbreak. The unit of time used in the construction of the graph depends on the disease, or the period covered by the outbreak. For example, use a scale in days or weeks for Hepatitis A; and a scale in hours for staphylococcal food poisoning.

The epidemic curve assists in determining whether the outbreak originated from a common-source, such as food, or person-to-person propagation. A common-source epidemic curve is characterized by a sharp rise to a peak; with the fall usually being less abrupt. The curve continues for a period approximately equal to the duration of one incubation period of the disease. A person-to-person curve is characterized by a relatively slow, progressive rise. The curve will continue over a period equivalent to the duration of several incubation periods of the disease. (Exhibit 8-9)

8.3.5.2 - Symptoms Determination

Determine predominant symptoms by constructing a table as illustrated below:

Frequency of symptoms

Symptoms	**Number of Cases**	**Percent with Symptoms (N = 20)**
Vomiting	17	85
Nausea	12	60
Diarrhea	12	60
Abdominal cramps	6	30
Headache	3	15
Fever	2	10

The percent of ill persons who manifest each symptom is obtained by dividing the number of individuals reporting a given symptom by the number of individuals reporting any symptom (twenty in this example), and multiplying by one-hundred.

This information helps determine whether the outbreak was caused by an agent that produces a neurological, enteric, or generalized illness. Either infections or intoxications will be suggested. Such information can identify suspect foods and indicate appropriate laboratory tests.

8.3.5.3 - Incubation Periods

The incubation period is the interval between ingestion of a food contaminated with enough pathogens to cause illness and the appearance of the initial symptom of the illness. Calculate this interval for each case. Individual incubation periods will vary because of individual resistance to disease, differing amounts of food eaten, uneven distribution of the infectious agent or toxin throughout the food, and other factors.

The shortest and longest incubation periods give a range. Calculate the median incubation period, the mid-value of a list of individual incubation periods when ordered in a series from the shortest to the longest or the average of the two middle values if such series contains an even number of values. The median, rather than the mean, is used because the former is not influenced by exceptionally short or long incubation periods which are sometimes reported in outbreaks of foodborne illness.

The median and range of the incubation period, coupled with information regarding predominant symptoms, form bases upon which to judge whether the disease in question is an infection or an intoxication and thereby determine what laboratory tests should be done. See Exhibit 8-6.

8.3.5.4 - Attack Rate Table

Complete the Food-Specific Attack Rate Table. It provides an easy way to compare the percentage of ill persons who ate each food with the percentage of ill persons who did not eat each food. The attack rate table is useful in identifying the food responsible for an outbreak or illness. This food will usually have the highest attack rate, percent ill, in the column for persons who ate the food and the lowest attack rate in the column for persons who did not eat the food; it will also have the greatest difference between the two rates. See IOM Exhibit 8-8.

8.3.5.5 - Tracebacks of Foods Implicated in Foodborne Outbreaks

Traceback investigations are important epidemiological tools that are used to determine the source of food implicated in foodborne outbreaks. Traceback investigations may prevent further sale and distribution of contaminated food. Commonly, states or local government agencies conduct the initial epidemiological investigation of foodborne outbreaks and identify suspect (interstate) product(s) requiring tracebacks. In some cases FDA may be asked to assist another agency with a traceback investigation.

If a request for an inter-state traceback investigation is received by a District Office, it should be referred to the OCM/OEO 301-443-1240. OCM/OEO and

CFSAN will review the epidemiological data and hazard analysis or environmental assessment before initiating a traceback investigation. OCM/OEO will issue traceback assignments to the appropriate district(s). The task of developing and issuing assignments for traceback investigations related to outbreaks may be delegated from OCM/OEO to CFSAN/OC as necessary. OCM/OEO will coordinate and issue inter-district assignments for traceback investigations. The field should use the FDA Guide to Tracebacks of Fresh Fruits and Vegetables Implicated in Epidemiological Investigations, dated April 2001, unless otherwise directed by DFI or OCM/OEO.

8.3.6 - Reporting

Your district will follow Field Management Directive FMD-119 for proper reporting of epidemiological investigations. Promptly submit a complete narrative of the investigation in English (IOM 1.1), including references to exhibits, samples, medical records, and laboratory reports. There is no prescribed reporting format, but it should be in a logical order. With the inclusion of investigative memos in Turbo EIR, Turbo can be utilized to prepare these memos. See the Turbo EIR Quick Reference Guide for detailed information. See also IOM 8.10.

Submit copies of any written reports and documents for all INJURY or ILLNESS complaints involving all CFSAN products (see section IOM 8.2andIOM 8.4.5) to:

Food and Drug Administration
CFSAN/OSAS
CAERS Staff (HFS-700)
5100 Paint Branch Pkwy
College Park, MD 20740
Attn: CAERS Monitor

Illness/injury complaints involving special nutritional products (refer to IOM 8.4.5.2) must be accompanied by a completed FACTS Adverse Event Questionnaire (Exhibit 8-1) when forwarded to CFSAN.

If additional follow-up on any complaint involving a CFSAN product is necessary, the Division of Field Program Planning and Evaluation (HFS-635) will issue an assignment.

8.3.7 - References

1. "Procedures to Investigate Foodborne Illness" Int'l Assoc. of Milk, Food and Environmental Sanitarians, Inc., Ames, Iowa 50010.
2. "Diseases Transmitted by Foods" CDC, Atlanta, GA. 30333.
3. "Procedures to Investigate Waterborne Illness" Int'l Assoc. of Milk, Food and Environmental Sanitarians, Inc., Ames, Iowa 50010.
4. "Epidemiology Man and Disease" J.P. Fox, M.D., and L.R. Elveback, PhD, MacMillan Publishing Co., N.Y., N.Y. - 1970.
5. FMD 119 - Consumer Product Complaints System.

6. Regulatory Procedures Manual Chapters 5 - 10.

7. "Control of Communicable Diseases Manual," American Public Health Association, Washington, D.C. 20001-3710.

8.4 - Investigation - Injury & Adverse Reaction

8.4.1 - Investigations

The purpose for investigating injury and adverse reactions to drugs, devices, biologics, foods, dietary supplements and cosmetics is to determine the cause of, and to prevent additional injury or adverse reaction to the consuming public.

Injury and adverse reaction complainants should receive a prompt, courteous response, and assurance their complaints will receive appropriate consideration. An immediate follow-up should be made when there is an indication of a serious injury or adverse reaction.

When investigating injuries or adverse reactions, do not make comments or enter into discussions with firms as to the involvement of particular products, unless specifically instructed to do so. Many adverse reactions come to FDA from consumers or health care professionals through the voluntary reporting branch of the MedWatch system. These reports are to be held confidential. Divulging information before the reports are confirmed or denied is inappropriate, and not to be done.

Whenever the press has been informed about a complaint, follow instructions found in Section IOM 1.6.1. When the responsible firm invites the news media to observe the inspectional process, follow instructions found in Section IOM 5.1.4.3.

Personnel routinely receiving complaints should be particularly sensitive to those involving recently approved drugs, devices and biologics. Clinical trials may not have identified all possible adverse reactions, and FDA's approving Center may want to reconsider current labeling, modify directions for use, establish registries for monitoring distribution, or withdraw approval based on the most recent information.

8.4.1.1 - Procedures

When investigating all injuries and adverse reactions:

1. Complete a FACTS Consumer Complaint Report and FACTS Follow-up Report (replaces the FDA 2516 and 2516a) to record and investigate all complaints, unless previously reported through one of FDA's other post marketing surveillance systems such as MedWatch. For special nutritionals, complete the FACTS Adverse Event Questionnaire. For cosmetics, complete the Cosmetics Adverse Event Report. See IOM Exhibits 8-1, 8-2, 8-3, 8-4.

2. Provide complete details on the product involved, including brand name and identity statement with all qualifiers appearing on the label and code marks. In device cases, obtain a wiring diagram or furnish a complete description. Take photographs, if appropriate.

3. Identify the source of the offending article.

4. Provide details of how the product was used, including frequency, in what amounts, other on-going treatments, any known previous adverse reactions or pre-existing allergies and whether applied by the user or someone else. Determine if label directions were followed. Obtain copies of all labeling/inserts. Also, be alert for medical research or literary reviews the reporting party may have conducted or relied upon, and collect copies of such research or reviews. The device community has various publications of frequency of types of adverse events investigated and findings.

5. Obtain a complete description of the incident (sequence of events) and the nature of the injury or adverse reaction, including date, time, location and symptoms or description of injury.

    a. Include any hospital or physician's records available, and identify pre-existing conditions which may have a bearing on the injury or adverse reaction.

    b. Obtain photographs of the victim's injuries, if significant. See IOM 8.2.6 for the procedures used to obtain medical records.

6. List names of other persons involved, such as beauty salon operators, medical personnel, lawyers, insurance agents. Obtain their views on the injury or adverse reaction. The views of an attending physician are important because they may vary markedly from those of the patient.

7. Ask the consumer if an attempt to report the adverse reaction to the product manufacturer has been made, and the nature of the manufacturer's response, if known.

8. Any other consumer complaints, injuries or alleged adverse reactions reported to the manufacturer concerning the product.

9. If necessary, obtain distribution information of the implicated lot(s) from the manufacturer.

8.4.2 - Drugs - Injury or Reactions

Drug injuries or reactions, either human or veterinary, result from the use of products which may:

1. Vary markedly from declared potency.

2. Contain deleterious substances.

3. Are mislabeled as to identity, warnings, or instructions.

4. Have been mistaken for other drugs despite proper labeling.

5. Have changed composition, or become contaminated after shipment.

6. Are dangerous when used according to directions.

7. Have not been used in accordance with label directions or directions from the prescriber.

8. Have been improperly administered, or administered without the necessary precautions.

9. Have been contaminated with objectionable microorganisms, soaps or cleaning solutions.

10. Have been misidentified.

11. Be labeled as sterile drugs, but are found to be non-sterile.

12. Have adverse effects that were not identified prior to marketing.

8.4.2.1 - Investigative Procedures

The following procedures should be followed for investigating suspected adverse drug reactions, including drug-induced birth defects:

1. If you are interviewing the consumer, conduct the normal complaint investigation and gather all pertinent information regarding the product, patient, adverse event, etc. If the consumer received medical treatment, obtain a medical records release (Exhibit 8-5). Reporting of drug adverse experiences is voluntary and you should encourage and assist complainants and health care providers to complete the FDA 3500 form (see Exhibit 8-10) and submit to MedWatch. Report your findings in FACTS Consumer Complaint Follow-up screens and in a memo of investigation.

2. If you are investigating an adverse reaction at the manufacturer, conduct your investigation in an attempt to determine whether the adverse event was caused by a drug quality defect. Determine if the manufacturer was aware of the complaint, has conducted an investigation and per IOM 5.5.7 Adverse Event Reporting has submitted the reportable event to FDA. Your findings will be reported through FACTS Consumer Complaint Follow-up screens and a memo of investigation or Establishment Inspection Report.

3. You may also be directed to conduct investigations at other establishments, such as a pharmacists or distributors. Conduct your normal complaint investigation determining each party's role and involvement. If individuals interviewed are not required to report adverse drug reactions, encourage and assist them to complete and submit the FDA 3500 form to MedWatch.

In all cases of suspect drug-induced adverse reactions, the Center will review the with information on the FDA 3500 form, and will issue assignments to the field if additional information is needed.

8.4.3 - Devices - Injury

The cause of medical device injuries may originate with the manufacturer, operator, user, or from other factors including, but not limited to the transportation or installation of the device.

8.4.3.1 - Mechanical, Electrical or Electromechanical Devices

Injuries caused by mechanical, electrical or electromechanical devices may result from devices that:

1. Do not conform to specifications due to:
    a. Mistreatment (e.g., damage in transit), or
    b. Failure to comply with good manufacturing practices.
2. Malfunction because:
    a. Of incorrect installation,
    b. Have not been used in accordance with labeled instructions,
    c. Have been used/installed with accessories or parts which are not compatible,
    d. Have been used under conditions which interfere with their ability to function (e.g., electromagnetic interference (EMI), fluid seepage into electrical circuits, etc.),
    e. Have been damaged during use, or
    f. Random failures.
3. Have not been adequately designed for intended use (e.g., unstable, poor structural integrity, sharp or pointed surfaces, electrical leakage, etc.).
4. Do not contain adequate directions or warnings.
5. Are intended to be sterile but are nonsterile.
6. Fail or deteriorate for any reason.

8.4.3.2 - Devices for Implant

Causes of injuries which may result from implanted devices include those listed in IOM 8.4.3.1. The term installation, as used above, does not include implantation. Injuries also may result because the materials used in the implant are not biocompatible, thereby causing an adverse tissue reaction and/or deterioration of the implant.

8.4.3.3 - In Vitro Diagnostic Devices

Certain In Vitro Diagnostics (IVD) are instruments, such as gas chromatographs and automated blood analyzers, and much of the information under IOM 8.4.3.1 is applicable.

Investigations

Injuries to patients from IVD products may, in many cases, be considered indirect, because they are due to complications resulting from misdiagnosis or delays in patient treatment due to incorrect test results. Examples of IVD failures include false positives, false negatives and erratic results. Poor performance or failure may be due to poor manufacturing practices or user error.

Manufacturing problems include:

1. Process errors and mix-ups. (e.g., varying fill in kit components, improper ingredient addition, etc.)

2. Labeling does not contain adequate directions or warnings, or contains incorrect information.

3. Labeling mix-ups

4. Contamination, making the product unusable or causing misdiagnosis.

User errors include:

1. Failure to follow label directions

2. Use of unclean or poorly calibrated laboratory equipment.

3. Improper storage of reagents

8.4.3.4 - Investigative Procedures

When investigating incidents implicating a medical device, you must first confirm whether or not the device was a contributing factor. An appropriate follow-up, such as inspection at the manufacturer, may be necessary.

Current agency policy defers regulation to the Department of Transportation (DOT) of automotive adaptive equipment which are medical devices. Consumer complaints or other reports concerning these devices should be referred to DOT.

Copies of EIR's, FACTS Consumer Complaint Report and Follow-Up Report, including documentation and related materials, for all device consumer complaints should be sent to HFZ-343.

Reports received through the Medical Device Reporting system are not considered to be consumer complaints and are tracked through a system maintained by CDRH. A FACTS Consumer Complaint Report should not be completed for any incident that CDRH has requested follow-up on via MDR, unless you originally were advised of the incident by a consumer and initiated a FACTS Consumer Complaint Report at that time. For additional information concerning MDR reports, see the applicable Compliance Program in the CPGM.

Interview the victim, physician(s), and any other individual(s) who witnessed or has knowledge of the incident. When conducting an investigation at a hospital, be sure to contact and inform the administrator of the purpose of the investigation.

8.4.3.4.1 - Devices

Obtain the following information for devices:

1. A complete description of the incident (sequence of events) and the injury, including:
    a. Type, model, serial number and manufacturer of the device.
    b. Details of the alleged incident, including: number of people involved; symptoms, onset time and duration and outcome; date and time of occurrence; reports of other investigating agencies and their conclusions, e.g., fire marshal or OSHA reports; similar incidents which may have resulted in injury; all operational SOP's, written or unwritten.

2. Copies of medical records and/or laboratory records. Use an FDA 461, Authorization for Medical Records Disclosure, IOM Exhibit 8-5, signed by the patient or other authorized person, when obtaining these records.

3. Official cause of death, death certificate and/or autopsy report, if indicated.

4. Determine if the device malfunctioned, and the cause.

5. The condition of the device at the time of use. Review its maintenance history, including responsibility for maintenance (past and present), special service calls, repairs, whether component warning or safety systems were functional, maintenance records, changes or corrections accomplished just prior to or immediately after the incident, and who performed the activity. An interview with bio-engineering department personnel may be indicated.

6. Who has access to the device, and if individuals using the device are familiar with its operation?

7. The results of any examination or inspection of the device by the hospital or other party to determine the cause of the incident.

8. Whether there are other devices of the same model number or lot number on the premises.

8.4.3.4.2 - In Vitro Diagnostics

For In Vitro Diagnostics, determine:

1. What are the results of the test used for? (Screening, therapeutic drug monitoring, epidemiological information, monitoring the course of disease, susceptibility testing, etc.)

2. The clinical value or worth of the test (is it diagnostic, does it only aid in diagnosis).

The report of the investigation and related documentation is extremely important and must be promptly submitted. The report will be used by CDRH Medical and Scientific Review Staff in their health hazard evaluation.

8.4.3.4.3 - Dialysis Injury or Deaths

For Dialysis Injury or Deaths, in addition to the general device investigative procedures,

1. Obtain the following information:
    a. Determine time of incident, i.e., at beginning of procedure, or after several hours of operation.
    b. Actions taken by staff, the number of patients normally treated, medications given, etc.
    c. Whether reuse of the dialyzer is practiced (manual or automated).
    d. Contact and interview maintenance personnel, where appropriate. Verify there is a maintenance schedule.
    e. Verify whether checks on alarm systems were performed prior to each start up and at any other critical stages in the operation, and how often. Determine the last time temperature and/or other alarm systems were calibrated.

2. Verify when the dialysis facility filed a User Facility Report (UFR) in compliance with the Safe Medical Devices Act of 1990.

3. Describe the type of water treatment devices used to make the dialysate. Verify who services and maintains the water treatment system, including off-site regeneration systems. Determine when these services were performed and recorded (name and times), in relationship to the incident. Report, for off-site regeneration systems, whether the resin bed regeneration was "medical use only" or mixed with other uses.

4. Where a dialysis center practices reuse of dialyzers, determine the type of disinfectant method used (manual or automated), type of disinfectant used (formaldehyde, renalin, glutaraldehyde, etc.) and review the service and maintenance records for proper procedure including names, dates and time.

8.4.4 - Biologics - Injury, Reaction Or Fatality

Reactions or symptoms of illness may occur in association with the administration of vaccines and other biological products. The Center for Biologics Evaluation and Research (CBER) is interested in all unexpected clinical responses to a biological product, as well as any expected responses of unusual frequency or severity. In some cases, a reaction or illness could occur because the product may:

1. Vary from declared potency.

2. Have been contaminated during manufacturing, shipment, or after shipment.

3. Be mislabeled.

4. Not have been given according to directions.

5. Not have been stored under proper conditions.

6. Have been provided to the wrong person.

7. Contain substances innocuous to most people, but which the recipient is unable to tolerate (anti-Kidd, anti-Duffy), or contains substances not usually present in such a product which stimulate an adverse response in the recipient (HLA antibodies).

8.4.4.1 - Professional Reporting System for Vaccine Adverse Reactions

The National Childhood Vaccine Injury Act of 1986, 42 USC 201, was passed to achieve optimal prevention of childhood infectious diseases through immunization. At the same time, it was intended to minimize the number and severity of adverse reactions to vaccines routinely administered to children. This law requires health care providers and vaccine manufacturers to report certain adverse events which occur following the administration of specific vaccines. The vaccines and reportable events are listed in the National Childhood Vaccine Injury Act Vaccine Injury Table. The Department of Health and Human Services (DHHS) has established a Vaccine Adverse Events Reporting System (VAERS) to accept all reports of suspected adverse events after the administration of any vaccine, in all age groups, including but not limited to those in the table.

The Vaccine Adverse Event Reporting System (VAERS) is administered under a joint FDA/CDC contract. The system utilizes a preaddressed and postage paid form (Form VAERS-1) for reporting adverse events which occur subsequent to vaccine administration. See IOM Exhibit 8-11.

8.4.4.2 - Investigation/Reporting

When a biologics reaction/injury complaint is received by the district office (DO), a preliminary investigation should be conducted. CBER should be consulted before initiating any follow-up which extends beyond the complainant, and in some cases even before the complainant interview.

All complaints initially received by the District Office must be recorded on the FACTS Consumer Complaint Report. When interviewing the complainant about a biologics complaint /injury, obtain:

1. Complete description of the complaint/injury.

2. Onset and duration of the reaction/injury.

3. Name of product administered, include date and time of administration.

4. Manufacturer and lot number of product, if available.

At this point, it is generally unnecessary to conduct interviews beyond the complainant, or obtain records, until a preliminary review has been conducted. It is important to rapidly communicate the basic information about the incident, implicated product, lot, license number, manufacturer, and presence of intact units to the Center and the OCM/OEO contact. Immediately, CBER offices will advise whether reactions are expected or unexpected, and the level of investigation, including sample collection and analysis, necessary. Further follow-up is unnecessary until it has been determined the reaction/injury is not unexpected, or has not already been reported through other channels.

Vaccine Products - If the complaint involves an adverse reaction of any kind, then a Form VAERS-1 (IOM Exhibit 8-11) should be sent to the complainant. The form should be completed by the complainant's physician, if at all possible, or by the complainant, if the physician will not cooperate. The completed VAERS Reporting Form should be mailed directly to the address on the form. When you send a VAERS form to a complainant, note this fact in the Remarks Section of the FACTS Consumer Complaint Report.

If the complaint does not involve an adverse reaction, obtain the necessary information to allow the Center to make an informed decision on follow-up at the manufacturer.

Biological Products - If the complaint is an adverse reaction to a product, an FDA 3500, MedWatch Form (See IOM Exhibit 8-10) must also be completed and forwarded to the complainant for completion by their physician. If the physician will not cooperate by completing the FDA-3500, request the complainant to do it. Assist the complainant in completing the FDA 3500, if necessary. Note in the "Remarks" section of the FACTS Consumer Complaints Report that the FDA 3500 was forwarded to the complainant.

If the complaint does not involve an adverse reaction, obtain information necessary to permit the Center or home district to make an informed decision on follow-up at the manufacturer. If a complainant desires further information, refer them to CBER, Office of Biostatistics and Epidemiology at 301-827-3974.

If the complaint is a fatality where blood or a blood component is implicated, notify CBER, Office of Compliance and Biologics Quality, as soon as possible (21 CFR 606.170). This is required of the collecting facility, in the event of a donor reaction, and by the facility which performed the compatibility tests, in the event of a transfusion reaction. An investigation of the incident shall be conducted by either HCFA or FDA, based on the type of facility involved, for example, transfusion service, blood bank, plasma center or hospital.

8.4.5 - Foods, Dietary Supplements and Cosmetics - Injury or Reaction

CFSAN regulates a wide variety of products including foods, seafood, wine beverages less than 7% alcohol (including wine coolers), bottled water, food additives, infant formulas, dietary supplements, and cosmetics. Each of these products is used differently and regulated under a different part of the Act and thus has slightly different investigational requirements. Background and common causes for adverse events are provided for selected products below.

Monitoring of complaints on CFSAN products is performed by the CAERS Staff. CFSAN investigations are generally limited to serious adverse events. Therefore, for serious adverse events (previously defined above in IOM 8.2.1.1) follow the specific investigation requirements below, in addition to the general investigation requirements above.

NOTE: Contact the CFSAN Adverse Events Reporting System (CAERS) Staff, HFS-845, 301-436-2405, Fax: 301-436-2452, or email CAERS@fda.hhs.gov for all questions pertaining to field follow-up requests or medical guidance on investigations of adverse reactions associated with CFSAN monitored products. CAERS will coordinate with the office experts.

8.4.5.1 - Cosmetics

It is important that FDA conducts appropriate investiga-tions and follow-up on adverse events attributed to cos-metic products.

Confusion regarding a product's legal status as a cos-metic, a drug or a combination drug/cosmetic may impede investigational use of complaint system information. For clarification of the distinction between cosmetics and drugs, refer to the document, "Is it a cosmetic, a drug or both? (or is it soap?)" at http://www.cfsan.fda.gov/~dms/cos-218.html. Questions may also be directed to the Office of Cosmetics and Colors at (301) 436-1130.

Injuries or adverse reactions may arise from cosmetics which:

1. Are inherently dangerous or which may prove harmful or injurious to a consumer;
2. Cause primary irritation of skin, eye, or mucous membranes (including the lungs and urinary tract) or which may be due to an indi-vidual sensitization reaction or allergic response; or due to ingestion;
3. Have undergone formulation changes, or been chemi-cally or microbiologically contaminated while in the pos-session of the manufacturer, dealer, distributor, or end user;
4. Are misbranded because they contain unlisted ingredi-ents, lack instructions for safe use for certain high risk products (e.g., depilatories, hair dyes), or lack any required warning statements;
5. Have been misused.

8.4.5.2 - Dietary Supplements

The Dietary Supplement Health and Education Act of 1994 (See DSHEA) defined the term "dietary supplement" to mean a product, intended to supplement the diet, that contains one or more dietary ingredients, i.e., vitamins, minerals, herbs or other botanicals, amino acids, and dietary substances for use by man to increase the total dietary intake, as well as a concentrate, metabolite, constituent, extract, or combination of any of the dietary ingredients. Under DSHEA, a dietary supplement is a food which must be labeled as a "dietary supplement", and cannot be represented for use as a conventional food or the sole item of a meal or diet.

DSHEA also removes dietary ingredients from coverage under the food additive provisions of the FD&C Act. Rather, DSHEA places the burden on the Agency to prove a dietary supplement or dietary ingredient is adulterated before the product can be removed from the marketplace.

Therefore, a crucial source of information on potentially unsafe products is the Agency's consumer complaint system. It is extremely important that FDA conduct appropriate investigations and follow-up on adverse events attributed to dietary supplement products.

The instruction and guidance provided in IOM 8.4.5.2.1/2 must be followed when conducting follow-up on complaints involving adverse reactions to special nutritional products.

8.4.5.2.1 - Causes

Injuries or other adverse reactions may be associated with the use of products which:

1. Vary markedly from the declared potency or concentration.
2. Contain deleterious substances accidentally included in their manufacture.
3. Have changed composition or become contaminated after shipment.
4. Are mislabeled as to identity, warnings or instructions for use.
5. Have not been used according to label instructions or the directions of the manufacturer or prescriber.
6. Are dangerous when used according to directions.

8.4.5.2.2 - Procedures

When investigating adverse events attributed to special nutritional products, direct attention to, and document:

1. Complete details on the product involved, including code marks.
2. The source of the offending article.
3. Details of how the product was used, including frequency, in what amounts, concomitant treatments, and whether administered by the user or someone else. Determine if label directions were followed. Obtain copies of all labeling/inserts.
4. Nature of the injury. Include any hospital or physician's records available, and identify pre-existing conditions which may have a bearing on the injury. Obtain photographs of the victim's injuries, if significant. See IOM 8.2.6 for the procedures used to obtain medical records.

5. Names of other persons involved, such as medical personnel, lawyers, insurance agents, etc. Obtain their views on the injury. The views of attending physician are important because they may vary markedly from those of the patient.

6. A complete description of the incident (sequence of events) and the injury.

Complete the FACTS Adverse Event Questionnaire (See IOM Exhibit 8-1) either during the initial consumer contact, e.g., telephone report of complaint, or soon thereafter. The Adverse Event Questionnaire contains additional information which must be obtained and forwarded to CFSAN. Information already contained in the FACTS Consumer Complaint Report need not be duplicated on the questionnaire.

NOTE: Contact the CFSAN Adverse Events Reporting System (CAERS) Staff, HFS-845, 301-436-2405, Fax: 301-436-2452, or email CAERS@fda.hhs.gov for questions pertaining to field follow-up requests related to foods, seafood, food additives, dietary supplements, infant formulas and medical foods. CAERS personnel will coordinate field guidance related to these products with CFSAN's experts.

Questions on compliance or other regulatory matters should be directed to the Office of Compliance, Division of Enforcement, HFS-605, 301-436-2417.

Investigations

8.4.5.3 - Investigation Requirements for Serious Adverse Events of CFSAN Regulated Products

If the suspect product is a Cosmetic, interview the injured person and/or the reporter of the event and complete the FACTS Consumer Complaint Cosmetic Report (IOM Exhibit 8-4).

If the suspect product is not a Cosmetic, interview the injured person and/or the reporter of the event and complete the Adverse Event Questionnaire (IOM Exhibit 8-1).

If suspect product is an Infant Formula or Baby Food, inform OCM/OEO 301-443-1240 immediately and investigate on a high-priority basis due to the continued sensitivity to these incidents. This will include follow-up with the doctor or hospital, sample collection and analysis of appropriate product. Refer complaints involving baby food regulated by USDA to USDA for appropriate follow-up. See IOM 8.3.1.3 and IOM 3.2.1.2.

Obtain Medical Records Release forms (FDA-461) from the injured person or guardian.

If the adverse event is a death, the following medical records should be considered for collection:

1. Admission History and Physical or Emergency Room/Clinic record of the event if the patient was not admitted

2. Discharge Summary

3. Autopsy Report

4. Death Certificate

Samples - If you believe a suspect product should be sampled, discuss with your Supervisor. See IOM 8.2.7 for guidance.

For all events, a memo of investigation will be completed. Send a complete copy, including copies of all labels and labeling, Medical Records Release (FDA 461) and medical records collected to the CAERS Staff.

8.4.5.4 - Undeclared Allergen/Allergic Reactions

We often receive complaints involving allergic reactions to food products containing suspected undeclared allergens. It is important to obtain specific information unique to these complaints. Suspected undeclared allergen complaints should receive high priority. Undeclared allergens in food products often result in recalls.

The following should be addressed with the consumer and recorded in the "Complaint Description" section of the FACTS consumer complaint report.

1. List all foods the person is allergic to.
2. List all foods consumed within approximately the hour prior to reaction.
3. Indicate how much was consumed of the suspect food(s).
4. Record the on-set time of the reaction.
5. List all symptoms experienced in the order they occurred.
6. Indicate treatment given.
7. Record the ingredient statement from product packaging on the complaint form ("Remarks"-page 1). (Look for hidden allergens within the ingredient statement.)
8. Indicate if the label includes a "may contain" statement and record the statement.
9. Indicate whether the consumer has a documented food allergy. (It may be necessary to collect the medical records as the investigation of the complaint progresses.)

Inspectional follow up at the manufacturing plant may be warranted to determine if suspect allergenic ingredient is added to the product; or if the possibility of cross-contact exists.

The Food Allergen Labeling and Consumer Protection Act (FALCPA) became effective 1/1/2006. See the FDA Website for additional background information related to it.

8.4.6 - Veterinary Products - Complaints/Adverse Reactions

Complaints and adverse reactions associated with veteri-nary products including animal drugs, medicated feeds, and medical devices for animals are handled through the Division of Surveillance (HFV-210). Veterinarians, animal owner and firms may report problems to their local FDA offices, OCM/OEO, or directly to the Center for Vet-erinary Medicine. The District and the OCM/OEO will complete a FACTS Consumer Complaint Report and ad-vise the complainant to complete a FDA 1932a "Veteri-nary Drug Adverse Experience, Lack of Effectiveness or Product Defect Report". The form and instructions are available at http://www.fda.gov/cvm/adetoc.htm

8.4.7 - Sample Collection

Collect a sample of the product which caused the injury and an official sample from the same lot. Collect the same and other lot codes, if available. Check with your supervisor if you have any doubt as to the appropriateness of collecting a particular sample.

See IOM 4.5.5.3 for routing of injury and complaint samples to the laboratory.

8.4.7.1 - Device Samples

Obtain Center concurrence prior to collecting any device samples.

8.4.7.2 - Biological Samples

Do not collect samples of the suspect product until an evaluation of the preliminary information on the injury/reaction has been made by CBER (Licensed products) or the Home District (Unlicensed Products, Plasma and Blood Products).

8.4.7.3 - Cosmetic Samples

Products such as depilatories, permanent hair dyes, home permanents, deodorants, hair straighteners, etc. are known to cause adverse reactions. Samples of these products should not be collected except in cases of alleged severe or unusual injury, e.g., multiple complaints. In case of obvious allergic type reactions, samples should not be collected. Most cosmetic products which get into the eye will cause temporary eye irritation and in such cases, a sample generally should not be collected.

8.4.7.4 - Microbiological Contamination

Collect samples associated with consumer complaints in which microbiological contamination is suspected.

8.4.7.5 - Allergen Samples

Sample if allergen is visible (i.e. nuts) and is not declared on label (and if deemed necessary by District management). In all other cases, only after consultation with OEO (e.g., National Consumer Complaint Coordinator) and

CFSAN. See IOM Sample Schedule Chart 13 for guidance on sample size. Note: the sample size may be modified depending on product availability.

8.4.8 - Reporting

Prompt reporting is essential. You may save the lives of others. See IOM 1.1 English language requirement.

8.4.8.1 - Reporting Forms

Field personnel should report all consumer complaints in FACTS. In addition, for adverse reactions or injury associ-ated with drugs, medical devices, cosmetics, biologics (except vaccines), provide complainants the MedWatch web address: www.fda.gov/medwatch or the FDA 3500 MedWatch form (IOM Exhibit 8-10). Prior to sending a MedWatch form to the complainant, enter the FDA FACTS consumer complaint number in the box below the Triage Unit Se-quence # in the upper right corner of form FDA 3500.

For veterinary product complaints, provide complainants with an FDA 1932a "Veterinary Drug Adverse Experience, Lack of Effectiveness or Product Defect Report" available at http://www.fda.gov/cvm/adetoc.htm.

For adverse reactions to vaccine products, provide com-plainants with form VAERS-1 (IOM 8.4.4.2, IOM Exhibit 8-11).

8.4.8.2 - Routing Reports

A copy of the FACTS consumer complaint report and your narrative report(s), including any copies of medical or injury reports obtained should be submitted by your district to the appropriate office. Fax transmission may be used.

8.4.8.2.1 - Drugs

Drug complaints and injuries to:

MedWatch
The FDA Medical Products Reporting Program (HFD-410)
Food and Drug Administration
5600 Fishers Lane
Rockville, MD 20857
Fax Number: 301-827-7241

8.4.8.2.2 - Medical Device and Radiological Products

Medical Device and Radiological Product complaints and injuries to:

Food and Drug Administration
Center for Devices and Radiological Health
Division of Surveillance Systems (HFZ-530)
1350 Piccard Drive
Rockville, MD 20850

8.4.8.2.3 - Foods and Cosmetics

If the online MedWatch form is not used for reporting adverse events, send both adverse events and product problems for CFSAN regulated products including cosmetics, infant formulas, dietary supplements and all other foods to:

Food and Drug Administration
Center for Food Safety and Applied Nutrition
CAERS Staff (HFS-845)
Attn: CAERS Monitor
5100 Paint Branch Pkwy
College Park, MD 20740

8.4.8.2.4 - Veterinary Products

Veterinary injuries or adverse reaction reports to:

Food and Drug Administration
Center for Veterinary Medicine
Division of Surveillance (HFV-210)
7500 Standish Place
Rockville, MD 20857

8.4.8.2.5 - Licensed Biological Products

For licensed biological products (includes vaccines), except for source plasma and blood products, the receiving district will complete the FACTS consumer complaint report and fax a copy to HFM-650 at 301-443-3874, select HFM-650 in the referrals box and then electronically forward to the home district. The home district will select "Surveillance for Next EI" as the final disposition and close the complaint. CBER will issue an assignment if follow-up is needed.

8.4.8.2.6 - Unlicensed Biologics Products

For unlicensed biological product, plasma, blood and blood products, the receiving district will complete and electronically forward the FACTS consumer complaint to the home district and send a hard copy to HFM-650. The home district will determine if any follow-up is needed and issue an appropriate assignment. Advice is available from HFM-650 at 301-594-1911.

8.4.8.2.7 - Biologics Injury/Adverse Reaction Reports

Biologics injury/adverse reaction narrative reports are forwarded to:

Food and Drug Administration
Center for Biologic Evaluation and Research
Office of Compliance
1401 Rockville Pike, Suite 400S
Rockville, MD 20852

NOTE: *In addition, check the "Notify EO/EMOPS?" box in FACTS for all injury and adverse reaction complaints. For serious injury/illness reports, please notify the OCM/OEO immediately at 301-443-1240.*

8.5 - Disaster Procedures

The objective of FDA investigations in the aftermath of non-attack disasters is to determine whether or not foods, drugs including biologics, cosmetics and devices affected by the catastrophe are safe for human and animal use; and if not, to effectively remove them from commerce.

In disaster operations, FDA will assist state, local and other federal agencies in removing contaminated or unfit merchandise from the market.

8.5.1 - Disaster Types

The types of natural and man-made disasters which affect FDA operations are:

Floods	Earthquakes
Hurricanes	Volcanoes
Tornadoes	Chemical Spills
Wrecks	Riots and Disorders
Fires Explosions	Bioterrorism

8.5.2 - Responsibility & Coordination

State and local officials usually assume direct responsibility, as their laws and regulations can be immediately invoked, however FDA assistance is often requested. Except in unusual circumstances, FDA responsibilities are to assist the state and local health agencies in removing, destroying or reconditioning affected merchandise.

In situations involving interstate movement of merchandise; large interstate firms; areas in which state or local political ramifications are anticipated; or when state or local health officials so request; FDA may assume the primary role in the operation.

8.5.3 - Preparation

Personal Safety - In a disaster or pending disaster the personal protection of yourself and your family is your primary concern. Provide for your own safety as you perform your FDA duties in a disaster area. Inoculations and protective clothing should be considered. See IOM 1.5.1 and IOM 1.5.1.3.

Disasters produce dangerous situations. e.g.; high water, escaping gases, fallen electrical lines, damaged buildings, falling rubble, etc., so care and extra safety precautions must be observed. If you become sick or injured, you become another problem to already overworked health officials.

CAUTION: In situations where electrical power has been out for an extended period of time, and firms attempt to salvage frozen or refrigerated products using dry ice, do not enter these areas without first providing for proper ventilation and/or obtaining oxygen breathing apparatus.

Inspectional and Investigational Preparation - After taking care of yourself and family, and being properly equipped and supplied, you are ready to begin disaster operation. Stock your car in the same manner as for any inspectional activities; however, consider the extra amounts of materials needed in the particular situation.

Extra gasoline and oil, drinking water, communication equipment (cellular and satellite phones, email, etc.), battery powered radios, lighting equipment (battery flashlights, propane or gasoline lanterns, etc), extra film, medical supplies and materials of an emergency nature must be provided if power facilities and normal distribution channels are disrupted. Consideration must also be given to your own sleeping and eating needs.

Review the Model Food Salvage Code, 1984 Recommendation of the Association of Food and Drug Officials and the U.S. Department of Health and Human Services for guidance.

8.5.4 - Preliminary Investigation

Initial Information - FDA usually learns of disasters, or impending disasters from weather agencies, news media, public health agencies, civil defense units, or law enforcement organizations. Initially, there is little anyone can do, other than monitor the course and severity of a disaster, until the situation becomes sufficiently stabilized for personnel to move into the area to survey damage.

Initial Procedures - FDA's initial course of action is to contact state and local officials, offer assistance, and begin to coordinate the mobilization of personnel and resources necessary to handle the emergency.

If you are in an area when a disaster strikes or is imminent, advise your supervisor on the situation by the fastest means possible. In the initial stage of the operation you may be the only FDA representative on the scene. If this is the case, contact the state or local officials and offer your services, advising them you have alerted or will alert your district as soon as possible. Keep your supervisor informed.

Each district has a disaster plan which will be implemented in applicable situations. As the situation develops, you will receive instructions from your supervisor.

8.5.5 - Field Operations

Inspectional and investigational activities will normally be conducted with other FDA personnel and state or local counterparts.

Once personnel are mobilized and assignments issued, your operational procedures will be similar, regardless of the type of disaster. You will be searching out, identifying and investigating foods, drugs, devices, and cosmetics for actual or possible contamination and taking the necessary steps to preclude their use until they are released, reconditioned, or destroyed.

A rapid physical survey must first be made of the disaster area to determine the extent of damage, and the amounts and kinds of merchandise involved.

CAUTION: Although procedures in this subchapter do not cover disasters resulting from nuclear attack, it is possible you may discover products suspected of contamination by radioactive materials in the disaster area. If you suspect the presence of radioactive materials, take no action on the materials yourself, but have the area cordoned off at once. Notify the command official and immediately contact your supervisor to alert the regional radiological health representative and the state radiation control agency. Follow their instructions.

When in doubt as to the condition of any materials affected, request holds or embargoes pending final outcome of further examinations. See IOM 8.5.5.2.

8.5.5.1 - Embargoes

See IOM 3.3.1 and IOM 2.7.1.

FDA has no embargo powers except as specified in:

1. The Federal Meat Inspection Act
2. The Poultry Products Inspection Act
3. The Egg Products Inspection Act
4. Certain parts of the FD&C Act, namely Section 304(g)[21U.S.C.334(g)]

In emergency situations, state and local embargoes are an effective tool. Embargoes can be employed immediately and, the merchandise held, destroyed, or reconditioned without time consuming delays. Some state and local embargo powers are limited as to time and/or amounts. In these cases, the use of federal injunction and seizure action must not be overlooked. State or local agencies may also confer their embargo authority to FDA personnel for the duration of the emergency.

8.5.5.2 - Field Examination & Samples

During all your investigational activities examine the lots affected for obvious adulteration, decomposition, contamination, or physical damage. Use your camera extensively, and collect samples whenever indicated. Judge the extent of field examination and sample collections necessary, based on the nature and magnitude of the disaster.

In major catastrophes, large numbers of samples may not be necessary because of obvious visible contamination and the emergency disposition powers invoked by state and local officials. In minor local disasters, such as fires, riots, train, truck, or shipwrecks, lots may be held pending outcome of examinations, so extensive sampling may be required.

Examine cans or jars for physical damage (rusty, burst seams, holes, ripped, etc.), and for visible adulteration from filth, oil or chemicals, and defaced labels. In addition, examine jars and bottles for sediment or other visible filth under cap crimps and cap lugs. When a lid is removed, sediment or micro-contamination may be drawn into the container by internal vacuum. Discard any jars you open for examination. Visible contamination under lids may be photographed or lids may be used as exhibits as conditions permit.

Plastic, paper, cloth bags, and cardboard containers must be examined for physical damage and contamination.

Stocks of devices must be examined for contamination, water, heat, mechanical, physical, electrical, or chemical damage. If any doubt exists as to whether or not devices have been affected, experts should be consulted or utilized.

Examine bulk containers and their contents, including underground storage tanks. Examine material in rail cars, truck trailers, and storage silos. Be especially alert for rail car and trailer movement. These quickly disappear, as clean-up crews arrive.

8.5.5.3 - Flooding

All flood water, regardless of its source, must be considered a polluting medium because of overflowing sewers, outhouses, decomposing livestock, street run-off water, etc.

Depending on the extent of the flood, first determine the locations of the major stocks of regulated products. Food and drugs will normally receive first priority. As stocks of goods are located, rapidly survey the extent of damage, then concentrate on affected materials. Use your camera extensively. Examine the walls of buildings and storage areas and the top and sides of stacked or tiered goods for flood water residue, debris, and the usually well defined high-water mark. Merchandise stacked above this line is still of concern because other problems probably exist, e.g. vermin defilement, failure of refrigeration, thawing of frozen items, etc.

Make arrangements to have any suspect material embargoed by local officials, or held pending final disposition. Management is usually cooperative and willing to do things it may not normally do to get back to normal operations as quickly as possible. Cooperate with management, but avoid hasty decisions.

Much merchandise is quickly rendered unsuitable for human consumption by water action. Items such as bread, cakes, cookies, candies, bulk flour, sugar, bulk liquids, and similar items not in jars or hermetically sealed containers can often be immediately hauled to disposable areas and destroyed.

Determine areas which have lost power. In facilities such as frozen food firms, frozen or refrigerated warehouses, etc., check the sites for length of down-power and condition of the merchandise. If power is restored in time to avoid thawing, or prevent spoilage of refrigerated items, and products were not inundated, or otherwise affected, there is no need for further examination.

Even though flood waters may not have inundated the firm, the situation may have caused sewer and waste lines to back-flush into basements and immediately drain out again. Debris or sewage particles along walls and on low floor surfaces or presence of sewage odors are evidence of backflushing.

Grain, cottonseed, soybeans, dried bean products, peanuts, and similar products may become flood damaged in terminal elevators, on farms, and in flat storage facilities. In addition to flood water contamination, molding products may develop mycotoxin contamination. Examine susceptible products and facilities for damage, inundation and mold.

Rodent activity may increase in flooded areas as the vermin seek food and shelter. Be alert to rodent defilement on products.

As lots of goods are checked, embargoed or released and the immediate situation returns to normal, firms will want to start operating. Prior to their beginning operations, examine equipment and processing facilities for pollution, and its aftermath. Plant operation must not be permitted unless proper cleanup and sanitizing is performed.

8.5.5.4 - Hurricanes & Tornadoes

Investigate following the guidance in IOM 8.5.5.3. In addition, examine merchandise for evidence of physical damage caused by flying particles and crushing by debris. Physical damage to product containers may be extensive. Broken or leaking containers of materials such as chemicals, oils, fertilizers, etc., may have contaminated materials subject to FDA coverage. Also see IOM 8.5.5.6 on chemical contamination from various sources.

8.5.5.5 - Fires, Explosions, Riots

FDA operations following these disasters are usually localized and do not normally involve a large number of personnel or extended resources.

Examine stocks for exposure to excessive heat, physical damage from flying particles and falling debris, and lack of refrigeration in down-power areas. Examine for water damage from fire fighting activities and handle these as a flooding situation. Also, be alert for possible pollution from using non-potable water in fire fighting.

Fire fighting often involves use of chemicals, so examine merchandize for residues from possible toxic fire extinguishing materials, and question fire authorities regarding this issue.

In addition, chemical contamination in fire disasters can also be present from other sources, including:

1. Stored chemicals rupturing from heat or from impact of falling debris.
2. Spraying or leaking chemicals (liquid, powder, dust, granules) as damaged containers are being removed or salvaged from the fire area.
3. Tracking of chemical material from contaminated areas to other areas by fire crews or others.
4. Burning or melting plastic containers and/or insulation and other building materials.
5. Leaking fuels, storage batteries, anti-freeze, etc., from burning, damaged or overheated equipment.
6. Chemicals from melting or vaporizing electrical insulation and, in particular, cooling chemicals from leaking or exploding electrical transformers. Large commercial transformers are often directly involved in the fire area and may leak or explode from the heat, spreading toxic liquid chemicals (some transformer oils contain concentrations of PCB) over a large area, even contaminating products in non-fire areas.

8.5.5.6 - Chemical Spills, Hazardous Waste Sites, Wrecks

See IOM 3.2.11 for information.

Chemical spills occurring on land or water can pose a serious threat to the environment and contaminate FDA regulated products both directly and indirectly.

In wrecks, the physical impact usually causes most damage. Toxic items in the same load may rupture and add to the contamination. In train wrecks, other railcars loaded with chemicals, oils or other contaminating materials may rupture and contaminate food and drug products in otherwise undamaged cars. Removal of the wreckage may cause further physical damage or chemical contamination. Exposure to weather may also adversely affect the products.

Do not overlook the possibility that runoff of toxic chemicals from wrecked and ruptured cars may contaminate adjacent or nearby streams supplying water to downstream firms under FDA jurisdiction.

Hazardous waste sites also pose a hazard to the immediate environment, as well as off-site, if runoff contaminates nearby surface waters or if leachate contaminates ground water supplies.

8.5.5.7 - Earthquakes

Extreme care must be exercised when working in earthquake areas. Do not enter severely damaged buildings.

Most damage from an earthquake comes from the after shocks, falling debris, and resulting fires and flooding. Items under FDA jurisdiction are most likely to suffer physical damage, spoilage from lack of refrigeration, and/or fire and flood damage.

8.5.6 - Bioterrorism

Guidance to the Field on Bioterrorism (10/17/2001)

When a District is notified of a suspected bioterrorism event (including anthrax events) involving an FDA regulated product, they will notify Office of Crisis Management/Office of Emergency Operations (OCM/OEO) (301-443-1240) and the local OCI office immediately. OCM/OEO will then notify the appropriate FDA Center, the HHS Office of Emergency Preparedness (OEP) and OCI headquarters. OCI will then notify FBI and/or local law enforcement. If OCM/OEO or any other FDA office gets a report, OCM/OEO will notify the offices above as well as the District Office involved. Notification of the state officials will occur at the direction of OCM/OEO or OCI.

It is vital that the person taking the initial report obtain complainant contact information as well as detailed information about the event. This is the same information that is regularly collected for consumer complaints and used to record the complaint in FACTS. Complainants should be instructed to call local police (911) and follow police instructions.

If a bioterrorism act is suspected, FDA staff should not collect or accept samples from any local, state, or law enforcement agency as such actions will be coordinated by OCI and the FBI, as appropriate. If an FDA product is suspected in a tampering, please call OCM/OEO immediately. In the event that FBI/OCI determine the product is not suspect, OCM/OEO will issue further guidance to the District Office.

8.5.7 - Product Disposition

In every disaster situation orderly disposition of affected merchandise poses problems. Lots under embargo, or voluntarily held pending examination or analysis, must be secured until the examination or analysis is completed, and a decision to release is made. If the material can be released, it is returned to the owner. If contamination is obvious and state or local officials condemn the lots, arrangements must be made for disposition. Mixed adulterated and non-adulterated materials must be held for segregation and disposition.

Depending on the circumstances and the magnitude of the disaster, segregation, destruction or reconditioning of affected goods may be accomplished in the immediate area. However, the materials may be moved to distant locations for further manipulation.

FDA normally opposes movement of affected goods since control of the lots is difficult. However, in cases of wide spread disasters, reconditioning centers established in non-disaster areas may be the most efficient way to handle the problem. Decisions of this nature will be made by command or headquarters officials. Should the materials be moved, arrangements must be made for their control. Short moves might necessitate guards on the vehicles to prevent diversion, while longer ones may be by regular carriers with control by shipping records, sealed railroad cars, bonded truckers, etc.

A situation not usually encountered during our normal operations is the problem of scavengers. Handling scavengers and preventing their activity is a police matter. Nevertheless, it ties in closely with your operations in disasters, and plans must be formulated for the protection of merchandise detained, released, or awaiting disposition at the disposition site.

In disasters, local police forces are usually augmented by State and County Police, National Guard, State Militia or private security forces. Arrangements should be made by the disaster command officials for guarding of affected merchandise. If this has not been done, you should make the recommendation.

8.5.7.1 - Segregation

The condition of certain goods may be difficult to ascertain since one often has no way of determining how excessive heat, humidity or disaster conditions affected package contents. Smoke damaged containers of one material may not be of concern, while for other materials, it may be cause for condemnation. Rules for each product in each situation are impossible. Your decisions in disaster areas should be based on experience, review of the laboratory results if possible, and input from your state/local counterparts and superiors.

The segregation process often creates a multitude of problems, especially when insurance claims-agents and salvage firms become involved. You are not to segregate materials yourself. This is the responsibility of the owner or his agent. You should advise them what constitutes releasable conditions.

After segregation, you may be instructed to advise them what can and cannot be released based on your examination and/or laboratory results.

8.5.7.2 - Destruction

It is not your responsibility to say how condemned goods are to be destroyed. This is a concern of the owner and the state or local health agencies who condemned the lots. Many times, however, FDA will be asked to aid in or recommend destruction methods. The most common destruction method is crushing and dumping in a land fill in approved areas. See IOM 2.6.1. Destruction methods usually are worked out with state or local officials. The final decision in major operations may be required of the command officials or higher headquarters, especially if the environmental impact is significant.

Control materials to be destroyed, and protect them from pilfering at destruction sites.

8.5.7.3 - Reconditioning

Often, merchandise affected may be reconditioned depending on the condition of the product, its container, type product, intended use, and extent and kind of contamination.

Any reconditioning must be closely supervised, with proper safeguards for merchandise accountability. Procedures must be such that control over the operation is complete, with proper disposition of the rejected portion and the material reconditioned to the satisfaction of all health officials.

Certain articles which cannot be salvaged for human or animal use might be of use in non-food or non-feed industries. Examples of such products are:

1. Butter for soap stock
2. Meat and Poultry products for technical oil production
3. Oils and nuts for technical oil production
4. Flour for glue or wall board construction
5. Grains and fruits (especially dried) for industrial alcohol
6. Fish for fertilizer
7. Eggs for tannery use

However, these must be denatured to render them unfit for food or feed use. Firms must be required to account for the amounts denatured and keep records as to whom sold and for what final use. Examination of the product at its final destination and/or a spot check may be required to assure it is utilized in non-food or non-feed products.

8.5.7.4 - Relabeling

Relabeling will be permitted, if all the following conditions are met.

1. The new label contains all mandatory information, is not misleading in any way, and conforms with the Act in all other aspects;
2. Label codes are carried over to the new label;
3. The product is not contaminated; and
4. The container has its original integrity.

8.5.7.5 - Ammonia Leaks

Refer to IOM 1.5.4.2.2 for guidance prior to entering any area where an ammonia leak has occurred.

If products involved in an ammonia leak are to be salvaged/reconditioned, cover the following points:

1. Cases of food should be removed from ammonia spill rooms as soon as possible.
2. Food packages should be removed from master corrugated cases as soon as possible. Ammonia appears to be absorbed by the corrugated cases.
3. Food products should be recased and moved to storage areas free of ammonia and other products.
4. When sampling ammonia contaminated products use IOM Sample Schedule Chart 3 for guidance.

The following barrier characteristics of packaging materials exposed to ammonia will help in deciding if food products may be salvaged or reconditioned.

1. Kraft and other types of paper are very permeable.
2. Plastic films (polyethylene, saran, cryovac, etc.) are fairly good barriers.
3. Water glaze (ice) on food will absorb ammonia and the washing action by melting ice may eliminate ammonia.
4. Waxed paper overwrap and waxed cardboard boxes are very permeable.
5. Loose packed Individually Quick Frozen (I.Q.F.) Foods are more susceptible than block frozen foods.
6. Glass, metal and heavy aluminum foil packages are excellent barriers.

8.5.7.6 - Perishable Products

Milk is extremely perishable, and is highly susceptible to bacterial contamination. Any attempts at salvage are risky. Retail cartons of milk are not to be salvaged. Storage vats or sealed tanks of milk in processing plants must be closely examined and tested before release. If milk has been affected by flood waters, it should be condemned.

Fresh fruits and vegetables which have been inundated by flood waters cannot be adequately cleaned. Most are subject to rapid spoilage.

Merchandise requiring refrigeration or freezing which has been immersed in flood waters cannot be reconditioned. The same applies to meats or poultry which have been without refrigeration and may be in a decomposing state.

The following is general guidance in determining when frozen or refrigerated products cannot be reconditioned.

1. Product is contaminated.
2. Products which have been thawed, and there is evidence of decomposition.
3. Products which have thawed and represent a potential public health hazard.
4. Products which have not been maintained at temperatures appropriate to individual product requirements.
5. Products meeting criteria in the following sections regarding types of containers.

8.5.7.7 - Reconditioning Plastic, Paper, Cardboard, Cloth and Similar Containers

Goods packed in these containers which have been water damaged usually cannot be reconditioned. (In some instances, sugar has been permitted to be returned to a refinery for reprocessing, but each case must be decided individually). Fire and/or smoke damaged material may be permitted to be relabeled if contents have not been affected.

General rules for reconditioning of products in these types of containers are:

1. The product is not contaminated and the product is not highly susceptible to bacteriological contamination.
2. If the external container is torn, the interior liner must be intact, and the external container must be repaired or replaced to eliminate possible contamination of the product.
3. Soiled containers may be cleaned, if the product is not damaged and the container can be cleaned.
4. Foods from torn packages, where the product has been exposed but not obviously subjected to contamination, may be repackaged.

5. Water, chemical or other liquid damage, where the exterior package may be replaced, providing the internal containers were not affected and the external containers can be replaced without contaminating the product.

6. Fire damaged goods (wet, burned, heavy smoke contamination, or toxic fumes) are generally not reconditionable.

NOTE: Foods for infants, the aged or infirm, and drug products must be strictly controlled to assure the product is acceptable.

8.5.7.8 - Reconditioning Screw-top, Crimped-cap, and Similar Containers

Products in containers with screw-caps, snap-lids, crimped-caps (soda pop bottles), twist-caps, flip-top, snap-open, and similar type closures must not be reconditioned. Sediment and debris from flood water becomes lodged under the cap lips, threads, lugs, crimps, snap-rings, etc. and is impossible to remove, especially after it has dried. If these container/closure systems are affected only by fire or smoke, but the contents are not affected by the heat, they may be relabeled.

General rules for reconditioning are:

1. Product is not contaminated, or rendered unfit for food.

2. Soiled containers may be reconditioned if soil can be removed, and it does not involve the closure or contents.

3. Rust on closure: No rust allowed; surface rust may be removed by buffing or other suitable means.

4. Cap or crown dents: slight indentations obviously not affecting the rim seal would be reconditionable.

5. If there is evidence of exposure to extreme temperatures or pressures (hurricanes-tornadoes), products are not reconditionable.

6. If there is soil around the closure, products are not reconditionable.

7. If submerged in water, chemicals, or other liquids, products are not reconditionable.

8. If container/closure are defective or not properly sealed, products are not reconditionable.

8.5.7.9 - Reconditioning Hermetically Sealed (Top & Bottom Double Seam) Cans

Products in this type container which have been exposed to fire and smoke, and which are not damaged by the heat or exposed to water contamination, may be relabeled.

This type container, having been immersed in water, may be reconditioned and relabeled under controlled conditions and supervision as follows:

1. Inspect cans;

2. Remove labels;

3. Wash containers in soap or detergent solution, brushing as necessary;

4. Rinse in potable water;

5. Buff to remove rust. Heavily rusted cans are to be discarded.

6. Disinfect by:
    1. Immersion in a solution of sodium hypochlorite containing not less than 100 ppm available chlorine or other equivalent disinfectant, or
    2. If product will stand it, immerse in 212°F water, bring the temperature of the water back to 212°F and maintain the temperature at 212°F for at least five minutes, then remove and cool to 95°F,

7. Dry thoroughly, and

8. Relabel.

General Rules for reconditioning canned foods are:

1. The product is not contaminated.

2. No rust is allowed. Surface rust may be removed, by buffing, electrolysis, or other suitable means.

3. Cans soiled by dirt, smoke, etc., may be reconditioned if the product is not contaminated and the container can be cleaned by an acceptable method.

4. Water contaminated cans may be reconditioned if subjected to an approved bactericidal treatment and dried promptly.

5. If can dents consist of insignificant paneling or slight dents not affecting the double seam, or cracking the can corrugation, and not causing the can end to bulge, reconditioning is possible.

6. Leaking cans, cans with open seams, severely damaged seams, cans which are abnormal (i.e., swollen or flipper) and cans with defective closures are not reconditionable.

7. Cans exposed to extreme temperatures are not reconditionable.

8. Cans crushed to the point that the can body is extensively creased, paneled or dented on the seams can not be reconditioned.

8.5.7.10 - Reconditioning Devices

Radiation Type Devices - Radiation producing products such as x-ray equipment, TV sets, and microwave ovens are relatively complex, expensive, sensitive devices. Any of these type devices which have been inundated by flood waters, exposed to fire, heat, mechanical or physical damage such as falling debris, chemically corroded, or electrically damaged must be checked by expert personnel. They will decide whether the device can be repaired or reconditioned by the manufacturer and/or re-tested for compliance.

Do not release any of these type devices, but report the situation to your supervisor so arrangements can be made for appraisal. The regional radiological health representative will normally be the individual contacted by your district in this type situation.

Medical Devices and Diagnostic Products - Do not attempt any reconditioning of these type products.

Any medical devices or diagnostic products which have been affected by disaster forces should not be released. Advise your supervisor of the facts so the district officials can obtain any necessary advice and guidance from the Center for Devices and Radiological Health.

8.5.8 - Reporting

See IOM 1.1 English language requirement. There is no prescribed format for narrative reporting of disaster operations. Consult with your supervisor as to your district's preference. The report should briefly describe the onset of the disaster, its magnitude, and your activities. Include cooperation with officials, planning operations, and the logical sequence of your activities.

Your report must contain exhibits consisting of photographs, diagrams, records, references to samples, and any other items necessary for proper presentation of the operation. Refer to RPM Chapter 8 "Emergency Procedures," for guidance on reporting natural disasters and civil disorders. Attach copies of any FDA forms issued, especially the use of FDA-2809 (exhibit 8-12), Natural Disaster Report, listing amounts of materials destroyed and the method of destruction. See IOM 2.6.4. Prepare charts and lists as necessary to provide documentation of all affected lots destroyed, reconditioned, or released. Include kinds and amounts of materials segregated, released, reconditioned, and destroyed and method of reconditioning and/or destruction.

Record operation and time in FACTS.

8.6 - Surveillance

8.6.1 - Surveillance Procedures

Instructions for planned surveillance activities are found in your Compliance Program Guidance Manual. During your inspectional, investigational, and other activities, be alert to anything which may be new or unusual or interesting from FDA's viewpoint such as:

1. New firms;

2. New products;

3. New production and distribution practices;
4. New equipment and industrial processes;
5. Seasonal practices;
6. Industry trends;
7. Recent or on-going construction and plans for future expansion;
8. Proposed products;
9. New ideas the firm is contemplating;
10. New products in the development stage;
11. Activities about a firm's competitor;
12. Plans for consolidation, mergers, diversification, etc.;
13. Equipment failures or malfunction possibly affecting other firms, faulty design of equipment, incompatibility of ingredients, faulty process design, equipment manufacturers' recommendations which violate proper manufacturing precautions, health fraud (quackery), etc.
14. Health Fraud (Quackery) is defined as "the deceptive promotion, advertisement, distribution or sale of articles, intended for human or animal use, which are represented as effective to diagnose, prevent, cure, treat or mitigate disease, or provide a beneficial effect on health, but which have not been scientifically proven safe and effective for such purposes." See CPG: Chapter 1.

Use the FDA-457, Product/Establishment Surveillance Report, to report any of the items listed above. Include any other ideas/observations you may consider worthy of reporting. FDA must keep abreast of new ideas, trends, or contemplated changes in the industries we regulate as well as problems with possible broad impact.

8.6.2 - FDA 457 Preparation

Report product or establishment surveillance on the FDA 457, Product/Establishment Surveillance Report, and submit it to your supervisor. See IOM Exhibit 8-13. Prospective new establishments must be verified for appropriateness before inclusion in the active FEI. See Field Management Directive(FMD) 130.

Complete blocks 1 through 18 and 22 through 26 of the FDA 457 for product surveillance or blocks 1,6, 8 through 10, and 18 through 26 of the FDA 457 for establishment surveillance. Your supervisor or reviewing official will complete blocks 27 through 30. For a human drug firm or product which has not actually entered the market, enter the information in the REMARKS Section.

The following number designations correspond to identically numbered blocks on the FDA 457.

1. "HOME DISTRICT" - Enter the name of the home district of the new firm or firm producing the product reported. See IOM 2.2.5.6 for definition of home district.

2. "REPORTING UNIT SYMBOL" - Enter your district symbol here, e.g., " ATL-DO", "BOS-DO", "LOS-DO", etc. If units other than field units report on the form, their mailing symbol goes here.

3. "CENTRAL FILE NO." - Enter the central file number if readily available. Otherwise, leave blank.

4. "J.D./T.A." - Leave blank.

5. "COUNTY" - Leave blank.

6. "DATE" - Enter date you prepare the FDA 457.

7. "PRODUCT CODE" - Enter the 7-character Product Code from the Data Codes Manual.

8. "OPERATION" - Enter operation code from the Data Codes Manual. For surveillance it is 13.

9. "PROGRAM ASSIGNMENT CODE" - Enter the Program/Assignment Code (PAC) from the Data Codes Manual.

10. "HOURS" - Enter the time spent on this operation, including time for preparing the report, through FACTS. Report time to the nearest 1/4 hour in fractions, not decimals. Do not report travel time.

11. "IDENTIFICATION" - Enter the generic name of the product and quote enough of the label to properly identify the item, including the firm name and address.

12. "MANUFACTURER CONTROL CODES" - Enter all codes, lot numbers, batch codes, etc., found on the containers, labels, wrappers, packages, cases, etc. and indicate whether the number is located on the label, containers, case, etc.

13. "AMOUNT ON HAND" - List lot size (amount of the products) on hand or available. If count cannot be made, make an estimate and so indicate.

14. "DATE LOT RECEIVED" - Determine and enter the date the dealer received the lot(s).

15. "ESTIMATED VALUE" - This is the invoice value of the amount on hand at the time you observed it. Estimate, if not readily available.

16. "SAMPLE NO(s)" - Enter sample number(s) of any relevant samples collected. If no samples are collected, enter "None".
17. "DEALER" - List name and complete address including the ZIP code of dealer who owns or has custody of the product.
18. "DISTRIBUTOR MANUFACTURER SHIPPER OTHER" - Check applicable box or boxes and list name, complete address, ZIP code and telephone number, including area code.
19. "ESTABLISHMENT TYPES/INDUSTRY CODES" - Enter up to three establishment types with up to six industry codes each for the establishment.
20. "ESTABLISHMENT SIZE" - Enter gross dollar value of the annual production of all FDA regulated products made or manipulated in the establishment.
21. "INFORMATION OBTAINED BY" - Check the applicable box to indicate how the FEI information was obtained.
22. "REMARKS" - Enter explanatory information here.
23. "REPORT PREPARED BY" - Type or print your name and title.
24. "EMPL NO." - Enter your employee number.
25. "PC" - Enter your Position Classification code.
26. "SIGNATURE" - Enter usual signature.
27. "REPORTING UNIT ACTION" - Your supervisor or reviewing official completes this section by checking the applicable box.
28. "NAME OF REVIEWING OFFICIAL" - Typed or printed name of person reviewing the report.
29. "TITLE" - Title of reviewing official.
30. "DATE REVIEWED" - The reviewing official enters date report was reviewed.

Complete reverse side of the FDA 457 by checking the appropriate box(s).

8.6.3 - FDA 457 Routing

Submit all FDA 457's to your supervisor for review, assignment, or routing as indicated:

1. *Human Drug Surveillance* - Submit a copy of the FDA 457 to the Center for Drug Evaluation and Research (HFD-323).

2. *Veterinary Drug Surveillance* - Submit a copy of the FDA 457 to the Center for Veterinary Medicine, (HFV-236).

3. *Device Surveillance* - Submit a copy of the FDA 457 to the Office of Medical Devices (HFZ-331).

4. *Foods Surveillance* - Submit a copy of the FDA 457 to the home district.

5. *Other Products* - Submit a copy of the FDA 457 to the home district.

8.7 - Investigational Research

8.7.1 - Research Assignments

"Investigational Research" is investigation to discover and interpret facts, or to revise accepted theories and practices in the light of new facts, to improve investigational operations.

Investigational Research may be proposed by you, or assigned by your supervisor, and must be submitted for approval on the FDA 1609, Research Project Record. To formally propose research, complete this form and submit the original and two copies to your supervisor. After branch approval, original is retained by the branch research coordinator; one copy to the researcher; and one copy to HFC-132. Approval authority, except for research under the Science Advisor Research Associate Program (SARAP), is at the branch director level. SARAP projects are considered on a competitive basis and approved at headquarters. Investigational personnel are eligible to compete for SARAP approvals. Instructions and conditions for SARAP proposals are provided in the "ORO Research Programs" booklet.

Numerical and alpha listings of active laboratory and investigational research projects will be computer generated at headquarters and supplied to the districts on a semi-annual basis. To prevent duplications, check these listings (in possession of the science branch research coordinator) prior to proposing projects.

8.7.2 - Joint Research Projects

Project proposals involving significant analytical requirements must be approved in advance by the appropriate laboratory. Whenever investigational research requires analysis of samples, consider submitting a joint investigational/laboratory project proposal and final report. In these instances, request your supervisor to assist in arranging such joint projects.

When proposed research projects involve engineering assistance beyond that which is available within the district, request this through your supervisor from the Domestic Operations Branch/Division of Field Investigations (HFC-130). DFI Engineers may be available to assist on a specific short term basis, and to work with field investigators on joint projects, or may initiate investigational research independently.

8.7.3 - Research Project Identification Code

Project Codes are assigned by the district investigations branch research coordinator after project approval. You should assure a correct code has been assigned before beginning work under the approved project. The project code will reveal the district, the research category, and sequential project number (1 through 99) within the category for the district.

8.7.4 - Research Project Progress Reports

You must submit semi-annual progress reports for each ongoing research project. Each researcher shall initiate this form for each active project in April and October to reach DFI (HFC-130) by April 15th and October 15th respectively.

8.7.5 - Termination of Research Projects

Report project termination on FDA 1609 and FDA 1609a. Enter a summary of the completed project on the FDA 1609, including actions taken and publication, if any. If a paper has been prepared for publication, include the abstract.

The complete project report, with supporting data, may be on plain-paper continuation sheets to the FDA 1609, or may be a separate memorandum attached to the FDA 1609. Submit FDA 1609a to accompany a termination FDA 1609, to summarize the concluding semi-annual period of work on the project and to report final time expenditures. The minimum number of termination forms and project report copies is original plus two. After branch action, original is retained by the branch research coordinator; one copy by researcher; and one copy by HFC-130.

8.7.6 - Priority

Investigational research, after project approval, will be considered in relative priority to other assignments. Always keep your supervisor apprised when you are working on research projects. Whenever possible, such work should be done with other assignments for efficient operations. When research projects are urgently needed, or of substantial scope and duration, you may request supervisory approval of appropriate continuous periods for uninterrupted work. The "Research Priority" entered in block # 9 of the FDA-1609a indicates relative priority to other research, not the priority relative to regulatory and compliance assignments. You should complete regulatory and compliance work while avoiding, as best you can, delays in completing approved research projects. See your supervisor to help determine priorities.

8.7.7 - Data Reporting

Investigational research time is reported into FACTS under the Miscellaneous Operations Accomplishment Hours screen (available under navigate on the tool bar), using a distinctive Program/Assignment Code (PAC), reporting as Operation 01, Research.

If laboratory personnel are working on investigational research projects, follow laboratory procedures for reporting time, while using the Investigational Research Project Identification Code.

8.8 - Counterfeiting/Tampering

8.8.1 - Reporting Contacts

All reports of counterfeiting, tampering or tampering threats must be immediately reported to the Office of Criminal Investigations (OCI) Headquarters' Office, SAIC-IOD (Special Agent in Charge- Investigative Operations Division) (301-294-4030) and the Office of Crisis Management (OCM)/Office of Emergency Operations (OEO), HFA-615, (301-443-1240).

If the complaint or report involves a USDA (United States Department of Agriculture) regulated product, the District office should report it directly to the USDA and notify OCI, SAIC-IOD and OCM/OEO immediately.

8.8.1.1 - OCM / OEO Responsibility

OCM/OEO is the focal point for communications; especially in those counterfeiting/tampering cases where regional/national coverage is necessary. Alert the OEO immediately to all suspected or confirmed counterfeiting/tampering incidents, whether or not there is an injury/illness involved, especially if media attention will be initiated by any source.

8.8.2 - Coordination With Other Government Agencies

Federal - The Federal Bureau of Investigations (FBI) and the USDA share enforcement of the Federal Anti-Tampering Act (FATA) with FDA as described below:

1. *FBI Responsibility* - The FBI has concurrent jurisdiction under the FATA over products regulated by FDA. The FDA understands the FBI's primary interest in the FATA matters will be to investigate; particularly, those cases which involve a serious threat to human life or a death. SAIC-IOD or the local OCI Field Office will coordinate all referrals to the FBI in accordance with agency policy.

2. *USDA Responsibility* - The USDA will investigate and interact with the FBI on counterfeiting/tamperings with products regulated by USDA. If a counterfeiting/tampering complaint or report is made to an FDA District office and involves a USDA regulated product, the District office should report it directly to the USDA and notify OCI, SAIC-IOD and OCM/OEO immediately.

State and Local - Isolated incidents of counterfeiting/tampering not investigated by OCI and not meeting the criteria for FBI or USDA follow-up, may be referred to the appropriate state or local investigative agencies, as outlined in IOM 8.8.3. Assistance should be provided to cooperating officials as necessary or where requested.

8.8.3 - Authority & Responsibility

FDA is authorized to investigate reported counterfeiting/tampering of FDA regulated consumer products under the FATA, Title 18, USC, Section 1365 and Title 18, USC, Section 2320. (See IOM Exhibit 8-14.) In most cases, the authority for such investigations is also found in the FD&C Act.

OCI has the primary responsibility for all criminal investigations of counterfeiting/tampering/threat incidents of FDA regulated products. Given that responsibility, OCI Field Offices will coordinate responses to counterfeiting/tampering reports with the District Offices they deem appropriate, to ensure initial investigative steps are taken in a timely and efficient manner.

In those incidents where OCI does not, or cannot, initiate a criminal investigation, they will inform the District Offices of their decision and the District Offices will determine the proper follow-up, which could include further investigation by the Districts or referral to local or state authorities. The District Offices will keep OCI informed of their follow-up activities and any relevant changes in its status. Prior to initiation of any tampering investigation, you and your supervisor should evaluate the situation from a personal safety perspective. You and your District management may also need to determine if a situational plan is warranted. Refer to IOM 5.2.1.2 – Personal Safety, and IOM 5.2.1.4 Situational Plan, for more information.

8.8.4 - Release of Information

Information on matters under investigation by OCI should not be released without prior discussion and concurrence of the OCI Field Office.

Information regarding open regulatory investigations should not be released without prior discussion and concurrence of the OCM/OEO office.

See IOM 1.6.1 and IOM 8.8.1.1 for additional information concerning dealing with the media in investigative matters.

8.8.5 - Investigation

The purpose of these investigations is to determine if counterfeiting/tampering has occurred; the seriousness of the problem; the quantity of affected products on the market; the source of the counterfeiting/tampering; and quick removal from consumers or commerce of any contaminated product. OCI will seek to identify and initiate criminal prosecution of those persons responsible for criminal activity associated with counterfeiting/tampering/threat incidents.

FDA will investigate reports of counterfeiting/tampering associated with FDA regulated products. Priority will be given to reports of death, illness, injury, or a potential health hazard. Adhere to existing procedures and instructions as outlined in the IOM and RPM when conducting counterfeiting/tampering investigations, inspections, sample collections, special investigations, and related activities including interviews, record examination, direct observation, affidavits, etc. Additional guidance on investigational authority under FATA can be found in IOM 8.8.3.

8.8.5.1 - General Procedures

Counterfeiting/Tampering incidents historically have occurred in unpredictable forms and products. Standard operating procedures (SOPS), in most cases, will suffice for these investigations. As events take place, specific instructions for some investigations may be provided by OCI headquarters and/or your District office. Expeditious resolution is important, especially when a health hazard may be involved.

Attempt to answer the following questions as rapidly as possible:

1. Has counterfeiting/tampering occurred, or can the condition of the product be explained by other means?

2. Is death, injury, or illness associated with the report and, if so, does it appear to be caused by the product counterfeiting/tampering?

3. Does the incident appear to be isolated, or widespread?

4. Is it likely other, similarly affected FDA regulated products remain in distribution, and if so, what is the extent and magnitude of distribution?

5. If not isolated, could the product counterfeiting/tampering have occurred at the production facility or in the distribution chain?

6. Can specific persons or points in the distribution chain be identified as possibly causing the problem?

When counterfeiting/tampering, threat or false reports are evident, or highly suspect, use the concepts listed below which are appropriate for the situation. Be sure to coordinate your efforts with OCI SAIC/IOD and OCM/OEO.

8.8.5.2 - Interviews

It is often advantageous to work in pairs during interviews with complainants. Conduct interviews in a location which reduces unnecessary interruptions or distractions. Establish rapport with the person or persons being interviewed to put them at ease. Listen to the person. Let them first tell the story in their own way. Listen carefully to each facet. Be genuine and at ease. After hearing the entire story, ask them for more information to fill in details. Ask for clarification of key points.

Obtaining details and requesting clarification of key points allows you to obtain an idea of the validity of the person's story through comparison of the accuracy of the details with previous information supplied.

Note-taking may put the person being interviewed on edge. If this appears to be the case, do not take notes until you request clarification of key points. For cases of counterfeiting/tampering, ask who was with the person, what happened in the store, any problems noted with the product at the store, and other questions which will provide you with more information on when, where, or why events took place, who was present, etc. If two investigators are involved in the interview, one should take notes while the other asks the questions.

During interviews, watch for changes in attitudes, body language, hesitation in speech, etc., as you observe and listen to the person being interviewed. Describe your observations of body language and personal characteristics in your report.

In most counterfeiting cases, ORA investigators and OCI agents conduct joint inspections/investigations at the distributors. It is the purpose of the ORA investigators to document receipt and distribution of counterfeit products and to discuss voluntary recall of those products by the wholesalers. OCI agents will at the same time conduct their investigation into the knowledge and source of the counterfeit products. It is NOT the purpose of the investigator to simply accompany the OCI agent during his/her investigation.

8.8.5.3 - Sampling

Tampering Cases: Follow these procedures:

Whenever a sample is collected for suspected tampering, you must collect an authentic sample of the same product. It should be from the same lot and code, if at all possible. The sample size for the authentic portion is at least 6 intact units.

Collect any containers a suspect may have handled as they placed the tampered product on the shelf. Preparation of the sample and the shipping method should be carefully selected to insure the integrity and security of the samples. Coordinate with the OCI and the Forensic Chemistry Center (FCC) on correct sample packaging.

When handling product containers or other evidence associated with tampering, take care to avoid adding or smearing fingerprints by wearing cotton gloves, using tongs, forceps, or by picking the container up by opposing corners. Identify product containers carefully and in as small an area as possible. Do not open outer containers to identify inner containers or inserts.

When sampling or handling product, be alert for traces of evidence such as hair, dust, paint chips, glass fragments, etc. Secure such evidence in a separate container such as a glass vial, small manila envelope or plastic bag.

Samples should be packed to avoid movement of the product container within the bag. Individual dosage units from previously opened containers can be protected by removing them from their container utilizing a spoon or forceps. Secure them in separate containers so they do not rub or smear possible evidence. Further guidance can be found in the FBI "HANDBOOK OF FORENSIC SCIENCE" http://www.fbi.gov/hq/lab/handbook/intro.htm which has been supplied to each district. As a precaution, rubber gloves may be worn inside of cotton gloves as protection against toxic or caustic substances.

Ship samples with extreme care to insure their integrity. Thoroughly describe your sample and its characteristics on the collection report (C/R) to facilitate the analysis. Include any descriptive terms used by individuals associated with the complaint. If special instructions to preserve fingerprints or for further handling are indicated, they should be noted on the C/R and FDA-525. If speed is imperative consider hand delivery to the lab.

Counterfeiting Cases: Follow these procedures:

The District office may be asked to pick up suspect counterfeit products. Normal procedures for handling suspected products and the preservation of evidence should be followed as outlined in the tampering section for sampling above. In most counterfeiting cases, investigators do not usually collect an authentic sample of the same product. Authentic samples should only be collected when requested by OCI in consultation with FCC.

8.8.5.4 - Complainants

When visiting the complainant, use the standard consumer complaint procedures set forth in the IOM. Plan and think through the reasons for and goals for your visit before approaching the complainant. Listen carefully to the complainant. Review background of the complainant for history of complaints or law suits filed. Background checks are appropriate when district management has strong suspicions concerning the validity of the complaint or the potential for the complaint being used to defraud. It is often advantageous to work in pairs while interviewing complainants.

When collecting samples from the complainant, document them as official samples, including an affidavit describing the circumstances involved in the purchase and use of the product.

When investigating at a complainant's residence, obtain permission from the occupant to examine trash containers for discarded product labeling and/or containers which can be utilized to further investigations. Be alert to sources of contamination in the residence which are similar to the contaminants found in the product. Be sure to examine other containers of the same product in the residence with the owner's permission and sample them if suspect. Obtain permission to examine medicine cabinets if a drug dosage form is involved.

It is possible individuals you contact may not be aware of the provisions of the FATA. A general discussion of the FATA, its provisions for investigation, filing of false reports, and counterfeiting/tampering can be useful and informative to those individuals. Prior to concluding your interview of the complainant, obtain a signed affidavit attesting to the circumstances of the complaint, as directed by IOM 4.4.8. Include a statement in the affidavit similar to the following, "I have been informed of the provisions of the Federal Anti-Tampering Act and also that the providing of false information to the federal government is illegal." It is permissible to pre-type this statement at the bottom of an Affidavit, FDA 463a, and photocopy it before use if you have a large number of counterfeiting/tampering complaints to investigate.

8.8.5.5 - Retail Stores

When investigating a counterfeiting/tampering report at a retail store or other source of product, the local police department can be of assistance and provide advice. Before instituting any activities at the scene, protect the area to preserve any evidence on the store shelves, floor or adjacent areas and products. Discuss with the firm's management, and/or the personnel doing the stocking of the shelves, how material is received and handled prior to being placed on shelves.

Document the area using photographs of the product shelves, surrounding area, and any shots which would provide information on the product, its location and store layout. Samples of materials in the area that may be applicable to the investigation are to be collected. Because suspects are thought to handle multiple product containers when placing a tampered product on a store shelf, a diagram of the container relationships to each other should be prepared and individual containers given subsample numbers.

Be observant of persons present in the store, as guilty parties are thought often to return to such location, especially when the agency or news media are present. Be alert to statements of store personnel about activities they have observed. Obtain descriptions of the actions, dress and physical characteristics of persons the employees have noted exhibiting unusual/notable behavior in the store. Ascertain if the firm has a closed circuit TV monitoring system and if they maintain tapes, if so, these may be a source of leads. Obtain information about employees terminated in past year, employee problems, or shoplifters who may wish to cause problems in the store.

8.8.5.6 - Manufacturer and Distribution System Follow-up

The key to a successful investigation or inspection is to clearly define the objectives of the operation and to examine each facet of the establishment in light of the objective(s). Aspects of the production/distribution system to inspect for leads may include, but not be limited to the following:

8.8.5.6.1 - Manufacturing Sites

Manufacturing Sites

1. Age of facility, and date when production of the first batch of the product under investigation was initiated.

2. List of other facilities which produce the product under investigation.

3. For drugs, list by strength, size of container, name, dosage form, and number of packages per shipping case, all products manufactured or processed at the facility. If products handled are repackaged at this facility, give the name and address and method of receipt from the product source.

4. Obtain the names, titles, addresses, office and residence telephone numbers of representatives of the company, including that of the Chief Executive Officer (CEO), who are specified as contacts for various aspects of the event under investigation. State whether these representatives are members of an established management team to deal with such events, or have they been identified for the particular instance at hand.

5. Contract packagers, if any, should be described by name, location and products handled.

6. For the suspect lot, give its lot number, the size of the lot, size and type of containers in which it was packaged, its history of production and distribution beginning with the date of weighing of the raw material, and the dates and description of steps in processing.

7. Describe any locations within the facility where an employee could have access to the contaminant being investigated.

8. Describe the characteristics of the suspected contaminant within the facility, its container type, its brand and generic name, its lot number, size of container, whether the container is full, or partially full and the approximate amount remaining.

9. Describe security for the suspected contaminant including limitations of access, where it is stored, and responsibility for controlling access to the material.

10. Describe what legitimate use, if any, the facility has for the suspected contaminant in each of the locations found.

11. Determine how often the material is used and whether or not a log of its use is maintained.

12. If a log is maintained, obtain a copy showing its use and discuss with plant management the legitimacy of each such use.

13. Determine whether the firm verifies use and use rates and has a method of determining explanations for any discrepancies noted.

14. Have samples of the suspect contaminant been obtained by the FDA or other agencies, and if so, what are the results of analysis?

15. Does the firm test for the contaminant under investigation?

16. What method is utilized for such testing, and at what frequency?

17. List the facility's sources of raw materials for the suspect lot/product.

18. Evaluate the raw material storage conditions to determine the potential for manipulation of materials.

19. Describe the lot numbering system, any plant identification numbers, and expiration dates placed on retail products and cases.

20. If any product for export is processed at this plant, describe any differences from domestic products.

21. If the product under investigation has tamper resistant packaging (TRP), determine the type of system utilized, and if the system utilized has been evaluated to determine if breaching is possible. If breaching is possible, describe. Describe lot numbers or code numbers placed on TRP and security measures taken for TRP materials on hand and those sent to contract packagers. Determine whether TRP materials are accountable.

22. If the plant process includes collection of samples for examination on the production line or by laboratory facilities, discuss where the samples are maintained, who has access to them, and their disposition.

23. Report dates and description of each step in processing, including identification of storage locations between steps. Obtain estimates of

flow rates and volume of materials in hoppers and drums at key stages. Determine distances between production areas or between processing equipment at critical points. This information can be useful for statistical evaluation of the likelihood of contamination at various points in the process.

24. Include a description of the in-process lot numbering systems for each phase of manufacturing, security for each process and/or product while in storage and during processing.

25. In some types of processes, there are provisions for an individual to ensure sufficient product is placed in each container being filled. If this is the case in the plant under inspection, describe the circumstances and security for this process.

26. Determine whether the facility hires part-time employees, or transfers employees from one location to another on a temporary basis. Were any were present during production of the suspect lot?

27. Describe provisions for determining reliability of employees.

28. Determine if employees can move from area to area within the facility. Describe any restrictions on their movements and if enforced.

29. Describe laboratory control tests and in-process tests performed on the finished packaged product and in-process materials. Determine if reserve samples are retained of all lots.

30. Determine how rejects and reworked materials are handled.

31. Describe any unusual events which may have taken place during the period when the suspect material was in the facility.

32. Determine if the firm has a plan to safeguard against counterfeiting/tampering as part of its quality assurance (Q.A.) program. If so, determine the implementation date of this plan and review any periodic assessment reports for potential problem areas.

8.8.5.6.2 - Distribution Facilities

It may be necessary to obtain the following information at each level in the distribution chain:

1. Amount of suspect lot on hand at time of inspection.

2. Obtain the turnover rate for the product under investigation.

3. Amount of suspect lot received, and any variations from amount consigned to the facility.

4. Date received.

5. How received.

6. Name and type of carrier which delivered the product. Determine security of the vehicle or container while in-transit.

7. Obtain distribution history of the suspect lots.

8. Describe the distribution area covered by the facility being inspected and the number of accounts served, whether they are retail or wholesale.

9. Determine if the facility handles any cash and carry orders.

10. Determine if the facility will accept returns and how are they handled.

11. Describe stock rotation practices and how they can be assured.

12. Determine if lot numbers of products distributed can be traced.

13. Describe the method of packing of shipments; for example, plastic tote bins sealed with nylon tape, intact cartons only, cases are split, etc.

14. Describe the methods of shipment utilized by the warehouse.

15. Describe personnel practices, problems and other information on visitors, contractors, etc.

It is often advantageous to chart a pictograph or a time line chart of the distribution system which shows basic information on each level in the distribution chain and distances between each link in the chain. It is also often worthwhile to prepare a time-line chart showing the progression of the suspect lot through the manufacturing process to the source of the complaint, including the significant steps in the manufacture and distribution of the suspect product.

8.8.5.6.3 - Security

Obtain the following information. However, when preparing the EIR, do not report the details of the security system, since an inadvertent release could compromise a facilities security system. Discuss with your supervisor how to report this information.

1. General security arrangements, including the number of guards, their shifts, locations, and whether or not they patrol the facility.

2. Describe any closed circuit TV systems, their locations, and any physical barriers to prevent access to the plant grounds and its facility.

3. Describe who is logged in and out of the facility and whether or not employees must display identification badges upon entry. If plant employees are issued uniforms by color or design, which designate their work station locations, also describe.

4. Determine whether visitors, contractor representatives, cleaning crews, etc., are subject to movement tracking or control, and if any were present during production of the suspect product.

5. If the suspect product was particularly vulnerable to in-plant tampering during certain stages of handling, identify particular employees who had access to product during these stages and interview them individually. There may be occasions when line employees may be able to remember suspicious activities on the part of co-workers or others working in the area when suspect lots were being produced.

6. Describe the security measures taken for the processing area after hours, during work breaks, and at meal times. Be alert to those periods when in-process containers are left unattended on a packing/production line.

7. Describe any employee relations problems such as layoffs, firings, probations, adverse actions, etc.

8.8.6 - Record Requests

Occasionally, your investigation may require you to obtain information not specifically authorized under the FD&C Act, e.g., distribution records of food products, production records for OTC drugs or foods, etc. Seek to obtain such records if the following criteria have been met, or if, in the opinion of your supervisor, district, or headquarters, it is necessary to do so:

1. The apparent counterfeiting/tampering incident may be serious and is assigned a high priority by your supervisor, district and/or agency, and;

2. The data sought is normally of the type FDA is trained to evaluate and have access to in other areas of routine FD&C Act activities, e.g., production records, formulas, distribution records, etc., and;

3. The requested data is likely to be necessary to the successful resolution of the investigation, and;

4. Other alternatives to obtain the information are not as readily available.

If a request for data is made, you should direct it to the most responsible individual at the location. Explain clearly and concisely your need for the data. Do not issue a written request unless you have specific supervisory/district concurrence to do so.

8.8.7 - Refusals

All refusals encountered during counterfeiting/tampering investigations should be documented using existing procedures. Refusals of requests should include documentation the criteria in IOM 8.8.6 were met and the firm was aware of the non-routine nature of the request. The lack of precedent in this area suggests thorough documentation to allow appropriate compliance review and follow-up. A search warrant, subpoena or other court order may be appropriate in some circumstances. The feasibility and necessity of these actions should be discussed with the OCI before such action is initiated.

8.8.8 - Reporting

See IOM 1.1 English language requirement. Complete the FACTS Consumer Complaint Report and the FACTS Complaint Follow-up Report for all counterfeiting/tampering complaints received. See IOM Exhibits 8-2 and 8-3.

All completed and/or resolved reports of counterfeiting/tampering incidents should be provided to the OCM/OEO (HFA-615) to develop background information for agency use. If the investigation is of a continuing nature, OCM/OEO may require interim reports on a case by case basis.

Note: *Time reporting should occur through FACTS.*

Counterfeiting/Tampering reports should be reported in FACTS using the following guidelines:

Counterfeiting: Use the Problem Keyword " OR" (for "Other") and " counterfeit " in the Problem Keyword Detail field when recording complaints about counterfeiting in FACTS."

Tampering: Use the Problem Keyword "TM." It should be followed by a brief description of the problem such as " tamper evident seal missing " or " foreign capsules in bottle ".

8.9 - Office of Criminal Investigations (OCI)

8.9.1 - OCI Procedures

The Office of Criminal Investigations (OCI) has the primary responsibility for all criminal investigations conducted by the FDA, including suspected tampering incidents and suspected counterfeit products. Similarly, OCI has primary responsibility and is the primary point of contact for all law enforcement and intelligence issues pertaining to threats or perceived threats against FDA regulated products. OCI participates in numerous law enforcement and intelligence task forces both nationally and internationally to include a full time representative to Interpol.

8.9.1.1 - Reports of Criminal Activity

All reports of suspected or confirmed criminal activity, including suspected tampering or counterfeiting incidents, must be reported to the appropriate OCI field office or resident office without delay. Additionally, all threats or perceived threats against FDA regulated products are to be referred immediately to the local OCI Field Office or to OCI Headquarters. In those instances where OCI does not, or cannot, initiate a criminal investigation in a timely manner, the District Offices will determine, in consultation with OCI, the proper follow-up.

8.9.1.2 - Liaison with Law Enforcement / Intelligence Community

OCI is the FDA's liaison component with the law enforcement community for criminal investigations and related matters. In addition OCI serves as the primary point of contact between the FDA and the Intelligence Community on all matters of mutual interest. All contacts regarding requests or questions received from federal, state, or local law enforcement agencies or intelligence agencies are to be referred without delay to the local OCI Field Office. Similarly, contacts to FDA Headquarters or Centers should be referred to OCI Headquarters. When FDA personnel receive information or requests from law enforcement or other agencies, they should obtain the caller's name, organization, request and refer the caller to the appropriate OCI component. After referring the caller to OCI, contact the affected OCI unit to provide them with the caller's information. This will ensure OCI is not caught by surprise. FDA personnel should not respond to inquiries concerning criminal investigations, including questions seeking confirmation FDA is or is not conducting a criminal investigation.

8.9.1.3 - Consensual Electronic Surveillance

OCI has been designated the authority to administer the consensual electronic surveillance program for the FDA. To comply with FDA Policy and Department of Justice requirements, all FDA personnel must contact the appropriate OCI Field Office SAIC to request approval before any electronic surveillance; this includes recording consensual telephone conversations. FDA Headquarters and Center personnel should contact OCI Headquarters, AD IOD for approval requests.

8.9.1.4 - Postal Mail Cover

OCI is also the point of contact for any request for a mail cover through the U.S. Postal Inspection Service. A mail cover provides a written record of all data appearing on the outside of any class of mail to obtain information for:

1. Protecting national security.
2. Locating a fugitive.
3. Obtaining evidence of the commission or attempted commission of a crime punishable by more than one year in prison. A mail cover may not be used in non-criminal investigations, except in those cases involving a civil forfeiture of assets related to violations of criminal laws.

Investigations

8.10 - General Investigation Reporting

The current Field Accomplishment and Compliance Tracking System (FACTS) Investigation (Operation 13) is used to capture the findings, endorsement and accomplishment time for investigations. FACTS does not provide for the generation of a hard copy memorandum. Limitations on data input also inhibit your ability to produce an investigative memo describing all relevant facts of your investigation. Therefore, in each case where a hard copy is required, use the reporting method described below. The FACTS Summary and Endorsement should be annotated to indicate the location of the actual report and endorsement, i.e., "see KAN-DO files," "see FACTS Consumer Complaint #," etc., along with minimal narrative text describing the findings of the investigation.

Following the completion of an investigation, you will prepare a written report in English (See IOM 1.1) of the investigation as directed by your supervisor, which records all pertinent data, including referencing of firms and attachments/exhibits, samples collected, etc. Use memorandum format, with appropriate supervisory endorsement and routing. For consumer complaints complete the FACTS Complaint Follow-Up Report. See IOM 8.2, IOM 8.2.8 and IOM 8.4.5. For surveillance activities, use Surveillance Report form (FDA 457). See IOM 8.6.2. In other situations use methods directed by your District.

In those instances where FACTS is used for simple data/time entry under the Investigation Operation, and when you may not need a written report (examples: OEI improvement or pesticide surveillance), then enter sufficient information in the appropriate FACTS fields. The fields are those necessary for your supervisor to endorse the entry.

FACTS Operation 13, Investigation, will be used for inspections where the firm is Out of Business (OOB), not Official Establishment Inventory (NOEI), or where no inspection was made. Currently, this requires a written, hard copy memorandum and supervisory endorsement for inclusion in your District's files. In the case of OOB and NOEI, this is required for the appropriate filing personnel to know to remove the active files and send to the record center or storage per District procedure. For "no inspection made" the information in the file, especially the reason, may be helpful to future investigators. When you have a FACTS assignment to conduct an inspection and you determine the firm is OOB, follow FACTS procedures for converting the operation 12 to an operation 13.

Part II

Exhibits, Appendix, and Samples

Exhibits, Appendix, and Samples

The Investigations Operations Manual (IOM) provides chapter-specific exhibits, appendixes, and samples that demonstrate and support the procedures detailed in the IOM.

Exhibits[17]

Exhibits supporting each chapter of the Investigations Operations Manual are available on the FDA website at http://www.fda.gov/ICECI/Inspections/IOM/ucm127372.htm.

The list of available exhibits for each chapter follows.

Chapter 1 - Exhibits

1-1 Allowable Expenses Chart

Chapter 2 - Exhibits

2-1 Interrogation; Advice of Rights

2-2 Form FDA 2289

2-3 Detention Tag

2-4 Form FDA 2291

Chapter 3 - Exhibits

3-1 FDA/USDA Jurisdictional Chart

3-2 History of Menu Items (2 Pgs)

3-3 Address Information Request (2 Pgs)

Chapter 4 - Exhibits

4-1 Facts Sample Collection Screen (5 Pgs)

4-2 Facts Sample Collection Screen (2 Pgs)

4-3 Affidavit (In-Transit) - FDA 1664b

4-4 Carrier's Receipt for Sample - FDA 472

4-5 Receipt for Samples - FDA 484 (2 Pgs Replace With 510c)

---

[17] Downloadable files are available on the FDA website at http://www.fda.gov/ICECI/Inspections/IOM/ucm127372.htm

Chapter 5 - Exhibits

Chapter 6 - Exhibits

6-2 Form FDA-766

6-3 Charges for Supervision Form FDA-790

6-4 Oasis Collection Report Form

6-5 Import Investigation Affidavit

Chapter 7 - Exhibits

7-1 Recall Communications - Examples

7-2 Form FDA-3177, Recall Audit Check Report

Chapter 8 - Exhibits

8-1 Facts Adverse Event Questionnaire

8-2 Facts Consumer Complaint Report

8-3 Facts Consumer Complaint Follow-Up Report

8-4 Facts Cosmetics Adverse Event

8-5 Form FDA-461

8-6 Classification of Illnesses Attributable to Foods

8-7 Form FDA-3042

8-8 Attack Rate Table

8-9 Epidemic Curve

8-10 Medwatch Form

8-11 Vaccine Adverse Event Report System

8-12 Natural Disaster Form FD - 2809

8-13 Form FDA-457

8-14 Federal Anti-Tampering Act

Appendixes

Appendixes supporting each chapter of the Investigations Operations Manual are available on the FDA website at http://www.fda.gov/ICECI/Inspections/IOM/ucm127497.htm.

The list of available appendixes for each chapter follows:

Appendix A - Insects

Appendix B - Calendars

Appendix C - Blood Values

Appendix D - Conversion Factors

Appendix E - ORA Map

Sample Schedules

Chapter 1 Exhibits

CONTENT

Exhibit 1-1: Allowable Expenses Chart

Below is a table of allowable expense items and the requirements that must be met to assure reimbursement. Unless "xx" appears in one or more of the columns at the right, there are no special requirements for reimbursement.

EXPENSE ITEM I	Specific authorization or approval	Receipt	Justification on voucher for any amount
BAGGAGE 1. Weight allowance on baggage transported free of charge by common carrier on ticket: a. Rail. Up to 150 lbs. (domestic) b. Air. Varies. Up to 70 lbs. per each of 2 bags within the continental U.S. on major trunk or regional carriers. c. Steamship. No specific limitation on baggage carried in traveler's stateroom. There is no additional allowance for free transportation of baggage for infants.			
2. Excess Baggage Charges for government property Note: Where air coach or air tourist accommodations are used, transportation of baggage up to the weight carried free on first-class service is allowed	XX	XX	XX1
3. Service Charge for checking baggage by checking agent where such charges for checking baggage in baggage rooms, or station or air terminal		XX	XX
4. Storage Charges (e.g., when traveler stores baggage or equipment not needed during a portion of his trip		XX	XX2
5. Transfer Charges - when necessary for official travel (e.g., when changing between stations where free transportation is not issued by common carrier.) CAUTION: Where the traveler's plans are changed he shall make sure that baggage that has been checked beyond the point where he leaves the train is stopped or transferred. If baggage cannot be intercepted or		XX	XX

EXPENSE ITEM I	Specific authorization or approval	Receipt	Justification on voucher for any amount
transferred and is carried to original destination on unused portion of ticket, the traveler shall give full explanation of facts when submitting unused portion of ticket. Failure to do so will result in any excess cost being charged to traveler.			
FEES OR TIPS 1. Parking Fees - charges for parking automobiles		XX	XX (over $75)
2. Porter - allowable only at transportation terminals for handling Government property carried by travelers. Porter fees for personal property, brief cases, etc. are not allowed.			XX3
3. Registration for attendance at local non-government sponsored meetings other	HHS-99		
4. Exchange of Currency a. Allowed i. fees for cashing U.S. Government checks or drafts reimbursing traveler for travel expenses only incurred in foreign countries ii. commissions for conversion of currency in foreign countries iii. Costs of travelers checks, money orders, certified checks purchased in connection with official travel. Costs may not exceed amount needed to cover reimbursable expenses. b. Not allowed: exchange fees for cashing checks or drafts issued in payment of salary.	XX XX XX	XX XX4	
5. For Foreign Travel - Passports, visa fees, costs of photographs for passports and visas, costs of certificates of birth, health, identity, and of affidavits, and charges for inoculations not obtainable through a Federal dispensary	XX	XX	
6. Not Allowed - Gratuities (tips) to Government employees			
HIRE OF ROOM 1. Allowed: When necessary to engage a room in a hotel or other place to transact official business	XX	XX	XX6
2. Not allowed: Hotel accommodations for personal use (cost included in subsistence allowance).			
PERSONAL SERVICES 1. Stenographic and typing services, guides, interpreters, drivers of vehicles, etc.	XX	XX	XX5
2. Rental of typewriter	XX	XX	XX5
POSTAGE Postage necessary for official airmail, foreign, or parcel post mail; and for official registered and special delivery mail.	XX	XX	XX7

EXPENSE ITEM I	Specific authorization or approval	Receipt	Justification on voucher for any amount
POST OFFICE BOX RENTAL Where necessary for official airmail, foreign, or parcel post mail; and for official registered and special delivery mail.	XX	XX	XX
STEAMER CHAIRS, RUGS, CUSHIONS, ETC. For official steamship travel, expenses incident thereto at customary rates actually charged			
STREETCARS AND BUSES WHILE IN TRAVEL STATUS 1. Allowed: Public transportation fares; a. from (or to) common carrier, or other terminals, to (or from) place of abode or place of business b. between place of abode and place of business, or between places of business	XX	XX (over $75)	XX9
2. Not allowed: Public transportation fares between places where meals are taken, and places of business or places of lodging, except where nature and location of work at temporary duty station is such that suitable meals cannot be procured there - allowance will be made for transportation to the nearest available place for such meals			
TAXICABS WHEN USED LOCALLY WHILE IN TRAVEL STATUS 1. Use allowed: a. from (or to) common carrier or other terminal to (or from) place of abode or place of business. b. between place of abode and place of business, or between places of business, where cheaper mode of transportation is not available, or is impracticable to use.	XX	XX (over $75) XX (over $75)	XX9
2. Use not allowed: between places where meals are taken, and places of business, except where nature and locations of suitable meals cannot be procured there - allowance will be made for transportation to the nearest available place for such meals.	XX	XX (over $75)	XX9
3. Fares and Tips (refer to IOM 1.2.1.3)			
CHARGES for limousine service plus taxicab tip rates between airport and limousine pick-up or discharge point.		XX (over $75)	
TELEGRAMS AND CABLEGRAMS 1. Allowed: Charges for telegrams, cablegrams, and radiograms on official business. (Note: traveler shall use government facilities where available. Where not available official messages may be sent collect via commercial facilities.		XX	XX10

EXPENSE ITEM I	Specific authorization or approval	Receipt	Justification on voucher for any amount
2. Not allowed: messages of a personal nature, including request for leave, information about salary check, expense voucher, hotel reservation, etc.; except that a request for hotel reservation incident to official business provided reference is made to official conference or official business involved is allowable.			
TELEPHONE CALLS 1. Allowed: charges for local and long distance calls when made on official business		xx10 & xx11	
2. Personal calls - see IOM 1.2.8			
RECORDS Charges for copies of records furnished by State officials, such as Clerks of Courts, etc., when necessary for performance of official business		xx	xx5
SHIPMENTS (FREIGHT OR EXPRESS) - see IOM 4.5.5		xx	xx12
EMERGENCY OR OTHER MISCELLANEOUS EXPENSES 1. Cash used in lieu of transportation request for passenger transportation and accommodations. 2. Purchase of emergency supplies. 3. Any other miscellaneous expenditures incurred by traveler in performance of official business, such as samples of drugs, cosmetics, etc. purchased by FDA inspectors and investigators.	xx xx	xx xx	xx5

FOOTNOTES:

1 Voucher must show weight of baggage and points between which moved.

2 State that storage is solely on account of official business.

3 State that porter fee was for handling Government property carried by traveler.

4 Voucher shall show rate of conversion and commission charges.

5 Voucher shall show date of service, quantity, unit, and unit price.

6 In addition to information required in footnote #5, state necessity for hire of room.

7 State that postage was used for official mail.

8 Omitted

9 State necessity for daily travel.

10 For telegrams, cablegrams, and long distance telephone calls, show points between which service was rendered, date, amount paid on each and "official business".

11 For local telephone, calls show number of calls, rate per call, total amount expended each day, and "official business".

12 When government Bill of Lading is not used, explain circumstances.

13 Continental United States (CONUS) is defined as the 48 contiguous states and the District of Columbia.

Chapter 2 Exhibits

CONTENT

Exhibit 2-1: Interrogation; Advice of Rights

INTERROGATION: ADVICE OF RIGHTS

YOUR RIGHTS

Place ______________ Date ______________ Time ______________

Before we ask you any questions, you must understand your rights.

You have the right to remain silent.

Anything you say can be used against you in court.

You have the right to talk to a lawyer for advice before we ask you any questions and to have him with you during questioning.

If you cannot afford a lawyer, one will be appointed for you before any questioning if you wish.

If you decide to answer questions now without a lawyer present, you will still have the right to stop answering at any time. You also have the right to stop answering at any time until you talk to a lawyer.

WAIVER OF RIGHTS

I have had read to me this statement of my rights and I understand what my rights are. I am willing to make a statement and answer questions. I do not want a lawyer at this time. I understand and know what I am doing. No promises or threats have been made to me and no pressure or coercion of any kind has been used against me.

Signed ____________________________

Witness: ____________________________

Witness: ____________________________

Time: ____________________________

INTERROGATORIO: NOTIFICCACION DE LOS DECECHOS

SUS DERECHOS

Lugar ______________ Fecha ______________ Hora ______________

Antes de hacerle pregunta alguna, Ud. debe entender lo que son sus derechos.

Ud. tiene el derecho de mantener silencio.

Culquier cosa que diga Ud. puede ser usada en su contra en un tribunal.

Ud. tiene el derecho de consultar con un abogado para que éste le aconseje antes de que le hagamos las preguntas y también tiene derecho a la presencia del abogado durante el interragatorio.

Si Ud. no puede pagar los gastos de un abogado, se le asignara uno antes de iniciarse el interragotorio, si así lo desea Ud.

Si Ud. se decide a contestar las preguntas ahora sin la presencia del abogado, Ud. tiene todavía el derecho de negarse a contestar en cualquier momento. Ud. tiene también el derecho de interrumpir las contestaciones en cualquier momento hasta que haya consultado con un abogado.

RENUNCIA A LOS DERECHOS

Me han leído esta declaración de mis derechos y entiendo lo que son. Estoy despuesto a hacer una declaración y a contestar las preguntas. No quiero que esté presente un abogado en este momento. Tengo conciencia de lo que hago. No se me han hecho ni promesas ni amenazas y no se has ejercido presión alguna en mi contra.

Firmado ____________________________

Testigo: ____________________________

Testigo: ____________________________

Hora: ______________________________

Exhibit 2-2: Form FDA 2289

DEPARTMENT OF HEALTH AND HUMAN SERVICES
FOOD AND DRUG ADMINISTRATION

DETENTION NOTICE

1a. DISTRICT ADDRESS	850 Third Ave. Brooklyn, NY 11232
1b. PHONE NUMBER	718-340-7000
1c. NAME OF DISTRICT DIRECTOR	Thomas Gardine
1d. EMAIL ADDRESS	tgardine@ora.fda.gov
1e. FAX NUMBER	718-340-7766
2. NAME OF CUSTODIAN	TO: Mr. William Jantz
3. DETENTION NOTICE NUMBER	DN 60006
4. TITLE OF CUSTODIAN	Warehouse Manager, Division II
5. TELEPHONE NO.	716- 843-7066
6. DATE AND HOUR DETAINED	12-29-05 10:45 a.m.
7. FIRM NAME	Amoure Cold Storage Co., Inc.
8. ADDRESS (Street, City, State, ZIP code)	245 Dockage St. Buffalo, NY 14206
9. MAXIMUM DETENTION	Twenty (20) DAYS

■ See Instructions on back of pages 4 and 5

Pursuant to Sections 402 and 409(b) of the Federal Meat Inspection Act; Sections 19 and 24(b) of the Poultry Products Inspection Act; Sections 19 and 23(d) of the Egg Products Inspection Act; or Section 304(g) of the Federal Food, Drug, and Cosmetic Act (FD&C Act); or Section 304(h) of the FD&C Act. The merchandise must not be used, moved, altered or tampered with in any manner during the detention period without the written permission of an authorized representative of the Secretary of the U.S. Department of Health and Human Services, except that a device may be moved and processed under 21 CFR 800.55(h)(2) pursuant to Section 304(g)(2)(B) of the FD&C Act. An article of food detained pursuant to Section 304(h) of the FD&C Act shall not be consumed, moved, altered or tampered with in any manner during the detention period, unless the detention order is first modified under 21 CFR 1.381(c).

10. NAME OF DETAINED ARTICLE	Beefy Brand Beef Pot Pie with Mushrooms
11. SIZE OF DETAINED LOT	1600cs/24 – 1 lb. 2 oz tins
12. DETAINED ARTICLE LABELED (Include Master Carton Label)	Tins lbld in part "Beefy Brand Pot Pie***ingredients: Selected beef, choice green peas, carrots, selected Idaho potatoes, Mushrooms*** Gravy***1 lb. 2 oz.***Packed by Burly Products Co.***Kansas City, MO EST 223" Tins in
13. REASON FOR DETENTION	Estimated 10% of tins swelled and/or leaking.
16. DETAINED ARTICLE STORED AT (Name, Address, ZIP code)	Amoure Cold Storage Co., Inc. Warehouse 3B, 321 Dockage St. Buffalo, NY 14206
17. NAME AND TITLE OF THE PERSON WHO APPROVED DETENTION ORDER	Sylvester B. Pearson, Compliance Officer
18. APPROVAL OF DETENTION ORDER	☐ Written ☒ Verbal

Sections 402 and 409(b) of the federal Meat Inspection Act is quoted below:

"Sec. 402. Whenever any carcass, part of a carcass, meat or meat food product of cattle, sheep, swine, goats, horses, mules, or other equines or any product exempted from the definition of a meat food product, or any dead, dying, disabled, or diseased cattle, sheep, swine, goat, or equine is found by any authorized representative of the Secretary upon any premises where it is held for purposes of, or during or after distribution in, commerce or otherwise subject to Title I or II of this Act, and there is reason to believe that any such article is adulterated or misbranded and is capable of use as human food, or that it has not been inspected, in violation of the provisions of Title I of this Act or of any other Federal law or the laws of any State or Territory or the District of Columbia, or that such article or animal has been or is intended to be, distributed in violation of any such provisions, it may be detained by such representative for a period not to exceed twenty days, pending action under Section 403 of this Act or notification of any Federal, State, or other governmental authorities having jurisdiction over such article or animal, and shall not be moved by any person, firm, or corporation from the place at which it is located when so detained, until release by such representative. All official marks may be required by such representative to be removed from such article or animal before it is released unless it appears to the satisfaction of the Secretary that the article or animal is eligible to retain such marks. (21 U.S.C. 672.)

Sec. 409.

(b) The detainer authority conferred by Section 402 of this Act shall apply to any authorized representative of the Secretary of Health and Human Services for purposes of the enforcement of the Federal, Food, Drug, and Cosmetic Act with respect to any carcass, part thereof, meat, or meat food product of cattle, sheep, swine, goats, or equines that is outside any premises at which inspection is being maintained under this Act, and for such purposes the first reference to the Secretary in Section 402 shall be deemed to refer to the Secretary of Health and Human Services. (21 U.S.C. 679)"

Sections 19 and 24(b) of the Poultry Products Inspection Act is quoted below:

"Sec. 19. Whenever any poultry product, or any product exempted from the definition of a poultry product, or any dead, dying, disabled, or diseased poultry is found by an authorized representative of the Secretary upon any premises where it is held for purposes of, or during or after distribution in, commerce or otherwise subject to this Act, and there is reason to believe that any such article is adulterated or misbranded and is capable of use as human food, or that it has not been inspected, in violation of the provisions of this Act or of any other Federal law or the Laws of any State or Territory, or the District of Columbia, or that it has been or is intended to be, distributed in violation of any such provisions, It may be detained by such representative for a period not to exceed twenty days, pending action under Section 20 of this Act or notification of Any Federal, State, or other governmental authorities having jurisdiction over such article or poultry, and shall not be moved by any person, from the place at which it is located when so detained, until released by such representative. All official marks may be required by such representative to be removed from such article or poultry before it is released unless it appears to the satisfaction of the Secretary that the article or poultry is eligible to retain such marks."

Sec. 24.

"(b) The detainer authority conferred by Section 19 of this Act shall apply to any authorized representative of the Secretary of Health and Human Services for purposes of the enforcement of the Federal Food, Drug and Cosmetic Act with respect to any poultry carcass, or part or product thereof, that is outside any official establishment, and for such purposes for first reference to the Secretary in Section 19 shall be deemed to refer to the Secretary of Health and Human Services."

(Continued on the reverse of this form)

NAME OF FDA EMPLOYEE (Type or Print)	TITLE (FDA Employee)	SIGNATURE (FDA Employee)
Sylvia A. Rogers	Investigator	Sylvia A. Rogers

FORM FDA 2289 (12/05) PREVIOUS EDITIONS MAY NOT BE USED **DETENTION NOTICE** **1**

Sections 19 and 23(d) of the Egg Products Inspection Act is quoted below:

"Sec. 19. Whenever any eggs or egg products subject to the Act, are found by any authorized representative of the Secretary upon any premises and there is reason to believe that they are or have been processed, brought, sold, possessed, used, transported, or offered or received for sale or transportation in violation of this Act or that they are in any other way in violation of this Act, or whenever any restricted eggs capable of use as human food are found by such a representative in the possession of any person not authorized to acquire such eggs under the regulations of the Secretary, such articles may be detained by such representative for a reasonable period but not to exceed twenty days, pending action under Section 20 of this Act or notification of any Federal, State, or other governmental authorities having jurisdiction over such articles and shall not be moved by any person from the place at which they are located when so detained until released by such representative. All official marks may be required by such representative to be removed from such articles before they are released unless it appears to the satisfaction of the Secretary that the articles are eligible to retain such marks."

"Sec. 23(d). The detainer authority conferred on representatives of the Secretary of Agriculture by Section 19 of this Act shall apply to any authorized representative of the Secretary of Health and Human Services for the purposes of paragraph (d) of Section 5 of this Act, with respect to any eggs or egg products that are outside any plant processing egg products."

Section 304(g) of the Food, Drug and Cosmetic Act is quoted below.

"(g)(1) If during an inspection conducted under Section 704 of a facility or a vehicle, a device which the officer or employee making the inspection has reason to believe is adulterated or misbranded is found in such facility or vehicle, such officer or employee may order the device detained (in accordance with regulations prescribed by the Secretary) for a reasonable period which may not exceed twenty days unless the Secretary determines that a period of detention greater than twenty days is required to institute an action under Subsection (a) or Section 302, in which case he may authorize a detention period of not to exceed thirty days. Regulations of the Secretary prescribed under this paragraph shall require that before a device may be ordered detained under this paragraph the Secretary or an officer or employee designated by the Secretary approve such order. A detention order under this paragraph may require the labeling or marking of a device during the period of its detention for the purpose of identifying the device as detained. Any person who would be entitled to claim a device if it were seized under Subsection (a) may appeal to the Secretary a detention of such device under this paragraph. Within five days of an appeal of a detention is filed with the Secretary, the Secretary shall after affording opportunity for an informal hearing by order confirm the detention or revoke it.

"(2)(A) Except as authorized by subparagraph (B), a device subject to a detention order issued under paragraph (1) shall not be moved by any person from the place at which it is ordered detained until -

"(i) released by the Secretary, or

"(ii) the expiration of the detention period applicable to such order, whichever occurs first.

"(B) A device subject to a detention order under paragraph (1) may be moved -

"(i) in accordance with regulations prescribed by the Secretary, and

"(ii) if not in final form for shipment, at the discretion of the manufacturer of the device for the purpose of completing the work required to put it in such form."

Section 304(h) of the Food, Drug and Cosmetic Act is quoted below:

"(h) Administrative Detention of Foods.

(1)Detention Authority

(A) In general. An officer or qualified employee of the Food and Drug Administration may order the detention, in accordance with this subsection, of any article of food that is found during an inspection, examination, or investigation under this Act conducted by such officer or qualified employee, if the officer or qualified employee has credible evidence or information indicating that such article presents a threat of serious adverse health consequences or death to humans or animals.

(B) Secretary's approval. An article of food may be ordered detained under subparagraph (A) only if the Secretary or an official designated by the secretary approves the order. An official may not be so designated unless the official is the director of the district under this Act in which the article involved is located, or is an official senior to such director

(2) Period of detention. An article of food may be detained under paragraph (1) for a reasonable period, not to exceed 20 days, unless a greater period, not to exceed 30 days, is necessary, to enable the Secretary to institute an action under subsection (a) or section 302. The Secretary shall by regulation provide for procedures for instituting such action on an expedited basis with respect to perishable foods.

(3) Security of detained article. An order under paragraph (1) with respect to an article of food may require that such article be labeled or marked as detained, and shall require that the article be removed to a secure facility, as appropriate. An article subject to such an order shall not be transferred by any person from the place at which the article is ordered detained, or from the place to which the article is so removed, as the case may be, until released by the Secretary or until the expiration of the detention period applicable under such order, whichever occurs first. This subsection may not be construed as authorizing the delivery of the article pursuant to the execution of a bond while the article is subject to the order, and section 801(b) does not authorize the delivery of the article pursuant to the execution of a bond while the article is subject to the order.

(4) Appeal of detention order.

(A) In general. With respect to an article of food ordered detained under paragraph (1), any person who would be entitled to be a claimant for such article if the article were seized under subsection (a) may appeal the order to the Secretary. Within five days after such an appeal is filed, the Secretary, after providing opportunity for an informal hearing, shall confirm or terminate the order involved, and such confirmation by the Secretary shall be considered a final agency action for purposes of section 702 of title 5, United States Code. If during such five-day period the Secretary fails to provide such an opportunity, or to confirm or terminate such order, the order is deemed to be terminated.

(B) Effect of instituting court action. The process under subparagraph (A) for the appeal of an order under paragraph (1) terminates if the Secretary institutes an action under subsection (a) or section 302 regarding the article of food involved."

Section 1.401 and 1.402 of Title 21, Code of federal Regulations, are quoted below as notice of opportunity for appeal and a regulatory hearing.

"Section 1.401 Who is entitled to appeal?

Any person who would be entitled to be a claimant for the article of food, if seized under section 304(a) of the FD&C Act, may appeal a detention order as specified in section 1.402. Procedures for establishing entitlement to be a claimant for purposes of section 304(a) of the FD&C Act are governed by Supplemental Rule C to the "Federal Rules of Civil Procedure."

Sec. 1.402 What are the requirements for submitting an appeal?

"(a) If you want to appeal a detention order, you must submit your appeal in writing to the FDA District Director, in whose district the detained article of food is located, at the mailing address, e-mail address, or fax number identified in the detention order according to the following applicable timeframes:

(1) Perishable food: If the detained article is a perishable food, as defined in section 1.377, you must file an appeal within 2 calendar days of receipt of the detention order.

(2) Nonperishable food: If the detained article is not a perishable food, as defined in section 1.377, you must file a notice of an intent to request a hearing within 4 calendar days of receipt of the detention order. If the notice of intent is not filed within 4 calendar days, you will not be granted a hearing. If you have not filed a timely notice of intent to request a hearing, you may file an appeal without a hearing request. Whether or not it includes a request for hearing, your appeal must be filed within 10 calendar days of receipt of the detention order.

(b) Your request for appeal must include a verified statement identifying your ownership or proprietary interest in the detained article of food, in accordance with Supplemental Rule C to the Federal Rules of Civil Procedure.

(c) The process for the appeal of a detention order under this section terminates if FDA institutes either a seizure action under section 304(a) of the FD&C Act or an injunction under section 302 of the FD&C Act (21 U.S.C. 276) regarding the article of food involved in the detention order.

(d) As part of the appeals process, you may request an informal hearing. Your request for a hearing must be in writing and must be included in your request for an appeal specified in paragraph (a) of this section. If you request an informal hearing, and FDA grants your request, the hearing will be held within 2 calendar days after the date the appeal is filed."

Any informal hearing on appeal of a detention order must be conducted as a regulatory hearing under 21 CFR section 1.403.

Section 800.55(g)(1)-(2) of Title 21, Code of Federal Regulations, is quoted below as notice of opportunity for appeal and a regulatory hearing.

"(g) Appeal of a detention order.

(1) A person who would be entitled to claim the devices, if seized, may appeal a detention order. Any appeal shall be submitted in writing to FDA District Director in whose district the devices are located within 5 working days of receipt of a detention order. If the appeal includes a request for an informal hearing, as defined in Section 201(y) of the Act, the appellant shall request either that a hearing be held within 5 working days after the appeal is filed or that the hearing be held at a later date, which shall not be later than 20 calendar days after receipt of the detention order.

(2) The appellant of a detention order shall state the ownership or proprietary interest the appellant has in the detained devices. If the detained devices are located at a place other than an establishment owned or operated by the appellant, the appellant shall include documents showing that the appellant would have legitimate authority to claim the devices if seized."

Any informal hearing on an appeal of a detention order shall be conducted as a regulatory hearing under 21 CFR Part 16, with certain exceptions Described in 21 CFR § 800.55(g)(3).

FORM FDA 2289 (12/05) (BACK)

DEPARTMENT OF HEALTH AND HUMAN SERVICES FOOD AND DRUG ADMINISTRATION **DETENTION NOTICE**	1a. DISTRICT ADDRESS 850 Third Ave. Brooklyn, NY 11232 1b. PHONE NUMBER 718-340-7000	1c. NAME OF DISTRICT DIRECTOR Thomas Gardine 1d. EMAIL ADDRESS tgardine@ora.fda.gov 1e. FAX NUMBER 718-340-7766
2. NAME OF CUSTODIAN TO: Mr. William Jantz		3. DETENTION NOTICE NUMBER **DN** 60006
4. TITLE OF CUSTODIAN Warehouse Manager, Division II	5. TELEPHONE NO. 716- 843-7066	6. DATE AND HOUR DETAINED 12-29-05 10:45 a.m. p.m.
7. FIRM NAME Amoure Cold Storage Co., Inc.		
8. ADDRESS (Street, City, State, ZIP code) 245 Dockage St. Buffalo, NY 14206		9. MAXIMUM DETENTION Twenty (20) DAYS

Pursuant to Sections 402 and 409(b) of the Federal Meat Inspection Act; Sections 19 and 24(b) of the Poultry Products Inspection Act; Sections 19 and 23(d) of the Egg Products Inspection Act, or Section 304(g), or Section 304(h) of the Federal Food, Drug, and Cosmetic Act, the merchandise listed below is hereby detained for the period indicated and must not be used, moved, altered or tampered with in any manner during that period (except that device may be moved and processed under 21 CFR 800 55(h)(2) pursuant to Section 304(g)(2)(B) of the latter Act) without the written permission of an authorized representative of the Secretary of the U.S. Department of Health and Human Services. An article of food detained pursuant to Section 304(h) of the FD&C Act shall not be consumed, moved, altered or tampered with in any manner during the detention period, unless the detention order is first modified under 21 CFR 1.381(c).

10. NAME OF DETAINED ARTICLE Beefy Brand Beef Pot Pie with Mushrooms	11. SIZE OF DETAINED LOT 1600cs/24 – 1 lb. 2 oz tins
12. DETAINED ARTICLE LABELED (Include Master Carton Label) Tins lbld in part "Beefy Brand Pot Pie***ingredients: Selected beef, choice green peas, carrots, selected Idaho potatoes, Mushrooms*** Gravy***1 lb. 2 oz.***Packed by Burly Products Co.***Kansas City, MO EST 223" Tins in	13. APPROXIMATE VALUE OF LOT $19,000.00 14. SAMPLE NUMBER 55566
15. REASON FOR DETENTION Estimated 10% of tins swelled and/or leaking.	16. DETAINED ARTICLE STORED AT (Name, Address, ZIP code) Amoure Cold Storage Co., Inc. Warehouse 3B, 321 Dockage St. Buffalo, NY 14206
17. NAME AND TITLE OF THE PERSON WHO APPROVED DETENTION ORDER Sylvester B. Pearson, Compliance Officer	18. APPROVAL OF DETENTION ORDER ☐ Written ☒ Verbal
19. NAME AND ADDRESS OF ARTICLE OWNER Big Midget Food Chains General Offices – Chicago, Illinois Local Agent – Big Midget, Division 132 2234 Lake drive, Buffalo, NY 14238	20. NAME AND ADDRESS OF INITIAL SHIPPER OR SELLER Burly Products Co. 1921 Packer Avenue Kansas City, MO 64309
21. NAME AND ADDRESS OF SUBSEQUENT SHIPPERS OR SELLERS (Continue in Remarks, if necessary) Big Midget Food Chains, Chicago, IL, lot shipped by Burly from KC to Chicago to Big Midget Warehouse 1st & 2nd Ave. Then shipped by Big Midget to Amoure, Buffalo.	22. NAME OF CARRIERS KC to Chicago via Overland Transport, KC, MO Chicago to Buffalo via IS Cartage, Chicago 23. DATE LOT SHIPPED 12-13-05 to Chicago; 11-20-05 to Buffalo
24. NAME AND ADDRESS OF PACKING PLANT Burly Products Co., Inc. 1921 Packer Avenue Kansas City, MO 64309	25. DATE LOT RECEIVED 12-23-05 in Buffalo 26. PACKING PLANT USDA NO. EST 223

27. DESCRIPTION OF SAMPLE
Sample consists of 2 cs/24/1 lb. 2 oz. tins taken at rate of 2 tins from each of 24 previously unopened cases selected at random from the lot. Of the 48 tins taken, 24 were swollen to some degree and 12 of these were leaking. The other 24 were normal.

28. REMARKS (List any recommendations made to custodian for special storage requirements, i.e., refrigeration, frozen, etc.)
Entire lot was removed from initial location at Amoure Cold Storage Warehouse #2A, 245 Dockage St. to same firm's warehouse #3B at 321 Dockage St., Buffalo, NY, where detention was placed in effect.

NAME OF FDA EMPLOYEE (Type or Print)	TITLE (FDA Employee)	SIGNATURE (FDA Employee)
Sylvia A. Rogers	Investigator	Sylvia A. Rogers

FORM FDA 2289 (12/05) PREVIOUS EDITION MAY NOT BE USED **DETENTION NOTICE 2**

Exhibit 2-3: Detention Tag

DEPARTMENT OF HEALTH AND HUMAN SERVICES
FOOD AND DRUG ADMINISTRATION

U.S. DETAINED

The Lot of goods to which this tag is affixed is

DETAINED BY THE UNITED STATES GOVERNMENT

In accordance with the provisions of Section 402 and 409(b) of the Federal Meat Inspection Act; Sections 19 and 24(b) of the Poultry Products Inspection Act; Sections 19 and 23(d) of the Egg Products Inspection Act; Section 304(g) of the Federal Food, Drug and Cosmetic Act (FD&C Act); or Section 304(h) of the FD&C Act, the merchandise listed below is hereby detained for the period indicated. The merchandise must not be used, moved, altered or tampered with in any manner during that period without the written permission of an authorized representative of the Secretary of the U.S. Department of Health and Human Services, except that a device may be moved and processed under 21 CFR 800.55(h)(2) pursuant to section 304(g)(2)(B) of the FD&C Act. An article of food detained pursuant to Section 304(h) of the FD&C Act shall not be consumed, moved, altered or tampered with in any manner during the detention period, unless the detention order is first modified under 21 CFR 1.381(C).

WARNING: Removal, alteration or mutilation of this Tag or Violation of any of the above conditions is punishable by fine or imprisonment or both.

SEE REVERSE OF THIS TAG FOR DESCRIPTION OF DETAINED MERCHANDISE

DETENTION DATE	& HOUR	DETENTION NOTICE NO.
12-29-2005	10:45 a.m. / p.m.	DN 60006

MAXIMUM DETENTION 20 DAYS

NAME FDA EMPLOYEE ISSUING DETENTION NOTICE (Print or type)
Sylvia A. Rogers

SIGNATURE FDA EMPLOYEE ISSUING DETENTION NOTICE
Sylvia A. Rogers

TITLE FDA EMPLOYEE ISSUING DETENTION NOTICE
Investigator

NAME FDA EMPLOYEE AFFIXING TAG (If different from issuing employee)

SIGNATURE FDA EMPLOYEE AFFIXING TAG

TITLE FDA EMPLOYEE AFFIXING TAG

FORM FDA 2290 (5/05) **Prev. Ed. May NOT Be Used**

DETENTION TAG

U.S. DETAINED

NAME OF DETAINED ARTICLE.

Beefy brand pot pie with mushrooms

DETAINED ARTICLE LABELED

"Beefy Brand Pot Pie net wt. 1 lb. 2 oz. packed by Burly Products Co. Inc.***Kansas City, MO. EST 223"

SIZE OF DETAINED LOT

1600 cs/28/1 lb. 2oz. tins

SEE REVERSE

FORM FDA 2290 (5/05)

Exhibit 2-4: Form FDA 2291

DEPARTMENT OF HEALTH AND HUMAN SERVICES FOOD AND DRUG ADMINISTRATION **DETENTION TERMINATION NOTICE**	1a. DISTRICT ADDRESS 850 Third Ave. Brooklyn, NY 11232 1b. PHONE NUMBER 718-340-7000	1c. NAME OF DISTRICT DIRECTOR Thomas Gardine

TO:	2. NAME OF CUSTODIAN Mr. William Jantz	3. DETENTION NOTICE NUMBER **DN** 60006

4. TITLE OF CUSTODIAN Warehouse Manager, Division II	5. DATE AND HOUR DETAINED 12-29-05	10:45 a.m. / p.m.
6. FIRM NAME Amoure Cold Storage Co., Inc.	7. DATE AND HOUR DETNTION TERMINATED 1-6-06	8:35 a.m. / p.m.

8. ADDRESS *(Street, City, and State)* 245 Dockage St. Buffalo, NY	9. ZIP CODE 14206

The merchandise listed below which, pursuant to Sections 402 and 409(b) of the Federal Meat Inspection Act; Sections 19 and 24(b) of the Poultry Products Inspection Act; Sections 19 and 23(d) of the Egg Products Inspection Act; or Section 304(g) of the Federal Food, Drug, and Cosmetic Act, was detained on the above date and bears the above detention number, is hereby released and the detention is terminated.

10. NAME OF DETAINED ARTICLE Beefy Brand Beef Pot Pie with Mushrooms	11. SIZE OF DETAINED LOT 1600cs/24 – 1 lb. 2 oz tins

12. DETAINED ARTICLE LABELED *(Include Master Carton Label)*

Tins labeled in part with paper labels: "Beefy Brand Pot Pie***ingredients: Selected beef, choice green peas, carrots, selected Idaho potatoes, Mushrooms***Gravy composed of: Water, beef stock, and flour***Net Wt. 1 lb. 2 oz.***Packed by Burly Products Co.***General Offices Kansas City, MO EST 223" Tins in cases labeled in part: "***24/ 1 lb 2 oz tins Beefy Pot Pies***EST 223***"

NAME OF FDA EMPLOYEE *(Type or Print)*	SIGNATURE *(FDA Employee)*	TITLE *(FDA Employee)*
Sylvia A. Rogers	*Sylvia A. Rogers*	Investigator

FORM FDA 2291 (12/05) PREVIOUS EDITION MAY NOT BE USED **DETENTION TERMINATION NOTICE**

DEPARTMENT OF HEALTH AND HUMAN SERVICES FOOD AND DRUG ADMINISTRATION **DETENTION TERMINATION NOTICE**	1a. DISTRICT ADDRESS 850 Third Ave. Brooklyn, NY 11232 1b. PHONE NUMBER 718-340-7000	1c. NAME OF DISTRICT DIRECTOR Thomas Gardine
TO: 2. NAME OF CUSTODIAN Mr. William Jantz		3. DETENTION NOTICE NUMBER **DN** 60006
4. TITLE OF CUSTODIAN Warehouse Manager, Division II		5. DATE AND HOUR DETAINED 12-29-05 10:45 a.m.
6. FIRM NAME Amoure Cold Storage Co., Inc.		7. DATE AND HOUR DETNTION TERMINATED 1-6-05 8:35 a.m.
8. ADDRESS *(Street, City, and State)* 245 Dockage St. Buffalo, NY		9. ZIP CODE 14206

The merchandise listed below which, pursuant to Sections 402 and 409(b) of the Federal Meat Inspection Act; Sections 19 and 24(b) of the Poultry Products Inspection Act; Sections 19 and 23(d) of the Egg Products Inspection Act; or Section 304(g) of the Federal Food, Drug, and Cosmetic Act, was detained on the above date and bears the above detention number, is hereby released and the detention is terminated.

10. NAME OF DETAINED ARTICLE	11. SIZE OF DETAINED LOT
Beefy Brand Beef Pot Pie with Mushrooms	1600cs/24 – 1 lb. 2 oz tins

12. DETAINED ARTICLE LABELED *(Include Master Carton Label)*

Tins labeled in part with paper labels: "Beefy Brand Pot Pie***ingredients: Selected beef, choice green peas, carrots, selected Idaho potatoes, Mushrooms***Gravy composed of: Water, beef stock, and flour***Net Wt. 1 lb. 2 oz.***Packed by Burly Products Co.***General Offices Kansas City, MO EST 223" Tins in cases labeled in part: "***24/ 1 lb 2 oz tins Beefy Pot Pies***EST 223***"

REMARKS

The Culmore County Health department assumed jurisdiction of the product at 8:35 AM on 1-6-06 when it was released from US detention. The entire 1600 case lot was hauled on 1-6-06 by the ACE Trucking Co., 2993 Longway Place, Buffalo, NY, from Amoure Cold Storage Co., Warehouse #3B, 321 Dockage St., Buffalo, NY, to the county landfill at Port Road and Culmore County Road #8 where the lot was dumped, crushed by bulldozers, buried in a ditch, and covered with approximately five feet of earth.

The entire operation was supervised by Culmore County Health Department Inspectors Robert J. Sandi and Henry D. Larky and FDA Investigator Sylvia A. Rogers.

FDA supervision time and expenses:
  Inspectional time – 6 hours
  Mileage – 22 miles in US Gov't car G11-396

Sylvia A. Rogers
Sylvia A. Rogers
Investigator

NAME OF FDA EMPLOYEE *(Type or Print)*	SIGNATURE *(FDA Employee)*	TITLE *(FDA Employee)*
Sylvia A. Rogers	*Sylvia A. Rogers*	Investigator

FORM FDA 2291 (12/05) PREVIOUS EDITION MAY NOT BE USED **DETENTION TERMINATION NOTICE**

Chapter 3 Exhibits

CONTENT

Exhibit 3-1: FDA/USDA Jurisdictional Chart

This table summarizes information concerning jurisdiction overlap for commercial products regulated by either or both FDA and USDA. It does not cover products made for on-site consumption such as pizza parlors, delicatessens, fast food sites, etc. Products carrying the USDA shield are USDA jurisdiction.

FDA JURISDICTION	**USDA JURISDICTION**		
21 USC 392(b) Meats and meat food products shall be exempt from the provisions of this Act to the extent of the application or the extension thereto of the Meat Inspection Act. FDA responsible for all non-specified red meats (bison, rabbits, game animals, zoo animals and all members of the deer family including elk (wapiti) and moose)). FDA responsible for all non-specified birds including wild turkeys, wild ducks, and wild geese.	The Federal Meat Inspection Act regulates the inspection of the following amenable species: cattle, sheep, swine, goats, horses, mules or other equines, including their carcasses and parts. It also covers any additional species of livestock that the Secretary of Agriculture considers appropriate. Mandatory Inspection of Ratites and Squab (including emu) announced by USDA/FSIS April 2001	The Poultry Products Inspection Act (PPIA) defines the term poultry as any domesticated bird. USDA has interpreted this to include domestic chickens, turkeys, ducks, geese and guineas. The Poultry Products Inspection Act states poultry and poultry products shall be exempt from the provisions of the FD&C Act to the extent they are covered by the PPIA. Mandatory Inspection of Ratites and Squab announced by USDA/FSIS April 2001	The Egg Products Inspection Act defines egg to mean the shell egg of domesticated chicken, turkey, duck, goose or guinea. Voluntary grading of shell eggs is done under USDA supervision. (FDA enforces labels/labeling of shell eggs.)

<table>
<tr><th>FDA JURISDICTION</th><th colspan="3">USDA JURISDICTION</th></tr>
<tr><td>Products with 3% or less raw meat; less than 2% cooked meat or other portions of the carcass; or less than 30% fat, tallow or meat extract, alone or in combination.
Products containing less than 2% cooked poultry meat; less than 10% cooked poultry skins, giblets, fat and poultry meat (limited to less than 2%) in any combination.*
Closed-face sandwiches.</td><td>Products containing greater than 3% raw meat; 2% or more cooked meat or other portions of the carcass; or 30% or more fat, tallow or meat extract, alone or in combination.*
Open-face sandwiches.</td><td>Products containing 2% or more cooked poultry; more than 10% cooked poultry skins, giblets, fat and poultry meat in any combination.*</td><td>Egg products processing plants (egg breaking and pasteurizing operations) are under USDA jurisdiction.</td></tr>
<tr><td colspan="2">FDA is responsible for shell eggs and egg containing products that do not meet USDA's definition of "egg product." FDA also has jurisdiction in establishments not covered by USDA; e.g. restaurants, bakeries, cake mix plants, etc.
Egg processing plants (egg washing, sorting, packing) are under FDA jurisdiction.</td><td colspan="2">Products that meet USDA's definition of "egg product" are under USDA jurisdiction. The definition includes dried, frozen, or liquid eggs, with or without added ingredients, but mentions many exceptions. The following products, among others, are exempted as not being egg products: freeze-dried products, imitation egg products, egg substitutes, dietary foods, dried no-bake custard mixes, egg nog mixes, acidic dressings, noodles, milk and egg dip, cake mixes, French toast, sandwiches containing eggs or egg products, and balut and other similar ethnic delicacies. Products that do not fall under the definition, such as egg substitutes and cooked products, are under FDA jurisdiction.</td></tr>
<tr><td>Cheese pizza, onion and mushroom pizza, meat flavored spaghetti sauce (less than 3% red meat), meat flavored spaghetti sauce with mushrooms, (2% meat), pork and beans, sliced egg sandwich (closed-face), frozen fish dinner, rabbit stew, shrimp-flavored instant noodles, venison jerky, buffalo burgers, alligator nuggets, noodle soup chicken flavor</td><td colspan="2">Pepperoni pizza, meat-lovers stuffed crust pizza, meat sauces (3% red meat or more), spaghetti sauce with meat balls, open-faced roast beef sandwich, hot dogs, corn dogs, beef/vegetable pot pie</td><td>Chicken sandwich (open face), chicken noodle soup</td></tr>
</table>

Jurisdiction for products produced under the School Lunch Program, for military use, etc. is determined via the same algorithm although the purchases are made under strict specifications so that the burden of compliance falls on the contractor. Compliance Policy Guide 565.100, 567.200 and 567.300 provide additional examples of jurisdiction. IOM 3.2.1 and 2.7.1 provide more information on our interactions with USDA and Detention Authority.

* These percentages are based on the amount of meat or poultry product used in the product at formulation.

Exhibit 3-2: History of Menu Items (2 Pgs)

HISTORY OF MENU ITEMS

DATE 4/25/03

PLACE Hyatt Hotel, St. Louis, MO

MENU ITEM	SUPPLIER	DATE REC'D	PRE-PARED	ADVANCE PREPARED	LOCATION	STEPS IN PROCESS	TEMP OF	TIMES	EMPLOYEE(S) INVOLVED
Egg Rolls (Appetizer)	Independent Foods St. Louis, MO	4/20	yes		freezer	bake	5°-230°F	1600-1730	R. Brown
Ravioli (Appetizer)	ITAL-AMER Foods St. Louis, MO	4/21	yes		freezer	deep fry	5°-300°F	1700 - 1730	B. Black
Cheeses (Appetizer)	Fox Dairy St. Louis, MO	4/24	yes		cooler	slice	40°F	1350 - 1450	C. White
Pate (Appetizer)	Joe's Butcher Shop E. St. Louis, IL (liver)	4/10		yes 4/10 Chef Welsh	freezer	thaw slice plate	5°-40°F 40°F 40°F	?-1600 1600-1630 1630-1700	K. Green " " " "
Produce (Salad)	Lombardi's St. Louis, MO	4/24			cooler	wash plate cool	55°F 75°F 75°-40°F	0730 0845-0945 0945-1730	B. Black & K. Green
Crown Potatoes	"	"			"	slice bake plate	75°F 75°-225°F 200°F	0900-1030 1030-1200 1700-1730	R. Brown & A. Smith
Prime Rib	Joe's Butcher Shop E. St. Louis, IL	4/24			"	roast slice plate	36°-140°F 135°F 130°F	1500-1800 1800-1830 1930-1900	Chef Welsh C. White Chef Welsh
Wine Chateau St. Juan 2001 2000 Marion Cabernet	Sonoma Valley CA "								

HISTORY OF MENU ITEMS

DATE PLACE

MENU ITEM	SUPPLIER	DATE REC'D	PRE-PARED	ADVANCE PREPARED	LOCATION	STEPS IN PROCESS	TEMP OF	TIMES	EMPLOYEE(S) INVOLVED

Exhibit 3-3: Address Information Request (2 Pgs)

DEPARTMENT OF HEALTH & HUMAN SERVICES

FOOD AND DRUG ADMINISTRATION

To: Postmaster

Agency Control Number:
Date:

ADDRESS INFORMATION REQUEST

Please furnish this agency with the new address, if available, for the following individual or verify whether or not the address given below is one at which mail for this individual is currently being delivered. If the following address is a post office box, please furnish the street address as recorded on the boxholder's application form.

Name:
Last Known Address:

I certify that the address information for this individual is required for the performance of this agency's official duties.

(Signature of Agency Official)

(Title)

FOR POST OFFICE USE ONLY

[ ] MAIL IS DELIVERED TO ADDRESS GIVEN
[ ] NOT KNOWN AT ADDRESS GIVEN
[ ] MOVED, LEFT NO FORWARDING ADDRESS
[ ] NO SUCH ADDRESS
[ ] OTHER (SPECIFY):

Agency return address

NEW ADDRESS

BOXHOLDER'S STREET ADDRESS

Postmark/Date Stamp

Instructions for Completing IOM Exhibit 3-3

If you have already attempted to locate the individual or firm by sending mail marked on the outside of the envelope "DO NOT FORWARD. ADDRESS CORRECTION REQUESTED", without results, then proceed with this form according to the instructions below.

Instructions

1. Address the request to the Postmaster at the post office of the last known address.

2. Insert FEI # if known; or assignment or sample number for Agency Control number.

3. On the lines provided, give the name and last known address, including zip code, of the individual or firm. Do not include any other identifying information such as race, date of birth, social security number, etc.

4. The Postal Service provides the service of address verification to Government agencies only. For this reason, the Postal Service requires the signature and title of an agency official to certify that the address information requested is required in the performance of the agency's official duties. The agency official should be if possible, the chief of the office requesting the information. In the interests of efficiency, the signature may be preprinted or rubber-stamped.

5. Type or stamp the agency's return mailing address in the space provided at the bottom of the request. Then, mail or deliver the request to the Postmaster at the post office of the last known address.

   You are not required to submit this request in duplicate or to furnish a return envelope.

Chapter 4 Exhibits

CONTENT

Exhibit 4-1: Facts Sample Collection Screen (5 Pgs)

This document is available on the FDA website at http://www.fda.gov/ICECI/Inspections/IOM/ucm127372.htm.

Exhibit 4-2: Facts Sample Collection Screen (2 Pgs)

This document is available on the FDA website at http://www.fda.gov/ICECI/Inspections/IOM/ucm127372.htm.

Exhibit 4-3: Affidavit (In-Transit) - FDA 1664b

AFFIDAVIT *(In-transit Sampling)*

SAMPLE NO. 55522

STATE OF UTAH

COUNTY OF UINTAH

Before me, Sylvia A. Rogers, an employee of the Department of Health and Human Services, Food and Drug Administration, designated by the Secretary under authority of the Act of January 31, 1925, 43 Statutes at Large 803; Reorganization Plan No. IV, Secs. 12-15, effective June 30, 1940; Reorganization Plan No. 1 of 1953, Secs. 1-9, effective April 11, 1953; and P.L. 96-88, Sec. 509, 93 Statutes at Large 965 (20 U.S.C. 3508), effective May 4, 1980, to administer or take oaths, affirmations and affidavits, personally appeared Wayne J. Ellmore, in the county and State aforesaid, who, being duly sworn, deposes and says: I am employed by

Trans-National Truck Lines, Tulsa, OK
(Carrier or firm name, city & state)

as Driver
(Title of position)

On October 14, 2001 *(Date)*, at Vernal, Utah *(City & state where sampled)*

The above named FDA employee collected a sample consisting of two crates (48 heads per crate) of Polar brand Iceberg lettuce packed by Delbert Brothers Lettuce Suppliers, Fresno, CA
(Description and number of units sampled)

from Tractor Trailer #321, Oklahoma Lic. #3672TR, 2001
(Enter type and number & License number of truck, bus, RR car, airplane, etc. or Firm name and shipping dock address if from dock), from shipment(s) of goods consigned to or being shipped to

Mid Central Distributors, 33 Front St., Minneapolis, Minnesota
(Consignee name and address)

The aforesaid sampled shipment(s) was (were) identified to the FDA collector by Wayne J. Ellmore *(Name of individual making identification)*, Truck Driver *(Title of person making identification)*.

(Copy of) Shipping Record(s) F/B *(Type record – B/L, Waybill, etc.)*, number A-32196,

dated 10/14/01, issued by Trans-National Truck Lines, which were identified by Wayne J. Ellmore, Driver *(Name & title of individual identifying records)*, and furnished to the FDA collector cover this (these) shipment(s).

AFFIANT'S SIGNATURE

Wayne J. Ellmore

Subscribed and sworn to before me at Vernal, Utah *(City and State)*

this 14th day of October, 2001.

Sylvia A. Roger
(Employee's Signature)

Employee of the Department of Health and Human Services designated under Act of January 31, 1925, Reorganization Plan IV effective Sylvia A. Rogers, June 30, 1940; Reorganization Plan No. 1 of 1953, effective April 11, 1953; and P.L. 96-88, effective May 4, 1980

FORM FDA 1664b (8/01) PREVIOUS EDITIONS MAY BE USED

Created by PSC Media Arts (301) 443-2454 XTF

Exhibit 4-4: Carrier's Receipt for Sample - FDA 472

DEPARTMENT OF HEALTH AND HUMAN SERVICES FOOD AND DRUG ADMINISTRATION	DISTRICT ADDRESS AND PHONE NO. 300 S. Riverside Plaza, Suite 550 South Chicago, IL 60606

TO	NAME AND TITLE OF INDIVIDUAL John B. Carr, Driver	DATE 11-6-04
	NAME AND ADDRESS OF CARRIER Transcontinental Trucking, 10 Front St. Dallas, TX 75204	SAMPLE NUMBER 27269

CONSIGNEE AND ADDRESS *(Street, City, State and ZIP Code)*	CONSIGNOR AND ADDRESS *(Street, City, State and ZIP Code)*
XYZ Wholesale 111 S. Water Market Chicago, IL 60601	Best Yet Packing Co. 3 First St. Young Town, TX 75002

SAMPLE(S) REMOVED FOR EXAMINATION		WAYBILL OR FREIGHT BILL NUMBER
AMOUNT OF SAMPLE	PRODUCT	
2 cases (48 ct)	Lettuce – Best Yet Brand	A-23764

SAMPLE COLLECTOR'S NAME	TITLE	SIGNATURE
Sylvia H. Rogers	Investigator	*Sylvia A. Rogers*

FORM FDA 472 (10/01) PREVIOUS EDITION MAY BE USED UNTIL SUPPLY IS EXHAUSTED. **CARRIER'S RECEIPT FOR SAMPLE**

Exhibit 4-5: Receipt for Samples - FDA 484 (2 Pgs Replace With 510c)

DEPARTMENT OF HEALTH AND HUMAN SERVICES
FOOD AND DRUG ADMINISTRATION

1. DISTRICT ADDRESS & PHONE NUMBER
850 Third Avenue
Brooklyn, NY 11232
718-340-7000

2. NAME AND TITLE OF INDIVIDUAL	3. DATE	4. SAMPLE NUMBER
Richard A. Frost, General Manager	12-4-06	25563

5. FIRM NAME	6. FIRM'S DEA NUMBER
Quality Wholesale Drug Co.	AB3632918
7. NUMBER AND STREET	**8. CITY AND STATE** *(Include Zip Code)*
3146 Front Street	Brooklyn, NY 11232

9. SAMPLE COLLECTED *(Describe fully. List lot, serial, model numbers and other positive identification)*

The following samples were collected by the Food and Drug Administration and receipt is hereby acknowledged pursuant to Section 704(c) of the Federal Food, Drug, and Cosmetic Act [21 U.S.C. 374(c)] and / or Section 532 (b) of the Federal Food, Drug, and Cosmetic Act [21 U.S.C 360ii(b)] and/or 21 Code of Federal Regulations (CFR) 1307.02. Excerpts of these are quoted on the reverse of this form.
(**NOTE**: *If you bill FDA for the cost of the Sample(s) listed below, please attach a copy of this form to your bill.*)

One Box of 25 - 1 cc ampules, Diloudid HCl (hydromorphine) 2 mg/cc, lot # 0103213 manufactured by Knoll Pharmaceutical Co., Orange NJ.

10. SAMPLES WERE	11. AMOUNT RECEIVED FOR SAMPLE	12. SIGNATURE *(Persons receiving payment for sample or person providing sample to FDA at no charge.)*
☐ PROVIDED AT NO CHARGE ☒ PURCHASED ☐ BORROWED *(To be returned)*	☒ CASH ☐ BILLED ☐ VOUCHER ☐ CREDIT CARD $15.00	Richard A. Frost

13. COLLECTOR'S NAME *(Print or Type)*	14. COLLECTOR'S TITLE *(Print or Type)*	15. COLLECTOR'S SIGNATURE
Sylvia A. Rogers	Investigator	Sylvia A. Rogers

FORM FDA 484 (3/06) PREVIOUS EDITION MAY BE USED **RECEIPT FOR SAMPLES** PAGE 1 OF 1 PAGES
PSC Media Arts (301) 443-1090 EF

Section 704 (c) of the Federal Food, Drug, and Cosmetic Act [21 U.S.C. 374(c)] is quoted below:

"If the officer or employee making any such inspection of a factory, warehouse, or other establishment has obtained any sample in the course of the inspection, upon completion of the inspection and prior to leaving the premises he shall give to the owner, operator, or agent in charge a receipt describing the samples obtained."

Section 532(b) of The Federal Food, Drug and Cosmetic Act [21 U.S.C 360 ii (b)] is quoted in part below:

"Section 532(b) In carrying out the purposes of subsection (a), the Secretary is authorized to-

(1) ****

(2) ****

(3) ****

(4) procure (by negotiation or otherwise) electronic products for research and testing purposes, and sell or otherwise

dispose of such products"

21 Code of Federal Regulations 1307.02 is quoted below:

"1307.02 Application of State law and other Federal law.

Nothing in this chapter shall be construed as authorizing or permitting any person to do any act which such person is not authorized or permitted to do under other Federal laws or obligations under international treaties, conventions or protocols, or under the law of the State in which he/she desires to do such an act nor shall compliance with such be construed as compliance with other Federal or State laws unless expressly provided in such other laws."

Therefore, in the event any samples of controlled drugs are collected by FDA representatives in the enforcement of the Federal Food, Drug, and Cosmetic Act, the FDA representative shall issue a receipt for such samples on FDA Form FDA 484, RECEIPT FOR SAMPLES, to the owner, operator, or agent in charge of the premises.

Report of analysis will be furnished only where samples meet the requirements of Section 704(d) of the Federal Food, Drug, and Cosmetic Act [21 U.S.C. 374(d)] which is quoted below:

"Whenever in the course of any such inspection of a factory or other establishment where food is manufactured, processed, or packed, the officer or employee making the inspection obtains a sample of any such food, and an analysis is made of such sample for the purpose of ascertaining whether such food consists in whole or in part of any filthy, putrid, or decomposed substance, or is otherwise unfit for food, a copy of the results of such analysis shall be furnished promptly to the owner, operator, or agent in charge."

Exhibit 4-6: Field Weight Sheet - FDA 485

DEPARTMENT OF HEALTH AND HUMAN SERVICES
FOOD AND DRUG ADMINISTRATION

1. DATE: 9-16-05
2. SAMPLE NUMBER: 55532
3. PRODUCT: Spaghetti in plastic bags: "Genoa Semolina Vermicelli***Delmonico Foods, Inc. San Francisco, Calif.***Net Weight 12 ozs."
4. TYPE OF BALANCE: Gurley
5. RESPONSIBLE FIRM AND ADDRESS *(Zip Code)*: Delmonico Foods, Inc.
4701 Canal Street
San Francisco, California
6. ADDRESS WHERE WEIGHED: Medicine Bow Wholesalers
23 Railroad Ave.
Cheyenne, Wyoming
7. WAREHOUSE — a. TYPE: Wholesale Grocery Warehouse; b. TEMPERATURE: 80° F; d. HUMIDITY: est. 20%
8. NO. OF — a. CASES IN LOT: 325 48/12 oz.; b. CASES SAMPLED: 12; c. SUBS WEIGHED FROM EACH CASE: 4 from each of 12 cases

9. GROSS WEIGHT *(Submit a minimum of 12 subs with at least one from each case examined. Submit the subs indicated by the asterisks adding others where necessary to identify additional subs submitted. Determine six tares. Where tares may vary widely, determine up to 12 where practical.)*

CASE NO.	SUB NO.	GROSS WEIGHT	CASE NO.	SUB NO.	GROSS WEIGHT	CASE NO.	SUB NO.	GROSS WEIGHT	CASE NO.	SUB NO.	GROSS WEIGHT
1	1	11.40	4	13	12.08	7	25	11.32	10	37	12.00
1	2	11.72	4	14	11.68	7	26	12.00	10	38	12.04
1	3*	11.60	4	15*	11.42	7	27*	11.34	10	39*	11.64
1	4	11.30	4	16	12.40	7	28	11.34	10	40	11.72
2	5	11.32	5	17	11.32	8	29	11.34	11	41	12.10
2	6	11.40	5	18	11.34	8	30	11.40	11	42	11.70
2	7*	12.00	5	19*	11.40	8	31*	11.40	11	43*	11.40
2	8	11.38	5	20	11.42	8	32	11.36	11	44	11.50
3	9	11.34	6	21	12.02	9	33	12.04	12	45	11.32
3	10	11.40	6	22	11.70	9	34	12.00	12	46	11.30
3	11*	11.42	6	23*	12.08	9	35*	11.38	12	47*	11.24
3	12	12.02	6	24	12.10	9	36	11.36	12	48	11.36
TOTAL		138.30			140.96			138.28			139.32
									GRAND TOTAL		556.86

10. PRELIMINARY TARE

TARE NO.	WEIGHT	TARE NO.	WEIGHT
1	0.22	4	0.23
2	0.22	5	0.21
3	0.21	6	0.22
TOTAL	0.65	TOTAL	0.66
		GRAND TOTAL	1.31
*NUMBER OF TARES WEIGHED			6
PRELIMINARY AVERAGE TARE			0.22

11. WEIGHING RESULTS

a. AVERAGE GROSS	11.60
b. PRELIMINARY AVERAGE TARE	.22
c. AVERAGE NET	11.38
d. DECLARED NET	12.00
e. SHORTAGE	.62

12. PRELIMINARY % SHORT: 5.2%

13. REMARKS *(List observations of lot or storage conditions affecting net weights)*: Lot has been in storage since 9-1-05.

14. DISTRICT: DEN-DO
15. EMPLOYEE SIGNATURE: Sidney H. Rogers
16. EMPLOYEE TITLE: Investigator

FD FORM 485 — PREVIOUS EDITION MAY NOT BE USED — FIELD WEIGHT SHEET

Exhibit 4-7: Affidavit - FDA 463a

AFFIDAVIT

SAMPLE NO. 55533

STATE OF: Kansas

COUNTY OF: Sedgwick

Before me, Sidney H. Rogers , an employee of the Department of Health and Human Services, Food and Drug Administration, designated by the Secretary, under authority of the Act of January 31, 1925, 43 Statutes at Large 803; Reorganization Plan No. IV, Secs. 12-15, effective June 30, 1940; Reorganization Plan No. 1 of 1953, Secs. 1-9, effective April 11, 1953; and P.L. 96-98, Sec. 509, 93 Statutes at Large 965 (20 U.S.C. 3508), effective May 4, 1980; to administer or take oaths, affirmations, and affidavits, personally appeared Joseph H. Roe in the county and State aforesaid, who, being duly sworn, deposes and says:

I am the Vice President in charge of production of the Doe Bottling Co., Inc., 123 Main, Thistown, Kansas 67201; and as such I have knowledge of the raw material receiving and use, and carbonated beverage production at this firm.

The sample consisting of two cases, 48- 10 ounce bottles, of Kola Cola, coded ABCD, collected by Investigator Rogers on November 15, 1999 was from a lot of 2668 cases produced by this firm on October 7, 1999. The copies of our production records for October 7, 1999 consist of a Syrup Room Report dated 10-6-99, a two-page Production Report dated 10-7-99, an undated in-line Control record, and a Finished Drink Control Record dated 10-7-99. Copies of these records were provided to the investigator and cover our production of this lot.

The above described lot was made in part from a portion of a lot of bulk liquid sugar received October 3, 1999 from the Sweet Sugar Co., Boise, Idaho, in railroad tank car ATSF 98765, unloaded October 6, 1999. The copies of the Sweet Sugar Co. invoice number 468 dated Sept. 26, 1999; freight waybill number UP-3579 dated Sept. 27, 1999 issued by the Union Pacific Railroad Co.; and our receiving report number 01-23 dated October 3, 1999 were provided to the investigator and cover this shipment.

The above described lot was also made in part from a portion of a lot of Kola Cola syrup base received September 23, 1999 from the Kola Cola Co., Thattown, Texas. The copies of Kola Cola Co. invoice number KCO1928 dated Sept. 20, 1999; freight bill number X-98125 dated Sept. 21, 1999 issued by Speedy Truck Line Co.; and our receiving report number 01-01 dated Sept. 23, 1999 were provide to the investigator and cover this shipment.

The above described lot of Kola Cola was identified to the investigator by William S. Doe, Production Supervisor. I identified and provided copies of the records to the investigator.

AFFIANT'S SIGNATURE AND TITLE

Joseph H. Roe, Production Vice President

FIRM'S NAME AND ADDRESS *(Include ZIP Code)*

Doe Bottling Co., Inc. 123 Main, Thistown, Kansas, 67201

Subscribed and sworn to before me at Thistown, Kansas this 15th day of November, 1999 .

Sidney H. Rogers

(Employee Signature)

Employee of the Department of Health and Human services designated under Act of January 31, 1925, Reorganization Plan IV effective June 30, 1940; Reorganization Plan No. 1 of 1953, effective April 11, 1953; and P.L. 96-88 effective May 4, 1980.

FORM FDA 463a (4/83) PREVIOUS EDITIONS ARE OBSOLETE PAGE 1 OF 1 PAGES

Exhibit 4-8: Copy of Invoice/Shipping Record - FD1662

1. LOCATION	2. NAME OF SAMPLE COLLECTOR	3. DATE COLLECTED	4. SAMPLE NUMBER
Pine Bluff, Arkansas	Sylvia A. Rogers	10-8-05	55566

SECTION I - COPY OF INVOICE

5. CONSIGNOR *(Name, Street, City, and State)*	6. CONSIGNEE *(Name, Street, City, and State)*
Captain Sam Seafood, Inc. 719 Butler Ave. New Orleans, LA	Razor Back Super Market 1207 Little Rock Dr. Pine Bluff, AR

7. GUARANTEE	8. INVOICE NUMBER	9. INVOICE DATE
-----see reverse-----	477	9-20-05

10 QUANTITY	11 UNIT SIZE	12 DESCRIPTION OF ARTICLE(S)	13 UNIT PRICE		14 TOTAL	
10 cs.	24/4.5 oz.	Horseshoe Brand Canned Medium Shrimp	2	84	56	80
5 cs.	10/5 lb.	Frozen Green Hills 21-25 Shrimp	1	10	275	00
		**************************				
5cs.	24/8 oz.	Horseshoe Brand Canned Cove Oysters	5	25	52	50
		***************************				
2 cs.	6/4 lb.	Frozen C&P Small Shrimp	1	50	72	00
			15. TOTAL		642	80

SECTION II - COPY OF SHIPPING RECORD

16. SHIPPER *(Name, Street, City, and State)*	17. CONSIGNEE *(Name, Street, City, and State)*
Captain Sam Seafood, Inc. NOLA	Razor Back Super Market 1207 Little Rock Dr. Pine bluff, AR

18. CARRIER *(Name, City, and State)*
Sea Breeze Trucking, Inc. NOLA

19. CAR OR EQUIPMENT NUMBER	20. WAYBILL DATE & NUMBER	21. TYPE OF RECORD *(Specify)*	22. RECORD NO.	23. RECORD DATE
Van 109	N/A	F/B	06641	9-20-05

24. SHIPPED FROM *(City and State)*	25. ROUTE	26. DATE SHIPPED
NOLA	N/A	9-20-05

27 DESCRIPTION OF ARTICLE(S)			28 NO. PKGS.	29 WEIGHT	30 RATE	31 CHANGES
Canned Food			20	300	172	5.16
Frozen Seafood			8	350	224	7.84
32. RECEIVED BY P. Monteux s/s	33. DATE REC'D 9-26-05	34. TOTAL	28	650		13.00

FORM FDA 1662 (4/86) PREVIOUS EDITION MAY BE USED **COPY OF INVOICE AND SHIPPING RECORD**

Exhibit 4-9: Affidavit (Parcel Post) - FDA 463

AFFIDAVIT *(Parcel Post/Parcel Service)*	SAMPLE NO. 2358
STATE OF Colorado	COUNTY OF Pueblo

Before me, Sidney H. Rogers an employee of the Department of Health and Human Services, Food and Drug Administration, designated by the Secretary, under authority of the Act of January 31, 1925, 43 Statutes at Large 803; Reorganization Plan No. IV, Secs. 12-15, effective June 30, 1940; Reorganization Plan No. 1 of 1953, Secs. 1-9, effective April 11, 1953; and P.L. 96-88, Sec. 509, 93 Statutes at Large 965 (20U.S.C.3508), effective May 4, 1980; to administer or take oaths, affirmations, and affidavits, personally appeared Joseph D. Bullard in the county and state aforesaid, who, being duly sworn, deposes and says: (I) (My firm) received on or about the day of July 10th, 2005, in response to an order previously given by me, two (packages, cartons, etc.) consisting in whole or in part of a product designated "4 ounces NET***Johnson's Eye Ease***Reservation Special" via: (parcel post, United States mail) (United Parcel Service) from Old Indian Herb Co. 294 N. Blackfoot St., Boise, Idaho 30854 and covered by attached copy of invoice number C-20 dated 7-2-05; after unpacking the goods the (parcel post) (parcel service) wrapper was destroyed; and on the 12th day of July, 2005, Inspector/Investigator Rogers obtained from me a sample consisting of 10-4 oz. bottles of Johnson's Eye Ease coded "J-638" on the bottle label, shipped and described as aforesaid and for which he paid me the sum of $25.00 in (cash) (voucher) (billed).

Remarks: I first learned of this product while reading the January 2005 issue of "The Retired Engineer." I use it to relieve the burning and itching in my eyes after working in the heat and dryness.

AFFIANT'S SIGNATURE AND TITLE

Joseph D. Bullard

FIRM'S NAME AND ADDRESS *(Include ZIP Code)*

Subscribed and sworn to before me at Crow, Colorado *(City & State)* this 13th day of July, 2005.

Sidney H. Rogers

(Employee's Signature)

Employee of the Department of Health and Human Services designated under Act of January 31, 1925, Reorganization Plan IV effective June 30, 1940; Reorganization Plan No. 1 of 1953, effective April 11, 1953; and P.L. 96-88, effective May 4, 1980.

FORM FDA 463(4/83) PREVIOUS EDITIONS ARE OBSOLETE

Exhibit 4-10: Affidavit - FDA 463a

AFFIDAVIT		SAMPLE NO. 55555
STATE OF Oregon	COUNTY OF Klamath	

Before me, Sidney H. Rogers, an employee of the Department of Health and Human Services, Food and Drug Administration, designated by the Secretary, under authority of the Act of January 31, 1925, 43 Statutes at Large 803; Reorganization Plan No. IV, Secs. 12-15, effective June 30, 1940; Reorganization Plan No. 1 of 1953, Secs. 1-9, effective April 11, 1953; and P.L. 96-98, Sec. 509, 93 Statutes at Large 965 (20 U.S.C. 3508), effective May 4, 1980; to administer or take oaths, affirmations, and affidavits, personally appeared George W. Hughes in the county and State aforesaid, who, being duly sworn, deposes and says:

I live at 482 Abricia Ave., Klamath Falls, Oregon. On October 18, 1999, my neighbor, Dr. Samuel Thompson, asked me to pick up some medical instruments from a firm in Santa Rosa, California for him. Later that same day I drove to Santa Rosa in my 1997 Dodge Ram pick-up truck which has Oregon license plates, number FAS 682.

The next morning, October 19, 1999, I drove to Charles Brown & Associates at 920 Grape St., Santa Rosa, California and picked up 4 cartons bearing the label: "Fancy Medical Device, quantity 1." Each carton contained a medical device.

I drove back to Klamath Falls, Oregon after picking up a load of wine for my wine cellar, and arrived home on or about 11:00 PM.

The next morning, October 20, 1999, I delivered the 4 cartons to Dr. Samuel Thompson at his office, 2209 Timberline Ave., Klamath Falls, Oregon.

I did not charge Dr. Thompson for the pick-up and delivery because I make regular trips to pick up wine in Santa Rosa for my wine cellar.

AFFIANT'S SIGNATURE AND TITLE

George W. Hughes, Owner

FIRM'S NAME AND ADDRESS *(Include ZIP Code)*

Hughes Wine Cellar, 483 Abrecia Ave., Klamath Falls, 97210

Subscribed and sworn to before me at Klamath Falls, Oregon this 4th day of November, 1999.

Sidney H. Rogers
(Employee Signature)

Employee of the Department of Health and Human services designated under Act of January 31, 1925, Reorganization Plan IV effective June 30, 1940; Reorganization Plan No. 1 of 1953, effective April 11, 1953; and P.L. 96-88 effective May 4, 1980.

FORM FDA 463a (4/83) PREVIOUS EDITIONS ARE OBSOLETE PAGE 1 OF 1 PAGES

Exhibits

Exhibit 4-11: Affidavit - FDA 463a

AFFIDAVIT

SAMPLE NO. 166455

STATE OF Florida

COUNTY OF Orange

Before me, Paul A. Revere, an employee of the Department of Health and Human Services, Food and Drug Administration, designated by the Secretary, under authority of the Act of January 31, 1925, 43 Statutes at Large 803; Reorganization Plan No. IV, Secs. 12-15, effective June 30, 1940; Reorganization Plan No. 1 of 1953, Secs. 1-9, effective April 11, 1953; and P.L. 96-98, Sec. 509, 93 Statutes at Large 965 (20 U.S.C. 3508), effective May 4, 1980; to administer or take oaths, affirmations, and affidavits, personally appeared Nicholas I. Herkimer in the county and State aforesaid, who, being duly sworn, deposes and says:

I am the Warehouse Manager at ABC Distribution Company, 200 Harding Street, Orlando, FL 32806 and have held this position for 3 months. Previously, I held the position of Traffic Manager here for 10 years. As such, I am familiar with and can identify records associated with the receipt, storage and shipment of goods at my firm.

On or about 3/1/01, my firm received a shipment of 500 cases, 24-½ fl. oz. bottles/case of Opti-One brand 0.12% Phenylephrine HCl Ophthalmic Drops from Sawyer Corporation, 51 Summer Street, Andover, MA 01810. This shipment was delivered to my firm by Yellow Freight Company, 1553 Fairlawn Street, St. Louis, MO 63126 and is covered by Sawyer Corporation invoice number 1500 dated 3/1/01 and bill of lading number 2000 dated 3/1/01.

On 4/1/01, I identified and provided Investigator Revere copies of the documents described in this statement. On 4/1/01, Investigator Revere collected a sample consisting of 96 - ½ fl. oz. bottles of Opti-One brand 0.12% Phenylephrine HCl Ophthalmic Drops, lot number 020101, from the shipment described above. This sample was provided to the FDA at a cost of $192.00, which will be billed.

I read this statement and agree it is true.

AFFIANT'S SIGNATURE AND TITLE Nicholas I. Herkimer, Warehouse Manager

FIRM'S NAME AND ADDRESS *(Include ZIP Code)*

ABC Distribution Company, 200 Harding Street, Orlando, FL 32806

Subscribed and sworn to before me at Orlando, FL this 1st day of April, 2001.

Paul A. Revere

(Employee Signature)

Employee of the Department of Health and Human services designated under Act of January 31, 1925, Reorganization Plan IV effective June 30, 1940; Reorganization Plan No. 1 of 1953, effective April 11, 1953; and P.L. 96-88 effective May 4, 1980.

FORM FDA 463a (4/83) PREVIOUS EDITIONS ARE OBSOLETE PAGE 1 OF 1 PAGES

Exhibit 4-12: Affidavit - FDA 1664

AFFIDAVIT *(Dealer/Warehouseman)*

SAMPLE NO 55563

STATE OF Arkansas

COUNTY OF Jefferson

Before me, Sidney H. Rogers, an employee of the Department of Health and Human Services, Food and Drug Administration, designated by the Secretary under authority of the Act of January 31, 1925, 43 Statutes at Large 803; Reorganization Plan No. IV, Secs. 12-15, effective June 30, 1940; Reorganization Plan No. 1 of 1953, Secs. 1-9, effective April 11, 1953; and P.L. 96-88, Sec. 509, 93 Statutes at Large 965 (20 U.S.C. 3508), effective May 4, 1980, to administer or take oaths, affirmations, and affidavits, personally appeared Henry O'Rourke, in the county and State aforesaid, who, being duly sworn, deposes and says: The sample consisting of Two Cases (24/8 oz. Each) Horseshoe Brand Canned Cove Oysters collected by the above FDA employee on 3-10-99 was from shipment(s) received by us from Captain Sam Seafood, Inc. New Orleans, LA on 3-7-99 and so identified to the collector:

That the copy of invoice(s):

NUMBER	DATE	NUMBER	DATE	NUMBER	DATE
1) 06641	3/6/99	2) 06643	3/7/99	3)	

and (copy of) shipping record(s):

TYPE (B/L, F/B)	NUMBER	DATE	ISSUING FIRM OR CARRIER
1) F/B	4778	3/6/99	Acme Freight Lines, Inc. NOLA
2) F/B	A-9321	3/7/99	Thru-Fast Lines, Little Rock, AR
3)			

which were identified and furnished the collector, cover this (these) shipment(s):

That said shipment(s) was (were) entered for the account of N/A

______________________ under Lot no.

The collector paid me the sum of $ 21.32 (in cash) ~~(by voucher)(to be billed)~~ for the sample.

REMARKS

AFFIANT'S SIGNATURE & TITLE

Henry O. O'Rourk, Warehouse Manager Plant #12

FIRM (Name and address, include ZIP Code)

Southeastern Seafood Distributors, Inc.
#4 Canal Street Dock Red River Basin Area, Little Rock, AR 72901

Subscribed and sworn to before me at Little Rock, AR (City and State)

this 10th day of March, 1999

Sidney H. Rogers
(Employee's Signature)

Employee of the Department of Health and Human Services designated under Act of January 31, 1925, Reorganization Plan IV effective June 30, 1940; Reorganization Plan No. 1 of 1953, effective April 11, 1953;and P.L. 96-88, effective May 4, 1980

FORM FDA 1664(4/83) PREVIOUS EDITIONS ARE OBSOLETE

Exhibit 4-13: Affidavit - FDA 463a

AFFIDAVIT

SAMPLE NO. 55545

STATE OF Tennessee

COUNTY OF Shelby

Before me Sidney H. Rogers, an employee of the Department of Health and Human Services, Food and Drug Administration, designated by the Secretary, under authority of the Act of January 31, 1925, 43 Statutes at Large 803; Reorganization Plan No. IV, Secs. 12-15, effective June 30, 1940; Reorganization Plan No. 1 of 1953, Secs. 1-9, effective April 11, 1953; and P.L. 96-98, Sec. 509, 93 Statutes at Large 965 (20 U.S.C. 3508), effective May 4, 1980; to administer or take oaths, affirmations, and affidavits, personally appeared George R. Applegate in the county and State aforesaid, who, being duly sworn, deposes and says:

I am manager of John's Curb Market, 342 East Johnson St., Memphis, Tennessee. As such, I have knowledge of purchasing and receipt of products at the market.

On September 2, 1999, FDA Investigator Sydney H. Rogers collected from my firm a sample consisting of six - 4 pound cans of Red River Brand Pure Sorghum. This sorghum was collected from a lot of six cases, each containing 4 - 4 pound buckets (cans) purchased by me from Ted Buymore who regularly sells sorghum in this area. Ted delivered this lot of six cases to my market on August 28, 1999 in a red panel GM truck with Alabama license plates. I do not know the license number.

AFFIANT'S SIGNATURE AND TITLE

George R. Applegate, Manager

FIRM'S NAME AND ADDRESS *(Include ZIP Code)*

John's Curb Market, 342 East Johnson St., Memphis, TN 38110

Subscribed and sworn to before me at Memphis, Tennessee this 2nd day of September 1999.

Sidney H. Rogers

(Employee Signature)

Employee of the Department of Health and Human services designated under Act of January 31, 1925, Reorganization Plan IV effective June 30, 1940; Reorganization Plan No. 1 of 1953, effective April 11, 1953; and P.L. 96-88 effective May 4, 1980.

FORM FDA 463a (4/83) PREVIOUS EDITIONS ARE OBSOLETE PAGE 1 OF 1 PAGES

Exhibit 4-14: Affidavit - FDA 1664a

AFFIDAVIT *(Jobber)*

SAMPLE NO: 55563

STATE OF: Arkansas

COUNTY OF: Jefferson

Before me, Sylvia A. Rogers, an employee of the Department of Health and Human Services, Food and Drug Administration, designated by the Secretary under authority of the Act of January 31, 1925, 43 Statutes at Large 803; Reorganization Plan No. IV, Secs. 12-15, effective June 30, 1940; Reorganization Plan No. 1 of 1953, Secs. 1-9, effective April 11, 1953; and P.L. 96-88, Sec. 509, 93 Statutes at Large 965 (20 U.S.C. 3508), effective May 4, 1980, to administer or take oaths, affirmations, and affidavits, personally appeared Patrick T. Palmer, in the county and State aforesaid, who, being duly sworn, deposes and says: The lot of The lot of 325 cases, (24/ 4 ½ oz. cans) of Jolly Miller Canned Mushrooms

which we invoiced and sold to Patriot Markets, Inc. Frankford, Pennsylvania

on 4-12-99

was a portion/all of a parcel shipped to us by Northern Light Foods, Inc. Duluth, Minnesota

and is covered by submitted (copy of) invoice(s):

	NUMBER	DATE		NUMBER	DATE		NUMBER	DATE
1)	3914	4/4/99	2)			3)		

and (copy of) shipping record(s):

	TYPE: (B/L, F/B)	NUMBER	DATE	ISSUING FIRM OR CARRIER
1)	B/L	20018	4/5/99	Northern Freight Carriers
2)				
3)				

REMARKS

AFFIANT'S SIGNATURE & TITLE

Patrick T. Palmer, Warehouse Manager Plant #12

FIRM (Name and address, include ZIP Code)

Liberty Wholesale Grocers
3210 11th Ave. Frankford, PA 19105

Subscribed and sworn to before me at Frankford, PA (City and State)

this 28th day of April, 1999

Sylvia A. Rogers
(Employee's Signature)

Employee of the Department of Health and Human Services designated under Act of January 31, 1925, Reorganization Plan IV effective June 30, 1940; Reorganization Plan No. 1 of 1953, effective April 11, 1953; and P.L. 96-88, effective May 4, 1980.

FORM FDA 1664a (4/83) PREVIOUS EDITIONS ARE OBSOLETE

Exhibit 4-15: Facts Sample Collection Screen

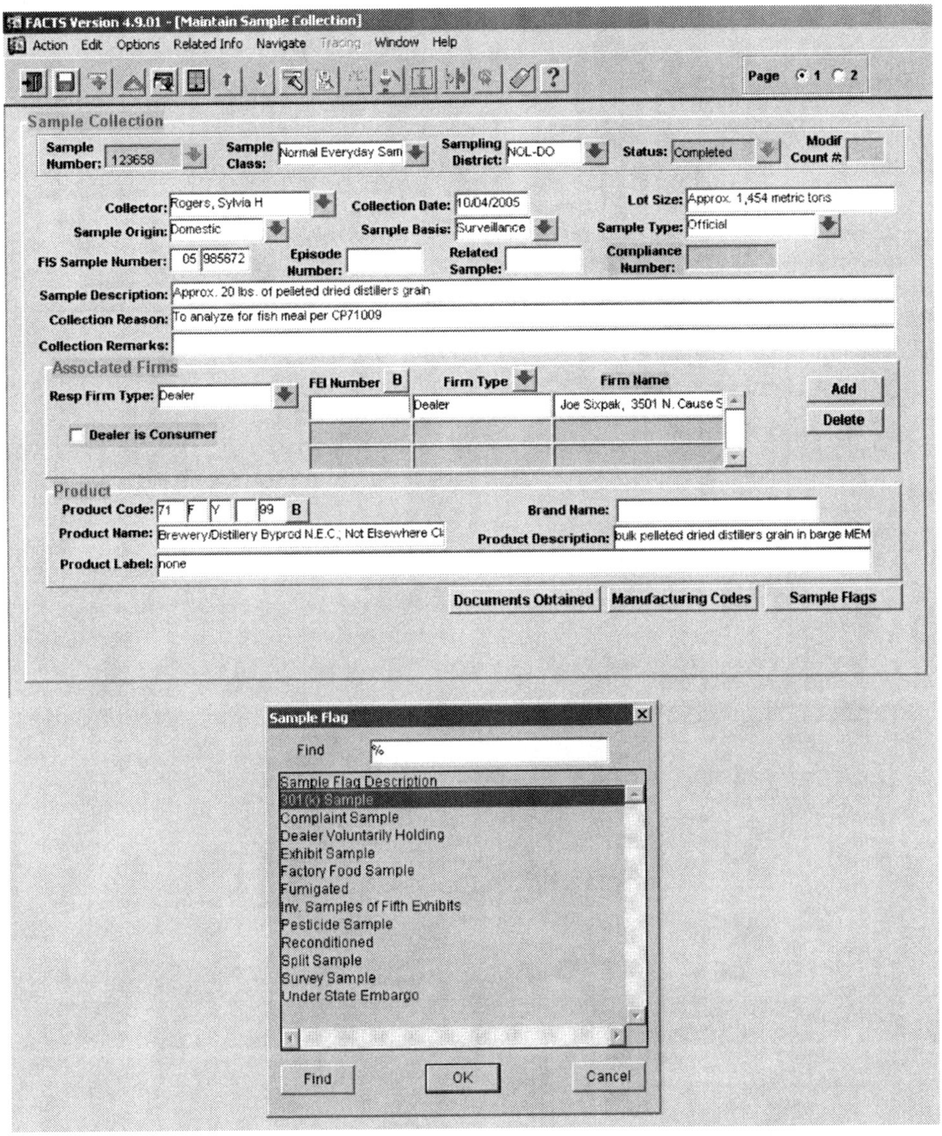

Exhibit 4-16: Facts Sample Collection Screen

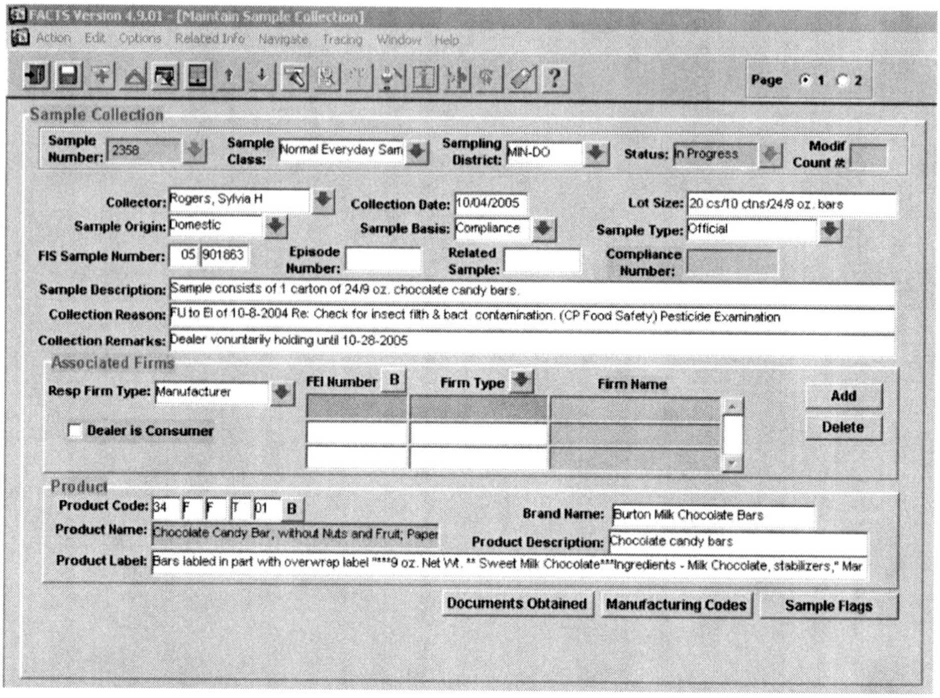

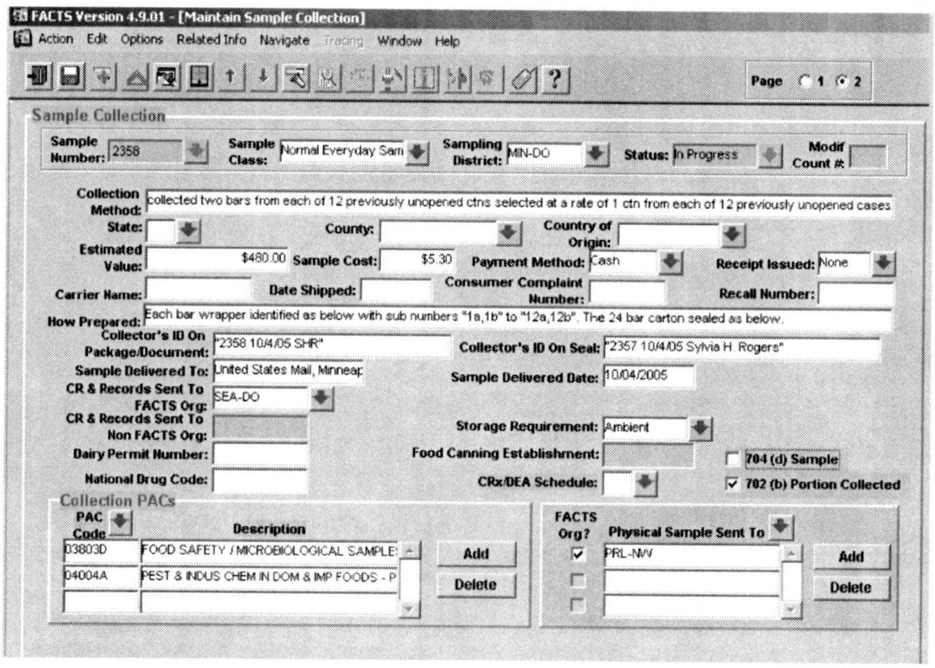

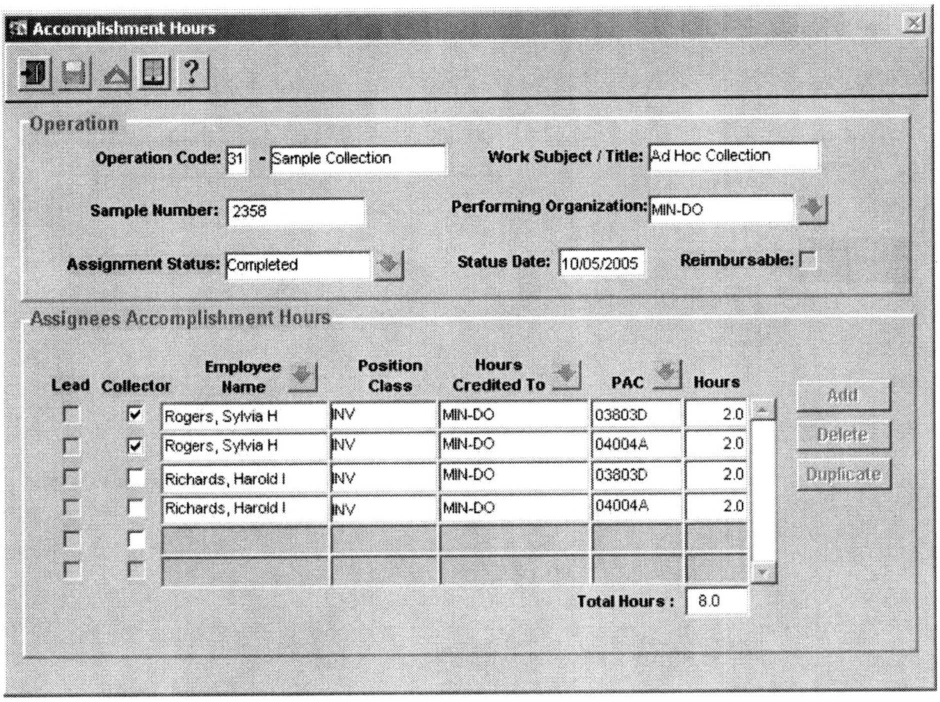
Accomplishment Hours
Operation
Operation Code: 31 - Sample Collection
Work Subject / Title: Ad Hoc Collection
Sample Number: 2358
Performing Organization: MIN-DO
Assignment Status: Completed
Status Date: 10/05/2005
Reimbursable:
Assignees Accomplishment Hours
Lead
Collector
Employee Name
Position Class
Hours Credited To
PAC
Hours
Rogers, Sylvia H | INV | MIN-DO | 03803D | 2.0
Rogers, Sylvia H | INV | MIN-DO | 04004A | 2.0
Richards, Harold I | INV | MIN-DO | 03803D | 2.0
Richards, Harold I | INV | MIN-DO | 04004A | 2.0
Total Hours : 8.0
Add
Delete
Duplicate

Exhibit 4-17: Official Seal - FDA 415a

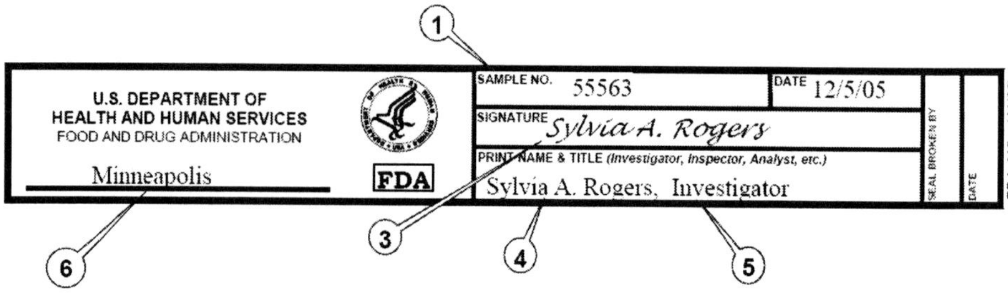

1. Insert sample number. When applicable, use prefix, e.g. “INV”, “FS”, “DOC”, “PS”, etc. (See IOM 4.4.10.2)

2. Insert date sealed. Use figures, month, day, year. (See # 7 below when seal is broken for any purpose.)

3. Sign your usual signature.

4. Print your name same as signature. (A rubber name stamp may be used if desired but use it carefully and do not smear.)

5. Print your title.

6. Print your district - spell out - do not use abbreviations or symbols. (A rubber stamp may be used.)

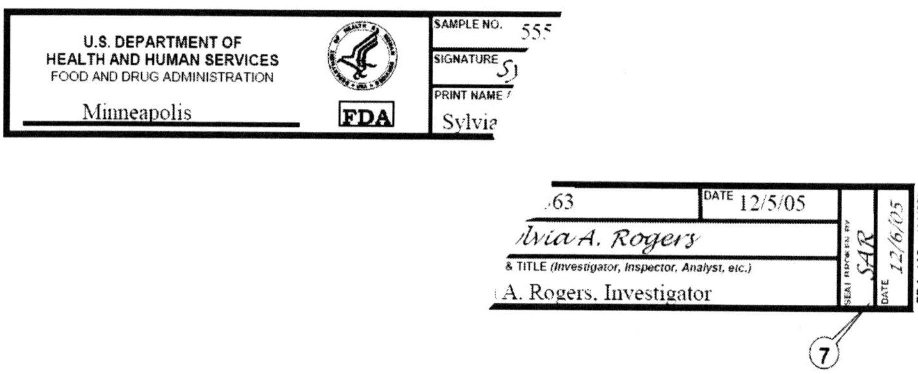

7. When seal is broken for any purpose, initial here and enter the date broken. Submit broken seal with sample records.

Exhibit 4-18: Declaration for Dangerous Goods

Shippers declaration for dangerous goods

Shipper	Air Waybill No.
U. S. FOOD & DRUG ADMINISTRATION 6601 N.W. 25th St. Room 236 Miami, FL 33122	Delta 7012-6140 Page 1 of 1 Pages Collection Report Number 2555

Consignee	
Food and Drug Administration 60 Eighth Street Atlanta, GA 30309	**U.S. GOVERNMENT SHIPMENT**
Two completed and signed copies of this Declaration must be handed to the operator	**WARNING** Failure to comply in all respects with the applicable Dangerous Goods Regulations may be in breach of the applicable law, subject to legal penalties. This Declaration must not, in any circumstances, be completed and/or signed by a consolidator, a forwarder or an IATA cargo agent.

TRANSPORTATION DETAILS

This shipment is within the limitations prescribed for *(delete non-applicable)*	Airport of Departure
PASSENGER AND CARGO AIRCRAFT / ~~CARGO AIRCRAFT ONLY~~	Miami, FL

Airport of Destination	Shipment type *(Delete non-applicable)*
Atlanta, GA	NON-RADIOACTIVE / ~~RADIOACTIVE~~

NATURE AND QUANTITY OF DANGEROUS GOODS

Dangerous Goods Identification: PROPER SHIPPING NAME OF ARTICLE as listed in the Restricted Articles Tariff Federal Aviation Regulations or IATA Restricted Articles Regulations	Class Or Division	UN Or ID No.	Subsidiary Risk	Quantity and Type of packing	Packing Inst.	Authorization
DRY ICE (CARBON DIOXIDE SOLID)	ORM A OR 9	UN 1845	N/A	5 Fiberboard cartons net weight 20 lbs. dry ice each carton	173.615 or 615	

Note: Include these notations on all Dry Ice shipments.

Additional handling Information

DO NOT OPEN THIS PACKAGE, IF PROBLEMS ARISE, CONTACT SHIPPER AT (305)555-3344

I hereby declare that the contents of this consignment are fully and accurately described above by proper shipping name and are classified, packed, marked and labeled, and are in all respects in the proper condition for transport by air according to the applicable International and National Government Regulations	Name/Title of Person Signing Sidney H. Rogers Investigator
	Place and Date Miami, FL (9-8-99)
	Signature *(See warning above)* *Sidney H. Rogers*

FORM FDA 3082 (3/83) PREVIOUS EDITION IS OBSOLETE

Exhibit 4-19: Dry Ice Sticker

Shipper's Declaration Not Required

Part B is required

Dry ice amount must be in kilograms

Note: 2.2 lbs = 1 kg

Airwaybills/airbills must have the following:

1. "Dangerous Goods – Shipper's Declaration not required."
2. Dry Ice, 9, UN 1845
3. _______ X _________ Kg 904 III
   (Number pkgs) (wt)

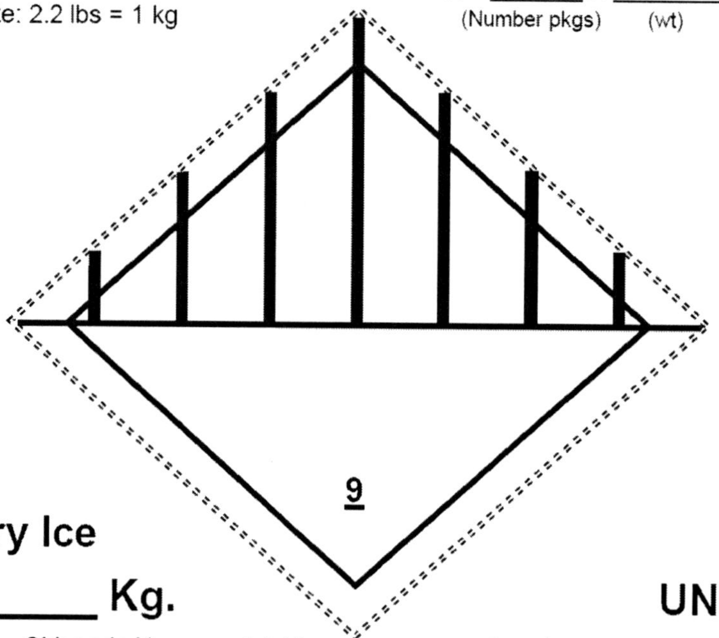

Dry Ice

______ Kg.

UN 1845

Shipper's Name and Address

____

____

____

Consignee Name and Address

____

____

____

Bottom portion of label must be completed by shipper.

Chapter 5 Exhibits

CONTENT

Exhibit 5-1: Form FDA 482 Notice of Inspection (2 Pgs)

DEPARTMENT OF HEALTH AND HUMAN SERVICES
FOOD AND DRUG ADMINISTRATION

1. DISTRICT OFFICE ADDRESS & PHONE NO.
1431 Harbor Bay Parkway
Alameda, CA 94502-7070
408-225-5332

TO

2. NAME AND TITLE OF INDIVIDUAL
Robert K. Thompson, Plant Manager

3. DATE
8-10-08

4. FIRM NAME
Garden City Nut Shellers

5. HOUR
8:30 a.m.
p.m.

6. NUMBER AND STREET
2704 Sellers Ave

7. CITY AND STATE & ZIP CODE
San Jose, CA 95131

8. PHONE # & AREA CODE
408-213-4567

Notice of Inspection is hereby given pursuant to Section 704(a)(1) of the Federal Food, Drug, and Cosmetics Act [21 U.S.C. 374(a)][1] and/or Part F or G, Title III of the Public Health Service Act [42 U.S.C. 262-264][2]

9. SIGNATURE *(Food and Drug Administration Employee(s))*
Sidney H. Rogers

10. TYPE OR PRINT NAME AND TITLE *(FDA Employee(s))*
Sidney H. Rogers, Investigator

[1] Applicable portions of Section 704 and other Sections of the Federal Food, Drug, and Cosmetic Act [21 U.S.C. 374] are quoted below:

Sec. 704. (a)(1) For purposes of enforcement of this Act, officers or employees duly designated by the Secretary, upon presenting appropriate credentials and a written notice to the owner, operator, or agent in charge, are authorized (A) to enter, at reasonable times, any factory, warehouse, or establishment in which food, drugs, devices, or cosmetics are manufactured, processed, packed, or held, for introduction into interstate commerce or after such introduction, or to enter any vehicle being used to transport or hold such food, drugs, devices, or cosmetics in interstate commerce; and (B) to inspect, at reasonable times and within reasonable limits and in a reasonable manner, such factory, warehouse, establishment, or vehicle and all pertinent equipment, finished and unfinished materials, containers, and labeling therein. In the case of any person (excluding farms and restaurants) who manufactures, processes, packs, transports, distributes, holds, or imports foods, the inspection shall extend to all records and other information described in section 414 when the Secretary has a reasonable belief that an article of food is adulterated and presents a threat of serious adverse health consequences or death to humans or animals, subject to the limitations established in section 414(d). In the case of any factory, warehouse, establishment, or consulting laboratory in which prescription drugs, nonprescription drugs intended for human use, or restricted devices are manufactured, processed, packed, or held, inspection shall extend to all things therein (including records, files, papers, processes, controls, and facilities) bearing on whether prescription drugs, nonprescription drugs intended for human use or, restricted devices which are adulterated or misbranded within the meaning of this Act, or which may not be manufactured, introduced into interstate commerce, or sold, or offered for sale by reason of any provision of this Act, have been or are being manufactured, processed, packed, transported, or held in any such place, or otherwise bearing on violation of this Act. No inspection authorized by the preceding sentence or by paragraph (3) shall extend to financial data, sales data other than shipment data, pricing data, personnel data (other than data as to qualifications of technical and professional personnel performing functions subject to this Act), and research data (other than data relating to new drugs, antibiotic drugs and devices and, subject to reporting and inspection under regulations lawfully issued pursuant to section 505(i) or (k), section 519, or 520(g), and data relating to other drugs or devices which in the case of a new drug would be subject to reporting or inspection under lawful regulations issued pursuant to section 505(j)). A separate notice shall be given for each such inspection, but a notice shall not be required for each entry made during the period covered by the inspection. Each such inspection shall be commenced and completed with reasonable promptness.

Sec. 704. (a)(2) The provisions of the third sentence of paragraph (1) shall not apply to (A) pharmacies which maintain establishments in conformance with any applicable local laws regulating the practice of pharmacy and medicine and which are regularly engaged in dispensing prescription drugs or devices, upon prescriptions of practitioners licensed to administer such drugs or devices to patients under the care of such practitioners in the course of their professional practice, and which do not, either through a subsidiary or otherwise, manufacture, prepare, propagate, compound, or process drugs or devices for sale other than in the regular course of their business of dispensing or selling drugs or devices at retail; (B) practitioners licensed by law to prescribe or administer drugs, or prescribe or use devices, as the case may be, and who manufacture, prepare, propagate, compound, or process drugs, or manufacture or process devices solely for use in the course of their professional practice; (C) persons who manufacture, prepare, propagate, compound, or process drugs, or manufacture or process devices solely for use in research, teaching, or chemical analysis and not for sale; (D) such other classes of persons as the Secretary may by regulation exempt from the application of this section upon a finding that inspection as applied to such classes of persons in accordance with this section is not necessary for the protection of the public health.

Sec. 704. (a)(3) An officer or employee making an inspection under paragraph (1) for purposes of enforcing the requirements of section 412 applicable to infant formulas shall be permitted, at all reasonable times, to have access to and to copy and verify any records (A) bearing on whether the infant formula manufactured or held in the facility inspected meets the requirements of section 412, or (B) required to be maintained under section 412.

Sec. 704. (b) Upon completion of any such inspection of a factory, warehouse, consulting laboratory, or other establishment, and prior to leaving the premises, the officer or employee making the inspection shall give to the owner, operator, or agent in charge a report in writing setting forth any conditions or practices observed by him which, in his judgment, indicate that any food, drug, device, or cosmetic in such establishment (1) consists in whole or in part of any filthy, putrid, or decomposed substance, or (2) has been prepared, packed, or held under insanitary conditions whereby it may have become contaminated with filth, or whereby it may have been rendered injurious to health. A copy of such report shall be sent promptly to the Secretary.

Sec. 704. (c) If the officer or employee making any such inspection of a factory, warehouse, or other establishment has obtained any sample in the course of the inspection, upon completion of the inspection and prior to leaving the premises he shall give to the owner, operator, or agent in charge a receipt describing the samples obtained.

Sec. 704. (d) Whenever in the course of any such inspection of a factory or other establishment where food is manufactured, processed, or packed, the officer or employee making the inspection obtains a sample of any such food, and an analysis is made of such sample for the purpose of ascertaining whether such food consists in whole or in part of any filthy, putrid, or decomposed substance, or is otherwise unfit for food, a copy of the results of such analysis shall be furnished promptly to the owner, operator, or agent in charge.

Sec. 704(e) Every person required under section 519 or 520(g) to maintain records and every person who is in charge or custody of such records shall, upon request of an officer or employee designated by the Secretary, permit such officer or employee at all reasonable times to have access to and to copy and verify, such records.

Section 704 (f)(1) An accredited person described in paragraph (3) shall maintain records documenting the training qualifications of the person

FORM FDA 482 (4/08) PREVIOUS EDITION IS OBSOLETE (Continued on Reverse) NOTICE OF INSPECTION

PSC Media Arts (301) 443-1090 EF

and the employees of the person, the procedures used by the person for handling confidential information, the compensation arrangements made by the person, and the procedures used by the person to identify and avoid conflicts of interest. Upon the request of an officer or employee designated by the Secretary, the person shall permit the officer or employee, at all reasonable times, to have access to, to copy, and to verify, the records.

Section 512 (l)(1) In the case of any new animal drug for which an approval of an application filed pursuant to subsection (b) is in effect, the applicant shall establish and maintain such records, and make such reports to the Secretary, of data relating to experience, including experience with uses authorized under subsection (a)(4)(A), and other data or information, received or otherwise obtained by such applicant with respect to such drug, or with respect to animal feeds bearing or containing such drug, as the Secretary may by general regulation, or by order with respect to such application, prescribe on the basis of a finding that such records and reports are necessary in order to enable the Secretary to determine, or facilitate a determination, whether there is or may be ground for invoking subsection (e) or subsection (m)(4) of this section. Such regulation or order shall provide, where the Secretary deems it to be appropriate, for the examination, upon request, by the persons to whom such regulation or order is applicable, of similar information received or otherwise obtained by the Secretary.

(2) Every person required under this subsection to maintain records, and every person in charge or custody thereof, shall, upon request of an officer or employee designated by the Secretary, permit such officer or employee at all reasonable times to have access to and copy and verify such records.

[2] Applicable sections of Parts F and G of Title III Public Health Service Act [42 U.S.C. 262-264] are quoted below:

Part F - Licensing - Biological Products and Clinical Laboratories and" * * * * *

Sec. 351(c) "Any officer, agent, or employee of the Department of Health and Human Services, authorized by the Secretary for the purpose, may during all reasonable hours enter and inspect any establishment for the propagation or manufacture and preparation of any virus, serum, toxin, antitoxin, vaccine, blood, blood component or derivative, allergenic product, or other product aforesaid for sale, barter, or exchange in the District of Columbia, or to be sent, carried, or brought from any State or possession into any other State or possession or into any foreign country, or from any foreign country into any State or possession."
Part F - * * * * *Control of Radiation.
Sec. 360 A (a) "If the Secretary finds for good cause that the methods, tests, or programs related to electronic product radiation safety in a particular factory, warehouse, or establishment in which electronic products are manufactured or held, may not be adequate or reliable, officers or employees duly designated by the Secretary, upon presenting appropriate credentials and a written notice to the owner, operator, or agent in charge, are thereafter authorized (1) to enter, at reasonable times any area in such factory, warehouse, or establishment in which the manufacturer's tests (or testing programs) required by section 358(h) are carried out, and (2) to inspect, at reasonable times and within reasonable limits and in a reasonable manner, the facilities and procedures within such area which are related to electronic product radiation safety. Each such inspection shall be commenced and completed with reasonable promptness. In addition to other grounds upon which good cause may be found for purposes of this subsection, good cause will be considered to exist in any case where the manufacturer has introduced into commerce any electronic product which does not comply with an applicable standard prescribed under this subpart and with respect to which no exemption from the notification requirements has been granted by the Secretary under section 359(a)(2) or 359(e)."

(b) "Every manufacturer of electronic products shall establish and maintain such records (including testing records), make such reports, and provide such information, as the Secretary may reasonably require to enable him to determine whether such manufacturer has acted or is acting in compliance with this subpart and standards prescribed pursuant to this subpart and shall, upon request of an officer or employee duly designated by the Secretary, permit such officer or employee to inspect appropriate books, papers, records, and documents relevant to determining whether such manufacturer has acted or is acting in compliance with standards prescribed pursuant to section 359(a)."

* * * * * *

(f) "The Secretary may by regulation (1) require dealers and distributors of electronic products, to which there are applicable standards prescribed under this subpart and the retail prices of which is not less than $50, to furnish manufacturers of such products such information as may be necessary to identify and locate, for purposes of section 359, the first purchasers of such products for purposes other than resale, and (2) require manufacturers to preserve such information. Any regulation establishing a requirement pursuant to clause (1) of the preceding sentence shall (A) authorize such dealers and distributors to elect, in lieu of immediately furnishing such information to the manufacturer to hold and preserve such information until advised by the manufacturer or Secretary that such information is needed by the manufacturer for purposes of section 359, and (B) provide that the dealer or distributor shall, upon making such election, give prompt notice of such election (together with information identifying the notifier and the product) to the manufacturer and shall, when advised by the manufacturer or Secretary, of the need therefore for the purposes of Section 359, immediately furnish the manufacturer with the required information. If a dealer or distributor discontinues the dealing in or distribution of electronic products, he shall turn the information over to the manufacturer. Any manufacturer receiving information pursuant to this subsection concerning first purchasers of products for purposes other than resale shall treat it as confidential and may use it only if necessary for the purpose of notifying persons pursuant to section 359(a)."

* * * * * *

Sec. 360 B.(a) It shall be unlawful-
(1) * * *
(2) * * *
(3) "for any person to fail or to refuse to establish or maintain records required by this subpart or to permit access by the Secretary or any of his duly authorized representatives to, or the copying of, such records, or to permit entry or inspection, as required or pursuant to section 360A."

* * * * * *

Part G - Quarantine and Inspection

Sec. 361(a) "The Surgeon General, with the approval of the Secretary, is authorized to make and enforce such regulations as in his judgment are necessary to prevent the introduction, transmission, or spread of communicable diseases from foreign countries into the States or possessions, or from one State or possession into any other State or possession. For purposes of carrying out and enforcing such regulations, the Surgeon General may provide for such inspection, fumigation, disinfection, sanitation, pest extermination, destruction of animals or articles found to be so infected or contaminated as to be sources of dangerous infection to human beings, and other measures, as in his judgment may be necessary."

(Reverse of Form FDA 482)

FORM FDA 482 (4/08)

Exhibit 5-2: FDA 482a Demand for Records

DEPARTMENT OF HEALTH AND HUMAN SERVICES FOOD AND DRUG ADMINISTRATION		1. DISTRICT ADDRESS AND PHONE NO. 6751 Steger Dr. Cincinnati, OH 45237 (513) 679-2700	
TO	2. NAME AND TITLE OF INDIVIDUAL Michael Campbell, President	3. DATE 8/20/2007	
	4. FIRM NAME ABC Soup Company	5. HOURS 8:30	
	6. NUMBER AND STREET 3114 Mapleleaf Ave	A.M. XXX	P.M.
	7. CITY AND STATE Cincinnati, OH	8. ZIP CODE 45213	

Written demand for examination and/or copying of the records required by 21 CFR 113.100, 21 CFR 114 and 21 CFR 500.23 is hereby given, pursuant to 21 CFR 108.25(g), 21 CFR 108.35(h) and 21 CFR 500 for the records described below in order to verify the pH, adequacy of processing, the integrity of container closures, and the coding of the products processed by your firm.

9. RECORDS NECESSARY

All thermal process and production records mandated by 21 CFR 113 and 114 for the manufacture of Mighty Good Vegetable Soup in 303 cans from May 1, 2004 to the present. This includes pH records, calibration record, formulation, batch records, etc.

10. SIGNATURE *(Food and Drug Administration Employee(s))*	11. TITLE FDA EMPLOYEE
Sydney H. Rogers	Investigator

FORM FDA 482a (10/03) PREVIOUS EDITION IS OBSOLETE DEMAND FOR RECORDS

Exhibit 5-3: FDA 482b Request for Information

DEPARTMENT OF HEALTH AND HUMAN SERVICES FOOD AND DRUG ADMINISTRATION		1. DISTRICT ADDRESS AND PHONE NO. 6751 Steger Dr. Cincinnati, OH 45237 (513) 679-2700	
TO	2. NAME AND TITLE OF INDIVIDUAL Michael Campbell, President	3. DATE 8/20/2007	
	4. FIRM NAME ABC Company	5. HOURS 8:00	
	6. NUMBER AND STREET 3114 Mapleleaf Ave.	A.M. XXX	P.M.
	7. CITY AND STATE Cincinnati, OH	8. ZIP CODE 45213	

Written request is hereby given pursuant to 21 CFR 108.25(c)(3)(ii), 21 CFR 108.35(c)(3)(ii) and 21 CFR 500.23 for the information described below, concerning processes and procedures which is deemed necessary by the Food and Drug Administration to determine the adequacy of the processes for products processed by your firm.

9. RECORDS NECESSARY

All written supporting documentation from a process authority or other source which specify the scheduled process and critical factors for the processing of Mighty Good Vegetable Soup in 303 cans to include pH records, calibration records, formulation and batch records, etc

10. SIGNATURE *(Food and Drug Administration Employee(s))*	11. TITLE FDA EMPLOYEE
Sydney H. Rogers	Investigator

FORM FDA 482b (10/03) PREVIOUS EDITION IS OBSOLETE. **REQUEST FOR INFORMATION**

Exhibit 5-4: Modified FDA 482

DEPARTMENT OF HEALTH AND HUMAN SERVICES FOOD AND DRUG ADMINISTRATION		1. DISTRICT OFFICE ADDRESS & PHONE NO. 22201 23rd Drive SE Seattle, WA 98021-4421 503-225-5332	
TO	2. NAME AND TITLE OF INDIVIDUAL Howard M. Allgreen, Pharmacist-Owner	3. DATE 8-10-08	
	4. FIRM NAME Darlings Drug Store	5. HOUR	a.m.
	6. NUMBER AND STREET 312 Main Street		2:00 p.m.
	7. CITY AND STATE & ZIP CODE Medford, OR 97501	8. PHONE # & AREA CODE 503-765-4321	

Notice of Inspection is hereby given to collect samples only pursuant to **Section 704(a)(1) of the Federal Food, Drug, and Cosmetics Act [21 U.S.C. 374(a)][1] and/or Part F or G, Title III of the Public Health Service Act [42 U.S.C. 262-264][2]**

9. SIGNATURE *(Food and Drug Administration Employee(s))*	10. TYPE OR PRINT NAME AND TITLE *(FDA Employee(s))*
Sidney H. Rogers	Sidney H. Rogers, Investigator

[1] **Applicable portions of Section 704 and other Sections of the Federal Food, Drug, and Cosmetic Act [21 U.S.C. 374] are quoted below:**

Sec. 704. (a)(1) For purposes of enforcement of this Act, officers or employees duly designated by the Secretary, upon presenting appropriate credentials and a written notice to the owner, operator, or agent in charge, are authorized (A) to enter, at reasonable times, any factory, warehouse, or establishment in which food, drugs, devices, or cosmetics are manufactured, processed, packed, or held, for introduction into interstate commerce or after such introduction, or to enter any vehicle being used to transport or hold such food, drugs, devices, or cosmetics in interstate commerce; and (B) to inspect, at reasonable times and within reasonable limits and in a reasonable manner, such factory, warehouse, establishment, or vehicle and all pertinent equipment, finished and unfinished materials, containers, and labeling therein. In the case of any person (excluding farms and restaurants) who manufactures, processes, packs, transports, distributes, holds, or imports foods, the inspection shall extend to all records and other information described in section 414 when the Secretary has a reasonable belief that an article of food is adulterated and presents a threat of serious adverse health consequences or death to humans or animals, subject to the limitations established in section 414(d). In the case of any factory, warehouse, establishment, or consulting laboratory in which prescription drugs, nonprescription drugs intended for human use, or restricted devices are manufactured, processed, packed, or held, inspection shall extend to all things therein (including records, files, papers, processes, controls, and facilities) bearing on whether prescription drugs, nonprescription drugs intended for human use or, restricted devices which are adulterated or misbranded within the meaning of this Act, or which may not be manufactured, introduced into interstate commerce, or sold, or offered for sale by reason of any provision of this Act, have been or are being manufactured, processed, packed, transported, or held in any such place, or otherwise bearing on violation of this Act. No inspection authorized by the preceding sentence or by paragraph (3) shall extend to financial data, sales data other than shipment data, pricing data, personnel data (other than data as to qualifications of technical and professional personnel performing functions subject to this Act), and research data (other than data relating to new drugs, antibiotic drugs and devices and, subject to reporting and inspection under regulations lawfully issued pursuant to section 505(i) or (k), section 519, or 520(g), and data relating to other drugs or devices which in the case of a new drug would be subject to reporting or inspection under lawful regulations issued pursuant to section 505(j)). A separate notice shall be given for each such inspection, but a notice shall not be required for each entry made during the period covered by the inspection. Each such inspection shall be commenced and completed with reasonable promptness.

Sec. 704. (a)(2) The provisions of the third sentence of paragraph (1) shall not apply to (A) pharmacies which maintain establishments in conformance with any applicable local laws regulating the practice of pharmacy and medicine and which are regularly engaged in dispensing prescription drugs or devices, upon prescriptions of practitioners licensed to administer such drugs or devices to patients under the care of such practitioners in the course of their professional practice, and which do not, either through a subsidiary or otherwise, manufacture, prepare, propagate, compound, or process drugs or devices for sale other than in the regular course of their business of dispensing or selling drugs or devices at retail; (B) practitioners licensed by law to prescribe or administer drugs, or prescribe or use devices, as the case may be, and who manufacture, prepare, propagate, compound, or process drugs, or manufacture or process devices solely for use in the course of their professional practice; (C) persons who manufacture, prepare, propagate, compound, or process drugs, or manufacture or process devices solely for use in research, teaching, or chemical analysis and not for sale; (D) such other classes of persons as the Secretary may by regulation exempt from the application of this section upon a finding that inspection as applied to such classes of persons in accordance with this section is not necessary for the protection of the public health.

Sec. 704. (a)(3) An officer or employee making an inspection under paragraph (1) for purposes of enforcing the requirements of section 412 applicable to infant formulas shall be permitted, at all reasonable times, to have access to and to copy and verify any records (A) bearing on whether the infant formula manufactured or held in the facility inspected meets the requirements of section 412, or (B) required to be maintained under section 412.

Sec. 704. (b) Upon completion of any such inspection of a factory, warehouse, consulting laboratory, or other establishment, and prior to leaving the premises, the officer or employee making the inspection shall give to the owner, operator, or agent in charge a report in writing setting forth any conditions or practices observed by him which, in his judgment, indicate that any food, drug, device, or cosmetic in such establishment (1) consists in whole or in part of any filthy, putrid, or decomposed substance, or (2) has been prepared, packed, or held under insanitary conditions whereby it may have become contaminated with filth, or whereby it may have been rendered injurious to health. A copy of such report shall be sent promptly to the Secretary.

Sec. 704. (c) If the officer or employee making any such inspection of a factory, warehouse, or other establishment has obtained any sample in the course of the inspection, upon completion of the inspection and prior to leaving the premises he shall give to the owner, operator, or agent in charge a receipt describing the samples obtained.

Sec. 704. (d) Whenever in the course of any such inspection of a factory or other establishment where food is manufactured, processed, or packed, the officer or employee making the inspection obtains a sample of any such food, and an analysis is made of such sample for the purpose of ascertaining whether such food consists in whole or in part of any filthy, putrid, or decomposed substance, or is otherwise unfit for food, a copy of the results of such analysis shall be furnished promptly to the owner, operator, or agent in charge.

Sec. 704(e) Every person required under section 519 or 520(g) to maintain records and every person who is in charge or custody of such records shall, upon request of an officer or employee designated by the Secretary, permit such officer or employee at all reasonable times to have access to and to copy and verify, such records.

Section 704 (f)(1) An accredited person described in paragraph (3) shall maintain records documenting the training qualifications of the person

FORM FDA 482 (4/08) PREVIOUS EDITION IS OBSOLETE (Continued on Reverse) NOTICE OF INSPECTION

PSC Media Arts (301) 443-1090 EF

Exhibit 5-5: Form FDA 483 (2 Pgs)

DEPARTMENT OF HEALTH AND HUMAN SERVICES
FOOD AND DRUG ADMINISTRATION

DISTRICT OFFICE ADDRESS AND PHONE NUMBER	DATE(S) OF INSPECTION
Minneapolis District 250 Marquette Ave. South, Suite 600 Minneapolis, MN 55401 Industry information: www.fda.gov/oc/industry	10/5-7/2008 FEI NUMBER 0000112233

NAME AND TITLE OF INDIVIDUAL TO WHOM REPORT IS ISSUED

TO: William S. Gundstrom, Vice President, Production

FIRM NAME	STREET ADDRESS
Topline Pharmaceuticals "T.L.P."	2136 Elbe Place
CITY, STATE AND ZIP CODE	TYPE OF ESTABLISHMENT INSPECTED
Jackson, MN 55326	Tablet Repacker

THIS DOCUMENT LISTS OBSERVATIONS MADE BY THE FDA REPRESENTATIVE(S) DURING THE INSPECTION OF YOUR FACILITY. THEY ARE INSPECTIONAL OBSERVATIONS, AND DO NOT REPRESENT A FINAL AGENCY DETERMINATION REGARDING YOUR COMPLIANCE. IF YOU HAVE AN OBJECTION REGARDING AN OBSERVATION, OR HAVE IMPLEMENTED, OR PLAN TO IMPLEMENT CORRECTIVE ACTION IN RESPONSE TO AN OBSERVATION, YOU MAY DISCUSS THE OBJECTION OR ACTION WITH THE FDA REPRESENTATIVE(S) DURING THE INSPECTION OR SUBMIT THIS INFORMATION TO FDA AT THE ADDRESS ABOVE. IF YOU HAVE ANY QUESTIONS, PLEASE CONTACT FDA AT THE PHONE NUMBER AND ADDRESS ABOVE.

DURING AN INSPECTION OF YOUR FIRM (I) ~~(WE)~~ OBSERVED:

List your observations in a logical manner

See IOM 5.2.3, 5.2.3.1, 5.2.3.2, and 5.2.3.3

SEE REVERSE OF THIS PAGE	EMPLOYEE(S) SIGNATURE	EMPLOYEE(S) NAME AND TITLE (*Print or Type*)	DATE ISSUED
	Sidney H. Rogers	Sidney H. Rogers, Investigator	10/7/2008

FORM FDA 483 (9/08) PREVIOUS EDITION OBSOLETE **INSPECTIONAL OBSERVATIONS** PAGE 1 of 1 PAGES

PSC Media Arts (301) 443-1090 EF

The observations of objectionable conditions and practices listed on the front of this form are reported: 1. Pursuant to Section 704(b) of the Federal Food, Drug and Cosmetic Act, or 2. To assist firms inspected in complying with the Acts and regulations enforced by the Food and Drug Administration.

Section 704(b) of the Federal Food, Drug, and Cosmetic Act (21 USC 374(b)) provides: "Upon completion of any such inspection of a factory, warehouse, consulting laboratory, or other establishment, and prior to leaving the premises, the officer or employee making the inspection shall give to the owner, operator, or agent in charge a report in writing setting forth any conditions or practices observed by him which, in his judgement, indicate that any food, drug, device, or cosmetic in such establishment (1) consists in whole or in part of any filthy, putrid, or decomposed substance, or (2) has been prepared, packed, or held under insanitary conditions whereby it may have become contaminated with filth, or whereby it may have been rendered injurious to health. A copy of such report shall be sent promptly to the Secretary."

Exhibit 5-6: Inserting Digital Photos into Turbo EIR (Resize Photo)

This document is available on the FDA website at http://www.fda.gov/ICECI/Inspections/IOM/ucm127372.htm.

Exhibit 5-7: Inserting Digital Photos into Turbo EIR (Insert Photo)

This document is available on the FDA website at http://www.fda.gov/ICECI/Inspections/IOM/ucm127372.htm.

Exhibit 5-8: Inserting Digital Photos into Turbo EIR (Resize Using MS Office Picture Manager)

This document is available on the FDA website at http://www.fda.gov/ICECI/Inspections/IOM/ucm127372.htm.

Exhibit 5-9: Facts Create Assignment Screen (1 Pg)

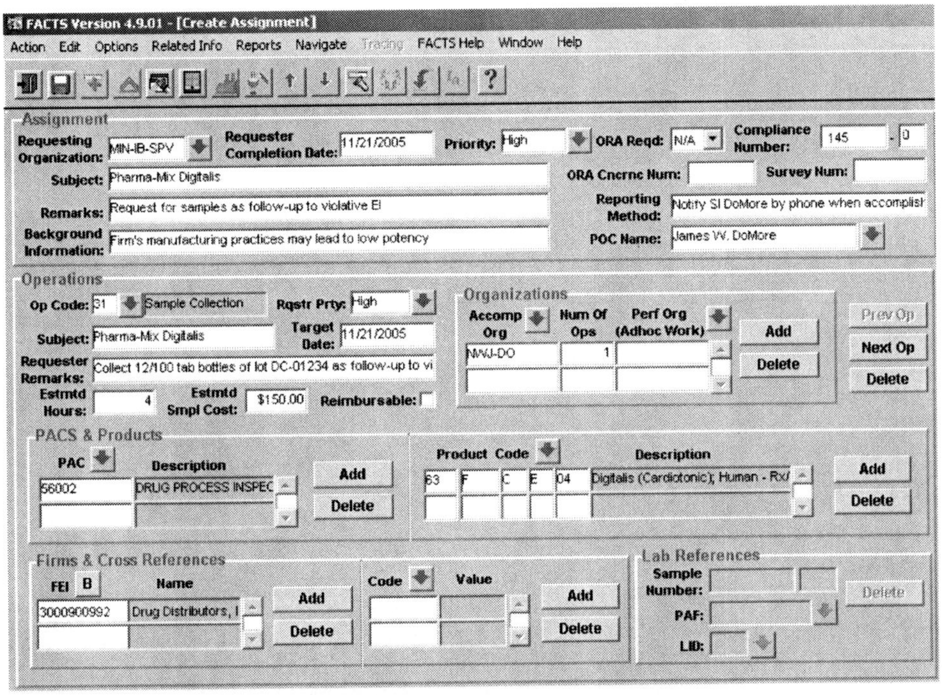

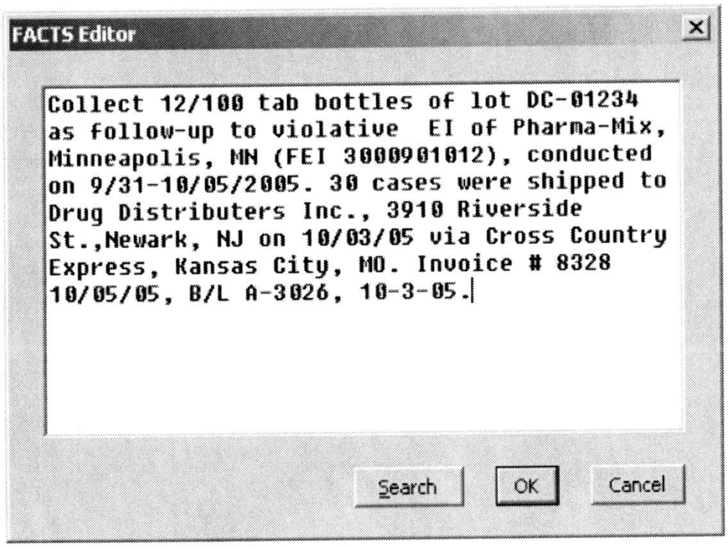

Exhibit 5-10: FDA 482(C) Notice of Inspection Request for Records

DEPARTMENT OF HEALTH AND HUMAN SERVICES FOOD AND DRUG ADMINISTRATION	1. DISTRICT OFFICE ADDRESS & PHONE NO. 212 3rd Avenue South Minneapolis, MN 55401 612-334-4100

TO		
	2. NAME AND TITLE OF INDIVIDUAL Howard P. Gunderson, Plant Manager	3. DATE 1/4/06
	4. FIRM NAME Happy Farms Cheese	5. HOUR 7:30 a.m.
	6. NUMBER AND STREET 123 County Road 23	p.m.
	7. CITY AND STATE & ZIP CODE Eau Claire, WI 54703	8. PHONE # & AREA CODE 715-223-4567

Notice of inspection is hereby given pursuant to Section 704(a)(1) of the Federal Food, Drug, and Cosmetic Act [21 U.S.C. 374(a)(1)][1]. Written request is hereby given to access and/or copy the records described below, pursuant to the Federal Food, Drug and Cosmetic Act, Section 414(a) [21 U.S.C. 350c][2] and Title 21 Code of Federal Regulations, Section 1.361[3].

9. SIGNATURE *(Food and Drug Administration Employee(s))*	10. TYPE OR PRINT NAME AND TITLE *(FDA Employee(s))*
Sidney H. Rogers	Sidney H. Rogers, Investigator

Applicable portions of Sections 704 and 414 of the Federal Food, Drug and Cosmetic Act (21 U.S.C. 374 and 350c) and Title 21 of the Code of Federal Regulations, are quoted below:

[1]Sec. 704.(a)(1) For purposes of enforcement of this Act, officers or employees duly designated by the Secretary, upon presenting appropriate credentials and a written notice to the owner, operator, or agent in charge, are authorized (A) to enter, at reasonable times, any factory, warehouse, or establishment in which food, drugs, devices, or cosmetics are manufactured, processed, packed, or held, for introduction into interstate commerce or after such introduction, or to enter any vehicle being used to transport or hold such food, drugs, devices, or cosmetics in interstate commerce; and (B) to inspect , at reasonable times and within reasonable limits and in a reasonable manner, such factory, warehouse, establishment, or vehicle and all pertinent equipment, finished and unfinished materials, containers and labeling therein. In the case of any person (excluding farms and restaurants) who manufactures, processes, packs, transports, distributes, holds, or imports foods, the inspection shall extend to all records and other information described in section 414 when the secretary has a reasonable belief that an article of food is adulterated and presents a threat of serious adverse health consequences or death to humans or animals, subject to the limitations established in section 414(d). In the case of any factory, warehouse, establishment, or consulting laboratory in which prescription drugs or restricted devices are manufactured, processed, packed, or held, the inspection shall extend to all things therein (including records, files, papers, processes, controls, and facilities) bearing on whether prescription drugs or restricted devices which are adulterated or misbranded within the meaning of this Chapter, or which may not be manufactured, introduced into interstate commerce, or sold, or offered for sale by reason of any provision of this Chapter , have been or are being manufactured, processed, packed, transported, or held in any such place, or otherwise bearing on violation of this Chapter. No inspection authorized by the preceding sentence or by paragraph (3) shall extend to financial data, sales data other then shipment data, pricing data, personnel data (other than data as to qualifications of technical and professional personnel performing functions subject to this Act), and research data (other than data, relating to new drugs, antibiotic drugs and devices and, subject to reporting and inspection under regulations lawfully issued pursuant to section 505(i) or (k), section 507(d) or (g), section 519, or 520(g), and data relating to other drugs or devices which in the case of a new drug would be subject to reporting or inspection under lawful regulations issued pursuant to section 505(k) of the title. A separate notice shall be given for each such inspection, but a notice shall not be required for each entry made during the period covered by the inspection. Each such inspection shall be commenced and completed with reasonable promptness.

[2]Sec. 414(a) Records Inspection. If the Secretary has a reasonable belief that an article of food is adulterated and presents a threat of serious adverse health consequences or death to humans or animals, each person (excluding farms and restaurants) who manufactures, processes, packs, distributes, receives, holds, or imports such article shall, at the request of an officer or employee duly designated by the Secretary, permit such officer or employee, upon presentation of appropriate credentials and a written notice to such person, at reasonable times and within reasonable limits and in a reasonable manner, to have access to and copy all records relating to such article that are needed to assist the Secretary in determining whether the food is adulterated and presents a threat of serious adverse health consequences or death to humans or animals. The requirement under the preceding sentence applies to all records relating to the manufacture, processing, packing, distribution, receipt, holding, or importation of such article maintained by or on behalf of such person in any format (including paper and electronic formats) and at any location).

[3]21 CFR 1.361 What are the record availability requirements? When FDA has a reasonable belief that an article of food is adulterated and presents a threat of serious adverse health consequences or death to humans or animals, any records and other information accessible to FDA under section 414 or 704(a) of the act (21 U.S.C. 350c and 374(a)) must be made readily available for inspection and photocopying or other means of reproduction. Such records and other information must be made available as soon as possible, not to exceed 24 hours from the time of receipt of the official request, from an officer or employee duly designated by the Secretary of Health and Human Services who presents appropriate credentials and a written notice.

FORM FDA 482c (12/05) **NOTICE OF INSPECTION - REQUEST FOR RECORDS**

PSC Media Arts (301) 443-1090 EF

Exhibit 5-11: Food Additives Nomographs

FOOD ADDITIVES NOMOGRAPH I

1. Additive and batch weight known. Apply a straight edge to appropriate points on outside columns. Read ppm and/or percent additive where straight edge intersects central column.

2. Tolerance and batch weight known. Apply a straight edge to appropriate points on central and right-hand columns. Read the amount of additive in lbs. or gals. where straight edge intersects the left-hand column.

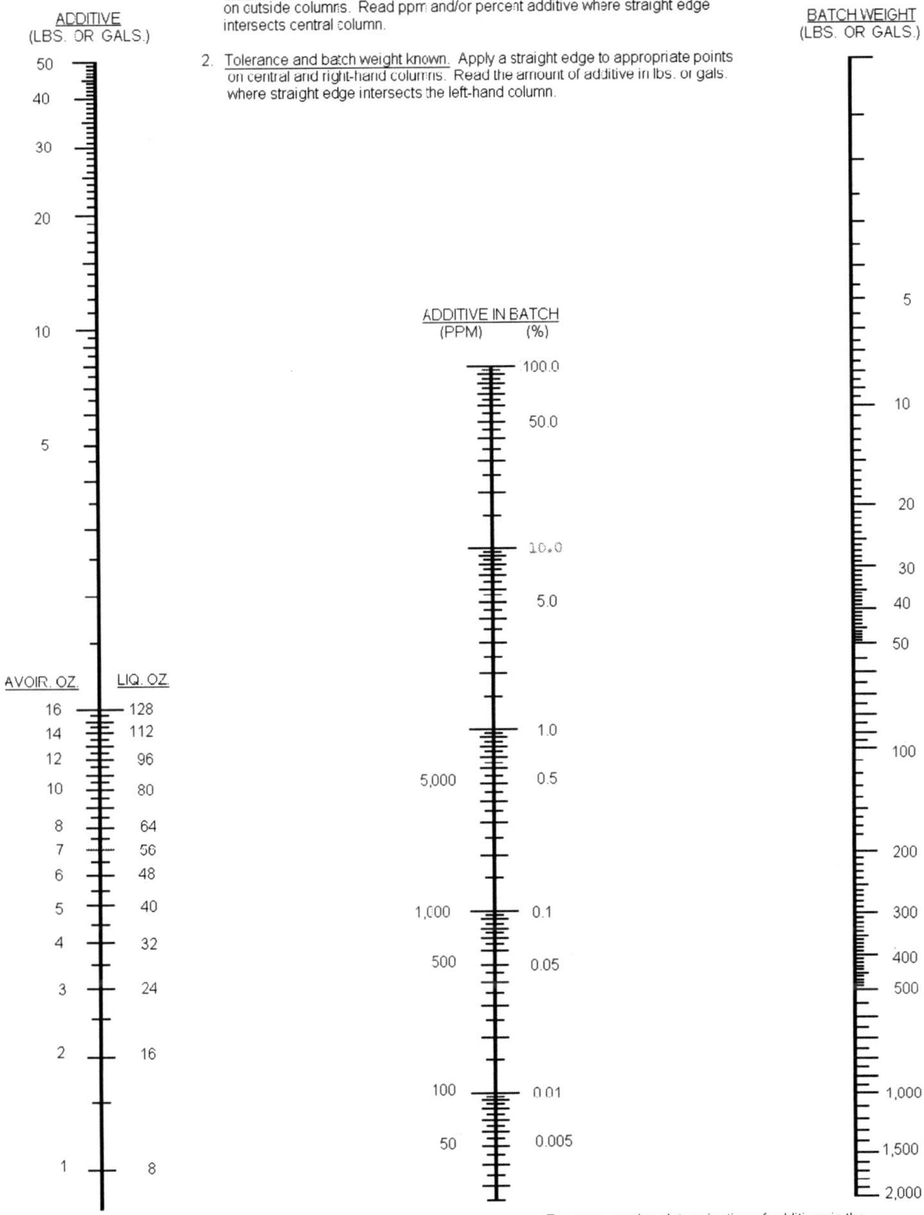

For more precise determination of additives in the 1-500 ppm range, use Nomograph II

FOOD ADDITIVES NOMOGRAPH II

1. Additive and batch weight known. Apply a straight edge to appropriate points on outside columns. Read ppm and/or percent additive where straight edge intersects central column.

2. Tolerance and batch weight known. Apply a straight edge to appropriate points on central and right-hand columns. Read the amount of additive in lbs. or gals. where straight edge intersects the left-hand column.

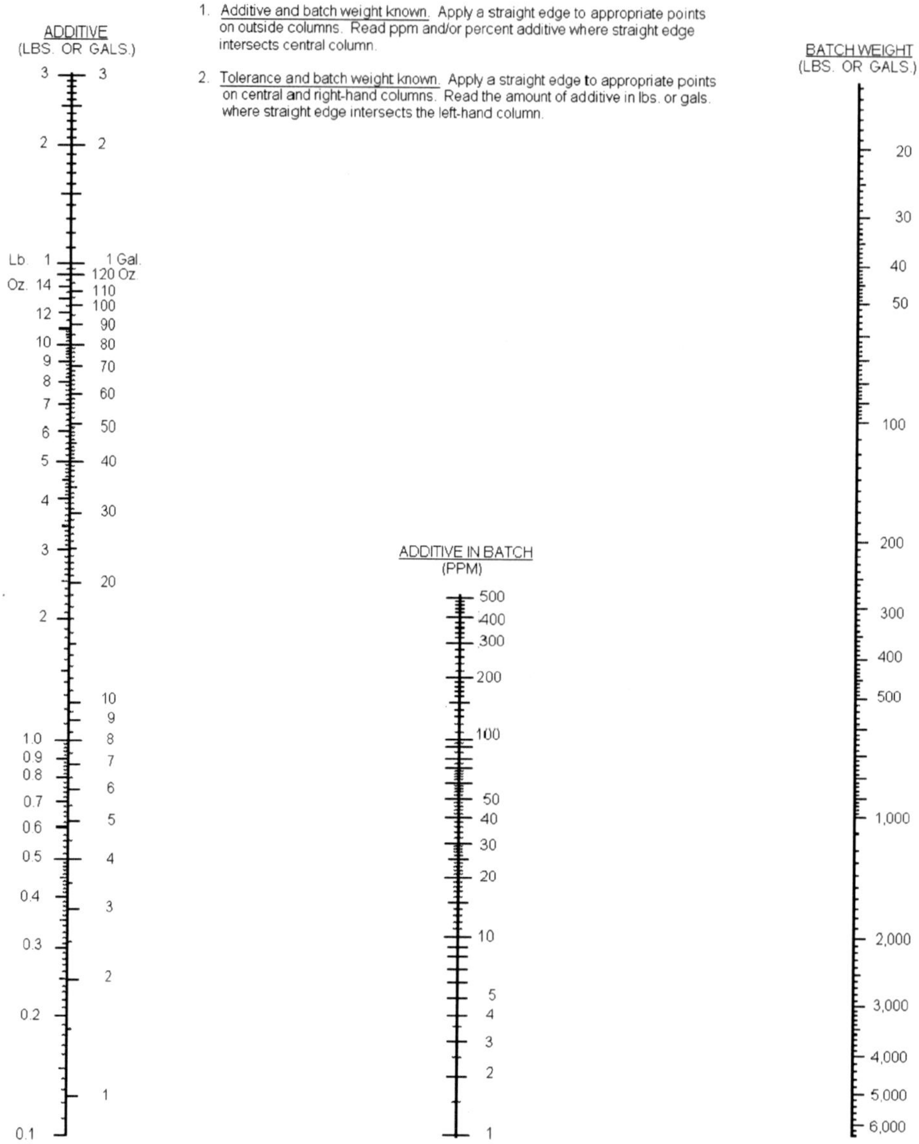

*Exhibit 5-12: Summary of Registration and Listing*** Human Pharmaceuticals (1 Pg)*

SUMMARY OF REGISTRATION AND LISTING REQUIREMENTS FOR THE MANUFACTURE OR DISTRIBUTION OF HUMAN PHARMACEUTICALS			
TYPE OF FIRM	**REGISTRATION STATUS**	**LISTING STATUS**	**FACTS CODE**
Manufacturer [including homeopathic & controlled drugs]	yes	yes	M
Contract Manufacturer	yes	yes	M
Own Label Distributor	no	yes	L
Wholesale Distributor	no	no	W-*
Own Label Repacker	yes	yes	R
Own Label Relabeler [including recirculizer]	yes	yes	Y
Contract Relabeler	yes	no	Y
Contract Testing Laboratory [dosage forms & active ingredient release]	yes	no	C
Contract Testing Lab [doing non-release tests]	no	no	C
Contract Sub-Manufacturer	yes	no	M
IND Manufacturer [Clinical Drugs]	no	no	M
NDA and ANDA Manufacturer	yes	yes	M
Sponsor/Monitors/Clinical Investigator	no	no	4, 5, 6, 7
Contract Sterilizer	yes	no	0
Fulfillment Packager [adding substantive labeling]	yes	no	Y
Mail Order House [adding insubstantial labeling]	no	no	D
Printing House	no	no	None
Medical Gas Transfiller	yes	yes	MG
First Aid/Rescue Squad [transfilling for own use]	no	no	MG
Medical Gas Transfiller [operating out of a van]	yes	yes	MG
Contract Assembler	yes	no	M
Active Drug Substance Manufacturer	yes	yes	M
Excipient Drug Manufacturer	no	no	M
Manufacturer of Research Drugs	no	no	M

SUMMARY OF REGISTRATION AND LISTING REQUIREMENTS FOR THE MANUFACTURE OR DISTRIBUTION OF HUMAN PHARMACEUTICALS			
TYPE OF FIRM	**REGISTRATION STATUS**	**LISTING STATUS**	**FACTS CODE**
Drug Importer	no	no	A
Foreign Drug Manufacturer	yes	yes	M
Methadone Clinic	no	no	T
Retail Pharmacy	no	no	D
Manufacturing Pharmacy	yes	yes	M
Regional Admixture Pharmacy	yes	no	M
Salvage Operation	yes	no	X
Biopharmaceutical Clinical Facility	no	no	2

*Includes W, WA, WF, WR, and/or WZ

Exhibit 5-13: Substantially Equivalent Medical Devices (1 Pg)

Operation		Submit 510(k)	Register	List	COMPLY W/GMP
1.	Manufacture and distribute device	YES: 807.81(a)	YES 807.20	YES 807.20(a)	YES
2.	Contract manufacturer who commercially distributes device for specifications developer	NO: 807.81(a)	YES if domestic: 807.20(a)(2), YES if foreign 807.40(a)	YES if domestic 807.20(a)(2), YES if foreign 807.40(a)	YES
3a.	Contract manufacturer who meets the definition of finish-ed device manufacturer per 21 CFR 820.3(l), but does not commercially distribute device for specifications developer	NO	NO: 807.20(c)(1)	NO: 807.20(c)(1)	YES
3b.	Contract manufacturer who does not meet the definition of finished device manufacturer per 21 CFR 820.3(l) (e.g., component manufacturer, subassembler) but does not commercially distribute device for specifications developer	NO	NO: 807.20(c)(1)	NO: 807.20(c)(1)	NO
4	Manufacturer modifies device or new intended use and distribute	NO: preamble no. 17 & 18 FR 8/23/77 YES: 807.81(a)(3) with signif. change in device or use	YES 807.20(a)	YES 807.20(a)	YES
5	Distribute U.S. Made device: no specification initiation (domestic distributor)	NO: 807:85(b)	NO: 510(g)(4) of act, 807.20(c)(3)	NO	NO

Operation		Submit 510(k)	Register	List	COMPLY W/GMP
6	Specification initiator and distribute only	YES: 807.81(a)	YES: 807.20(a)(1) preamble no. 5, FR 8-23-77	YES: 807.20(a)(1)	YES: 820.181, etc.
7	Specification consultant only; no distribution	NO	NO: preamble no, 5, FR 8-3-77	NO	NO
8	Relabeler or repacker: distribute under own name	NO: 807.85(b): no change to device or existing labeling	YES: 807.20(a)(3)	YES: 807.20(a)(3) preamble no. 7, FR 8-25-78	YES
9	Kit assembler using prelabeled & prepackaged devices only	NO: no change in device or existing labeling other than adding dist. name & address 807.81(a)(3)	YES: 807.20(a)	YES: 807.20(a)	NO
10	Kit assembler changes intended use (801.4) of prepackaged/prelabeled devices	YES: 807.81(a)	YES: 807.20(a)(2)	YES: 807.20(a)(2)	YES: 820.120, 820.130, etc.
11	Kit assembler changes prepackaged/prelabeled devices	NO: if no significant change to labeling or device: otherwise YES: 807.81(a)(3)(i)	YES: 807.20(a)(3)	YES: 807.20(a)(3)	YES
12	Manuf. Accessory, component and package & label for health purpose to end user.	YES: 807.81(a)	YES: 807.20(a)(5) preamble no. 77, FR 8-25-78	YES: 807.20(a)(5)	YES
13	Manuf. Components & dist. Only to finished device mfr.	NO: 807.81(a)	NO: 807.65(a)	NO	Use as guide: 820.1
14	Contract mfr. Of subassembly or component (see no. 12, accessory)	NO	NO	NO	Primary mfr. must see that GMP is met preamble no. 33, FR 7-21-78
15	Contract packager or labeler	NO	NO	NO	Primary mfr. must see that GMP is met preamble no. 33, FR 7-21-79
16	Contract sterilizer who commercially distributes device	NO	YES if domestic 807.20(a)(2), YES if foreign 807.40(a)	YES if domestic 807.20(a)(2), YES if foreign 807.40(a)	YES
17	Contract sterilizer who does not commercially distribute device	NO	NO: 807.20(c)(2)	NO: 807.20(c)(2)	YES
18	Manufacture custom device	NO:	YES	YES	YES: also

	Operation	Submit 510(k)	Register	List	COMPLY W/GMP
	(domestic or foreign)	807.85(a)(1)& (2)	807.20(a)(2)	807.20(a)(2)	see 520(b); 520(f)
19	U.S. Establishment who manufactures for export only	NO	YES 807.20(a)(2)	YES 807.20(a)(2)	YES
20	Foreign manufacturers and all foreign establishments	YES: 807.81 foreign mfr. has primary responsibility, but may delegate to an init. Dist.	YES, 807.40(a)	YES 807.40(a)	YES
21	Initial distributor/importer of device	YES: 807.81(a) or 807.85(b) unless 510(k) has been filed by foreign manufacturer or another init. Dist	YES: 807.40(a)	NO: enforcement discretion used for 807.22(c)	YES: 807.3(d), 820.198, 820.100, 820.200, etc.
22	Installer-mfr.'s agent	NO	NO	NO	YES: 820.170
23	Installer-user	NO	NO	NO	NO: for x-ray see 1020.30(d) report
24	Device being investigated under ide	Exempt: 812.1(a)	NO	NO: 807.40(c)	Exempt per 812.1(a), except for Design Control per 820.30
25	Mfr. Buys manufacturing rights for device (see no. 4)	NO: preamble 18 FR 8-23-77 only if same type of manuf. equip. is used and no signif. change to device	YES: 807.20(a)(2) if not already registered	Send letter to FDA per 807.30(b)(5) & 807.26	YES
26	Reprocessor of single use device	YES	YES: 807.20	YES: 807.20	YES
27	Foreign exporter of device (device manufactured in foreign country)	YES: (original manufacturer 's 510(k) maybe used)	YES: 807.40 (a)	YES: 807.40 (a)	

Exhibit 5-14: Facts - Profile - Comstat (6 Pgs)

This document is available on the FDA website at http://www.fda.gov/ICECI/Inspections/IOM/ucm127372.htm.

Exhibits

Exhibit 5-15: Compliance Achievement Report

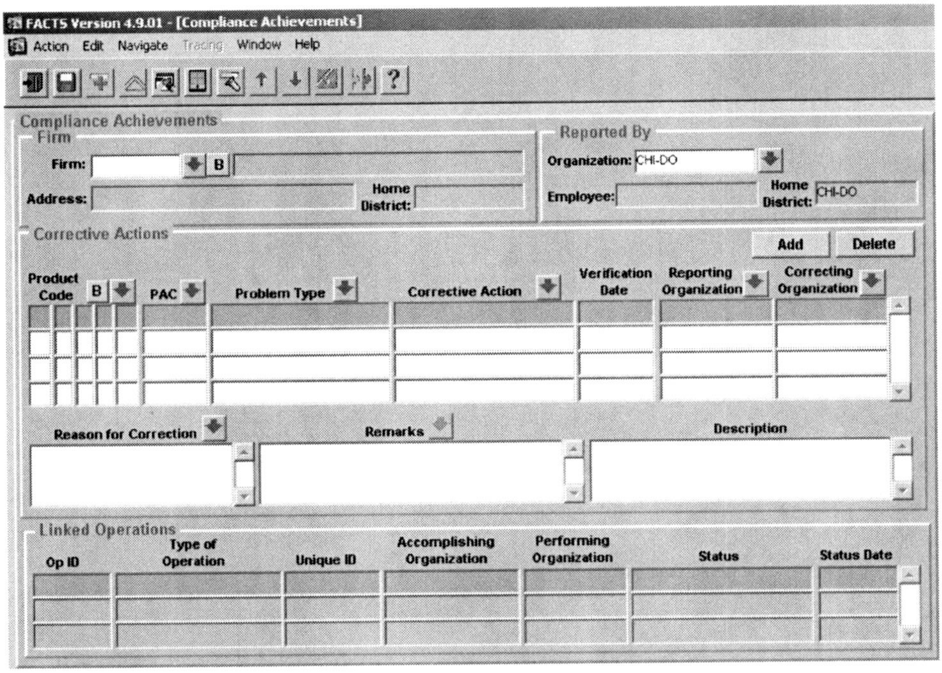

Exhibit 5-16: Facts EI Record (3 Pgs)

This document is available on the FDA website at http://www.fda.gov/ICECI/Inspections/IOM/ucm127372.htm.

Chapter 6 Exhibits

CONTENT

Exhibit 6-1: Notice of FDA Action

EXAMPLE

United States Food and Drug Administration
Los Angeles District Office

Notice of FDA Action[1]

Entry Number: 112-9861457-6

Notice Number: 2
November 6, 1996

Filer:
FBN Freight Services Attention: George
500 Canal St.
New Orleans LA 70130

:>

Port of Entry: 2704, Los Angeles,
Carrier: NOL RUBY
Entry Date: November 2, 1996
Arrival Date: November 4, 1996

Importer of Record: Shipley's Donut Shop Inc., Lafayette, LA
Consignee: a: Shipley's Donut Shop Inc., Lafayette, LA
b: Specialty Commodities Inc., Fargo, ND

HOLD DESIGNATED

Notify FDA of Availability

Summary of Current Status of Individual Lines

Document: 1 Invoice: PRAC004

@ LINE ACS/FDA	Product Description	Quantity	Current Status
* a 001/001	PINEAPPLE, DEHYDRATED	500 CT	RELEASED 11-6-96
* a 002/001	DEHYDRATED GINGER SLICES	10 KG	Product Collected by FDA 11-06-96
* b 003/001	PAPAYA, DEHYDRATED	10 KG	Detained 11-06-96

* = Status change since the previous notice. Read carefully the sections which follow for important information regarding these lines.
@ = Consignee id

[1] This example of a Notice of FDA Action is a model and should not be considered all inclusive. The format and wording in the actual Notice of FDA Action issued by districts from the Operational and Administrative System for Import Support (OASIS) may appear different.

Notice of FDA Action
Entry Number: 112-9861457-6

Notice Number: 2
Page: 2

FDA will not request redelivery for examination or sampling, if the products not released by FDA are moved, following USCS conditional release to a location within the local metropolitan area or to a location approved by the FDA office at the number below.

All products in this entry not listed above may proceed without FDA examination. This notice does not constitute assurance the products involved comply with provisions of the Food, Drug, and Cosmetic Act or other related acts, and does not preclude action should the products later be found violative.

Please provide documentation concerning all products in this entry to the FDA office below. Include the USCS document (e.g., CF-3461 or CF-7501) and commercial invoice for these products, annotated to show the ACS/FDA line numbers sent electronically.

Also, advise FDA upon actual availability, and include date, location, and warehouse control number, where applicable, for all lines in this entry.

Jennifer A Thomas, Inspector
U.S. Food & Drug Administration (213) 555-1212
2nd and Chestnut Streets (HFR-MA100)
Philadelphia, PA 19106

DETENTION WITHOUT EXAMINATION

The following products are subject to refusal pursuant to the Federal Food Drug and Cosmetic Act (FD&CA), Public Health Service Act (PHSA),or other related acts in that they appear to be adulterated, misbranded or otherwise in violation as indicated below:

LINE ACS/FDA	Product Description Respond By
003/001 DEHYDRATED	Product: PAPAYA, November 26, 1996

FD&CA Section 402(a)(1), 801(a)(3); ADULTERATION
The article appears to be held in a container containing a poisonous or deleterious substance which may render it injurious to health.

FD&CA Section 402(a)(2)(B), 801(a)(3); ADULTERATION
The article appears to be a raw agricultural commodity that bears or contains a pesticide chemical which is unsafe within the meaning of Section 408(a). The article appears to contain quinalphos.

Jennifer A Thomas, Inspector
U.S. Food & Drug Administration (213) 555-1212
2nd and Chestnut Streets (HFR-MA100)
Philadelphia, PA 19106

You have the right to provide oral or written testimony, to the Food & Drug Administration, regarding the admissibility of the article(s) or the manner in which the article(s) can be brought into compliance. This testimony must be provided to FDA on or before the dates shown above.

Notice of FDA Action
Entry Number: 112-9861457-6

Notice Number: 2
Page: 3

SAMPLES COLLECTED

LINE ACS/FDA	Product Description Est. Cost
001/001 $ 15.00	PINEAPPLE, DEHYDRATED

Sample: 10 KG Collected 1 KG from each of 10 cartons

LINE ACS/FDA	Product Description Est. Cost
002/001 $ .23	DEHYDRATED GINGER SLICES

Sample: .1 KG Collected approximately 4 ounces from one carton.

LINES RELEASED

LINE ACS/FDA	Product Description
001/001	PINEAPPLE, DEHYDRATED

These products are released. This notice does not constitute assurance that the product released complies with all provisions of the Food, Drug, and Cosmetic Act, or other related Acts, and does not preclude action should the product later be found violative.

Notice Prepared by: Thomas J. DiNunzio (QA5)
U. S. Food and Drug Administration

Exhibits

Exhibit 6-2: Form FDA-766

SUBMIT IN TRIPLICATE *(Submit in QUADRUPLICATE if you desire copy returned to you.)*

APPLICATION FOR AUTHORIZATION TO RELABEL OR TO PERFORM OTHER ACTION OF THE FEDERAL FOOD, DRUG, AND COSMETIC ACT AND OTHER RELATED ACTS

FORM APPROVED: OMB No. 0910-0025
EXPIRATION DATE: 12/31/08

Paper work Reduction Act Statement An agency may not conduct or sponsor, and a person is not required to respond to, a collection of information unless it displays a currently valid OMB control number. Public reporting burden for this collection of information is estimated to average 25 hours per response, including time for reviewing instructions, searching existing data sources, gathering and maintaining the necessary data, and completing of review of the collection of information. Send comments regarding the burden estimate or any other aspect of this collection of information to:

Department of Health and Human Services
Food and Drug Administration
15800CrabbsBranchParkway
Rockville, MD 20855-2613

TO: DIRECTOR

_______________________ District

Food and Drug Administration

Application is hereby made for authorization to bring the merchandise Below into compliance with the Act.

DATE | SAMPLE NO.

PRODUCT

ENTRY NO. | ENTRY DATE

CARRIER | AMOUNT AND MARKS

Redelivery bond has been posted by the applicant. The merchandise will be kept apart from all other merchandise and will be available for inspection at all reasonable times. The operations, if authorized, will be carried out at:

____ and will require about ________ days to complete. A detailed description of the method by which the merchandise will be brought into compliance is given in the space below:

We will pay all supervisory costs in accordance with current regulations.

FIRM NAME | ADDRESS OF FIRM

APPLICANT'S SIGNATURE

ACTION ON APPLICATION

TO: *(Name and Address)* | DATE

Your application has been: ☐ Denied because: ☐ Approved with the following conditions:

Time limit within which to complete authorized operations:_______________________

When the authorized operations are completed, fill in the importer's certificate on the reverse side and return this notice to this office.

SIGNATURE OF DISTRICT DIRECTOR | DISTRICT | DATE

FORM FDA 766 (12/04) *(See Back)* **FRONT**

PSC Media Arts (301)443-1090 EF

IMPORTER'S CERTIFICATE

PLACE	DATE

I certify that the work to be performed under the authorization has been completed and the goods are now ready for inspection at: ____

____

The rejected portion is ready for destruction under Customs' supervision and is held at: ____________________

____

TYPED NAME OF APPLICANT	SIGNATURE

REPORT OF INVESTIGATOR / INSPECTOR

TO PORT DIRECTOR OR DISTRICT DIRECTOR	DATE

I have examined the within-described goods and find them to be the identical goods described herein, and that they have been: ____ on: ____________________ , 20____, as authorized, except:

DATA ON CLEANED GOODS

Good Portion:

Rejections:

Loss (if any)

Did importer clean entire shipment?

Time and cost of supervision

INSPECTING OFFICER	DATE

DIRECTOR OF DISTRICT

Disposed of as noted above.

DIRECTOR OF CUSTOMS	DATE

FORM FDA 766 (12/04) BACK

Exhibit 6-3: Charges for Supervision Form FDA-790

CHARGES FOR SUPERVISION

☐ Federal Food, Drug and Cosmetic Act, Section 801 (b) and (c)
☐ 21 CFR 1005.24

TO: *(Insert Address)* DISTRICT DIRECTOR OF CUSTOMS	**FROM:** *(Insert Address)* DHHS FOOD AND DRUG ADMINISTRATION

PRODUCT	FDA SAMPLE NO.
CARRIER	ENTRY NO.
IMPORTER OF RECORD	ENTRY DATE
CONSIGNEE	

The following is a list of charges incurred by this Agency for supervision of operations performed in accordance with the above-designated Act or Regulation. You are requested to collect payment, including any expenses incurred by your Department,
for deposit into Treasury Miscellaneous Receipts.
Under Section 801(c), default of payment shall constitute a lien against any future importation made by the owner or consignee.

TYPE OF CHARGES	UNIT			CHARGE PER UNIT	TOTAL CHARGE
	HOURS	DAYS	MILES		
INVESTIGATORS TIME					
ANALYSTS TIME					
PER DIEM, PAID PER GOVERNMENT TRAVEL REGULATIONS					
AUTOMOBILE USE					
OTHER TRANSPORTATION EXPENSES *(itemize)*					
MISCELLANEOUS EXPENSES *(itemize)*					
GRAND TOTAL					

REMARKS

FORM FDA 790 (7/82) PREVIOUS EDITION MAY BE USED UNTIL SUPPLY IS EXHAUSTED. PSC Media Arts (301) 443-1090 EF

Exhibit 6-4: Oasis Collection Report Form

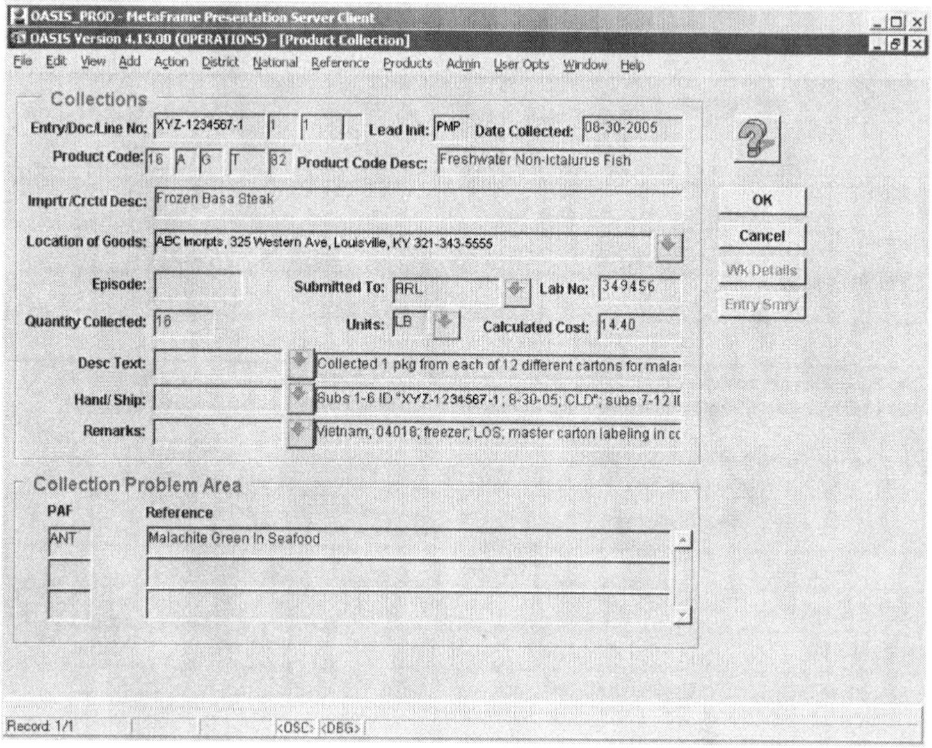

Exhibit 6-5: Import Investigation Affidavit

AFFIDAVIT	SAMPLE NO.
STATE OF Texas	COUNTY OF Hunt

Before me, Sydney H. Rogers , an employee of the Department of Health and Human Services, Food and Drug Administration, designated by the Secretary, under authority of the Act of January 31, 1925, 43 Statutes at Large 803; Reorganization Plan No. IV, Secs. 12-15, effective June 30, 1940; Reorganization Plan No. 1 of 1953, Secs. 1-9, effective April 11, 1953; and P.L. 96-98, Sec. 509, 93 Statutes at Large 965 (20 U.S.C. 3508), effective May 4, 1980; to administer or take oaths, affirmations, and affidavits, personally appeared Felicia M. Rodriguez in the county and State aforesaid, who, being duly sworn, deposes and says:

I am the Import Manager for ABC Foods Warehouse, 234 Industry Avenue, Commerce, TX, where I have worked for about 3 years, and as such have knowledge of products imported, held, processed and/or shipped by my firm.

On 8/12/04, we received a shipment consisting of five 200 kg burlap bags of dried Ancho Peppers, manufactured by Del Campo, Extension Del Mina #4, Guadalajara, Mexico, covered by entry BAD-1234565-7.

On 8/13/04, my firm repacked this shipment of peppers into 25 kg burlap bags for distribution to restaurants and other customers.

On 8/17/04, Investigator Rogers visited my firm and showed me copies of documents including Customs form 3461 marked with the entry number of Entry BAD-1234565-7, Bill of Lading #2345RRR678, dated 8/10/04 and invoice 45678, dated 8/8/04. I am familiar with these documents and they cover the shipment of peppers my firm received.

Part of the repackaged peppers from Entry BAD-123456-7 were sold and distributed by my firm on 8/16/04. Three 25 kg burlap bags were shipped to John's Pepper House, 3456 First Avenue, Dallas, Texas; and two 25 kg bags were shipped to Casa De Juanita, 5678 Mulberry Drive, Fort Worth, Texas. I have identified and provided copies of the shipping documents that cover this distribution to Investigator Rogers. These documents are invoice 999888, dated 8/14/04 and UPS B/L 787878000009, dated 8/16/04 which covers the shipment to John's Pepper House and invoice 757575, 8/14/04 and UPS B/L 2323232323, 8/16/04 which covers the shipment to Casa De Juanita. The rest of the repackaged peppers remain at my firm.

I received the Customs and Border Protection release for this entry on 8/12/04 and I believed I could ship the product. I was informed by Investigator Rogers I was not supposed to ship the product until I received the FDA release. I will keep the remainder of the shipment intact.

I read this statement and agree it is true.

AFFIANT'S SIGNATURE AND TITLE *Felicia M. Rodriquez*, Import Manager

FIRM'S NAME AND ADDRESS *(Include ZIP Code)*

ABC Foods Warehouse, 234 Industry Avenue, Commerce, TX 75428

Subscribed and sworn to before me at ABC Foods Warehouse, 234 Industry Avenue, Commerce, TX 75428 this 17th day of August, 2004.

Sydney H. Rogers
(Employee Signature)

Employee of the Department of Health and Human services designated under Act of January 31, 1925, Reorganization Plan IV effective June 30, 1940; Reorganization Plan No. 1 of 1953, effective April 11, 1953; and P.L. 96-88 effective May 4, 1980.

FORM FDA 463a (4/83) PREVIOUS EDITIONS ARE OBSOLETE PAGE 1 OF 1 PAGES

Chapter 7 Exhibits

CONTENT

Exhibit 7-1: Recall Communications - Examples

MODEL DRUG RECALL LETTER

John Doe Laboratories
Somewhere, U.S.A. 12345

Control Division
Date ______________

(red print) --URGENT: DRUG RECALL -- Nonsterile injectable

Re: List 1234, Cyanocobalamin Injection Lot No. 4321

Recent tests showed that the above lot number of this product is not sterile and therefore, represents a potential public health hazard. Consequently, we are recalling this lot from the market. Other lot numbers are not involved.

Please examine your stocks <u>immediately</u> to determine if you have any of Lot 4321 on hand. If so, <u>discontinue dispensing the lot</u> and promptly return via parcel post, to our New York City Plant; ATENTION RETURNED GOODS.

(<u>NOTE</u>: If a sub-recall is indicated in a particular situation, the following paragraph should be added:)

> "If you have distributed any of lot 4321, please immediately contact your accounts, advise them of the recall situation, and have them return their outstanding recalled stocks to you. Return these stocks as indicated above."

You will be reimbursed by check or credit memo for the returned goods and postage.

<u>Please return the enclosed card immediately</u> providing the requested information.

This recall is being made with the knowledge of the Food and Drug Administration. The FDA has classified this recall as class __________ (if classified).

We appreciate your assistance.

John Doe
President

PLEASE FILL OUT AND RETURN

We do not have any stock of List 1234, Cyanocobalamin

Injection Lot No. 4321 on hand

We have requested our accounts to return their stocks of this

merchandise to us.

We are returning _________ bottles of List 1234, Lot No. 4321

Name ______________________________

Address ______________________________

First Class
Permit No. 2

BUSINESS REPLY MAIL

No Postage Stamp Necessary if mailed in U.S.A.

Postage will be paid by:

JOHN DOE LABORATORIES
Somewhere, U.S.A. 12345-0909

Henry Doe

FIRST CLASS MAIL

JOHN DOE LABORATORIES

A. B. C. Pharmacy
Anywhere U. S. A.

(red print) **URGENT DRUG RECALL**

Exhibits

Exhibit 7-2: Form FDA-3177, Recall Audit Check Report

1. RECALL INFORMATION

a. RECALL NUMBER

b. RECALLING ESTABLISHMENT

c. RECALLED CODE(S) | d. PRODUCT

2. PROGRAM DATA (CHECK BOX IF PREVIOUSLY SUBMITTED)
(DO NOT COMPLETE IF REPORTED UNDER FDA 2123)

a. ACCOMP DISTRICT CODE	b. HOME DISTRICT CODE	c. OPERATION CODE	d. OPERATION DATE (MM/DD/YY)
		17	

e. CENTRAL FILE NUMBER OF RECALLING ESTABLISHMENT	f. PAC CODE

g. EMPLOYEE			h. TYPE	# OF CHECKS	HOURS
HOME DIST.	POS. CLASS	NUMBER	VISITS		
			PHONE		

3. AUDIT ACCOUNTS

a. DIRECT	b. SUB-ACCOUNT (SECONDARY)	c. SUB-ACCOUNT (TERTIARY)
PHONE NO.	PHONE NO.	PHONE NO.

4. CONSIGNEE DATA Contacted by: ☐ Phone ☐ Visit ☐ Other

a. NAME OF PERSON CONTACTED, TITLE & DATE

b. TYPE CONSIGNEE
☐ Wholesaler ☐ Physician
☐ Retailer ☐ Hospital ☐ Other
☐ Processor ☐ Pharmacy
☐ Consumer ☐ Restaurant

c. DOES (DID) THE CONSIGNEE HANDLE RECALLED PRODUCT?
☐ YES ☐ NO

5. NOTIFICATION DATA

a. FORMAL RECALL NOTICE RECEIVED?
(If "No" skip to item 6c.)
☐ YES ☐ NO ☐ CANNOT BE DETERMINED

b. RECALL NOTIFICATION RECEIVED FROM:
☐ Recalling Firm
☐ Direct Account
☐ Sub-Account
☐ Other *(Specify)*

c. DATE NOTIFIED

d. TYPE OF NOTICE RECEIVED (e.g. letter, phone)

6. ACTION AND STATUS DATA

a. DID CONSIGNEE FOLLOW THE RECALL INSTRUCTIONS? *(If "No", discuss in item 10 action taken upon FDA contact)*
☐ YES ☐ NO

b. AMOUNT OF RECALLED PRODUCT ON HAND AT TIME OF NOTIFICATION

c. CURRENT STATUS OF RECALLED ITEMS
☐ Returned ☐ Destroyed
☐ Corrected ☐ None on Hand
☐ Was Still Held for Sale/Use *
☐ Held For Return/Correction *
* = Ensure Proper Quarantine/Action

d. DATE AND METHOD OF DISPOSITION

7. SUB-RECALL NEEDED?
Did Consignee Distribute to any other Accounts? (If "Yes" give Details in "Remarks" or Memo)
☐ YES ☐ NO

8. AMOUNT OF RECALLED PRODUCT NOW ON HAND

9. INJURIES/COMPLAINTS

IS CONSIGNEE AWARE OF ANY INJURIES, ILLNESS, OR COMPLAINTS?
☐ INJURY ☐ COMPLAINT
☐ ILLNESS ☐ NONE

If answer is other than "None", report details in a separate memo to monitoring district and copy to E.O.B (HFC-162)

10. REMARKS *(Include action taken if product was still available for sale or use)*

SIGNATURE OF CSO/CSI		TO:	DATE	ENDORSEMENT
DISTRICT	DATE OF CHECK	SIGNATURE OF SCSO OR R&E COORDINATOR		

FORM FDA 3177 (11/91) **RECALL AUDIT CHECK REPORT**
Circle Appropriate Copy: Home District (White) Accomplishing District DPU (Pink) Accomplishing District (Yellow)

Chapter 8 Exhibits

CONTENT

Exhibit 8-1: Facts Adverse Event Questionnaire

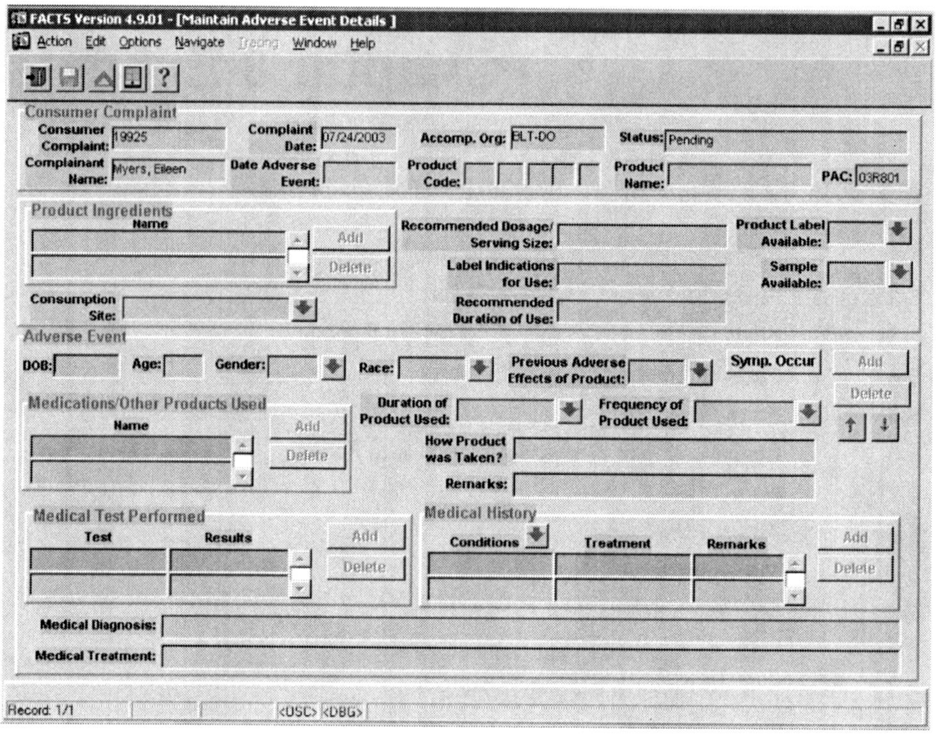

Exhibit 8-2: Facts Consumer Complaint Report

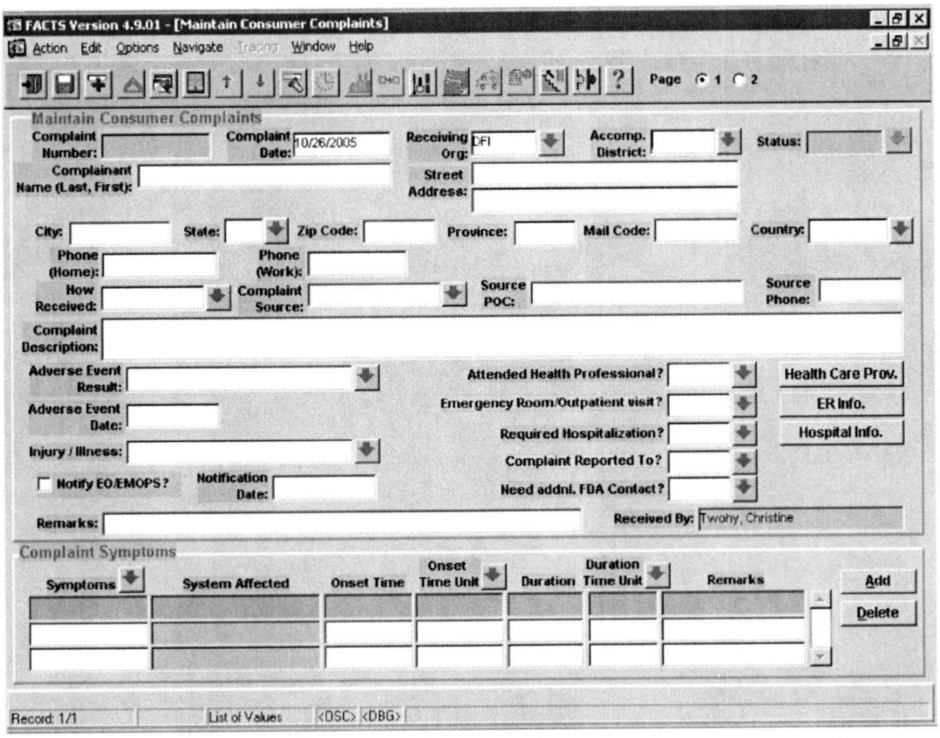

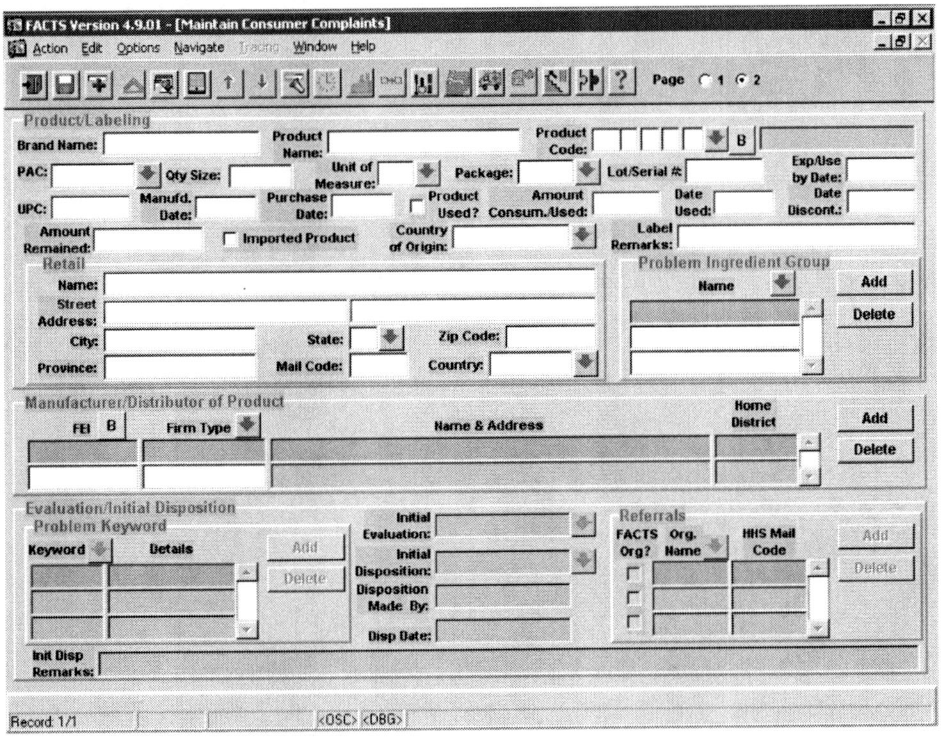

Exhibit 8-3: Facts Consumer Complaint Follow-Up Report

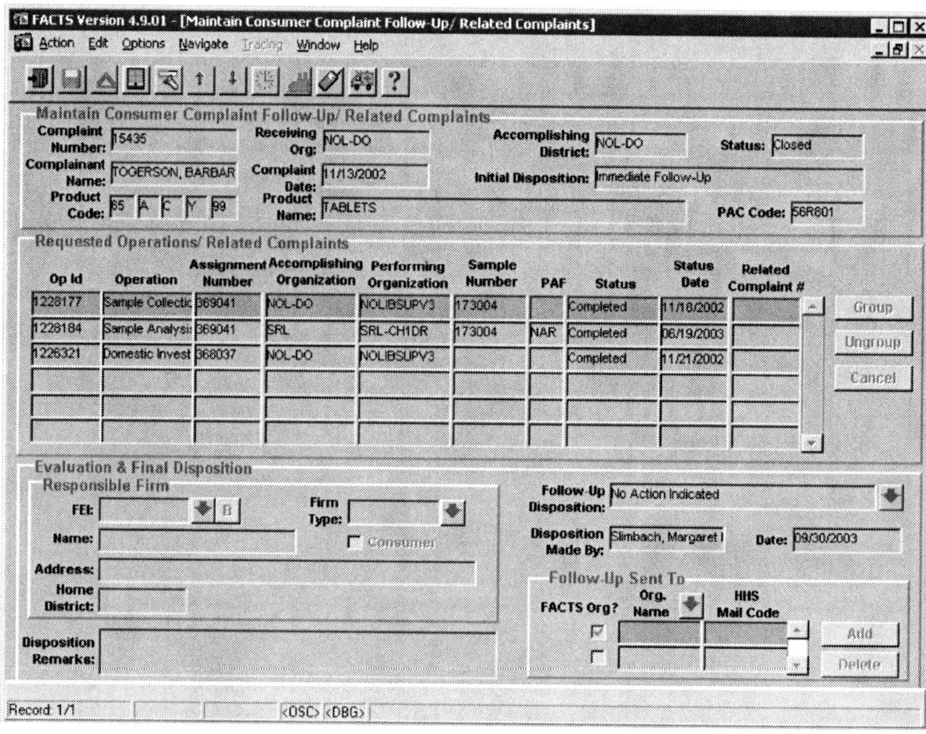

Exhibit 8-4: Facts Cosmetics Adverse Event

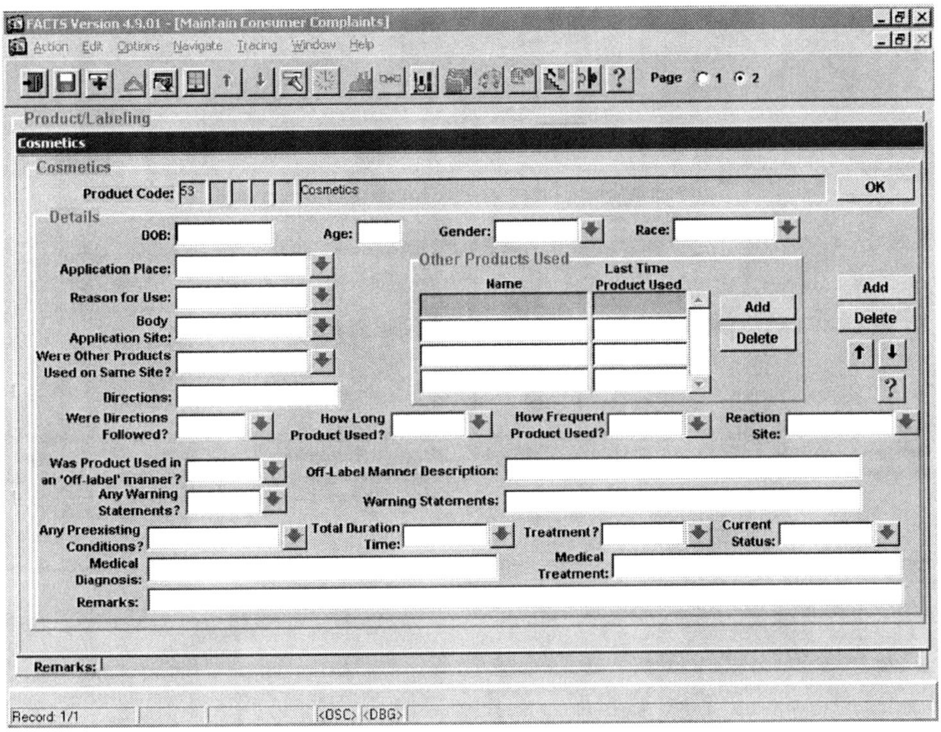

Exhibit 8-5: Form FDA-461

DEPARTMENT OF HEALTH AND HUMAN SERVICES
FOOD AND DRUG ADMINISTRATION

158-15 Liberty Ave.
Jamaica, NY 11433

AUTHORIZATION FOR MEDICAL RECORDS DISCLOSURE

Authorización Para Revelar Expediente Medico

TO WHOM IT MAY CONCERN:

You are hereby authorized to furnish the United States Food and Drug Administration all information and copies of any and all records you may have pertaining to ~~(my case)~~ (the case of

Miss Mary Ellen Pertillo
(Name)

Daughter),
(Relationship to you)

including, but not limited to, medical history, physical reports, laboratory reports and pathological slides, and X-ray reports and films. FDA may provide the public access to the content of the information obtained through this form, except to the extent that the information relating to personal privacy is protected from disclosure by law.

A Quien Pueda Interesar:

Por la presente se le authoriza proveer a la Administracion de Drogas y Alimentos de Estados Unidos toda información y copias de cualquira y todos los documentos que usted pueda tener con relacción a ~~(mi caso)~~ (el caso de

(Nombre)

),
(Parentesco)

incluyendo, pero no limitado a, historial medico, examenes fisicos, informes de laboratorio, laminillas de patologia, placas e informes de radiologia. La Administración de Drogas y Alimentos puede proveer acceso público al contenido de la información obtenida mediante este formulario, a excepción de información relacionada a la privacidad persona, la cual esta protegida y no puede ser divulgada por ley.

Anthony Oliver Pertillo — 10-26-05
(Signature) (Firma) — *(Date) (Fecha)*

Sidney H. Rogers — 10-26-05
(Witness) (Testiso) — *(Date) (Fecha)*

FORM FDA 461 (2/03) PREVIOUS EDITION MAY BE USED PSC Media Arts (301 443-1090 EF

Exhibit 8-6: Classification of Illnesses Attributable to Foods

CLASSIFICATION OF ILLNESSES ATTRIBUTABLE TO FOODS

(A CLASSIFICATION BY SYMPTOMS, INCUBATION PERIODS, AND TYPES OF AGENTS[1, 2])

DISEASE	ETIOLOGIC AGENT AND	INCUBATION OR LATENCY	SIGNS & SYMPTOMS	FOODS INVOLVED3	SPECIMENS TO COLLECT	FACTORS THAT CONTRIBUTE OUTBREAKS
UPPER GASTROINTESTINAL TRACT SIGNS AND SYMPTOMS (NAUSEA, VOMITING) OCCUR FIRST OR PREDOMINATE						
INCUBATION (LATENCY) PERIOD USUALLY LESS THAN ONE HOUR						
FUNGAL AGENTS						
Gastrointest-inal irritating group mush-room poisoning	Possibly resin-like substances in some mushrooms (mushroom species are different than those cited on pp. -- & --)	30 minutes to 2 hours	Nausea, vomiting, retching, diarrhea, abdominal cramps	Many varieties of wild mushrooms	Vomitus	Eating unknown varieties of mushrooms, mistaking toxic mushrooms for edible varieties
CHEMICAL AGENTS						
Antimony Poisoning	Antimony in gray enamelware	Few minutes to 1 hour	Vomiting, abdominal pain, diarrhea	High-acid foods and beverages	Vomitus, stools, urine	Using/buying antimony-containing utensils, storing high-acid foods in gray enamelware
Cadmium Poisoning	Cadmium in plated utensils	15 to 30 minutes	Nausea, vomiting, abdominal cramps, diarrhea, shock	High-acid foods & beverages, candy love beads or cake decorations	Vomitus, stools, urine, blood	Using/buying cadmium-containing utensils, storing high-acid foods in cadmium-containers, ingesting cadmium-containing foods
Copper Poisoning	Copper in pipes and utensils, old dairy white metal	Few minutes to few hours	Metallic taste, nausea, vomiting (green vomitus), abdominal pain, diarrhea	High-acid foods and beverages, ice cream (ices) and beverages	Vomitus, gastric washings, urine, blood	Storing high-acid foods in copper utensils or using copper pipes for dispensing high-acid beverages, faulty back-flow prevention valves in vending machines
Fluoride poisoning	Sodium fluoride in insecticides	Few minutes to two hours	Salty or soapy taste, numbness of mouth, vomiting, diarrhea, abdominal pain, pallor, cyanosis dilated pupils, spasms, collapse, shock	Any accidentally contaminated food, particularly dry foods, such as dry milk, flour, baking powder & cake mixes	Vomitus, gastric washings	Storing insecticides in same area as foods, mistaking pesticides for powdered foods
Lead poisoning	Lead in earthenware pesticides, putty, plaster, cans with lead solder seams	30 minutes or longer	Mouth and abdominal pain, milky vomitus, black or bloody stools, foul breath, shock blue gum line	Beverages stored in lead containing vessels, any accidentally conta-minated food	Washings, stools, blood, urine	Storing high-acid foods in lead-con-taining vessels, storing pesticides in same area as food, imported canned high-acid foods with faulty seams
Tin poisoning	Tin in tinned cans	30 minutes to two hours	Bloating, nausea, vomiting, abdominal cramps, diarrhea, headache	High-acid foods and beverages	Vomitus, stools, urine, blood	Using uncoated tin containers for storing acidic foods. Very high tin concentrations are required to cause illness.
Zinc poisoning	Zinc in galvanized containers	Few minutes to few hours	Mouth and abdominal pain, nausea, vomiting, dizziness	High-acid foods and beverages	Vomitus, gastric washings, urine, blood, stools	storing high-acid foods in galvanized cans
INCUBATION (LATENCY) PERIOD 1 TO 6 HOURS						
BACTERIAL AGENTS						
Bacillus cereus Gastroenteritis (emetic form, mimics staphylococcal intoxication)	Exotoxin of B. cereus organism in soil (strains differ from diarrheal form)	0.5 to 5 hours	Nausea, vomiting, occasionally diarrhea	Boiled or fried rice, pasta, cooked corn-meal dishes, porridge	Vomitus, stool	Storing cooked foods at room temp-erature, storing cooked foods in large containers in refrigerators, preparing foods several hours before serving
Staphylococcal intoxication	Exo-enterotoxins A, B, C, D & E of Staphylococcus aureus, staphylococci from skin, nose & lesions of infected humans and animals and from udders of cows	1 to 8 hours, mean 2 to 4 hours	Nausea, vomiting, retching, abdominal pain, diarrhea, prostration	Lower water activity foods (aw), e.g. cheese, whipped butter, ham, meat & poultry products, cream filled pastry, food mixtures, leftovers, dry milk	Vomitus, stools, rectal swabs, carriers nasal swabs, swabs of lesions, anal swab	Inadequate refrigeration, workers touching cooked food, preparing food several hours before serving, workers with infections containing pus, holding foods at warm (bacterial incubating) temperatures, fermentation of abnormally low-acid foods

CHEMICAL AGENTS

Nitrite poisoning4	Nitrites or nitrates used as meat curing compounds or ground water from shallow wells	1 to 2 hours	Nausea, vomiting, cyanosis, headache, dizziness, weakness, loss of consciousness, chocolate brown colored blood4	Cured meats, any accidentally contaminated food exposed to excessive nitrification	Blood	Using excessive amounts of nitrites or nitrates in foods for curing or for covering up spoilage, mistaking nitrites for common salt and other condiments, improper refrigeration of fresh foods.

TOXIC ANIMALS

Diarrhetic shellfish poisoning (DSP)	Okadaic acid and other toxins produced by dinoflagellates, Dinophysis acuminata and other species	0.5 to 12 hours commonly < 3 hrs	Diarrhea, nausea, vomiting, abdominal cramps, chills, fever, headache	Mussels, clams, scallops	Gastric washings	Harvesting shellfish from waters with high concentration of Dinophysis

INCUBATION (LATENCY) PERIOD USUALLY 7 TO 12 HOURS
FUNGAL AGENTS

Cyclopeptide and Gyromitrin groups of mushroom poisoning	Cyclopeptides and Gyromitrin in some mushrooms	6 to 24 hours average 6 - 15 h	Abdominal pain, feeling of fullness, vomiting, protracted diarrhea, loss of strength, thirst, muscle cramps, feeble rapid pulse, collapse, jaundice, drowsiness, dilated pupils, coma, death	Amanita phalloides A. verna, Galerina autumnalis, Gyromitra esculenta (false morels) and similar species of mushrooms	Urine, blood, vomitus	Eating certain species of Amanita, Galerina, and Gyromitra mushrooms, eating unknown varieties of mushrooms, mistaking toxic mushrooms for edible varieties

BURNING MOUTH, SORE THROAT AND RESPIRATORY SIGNS AND SYMPTOMS OCCUR

INCUBATION (LATENCY) PERIOD LESS THAN 1 HOUR
CHEMICAL AGENTS

Calcium chloride Poisoning	Calcium chloride freezing mixture for Frozen dessert bars	Few minutes	Burning lips, mouth, throat, vomiting	Frozen dessert bar	Vomitus	Splashing of freezing mixture onto popsicles while freezing; cracks in molds allowing $CaCl_2$ to penetrate popsicle syrup
Sodium hydroxide poisoning	Sodium hydroxide in bottle washing compounds, detergents, drain cleaners or hair straighteners	Few minutes	Burning of lips, mouth, and throat; vomiting, diarrhea, abdominal pain	Bottled beverages	Vomitus	Inadequate rinsing of bottles cleaned with caustic

INCUBATION (LATENCY) PERIOD 12 TO 72 HOURS
BACTERIAL AGENTS

Beta-hemolytic streptococcal infections	Streptococcus pyrogenes from throat and lesions of infected humans	1 to 3 days	Sore throat, fever, nausea, vomiting, rhinorrhea, sometimes a rash	Raw milk, foods containing eggs	Throat swabs, vomitus	Workers touching cooked foods, workers with infections containing pus, inadequate refrigeration, inadequate cooking or reheating, preparing foods several hours before serving

LOWER GASTROINTESTINAL TRACT SIGNS AND SYMPTOMS (ABDOMINAL CRAMPS, DIARRHEA) OCCUR FIRST OR PREDOMINATE

INCUBATION (LATENCY) PERIOD USUALLY 7 TO 12 HOURS
BACTERIAL AGENTS

Bacillus cereus enteritis (diarrheal form, mimics C. perfringens)	Enterotoxin of B. cereus, soil organism (strain differs from emetic form)	6 to 16 hours	Nausea, abdominal pain, diarrhea, some reports of vomiting	Cereal products, custards, sauces, starchy foods, e.g. pasta, potatoes, and meatloaf	Stools, vomitus	Inadequate refrigeration, holding of foods at warm (bacterial incubation) temperatures, preparing foods several hours before serving, inadequate reheating of leftovers
Clostridium perfringens gastroenteritis	Endo-enterotoxin formed during sporulation of C. perfringens in intestines, organism in feces of infected humans, other animals, and in soil	8 to 22 hours, mean 10 hours	Abdominal pain, diarrhea	Cooked meat, poultry, gravy, sauces and soups	Stools	Inadequate refrigeration, holding foods at warm (bacterial incubation) temperatures, preparing foods several hours before serving, inadequate reheating of leftovers

INCUBATION (LATENCY) PERIOD USUALLY 12 TO 72 HOURS
BACTERIAL AGENTS

Aeromonas diarrhea	Aeromonas hydrophila	1 to 2 days	Water diarrhea, abdominal pain, nausea, chills, headache	Fish, shellfish, snails, water	Stools	Contamination of foods by sea or surface water
Campylobacteriosis	Campylobacter jejuni	2 to 7 days, mean 3 to 5 days	Diarrhea, (often bloody), severe abdominal pain, fever anorexia, malaise, headache, vomiting	Raw milk, raw clams and shellfish, water poultry and meat	Stools, rectal swab, blood	Drinking raw milk, eating raw or undercooked shellfish, inadequate cooking or pasteurization
Cholera	Endemic in temperate U.S. coastal sea water. V.cholerae serogroup 01 classical and El Tor biotypes; serogroup O139	1 to 5 days, usually 2 - 3 days	Profuse, watery diarrhea (rice-water stools), vomiting abdominal pain, dehydration, thirst, collapse, reduced skin turgor, wrinkled fingers, sunken eyes, acidosis	Raw fish & shellfish foods washed or prepared with contaminated water	Stools, rectal swabs	Obtaining fish & shellfish from sewage contaminated waters in endemic areas, poor personal hygiene, infected workers touching foods, inadequate cooking, using contaminated water to wash or freshen foods, inadequate sewage disposal, using night soil as fertilizer
Cholera-like vibrio gastroenteritis	Non 01/O139 V. cholerae ,& related species, eg, V. mimicus, V. fluvialis, V hollisae	2 to 3 days	Watery diarrhea (varies from loose stools to cholera-like diarrhea)	Raw shellfish, raw fish	Stools, rectal swabs	Eating raw shellfish or raw fish, inadequate cooking, cross contamination
Pathogenic Escherichia coli Diarrhea (THREE FORMS):						
Enterotoxigenic E. coli (ETEC) Gastroenteritis	Enterotoxigenic strains E. coli	10 to 72 hours, usually 24 to 72 hrs	Watery diarrhea, abdominal cramps, nausea, malaise, low grade fever	Water, semi-soft cheeses, foods requiring no further heating	Stools, rectal swab	Infected workers touching foods, inadequate refrigeration, inadequate cleaning and disinfection of equipment
Enterohemorrhagic E. coli (EHEC) Gastroenteritis	O157:H7 E. coli Verotoxins	3 to 9 days, mean 4 days	Bloody diarrhea, severe abdominal cramping, complications- Hemolytic Uremic Syndrome (HUS), kidney failure	Raw ground beef, raw milk, cheese	Stools, rectal swabs	Infected workers touching foods, inadequate refrigeration, inadequate cooking, inadequate cleaning and disinfection of equipment
Enteroinvasive E. coli (EIEC) Gastroenteritis	Enteroinvasive strains of E. coli	10 to 72 hours	Severe abdominal cramps, watery diarrhea, vomiting malaise, complications – HUS, kidney failure	Raw milk, raw ground beef, cheese	Stools, rectal swabs	Infected workers touching foods, inadequate refrigeration, inadequate cooking, inadequate cleaning and disinfection of equipment
Salmonellosis	Various serotypes of Salmonella from feces of infected humans and other animals	6 to 72 hours, mean 18 to 36 hours	Abdominal pain, diarrhea, chills, fever, nausea, vomiting, malaise	Poultry, meat and their products, egg products, other foods contaminated by salmonellae	Stools, rectal swabs	Inadequate refrigeration, holding foods at warm (bacterial incubation) temperatures, inadequate cooking and reheating, preparing foods several hours before serving, cross contamination, inadequate cleaning of equipment, infected workers touching cooked foods, obtaining foods from contaminated sources
Shigellosis	Shigella flexneri, S. dysenteriae, S. sonnei, & S. boydii from feces of infected humans	24 to 72 hours	Abdominal pain, diarrhea, bloody & mucoid stools, fever	Any contaminated foods, frequently salads, water	Stools & rectal swab	Infected workers touching foods, inadequate refrigeration, inadequate cooking and reheating
Vibrio parahaemolyticus Gastroenteritis	V. parahaemolyticus from sea water or seafoods	2 to 48 hours, mean 12 hours	Abdominal pain, diarrhea, nausea, vomiting, fever, chills, headache	Raw seafoods, shellfish	Stools, rectal swabs	Inadequate cooking, inadequate refrigeration, cross contamination, inadequate cleaning of equipment, using seawater in food preparation
Yersiniosis	Yersinia enterocolitica, Y. psuedotuberculosis	24 to 36 hours	Severe abdominal pain, fever, headache malaise, sore throat may mimic appendicitis	Milk, tofu, water, pork	Stools, blood	Inadequate cooking, contamination after pasteurization, contamination of foods by water, rodents, other animals

VIRAL AGENTS

Astrovirus gastro-enteritis	Astroviruses from human feces	1 to 2 days	Diarrhea, some-times accompanied by one or more en-teric signs or symp-toms	Ready-to-eat foods	Stools, acute and convalescent blood	Failure to wash hands after defecation, infected person touching ready-to-eat foods, inadequate cooking or reheating
Acute viral Gastroenteritis (Small round structured virus)	Norwalk-like viruses, Calici-viruses	1 to 3 days (Norwalk-like virus mean 36 hours)	Nausea, vomiting, abdominal pain, diarrhea, low grade fever, chills, malaise, anorexia, headache	Clams, oysters cockles, green salad pastry, frostings, ice, cut fruit salads	Stools, acute and convalescent blood sera	Polluted shellfish growing waters, poor personal hygiene, infected persons touching prepared foods, foods not requiring further cooking, contamin-ated waters

PARASITIC AGENTS

Amebic Dysentery (Amebiasis)	Entamoeba histolytica from feces of infected humans	5 days to several months, mean 3 to 4 weeks	Abdominal pain, constipation or diarrhea	Raw vegetables and fruit	Stools	Poor personal hygiene, infected workers touching food, inadequate cooking
Anisakiasis	Anisakis simplex Pseudoterranova decipiens	4 to 6 hours	Stomach pain, nausea, vomiting, abdominal pain, diarrhea, fever	Rock fish, herring, cod, squid	Stools	Ingestion of raw fish, inadequate cooking
Beef tapeworm infection (Taeniasis)	Taenia saginata from flesh of infected cattle	3 to 6 months	Vague discomfort, hunger pain, loss of weight, abdominal pain	Raw or insufficiently cooked beef	Stools	Lack of meat inspection, inadequate cooking, inadequate sewage disposal, sewage contaminated pastures
Cryptospondiosis	Cryptosporidium parvum	1 – 12 days, usually 7 days	Profuse watery dia-rrhea, abdominal pain, anorexia, low grade fever, vomiting	Apple cider, water	Stools, intestinal biopsy	Inadequate sewage or animal waste dis-posal, contamination by animal manure, contaminated water, inadequate filtration of water
Cyclosporiasis	Cyclopsora cayetanensis	1 – 11 days, typically 7 days	Prolonged watery diarrhea, weight loss, fatigue, nau-sea, anorexia, ab-dominal cramps	Raspberries, lettuce, basil, water	Stools	Sewage contaminated irrigation or spraying water suspected; washing fruits with contaminated water; possibly handling foods that are not subsequently heated
Fish tapeworm infection (Diphyllobothriasis)	Diphyllobothrium latum from flesh of infected fish	5 to 6 weeks	Vague gastrointest-inal discomfort anemia may occur	Raw or insufficiently cooked fresh water fish	Stools	Inadequate cooking, inadequate sewage disposal, sewage contamin-ated lakes
Giardiasis	Giardia lamblia from feces of humans	1 to 6 weeks	Abdominal pain, mucoid diarrhea, fatty stools	Raw vegetables and fruits, water	Stools	Poor personal hygiene, infected workers touching foods, inadequate sewage disposal
Pork tapeworm infection (Taeniasis)	Taenia solium from flesh of infected swine	3 to 6 months	Vague discomfort, hunger pains, loss of weight	Raw or insufficiently cooked pork	Stools	Lack of meat inspection, inadequate cooking, inadequate sewage disposal, sewage contaminated pastures

NEUROLOGICAL SIGNS & SYMPTOMS (VISUAL DISTURBANCES, TINGLING, PARALYSIS) OCCUR

INCUBATION (LATENCY) PERIOD USUALLY LESS THAN 1 HOUR

FUNGAL AGENTS

Ibotenic acid group of mush-room poisoning	Ibotenic acid and and muscimol in some mushrooms	0.5 to 2 hours	Drowsiness and dizziness, state of intoxication, confu-sion, muscular spasms, delirium, visual disturbances	Amanita muscaria, A. pantherina and related species of mushrooms	Vomitus	Eating Amantia muscaria and related species of mushrooms, eating unknown varieties of mushrooms, mistaking toxic mushrooms for edible varieties
Muscarine group of mushroom poisoning	Muscarine in some mushrooms	15 minutes to 2	Excessive salivation, perspiration, tearing, reduced blood pres-sure, irregular pulse, pupils constricted, blurred vision, asth-matic breathing	Clitocybe dealbata, C. rivulosa, and many other species of Inocybe and Boletus mushrooms	Vomitus	Eating muscarine group of mush-rooms, eating unknown varieties of mushrooms, mistaking toxic mush-rooms for edible varieties
Organophos-phorous poisoning	Organic phosphorous insecticides such Parathion, TEPP, Diazinon, Malathion	Few minutes to few hours	Nausea, vomiting, abdominal cramps, diarrhea, headache, nervousness, blurred vision, chest pain, cyanosis, confusion, twitching, convulsions	Any accidentally contaminated food	Blood, urine, fat biopsy	Spraying foods just before harvesting, storing insecticides in same area as foods, mistaking pesticides for powdered foods

TOXIC ANIMALS

Paralytic shellfish Poisoning (PSP)	Saxitoxin and similar toxins from plankton Alexandrium species which are consumed by shellfish	Few minutes to 30 minutes on average, may take up to 2 hrs	Tingling, burning, numbness around lips and finger tips, giddiness, incoherent speech, respiratory paralysis, sometimes fatal	Bivalve molluscan shellfish, e.g., clams mussels, viscera of crabs and lobsters	N/A	Harvesting shellfish from waters with a high concentration of Alexandrium
Tetradon poisoning Aka Fugu (puffer Fish) poisoning	Tetrodotoxin from intestines and gonads of puffer type fish	10 minutes to 3 hrs	Tingling sensation of fingers & toes, dizziness, pallor, numbness of mouth and extremities, gastrointestinal symptoms hemorrage and desquamation of skin, eyes fixed, twitching, paralysis, cyanosis sometimes fatal	Puffer-type fish	N/A	Eating puffer-type fish, failure to effectively remove intestines and gonads from puffer-type fish if they are to be eaten
Neurotoxic shellfish Poisoning (NSP)	Brevetoxins from from Gymnodinium species	few minutes to few hours	Paresthesia, reversal of hot and cold temperature sensations, nausea, vomiting, diarrhea	Shellfish (mussels, clams) from S.E. coastal waters	Gastric washings	Harvesting shellfish from waters with high concentration of Gymnodinium species of dinoflagellates
Amnesic Shellfish Poisoning (ASP) or Domoic Acid	Domoic acid from diatoms (Toxin is heat stable)	30 min. to 24 hrs for gastrointestinal symptoms, neurolog-Ical symptoms within 48 hrs	Initially nausea, vomiting, abdominal pain, diarrhea, neurological signs include: confusion, memory loss, disorientation, seizure, coma, death may occur	Shellfish (mussels, clams), finfish (anchovies), viscera of crabs and lobsters	N.A.	Harvesting shellfish, crabs and finfish from waters which experience plankton blooms releasing domoic acid in the harvesting area
Diarrhetic shellfish Poisoning (DSP)	LISTED PREVIOUSLY					THIS IS NOT A NEUROLOGICAL ILLNESS, BUT IS INCLUDED HERE FOR EASE OF REFERENCE WITH ALL SHELLFISH POISONINGS.

PLANT TOXICANTS

Jimson weed	Tropane alkaloids in Jimson weed	Less than 1 hour	Abnormal thirst, photophobia, distorted sight, difficulty in speaking, flushing, delirium, coma, rapid heart beat	Any part of a plant, tomatoes grafted to Jimson weed stock	Urine	Eating any part of Jimson weed or eating tomatoes from tomato plant grafted to Jimson weed stock
Water hemlock Poisoning	Resin and cicutoxin in hemlock root	15 to 60 minutes	Excessive salivation, nausea, vomiting, Stomach pain, frothing at mouth, irregular breathing, convulsions, respiratory paralysis	Root of water hemlock Cicuta virosa and C. masculate	Urine	Eating water hemlock, mistaking water hemlock root for wild parsnip, sweet potato or carrot

INCUBATION (LATENCY) PERIOD 1-6 HOURS
CHEMICAL AGENTS

Chlorinated hydrocarbon poisoning	Chlorinated hydrocarbon insecticides such as aldrin, chlordane, ddt, endrin, lindane, & toxaphene	30 minutes to 6 hrs	Nausea, vomiting, paresthesis, dizziness muscular weakness, anorexia, weight loss, confusion	Any accidentally contaminated food	Blood, urine, stools gastric washings	Storing insecticides in same area as food, mistaking insecticides for powdered food

TOXIC ANIMALS

Ciguatera Poisoning	Ciguatoxin in intestines, roe, gonads & flesh of tropical marine fish	3 to 5 hours, sometimes longer	Tingling & numbness about mouth, metallic taste, dry mouth, gastrointestinal symptoms, watery stools, muscular pain, dizziness, dilated eyes, blurred vision, prostration, paralysis, reversal of hot and cold temperature sensations sometimes fatal	Numerous species of tropical fish		Eating liver, intestines, roe, gonads, or flesh of barracuda, large jacks & amberjacks, grouper and other species of tropical reef fish: usually large reef fish are more commonly toxic

INCUBATION (LATENCY) PERIOD USUALLY 12 TO 72 HOURS
BACTERIAL AGENTS

Botulism	Neurotoxins A, B, E & F of Clostridium botulinum spores found in soil & animal intestines	2 hours to 8 days, mean 18 to 36 hrs	Vertigo, double or blurred vision, dryness of mouth, difficulty in swallowing, speaking and breathing, descending muscular weakness, constipation, pupils dilated or fixed, respiratory paralysis, gastrointestinal symptoms may precede neurological symptoms, frequently fatal	Home canned low acid foods, vacuum packed fish; fermented fish eggs, fish and marine mammals	Blood, stool	Inadequate heat processing of canned foods and smoked fish, uncontrolled fermentation

INCUBATION (LATENCY) PERIOD GREATER THAN 72 HOURS
CHEMICAL AGENTS

Mercury poisoning	Methyl & ethyl mercury compounds from industrial waste and organic mercury in fungicides	1 week or longer	Numbness, weakness of legs, spastic paralysis, impairment of vision, blindness, coma	Grains treated with mercury containing fungicide; pork, fish, & shellfish exposed to mercury compounds	Urine, blood, hair	Streams polluted with mercury compounds, feeding animals grains treated with mercury fungicides, eating mercury treated grains or animals fed such grains
Triorthocresyl Phosphate Poisoning	Triorthocresyl phosphate used as extracts or as substitute cooking oil	5 to 21 days, mean 10 days	Gastrointestinal symptoms, leg pain, ungainly high stepping gait, foot and wrist drop	Cooking oils, extracts and other foods contaminated with triorthocresyl phosphate	N/A	Using compound as food extractant or as cooking or salad oil

<u>GENERALIZED INFECTION SIGNS AND SYMPTOMS (FEVER, CHILL, MALAISE, ACHES) OCCUR</u>

INCUBATION (LATENCY) PERIOD GREATER THAN 72 HOURS
BACTERIAL AGENTS

Brucellosis	Brucella abortus, B. melitensis, and B. suis from tissues & milk of infected animals	7 to 21 days	Fever, chills, sweats, weakness, malaise, headache, muscle and joint pain, loss of weight	Raw milk, goat cheese	Blood	Failure to pasteurize milk, livestock infected with brucellae
Typhoid fever	Salmonella Typhi from feces of infected humans	7 to 28 days, mean 14 days	Malaise, headache, fever, cough, nausea, vomiting, constipation, abdominal pain, chills, rose spots, bloody stools	Shellfish, foods contaminated by workers, raw milk, cheese, watercress, water	Stools, rectal swabs blood	Infected workers touching foods, poor personal hygiene, inadequate cooking, inadequate refrigeration, inadequate sewage disposal, obtaining foods from unsafe sources, harvesting shellfish from sewage contaminated areas
Listeriosis	Listeria monocytogenes from soil, manure, silage and environment	3 to 21 days, maybe longer	Low grade fever, flu-like illness, stillbirths, meningitis, encephalitis, sepsis, fatalities occur	Cole slaw, milk, cheese, animal products	Blood, urine, cerebrospinal fluid	Inadequate cooking, failure to properly pasteurize milk, prolonged refrigeration, immunosuppressed, pregnant, aged persons, and neonates are at high risk
Vibrio vulnificus Septicemia	Vibrio vulnificus from sea water	16 hr mean = 24 hr	Malaise, chills, fever, prostration, cutaneous lesions, fatalities occur	Raw shellfish and crabs	Blood	Eating raw shellfish, inadequate cooking, persons with liver damage are at high risk

VIRAL AGENTS

Hepatitis A (Infectious hepatitis)	Hepatitis A virus from feces, urine, blood of infected humans and other primates	10 to 50 days, mean 25 days	Fever, malaise, lassitude, anorexia, nausea, abdominal pain, jaundice	Shellfish, any food contaminated by hepatitis viruses, water	Urine, blood	Infected workers touching foods, poor personal hygiene, inadequate cooking, harvesting shellfish from sewage contaminated waters, inadequate sewage disposal

(Note: Hepatits E is an emerging viral pathogen. It has similar incubation periods and symptoms as Hepatitis A and can be transmitted in foods.)

PARASITIC AGENTS

Angiostrongylaisis (eosinophilic meningoencelplalitis)	Angiostrongylus cantonensis (rat lung worm) from rodent feces and soil	14 to 16 days	Gastroenteritis, headache, stiff neck and back, low-grade fever	Raw crabs, prawns, slugs, shrimp & snails	Blood	Inadequate cooking, ingesting raw food
Toxoplasmosis	Toxoplasma gondii from tissue and flesh of infected animals	10 to 13 days	Fever, headache, myalgia, rash	Raw or insufficiently cooked meat (rare)	Biopsy of lymph nodes, blood	Inadequate cooking of meat of sheep, swine and cattle
Trichinosis	Trichinella spiralis (roundworm) from flesh of infected	4 to 28 days, mean 9 days	Gastroenteritis, fever, edema about eyes, muscular pain, chills,	Pork, bear meat, walrus flesh	Muscle biopsy	Eating raw or inadequately cooked pork or bear meat, inadequate cooking or heat processing, feeding

	swine or bear		prostration, labored breathing			uncooked or inadequately heat processed garbage to swine

ALLERGIC TYPE SYMPTOMS (FACIAL FLUSHING, ITCHING) OCCUR

INCUBATION (LATENCY) PERIOD LESS THAN 1 HOUR BACTERIAL (AND ANIMAL) AGENTS

Scombroid Poisoning or Histaminosis	Histamine-like substance produced by proteus sp. or other bacteria from histidine in fish flesh	Few minutes to 1 hr	Headache, dizziness, nausea, vomiting, peppery taste, burning throat, facial swelling and flushing, stomach pain, itching of skin	Tuna, mackerel, Pacific dolphin (known as the mahi on the Pacific coast of the U.S.), jack, anchovy, marlin, swordfish, bluefish, sometimes from ripened cheese	Vomitus	Inadequate refrigeration of scombroid fish and improper curing of cheese

CHEMICALS

Monosodium glutamate (MSG) poisoning	Excessive amounts of monosodium glutamate (MSG)	Few minutes to 1 hr	Burning sensation in back of neck, forearms chest, feeling of tightness, tingling, flushing, dizziness, headache, nausea	Foods seasoned with MSG	N/A	Using excessive amounts of MSG as flavor intensifier.
Nicotinic acid (niacin) poisoning	Sodium nicotinate used as a color preservative	Few minutes to 1 hr	Flushing, sensation of warmth, itching abdominal pain, puffiness of face and knees	Meat or other food in which sodium nicotinate has been added	N/A	Using sodium nicotinate as color preservative
	Dietary supplements of niacin used chronically	A few days to a few a few months	Impairment of liver function (elevated transaminases), can result in fulminant liver failure	High potency dietary supplements, especially when used in multiples (500mg or more per day)	N/A	Dietary supplements of niacin can cause similar acute symptoms as niacin, but seldom does because of infrequent use at high doses

INCUBATION (LATENCY) PERIOD 1 TO 6 HOURS TOXIC ANIMALS

Hypervitaminosis A	Vitamin A containing foods or dietary supplements	Acute: 1 to 6 hours	Headache, gastrointestinal symptoms, dizziness, collapse, convulsions, desquamation of skin	Liver & kidney of arctic mammals	Blood	Eating liver & kidney from cold region animals
		Chronic: days to months or years	Chronic use can cause liver disease, including cirrhosis	High potency dietary supplements, especially with chronic use	N/A or Blood?	Chronic usage of dietary supplements containing 25,000 IU vitamin A or more per day

1. Symptoms and incubation periods will vary with the individual and group exposed because of resistance, age, and nutritional status of individuals, number of organism or concentration of poison in ingested foods, amount of food ingested, pathogenicity and virulence of strains of microorganisms or toxicity of chemical involved. Several of the illnesses are manifested by symptoms in more than one category and have an incubation range that overlaps the generalized categories.
2. A more detailed review can be found in:
   A. Bryan, F.L. 1982, Diseases Transmitted by Foods (A classification and summary), second edition, Centers for Disease Control, Atlanta, GA.
   B. Rhodehamel, E.J., Editor, 1992, "Foodborne Pathogenic Microorganisms and Natural Toxins", Third Edition, Food and Drug Administration, Washington, D.C.
   C. Bryan, F.L., Chairman, Committee on Communicable Diseases Affecting Man, 1999, "Procedures to Investigate Foodborne Illness" Fifth edition, International Association of Milk, Food, and Environmental Sanitarians, Inc., Ames, IA
3. Samples of any of the listed foods that have been ingested during the incubation period of the disease should be collected.
4. Carbon monoxide poisoning may simulate some of the diseases listed in this category. Patients who have been in closed care with motors running or have been in rooms with improperly vented heaters are subject to exposure to carbon monoxide.

Exhibit 8-7: Form FDA-3042

DEPARTMENT OF HEALTH AND HUMAN SERVICES
FOOD AND DRUG ADMINISTRATION

FOOD ILLNESS INVESTIGATION

1. NAME OF PERSON	3. OCCUPATION		
Jon R. Roe	Teacher - High School		
2. ADDRESS a. STREET	4. TELEPHONE NO.	5. AGE	6. SEX
321 Main St. N.W.	515-557-2145	35	M
b. CITY, STATE, & ZIP CODE	7. DID THE PERSON EAT ANY OF THE SUSPECT MEAL? ☒ YES ☐ NO		
Centerville, IA 52411	8. DID THE PERSON BECOME ILL? ☒ YES ☐ NO		

9. FOOD INJESTED (Names and types, Trade names, frozen, canned, dried, etc.)	10. METHOD OF FOOD PREPARATION	11. QUANTITY INJESTED	12. INJESTED a. DATE	12. INJESTED b. TIME	13. CODES OF SUSPECT CONTAINER
"Yummy Brand"	Consumed as purchased	2 oz.	11-8-05	6:30 am	XYZ-74
Cream-filled Donut					
"Better Brand" canned	" " "	4 oz.	11-8-05	6:30 am	3-2-3-A
Orange Juice					
"ABC" Corn Flakes	" " "		11-8-05	6:30 am	None
"Best" Dairy Grade A Milk	" " "		11-8-05	6:30 am	None

(Continue on additional forms if necessary)

14. SYMPTOMS a. SYMPTOMS (check)	b. DATE BEGAN	c. TIME BEGAN	d. HOURS DURATION
☐ NAUSEA			
☐ VOMITING			
☒ DIARRHEA	11-8-05	2:30 pm	6
☒ FEVER	11-8-05	2:30 pm	6
☒ PROSTRATION	11-8-05	2:30 pm	6
☐ PARALYSIS			
☒ OTHER (See Remarks)	11-8-05	2:30 pm	6

15. PHYSICIAN
- a. NAME: Thomas Meedic, M.D.
- b. STREET ADDRESS: 323 Broad St. N.W.
- c. CITY: Centerville
- d. STATE: IA
- e. ZIP CODE: 52412
- f. TELEPHONE NO.: 515-532-3334

16. HOSPITAL
- a. NAME: N/A
- b. STREET ADDRESS: --------
- c. CITY: --------
- d. STATE: --------
- e. ZIP CODE: --------
- f. TELEPHONE NO.: --------

17. REMARKS (Use reverse side if necessary)

Only product available for sampling was the cream filled donuts which sampled as INV 361245

14. cramps

18. DATE OF INVESTIGATION	19. OFFICE	20. EMPLOYEE(S) NAME	21. TITLE
11-9-05	KAN-DO	Sidney H. Rogers	Investigator

FORM FDA 3042 (10/05) PREVIOUS EDITION MAY BE USED

Exhibits

Exhibit 8-8: Attack Rate Table

ATTACK RATE TABLE

Food or Beverage	Group A Persons Who Ate Specified Foods				Group B Persons Who Did Note Eat Specified Foods			
	Ill	Not Ill	Total	Attack Rate %	Ill	Not Ill	Total	Attack Rate %
Baked ham............	29	17	46	63	17	12	29	59
Spinach................	26	17	43	60	20	12	32	62
Mashed potato......	23	14	37	62	23	14	37	62
Cabbage salad.......	18	10	28	64	28	19	47	60
Jell-O..................	16	7	23	70	30	22	52	58
Rolls....................	21	16	37	57	25	13	38	66
Brown bread.........	18	9	27	67	28	20	48	58
Milk.....................	2	2	4	50	44	27	71	62
Coffee..................	19	12	31	61	27	17	44	61
Water...................	13	11	24	54	33	18	51	65
Cakes...................	27	13	40	67	19	16	35	54
Ice cream (van.)....	43	11	54	(80)	3	18	21	(14)
Ice cream (choc.)..	25	22	47	53	20	7	27	74
Fruit salad............	4	2	6	67	42	27	69	61

To compute the attack rate in per cent, divide the number who became ill by the number who ate the food item and multiply by 100. (In the above example, baked ham 29 ÷ 46 x 100 = 63%). The offending food will show the greatest difference between the two attack rate percentages. The offending food should have a higher attack rate in "Group A" and a lower attack rate in "Group B". For example, in the table above, the attack rate for persons who ate vanilla ice cream (the offending food in the outbreak cited) was 80% while the attack rate for persons who did not eat vanilla ice cream was 14%. The disparity between the persons in "Group A" and "Group B" is the important point.

Exhibit 8-9: Epidemic Curve

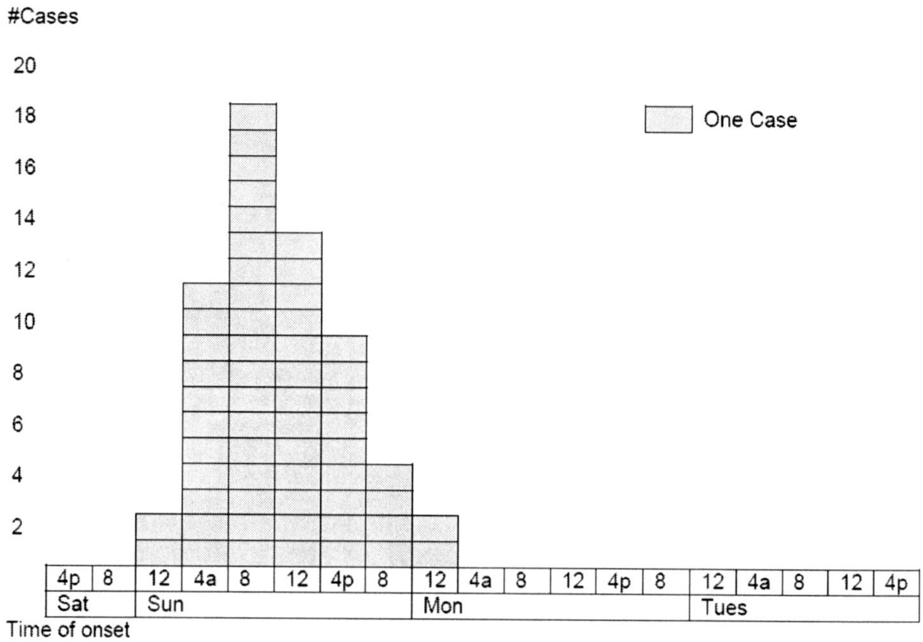

Epidemic curve of a common-source outbreak

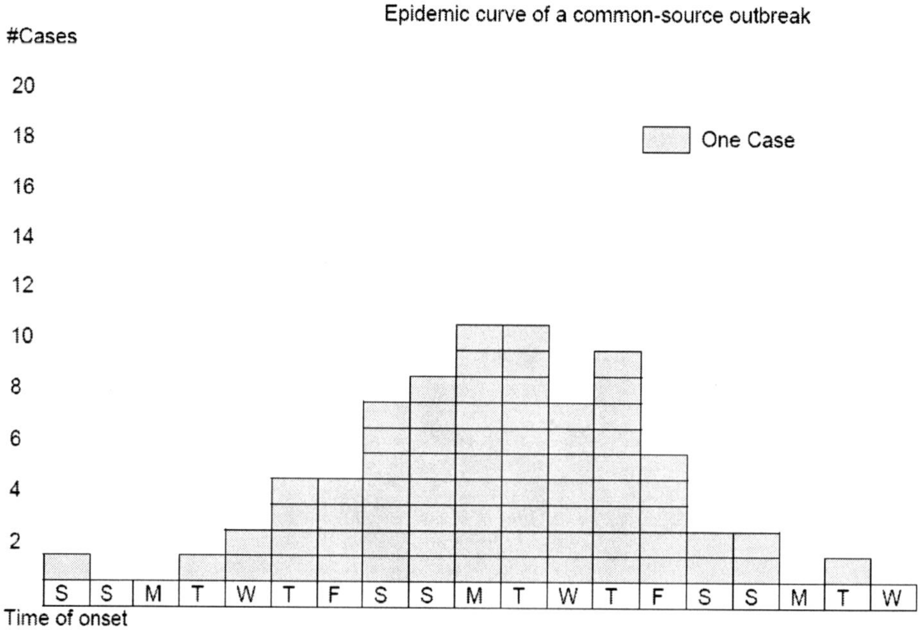

Epidemic curve of a person-to-person transmitted outbreak

Exhibits

Exhibit 8-10: Medwatch Form

U.S. Department of Health and Human Services

MEDWATCH

The FDA Safety Information and Adverse Event Reporting Program

For VOLUNTARY reporting of adverse events, product problems and product use errors

Page ____ of ____

Form Approved: OMB No. 0910-0291, Expires: 10/31/08
See OMB statement on reverse.

FDA USE ONLY

Triage unit sequence #

PLEASE TYPE OR USE BLACK INK

A. PATIENT INFORMATION

1. Patient Identifier	2. Age at Time of Event, or Date of Birth:	3. Sex	4. Weight
In confidence		☐ Female ☐ Male	____ lb or ____ kg

B. ADVERSE EVENT, PRODUCT PROBLEM OR ERROR

Check all that apply:

1. ☐ Adverse Event ☐ Product Problem *(e.g., defects/malfunctions)*
   ☐ Product Use Error ☐ Problem with Different Manufacturer of Same Medicine

2. Outcomes Attributed to Adverse Event *(Check all that apply)*

☐ Death: ____________ *(mm/dd/yyyy)*
☐ Disability or Permanent Damage
☐ Life-threatening
☐ Congenital Anomaly/Birth Defect
☐ Hospitalization - initial or prolonged
☐ Other Serious (Important Medical Events)
☐ Required Intervention to Prevent Permanent Impairment/Damage (Devices)

3. Date of Event *(mm/dd/yyyy)*

4. Date of this Report *(mm/dd/yyyy)*

5. Describe Event, Problem or Product Use Error

6. Relevant Tests/Laboratory Data, Including Dates

7. Other Relevant History, Including Preexisting Medical Conditions *(e.g., allergies, race, pregnancy, smoking and alcohol use, liver/kidney problems, etc.)*

C. PRODUCT AVAILABILITY

Product Available for Evaluation? *(Do not send product to FDA)*

☐ Yes ☐ No ☐ Returned to Manufacturer on: ____________ *(mm/dd/yyyy)*

D. SUSPECT PRODUCT(S)

1. Name, Strength, Manufacturer *(from product label)*

#1

#2

2.	Dose or Amount	Frequency	Route
#1			
#2			

3. Dates of Use *(If unknown, give duration) from/to (or best estimate)*

#1

#2

4. Diagnosis or Reason for Use *(Indication)*

#1

#2

5. Event Abated After Use Stopped or Dose Reduced?

#1 ☐ Yes ☐ No ☐ Doesn't Apply

#2 ☐ Yes ☐ No ☐ Doesn't Apply

6. Lot #

#1

#2

7. Expiration Date

#1

#2

8. Event Reappeared After Reintroduction?

#1 ☐ Yes ☐ No ☐ Doesn't Apply

#2 ☐ Yes ☐ No ☐ Doesn't Apply

9. NDC # or Unique ID

E. SUSPECT MEDICAL DEVICE

1. Brand Name

2. Common Device Name

3. Manufacturer Name, City and State

4. Model #	Lot #
Catalog #	Expiration Date *(mm/dd/yyyy)*
Serial #	Other #

5. Operator of Device

☐ Health Professional
☐ Lay User/Patient
☐ Other:

6. If Implanted, Give Date *(mm/dd/yyyy)*

7. If Explanted, Give Date *(mm/dd/yyyy)*

8. Is this a Single-use Device that was Reprocessed and Reused on a Patient?

☐ Yes ☐ No

9. If Yes to Item No. 8, Enter Name and Address of Reprocessor

F. OTHER (CONCOMITANT) MEDICAL PRODUCTS

Product names and therapy dates *(exclude treatment of event)*

G. REPORTER *(See confidentiality section on back)*

1. Name and Address

Phone #

E-mail

2. Health Professional? ☐ Yes ☐ No

3. Occupation

4. Also Reported to:

☐ Manufacturer
☐ User Facility
☐ Distributor/Importer

5. If you do NOT want your identity disclosed to the manufacturer, place an "X" in this box: ☐

FORM FDA 3500 (10/05) Submission of a report does not constitute an admission that medical personnel or the product caused or contributed to the event.

Exhibit 8-11: Vaccine Adverse Event Report System

WEBSITE: www.vaers.org E-MAIL: info@vaers.org FAX: 1-877-721-0366

VACCINE ADVERSE EVENT REPORTING SYSTEM
24 Hour Toll-Free Information 1-800-822-7967
P.O. Box 1100, Rockville, MD 20849-1100
PATIENT IDENTITY KEPT CONFIDENTIAL

VAERS

For CDC/FDA Use Only
VAERS Number ______
Date Received ______

Patient Name: ______
Last First M.I.
Address ______
City State Zip
Telephone no. (___) ______

Vaccine administered by (Name): ______
Responsible Physician ______
Facility Name/Address ______
City State Zip
Telephone no. (___) ______

Form completed by (Name): ______
Relation to Patient ☐ Vaccine Provider ☐ Patient/Parent ☐ Manufacturer ☐ Other
Address *(if different from patient or provider)* ______
City State Zip
Telephone no. (___) ______

1. State
2. County where administered
3. Date of birth __/__/__ mm dd yy
4. Patient age
5. Sex ☐M ☐F
6. Date form completed __/__/__ mm dd yy

7. Describe adverse events(s) (symptoms, signs, time course) and treatment, if any

8. Check all appropriate:
☐ Patient died (date __/__/__ mm dd yy)
☐ Life threatening illness
☐ Required emergency room/doctor visit
☐ Required hospitalization (____days)
☐ Resulted in prolongation of hospitalization
☐ Resulted in permanent disability
☐ None of the above

9. Patient recovered ☐YES ☐NO ☐UNKNOWN

10. Date of vaccination __/__/__ mm dd yy Time ____ AM PM

11. Adverse event onset __/__/__ mm dd yy Time ____ AM PM

12. Relevant diagnostic tests/laboratory data

13. Enter all vaccines given on date listed in no. 10

	Vaccine (type)	Manufacturer	Lot number	Route/Site	No. Previous Doses
a.					
b.					
c.					
d.					

14. Any other vaccinations within 4 weeks prior to the date listed in no. 10

	Vaccine (type)	Manufacturer	Lot number	Route/Site	No. Previous doses	Date given
a.						
b.						

15. Vaccinated at:
☐ Private doctor's office/hospital ☐ Military clinic/hospital
☐ Public health clinic/hospital ☐ Other/unknown

16. Vaccine purchased with:
☐ Private funds ☐ Military funds
☐ Public funds ☐ Other/unknown

17. Other medications

18. Illness at time of vaccination (specify)

19. Pre-existing physician-diagnosed allergies, birth defects, medical conditions (specify)

20. Have you reported this adverse event previously? ☐ No ☐ To health department ☐ To doctor ☐ To manufacturer

21. Adverse event following prior vaccination (check all applicable, specify)

	Adverse Event	Onset Age	Type Vaccine	Dose no. in series
☐ In patient				
☐ In brother or sister				

Only for children 5 and under
22. Birth weight ____ lb. ____ oz.
23. No. of brothers and sisters

Only for reports submitted by manufacturer/immunization project
24. Mfr./imm. proj. report no.
25. Date received by mfr./imm.proj.
26. 15 day report? ☐ Yes ☐ No
27. Report type ☐ Initial ☐ Follow-Up

Health care providers and manufacturers are required by law (42 USC 300aa-25) to report reactions to vaccines listed in the Table of Reportable Events Following Immunization. Reports for reactions to other vaccines are voluntary except when required as a condition of immunization grant awards.

Form VAERS-1(FDA)

"Fold in thirds, tape & mail — DO NOT STAPLE FORM"

NO POSTAGE NECESSARY IF MAILED IN THE UNITED STATES OR APO/FPO

BUSINESS REPLY MAIL

FIRST-CLASS MAIL PERMIT NO. 1895 ROCKVILLE, MD

POSTAGE WILL BE PAID BY ADDRESSEE

VAERS
P.O. Box 1100
Rockville MD 20849-1100

DIRECTIONS FOR COMPLETING FORM

(Additional pages may be attached if more space is needed.)

GENERAL

- Use a separate form for each patient. Complete the form to the best of your abilities. Items 3, 4, 7, 8, 10, 11, and 13 are considered essential and should be completed whenever possible. Parents/Guardians may need to consult the facility where the vaccine was administered for some of the information (such as manufacturer, lot number or laboratory data.)
- Refer to the Reportable Events Table (RET) for events mandated for reporting by law. Reporting for other serious events felt to be related but not on the RET is encouraged.
- Health care providers other than the vaccine administrator (VA) treating a patient for a suspected adverse event should notify the VA and provide the information about the adverse event to allow the VA to complete the form to meet the VA's legal responsibility.
- These data will be used to increase understanding of adverse events following vaccination and will become part of CDC Privacy Act System 09-20-0136, "Epidemiologic Studies and Surveillance of Disease Problems". Information identifying the person who received the vaccine or that person's legal representative will not be made available to the public, but may be available to the vaccinee or legal representative.
- Postage will be paid by addressee. Forms may be photocopied (must be front & back on same sheet).

SPECIFIC INSTRUCTIONS

Form Completed By: To be used by parents/guardians, vaccine manufacturers/distributors, vaccine administrators, and/or the person completing the form on behalf of the patient or the health professional who administered the vaccine.

Item 7: Describe the suspected adverse event. Such things as temperature, local and general signs and symptoms, time course, duration of symptoms, diagnosis, treatment and recovery should be noted.

Item 9: Check "YES" if the patient's health condition is the same as it was prior to the vaccine, "NO" if the patient has not returned to the pre-vaccination state of health, or "UNKNOWN" if the patient's condition is not known.

Item 10 and 11: Give dates and times as specifically as you can remember. If you do not know the exact time, please indicate "AM" or "PM" when possible if this information is known. If more than one adverse event, give the onset date and time for the most serious event.

Item 12: Include "negative" or "normal" results of any relevant tests performed as well as abnormal findings.

Item 13: List ONLY those vaccines given on the day listed in Item 10.

Item 14: List any other vaccines that the patient received within 4 weeks prior to the date listed in item 10.

Item 16: This section refers to how the person who gave the vaccine purchased it, not to the patient's insurance.

Item 17: List any prescription or non-prescription medications the patient was taking when the vaccine(s) was given.

Item 18: List any short term illnesses the patient had on the date the vaccine(s) was given (i.e., cold, flu, ear infection).

Item 19: List any pre-existing physician-diagnosed allergies, birth defects, medical conditions (including developmental and/or neurologic disorders) for the patient.

Item 21: List any suspected adverse events the patient, or the patient's brothers or sisters, may have had to previous vaccinations. If more than one brother or sister, or if the patient has reacted to more than one prior vaccine, use additional pages to explain completely. For the onset age of a patient, provide the age in months if less than two years old.

Item 26: This space is for manufacturers' use only.

Exhibit 8-12: Natural Disaster Form FD - 2809

NATURAL DISASTER REPORT

ESTABLISHMENT *(Name and Address)*	DATE OF VISIT
	KIND OF DISASTER *(Fire, flood, etc. If hurricane give name)*
TYPE OF BUSINESS *(Warehouse, coldstorage, candy manufacturer, etc.)*	DISPOSITION CODE *A – State or local seizure* *B – Destruction* *C – Converted to animal feed* *D – Converted to industrial use* *E – Further follow-up needed (Give date)*

PRODUCTS REQUIRING DESTRUCTION, CONVERSION, OR SEGREGATION

	DESCRIPTION *(E.g. 20, 100 lb. cloth bags flour)*	APPROXIMATE VALUE	DISPOSITION CODE *(More than one letter may be used where necessary)*
1			
2			
3			
4			
5			
6			
7			
8			
9			
10			
11			
12			
13			
14			
15			

SAMPLE NOS. *(If any)*	SUMMARY	
	DESTROYED	CONVERTED TO NON-HUMAN USE
REMARKS *(Include comments on method of destruction, denaturing, etc.)*	Food *(Lbs.)*	
	Drug	
	Cosmetic	
	Device	
	Sundry	
INSPECTOR	AGENCY	
INSPECTOR	AGENCY	

FORM FDA 2809 (9/05)

Exhibits

Exhibit 8-13: Form FDA-457

1. HOME DISTRICT	2. REPORTING UNIT SYMBOL	3. CENTRAL FILE NO.	4. J.D./T.A.	5. COUNTY	6. DATE
NWE	NOL	1234567	----	----	8-2-99

7. PRODUCT CODE	8. OPERATION	9. PROGRAM ASSIGNMENT CODE	10. HOURS
45AF-19	13	09001	1/2

11. IDENTIFICATION *(Quote pertinent labeling including Establishment name and address)*
"NO CLUMP" BRAND ANTI-CAKING AGENT
CLUMPLESS CORP. 3214 WHARF AVE.
WALTHAM, MA 02154

12. MANUFACTURER CONTROL CODES *(Labels, packaging and shipping containers)*	13. AMOUNT ON HAND	14. DATE LOT RECEIVED
BAGS CODED: "AC 123171"	1200/100# BAGS	7-15-99
	15. ESTIMATED VALUE	16. SAMPLE NO(s).
	$ 24,000.00	NONE

17. DEALER *(Name, street address, city, state, and ZIP code)*
CREOLE INDUSTRIES
239 CANAL ST.
NEW ORLEANS, LA 70130

18. ☐ DISTRIBUTOR ☐ SHIPPER ☒ MANUFACTURER ☐ OTHER
(Name, street address, city, state, ZIP code, and telephone)
CLUMPLESS CORP.
3214 WHARF AVE.
WALTHAM, MA 02154
(617) 765-4321

19. ESTABLISHMENT TYPE(S)	INDUSTRY CODE 1	2	3	4	5	6
a. Manufacturer	4 5					
b.						
c.						

20. ESTABLISHMENT SIZE *($ VOLUME)*

21. INFORMATION OBTAINED BY *(Check one)*	
	MAIL
	TELEPHONE
XXX	VISIT

22. REMARKS

23. REPORT PREPARED BY *(Type or print name and title)*	24. EMPLOYEE NO.	25. PC	26. SIGNATURE
Sidney H. Rogers, Investigator	075	2	*Sidney H. Rogers*

27. REPORTING UNIT ACTION
☒ REFERRED TO HOME DISTRICT ☒ ADD TO ACTIVE OEI
☐ COLLECT OFFICIAL SAMPLE ☐ ROUTINE FOLLOW-UP
☐ REFERRED TO STATE OR OTHER FEDERAL AUTHORITIES ☐ INSPECT
☐ REINSPECT ☐ MAKE INVESTIGATION ☐ NO ACTION
☐ REFERRED TO HDQTRS ____________ (Routing Symbol)

28. NAME OF REVIEWING OFFICIAL *(Type or print)*
Harry Abelman

29. TITLE	30. DATE REVIEWED
Supervisory Investigator	9-2-99

FORM FDA 457 (5/90) PREVIOUS EDITION MAY BE USED **PRODUCT/ESTABLISHMENT SURVEILLANCE REPORT**

Exhibit 8-14: Federal Anti-Tampering Act

Federal Anti-Tampering Act

Public Law 98-127 - OCT. 13, 1983

98th Congress

An Act

To amend title 18 of the United States Code to prohibit certain tampering with consumer products, and for other purposes. (Oct. 13, 1983, [S. 216])

Be it enacted by the Senate and House of Representatives of the United States of America in Congress assembled, That this Act may be cited as the "Federal Anti-Tampering Act". (Federal Anti-Tampering Act. 18 USC 1365 note.)

SEC. 2 Chapter 65 of title 18 of the United States Code is amended by adding at the end thereof the following new section:

"§ 1365. Tampering with consumer products

"(a) Whoever, with reckless disregard for the risk that another person will be placed in danger of death or bodily injury and under circumstances manifesting extreme indifference to such risk, tampers with any consumer product that affects interstate or foreign commerce, or the labeling of, or container for, any such product, or attempts to do so, shall-

"(1) in the case of an attempt, be fined not more than $25,000 or imprisoned not more than ten years, or both;

"(2) if death of an individual results, be fined not more than $100,000 or imprisoned for any term of years or for life, or both;

"(3) if serious bodily injury to any individual results, be fined not more than $100,000 or imprisoned not more than twenty years, or both; and

"(4) in any other case, be fined not more than $50,000 or imprisoned not more than ten years, or both.

"(b) Whoever, with intent to cause serious injury to the business of any person, taints any consumer product or renders materially false or misleading the labeling of, or container for, a consumer product, if such consumer product affects interstate of foreign commerce, shall be fined not more than $10,000 or imprisoned not more than three years, or both.

"(c)(1) Whoever knowingly communicates false information that a consumer product has been tainted, if such product or the results of such communication affect interstate or foreign commerce, and if such tainting, had it occurred, would create a risk of death or bodily injury to another person, shall be fined not more than $25,000 or imprisoned not more than five years, or both.

"(2) As used in paragraph (1) of this subsection, the term 'communicates false information' means communicates information that is false and that the communicator knows is false, under circumstances in which the information may reasonably be expected to be believed.

"(d) Whoever knowingly threatens, under circumstances in which the threat may reasonably be expected to be believed, that conduct that, if it occurred, would violate subsection (a) of this section will occur, shall be fined not more than $25,000 or imprisoned not more than five years, or both.

"(e) Whoever is a party to a conspiracy of two or more persons to commit an offense under subsection (a) of this section, if any of the parties intentionally engages in any conduct in furtherance of such offense, shall be fined not more than $25,000 or imprisoned not more than ten years, or both.

"(f) In addition to any other agency which has authority to investigate violations of this section, the Food and Drug Administration and the Department of Agriculture, respectively, have authority to investigate violations of this section involving a consumer product that is regulated by a provision of law such Administration or Department, as the case may be, administers.

"(g) As used in this section-

"(1) the term 'consumer product' means-

"(A) any 'food', 'drug', 'device', or 'cosmetic', as those terms are respectively defined in section 201 of the Federal Food, Drug, and Cosmetic Act (21 U.S.C. 321); or

"(B) any article, product, or commodity which is customarily produced or distributed for consumption by individuals, or use by individuals for purposes of personal care or in the performance of services ordinarily rendered within the household, and which is designed to be consumed or expended in the course of such consumption or use;

"(2) the term 'labeling' has the meaning given such term in section 201(m) of the Federal Food, Drug, and Cosmetic Act (21 U.S.C. 321(m));

"(3) the term 'serious bodily injury' means bodily injury which involves-

"(A) a substantial risk of death;

"(B) extreme physical pain;

"(C) protracted and obvious disfigurement; or

"(D) protracted loss or impairment of the function of a bodily member, organ, or mental faculty; and

"(4) the term 'bodily injury' means-

"(A) a cut, abrasion, bruise, burn, or disfigurement;

"(B) physical pain;

"(C) illness;

"(D) impairment of the function of a bodily member, organ, or mental faculty; or

"(E) any other injury to the body, no matter how temporary.".

SEC. 3. The table of sections at the beginning of chapter 65 of title 18 of the United States Code is amended by adding at the end thereof the following new item:

"1365. Tampering with consumer products."

Sample Schedules

CONTENT		VERSION DATE
Sample Schedule 1:	Salmonella Sampling Plan	June 11, 2009
Sample Schedule 2:	Sample Scheduling For Canned And Acidified Foods	June 11, 2009
Sample Schedule 3:	Pesticide Samples	June 11, 2009
Sample Schedule 4:	Wheat Carload Sampling	June 11, 2009
Sample Schedule 5:	Imported Whitefish Sampling Schedule	June 11, 2009
Sample Schedule 6:	Mycotoxin Sample Sizes	June 11, 2009
Sample Schedule 7:	Canned Fruit - Fill Of Container - Authentic Pack	June 11, 2009
Sample Schedule 8:	Imports - Coffee, Dates, and Date Material	June 11, 2009
Sample Schedule 9:	Sampling Schedule For Color Containing Products Color Additives	June 11, 2009
Sample Schedule 10:	Drug Sampling Schedules (Does not include Antibiotic Preparations)	June 11, 2009
Sample Schedule 11:	Veterinary Products, Feeds, & By-Products For Animal Feeds	June 11, 2009
Sample Schedule 12:	Medicated Animal Feeds Sampling	June 11, 2009
Sample Schedule 13:	Allergen Sample Schedule	June 11, 2009

Sample Schedule 1: Salmonella Sampling Plan

Purpose:

To determine the presence of Salmonella in processed foods intended for human consumption.

Applicability

This sampling plan is applicable to the inspection of either a continuing series of production lots or to isolated lots consisting of an identifiable collection of process units (cans, bags, packages, or similar units). This plan is for use by FDA for regulatory purposes.

Food Categories:

Foods are listed in three categories based on the number of Salmonella hazards and whether a food is to be consumed by infants, the aged, or infirm.

The three defined Salmonella Hazards of foods are:

1. The food or an ingredient of the food is a significant potential source of Salmonella;.

2. The manufacturing process does not include a controlled step that destroys Salmonella; and

3. The food has significant potential for microbiological growth if "abused" in distribution or by consumers.

Classification of Foods:

Foods have been classified into three food Categories for regulatory sampling purposes. The foods are listed in the Categories by Product Code sequence.

NOTE: *For products not listed, check with your supervisor. The District will request categorization from the Office of Field Programs/Center for Food Safety and Applied Nutrition (HFS-600), or, when time is of essence, the District will make the categorization and obtain later concurrence from CFSAN.*

Category I

This includes all foods that would normally be in Category II except that they are intended for consumption by the aged, the infirm, and infants.

Category II

This includes the foods that would not normally be subjected to a process lethal to Salmonella between the time of sampling and consumption. Examples are as follows:

PRODUCT CODE	FOOD ITEM
03	Bread, rolls, buns, sugared breads, crackers, custard and cream filled sweet goods
05	Breakfast cereals, ready to eat
07	Pretzels, chips and specialty items
09	Butter and butter products; pasteurized milk and raw fluid milk and fluid milk products for consumption; pasteurized and unpasteurized concentrated liquid milk products for consumption; dried milk and dried milk products for consumption

12	Cheese and Cheese products
13	Ice cream from pasteurized milk and related products that have been pasteurized; raw ice cream mix and related unpasteurized products for consumption.
14	Pasteurized and unpasteurized imitation dairy products for consumption
15	Pasteurized eggs, egg products from pasteurized eggs; unpasteurized eggs and egg products from unpasteurized eggs for consumption without further cooking
16	Canned and cured fish, vertebrates; other fish products; fresh and frozen raw oysters and raw clams, shellfish and crustacean products; smoked fish, shellfish and crustaceans for consumption
17	Unflavored gelatin
20-22	Fresh, frozen and canned fruits and juices, concentrates and nectars; dried fruit for consumption; jams, jellies, preserves and butters
23	Nuts and nut products for consumption
26	Oils consumed directly without further processing and oleomargarine
27	Dressings and condiments (including mayonnaise) salad dressing and vinegar
28	Spices including salt; flavors and extracts
29	Soft drinks and water
30	Beverage bases
31	Coffee and tea
33	Chewing gum and candy
34	Chocolate and cocoa products
35	Pudding mixes not cooked prior to consumption, gelatin products
36	Syrups, sugars and honey
38	Soups
39	Prepared salads

Category III

This includes the following foods that would normally be subjected to a process lethal to Salmonella between the time of sampling and consumption. Examples are as follows:

PRODUCT CODE	FOOD ITEM
02	Whole grain, processed grain and starch products for human use
04	Macaroni and noodle products
16	Fresh and frozen fish; vertebrates (except that eaten raw); fresh and frozen shellfish and crustaceans (except raw oysters and raw clams for consumption); other aquatic animals (including frog legs)
24	Fresh vegetables, frozen vegetables, dried vegetables, cured and processed vegetable products normally cooked before consumption
26	Vegetable oils, oil stock and vegetable shortening
35	Dry dessert and pudding mixes that are cooked prior to consumption
37	Frozen dinners, multiple food dinners
45-46	Food chemicals (direct additives)

Sample Collection

Each sub will consist of a minimum of 100 gm (approx 3.53 oz). The usual subsample is a consumer size container of a product. Subsamples should be obtained at random to insure that the total sample is representative of the lot. When a lot consists of identifiable subdivisions (e.g., different codes), sub samples should be obtained from subdivisions in the proportion that the subdivisions are to the whole lot.

More than one subsample may be collected from large institutional or bulk containers when the number of sub samples required exceeds the number of containers in the lot. A subsample will consist of more that one container when the lot consists of containers smaller than 100 gm (e.g., 4 - 25 gm containers is a subsample).

When a sample is collected by transferring it to sample containers, a sample control must be submitted which consists of an empty sample container that is exposed to the same conditions under which the sample is collected. See IOM 4.3.6.2 and 4.3.6.4 on controls. Use aseptic technique when sampling from bulk containers.

Sample Size

The following sample sizes also apply to the finished product portion of in-line samples when analyzed for Salmonella. Each subsample will consist of at least 100 gm (approx 3.5 oz).

The 702(b) [21 U.S.C. 372(b)] portion is included in these subsamples, however all subs must be collected for proper analysis. Do not reduce the number of subsamples when collecting import samples.

FOOD CATEGORY	NUMBER OF SAMPLE UNITS (SUBS)
I	60
II	30
III	15

Sample Submission

Submit all samples collected to your district's microbiological servicing laboratory unless directed otherwise by your supervisor or assignment. See IOM 4.5.5.2.

Sample Schedule 2: Sample Scheduling For Canned And Acidified Foods

Canned Foods

Field Examination

1. At the beginning of the inspection, conduct visual exams of warehouse stock for evidence of abnormal cans including swollen and leaking cans, wet cases, swarms of fruit flies around isolated pallets, etc.

2. If the visual exam or inspectional evidence indicates possible problems, such as under processed lots, lots with questionable seam integrity, or abnormal cans, exam the affected lots. Preferably field examine lots that have been warehoused at least 14 days.

3. A lot to be examined will be one production code.

4. Follow the chart below for the field examination. If abnormal containers are found, always collect an official sample of the lot, if possible. For lots with abnormal cans collect an investigational sample ONLY when there is not enough product available to collect an official sample. In all cases, include on the collection report: the lot size, the number of containers examined, and the number of abnormal containers found by type (e.g., hard swells).

5. The chart provides instructions on the number of cans/cases to examine depending on the size of the lot. When the maximum number of containers / cases have been examined for the specified lot size, collect a sample if one or more abnormal containers are found. The exam can be discontinued early based on the number of abnormal containers found. For example, if examining a lot consisting of 3409 or more cans, if 11 abnormal cans are found after examining 1000 cans, discontinue the exam and collect a sample

a. *Flippers.* Only one end is slack or slightly bulged and the end remains flat if pressed in. Cans which bulge when sharply and squarely struck end-down on a flat surface are flippers, provided that the bulged end remains flat when pressed. Flippers result from a lack of vacuum.

b. *Springers.* One end of a can bulges. Manual pressure on the bulged end forces the opposite and out or the same end will spring out with release of pressure. If both ends bulge, but only one will remain flat when pressed, the can is a springer. Springers result from moderate positive pressure in the can. Buckling or extensive denting of the side wall may produce a springer.

c. *Swells.* Both ends of the can are bulged. Neither end will remain flat without pressure. Soft swells yield to manual pressure, but no impression can be made manually on hard swells. Swells result from positive pressure in the can usually because of spoilage of the contents. Some swells, especially in acid products, may result from chemical reaction between the contents and the container. NOTE: Other abnormalities or defects, should be reported on C/R, but not counted as "abnormal containers" for the purposes of the sequential field examination. These other defects include visibly leaking cans, severe dents around seams, gross seam defects, severely rusted containers.

NOTE: Other abnormalities or defects, such as visibly leaking cans, severe dents around seams, gross seam defects, severely rusted containers should be reported on C/R, (with numbers of cans defective cans observed) but not counted as "abnormal containers" for the purposes of the sequential field examination. Do not collect leakers, but report the number observed. It may be necessary to collect samples of other defects (e.g. seam defects) to support observations and document the severity of the defects. In some cases photographs may be a suitable substitute for collection of physical samples.

If a sample is collected, on the C/R. Identify, by sub-sample number, the condition of each container in the sample (e.g., sub-sample 1 - flipper; sub-sample 2 - hard swell;- sub-sample x - normal). Report the results of the warehouse stock examination in the EIR and in FACTs.

See IOM 5.1.5.3

Special Sample Handling: If you are shipping swollen cans, double bag and ground ship the sample. If the cans are moderately swollen or worse you should ship the sample with ice packs.

Uncased Containers		Packed 48/Case		Packed 24/Case		Packed 12/Case		Packed 6/Case		
Lot Sz Contain.	**No. To Examine**	**Lot Size (Cases)**	**Cases To Examine**	**Lotsize (Cases)**	**Cases To Examine**	**Lotsize (Cases)**	**Cases To Examine**	**Lot Size (Cases)**	**Cases To Examine**	**Number Abnormal Containers To Discontinue Examination Early***
192 or less	all	1 - 4	all	1 - 8	all	1 - 16	all	1 - 32	all	3
193 - 288	192	4 - 6	4	8 - 12	8	16 - 24	16	32 - 48	32	5
289 - 384	all for< 298 298 if greater	6 - 8	6	12 - 16	12	24 - 32	25	48 - 64	all < 50 50 if greater	6
385 - 576	363	8 - 12	8	16 -24	15	32 - 48	30	64 - 96	61	7
577 - 912	433	12 - 19	9	24 - 38	18	48 - 76	36	96 - 152	72	8
913 - 1488	480	19 -31	10	38 - 62	20	76 - 124	40	152 - 248	80	9
1489 - 3408	529	31 - 71	11	62 - 142	22	124 - 284	44	248 - 568	88	10
3409 or more	576	71 or more	12	142 or more	24	284 or more	48	568 or more	96	11

Sample Schedules

1. Sample Size for Samples Collected as a Result of a Field Exam:

   a. Official Sample

      The sample will consist of all abnormal containers and the number of normal cans specified under 2. Official Samples below (e.g., if 8 abnormal containers are observed during the examination of a lot containing 696/ 2 lb. cans the sample will consist of the 8 abnormal cans and 48 normal cans, collected 2 cans from each of 24 cases). Open additional cases, if necessary to meet this requirement. This will provide enough product for complete analysis, including: can seam, incubation, aerobic and anaerobic growth, pH and water. Note that the sample size given for normal cans includes the 702(b) portion.

b. Investigational Sample

Samples for laboratory examination will consist of all abnormal and 12 normal containers

2. Other Sampling

Official Samples

a. Filth, Micro, etc. (Includes 702(b) [21U.S.C.372 (b)]portion)

Collect each subdivision to duplicate from a separate case, if possible. Mark subs 1a, 1b, 2a, 2b, etc. Collect as follows:

	Size of Lot	**Min total cans**	**Cans/case**
906 gm (2 lbs.) Net weight and smaller	Up to 50 cases	48	2 from 24
More than 50 cases	96	2 from 48	
Over 906 gm (2 lbs)	Up to 600 cases	48	2 from 24
	More than 600 cases	72	2 from 36

b. Standards Assay (Includes 702(b) portion)

NOTE: Sample sizes listed below are based upon the requirements of the Standards (21 CFR 145.3) When sampling products, which are likely to be non-uniform throughout the lot because of variations from standards of quality, identity, fill-of-container, grade, etc., collect each subdivision in the triplicate from a separate case. Mark subs 1a, 1b, 1c, 2a, 2b, 2c, etc. Collect as follows:

	Number of cans or packages	**Min total cans**	**Cans/case**
1 kg (2.2 lbs) Net weight or less	4800 or less	48	3 from 16
	4801 to 24,000	72	3 from 24
	24,001 to 48,000	96	3 from 32
	48,001 to 84,000	144	3 from 48
	84,001 to 144,000	264	3 from 88
	144,001 to 240,000	384	3 from 128
	Over 240,000	600	3 from 200
Greater than 1 kg (2.2lbs), but less than 4.5 kg (10 lbs.)	2400 or less	48	3 from 16
	2401 to 15000	72	3 from 24
	15001 to 24000	96	3 from 32
	24001 to 42000	144	3 from 48
	42001 to 72000	252	3 from 88

	72001 to 120,000	384	3 from 128
	Over 120,000	600	3 from 200
Greater than 4.5 kg (10 lbs)	600 or less	48	3 from 16
	601 to 2000	72	3 from 24
	2001 to 7200	96	3 from 32
	7201 to 15000	144	3 from 48
	15001 to 24000	252	3 from 88
	24001 to 42000	384	3 from 128
	Over 42000	600	3 from 200

Acidified Foods (Metal or Glass)

A lot is defined as one production code.

Samples must be collected randomly from the entire lot. Sample size does not include 702(b) portion .

1. # 10 size containers - Randomly select 1 normal container from each of 12 randomly selected cases (if available) in the lot.

2. # 2 and smaller - Randomly select 2 normal containers from each of 12 randomly selected cases (if available) in the lot. Sample size is 24 containers.

For acidified products, the equilibrium pH determines whether the product will support organisms of public health significance. Spoilage in such products is usually due to inadequate heat treatment to kill spoilage organisms. Spoilage may be significant because high numbers of microorganisms may affect the adequacy of the thermal process. Molds and some bacteria can grow in an acid environment and actually utilize acid as one of their nutrients; and thus, raise the pH to a level above 4.6 where Clostridium botulinum or other toxin-producing microorganisms can grow.

Microbial spoilage can be detected by observing swollen lids on jars or swollen can ends. The liquid may be turbid and a whitish deposit may be visible on the product or in the bottom of the jar. See DFI Guide to Inspection of Acidified Food Manufacturers for additional information:

http://www.fda.gov/ora/inspect_ref/igs/iglist.html

If you observe abnormal containers conduct an examination following the sequential plan provided for canned foods. Collect all abnormal containers (up to a maximum of 24) in addition to the normal containers collected for pH determination referenced in the table above. Indicate on the C/R the total number of containers examined and the number of each type of abnormality and defect observed. Also indicate the estimated percentage of abnormal containers in the lot.

Sample Schedule 3: Pesticide Samples

DO NOT FUMIGATE PESTICIDE SAMPLES

Introduction

The objectives of FDA's pesticide monitoring program are to gather information on levels and incidence of pesticide residues in the nation's food supply and to initiate enforcement action against shipments of food and feed found to contain illegal pesticide residues. To meet both objectives, it is necessary to collect samples of food and feed for pesticide residue analysis. These instructions describe procedures for collecting samples of raw agricultural commodities and processed commodities. The procedures apply to domestic and import shipments. The instructions include a separate set of procedures for collecting samples for special investigations such as determining levels of pesticide residues in soil, water, and growing crops.

For pesticide samples, the laboratory will maintain a portion of the composited sample as the 702(b) [21U.S.C.372(b)] portion.

Pesticide sample sizes no longer differentiate between Surveillance and Compliance Samples. All pesticide samples will be collected as directed below. Remember to include the state and county or country of origin in the Flag. See IOM 4.4.10.1.8.

For appraisal purposes, you must Flag each Domestic as to the basis for sampling in accordance with the definitions below.

Pesticide Compliance Sample. Collected on a selective basis as a result of inspectional or other evidence of suspected misuse of a pesticide on a food or feed commodity or as a follow-up to a "Pesticide Surveillance Sample" that was found to contain actionable levels of pesticide residues. Flag "Pesticide Compliance".

Pesticide Surveillance Sample. Collected on an objective basis where there is no evidence or suspicion of pesticide misuse on a food or feed commodity. Flag "Pesticide Surveillance".

Districts have the option to collect 1 intact shipping case of fresh produce from packing sheds or large produce warehouses. The one case must meet the minimum sample size specified below. This "one case" option may be used on any import sample or on domestic Pesticide Surveillance Samples, if the collector can be assured that the "one case" collected is representative of the lot or field. If the collector is not assured of this, collect the samples according to the instructions below. This "one case" sampling does not apply to large items such as melons.

NOTE: *If "one case" option is used for surveillance samples of domestic produce, describe in the Remarks Section of the CR, the basis for determining that the sample is representative of the lot or field.*

Plant products: description of primary samples and minimum size of laboratory samples (total weight of all subs or units collected).

	Commodity classification	Examples	Nature of primary samples to be taken	Minimum size of each laboratory sample
Primary Food Commodities of Plant Origin				
1 All fresh fruits, All fresh vegetables, Frozen bulk produce (not retail) except dry pulses				
1.1	small sized products **units generally < 25 g**	berries peas olives	whole units, or packages, or units taken with sampling device	1 kg (2.2 lbs)
1.2	medium sized products **units generally 25 - 250 g**	apples oranges corn on the cob potatoes	whole units, or units taken with sampling device	1 kg (2.2 lbs) (at least 10 units)
1.3	large sized products **units generally > 250 g**	cabbages lettuce cucumbers grapes (bunches, except for sulfites) sweet potatoes	whole units, units taken with sampling device	2 kg(4.4 lbs) (at least 5 units)
2	Pulses, Cereal grains,	soy beans, peas, lentils		1 kg (2.2 lbs)
		rice, wheat (except from rail carloads)		1 kg (2.2 lbs)
	Tree nuts,	(except coconuts)		1 kg (2.2 lbs)
		coconuts		5 units
	Oilseeds,	peanuts		0.5 kg (1.1 lb)
	Seeds for beverages and sweets	coffee beans		0.5 kg (1.1 lb)
3	Herbs(***for dried herbs see section 5 of this Table***)	fresh parsley	whole units or units taken with sampling device	0.5 kg (1.1 lb)
		others, fresh		0.2 kg (0.5 lb)
	Spices	dried	whole units or units taken with sampling device	0.1 kg (0.25 lb)

Primary Animal Feed Commodities			
4.	Primary feed commodities of plant origin		
4.1	Legume animal feeds, and other forages and fodders	whole units, or units taken with sampling device	1 kg (2.2 lbs) (from least 10 units)
4.2	Straw, hay and other dried products	whole units, or units taken with sampling device	0.5 kg(1.1 lbs) (at least 10 units)

See IOM Sample Schedule Chart 4, Wheat Carload Sampling for guidance in the collection of samples by trier from railcars and trucks.

Processed Foods of Plant Origin				
5.	Secondary food commodities of plant origin, **dried fruits, vegetables, herbs, milled cereal products** Derived products of plant origin, **teas, vegetable oils, juices, by-products for animal feed and miscellaneous products** Manufactured foods (single ingredient) of plant origin, Manufactured foods (multi-ingredient) of plant origin, **including products with ingredients of animal origin where the ingredient(s) of plant origin predominate(s), and breads**			
5.1	Products of high unit value		packages or units taken with a sampling device	0.1 kg* (0.25 lb)
5.2	Solid products of low bulk density	Hops, Tea	packaged units, or units taken with a sampling device	0.2 kg(0.5 lbs)
5.3	Other solid products	bread, flour, apple pomace, dried fruit	packages or other whole units, or units taken with a sampling device	0.5 kg (1.1 lbs)
5.4	Liquid products	vegetable oils, juices	packaged units, or units taken with a sampling device	0.5 L or 0.5 kg

* A smaller laboratory sample may be taken from a product of exceptionally high value but the reason for doing so should be noted in the collection report.

Eggs and Dairy Products			
6.	Poultry eggs		
6.1	Eggs, except quail and similar	whole eggs	12 whole chicken eggs, 6 whole goose or duck eggs
6.2	Eggs, quail and similar	whole eggs	24 whole eggs
7	Milks	whole unit(s), or unit(s) taken with a sampling device	0.5 L
Processed Foods of Animal Origin			
8.	Secondary food commodities of animal origin, **skimmed milks, evaporated milks and milk powders** Derived edible products of animal origin, **milk fats, butters, butter oils, creams, cream powders, caseins, etc.** Manufactured food (single ingredient) of animal origin, Manufactured food (multi-ingredient) of animal origin, **(including products with ingredients of plant origin where the ingredient(s) of animal origin predominates(s))**		
8.1	Liquid milk, milk powders, evaporated milk and cream, cream, dairy ice cream, yogurt	packaged unit(s), or unit(s) taken with a sampling device	0.5 L (liquid) or 0.5 kg (solid)
Notes. (i) Evaporated milks and evaporated cream in bulk must be mixed thoroughly before sampling aseptically. *(ii) Milk powder in bulk should be sampled aseptically, passing a dry borer tube through the powder at an even rate.* *(iii) Creams in bulk should be mixed thoroughly with a plunger before sampling but foaming, whipping and churning must be avoided.*			
8.2	Butter and butter oils **(butter, whey butter, low fat spreads containing butter fat, anhydrous butter oil, anhydrous milk fat)**	whole or parts of packaged unit(s), **or** unit(s) taken with a sampling device	0.2 kg or 0.2 L
8.3	Cheeses, including processed cheeses **units 0.3 kg or greater**	Whole unit(s) or units taken aseptically with a sampling device	0.5 kg
	units < 0.3 kg	whole unit(s)	0.3 kg
Note. Cheeses with a circular base should be sampled by making two cuts radiating from the center. Cheeses with a rectangular base should be sampled by making two cuts parallel to the sides.			
8.4	Liquid, frozen or dried egg products	unit(s) taken aseptically with a sampling device	0.5 kg

9. Grapes for Sulfites

Collect approximately 900 - 1800 g (2 - 4 lbs) of grapes [10/100 - 200 g (1/4 to 1/2 lb) subs]. Each subsample will consist of individual grapes, not bunches, and will be collected from different lugs (cases) on as many different pallets in the lot as possible. No grapes that are damaged during the sampling procedure should be included in the sample. However, grapes with damage prior to sampling may be included in the sample.

If sulfiting pads are present, grapes sampled should be selected from areas closest to and directly under the pad.

Monitoring activities should be focused upon lots of grapes with the highest potential for violative sulfite residues.

Direct efforts to lots of grapes sulfited through fumigation or to lots with multiple fumigations especially towards the end of the harvesting season and also to lots with significant numbers of damaged grapes (split, crushed, or unusually wet, if such damage is apparent).

Sample lots of grapes sulfited through use of sulfiting pads, with or without additional fumigation. If at all possible, sample lots subjected to the following conditions, which could cause high sulfite residues:

Lots subjected to un-refrigerated storage of 2 or more hours during warm weather.

Unusual shipping conditions (ships at sea during heavy storms).

Lots with significant numbers of damaged grapes.

Lots containing evidence of sulfite pad damage sufficient to cause spilling of sulfiting agent onto grapes.

Special Sample Handling

Place sample in tightly closed airtight glass mason jar(s) or sealed plastic bag(s). Although no effort should be made to commingle subsamples, more than one subsample may be placed in the same container for shipping convenience.

Appropriate cooling procedures are:

Place samples in shipping container or cooler with sufficient ice or other refrigerant to keep sample refrigerated until arrival at the laboratory. Sample should be placed immediately in a refrigerator at or below 7 degrees C. If sample is not to be analyzed within a few hours, the sample should be placed in a freezer, which is maintained at or below -20 degrees C.

or

Place sample in container with sufficient dry ice to keep sample frozen until arrival at the lab, sample should be placed in freezer upon arrival at laboratory.

10. Fish and Shellfish Products

NOTE: THIS SAMPLE SIZE FURNISHES SUFFICIENT FISH FOR HEAVY METAL ANALYSIS.

Packaged Fish, fresh, frozen, smoked, cured, or shellfish (except oysters)
Collect 12 subs - minimum sub size is 453 g (1 lb)

Bulk Fish - .453 - 1.35 kg (1 - 3 lb)/fish
Collect 12 subs, each sub to consist of 453 g (1 lb) of edible fish

Bulk Shellfish (except oysters)
Collect 12 - 453 g (1 lb) subs

Canned Fish and Shellfish Products (except oysters)
Collect 12 subs - 5 cans per sub

Other Fish and Shellfish Products
Oysters - Collect 12 1 pint subs

Fish Flour and Meal
Follow the guidance in section 5 above.

Swordfish for Heavy Metals

These sample sizes must be used whenever sampling swordfish, either for audit, surveillance, or compliance purposes.

Whole Fish (dressed, head removed)

Characterize lot in terms of fish sizes, i.e., small, medium, and large. The following dressed weight ranges are used for classification:

Small Fish - Weighs less than 36.4 kg (80 lbs)

Medium Fish - Weighs 36.4 - 54.5 kg (80 - 120 lbs)

Large Fish - Weighs more than 54.5 kg (120 lbs)

For lots consisting of 12 or more fish, the representative sample to be collected will be determined by the following formula:

ns = (n) (Ns)/N

ns = the number of fish in a given weight range from which subsamples must be taken

n = total number of subsamples to be collected from the lot. (In using this formula n will always equal 12)

Ns = the number of fish in a given weight range in the lot

N = the total number of fish in the lot

Example: If a lot consists of 25 fish and is characterized as: 5 small fish [less than 36.4 kg(80 lbs)], 15 medium fish [36.4 - 54.5 kg (80 - 120 lbs)], and 5 large fish [greater than 54.5 kg (129 lbs)], the sample should be collected as follows:

small fish $\frac{(12)(5)}{25} = 2.4 = 2$

medium fish $\frac{(12)(15)}{25} = 7.2 = 7$

large fish $\frac{(12)(5)}{25} = 2.4 = 2$

TOTAL SAMPLE: 11 sub samples

Usually, the total sample will consist of 12 subsamples. However, due to rounding numbers of subsamples determined by the formula may be 11 or 13 in some instances. The total sample should consist of the specific number of sub samples determined by the formula in all cases.

Each sub sample should consist of approximately a 0.5 kg (1 lb) steak cut from just below the nape of the fish. Care should be taken to avoid mutilation of fish. The sub must consist of edible flesh. If a private laboratory is conducting the analysis, individual fish from which the sub sample is taken should be identified with a tag or other suitable method. This will permit FDA to take audit samples from the same fish sampled by the private laboratories.

For lots consisting of 12 or less fish, collect 1 sub from each fish.

Swordfish Loins (slabs or sides cut from dressed whole fish which has been boned or trimmed).

Use the same formula stipulated for whole fish, with the exception that the following weight ranges should be used to characterize the lot:

Small fish loins = weighs 9.1 - 18.2 kg (20 - 40 lbs)

Medium fish loins) = weighs 18.2 - 36.4 kg (40 - 80 lbs)

Large fish loins = weighs over 36.4 kg (80 lbs)

Swordfish Steaks

Collect 12 sub samples, i.e., 12 steaks, at random from different containers in the lot (as many as possible)

Canned Swordfish

Collect 12/453 g (1 lb) sub samples at random

11. Retail Containers Canned, Frozen and Dried Foods

Collect retail containers equal to the number of primary units specified above.

12. Special Investigations

Growing Crops

Superimpose an imaginary grid on the field dividing it into approximately 100 areas. Randomly select 10 areas to form a representative sample of the field. Collect one pound subs from each area. Combine to form a composite. If a sample is being collected to document drift, etc. DO NOT composite subs. In addition, diagram the field in the Remarks Section of the C/R and indicate sub number where each sub was collected.

For leafy vegetables, such as lettuce, cabbage, etc. INV Samples collected in the growing field should be representative of local commercial harvesting practices If the local practice is to strip outer leaves at the time of harvest, this practice should be followed when collecting field samples. In head lettuce, for example, the lettuce may be packed directly into shipping cartons in the field, in which case 6 or 8 outer leaves are left on the head to be removed at the retail outlet. In other instances, each head is stripped of 2 or 3 outer leaves and individually wrapped in plastic, placed in shipping cartons, and the consumer receives the produce in this condition. Describe sampling method on C/R and describe how packing shed handles produce prior to shipping (e.g., washing, waxing, stripping, etc.).

Soil Samples

Collect soil samples from fields according to the following 3x3 grid diagram:

	a	b	c
1	o	o	o
2	o	o	o
3	o	o	o

Sample at the 9 locations indicated by the "o". If the field being sampled is very large, you may have to sample it using a 4x4, 5x5, or even larger grid pattern.

Subs are to be placed in clean quart glass jars, which have been washed in water, rinsed in methanol, and air dried. If methanol is not available, use washed, air dried jars and submit an empty jar as a control. Note on CR that jars were or were not rinsed with methanol.

Obtain two "6 in" deep plugs (1-2 in. in diameter from each sampling location. Place two plugs from each location in cleaned glass jars, place clean aluminum foil over top of jar and seal with screw cap.

Soil samples should be submitted to the lab at 4 degrees C (39 degrees F) or below.

Water Samples - Collect 3 quarts of water from the same sampling source (e.g., faucet, stream, lake, etc.) and place in cleaned, washed and methanol rinsed jars as described under "Soil Samples".

Submit water samples to lab at 4 degrees C (39 degrees F) or below.

General

Official Samples shall be collected whenever feasible unless they are not required to accomplish the objective of the assignment. Investigational Samples shall be collected only when Official Samples are not readily available.

Consult with your supervisor in cases of doubt as to sample cost, size, or collection technique.

When collecting samples in glass jars, line the lids with aluminum foil which has been certified by the laboratory as contaminant free or use teflon lined lids.

If shipment of shell eggs is required and breakage may result during transit, subs may be broken, shells discarded, and liquid magma collected in clean glass jars. Each sub jar should be properly identified.

Samples collected at Packing Sheds should be representative of the produce as shipped in commerce. DO NOT strip outer leaves from subs collected at packing sheds from bulk lots, shipping cartons ready for shipment, in-transit lots or at final destination. If the packing shed practice is to strip outer leaves prior to shipment, follow this practice when collecting the samples. Describe the sampling method on the C/R.

DO NOT USE magic markers, etc. to identify sub bags, because the ink may affect assay results. Use stick on labels to identify sub bags.

Collect samples in the container in which the dealer is packaging the product. If the dealer is packaging the product in plastic bags, collect sample in these bags. If the firm is not packing the product, collect the samples in paper bags, cardboard cartons, etc. Do not use plastic bags as this may interfere with the analysis, unless the bags are certified as contaminant free by your district laboratory.

Samples must be delivered as promptly as possible to the laboratory if regulatory action is to be taken against actionable lots.

Hold samples in cold storage until ready to be shipped or delivered to the laboratory. If the sample is of a hard fruit or vegetable (such as apples, pears, butternut squash), and is shipped overnight delivery, it can be shipped to the laboratory unrefrigerated, but the FDA 525 should direct refrigeration upon receipt.

Use aseptic technique, where applicable, when collecting samples of finished products from bulk containers.

Sample Schedule 4: Wheat Carload Sampling

I. Sampling Normalcars

CAUTION: WHEN USING A GRAIN PROBE, BE CAREFUL NOT TO CLOSE THE TRIER COMPARTMENT DOORS ON YOUR FINGERS.

Collect samples only of specific assignment.

A. Equipment

1. Double tube compartmented trier, 60 in. long
2. Sampling cloth at least 60 in. long
3. 1000 ml plastic graduate
4. Paper bags or other suitable containers capable of holding more than one quart of sample and do not use canvas bags.
5. FDA Metal Car Seals for resealing railroad cars
6. Aluminum ladder
7. Block and tackle to open railcar door

B. Drawing Sample

Principal sources of grain samples are railcars, barges, and trucks. Draw 5 probes (in duplicate) for each sample taken as described below. However, if the sample is to be Field Examined, an initial sample of 5 probes drawn as indicated below will be sufficient.

Probe samples from railcars and trucks as follows:

Probe #1 - From Center of car

Probe #2 - From 3-5 feet back from door post toward end of the car and approximately 2 feet from the side of the car.

Probe #3 - From 3-5 feet from the same end of the car, but approximately 2 feet from the opposite side of car as Probe #2.

Probe #4 - Same as Probe #2, but opposite end of car.

Probe #5 - Same as Probe #3, but opposite end of car.

Sketches I and II below are alternatives showing the approximate sampling locations.

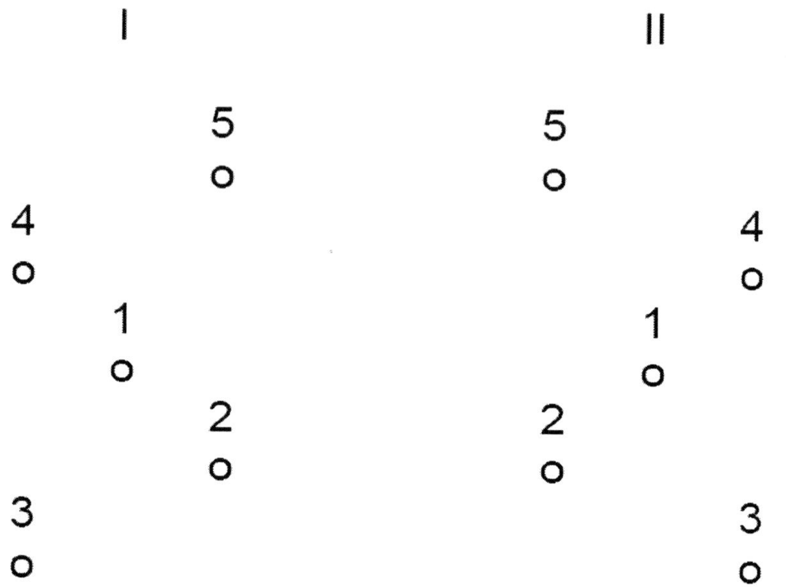

Insert trier in the grain at an angle of about 10° from the vertical, with the slot up and closed. Open slots, give trier 2 or 3 short up and down motions, so that the openings will fill. Close slots (SEE CAUTION AT BEGINNING OF SCHEDULE), withdraw trier and carefully empty over sampling cloth. The cloth should be long enough to catch product from each compartment separately when you open the trier compartment doors; e.g. about 6 feet long.

C. Field Examination

Examine each pocket of the probe separately, looking for evidence of pink wheat, rodent pellets, insect damage and uneven loading or plugging. Note any insect infestation and record types of insects and whether live or dead. Count and report for each probe the number of rodent pellets, or rodent pellet fragments. Follow procedure in I.C.2 below. Count as pellets any that are sufficiently large to be readily identified by size, shape, surface coating, and/or presence of rodent hairs. Report the number of rodent pellets per sub. Measure the volume of each sub (probe) in quarts and calculate the average number of pellets per quart per I.C.2.a below. Place pellets from each sub in separate vials and submit with each wheat sub. Place each of the wheat subs in clean, paper bags.

Do not use canvas bags or take glass jars into railcars.

Substantially larger loads will require additional probing or larger samples taken from falling grain during loading or unloading operations.

Submit all suspect samples to laboratory for confirmatory analysis.

1. **Non-Violative Samples.** When field examination shows sample as non-violative, return grain to the car, unless collected for pesticide analysis. Report results in the Remarks Section of the C/R.

2. **Violative Samples**

    1. **Rodent Pellet Contamination.** The guideline for determining whether wheat is violative due to rodent contamination is: "9 mg or more rodent excreta pellets and/or fragments of rodent excreta pellets per kg of wheat."

NOTE: Since it is impractical to weigh rodent pellets and wheat in the field, the following estimations can be used. Mouse pellets average approximately 8.7 mg each and a kilogram of wheat about 2.35 pints. This translates roughly as 1 pellet per quart of wheat or 1/2 pellet per pint.

Where your field examination reveals one or more rodent pellets (or you can estimate that sufficient fragments of rodent pellets exist to equal one pellet) in a quart of wheat, take duplicate probes to furnish the claimants portion. Take the duplicate probes from the same locations as the original probes. Place the duplicates in separate containers and identify these to correspond with the original probes.

    2. **Pink Wheat.** Where evidence of pink wheat or other fungicide treated wheat is found, collect 15 probe samples. Take 5 probes from each end of the car and 5 probes from the center of the car. Submit the three 5-probe portions separately, using new clean containers.

    3. **Insect Damaged Kernels.** The violative status of these samples should be established by laboratory analysis. When any evidence of insect damage is revealed by cursory examination, collect duplicate samples and submit for laboratory analysis.

3. **Resealing Cars** See IOM 4.3.4.

4. **Procedures for Actionable Cars.** If field examination reveals an average of one or more rodent pellets per quart or gross evidence of insect-damaged kernels, evidence of plugging, or "pink wheat" contamination, determine any movement of the car or other disposition of the grain and notify your supervisor immediately.

5. **Preparation of Sample for Laboratory Analysis.** If a sample can be delivered to the laboratory promptly and confirmatory analysis handled expeditiously, freezing of the FDA subsamples is not necessary. The claimant's (702(b)) portion of the sample, however, must be frozen. It is preferable to freeze the subsamples in paper bags. If a freezer is not available, the subsamples (in paper bags) can be placed in a cooler box with dry ice. Do not use glass jars with dry ice. Officially seal all subsamples. If dry ice is used, you must label the shipping container as described in IOM 4.5.5.8.6 no. 6. See Exhibit 4-19. Indicate frozen storage on the FDA 525.

D. Special Reporting

Submit an Analyst Worksheet (FDA-431) for each sample analyzed and found in compliance. See IOM 4.3.7.1. If field examination shows the sample is possibly actionable, report analytical results in Remarks Section of the C/R.

II. Sampling Plugged Car

If uneven loading, layering or "plugging" is suspected, contact your supervisor as to whether to sample or not. A 'plugged" car is a railcar, truck, or barge load of grain where the contamination is suspected of being in only one portion or layer of grain. Plugging is usually the deliberate mixing of violative grain below the surface or in isolated pockets of grain.

A. Equipment

Equipment needed is the same as in 1.A. above except:

1. Double tube grain probe must have individual compartments permanently separated.

2. Small containers of sufficient size to hold the contents of each compartment of each grain probe.

B. Procedure

1. In the Remarks Section of the C/R, draw a diagram showing actual "plugging" pattern suspected.

2. Each sample consists of thirty probes of grain with each probe compartment maintained as a separate sub. Each sample thus consists of 300-330 subs depending on whether a 10 or 11 compartment probe is used and if grain depth is sufficient to insert the probe to fully cover all compartments of the probe.

3. Probe each load and number the probes as follows:

   1 4 7 10 13 16 19 22 25 28

   2 5 8 11 14 17 20 23 26 29

   3 6 9 12 15 18 21 24 27 30

4. Identify the subs by probe number plus compartment letter starting with small "a" as the compartment nearest the tip of the probe.

Example:

Probe #1

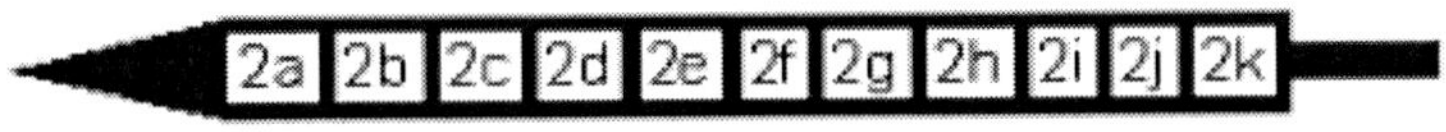

Probe #2

5. Submit sample to your district's servicing laboratory. See IOM 4.5.5.2.

Sample Schedule 5: Imported Whitefish Sampling Schedule

General

This Sample Schedule objective is to maintain import lot integrity from time of importation thru FDA inspection or examination and final action.

Shipments will be special manifested from non-lab ports to DO cities and other cities designated by the DD as FDA inspection points. These shipments will arrive in Customs bonded trucks under seal applied by Customs at the port of entry. Customs Entry documents and commercial invoice will accompany each shipment. The commercial invoice contains a description of the lots in the shipment and will serve as a guide in the selection of the lots to be sampled.

1. Special Manifested Shipments:
    a. Determine if seals are intact and record seal number.
    b. FDA metal seals may be broken and lots checked against invoice.
    c. Customs seals may be broken only if authorized by Customs.
    d. Lots which are not to be examined will be released by completing the "MAY PROCEED" block of the FDA-701.
    e. Sample lots to be examined by using either the Single or Sequential Sampling Plan depending on whether examination is made at the DO Lab or at the dock. The Sequential Plan can only be used where additional fish are immediately available for cutting.

2. Definition of a Lot & Selection for Examination.
    a. A lot is defined as "Each group of fish of a distinct size, listed in the invoice as from a distinct lake, will be considered as a separate lot. Where an invoice does not list lakes of origin of boxes of fish in a shipment, fish of the same size and kind will be considered to comprise a single lot. When the size of the fish or lakes of origin in a

shipment are not specified, the shipment will be treated as a single lot."

b. Limit sampling to lots containing 5 or more boxes unless deliberate splitting up of lots is suspected.

c. Basis for Sampling. Select lots for sampling on either a "selective" or "objective" (random) basis. The criteria in selective sampling may be prior knowledge or suspicion that fish listed as from a given lake are likely to have excess cysts; that the shipper has been known to manipulate shipments; etc. Regardless of the reason for selective sampling, record the basis for sampling each lot in your examination report. Simply list the basis as "selective" or "objective" next to the results of each lot sampled.

d. Normally, select boxes in a lot for sampling at random. However, where there's evidence of layering, selectively sample the suspect boxes.

3. Sampling Schedule.

a. Imported samples of whitefish & related fish for parasites. The sampling schedules estimate lot quality more precisely, thereby reducing the likelihood of passing a lot which should be detained, or vice versa, due to an inadequate sample.

SCHEDULE A below is a single sample plan for use in collecting samples for examination in the district lab or other location where it is impossible or undesirable to return and obtain additional fish.

SCHEDULE B below contains sequential sampling plans for use when the exam is made at a customs office or a carrier's dock where you have immediate access to the lot and can obtain additional fish, if necessary.

The sequential plan for lots of 20 to 100 boxes is presented in tabular form. the sequential sample plan for lots of 100 or more boxes is presented in a sampling chart. For small lots of 5-20 boxes, a sequential sample plan is not feasible. All import sampling plans are based on lot size and the sizes of the fish in the lot. When lots are very good or very poor quality, in terms of cyst infestation, double sample plans require a smaller sample size on the average than single sampling plans, to reach a decision.

b. Domestic Samples for Parasites.

i. For Laboratory Examination. Lots of 11 or more boxes; Collect at least 25 fish from a representative number of boxes. For small lots, under 11 boxes; Collect 12 fish from a representative number of boxes.

ii. For Examination in Other Than Laboratory. Cut a preliminary sample in accordance with the appropriate double sampling plan, Schedule B. Cut the additional sample where indicated or bring the additional sample to the laboratory for examination.

Schedule A - Single Sample Plan

Number of Boxes in Lots	NUMBER OF KG'S (POUNDS) IN A SAMPLE 1/		
	Jumbo or Large 2/	Medium 2/	Small 2/
5 - 19 boxes	12.7 Kg (28lbs)	10.5 Kg (23lbs)	7.3 Kg (16lbs)
20 - 100 boxes	24 Kg (73lbs)	20.5 Kg (45lbs)	15 Kg (33lbs)
100 or over	32 Kg (70lbs)	25.5 Kg (56lbs)	17.8 Kg (39lbs)

1/ When an invoice does not designate the size of the fish in the shipment and inspection reveals more than one size in the lot, use sampling plan for medium fish.

2/ RANGE OF WEIGHT OF FISH IN EACH SIZE CLASS:

SMALL Under 675 gms (1 1/2lbs)

MEDIUM 675 gms (1 1/2lbs) & under 1.4 Kg (3lbs)

LARGE 1.4 Kg (3lbs) & under 1.8 Kg (4lbs)

JUMBO Over 1.8 Kg (4lbs)

SCHEDULE B - SEQUENTIAL SAMPLE PLAN

1. Limited to lots of 20 - 100 boxes. 454 Kg (1000lbs) to 2272 Kg (5000lbs)

Size of Fish 1/	**Size of preliminary Sample**	**Cysts/45.5 Kg (100lbs) in Preliminary Sample**			**Size of ADD'L SMPL**	**Cysts/45.5 Kg (100lbs) in sample**	
		PASS	**DETAIN**	**TAKE ADD'L SMPL**		**PASS**	**DETAIN**
Large & Jumbo	16 Kg (35lbs)	30 or less	70 or more	31-69	28.6Kg (63lbs)	49 or less	50 or more
Medium	12.3 Kg (27lbs)	26 or less	67 or more	27-66	19.5 Kg (43lbs)	49 or less	50 or more
Small	8.2 Kg (18lbs)	38 or less	61 or more	39-61	11.8Kg (26lbs)	49 or less	50 or more

1/ When an invoice does not designate the size of the fish in the shipment and inspection reveals more than one size in the lot, use sampling plan for medium fish.

2/ For lots of 100 boxes or over, use the Sequential Sampling Chart for the particular size fish in the lot.

WHITEFISH SEQUENTIAL SAMPLING PLAN (WHEN LOT SIZE EXCEEDS 100 BOX

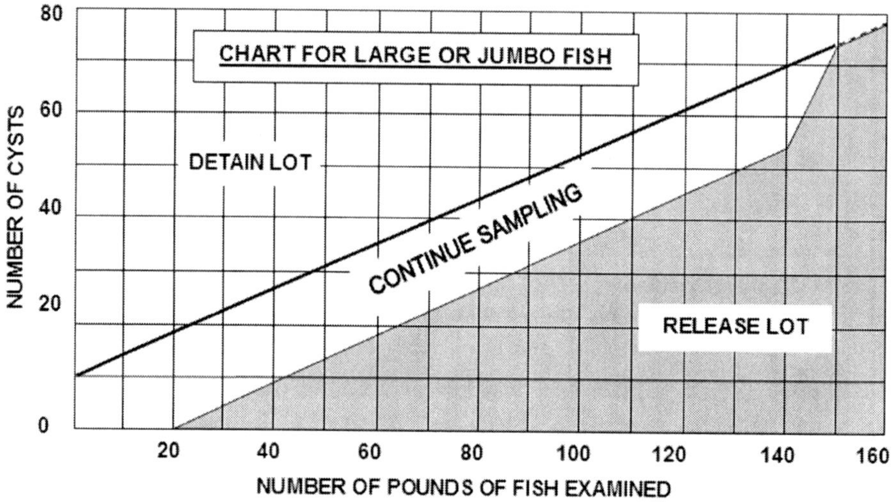

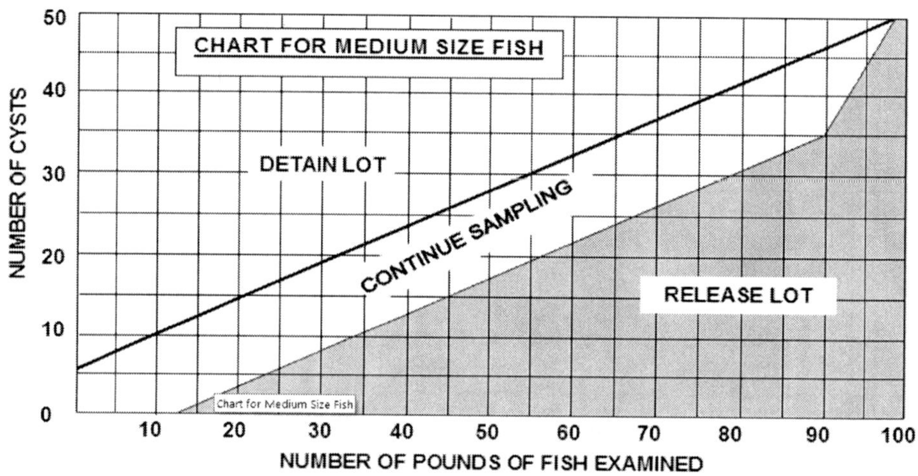

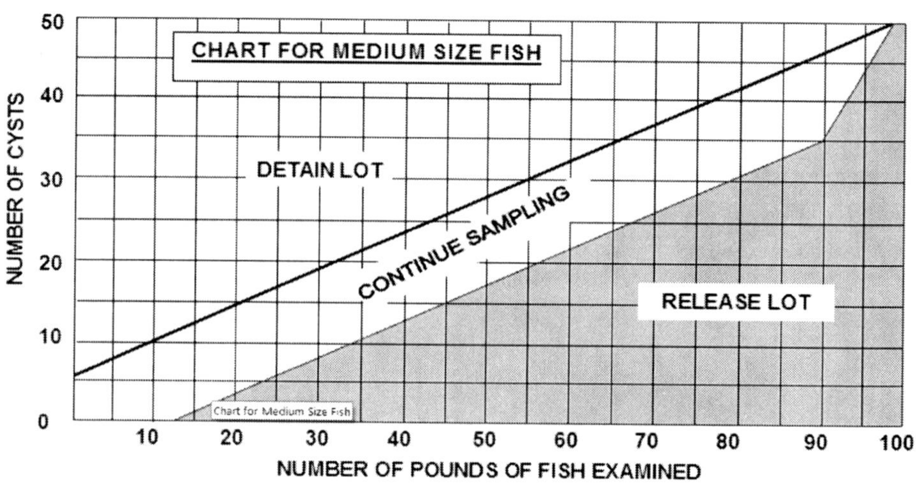

Sample Schedule 6: Mycotoxin Sample Sizes

Aflatoxin Sample Sizes

Sample sizes for all other mycotoxins can be found in CP7307.001 Domestic & Import Mycotoxin Compliance Program

Product Sample Sizes for Aflatoxin Analysis

(Includes 702(b) [21U.S.C. 372(b)] portion - each sample unit, contains product for the reserve portion, no duplicate subs are necessary)

NOTE: COMPLIANCE SAMPLE SIZES MAY DIFFER FROM SURVEILLANCE SAMPLE SIZES.

PRODUCT	PACKAGE TYPE	LOT SIZE	NUMBER OF SAMPLE UNITS*	UNIT SIZE (minimum)	TOTAL SAMPLE SIZE (minimum)
Peanut Butter (smooth)	Consumer or bulk	NA	24	225 gm (8 oz)	5.4 Kg (12 lbs)
			12	454 gm (1 lb)	5.4 kg (12 lbs)
Peanut Butter (Crunchy) Peanuts shelled roasted, or unroasted, Peanuts ground for topping	Consumer or bulk	NA	SURVEILLANCE		
			10	454 gm (1 lb)	4.5 kg (10 lb)
			COMPLIANCE SAMPLE		
			48	454 gm (1 lb)	21.8 kg (48 lbs)
Peanuts, roasted in shell (only for domestic runner variety)	Consumer or bulk	NA	SURVEILLANCE		
			15	454 gm (1 lb)	6.8 kg (15 lbs)
			COMPLIANCE SAMPLE		
			75	454 gm (1 lb)	34 kg (75 lbs)
Tree nuts (except in-shell Brazil Nuts and all pistachio nuts in import status) shelled, in-shell slices, pieces, or flour	Consumer or bulk	NA	SURVEILLANCE		
			10	454 gm (1 lb)	4.5 kg (10 lb)

PRODUCT	PACKAGE TYPE	LOT SIZE	NUMBER OF SAMPLE UNITS*	UNIT SIZE (minimum)	TOTAL SAMPLE SIZE (minimum)
			COMPLIANCE SAMPLE		
			50	454 gm (1 lb)	22.7 kg (50 lbs)
Tree nuts - paste			12	454 gm (1 lb)	5.4 kg (12 lbs)
Brazil Nuts in-shell (in import status)	Bulk	< 200 bags 201-800" 801-2000"	20 40 60	454 gm (1 lb) " "	9 kg(20 lbs) 18 kg (40 lbs) 27 kg (60 lbs)
Pistachio nuts in-shell (in import status)	Bulk	multiples of 34,100 kg (75,000 lbs)	20 % of units	---	50 lbs for each multiple of 34,100 kg (75,000 lbs) or less
Pistachio nuts shelled (in import status)		SAME	SAME	---	25 lbs for each multiple of 34,100 kg (75,000 lbs) or less
Corn - shelled, meal flour or grits	Consumer or bulk	NA	10	454 gm (1 lb)	4.5 kg (10 lbs)
Oil seed meals - Peanut meal, cottonseed meal	Bulk	NA	20	454 gm (1 lb)	9 kg (20 lbs)
Edible seeds** melon pumpkin, sesame, etc	Bulk	NA	**SURVEILLANCE**		
			10	454 gm (1 lb)	4.5 kg (10 lb)
			COMPLIANCE SAMPLE		
			50	454 gm (1 lb)	22.7 kg (50 lb)
Ginger Root dried whole	Bulk	"n" units	Sq root "n"	---	6.8 kg (15 lbs)
ground	Consumer	NA	16	16-28 gm (1 oz)	4.5 kg (10 lbs)

PRODUCT	PACKAGE TYPE	LOT SIZE	NUMBER OF SAMPLE UNITS*	UNIT SIZE (minimum)	TOTAL SAMPLE SIZE (minimum)
Milk - whole, skim low fat	Consumer	NA	10	454 gm (1 lb)	4.5 kg (10 lbs)
	Bulk	NA	---	---	4.5 kg (10 lbs)
Small grains - wheat sorghum, barley, etc	Bulk	NA	10	454 gm (1 lb)	4.5 kg (10 lbs)
Dried fruit** - e.g.: Figs	Consumer or bulk	NA	**SURVEILLANCE**		
			10	454 gm (1 lb)	4.5 kg (10 lb)
			COMPLIANCE SAMPLE		
			50	454 gm (1 lb)	22.7 kg (50 lb)
Mixtures containing commodities susceptible to mycotoxin contamination	Consumer	NA			
Commodity particles relatively large			50	454 gm (1 lb)	22.7 kg (50 lbs)
Commodity particles relatively small			10	454 gm (1 lb)	4.5 kg (10 lbs)

NOTE: Containers for samples of unprocessed, intact nuts, seeds, or grains must be sufficiently porous to provide for dissipation of moisture produced by respiration of the nut, seed, or grain.

* To be collected from as many random sites in the lot as possible. For surveillance samples, you may combine subs prior to shipping to the laboratory. For compliance samples, you must maintain sub integrity.

** Optional sampling program for seeds or dried fruit with a low incidence of contamination. Take initial 10 x 454 gm (1 lb) sample. If any aflatoxin is detected, resample 50 x 454 gm (1 lb) sample for determination of contamination level on which to base regulatory judgment.

Sample Schedule 7: Canned Fruit - Fill Of Container - Authentic Pack

Collect samples only on a specific assignment or during inspections when it appears that the firm is not filling the containers to capacity.

1. INVESTIGATIONAL SAMPLES: Authentic Pack Preparation . Procedure for preparing authentic factory packs.
   a. Remove 72 cans, 3 at a time, from packing line after fruit has been added and before syruping.
   b. Mark 24 cans with the sub numbers A-1, A-2, A-3, etc.; 24 cans with sub numbers B-1, B-2, B-3; and 24 cans with sub numbers C-1, C-2, C-3, etc. See IOM 4.5.2.3.
   c. Drain water from the "B" subs by inverting each can for 10 seconds, holding the fruit so it doesn't fall out.
   d. Obtain gross weight of each can and record data for each series of sub on 3 separate FDA-485 - Field Weight Sheets.
   e. Add additional fruit of the same kind and style to the "C" subs until the cans are filled to capacity. Do not tamp the contents or crush the fruit.
   f. Record the number of fruit pieces added where the size of the fruit makes the procedure reasonable. Do not make time consuming counts of small pieces of fruit or berries.
   g. Obtain the gross weight of the "C" subs after additional fruit is added and record on "C" series Field Weight Sheet.
   h. Return all 72 cans to the filling line for syruping, exhausting, sealing, etc. in normal cannery operation.
   i. Remove cans after cooking and cooling.
   j. Identify cans with a single INV Sample number.
   k. Attach FDA-485 - Field Weight Sheets to C/R.

2. OFFICIAL SAMPLES
   a. See Sample Schedule Chart 2 for sample size.

3. SPECIAL REPORTING AND PRECAUTIONS
   a. Report coding of cans and shipping cases.
   b. Obtain label specimen(s) for the slack filled products.
   c. Report shipments made before the inspection or since previous inspection in the same canning season.
   d. Do not prepare Authentic Factory Samples when the cannery is packing for USDA fill-of-container certification unless:
      i. USDA inspection is not continuous.
      ii. USDA Certification is for quality only.

iii. USDA recommendations for weights are not being followed.

4. SAMPLE SUBMISSION

   Submit samples to your district's designated workplan servicing laboratory

Sample Schedule 8: Imports - Coffee, Dates, and Date Material

1. Coffee - Import Field Examination - Note: Examine a minimum of six bags of coffee beans regardless of lot size. If a significant number of defective beans or significant contamination is found during the examination of these six bags, continue the examination using the following schedule, which applies for both Import Field Examination and samples for laboratory analysis:

LOT SIZE	NO. BAGS TO BE SAMPLED
100 or less	6 bags
101 - 200	10 bags
201 - 1000	15 bags
over 1000	20 bags

a. Sample each bag with a trier, collecting 1/2 pt. of beans from the top and 1/2 pt. from the bottom of the bag. The total quantity of beans taken from each bag must be the same, since both wharf and laboratory examinations are to be performed on a composite sample of all beans collected. Shake each sub on a #8 sieve nested in a pan. Dump the sifted beans from each sub into a bag of sufficient size to hold and permit mixing all of the subs collected from the lot. Composite the subs. Do not maintain individually.

b. Macroscopic Filth Examine the siftings for macroscopic filth (live and dead whole insects, excreta pellets, extraneous material and sweepings), reporting findings for each sub separately. See IOM 4.3.7.4. Transfer macroscopic filth, including all sifted material to a second bag and submit to the laboratory for confirmation. If live insect infestation is encountered, freeze the filth portion containing the insects and the composite coffee bean sample. The lot will be detained if a live insect infestation is encountered, however, proceed with the defect bean examination since the reconditioning process will depend on the results.

c. Defect Bean Examination Thoroughly mix the composite sample of coffee beans and remove three-hundred beans at random. Examine each individual bean visually (or at a 5X magnification) for insect tunneling and mold damage. Count as moldy only those beans with 1/4 or more of the surface being moldy. Note: Each district office has examples of the various types of reject beans.

Accept the lot if twenty or less rejects are found and discard the sample. Report your wharf examination into FACTS or OASIS, depending on your assignment; no Sample Collection Report is necessary.

d. If twenty-one or more rejects are detected, return beans examined to the composite and submit to the laboratory. You may discontinue the examination when twenty-one rejects are detected. When a sample is submitted to the laboratory, all import field examination time is reported as a field exam in FACTS and the sample collection time is reported as an import sample collection. All necessary documents for an import sample collection must be completed.

2. Dates & Date Material – Filth

In the laboratory, dates, like in-shell nuts are sampled in accordance with a sequential sampling program, i.e. all subsamples are composited, and 100 dates are sampled at a time, repetitively, until such time they either exceed or fall under certain reject numbers. It is not uncommon to have to examine 3 to 6 (100 date) repetitions. It is therefore important for each subsample to contain at least 200-300 dates or 2 lbs of date material. Sample according to the following schedule:

NUMBER OF SUBSAMPLES REQUIRED		
NO. CONTAINERS IN LOT*	**WHOLE DATES**	**DATE MATERIAL**
100 or less	3	4
101 - 600	8	6
601 - 1,200	14	8
1,201 - 2,000	26	10
2,001 - 2,800	36	12
2,801 - 6,000	44	14
6,001 - 9,600	56	16
9,601 - 15,000	68	18
Over 15,000	82	22

* Schedule is based upon unit containers weighing between twenty and one-hundred pounds. For containers exceeding one-hundred pounds each, consider as two or more containers. For example, a one-hundred and fifty pound container is considered as two containers; a three-hundred pound container as three containers, etc.

a. Identify each subsample separately.

b. Each lot will be a separate sample. Reconditioning, if possible, will be based on lot numbers.

c. Jujube sampling - collect according to the above schedule for dates and date material. Do not identify jujube samples as dates, Phoenix dactyllifera. Jujubes, Zizphus jujuba, are usually labeled as Chinese

Red Dates, Dried Red Dates, or Honey Dates and are not misbranded when labeled as such due to long standing use of these names.

d. If live insects are noted, include these as part of the sample collected and report on the C.R. which subs contained the insects and how many insects, adult or larvae, were noted. If live infestation is noted, place all subs from the lot sampled in large plastic whirlpak bags and freeze or place in a cooler on dry ice.

Sample Schedule 9: Sampling Schedule For Color Containing Products Color Additives

The following schedule provides general guidance for collecting samples of foods and cosmetics to determine whether non-permitted colors are present, rather than to determine the actual level of a particular color. This schedule was developed with the assumption that color distribution in the lot will be homogeneous. In the case of heterogeneous products, your supervisor should contact Center for Food Safety and Applied Nutrition, Office of Field Programs, Division of Enforcement (HFS-605) to determine sample size.

<table>
<tr><th>INDUSTRY CODE</th><th colspan="2">SAMPLE SIZE
(DO NOT COMMINGLE CODES) (Min. 225 gm (8 oz)/pkg Unless otherwise specified)</th></tr>
<tr><td colspan="3">GRAIN AND BAKING</td></tr>
<tr><td>02</td><td>Whole grains, Milled Grain Products and Starch</td><td>2 retail packages</td></tr>
<tr><td>03</td><td>Bakery Products, Doughs, Bakery Mixes, and Icings</td><td>2 retail packages</td></tr>
<tr><td>04</td><td>Macaroni and Noodle Products</td><td>2 retail packages</td></tr>
<tr><td>05</td><td>Cereal Preparations Breakfast Foods</td><td>2 retail packages</td></tr>
<tr><td>07</td><td>Snack Food Items (Flour, Meal, or Vegetable Base)</td><td>2 retail packages</td></tr>
<tr><td colspan="3">DAIRY</td></tr>
<tr><td>09</td><td>Milk, Butter, and Dried Milk Pdts</td><td>Liquid Pdts: 2 pts where possible
Solid: 2 packages</td></tr>
<tr><td>12</td><td>Cheese and Cheese Products</td><td>2 retail packages</td></tr>
<tr><td>13</td><td>Ice Cream and Related Products</td><td>6 items per sample (If item is single serving; i.e., cup, popsicle, bar, etc.) 2 pt</td></tr>
</table>

INDUSTRY CODE	SAMPLE SIZE (DO NOT COMMINGLE CODES) (Min. 225 gm (8 oz)/pkg Unless otherwise specified)	
		containers where possible, or 1 quart or 1/2 gal
14	Filled Milk and Imitation Milk Products	2 pints
EGGS		
15	Egg and Egg Pdts	2 dozen whole eggs (e.g. colored hard boiled Easter eggs) 2 retail pkg of egg pdts
FISH		
16	Fishery/Seafood Pdts	2 retail packages. Any collection of smoked salmon should be selective, based on inspectional evidence
MEAT & SIMULATED MEAT PRODUCTS		
17	Meat, Meat Products and Poultry	2 retail packages
18	Vegetable Protein Pdts	2 retail packages
FRUIT, NUT AND VEGETABLE PRODUCTS		
20-22	Fruit & Fruit Pdts	2 retail packages canned or glazed. 12 fresh fruit (e.g., oranges, etc.).
23	Nuts & Edible Seeds	2 retail packages
24-25	Vegetable & Vegetable Products	2 retail packages
26	Vegetable Oils & Olive Oil	Liquids - 2 pints Solids - 2 retail packages
DRESSINGS AND SPICES		
27	Dressings & Condiments	2 retail packages
28	Spices, Flavors, & Salts	Extracts - 2 pints Solids - 2 retail packages
BEVERAGES		
29	Soft Drinks & Waters	6 Retail Units (Cans, Bottles,

INDUSTRY CODE	SAMPLE SIZE (DO NOT COMMINGLE CODES) (Min. 225 gm (8 oz)/pkg Unless otherwise specified)	
		Packets)
30	Beverage Bases, Concentrates, and Nectars	Liquids - 1 pint Solids (Powder mix, packets) - 6 Consumer Pkg Solids - 2/225 gm (8 oz) or larger containers
31	Coffee and Tea	2 retail packages
32	Alcoholic Beverages	2 pints or 1 quart
CONFECTIONS AND DESSERTS		
33	Candy w/o chocolate, Candy Specialties, and Chewing Gum	2 retail packages
34	Chocolate & Cocoa Pdts	2 retail packages
35	Gelatin, Rennet, Pudding Mixes, & Pie Fillings	6 pkgs - smallest consumer size
36	Food Sweeteners (Nutritive)	2 pints
MULTIPLE FOODS, SOUPS, SALADS, BABY FOOD AND DIETARY		
37	Multiple Food Dinners Gravies, Sauces and Specialties (Total	Single Serving Dinners, etc - 4 pkgs Two Consumer Pkgs when 1 pkg serves more than 2
38	Soups	Same as 37 Above
39	Prepared Salad Products	Same as 37 Above
40	Baby (Infant and Junior) Food Pdts	Sufficient retail pkgs to total at least 454 gm (1 lb) of food
41	Dietary Conventional Foods and Meal Replacements	Same as 37 Above
COLORS AND COSMETICS		
50	Color Additives for Foods Drugs, and Cosmetics	1. Straight Color 28 gm (1 oz) powder. 2. Color Mixtures 110 gms (4

Sample Schedules

INDUSTRY CODE	SAMPLE SIZE (DO NOT COMMINGLE CODES) (Min. 225 gm (8 oz)/pkg Unless otherwise specified)	
		oz) Liq, paste or powder. If mixture contains over 50% pure dye, 55 gm (2 oz) is sufficient Four retail packages of the same lot code for each shade (color) in the product line, if the product is strongly colored. (e.g., Lipsticks, hair coloring products, eye mascara, eye liners, make up pencils of all types)
53	Cosmetics	Sufficient number of retail packages to equal 1 lb or 1 pt of sample if the product is lightly colored. (e.g., creams, lotions, shampoos, bath products, shaving preparations, and perfumes.) Note: Always collect a minimum of two retail units of each product.
MISCELLANEOUS		
	Bulk Items (Any bulk food or cosmetic)	Dry - 454 gm (1 lb) Liquid - Min 36 fl oz

Sample Schedule 10: Drug Sampling Schedules (Does not include Antibiotic Preparations)

STERILITY TESTING VITAMINS, DEVICES, & DRUGS

Type of Product		Sample Size[1]
	INV Sample[2]	Official [702(b) & Check][3]
DRUGS	36	86
DEVICES	46	106

LEGEND:

1. Double sample size requirements when individual containers are 2 ml (2 gm) or smaller.

2. INV sample includes units (30 for Drugs & 40 for devices) for examination and 6 units for bacteriostasis.

3. Official Sample includes units (30 for drugs & 40 for devices) for examination, units (30-40) for check, 20 units for 702(b) [21 U.S.C. 372(b)] and 6 for bacteriostasis.

Note: If a lot is aseptically filled into 200 finished units or less, sample no less than 10% of lot.

Dissolution Test - USP & NF

Unless directed otherwise by your assignment or supervisor, submit samples to your normal servicing laboratory.

Sample Size

Collect a 200 tablet portion for drug potency analysis by the collecting district lab, plus a separate 100 tab portion to be split for dissolution testing

Microbiological Examination Of Drugs (Other than for Sterility)

PRODUCT	-	MINIMUM SAMPLE SIZE (Includes 702(b) portion)	
	-	**Sub Size**	**Nos. of Subdivisions**
Dosage Form Drugs (See #1 below), Bulk Drugs, or Raw Materials for Manufacturing	-	90 gm or 90 ml	10

Sampling Instructions

1. Contact the laboratory (which has microbiological testing capabilities) serving your district for sample size requirements before sampling dosage form drugs containing less than 3 grains, 200 mg, or 25% of the suspect ingredient.

2. Use aseptic technique when collecting samples from raw materials or bulk containers. Implements and sample containers used must be sterile. Submit controls. See IOM 4.3.6 through 4.3.6.5.

3. Submit samples to the laboratory with microbiological testing capabilities which serves your district unless directed otherwise.

Sample Schedule 11: Veterinary Products, Feeds, & By-Products For Animal Feeds

1. GENERAL

   This sampling schedule may be used as a guide in the collection of surveillance or compliance samples resulting from district assignments or as a follow-up to violative inspections and/or investigations. Before collecting follow-up samples to violative inspections or investigations, contact your supervisor since it may be necessary for your district to consult with the Atlanta Center for Nutrient Analysis (HFR-SE680) when unscheduled compliance sampling is contemplated.

2. SAMPLE PRODUCT, SIZE, & SPECIAL INSTRUCTIONS

   Vitamin-mineral testing, sampling instructions and information. Sample size includes 702(b) portion.

   Unless excessive cost is a factor, collect at least 3 intact containers from each lot or control number. When sampling from bulk lots, collect appropriate subs from a minimum of 3 different bulk containers in the lot.

DOSAGE FORM VITAMIN-MINERAL PREPARATIONS (Single/Multiple Ingredients)			
1. PRODUCT	**NO. SUBSAMPLES**	**MINIMUM TOTAL SAMPLE SIZE**	**REMARKS**
Injectables	3 vials/amps	30 ml	Split samples for sterility testing (60 vials/amps)
Tabs/Caps	3 retail units	300 Tabs/Caps	Split sample for micro tests (10/50 tab/cap subs)
Liquids	3 retail units	4 fl. oz.	Split sample for micro tests (10/2 fl. oz. subs)
Powders	3 retail units	112 gm (4 oz)	Same as above

FEEDS & BY-PRODUCTS FOR ANIMAL FEEDS (Vitamin-Mineral Claims)			
Vitamin A & D Concentrates, Supplements & (A&D feeding	3 retail units(1/2 gal or less)	3 lbs (1.4 kg) 3 pints	Limit samples to those products containing at least 800 units/g Vit A and/or 80 Feeds units/g Vit D
Vitamin B2 (Riboflavin) Concentrates, Supplements, & feeds	Same	Same	Limit samples to those products containing at least 20 mg/lb
Vitamin B12 (Cyanocobalamin) Concentrates, Supplements & feeds	Same	Same	Limit samples to those products containing at least 1 mg/lb

Multiple Vitamins Concentrates, Supplements, & feeds.	Same	Same	Limit samples to those products meeting vitamin levels listed above.

Sample Submission

Submit all samples for Vitamin Potency analysis to the Atlanta Center for Nutrient Analysis (HFR-SE680).

Submit samples for filth analysis, microbiological examination, sterility, etc. to your district servicing laboratory.

Sample Schedule 12: Medicated Animal Feeds Sampling

Medicated Premixes

1. Investigational Samples (INV Samples)

   To demonstrate suspected drug carryover or other chemical contamination during manufacturing, collect 1-900 gm (2 lbs) of static residual material in the equipment, and the finished product premixes.

2. Official Physical Samples 702(b) [21U.S.C.372(b)] Portion Included

   For expensive premixes or components, collect a total of 3/170 gm(6 oz) subs; One sub from each of 3 containers. In the case of premixes packaged in plastic; e.g., mini-packs, follow instructions under bagged premixes.

   a. Bagged Premixes

      Collect 10 - 454 gm (1 lb) subs from each lot. Sample all bags in lots under 10 bags, for a total of 10 subs from the lot.

      Collect 454 gm (1 lb) subs from at least 10 different bags selected at random in lots of more than 10 bags.

   b. Bulk Premixes

      Collect at least 10 - 454 gm (l lb) subs, from different locations in the lot providing a minimum total sample of 4.5 Kg (10 lbs).

      Documentary Samples (DOC Sample) - Refer to IOM 4.1.4.2 for guidance on the collection of DOC Samples.

Medicated Feeds

1. Investigational Samples (INV Sample)

Collect 1 - 900 gm (2 lb) of static residual material in the equipment and correlate with finished feed samples to show that residues are being carried over into the finished product.

2. Official Samples (Includes 702(b) portion)

   a. Bagged Complete Feed

      Collect a total sample of not less than 2.3 Kg (5 lbs) from each lot. Collect 454 gm (1 lb) subs sampling all available bags from lots of 10 bags or less. If lot size is greater than 10 bags, collect 454 gm (1 lb) from each of 10 bags selected at random.

   b. Bulk Complete Feed

      Collect at least 10 - 454 (1lb) subs from different points in the bulk lot to obtain a minimum total sample of 4.5 kg (10 lbs).

   c. Concentrates/Supplements

      If the concentrate or supplement is relatively inexpensive, follow the sampling procedures for complete feeds. Limit sampling of more expensive drug materials, concentrates, or supplements to no more than 3 containers taking a 170 gm (6 oz) or 6 fl. oz. sub from each of the 3 containers.

3. Documentary Samples (DOC Sample)

   a. Feed Subject to MFA Approval - Collect DOC Samples of products processed without required MFA approval. Where the plant does not ship in IS commerce, but ingredients are received from IS sources, document the IS nature of drug ingredients and the "Held For Sale" status of the finished feed. Labeling of drug ingredients must be submitted.

   b. Misbranded Products - Collect a DOC Sample for misbranding or labeling deficiencies. The failure to provide warning and/or withdrawal statements which could present danger to animals or man, or gross evidence of false and misleading therapeutic claims, are factors for consideration.

Sampling Precautions (See IOM Sample Schedule Chart 4)

1. Insert the trier the full length of the bag when sampling bagged premixes, or complete feeds.

2. Clean trier between sampling the different lots of premixes or complete feeds.

3. Place subs in clean airtight container, preferably clean glass jars.

4. DO not fumigate samples intended for potency analysis, drug carryover or cross-contamination.

Sample Submission

Submit samples to your district's servicing laboratory or as directed by your assignment or supervisor. See IOM 4.5.5.2.

Sample Schedule 13: Allergen Sample Schedule

Sample Sizes With Application To Food Products For Allergens[18]

(Listed below is the sample size needed for lab analysis. Collect all samples in duplicate, with the duplicate serving as the 702 (b) reserve sample)

Product	Package type	Number of sample units	Unit size	Total sample
Non-liquefied foods, i.e., cereals, cookies	Consumer	20	1 lb	20 lbs
Pre-liquefied foods, i.e., ice cream, chocolates	Consumer	10	1 lb	10 lbs
Paste or slurry type	Consumer	24 12	8 oz 1 lb	12 lbs 12 lbs
Fluid, i.e., beverages	Consumer	10	16 fl. oz	160 fl. oz

IMPORTANT! WHEN TO SAMPLE: At the time of submission of this table to the IOM, only “for cause” allergen samples for peanut contamination should be collected. Test methods for additional allergens are under development and the field will be notified when they are available for regulatory purposes. The allergen compliance program, when issued, will provide additional sampling guidance. “For cause” sampling should be limited to instances where a consumer, medically determined to have a food allergy, experiences an adverse event believed due to the allergenic food, and the labeling of the suspect product does not indicate the presence of the allergen.

Note: *To be collected from random sites. May combine subs or maintain sub integrity depending on purpose of sampling*

Note: *Prepare composite following proper grinding and mixing procedures. Separate four 1-lb portions from composite.*

Adapted from U.S. Food and Drug Administration, Office of Regulatory Affairs, Investigations Operations Manual, Chapter 4, Sample Schedule 6, Mycotoxin Sample Sizes, http://www.fda.gov/ora/inspect_ref/iom/ChapterText/sschedule6.html

[18] See Laboratory Information Bulletin (LIB) # 4341, Application of Validated, Multiple Laboratory Performance Test MethodsSM for the Detection of Peanuts in Food, Vol 21(2) 2005 for details regarding the analysis and quantitation of analytical samples.

Part III

Combined Glossary and Index

Combined Glossary

A, B

Advanced Prepared Food

Food that was prepared on location at the food service establishment prior to arrival of the Lead Investigator. [Chapter 3]

Bacteriological Samples

During inspections of firms producing products susceptible to microbial contamination (e.g., frozen precooked; ready to eat seafood, creme filled goods, breaded items, egg rolls, prepared salads, etc.), proof of adulteration, with fecal organisms, or elevated levels of non-pathogenic microorganisms, must be established. Sampling of raw materials, in-line and finished product is warranted. Follow instructions under IOM 4.3.7.7 - Products Susceptible to Contamination with Pathogenic Microorganisms, Sampling During Inspection. [Chapter 4]

Biological Product

A virus, therapeutic serum, toxin, antitoxin, vaccine, blood, blood component or derivative, allergenic product, or analogous product, or arsphenamine or derivative of arsphenamine (or any other trivalent organic arsenic compound), applicable to the prevention, treatment, or cure of a disease or condition of human beings (Public Health Service Act Sec. 351(i)). Additional interpretation of the statutory language is found in 21 CFR 600.3. Biological products also meet the definition of either a drug or device under Sections 201(g) and (h) of the Federal Food, Drug, and Cosmetic Act (FD&C Act).

Veterinary biologicals are subject to the animal Virus, Serum, and Toxin Act which is enforced by USDA (21 U.S.C. 151-158). [Chapter 5]

C

Citation (Cite)

The section 305 Notice is a statutory requirement of the FD&C Act. It provides a respondent with an opportunity to show cause why he should not be prosecuted for an alleged violation. Response to the notice may be by letter, personal appearance, or an attorney(s). [Chapter 2]

Civil Number

A docket number used by US district courts to identify civil cases (seizure and injunction). [Chapter 2]

Complaint for Forfeiture

A document furnished to the U.S. attorney for filing with the clerk of the court to initiate a seizure. [Chapter 2]

Complaint Samples, Certain

Injury and illness investigation samples from certain complaints where there is no Federal jurisdiction, or where the alleged violation offers no basis for subsequent regulatory action. Complaint samples from lots for which Federal jurisdiction is clear should be submitted as Official Samples. [Chapter 4]

Comprehensive Inspection

Directs coverage to everything in the firm subject to FDA jurisdiction to determine the firms compliance status. [Chapter 5]

Criminal Number

A docket number used by the US district courts to identify criminal cases (prosecutions). [Chapter 2]

D

Dealer

For sample collection purposes, the dealer is the person, firm (which could include the manufacturer), institution or other party, who has possession of a particular lot of goods. The dealer does not have to be a firm or company, which is in the business of buying or selling goods. The dealer might be a housewife in her home, a physician, or a public agency; these dealers obtain products to use but not to sell. The dealer may be a party who does not own the goods, but has possession of them, such as a public storage warehouse or transportation agency. [Chapter 4]

Directed Inspection

Directs coverage to specific areas to the depth described in the program, assignment, or as instructed by your supervisor. [Chapter 5]

District Contact

The Director, Investigations Branch. [Chapter 3]

Denaturing

Decharacterization of a product, whereby it is made unusable for its originally intended purpose. [Chapter 2]

Destruction

The procedures involved in rendering a product unsalvageable. Destruction may be accomplished by burning, burial, etc. [Chapter 2]

Device

Section 201(h) of the FD&C Act [21 U.S.C. 321 (h)] defines a device as follows: "The term "device" *** means an instrument, apparatus, implement, machine, contrivance, implant, in-vitro reagent, or other similar or related article, including any component, part, or accessory, which is: [Chapter 2]

1. Recognized in the official National Formulary, or the United States Pharmacopoeia, or any supplement to them,

2. Intended for use in the diagnosis of disease or other conditions, or in the cure, mitigation, treatment, or prevention of disease, in man or other animals, or

3. Intended to affect the structure or any function of the body of man or other animals, and which does not achieve its primary intended purposes through chemical action within or on the body of man or other animals and which is not dependent upon being metabolized for the achievement of any primary intended purposes."

Document

Official records which are considered to be U.S. Government property regardless of the media e.g. Regulatory notes (electronic and hardcopy), memoranda, inspection reports, e-mails, and official government forms (e.g. SF-71, FDA-482, FDA-483, etc.) [Chapter 1]

E

Egg and Egg Products (Dual Jurisdiction)

The term "egg" means the shell egg of the domesticated chicken, turkey, duck, goose, or guinea.

The term "egg product" means any dried, frozen, or liquid eggs, with or without added ingredients, excepting products which contain eggs only in relatively small proportion or historically have not been, in the judgment of the Secretary, considered by consumers as products of the egg food industry, and which may be exempted by the Secretary under such conditions as he may prescribe to assure the egg ingredients are not adulterated and such products are not represented as egg products. This would be done on a case by case basis by USDA. [Chapter 2]

Ethylene Oxide (EO)

EO is a colorless gas or volatile liquid with a characteristic ether-like odor above 500 ppm. Unmonitored and inadequate ventilation will allow EO buildup of extremely high concentrations, especially in facilities utilizing malfunctioning or leaking equipment. [Chapter 1]

Exhibits

Filth exhibits and other articles taken for exhibit purposes during inspections to demonstrate manufacturing or storage conditions, employee practices, and the like. Typically filth exhibits submitted as part of an INV sample are not tied to any specific lot of product, but are meant to illustrate the conditions at a firm. An example of an INV filth sample would be rodent excreta pellets, apparent nesting or other rodent gnawed material, and other evidence of rodent activity collected from the perimeter and at multiple locations throughout a manufacturing facility or warehouse in order to document widespread rodent infestation. [Chapter 4]

F

Factory Samples

Raw materials, in-process and finished products to demonstrate manufacturing conditions. Note: Photographs taken in a firm are not samples. They are exhibits except when they are part of a DOC Sample. See IOM 4.5.2.4, 5.3.3, and 5.3.4. [Chapter 4]

FDC and INJ Numbers

The number used by the Chief Counsel's office to identify FDA cases. [Chapter 2]

Food

For the purpose of detention of food under section 304(h) of the FD&C Act, see section 201(f) of the FD&C Act, which defines food as follows: "(1) articles used for food or drink for man or other animals, (2) chewing gum, and (3) articles used for components of any such article."

Examples of food include, but are not limited to, fruits, vegetables, fish, dairy products, eggs, raw agricultural commodities for use as food or components of food, animal feed, including pet food, food and feed ingredients and additives, including substances that migrate into food from food packaging and other articles that contact food, dietary supplements and dietary ingredients, infant formula, beverages, including alcoholic beverages and bottled water, live food animals, bakery goods, snack foods, candy, and canned foods. [Chapter 2]

Food Service Function

A public event where food will be provided to a protectee. [Chapter 3]

G – L

Home District

The Home District is the district in whose territory the alleged violation of the Act occurs, or in whose territory the firm or individual responsible for the alleged violation is physically located. The original point from which the article was shipped, or offered for shipment, as shown by the interstate records, is usually considered the point where the violation occurred; and the shipper of such article, as shown by such records, may be considered to be the alleged violator.

Where actions against a firm are based on goods which became violative after interstate shipment was made, or after reaching its destination (such as 301(k) violations), the dealer in whose possession the goods are sampled may be considered the violator, and the location of this dealer determines the "Home District". [Chapter 2]

Lead Advance Agent

The Secret Service Agent in charge of all security arrangements. This person is responsible for all sites to be visited by the protectee, and is a representative of the Office of Protective Operations (Secret Service Headquarters). [Chapter 3]

Lead Investigator

The FDA person designated by the FDA district/region to coordinate the investigational activities at the site of a food service function. [Chapter 3]

M

May Proceed

Product may proceed without FDA examination. FDA has made no determination the product complies with all provisions of the Food, Drug, and Cosmetic Act, or other related acts. This message does not preclude action should the products later be found violative." (No compliance decision has been made.) [Chapter 6]

Meat Products and Poultry Products (Dual Jurisdiction)

For FDA purposes, meat products and poultry products are defined as the carcasses of cattle, sheep, swine, goats, horses, mules, other equines, or domesticated birds, parts of such carcasses, and products made wholly or in part from such carcasses, except products exempted by U.S.D.A. because they contain a relatively small amount of meat or poultry products (e.g.; meat flavored sauces, pork and beans, etc.). Examine labels for USDA Shield or coding information to help determine if it is a USDA product. [Chapter 2]

Medical Device Notification

A communication issued by the manufacturer, distributor, or other responsible person in compliance with a Notification Order. It notifies health professionals and other appropriate persons of an unreasonable risk of substantial harm to the public health presented by a device in commercial distribution. [Chapter 7]

Medical Device Notification Order

An order issued by FDA requiring notification under section 518(a) of the FD & C Act [21 U.S.C. 360h (a)]. The directive issues when FDA determines a device in commercial distribution, and intended for human use, presents an unreasonable risk of substantial harm to the public health. The notification is necessary to eliminate the unreasonable risk of such harm, and no more practicable means is available under the provisions of the Act to eliminate such risk. [Chapter 7]

Medical Device Safety Alert

This is a communication voluntarily issued by a manufacturer, distributor, or other responsible person (including FDA). It informs health professionals and other appropriate persons of a situation which may present an unreasonable risk to the public health by a device in commercial distribution. [Chapter 7]

Mold Samples

During inspections of manufacturers such as canneries, bottling plants, milling operations, etc., it may be necessary to collect scrapings or swabs of slime or other material to verify the presence of mold. The sample should represent the conditions observed at the time of collection and consist of sufficient material to confirm and identify mold growth on the equipment. If possible, take photographs and obtain scrapings or bits of suspect material. Describe the area scraped or swabbed, e.g., material was scraped or swabbed from a 2" x 12" area. [Chapter 4]

N, O

Nolle Prosequi (Nol-Pros)

The prosecutor or plaintiff in a legal matter will proceed no further in prosecuting the whole suit or specified counts. [Chapter 2]

Nolo Contendere (Nolo)

A plea by a defendant in a criminal prosecution meaning "I will not contest it". [Chapter 2]

Official Sample

An Official Sample is one taken from a lot for which Federal jurisdiction can be established. If violative, the Official Sample provides a basis for administrative or legal action. Official Samples generally, but not always, consist of a physical portion of the lot sampled. [Chapter 4]

P, Q

Perishable Food

For the purpose of detention of food under section 304(h) of the FD&C Act, the term "perishable food" means food that is not heat-treated; not frozen; and not otherwise preserved in a manner so as to prevent the quality of the food from being adversely affected if held longer than 7 calendar days under normal shipping and storage conditions. See 21 CFR 1.377. [Chapter 2]

Person-in-Charge

The available person in the food service establishment authorized to make necessary changes/decisions such as the general manager, executive chef, banquet manager, caterer's representative or other management person. [Chapter 3]

Pesticide Episode

An "episode" is defined as a violative pesticide (or other chemical contaminant) finding and all samples collected in follow-up to that finding. All samples must be associated with one responsible firm (grower, pesticide applicator, etc.) and one specific time period (e.g. growing season). [Chapter 4]

Pre-prepared Food

Potentially hazardous food that was received at the food service establishment in a prepared form. Examples would include chicken salad, liver pate, gefilte fish, hors d'oeuvres, etc. which were prepared at another location, and then transported to the food service establishment providing food for the event. [Chapter 3]

Protectee

Any person eligible to receive the protection authorized by law. [Chapter 3]

Protective Detail

A team of Secret Service agents responsible for security surrounding public events to be attended by a protectee during a trip. Protective details are assigned and coordinated by Secret Service Headquarters, but may include Secret Service field representatives. [Chapter 3]

R

Recall

A Recall is a firm's removal or correction of a marketed product that FDA considers to be in violation of the laws it administers, and against which the Agency would initiate legal action (e.g., seizure). Recall does not include a market withdrawal or a stock recovery. See the Agency recall policy outlined in 21 CFR 7.1/7.59 - Enforcement Policy - General Provisions, Recalls (Including Product Corrections) - Guidance on Policy, Procedures, and Industry Responsibilities. [Chapter 7]

Recall Audit Check

A personal visit, telephone call, letter, or a combination thereof, to a consignee of a recalling firm, or a user or consumer in the chain of distribution. It is made to verify all consignees at the recall depth specified by the strategy have received notification about the recall and have taken appropriate action. [Chapter 7]

Recall Classification

Means the numerical designation, i.e., I, II, or III, assigned by the FDA to a particular product recall to indicate the relative degree of health hazard presented by the product being recalled. [Chapter 7]

Class I Recall

A situation in which there is a reasonable probability that the use of, or exposure to, a violative product will cause serious adverse health consequences or death.

Class II Recall

A situation in which use of, or exposure to, a violative product may cause temporary or medically reversible adverse health consequences or where the probability of serious adverse health consequences is remote.

Class III Recall

A situation in which use of, or exposure to, a violative product is not likely to cause adverse health consequences.

Recall Completed

For monitoring purposes, the FDA classifies a recall action "Completed" when all outstanding product, which could reasonably be expected is recovered, impounded, or corrected. [Chapter 7]

Recall, Depth of

Depending on the product's degree of hazard and extent of distribution, the recall strategy will specify the level in the distribution chain to which the recall is to extend, i.e., wholesaler, retailer, user/consumer. [Chapter 7]

Recall Number

Number assigned by a responsible Center for each re-called product they initiate. This number consists first of a letter designating the responsible Center (see letter Codes below), a 3-digit sequential number indicating the number of recalls initiated by that Center during the fiscal year, and a 1-digit number (the Center for Devices and

Radiological Health (CDRH) uses 2-digit numbers) indicating the fiscal year the recall was initiated. For example: F-100-2 identifies the 100th recall initiated by the Center for Food Safety and Applied Nutrition (CFSAN) in FY-2002. [Chapter 7]

Recall Strategy

A planned specific course of action to be taken in conducting a specific recall, which addresses the depth of recall, need for public warnings, and extent of effectiveness checks for the recall. [Chapter 7]

Recall Terminated

A recall will be terminated when the FDA determines that all reasonable efforts have been made to remove or correct the violative product in accordance with the recall strategy, and when it is reasonable to assume that the product subject to the recall has been removed and proper disposition or correction has been made commensurate with the degree of hazard of the recalled product. Written notification that a recall is terminated will be issued by the appropriate District office to the recalling firm. [Chapter 7]

Recall Type

A designation based on whether the recall is Voluntary, FDA Requested (at the request of the Commissioner or his designee), or ordered under section 518(e) of the FD & C Act [21 U.S.C 360h (e)]. [Chapter 7]

Reconditioning

The reworking, relabeling, segregation, or other manipulation which brings a product into compliance with the law, whether or not for its original intended use. [Chapter 2]

Reconditioning Samples

These are taken from lots reconditioned under a Decree or other agreement to bring the lots into compliance with the law. The sample is taken to determine if reconditioning was satisfactorily performed. These samples should be submitted as Official Samples, rather than INV. [Chapter 4]

Release

The product is released after FDA examination. This message does not constitute assurance the product complies with all provisions of the Food, Drug and Cosmetic Act, or other related Acts, and does not preclude action should the product later be found violative." (A compliance decision has been made.) [Chapter 6]

S

Seizing District

The district where seizure is actually accomplished. The seizing district is not necessarily the collecting district, as in the case of intransit samples. [Chapter 2]

Subpoena Duces Tecum

A writ commanding a person to appear in court bringing with him certain designated documents or things pertinent to the issues of a pending controversy. [Chapter 2]

Supervising District

The district which exercises supervision over reconditioning lots in connection with seizure actions. [Chapter 2]

Seizure

Seizure is a judicial civil action directed against specific offending goods, in which goods are "arrested." Originally designed to remove violative goods from consumer channels, it was intended primarily as a remedial step; however, the sanction often has a punitive and deterrent effect. [Chapter 2]

Site Advance Agent

The Secret Service person responsible for security arrangements at a specific site to be visited by the protectee. This person is part of the protective detail headed by the Lead Advance Agent. Note: the term Site Advance Agent will include any agent designated by the Site Advance Agent to be the contact with the FDA Lead Investigator. [Chapter 3]

Support Personnel

FDA persons deemed necessary by FDA in order to properly inspect a food service function. [Chapter 3]

T – Z

Verified

To confirm; to establish the truth or accuracy. [Chapter 5]

Voluntary Corrective Action

The observed voluntary repair, modification, or adjustment of a violative condition, or product. For purposes of this definition, violative means the product or condition does not comply with the Acts or associated regulations enforced by the Agency. [Chapter 2]

Index

B

C

D

E

F

H

I

J, K, L

M

O

P

Q, R

S

U

V

W, X, Y, Z

About the author

Mindy Allport-Settle has served as a key executive, board member, and consultant for some of the best companies in the pharmaceutical and FDA-regulated industry. As CEO of PharmaLogika, Inc. since 2008 and over the course of her career, she has provided informed guidance in regulatory compliance, corporate structuring, restructuring and turnarounds, new drug submissions, research & development and product commercialization strategies, operational, project and contract management, and new business development. Her experience and dedication have resulted in international recognition as the developer of the only FDA-recognized and benchmarked quality systems training and development business methodology designed for regulated industries. Her education includes a Bachelor's degree from the University of North Carolina, an MBA in Global Management from the University of Phoenix, and completion of the corporate governance course series in audit committees, compensation committees, and board effectiveness at Harvard Business School.

About PharmaLogika

Since 2002, PharmaLogika, Inc has established itself as one of the world's premier consulting firms for Pharmaceutical, Biotech, and Medical Device companies across the globe. In so doing, it has earned the trust of executives in Life Sciences for its integrity, accuracy, and unwavering commitment to independent thought with regard to its products and services as well as those of its customers. Through www.PharmaLogika.com, its involvement in sponsored events, and personal references it has reached millions in print and online. Its mission, to provide flawlessly designed and executed products and services to startups as well as established industry leaders to facilitate their growth from discovery and clinical trial navigation to the commercialization and marketing of their products.

PharmaLogika consults with pharmaceutical, biotech, and medical device quality units to provide third party audits, training, pre approval inspections (PAIs), compliance remediation, and a portfolio of related quality and regulatory affairs products and services. Those products include but are not limited to Quality Assurance Forms, SOP and clinical templates, and the highly successful Integrated Development Training System.

Regulatory action guidance as well as quality systems guidance are delivered as part of its standard products and services. Through the use of highly skilled resources throughout the process, each offering is designed to enact a comprehensive quality systems approach in addressing Quality Assurance (QA) issues. The results insure a close adherence to current Good Manufacturing Practice (cGMP) standards.

PharmaLogika also has a Research and Development OTC line for human consumption that targets alpha 1-antitrypsin deficiency, Fibromyalgia, Restless Legs Syndrome, and Attention Deficit Disorder. A veterinary OTC is currently available that provides canine and feline oral debriding and cleansing agents as well as a stain remover and topical antiseptic. These products combine to provide a strong pipeline of both current and future deliverables.

PharmaLogika, Inc.

PO Box 461

Willow Springs, NC 27592

www.PharmaLogika.com

Other books available

Current Good Manufacturing Practices: Pharmaceutical, Biologics, and Medical Device Regulations and Guidance Documents Concise Reference

Good Manufacturing Practice (GMP) Guidelines: The Rules Governing Medicinal Products in the Eurpean Union, EudraLex Volume 4 Concise Reference

FDA Acronyms, Abbreviations and Terminology: Human and Veterinary Regualtory Reference

Course Development 101: Developing Training Programs for Regulated Industries

Compliance Remediation for Pharmaceutical Manufacturing: A Project Management Guide for Re-establishing FDA Compliance

Please visit www.PharmaLogika.com for additional titles

LaVergne, TN USA
14 January 2011

212459LV00003B/3/P

9 780982 147627